Privacy is for Wussies

Book Eleven of the Syndicated Cartoon **Stone Soup**

by
Jan Eliot

FOUR PANEL PRESS

Eugene, Oregon

Published by Four Panel Press, P.O. Box 50032, Eugene, OR 97405.

Stone Soup® is distributed by Universal Uclick.

ISBN-13: 978-0-9674102-4-1

Library of Congress Control Number: 2015959541

First Edition

fourpanelpress.com

A portion of the profits from this book will go to alleviate hunger through our local food bank, Food for Lane County.

For Alec, Eliot, and Asa— superboys.

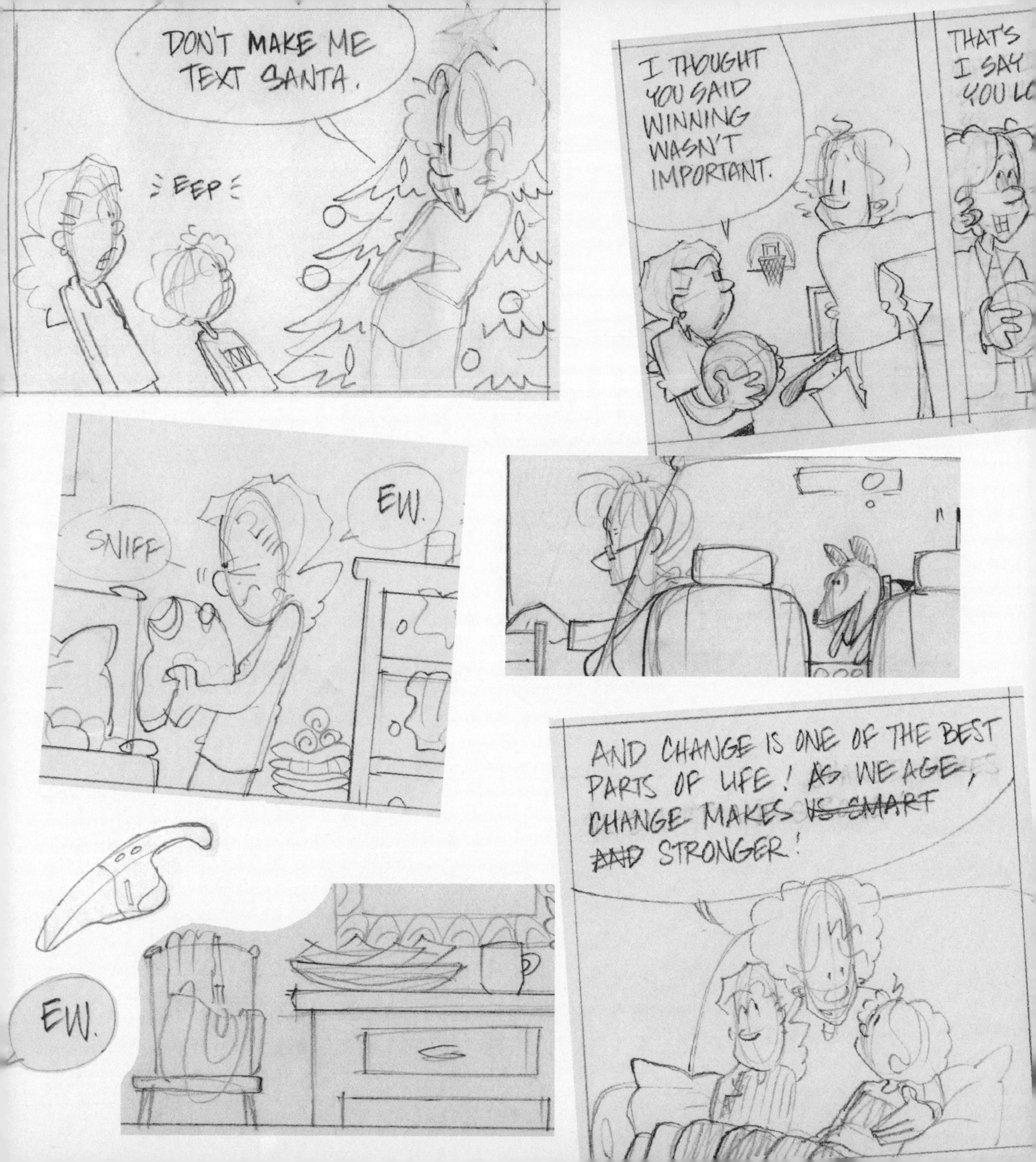
DON'T MAKE ME TEXT SANTA.
EEP
I THOUGHT YOU SAID WINNING WASN'T IMPORTANT.
THAT'S
I SAY
SNIFF
EW.
EW.
AND CHANGE IS ONE OF THE BEST PARTS OF LIFE! ~~AS WE AGE,~~ ~~CHANGE~~ MAKES ~~US SMART~~ ~~AND~~ STRONGER!

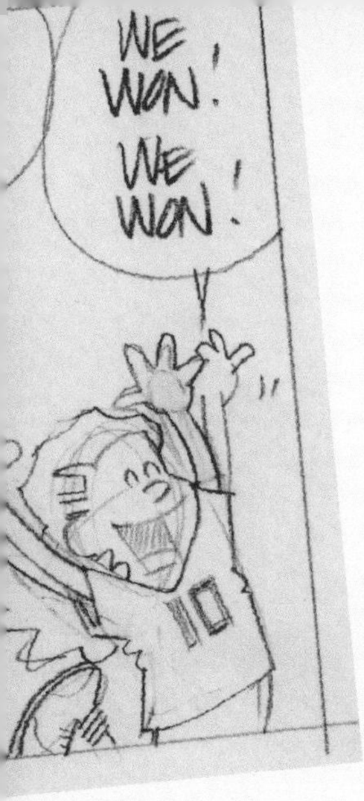
WE WON! WE WON!

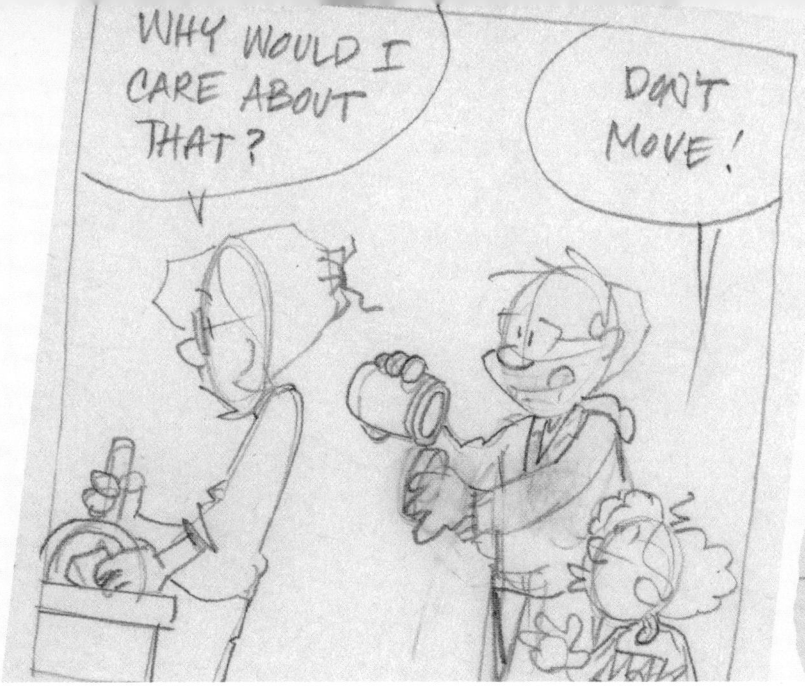
WHY WOULD I CARE ABOUT THAT?
DON'T MOVE!

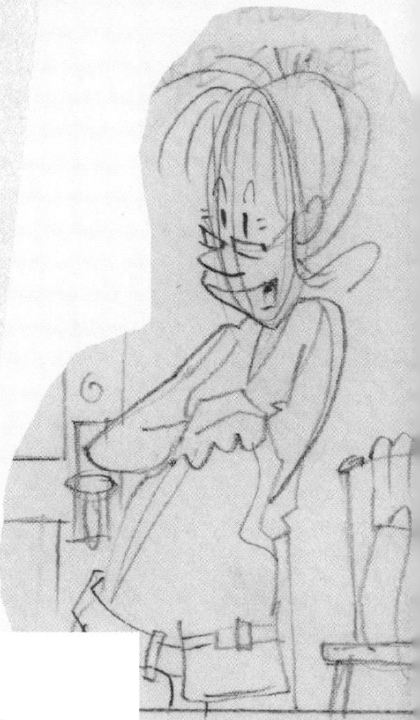

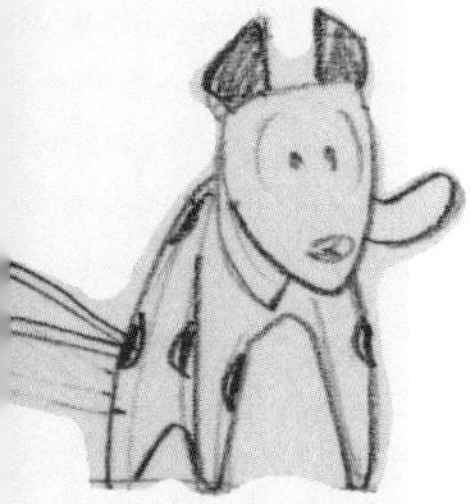

For the last 20 years I have devoted myself to creating a daily comic strip. It has been a privilege and a joy, and I count myself as one of the lucky humans who gets to do work they love. On these pages I share my love of the comic strip form, my love of my comic strip family, and my appreciation for all my faithful readers. I hope you find yourself, your family and your friends reflected in my stories, and that you smile, chuckle, belly laugh and roar your way through them.

Jan Eliot

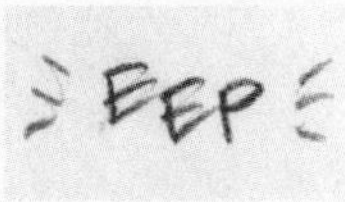
EEP

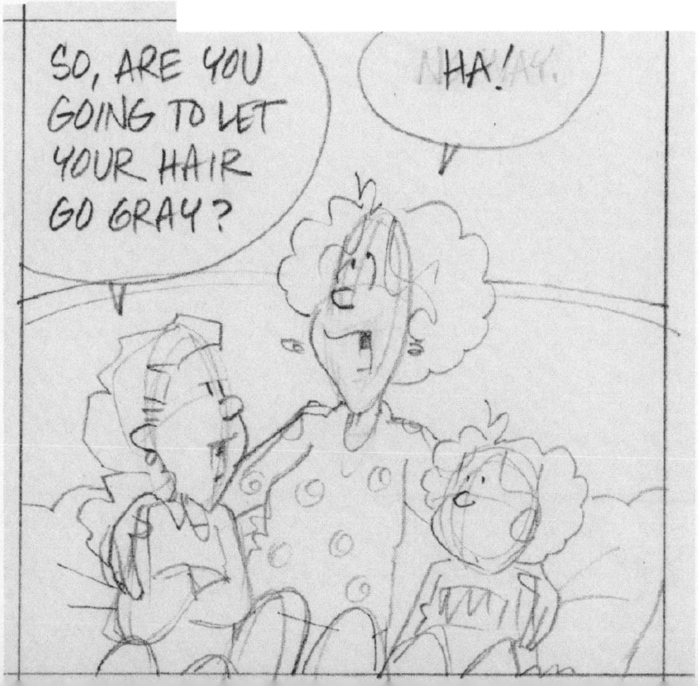
SO, ARE YOU GOING TO LET YOUR HAIR GO GRAY?
HA!

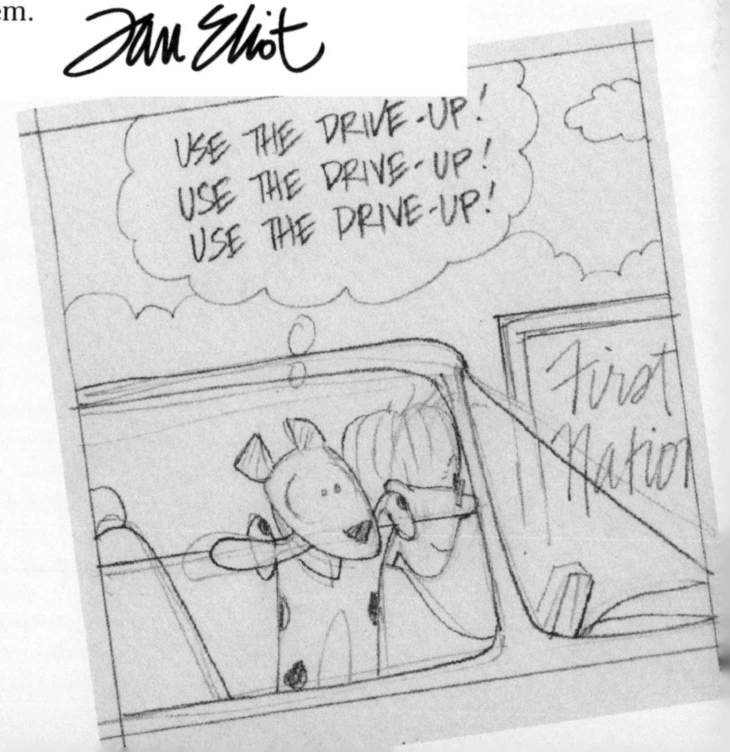
USE THE DRIVE-UP! USE THE DRIVE-UP! USE THE DRIVE-UP!
First Nation

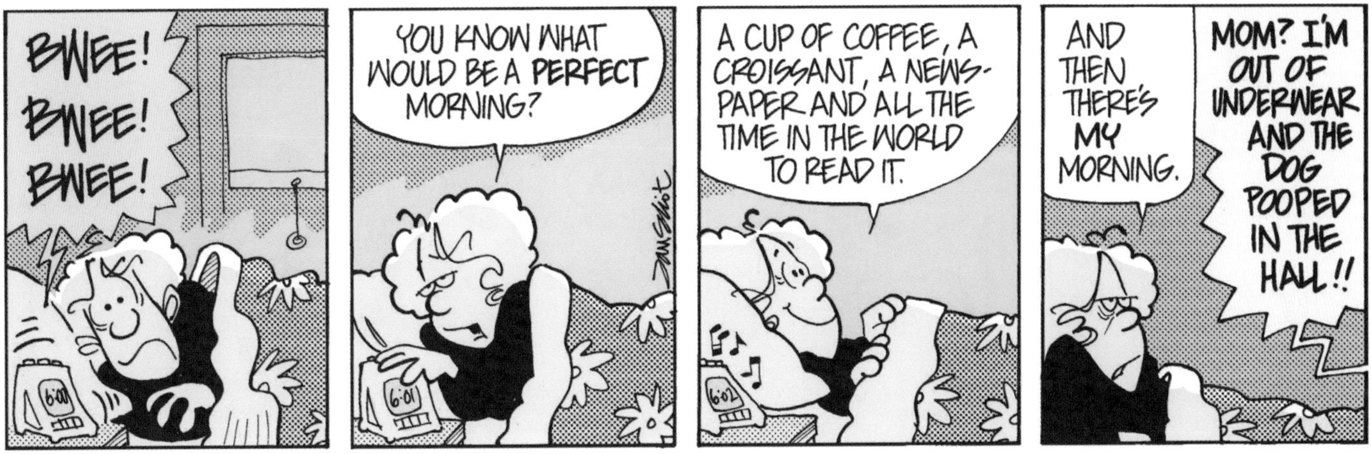
BWEE! BWEE! BWEE!
YOU KNOW WHAT WOULD BE A **PERFECT** MORNING?
A CUP OF COFFEE, A CROISSANT, A NEWSPAPER AND ALL THE TIME IN THE WORLD TO READ IT.
AND THEN THERE'S **MY** MORNING.
MOM? I'M OUT OF UNDERWEAR AND THE DOG POOPED IN THE HALL!!

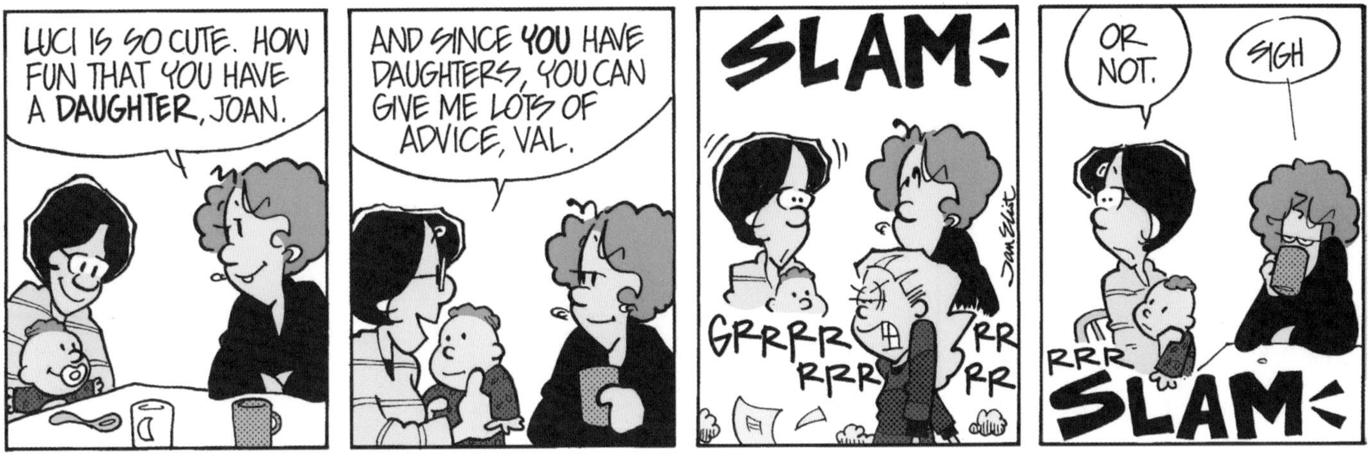
LUCI IS SO CUTE. HOW FUN THAT YOU HAVE A **DAUGHTER**, JOAN.
AND SINCE **YOU** HAVE DAUGHTERS, YOU CAN GIVE ME LOTS OF ADVICE, VAL.
SLAM
GRRRR RRR RR RR
OR NOT.
SIGH
RRR
SLAM

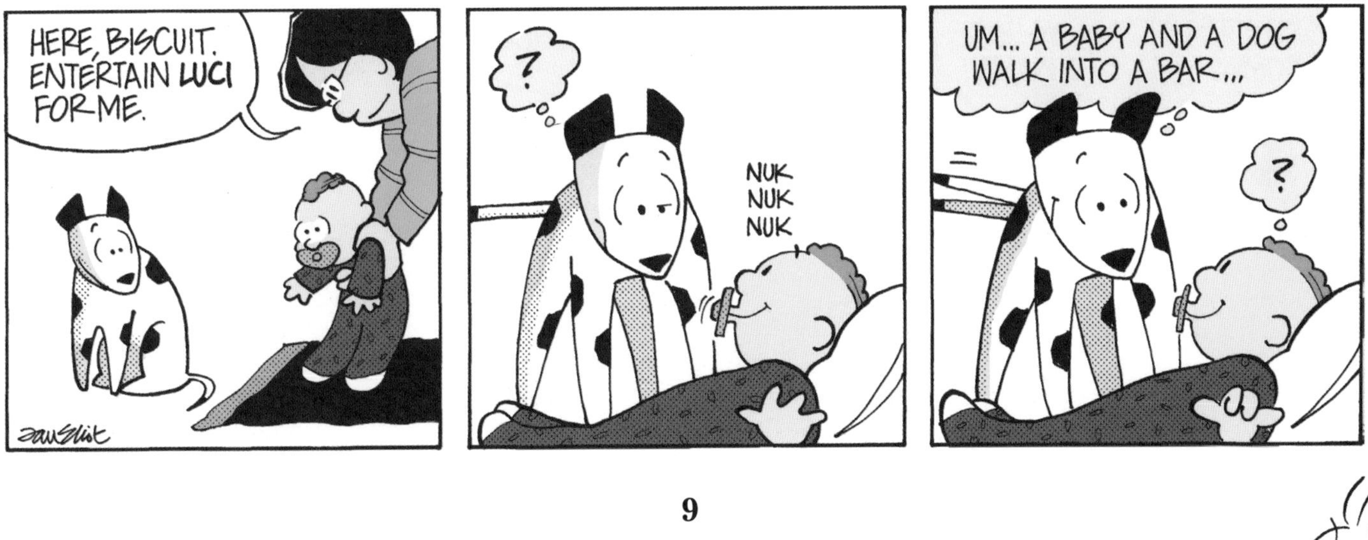
HERE, BISCUIT. ENTERTAIN **LUCI** FOR ME.
?
NUK NUK NUK
UM... A BABY AND A DOG WALK INTO A BAR...
?

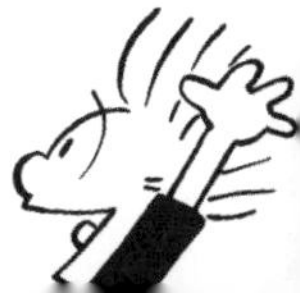

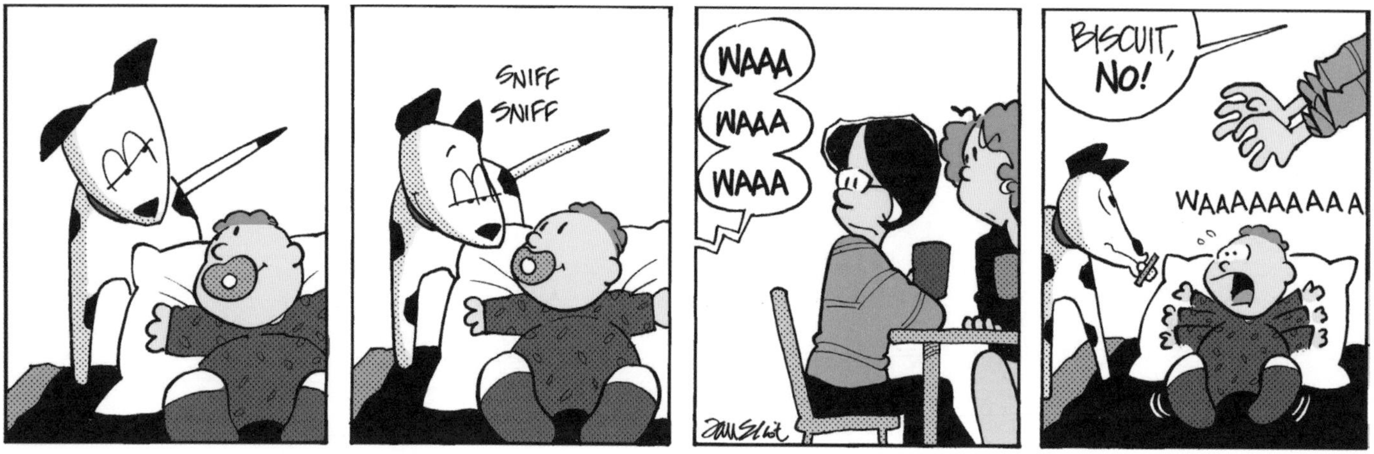
SNIFF
SNIFF
WAAA
WAAA
WAAA
BISCUIT, NO!
WAAAAAAAAA

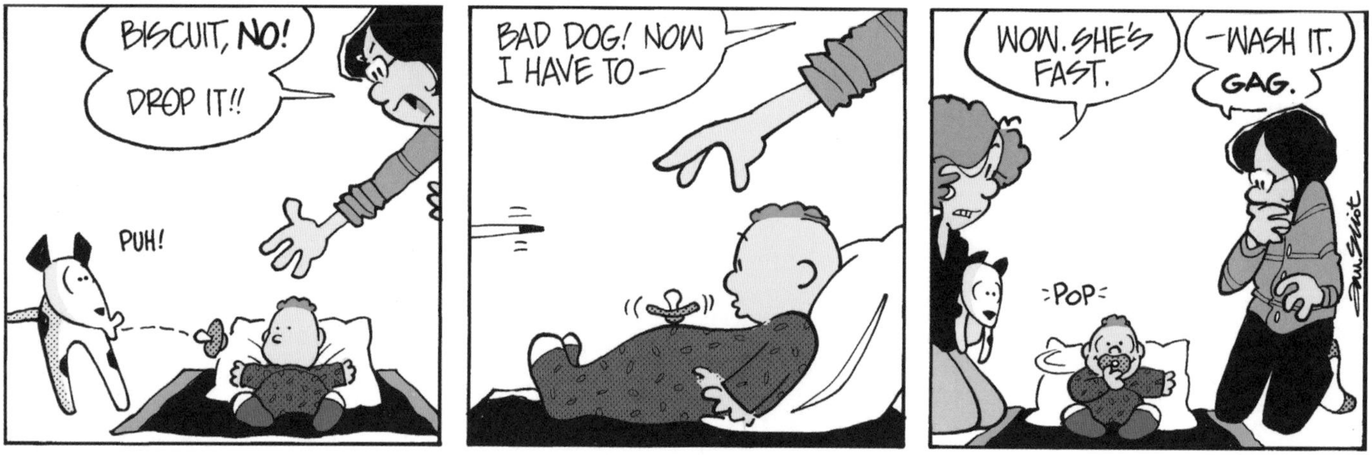
BISCUIT, NO!
DROP IT!!
PUH!
BAD DOG! NOW I HAVE TO—
WOW. SHE'S FAST.
—WASH IT. GAG.
POP

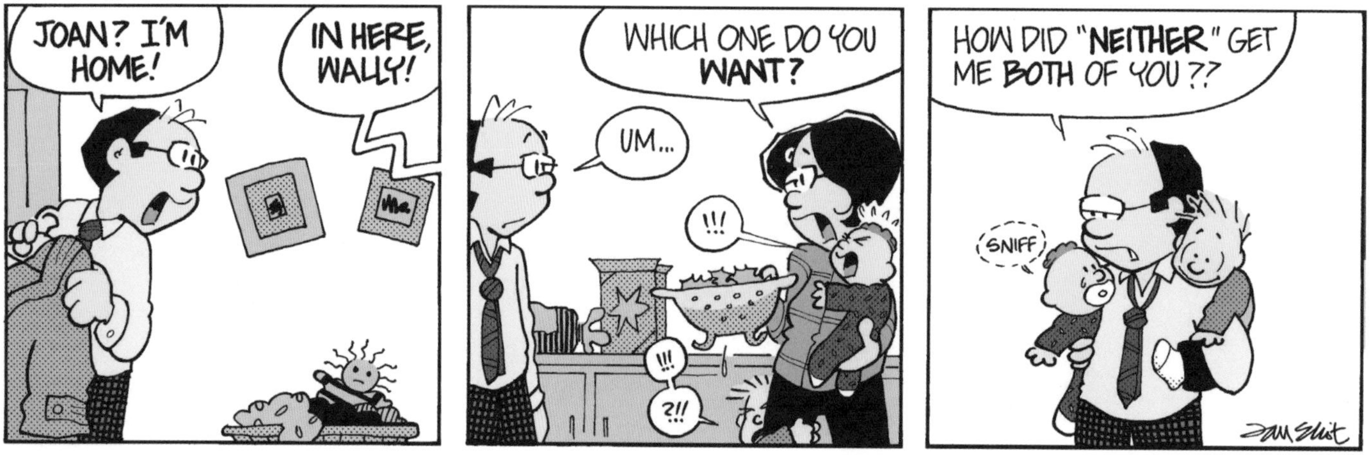
JOAN? I'M HOME!
IN HERE, WALLY!
WHICH ONE DO YOU WANT?
UM...
!!!
!!!
?!!
HOW DID "NEITHER" GET ME BOTH OF YOU??
SNIFF

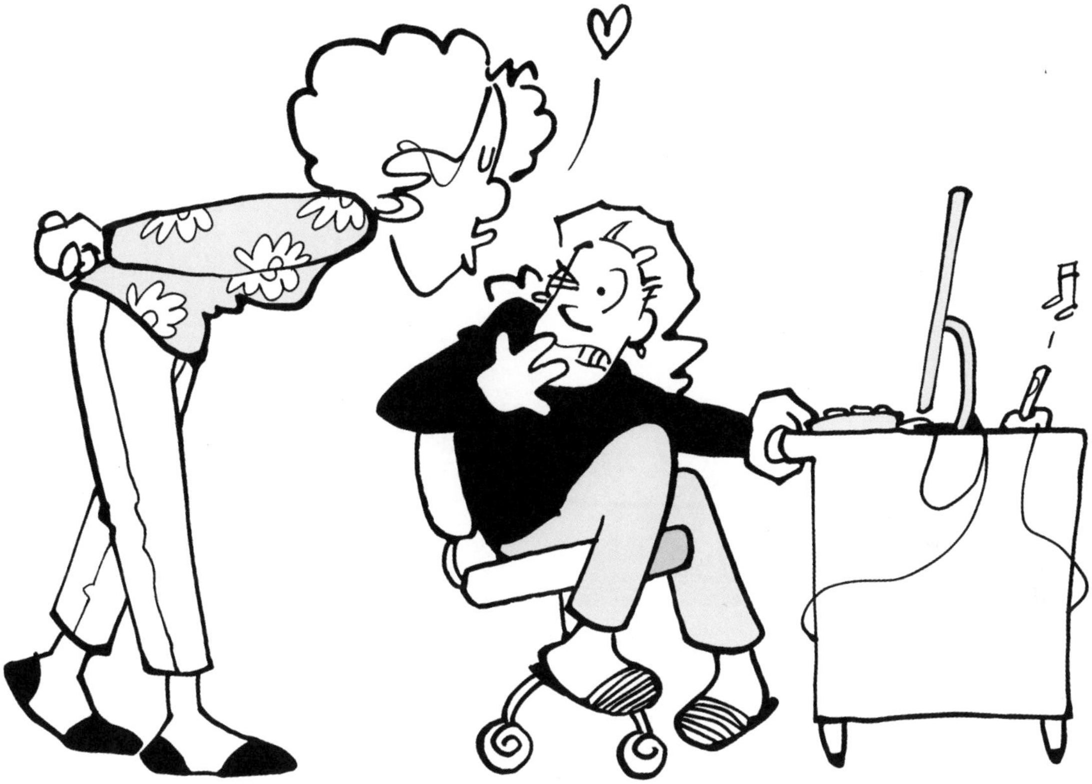

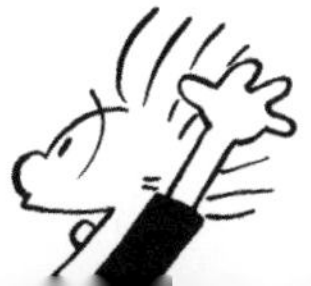

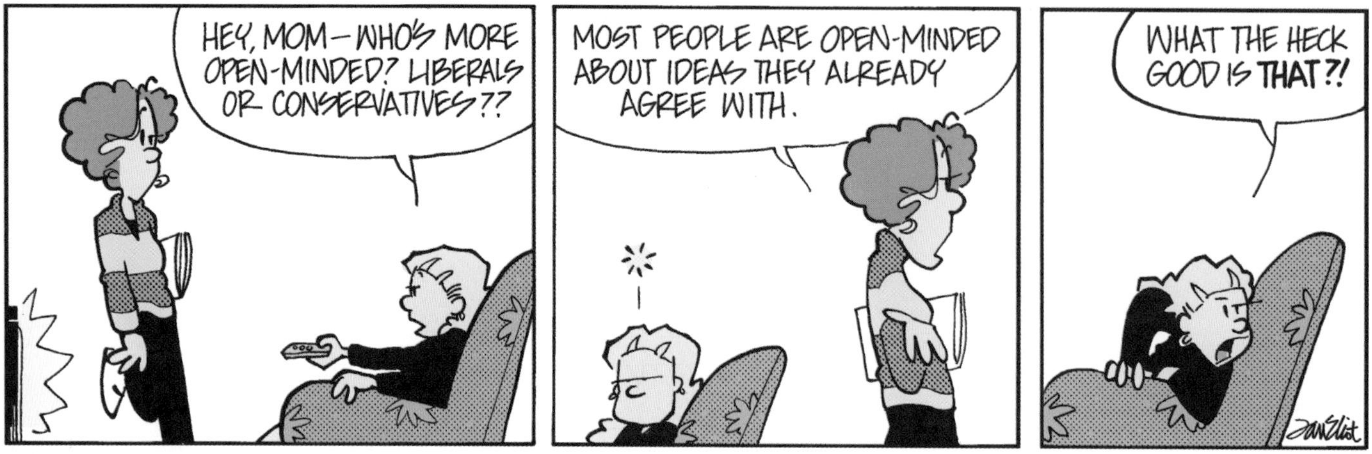
HEY, MOM—WHO'S MORE OPEN-MINDED? LIBERALS OR CONSERVATIVES??
MOST PEOPLE ARE OPEN-MINDED ABOUT IDEAS THEY ALREADY AGREE WITH.
WHAT THE HECK GOOD IS **THAT**?!

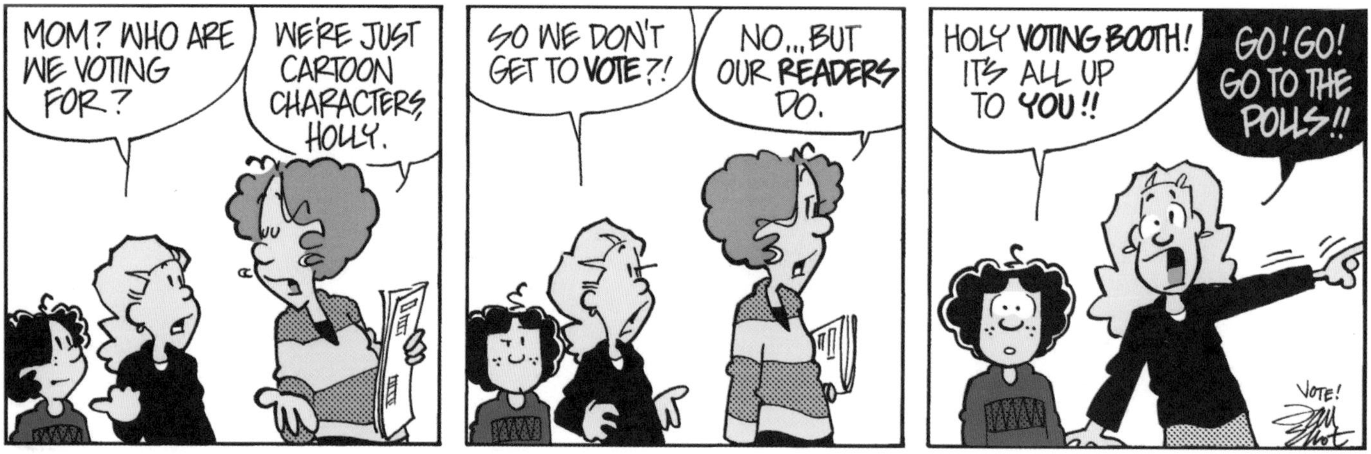
MOM? WHO ARE WE VOTING FOR?
WE'RE JUST CARTOON CHARACTERS, HOLLY.
SO WE DON'T GET TO **VOTE**?!
NO... BUT OUR **READERS** DO.
HOLY **VOTING BOOTH**! IT'S ALL UP TO **YOU**!!
GO! GO! GO TO THE POLLS!!
VOTE!

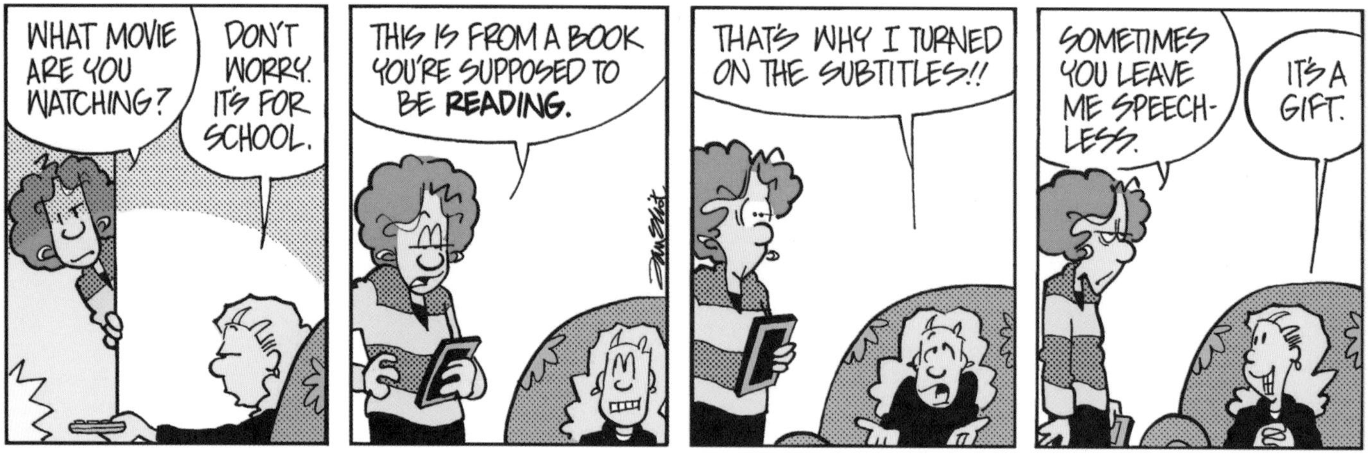
WHAT MOVIE ARE YOU WATCHING?
DON'T WORRY. IT'S FOR SCHOOL.
THIS IS FROM A BOOK YOU'RE SUPPOSED TO BE **READING.**
THAT'S WHY I TURNED ON THE SUBTITLES!!
SOMETIMES YOU LEAVE ME SPEECHLESS.
IT'S A GIFT.

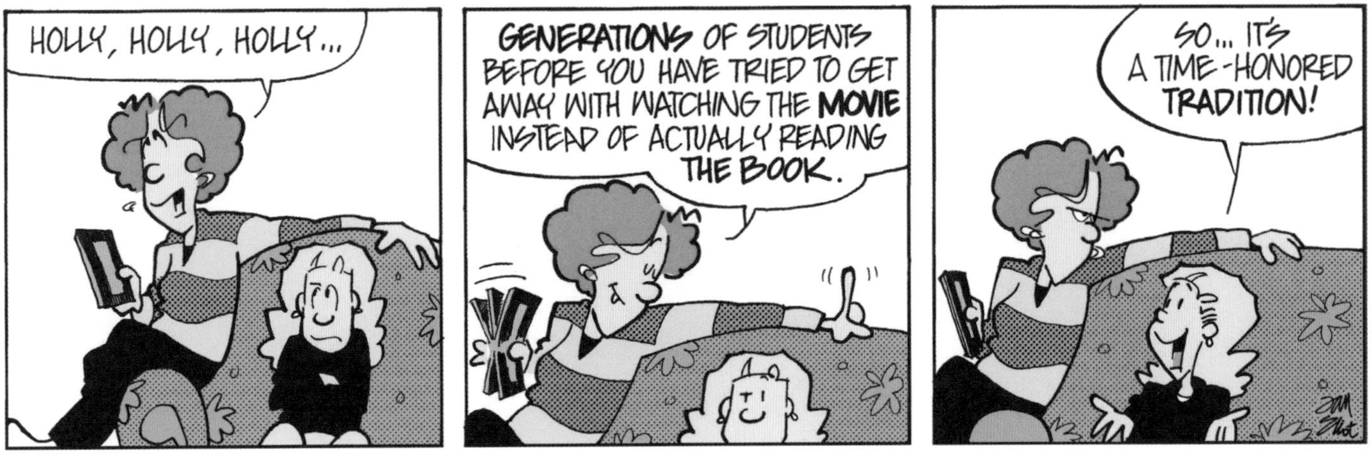
HOLLY, HOLLY, HOLLY...
GENERATIONS OF STUDENTS BEFORE YOU HAVE TRIED TO GET AWAY WITH WATCHING THE MOVIE INSTEAD OF ACTUALLY READING THE BOOK.
SO... IT'S A TIME-HONORED TRADITION!

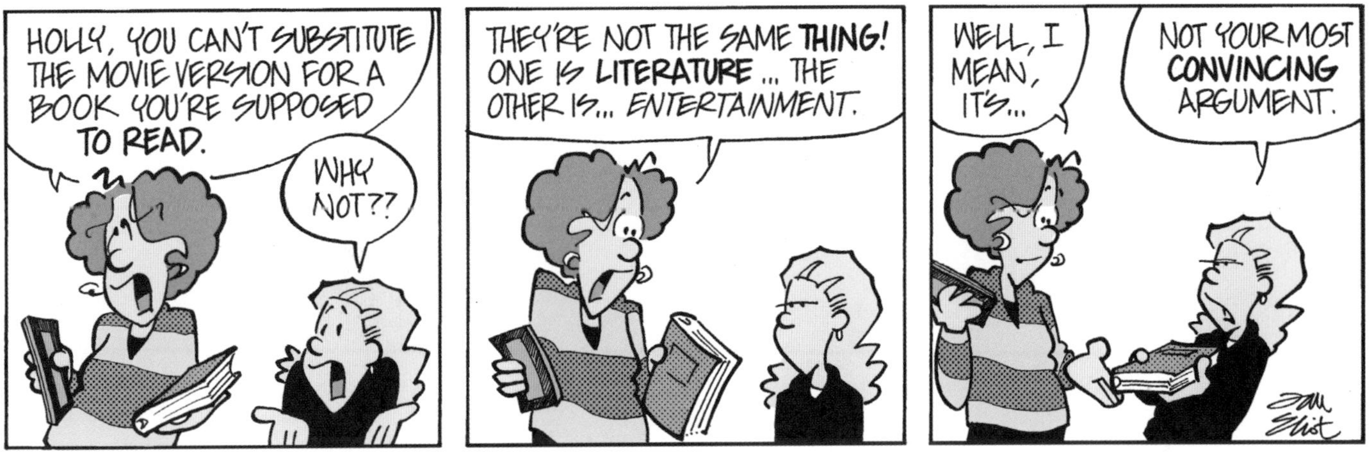
HOLLY, YOU CAN'T SUBSTITUTE THE MOVIE VERSION FOR A BOOK YOU'RE SUPPOSED TO READ.
WHY NOT??
THEY'RE NOT THE SAME THING! ONE IS LITERATURE ... THE OTHER IS... ENTERTAINMENT.
WELL, I MEAN, IT'S...
NOT YOUR MOST CONVINCING ARGUMENT.

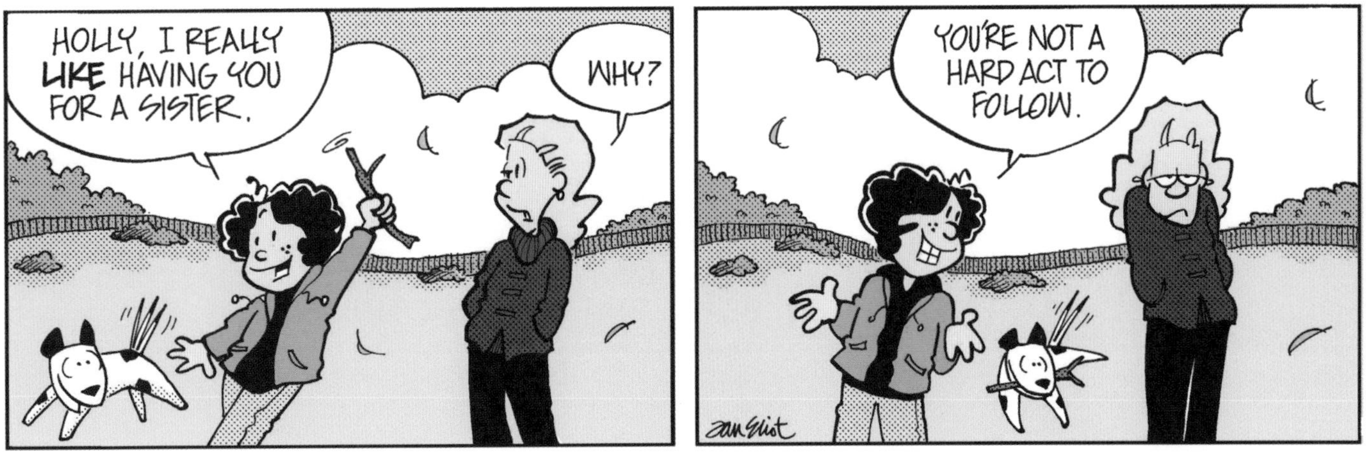
HOLLY, I REALLY LIKE HAVING YOU FOR A SISTER.
WHY?
YOU'RE NOT A HARD ACT TO FOLLOW.

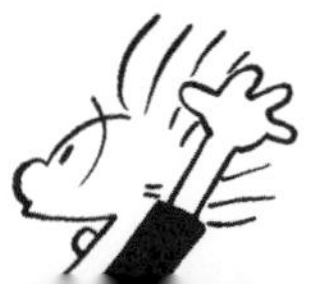

Stone Soup

MAAAAAMAAAAAAAAA
MA- MA!
MAMA MAMA MA- MA!!
MO O OM
MU- THUR!
MOMMY?!
?
!!
!!
GRANDMOTHER: THE MOTHER OF ALL MOTHERS.
?!
!!!
?!
!!?
!!
??
SIGH

Stone Soup

HOLLY?

TAKE OFF THE HEAD-PHONES AND TALK TO ME!

ABOUT **WHAT?**

ANYTHING. LET'S JUST TALK! WHAT'S **UP** WITH YOU??

UM...WELL... I WASN'T GOING TO **SAY** ANYTHING, BUT...

YOU TREAT ME LIKE A **CHILD.** NO ONE RESPECTS ME! **ALIX** GETS AWAY WITH **MURDER** BECAUSE SHE'S **LITTLE,** AND YOU ALL THINK SHE'S...

INNOCENT! **HA!** YOU SAY YOU UNDER-STAND BUT YOU **DON'T,** AND ANY-WAY...

I THINK 13 IS WAY OLD ENOUGH TO STAY OUT PAST ...

YADA YADA ...

?!   !!!

?#

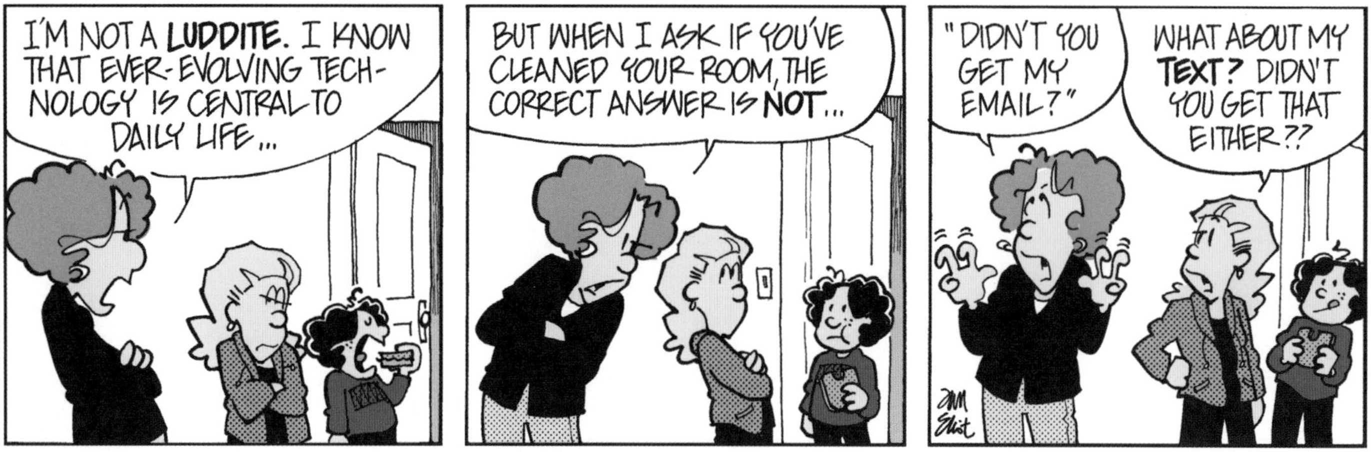
I'M NOT A **LUDDITE.** I KNOW THAT EVER-EVOLVING TECH-NOLOGY IS CENTRAL TO DAILY LIFE...
BUT WHEN I ASK IF YOU'VE CLEANED YOUR ROOM, THE CORRECT ANSWER IS **NOT**...
"DIDN'T YOU GET MY EMAIL?"
WHAT ABOUT MY **TEXT?** DIDN'T YOU GET THAT EITHER??

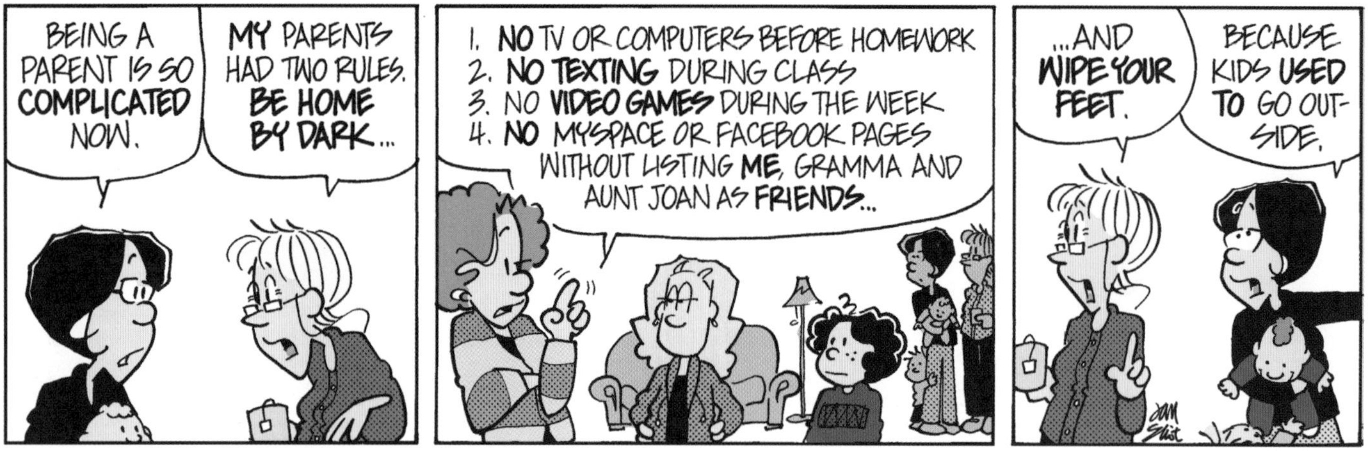
BEING A PARENT IS SO **COMPLICATED** NOW.
MY PARENTS HAD TWO RULES. **BE HOME BY DARK**...
1. **NO** TV OR COMPUTERS BEFORE HOMEWORK
2. **NO TEXTING** DURING CLASS
3. NO **VIDEO GAMES** DURING THE WEEK
4. **NO** MYSPACE OR FACEBOOK PAGES WITHOUT LISTING **ME**, GRAMMA AND AUNT JOAN AS **FRIENDS**...
...AND **WIPE YOUR FEET**.
BECAUSE KIDS **USED TO** GO OUT-SIDE.

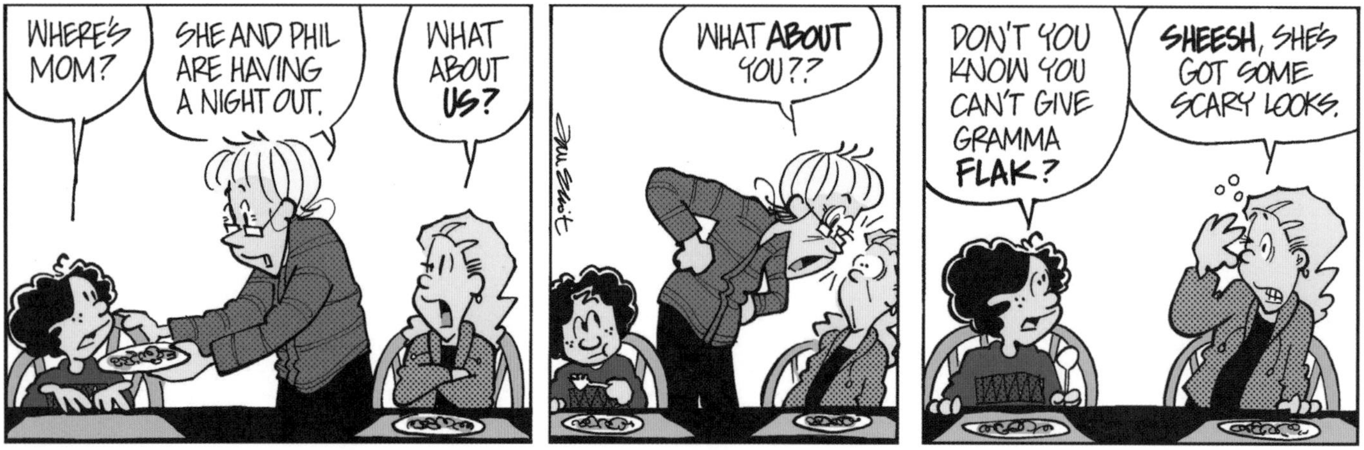
WHERE'S MOM?
SHE AND PHIL ARE HAVING A NIGHT OUT.
WHAT ABOUT **US?**
WHAT **ABOUT** YOU??
DON'T YOU KNOW YOU CAN'T GIVE GRAMMA **FLAK?**
SHEESH, SHE'S GOT SOME SCARY LOOKS.

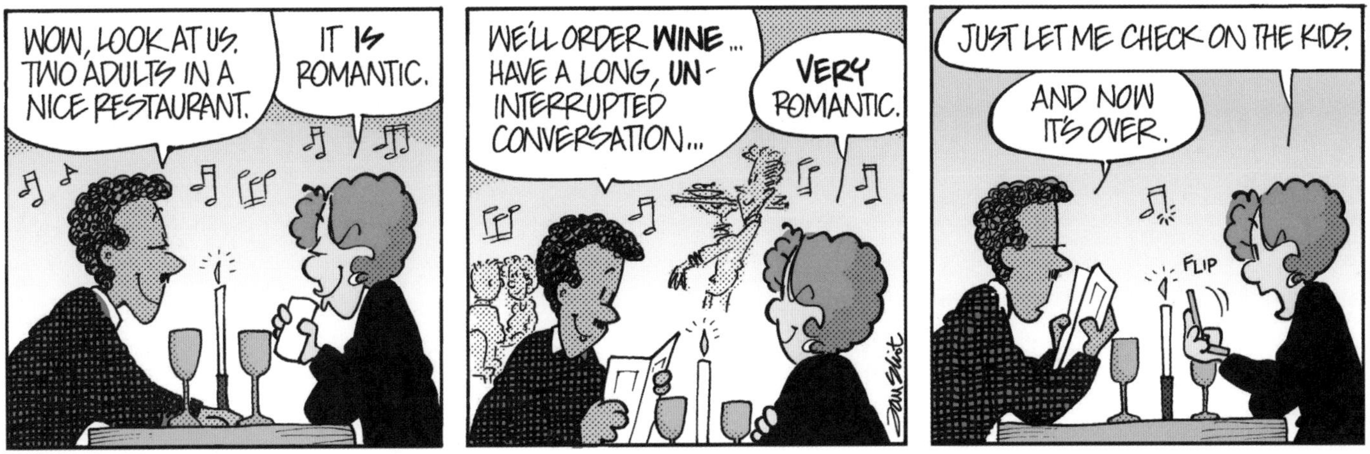
WOW, LOOK AT US. TWO ADULTS IN A NICE RESTAURANT.
IT IS ROMANTIC.
WE'LL ORDER WINE... HAVE A LONG, UN-INTERRUPTED CONVERSATION...
VERY ROMANTIC.
JUST LET ME CHECK ON THE KIDS.
FLIP
AND NOW IT'S OVER.

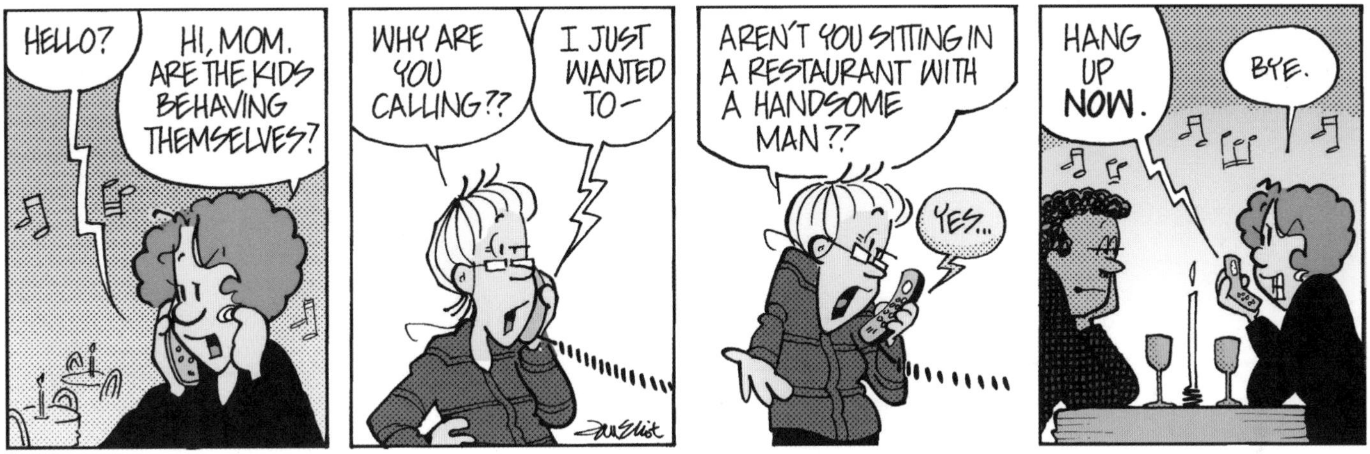
HELLO?
HI, MOM. ARE THE KIDS BEHAVING THEMSELVES?
WHY ARE YOU CALLING??
I JUST WANTED TO–
AREN'T YOU SITTING IN A RESTAURANT WITH A HANDSOME MAN??
YES...
HANG UP NOW.
BYE.

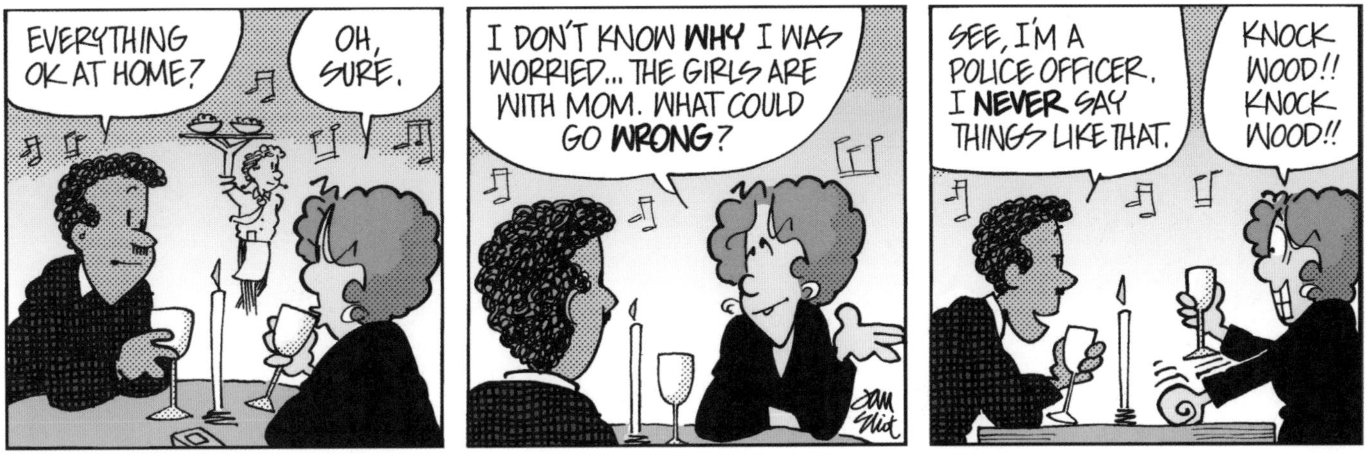
EVERYTHING OK AT HOME?
OH, SURE.
I DON'T KNOW WHY I WAS WORRIED... THE GIRLS ARE WITH MOM. WHAT COULD GO WRONG?
SEE, I'M A POLICE OFFICER. I NEVER SAY THINGS LIKE THAT.
KNOCK WOOD!! KNOCK WOOD!!

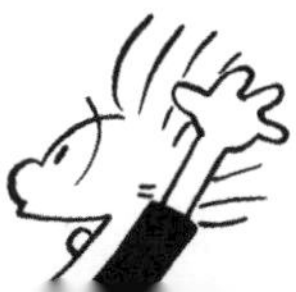

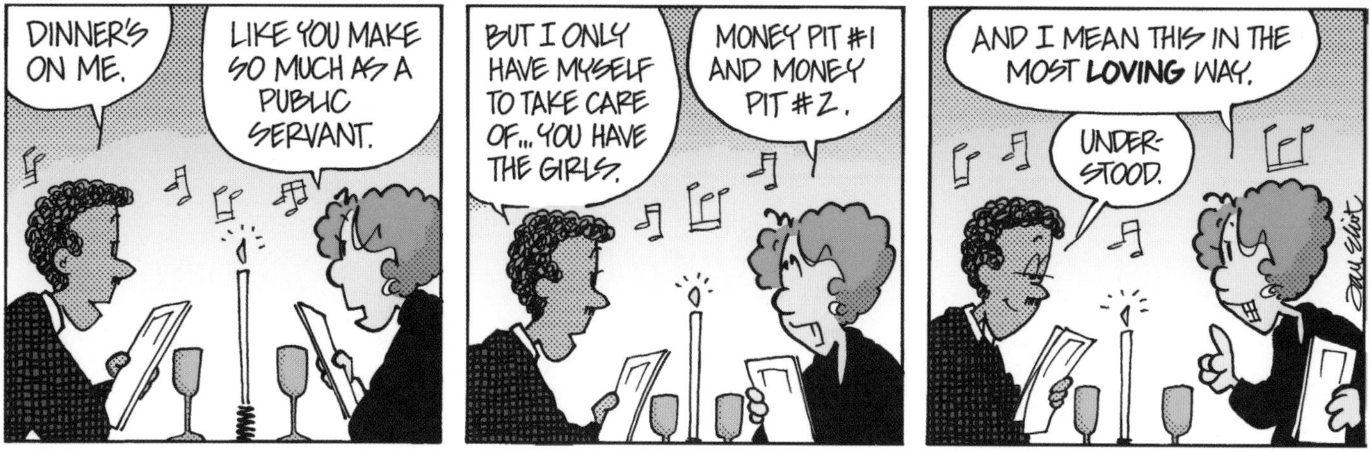
DINNER'S ON ME.
LIKE YOU MAKE SO MUCH AS A PUBLIC SERVANT.
BUT I ONLY HAVE MYSELF TO TAKE CARE OF... YOU HAVE THE GIRLS.
MONEY PIT #1 AND MONEY PIT #2.
AND I MEAN THIS IN THE MOST **LOVING** WAY.
UNDER-STOOD.

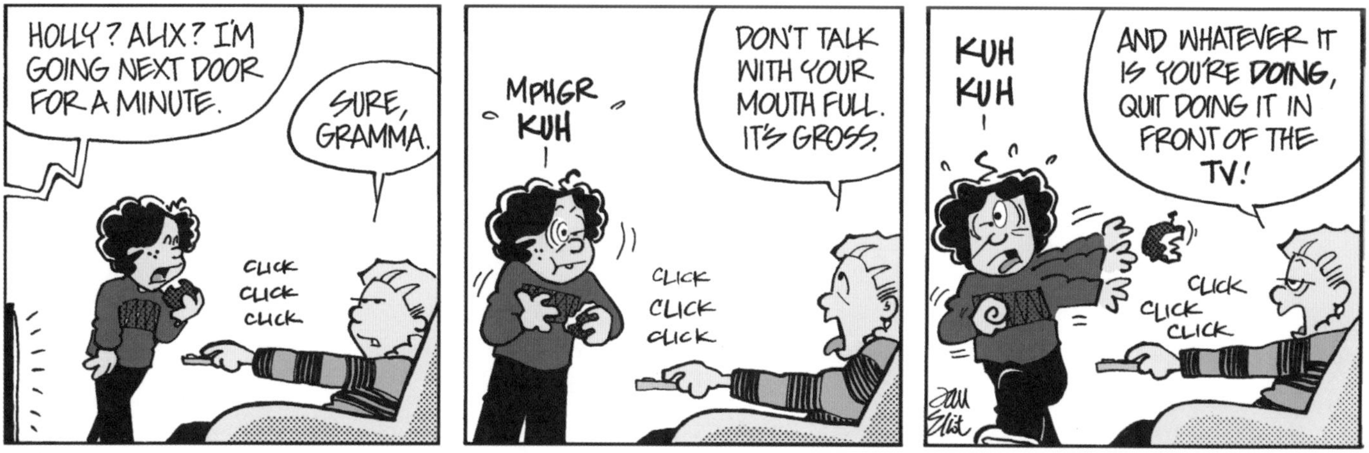
HOLLY? ALIX? I'M GOING NEXT DOOR FOR A MINUTE.
SURE, GRAMMA.
CLICK CLICK CLICK
MPHGR KUH
DON'T TALK WITH YOUR MOUTH FULL. IT'S GROSS.
CLICK CLICK CLICK
KUH KUH
AND WHATEVER IT IS YOU'RE **DOING**, QUIT DOING IT IN FRONT OF THE **TV**!
CLICK CLICK CLICK

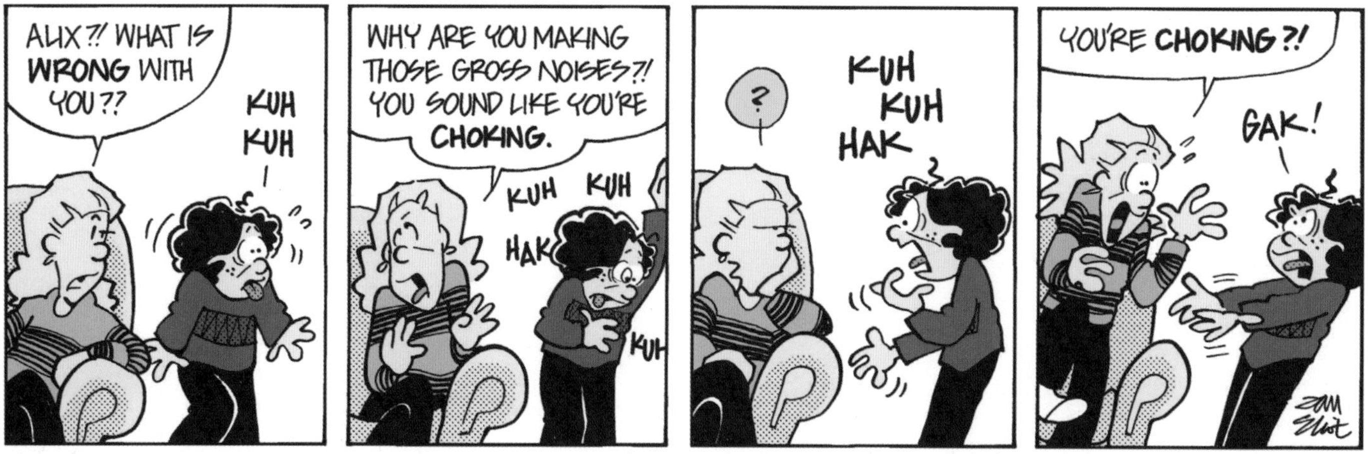
ALIX?! WHAT IS **WRONG** WITH YOU??
KUH KUH
WHY ARE YOU MAKING THOSE GROSS NOISES?! YOU SOUND LIKE YOU'RE **CHOKING**.
KUH KUH HAK KUH
?
KUH KUH HAK
YOU'RE **CHOKING**?!
GAK!

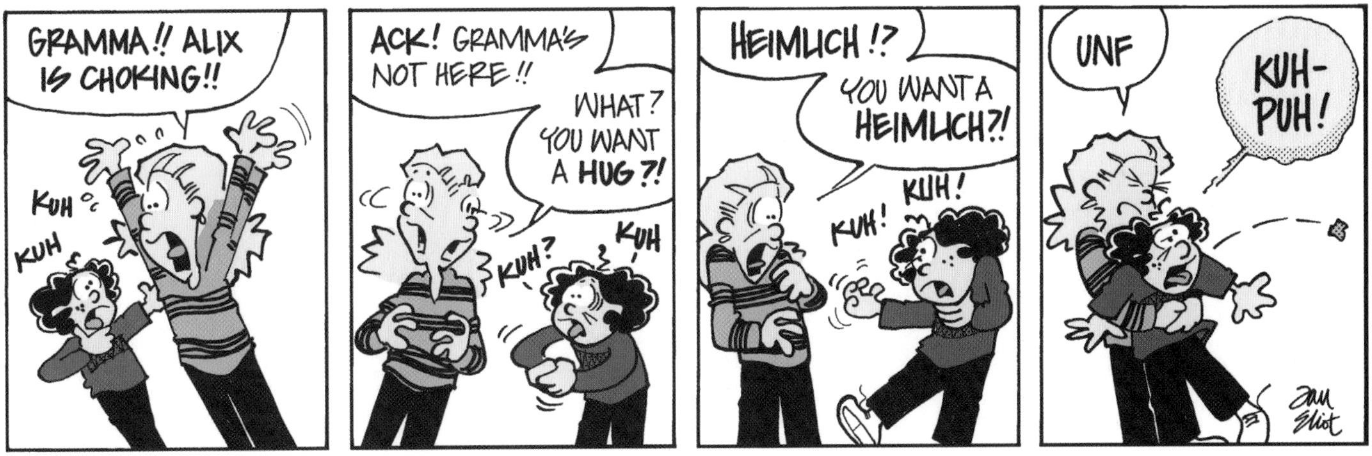
GRAMMA!! ALIX IS CHOKING!!
KUH
KUH
ACK! GRAMMA'S NOT HERE!!
WHAT? YOU WANT A HUG?!
KUH?
KUH
HEIMLICH!?
YOU WANT A HEIMLICH?!
KUH!
KUH!
UNF
KUH-PUH!
Jan Eliot

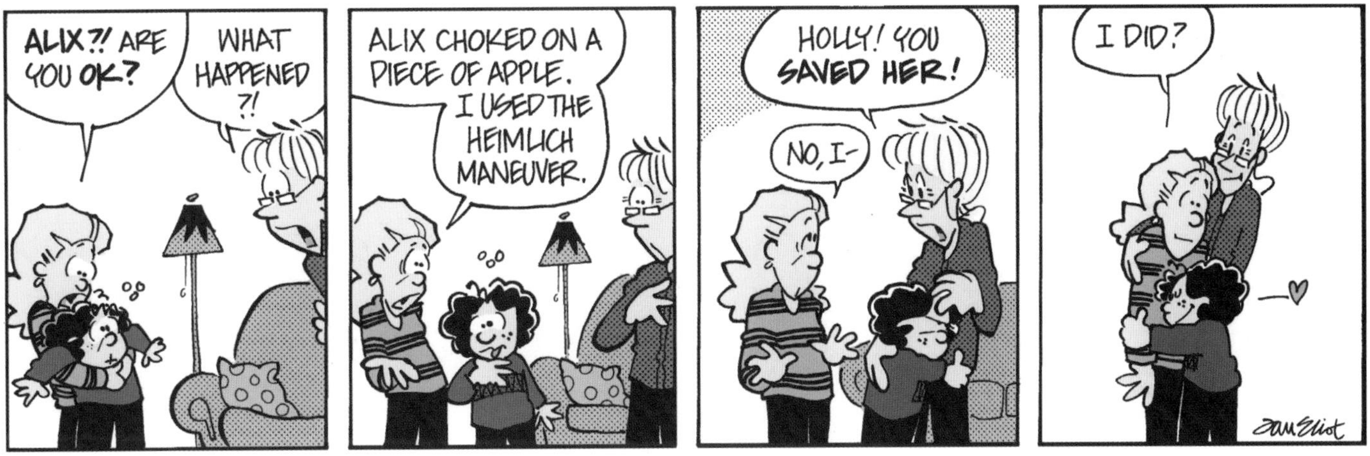
ALIX?! ARE YOU OK?
WHAT HAPPENED?!
ALIX CHOKED ON A PIECE OF APPLE.
I USED THE HEIMLICH MANEUVER.
HOLLY! YOU SAVED HER!
NO, I-
I DID?
Jan Eliot

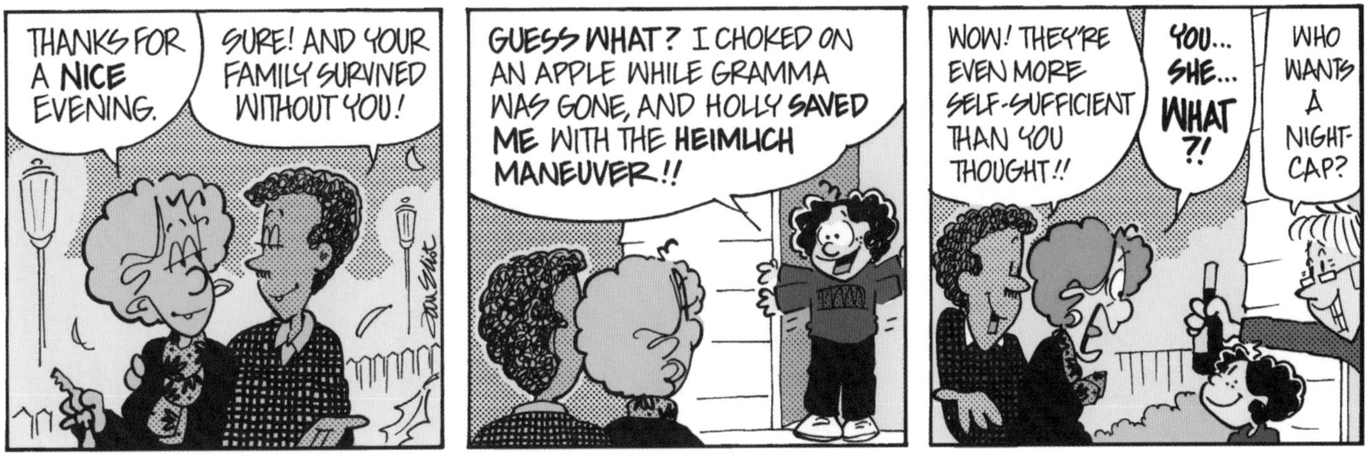
THANKS FOR A NICE EVENING.
SURE! AND YOUR FAMILY SURVIVED WITHOUT YOU!
Jan Eliot
GUESS WHAT? I CHOKED ON AN APPLE WHILE GRAMMA WAS GONE, AND HOLLY SAVED ME WITH THE HEIMLICH MANEUVER!!
WOW! THEY'RE EVEN MORE SELF-SUFFICIENT THAN YOU THOUGHT!!
YOU... SHE... WHAT?!
WHO WANTS A NIGHT-CAP?

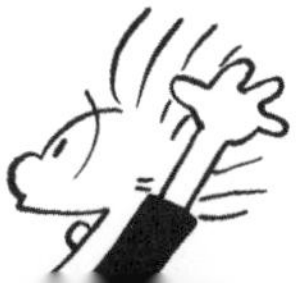

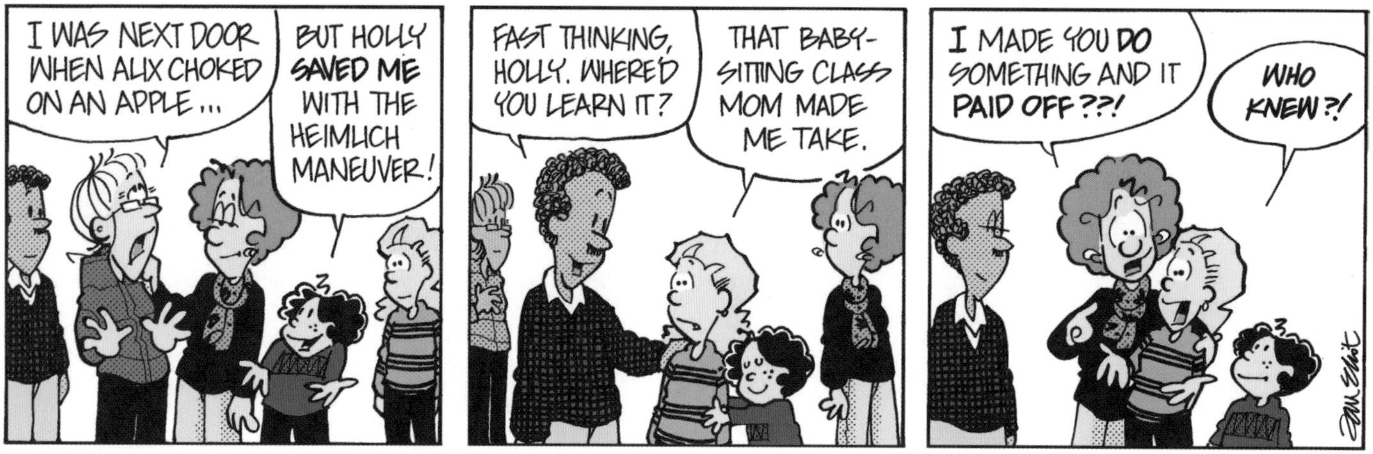
I WAS NEXT DOOR WHEN ALIX CHOKED ON AN APPLE ...
BUT HOLLY SAVED ME WITH THE HEIMLICH MANEUVER!
FAST THINKING, HOLLY. WHERE'D YOU LEARN IT?
THAT BABY-SITTING CLASS MOM MADE ME TAKE.
I MADE YOU DO SOMETHING AND IT PAID OFF??!
WHO KNEW?!

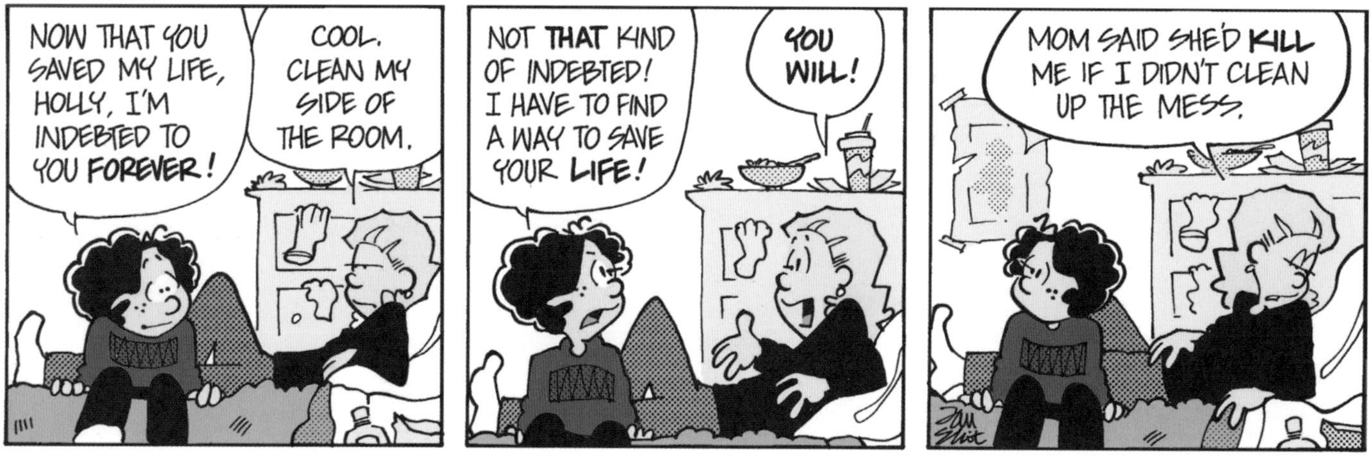
NOW THAT YOU SAVED MY LIFE, HOLLY, I'M INDEBTED TO YOU FOREVER!
COOL. CLEAN MY SIDE OF THE ROOM.
NOT THAT KIND OF INDEBTED! I HAVE TO FIND A WAY TO SAVE YOUR LIFE!
YOU WILL!
MOM SAID SHE'D KILL ME IF I DIDN'T CLEAN UP THE MESS.

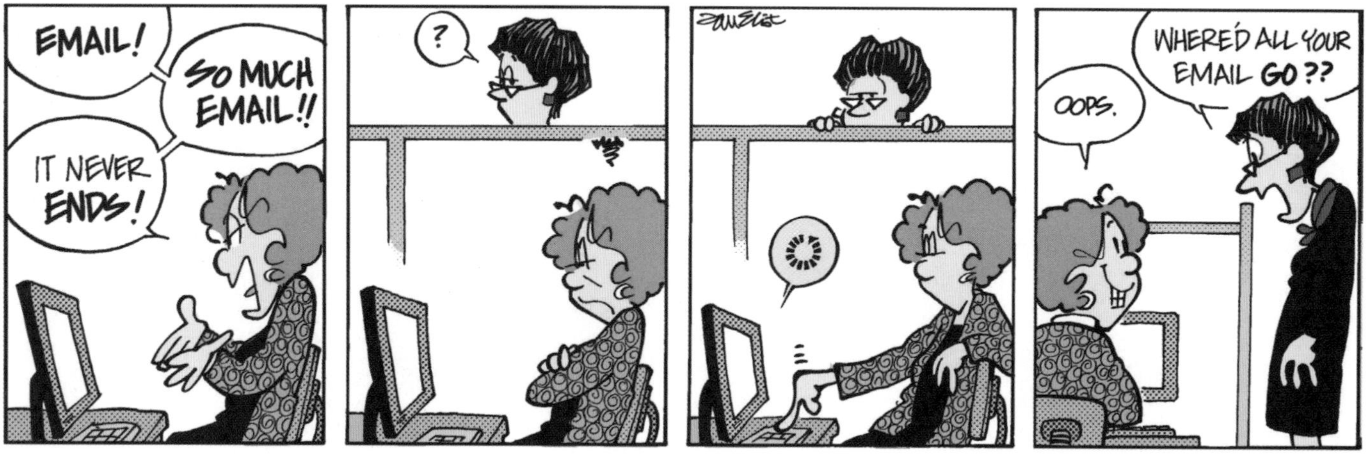
EMAIL!
SO MUCH EMAIL!!
IT NEVER ENDS!
?
OOPS.
WHERE'D ALL YOUR EMAIL GO??

Stone Soup

THAT PROJECT HAS BEEN STARING ME IN THE FACE FOR **WEEKS**...

SOMEHOW I ALWAYS FIND SOMETHING ELSE TO DO.

MAYBE I NEED A **LIST**.

SKRITCH SKRITCH

OOH! "THE TOP 10 THINGS I DO TO PROCRASTINATE!"

TIKKA TIKKA TIKKA

10. **FILE NAILS** (CAN'T THINK WITH RAGGED NAILS)
9. MAKE **COFFEE** (CAFFEINE HELPS ME THINK.)
8. CLEAN CUBICLE (**CLUTTER!**)
7. DUST (ALLERGIES)

TIKKA TIKKA TIKKA   TIKKA   TIKKA

6. CLEAN OUT EMAIL (AGAIN)
5. SURF WEB FOR INFO RELEVANT TO PROJECT

TIKKA TIKKA   TIK TIK-TIK   TIKKA TIKKA

4. CHECK MEDICAL SITES FOR CLUE TO **ELBOW PAIN** (WORK RELATED?)
3. TAKE SHORT **WALK** (CLEAR HEAD)
2. 10-MINUTE **STRETCH BREAK** (FOR BACK)

TIKKA TIKKA TIKKA TIK

AND THE NUMBER **ONE** THING I DO TO **PRO-CRAS-TINATE IS**...

MAKE A **TOP 10 LIST** OF THINGS YOU DO TO PROCRASTINATE...

DO YOU MIND? I'M BUSY.

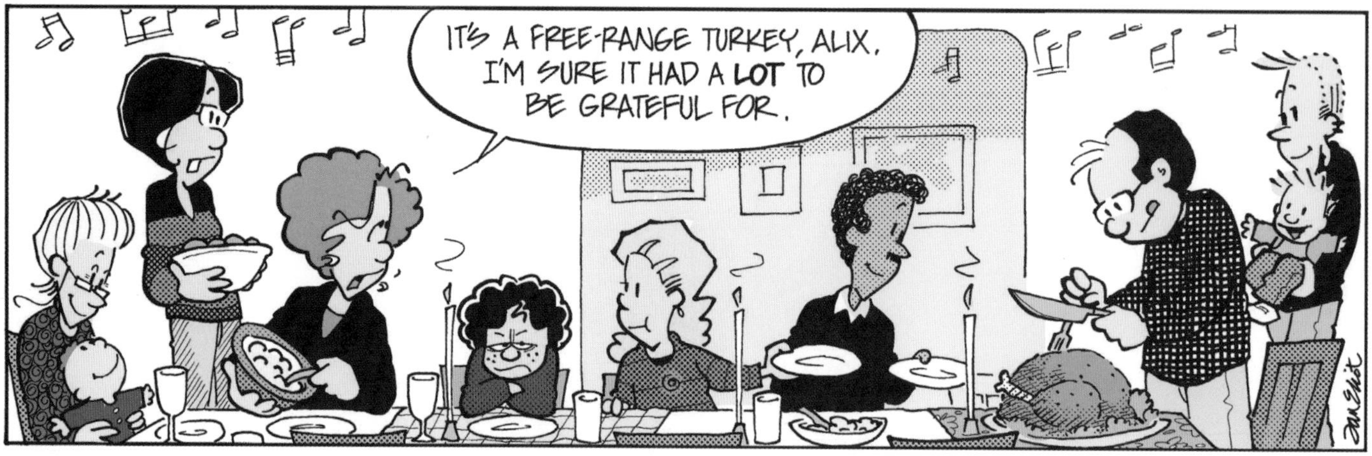
IT'S A FREE-RANGE TURKEY, ALIX. I'M SURE IT HAD A **LOT** TO BE GRATEFUL FOR.

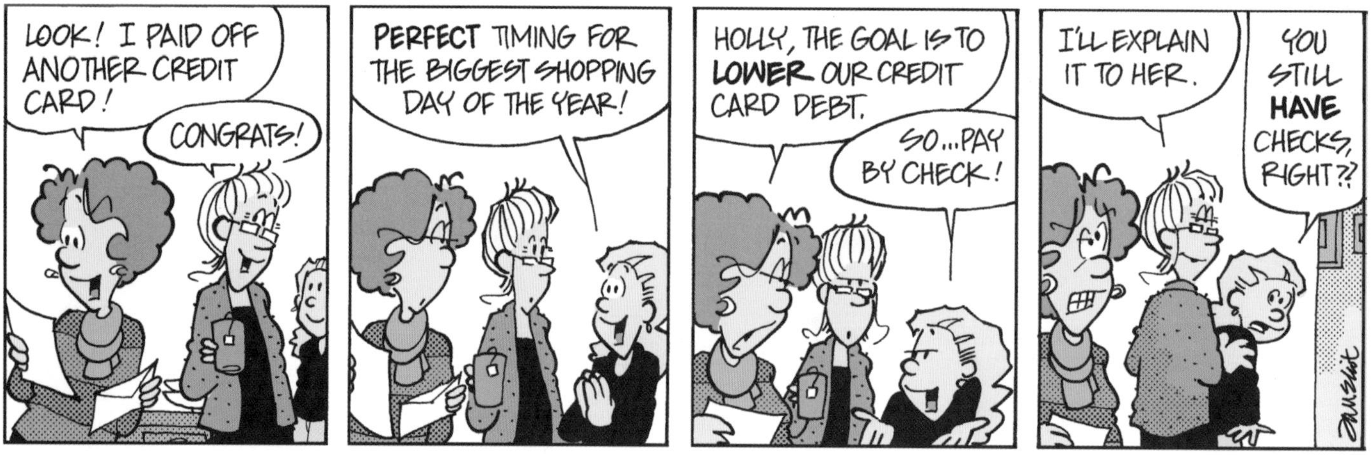
LOOK! I PAID OFF ANOTHER CREDIT CARD!
CONGRATS!
PERFECT TIMING FOR THE BIGGEST SHOPPING DAY OF THE YEAR!
HOLLY, THE GOAL IS TO **LOWER** OUR CREDIT CARD DEBT.
SO...PAY BY CHECK!
I'LL EXPLAIN IT TO HER.
YOU STILL **HAVE** CHECKS, RIGHT??

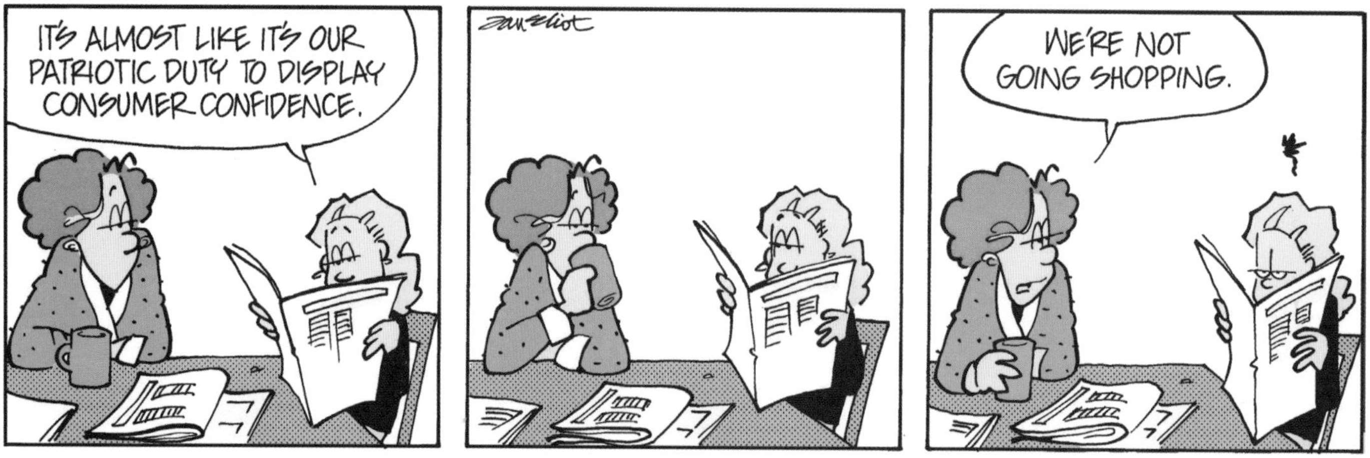
IT'S ALMOST LIKE IT'S OUR PATRIOTIC DUTY TO DISPLAY CONSUMER CONFIDENCE.
WE'RE NOT GOING SHOPPING.

WALLY? I NEED YOUR HELP.

SURE! SHOULD I GET MY TOOLBOX?

NO...NO... I'M CLEANING OUT MY CLOSET AND I CAN'T DECIDE IF I SHOULD KEEP THESE **PANTS**...

THEY'RE **WOOL** ... THE COLOR WORKS WITH ALL MY JACKETS... BUT DO THE PLEATS **DATE THEM?**

MAYBE IF I SHORTENED THEM AND ADDED A CUFF...

OR IS IT **HOPELESS** AND I SHOULD JUST GIVE THEM AWAY...?

THE TOWEL RACK IN THE BATHROOM IS LOOSE.

GREAT! I'LL GET MY TOOLBOX!!

23

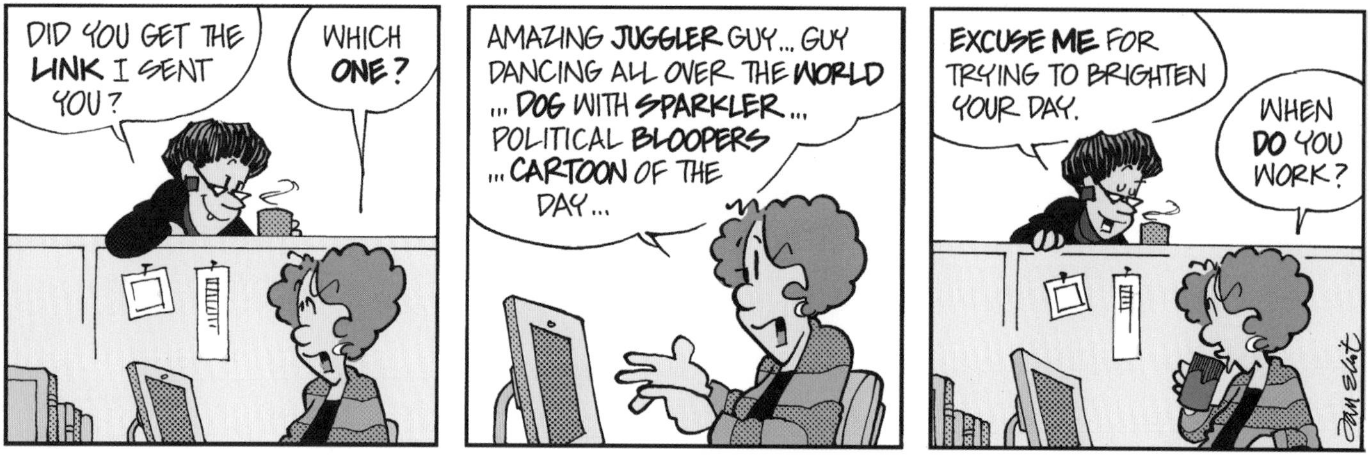
DID YOU GET THE **LINK** I SENT YOU?
WHICH **ONE?**
AMAZING **JUGGLER** GUY... GUY DANCING ALL OVER THE **WORLD** ... **DOG** WITH **SPARKLER**... POLITICAL **BLOOPERS** ...**CARTOON** OF THE DAY...
EXCUSE ME FOR TRYING TO BRIGHTEN YOUR DAY.
WHEN **DO** YOU WORK?

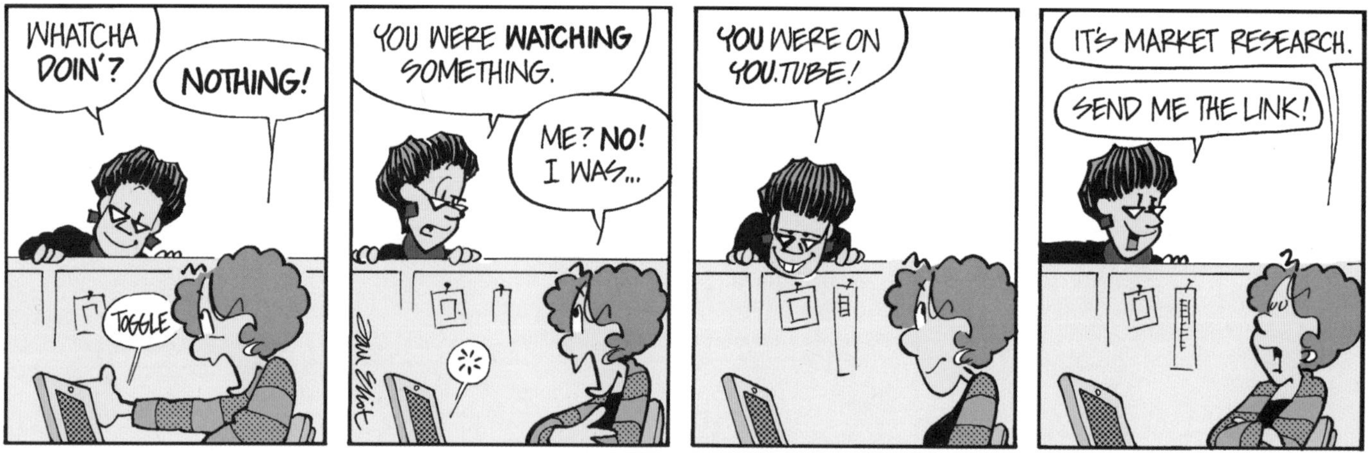
WHATCHA **DOIN'?**
NOTHING!
TOGGLE
YOU WERE **WATCHING** SOMETHING.
ME? **NO!** I WAS...
YOU WERE ON **YOU**.TUBE!
IT'S MARKET RESEARCH.
SEND ME THE LINK!

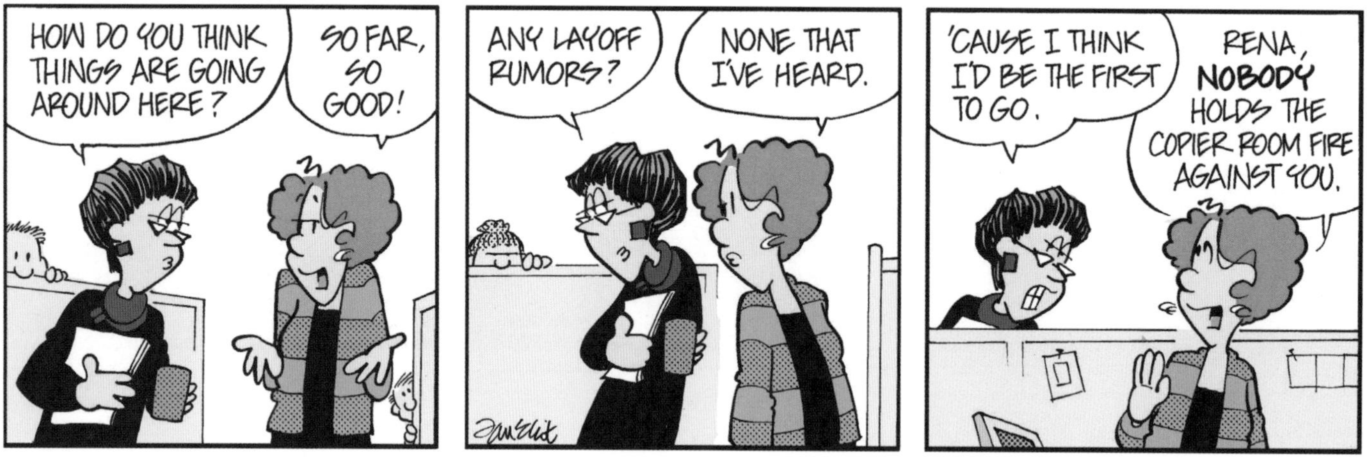
HOW DO YOU THINK THINGS ARE GOING AROUND HERE?
SO FAR, SO GOOD!
ANY LAYOFF RUMORS?
NONE THAT I'VE HEARD.
'CAUSE I THINK I'D BE THE FIRST TO GO.
RENA, **NOBODY** HOLDS THE COPIER ROOM FIRE AGAINST YOU.

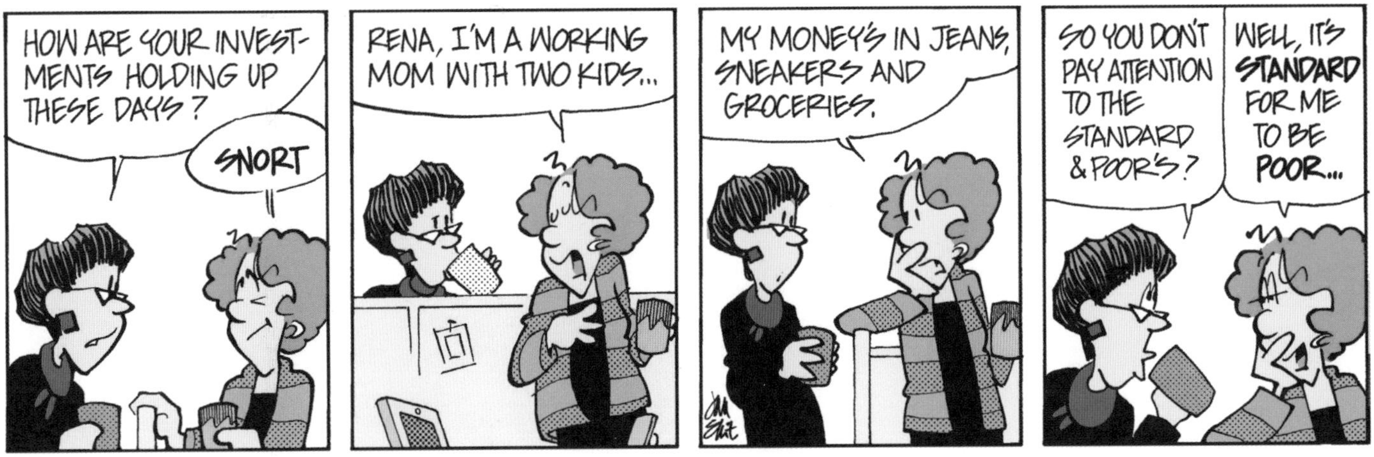
HOW ARE YOUR INVEST-MENTS HOLDING UP THESE DAYS?
SNORT
RENA, I'M A WORKING MOM WITH TWO KIDS...
MY MONEY'S IN JEANS, SNEAKERS AND GROCERIES.
SO YOU DON'T PAY ATTENTION TO THE STANDARD & POOR'S?
WELL, IT'S **STANDARD** FOR ME TO BE **POOR...**

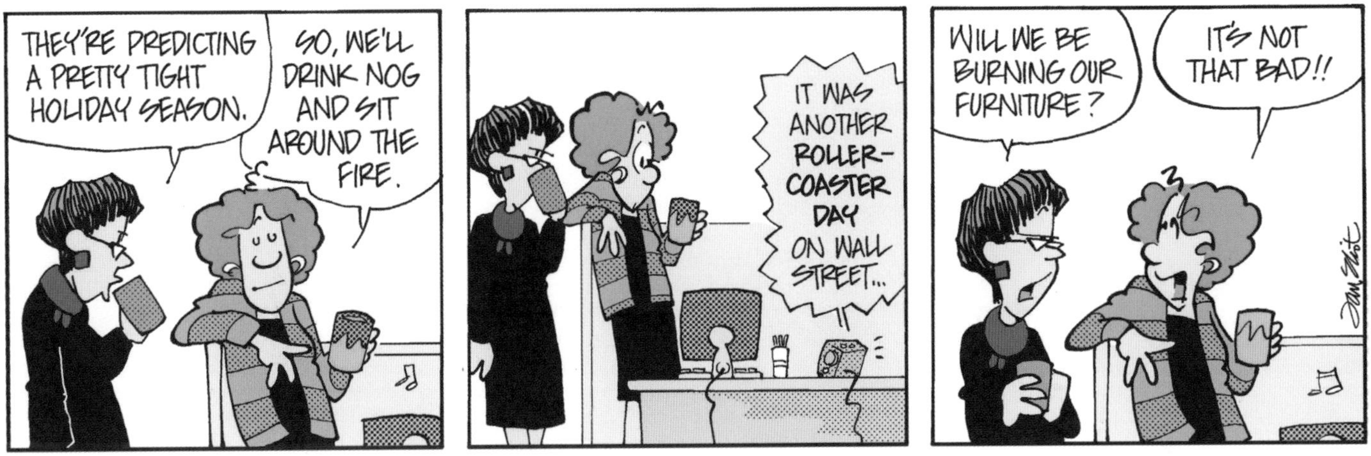
THEY'RE PREDICTING A PRETTY TIGHT HOLIDAY SEASON.
SO, WE'LL DRINK NOG AND SIT AROUND THE FIRE.
IT WAS ANOTHER **ROLLER-COASTER DAY** ON WALL STREET...
WILL WE BE BURNING OUR FURNITURE?
IT'S NOT THAT BAD!!

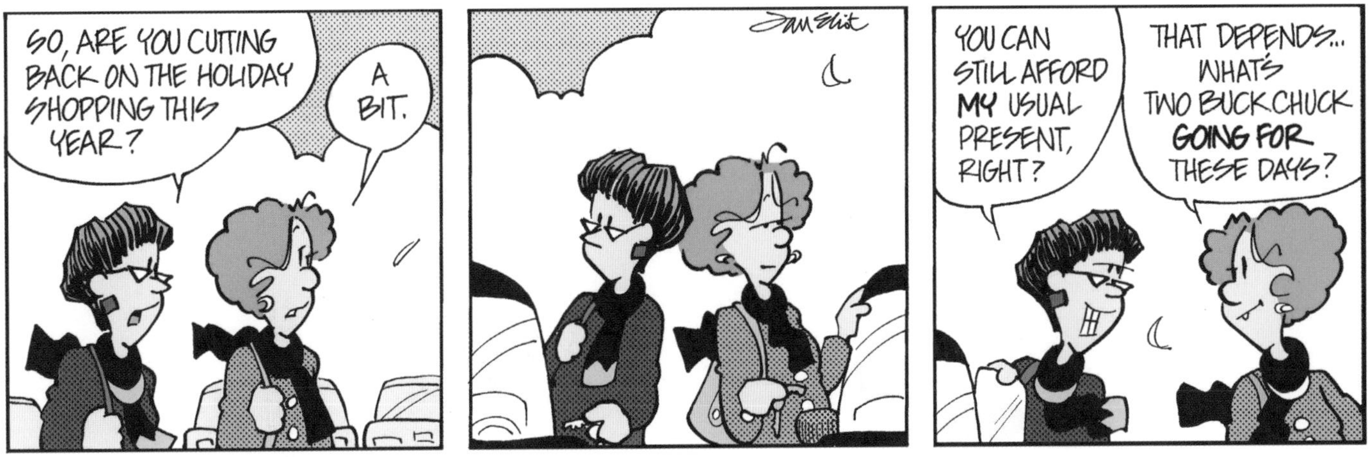
SO, ARE YOU CUTTING BACK ON THE HOLIDAY SHOPPING THIS YEAR?
A BIT.
YOU CAN STILL AFFORD **MY** USUAL PRESENT, RIGHT?
THAT DEPENDS... WHAT'S TWO BUCK CHUCK **GOING FOR** THESE DAYS?

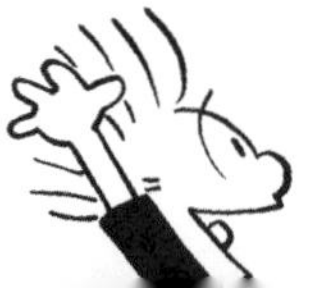

Stone Soup

WHAT'S... UP?
VALERIE, WE'RE ALL HERE BECAUSE WE LOVE YOU.
YOU HAVE A PROBLEM.
BUT... IT MAKES ME FEEL GOOD.
WE UNDERSTAND, BUT... YOU DON'T SEEM TO BE ABLE TO SET LIMITS.
BEFORE WORK...
AFTER WORK...
AT WORK...
LATE AT NIGHT...
HOURS OF YOUR LIFE YOU CAN'T GET BACK!
IT'S TIME TO FACE IT...SET AN EXAMPLE FOR YOUR CHILDREN.
OK.
SNIFF
MY NAME IS VAL, AND I'M ADDICTED TO YOUTUBE.
I THINK I MIGHT BE AN ENABLER.

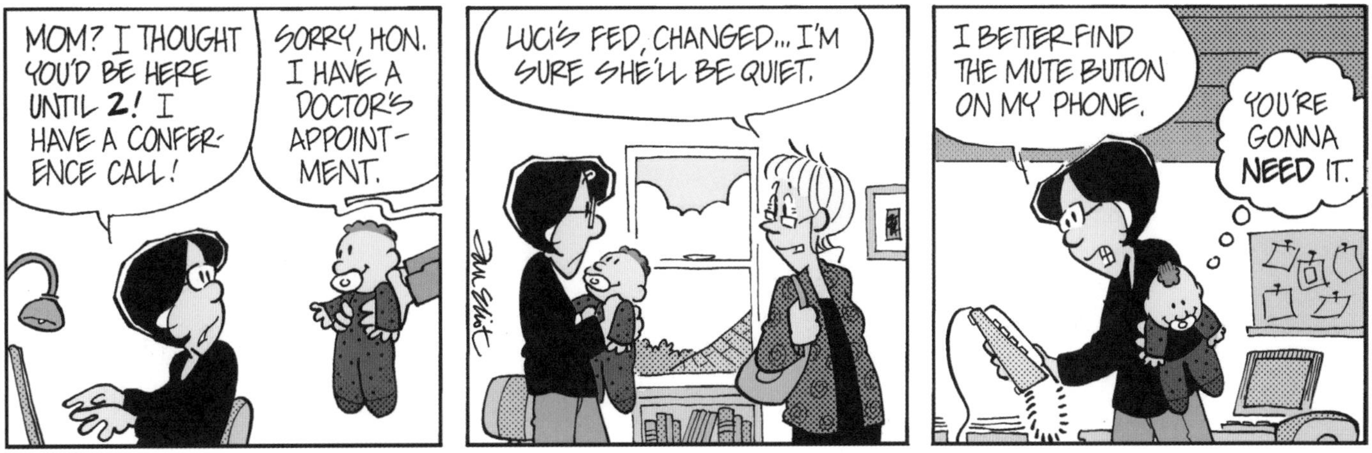
MOM? I THOUGHT YOU'D BE HERE UNTIL 2! I HAVE A CONFERENCE CALL!
SORRY, HON. I HAVE A DOCTOR'S APPOINTMENT.
LUCI'S FED, CHANGED... I'M SURE SHE'LL BE QUIET.
I BETTER FIND THE MUTE BUTTON ON MY PHONE.
YOU'RE GONNA NEED IT.

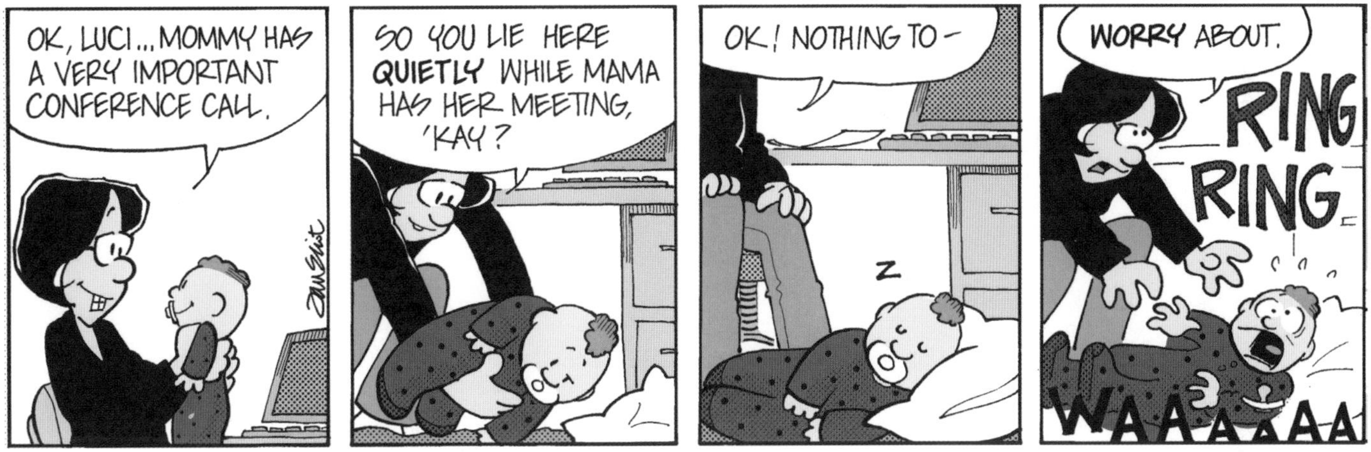
OK, LUCI... MOMMY HAS A VERY IMPORTANT CONFERENCE CALL.
SO YOU LIE HERE QUIETLY WHILE MAMA HAS HER MEETING, 'KAY?
OK! NOTHING TO—
Z
WORRY ABOUT.
RING
RING
WAAAAAA

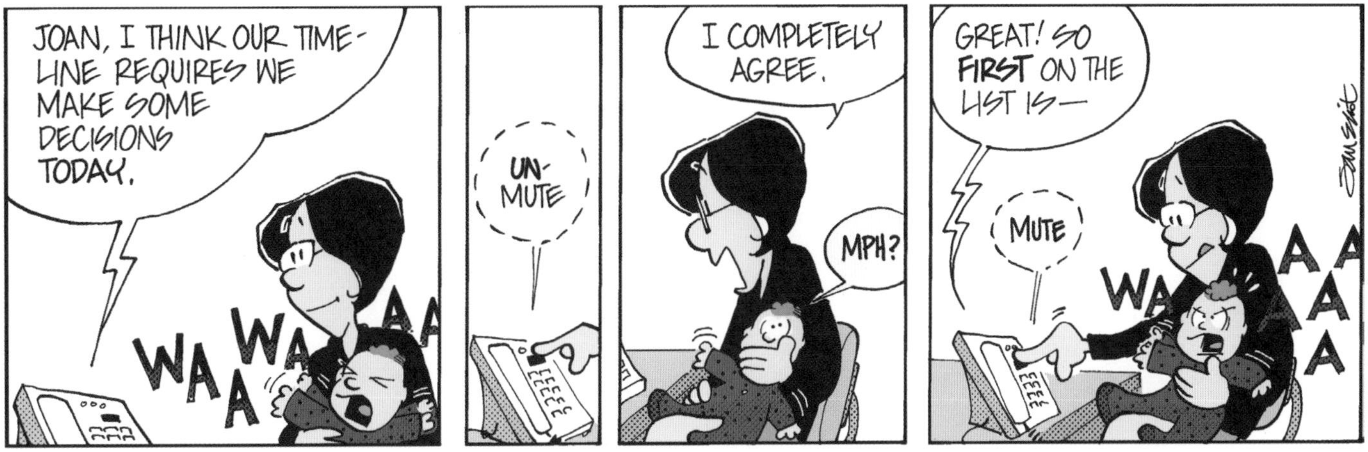
JOAN, I THINK OUR TIMELINE REQUIRES WE MAKE SOME DECISIONS TODAY.
WA
WA
A
WA
AA
UN-MUTE
I COMPLETELY AGREE.
MPH?
GREAT! SO FIRST ON THE LIST IS—
MUTE
WA
AA
AA
A

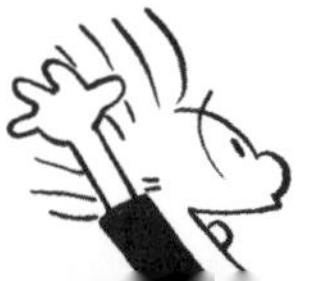

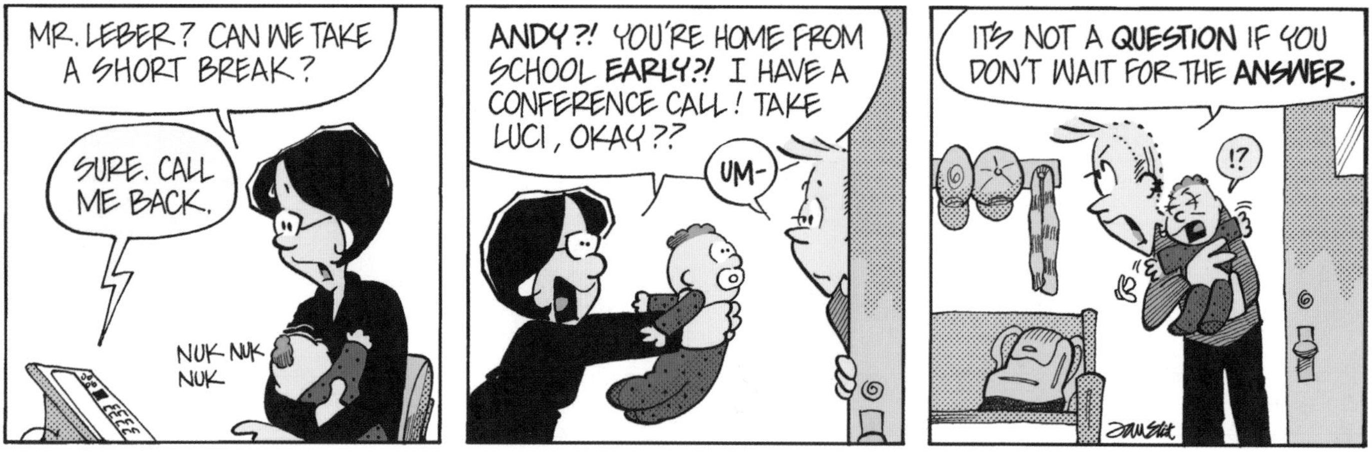
MR. LEBER? CAN WE TAKE A SHORT BREAK?
SURE. CALL ME BACK.
NUK NUK NUK
ANDY?! YOU'RE HOME FROM SCHOOL EARLY?! I HAVE A CONFERENCE CALL! TAKE LUCI, OKAY??
UM-
IT'S NOT A QUESTION IF YOU DON'T WAIT FOR THE ANSWER.
!?

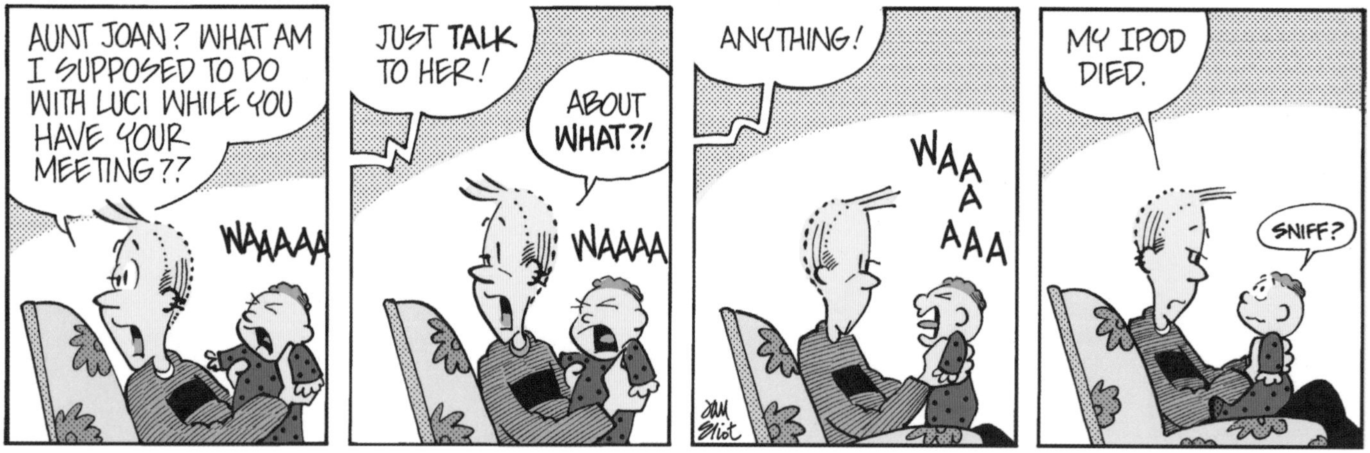
AUNT JOAN? WHAT AM I SUPPOSED TO DO WITH LUCI WHILE YOU HAVE YOUR MEETING??
WAAAAA
JUST TALK TO HER!
ABOUT WHAT?!
WAAAA
ANYTHING!
WAAAAAA
MY IPOD DIED.
SNIFF?

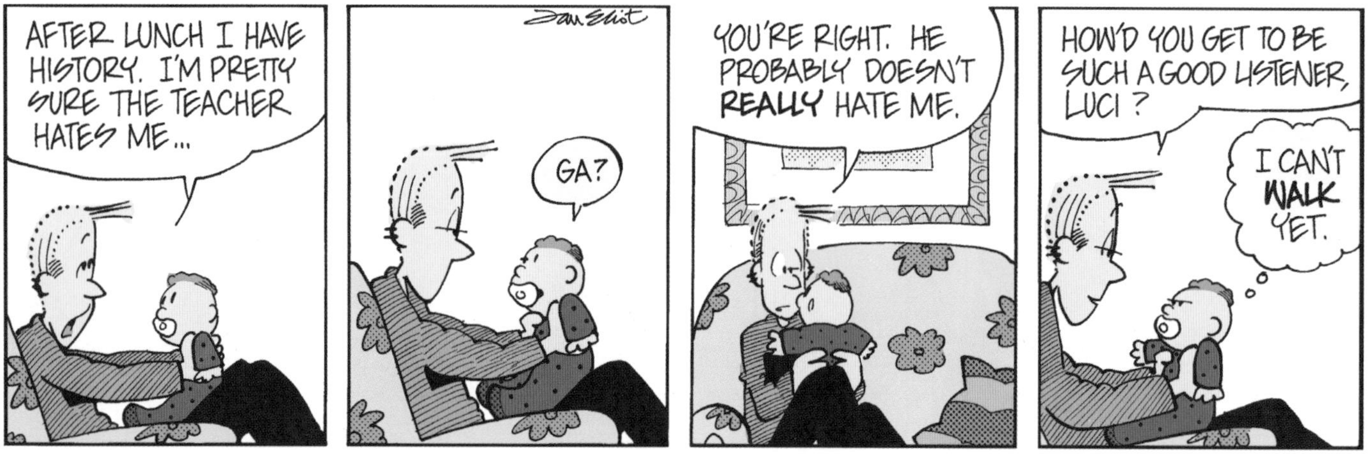
AFTER LUNCH I HAVE HISTORY. I'M PRETTY SURE THE TEACHER HATES ME...
GA?
YOU'RE RIGHT. HE PROBABLY DOESN'T REALLY HATE ME.
HOW'D YOU GET TO BE SUCH A GOOD LISTENER, LUCI?
I CAN'T WALK YET.

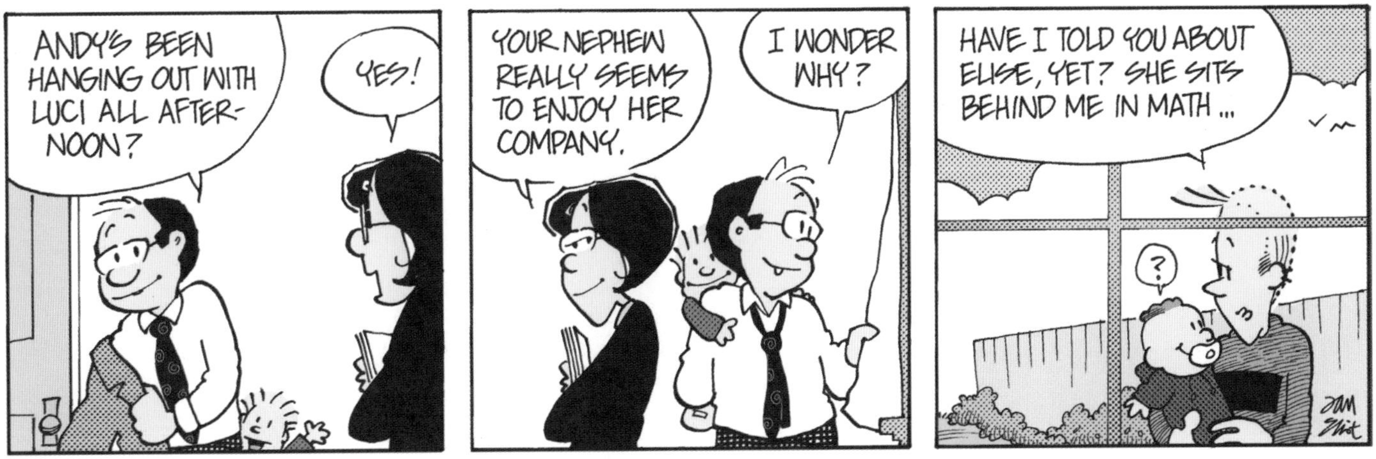
ANDY'S BEEN HANGING OUT WITH LUCI ALL AFTER-NOON?
YES!
YOUR NEPHEW REALLY SEEMS TO ENJOY HER COMPANY.
I WONDER WHY?
HAVE I TOLD YOU ABOUT ELISE, YET? SHE SITS BEHIND ME IN MATH ...
?

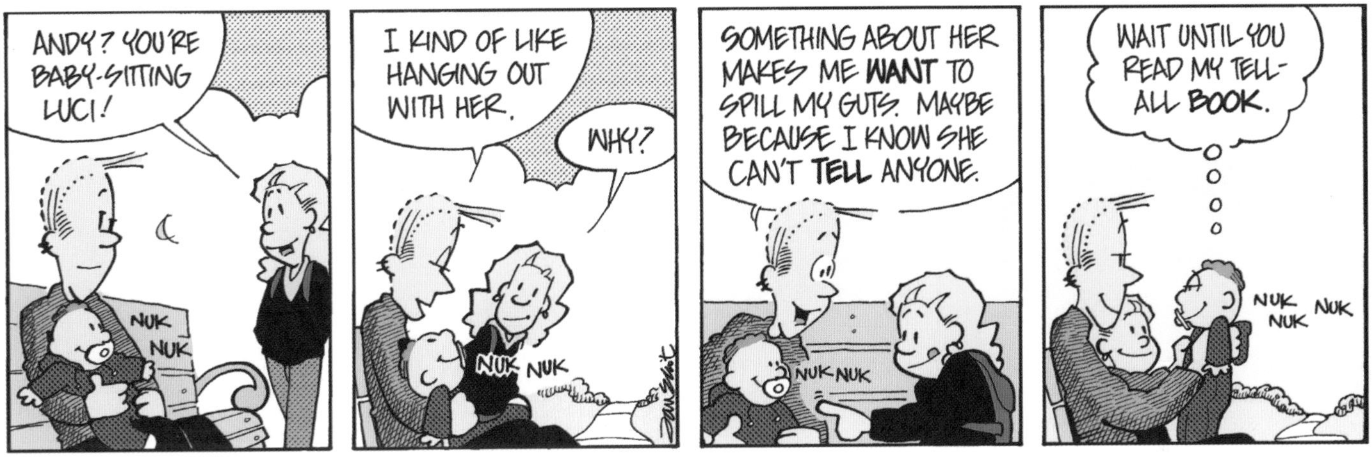
ANDY? YOU'RE BABY-SITTING LUCI!
NUK NUK
I KIND OF LIKE HANGING OUT WITH HER.
WHY?
NUK NUK
SOMETHING ABOUT HER MAKES ME **WANT** TO SPILL MY GUTS. MAYBE BECAUSE I KNOW SHE CAN'T **TELL** ANYONE.
NUK NUK
WAIT UNTIL YOU READ MY TELL-ALL **BOOK**.
NUK NUK NUK

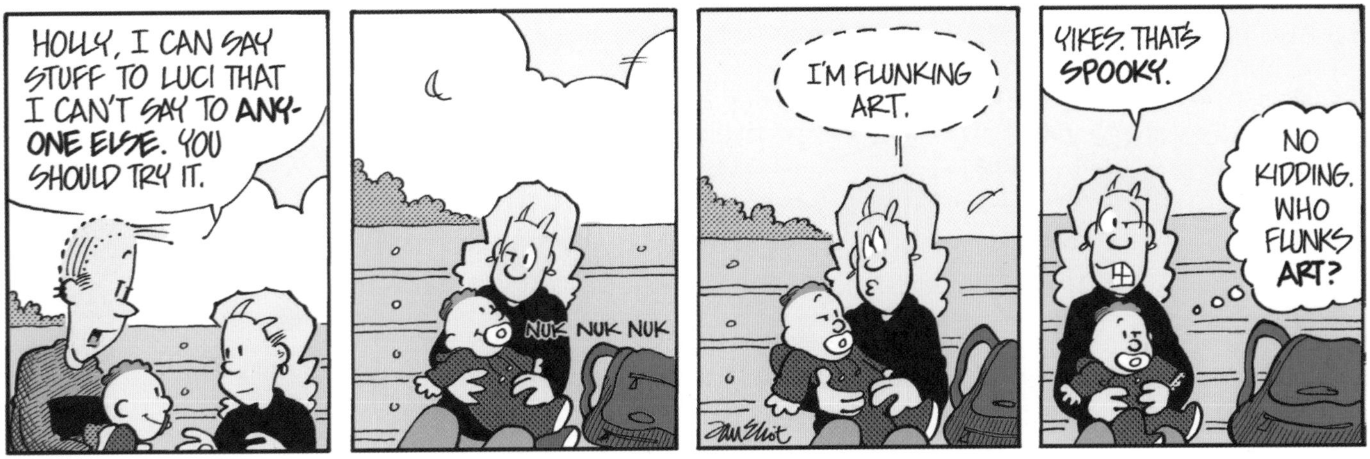
HOLLY, I CAN SAY STUFF TO LUCI THAT I CAN'T SAY TO **ANY-ONE ELSE**. YOU SHOULD TRY IT.
NUK NUK NUK
I'M FLUNKING ART.
YIKES. THAT'S **SPOOKY**.
NO KIDDING. WHO FLUNKS **ART**?

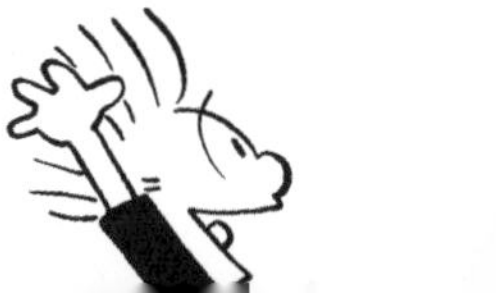

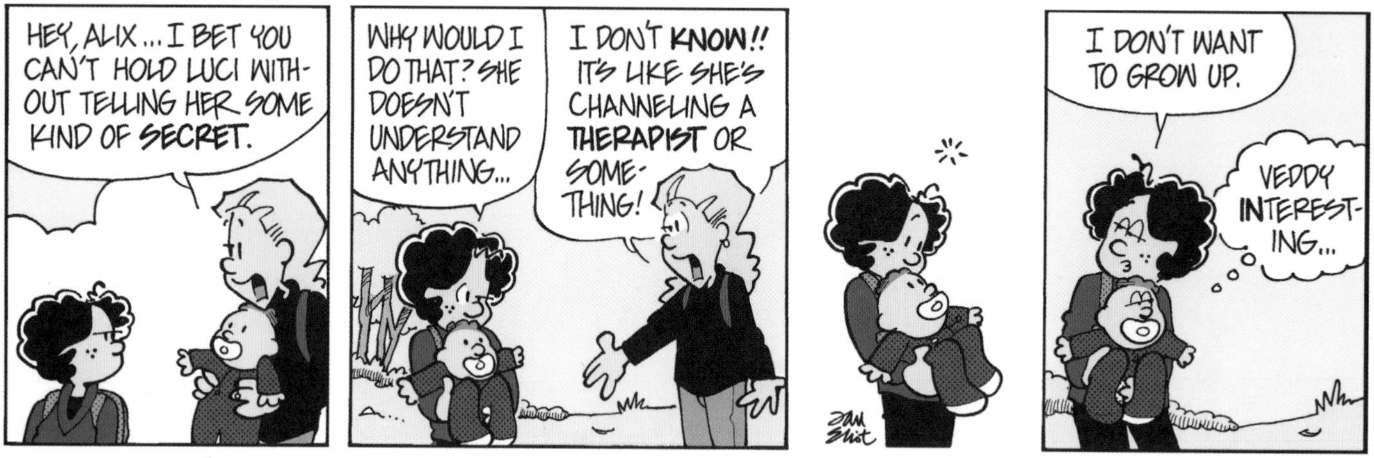
HEY, ALIX... I BET YOU CAN'T HOLD LUCI WITHOUT TELLING HER SOME KIND OF SECRET.
WHY WOULD I DO THAT? SHE DOESN'T UNDERSTAND ANYTHING...
I DON'T KNOW!! IT'S LIKE SHE'S CHANNELING A THERAPIST OR SOMETHING!
I DON'T WANT TO GROW UP.
VEDDY INTERESTING...

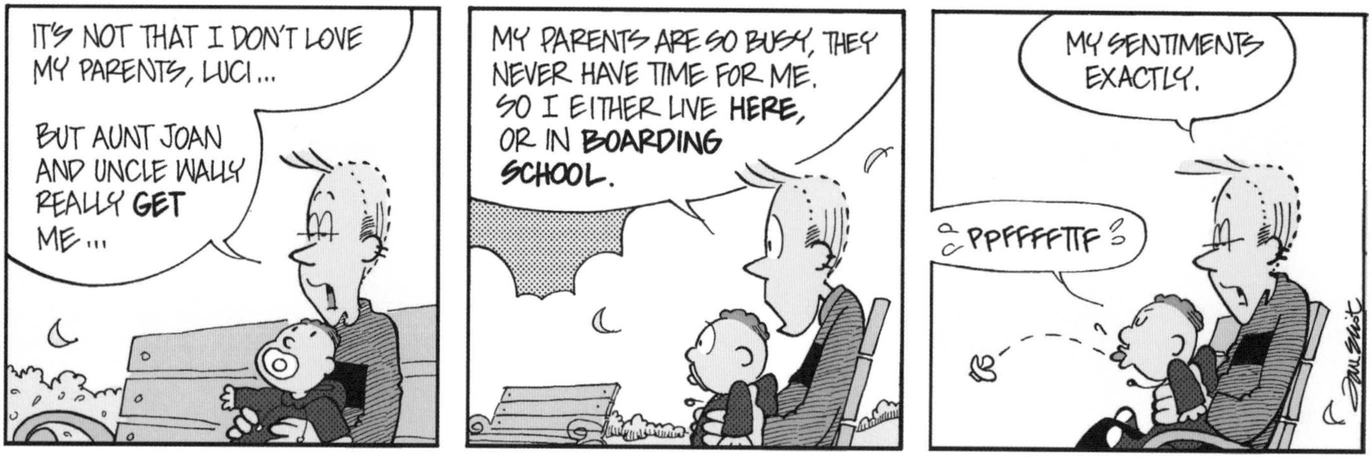
IT'S NOT THAT I DON'T LOVE MY PARENTS, LUCI...
BUT AUNT JOAN AND UNCLE WALLY REALLY GET ME...
MY PARENTS ARE SO BUSY, THEY NEVER HAVE TIME FOR ME. SO I EITHER LIVE HERE, OR IN BOARDING SCHOOL.
MY SENTIMENTS EXACTLY.
PPFFFFTTF

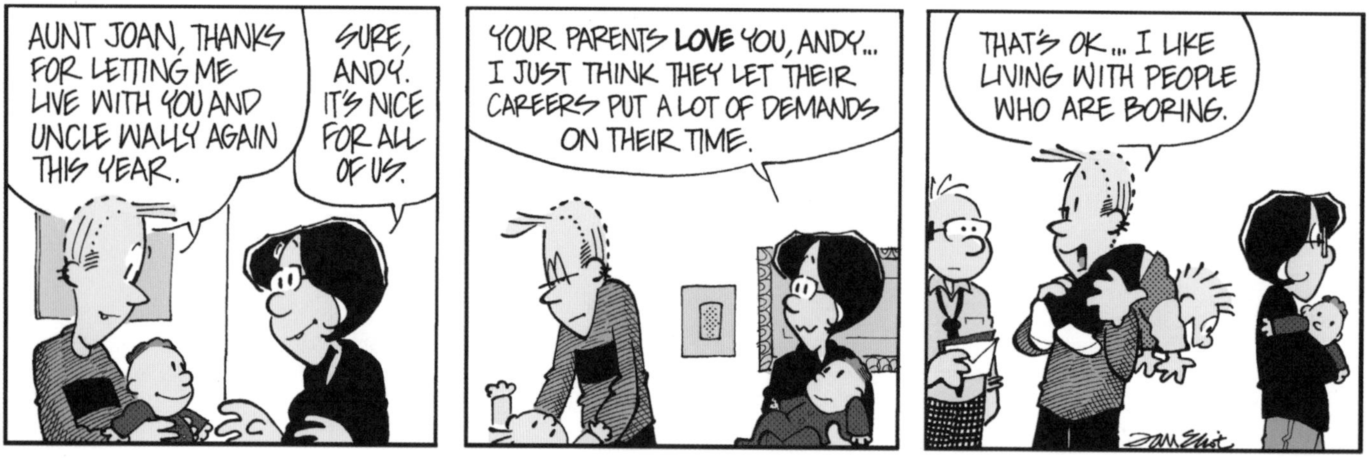
AUNT JOAN, THANKS FOR LETTING ME LIVE WITH YOU AND UNCLE WALLY AGAIN THIS YEAR.
SURE, ANDY. IT'S NICE FOR ALL OF US.
YOUR PARENTS LOVE YOU, ANDY... I JUST THINK THEY LET THEIR CAREERS PUT A LOT OF DEMANDS ON THEIR TIME.
THAT'S OK... I LIKE LIVING WITH PEOPLE WHO ARE BORING.

Stone Soup

OOF!
GIGGLE GIGGLE
GIGGLE GIGGLE
DA?
DA?!
ARR
SHREEEEEK
RRA!
WHAT ARE THEY **DOING**?
GETTING MAX READY FOR BED.

Stone Soup

SNIFF?
SNIFF?
SNIFF?
SNIFF?
SNIFF?
SNIFF ?
SNIFF?
SNIFF
SNIFF
SNIFF
SKOOTCH
CLICK
SNIFF ?
SNIFF
SNIFF
SNIFF
SNIFF
HERE!
WHERE?
SOMEBODY MADE GINGERBREAD COOKIES RIGHT... HERE...
ABOUT...
90 MINUTES AGO!
QUIT SNOOPING!
OOH! AND THERE WAS ICING!!

COOKIE?

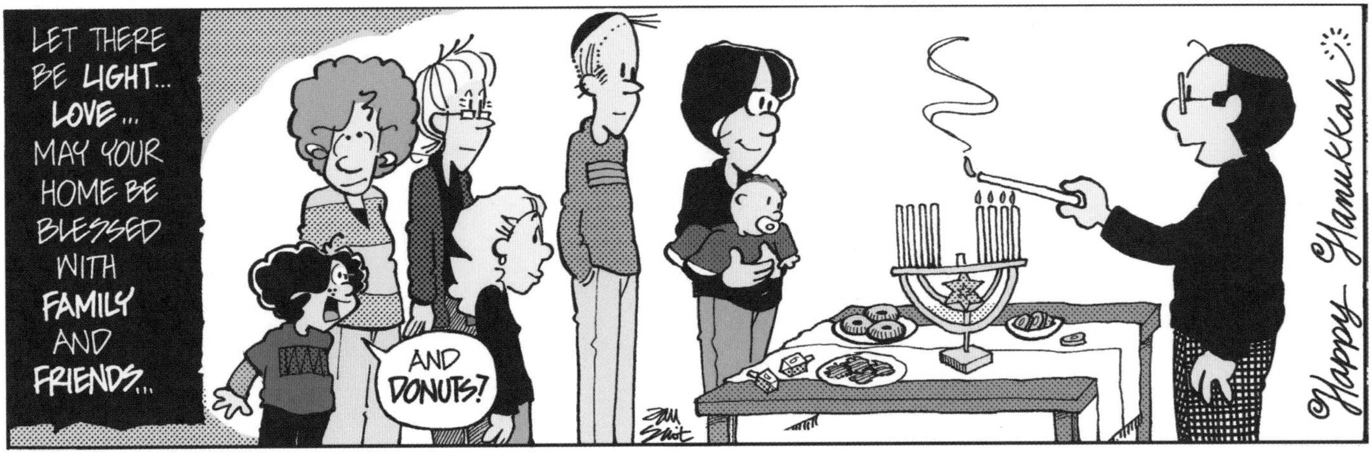
LET THERE BE **LIGHT**... **LOVE**... MAY YOUR HOME BE BLESSED WITH **FAMILY** AND **FRIENDS**...
AND **DONUTS**?
Happy Hanukkah

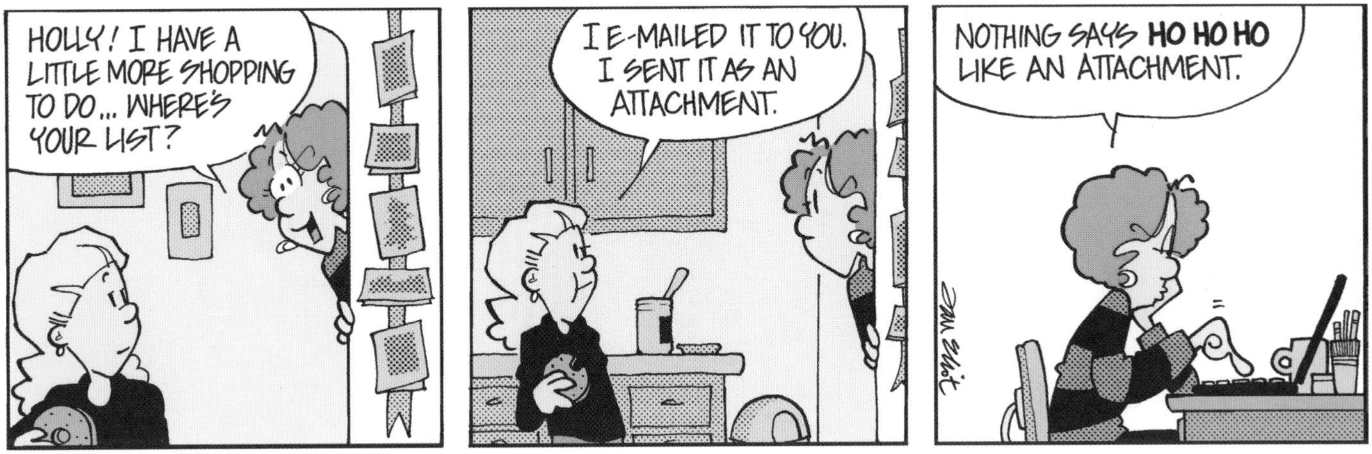
HOLLY! I HAVE A LITTLE MORE SHOPPING TO DO... WHERE'S YOUR LIST?
I E-MAILED IT TO YOU. I SENT IT AS AN ATTACHMENT.
NOTHING SAYS **HO HO HO** LIKE AN ATTACHMENT.

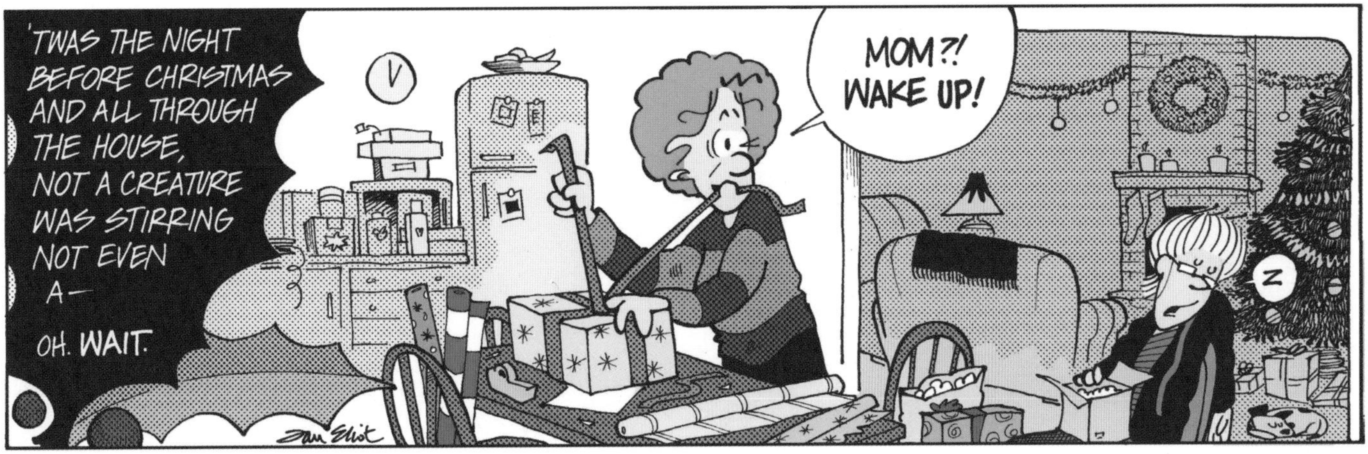
'TWAS THE NIGHT BEFORE CHRISTMAS AND ALL THROUGH THE HOUSE, NOT A CREATURE WAS STIRRING NOT EVEN A—
OH. **WAIT**.
MOM?! **WAKE UP!**
Z

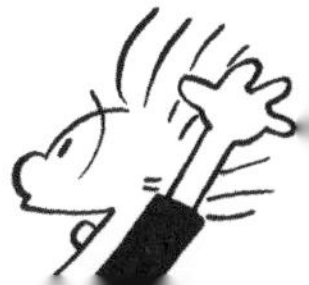

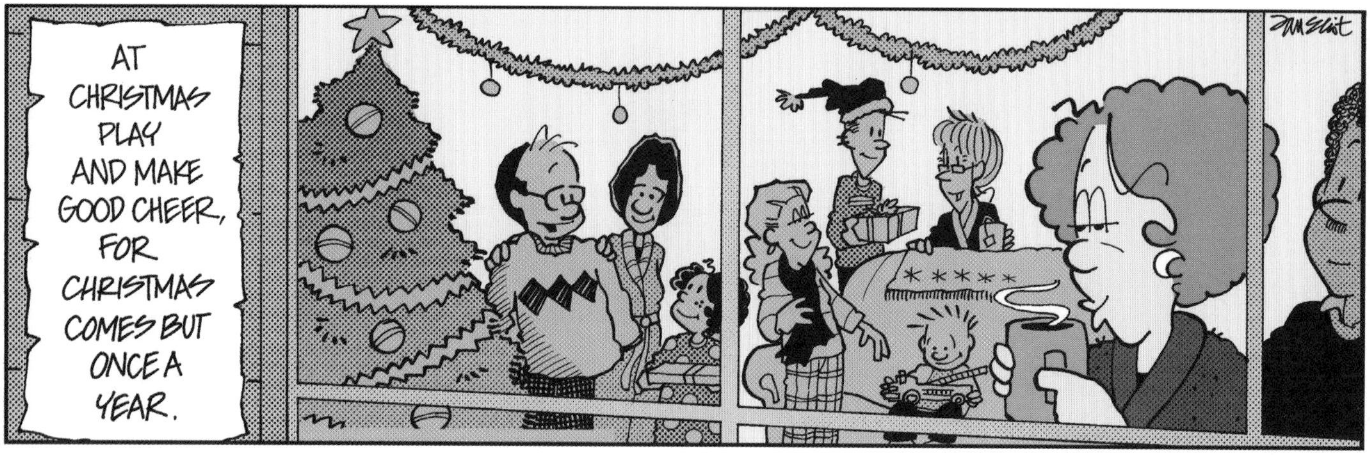
AT CHRISTMAS PLAY AND MAKE GOOD CHEER, FOR CHRISTMAS COMES BUT ONCE A YEAR.

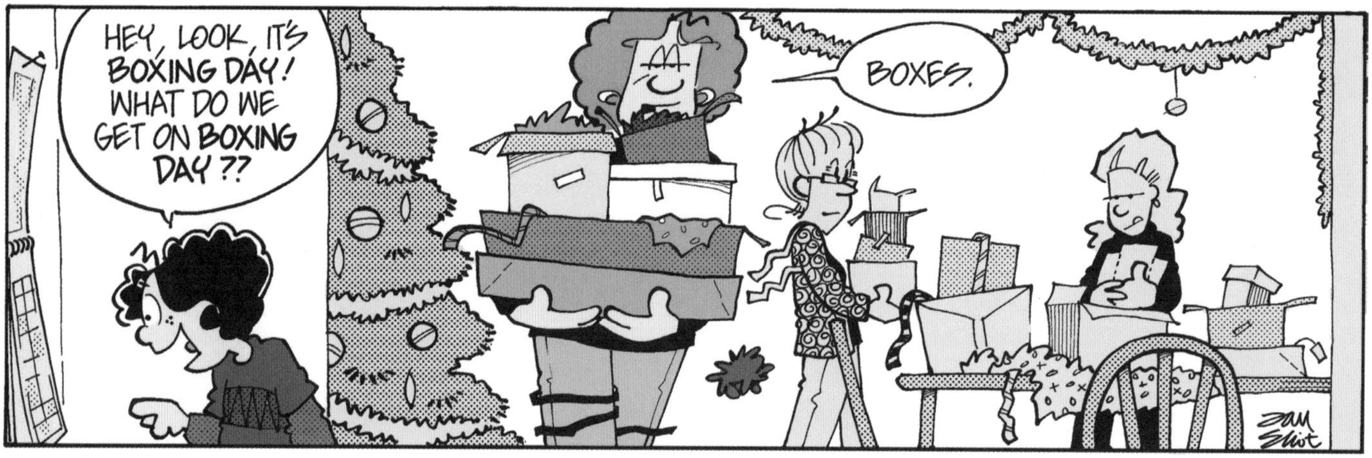
HEY, LOOK, IT'S BOXING DAY! WHAT DO WE GET ON BOXING DAY??
BOXES.

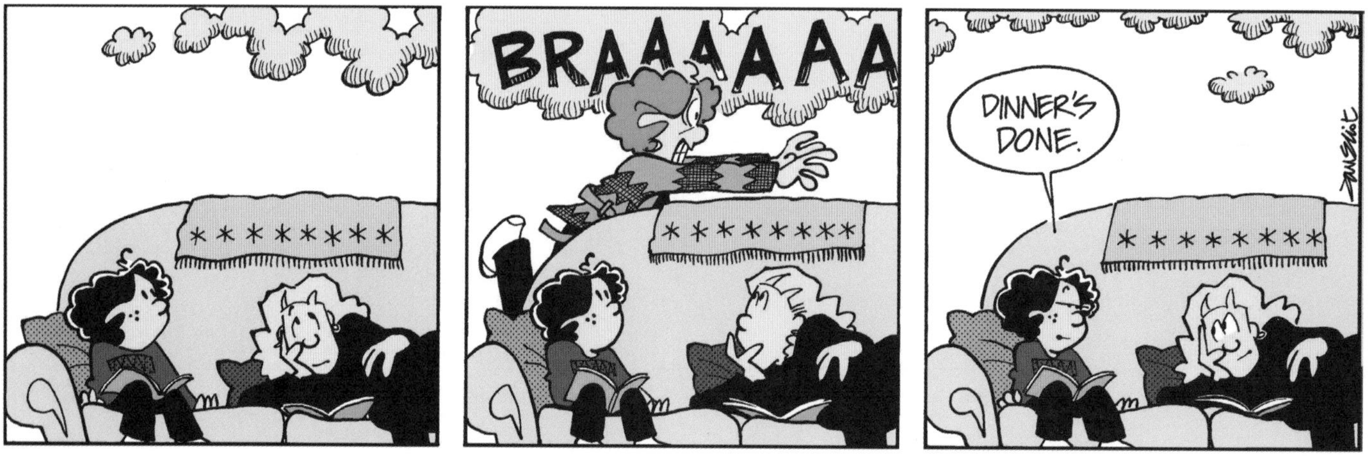
BRAAAAAA
DINNER'S DONE.

Stone Soup

ALL YOU GOT FOR HANUKKAH AND CHRISTMAS WERE **BOOKS**, UNCLE WALLY...

ISN'T IT GREAT?!

WHY DO YOU LIKE TO READ SO MUCH?

I LIKE ESCAPING INTO OTHER WORLDS...

THAT'S WHY I PLAY **VIDEO GAMES**.

MAYBE WE SHOULD TRADE.

UM...

FLIP FLIP

BIP BIP

FLIP

BIP

HEY, GUYS? IT'S LATE.

HMM?

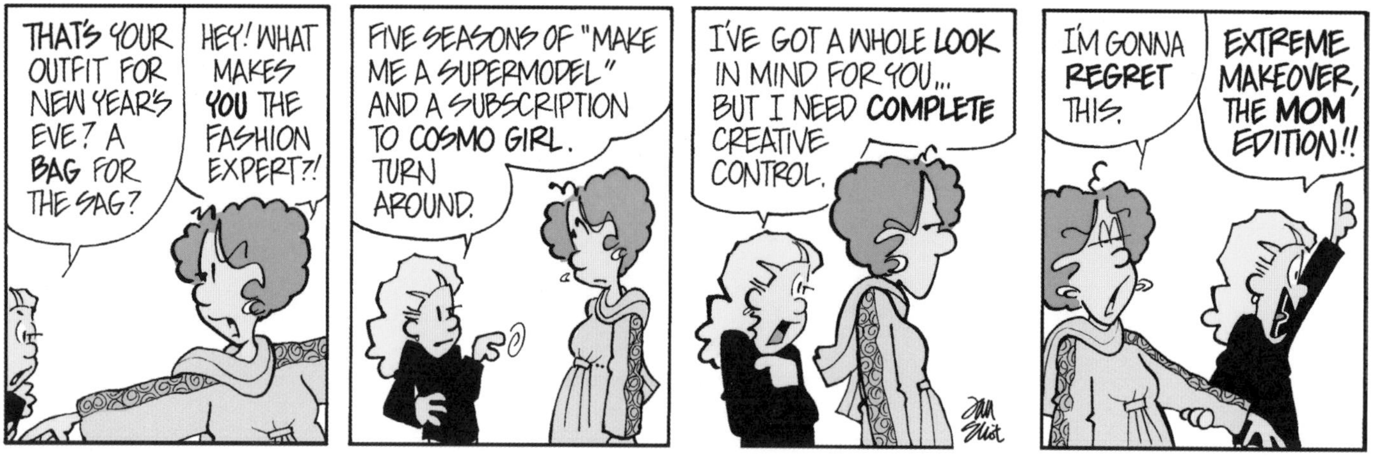
THAT'S YOUR OUTFIT FOR NEW YEAR'S EVE? A **BAG** FOR THE SAG?
HEY! WHAT MAKES **YOU** THE FASHION EXPERT?!
FIVE SEASONS OF "MAKE ME A SUPERMODEL" AND A SUBSCRIPTION TO **COSMO GIRL**. TURN AROUND.
I'VE GOT A WHOLE **LOOK** IN MIND FOR YOU... BUT I NEED **COMPLETE** CREATIVE CONTROL.
I'M GONNA **REGRET** THIS.
EXTREME MAKEOVER, THE MOM EDITION!!

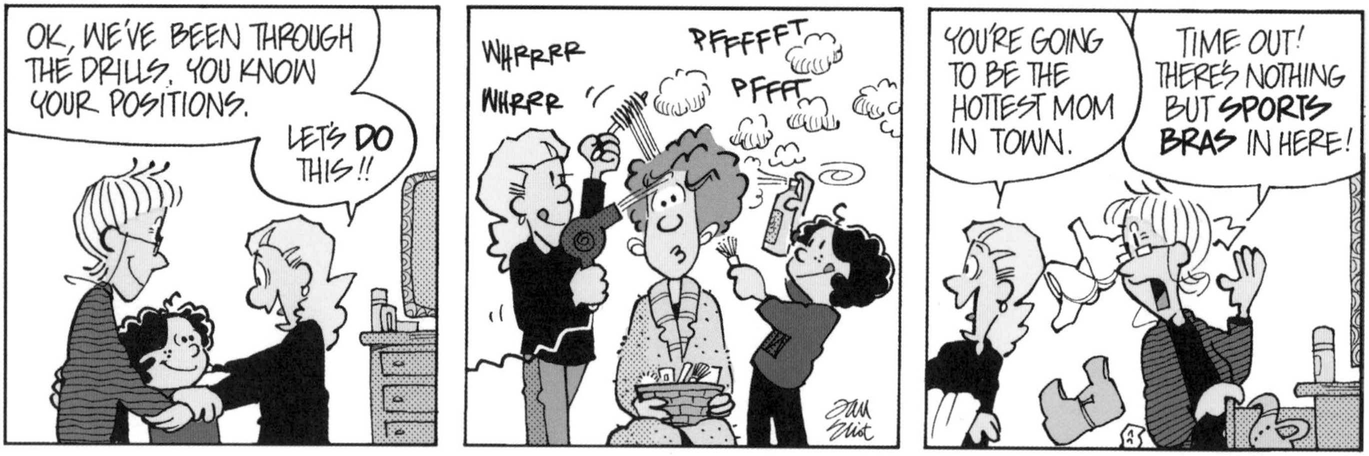
OK, WE'VE BEEN THROUGH THE DRILLS. YOU KNOW YOUR POSITIONS.
LET'S **DO** THIS!!
WHRRRR
WHRRR
PFFFFFT
PFFFT
YOU'RE GOING TO BE THE HOTTEST MOM IN TOWN.
TIME OUT! THERE'S NOTHING BUT **SPORTS BRAS** IN HERE!

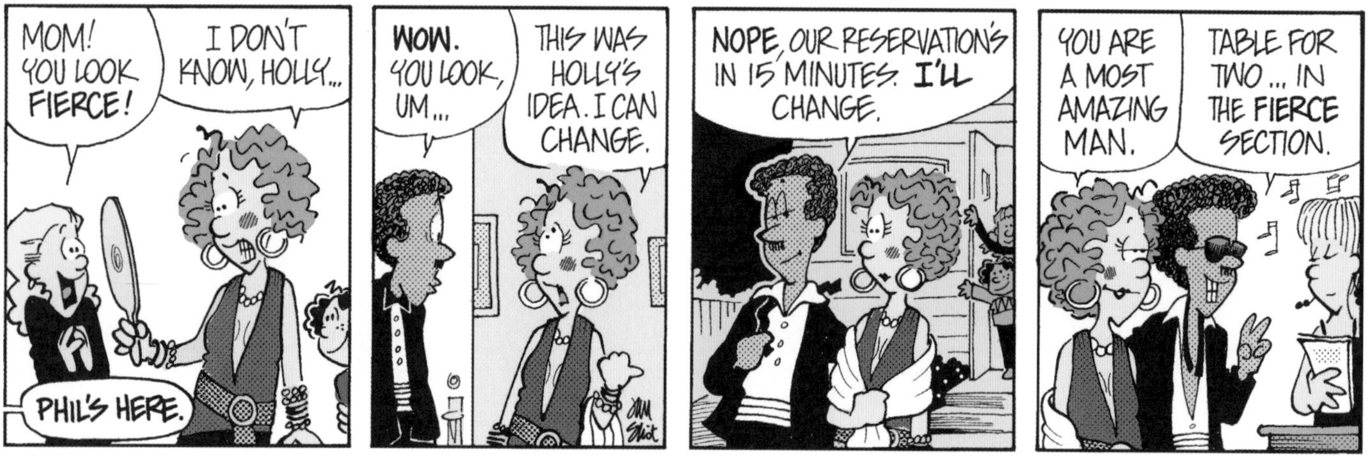
MOM! YOU LOOK **FIERCE**!
I DON'T KNOW, HOLLY...
PHIL'S HERE.
WOW. YOU LOOK, UM...
THIS WAS HOLLY'S IDEA. I CAN CHANGE.
NOPE, OUR RESERVATION'S IN 15 MINUTES. **I'LL** CHANGE.
YOU ARE A MOST AMAZING MAN.
TABLE FOR TWO ... IN THE **FIERCE** SECTION.

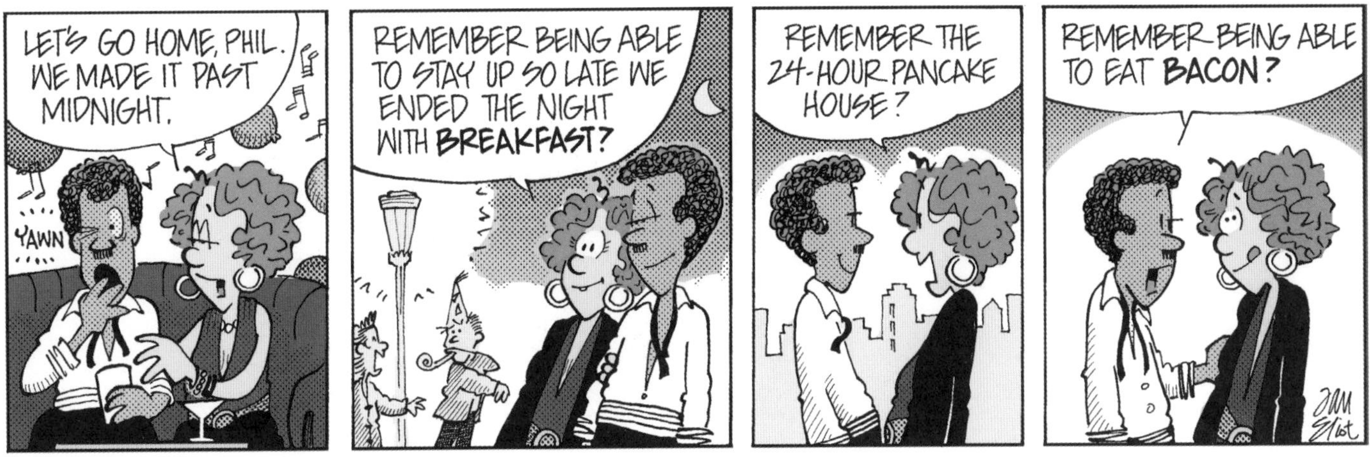
LET'S GO HOME, PHIL. WE MADE IT PAST MIDNIGHT.
YAWN
REMEMBER BEING ABLE TO STAY UP SO LATE WE ENDED THE NIGHT WITH **BREAKFAST?**
REMEMBER THE 24-HOUR PANCAKE HOUSE?
REMEMBER BEING ABLE TO EAT **BACON?**

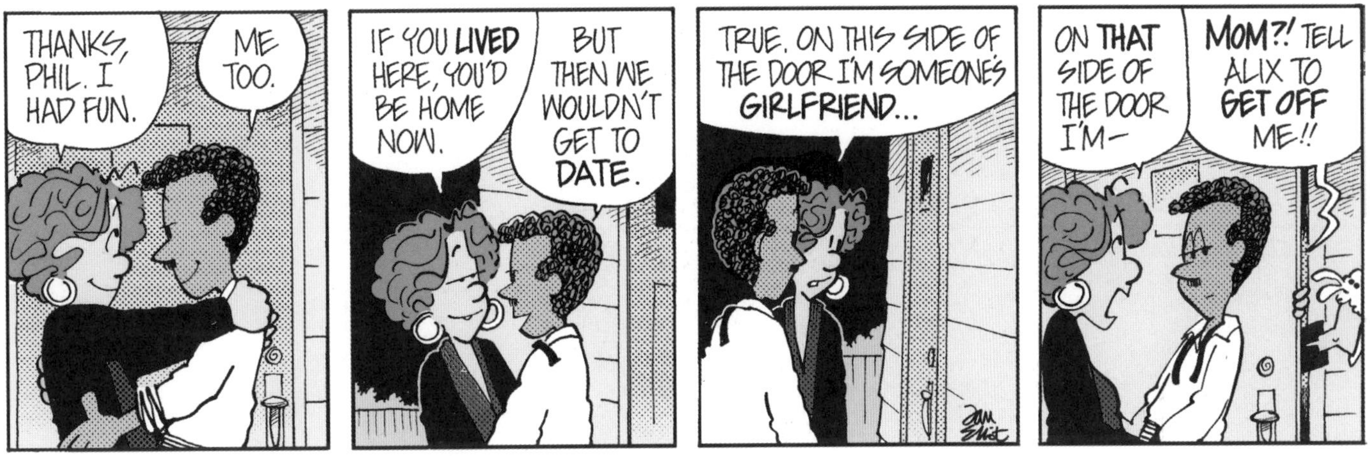
THANKS, PHIL. I HAD FUN.
ME TOO.
IF YOU **LIVED** HERE, YOU'D BE HOME NOW.
BUT THEN WE WOULDN'T GET TO **DATE**.
TRUE. ON THIS SIDE OF THE DOOR I'M SOMEONE'S **GIRLFRIEND**...
ON **THAT** SIDE OF THE DOOR I'M–
MOM?! TELL ALIX TO **GET OFF** ME!!

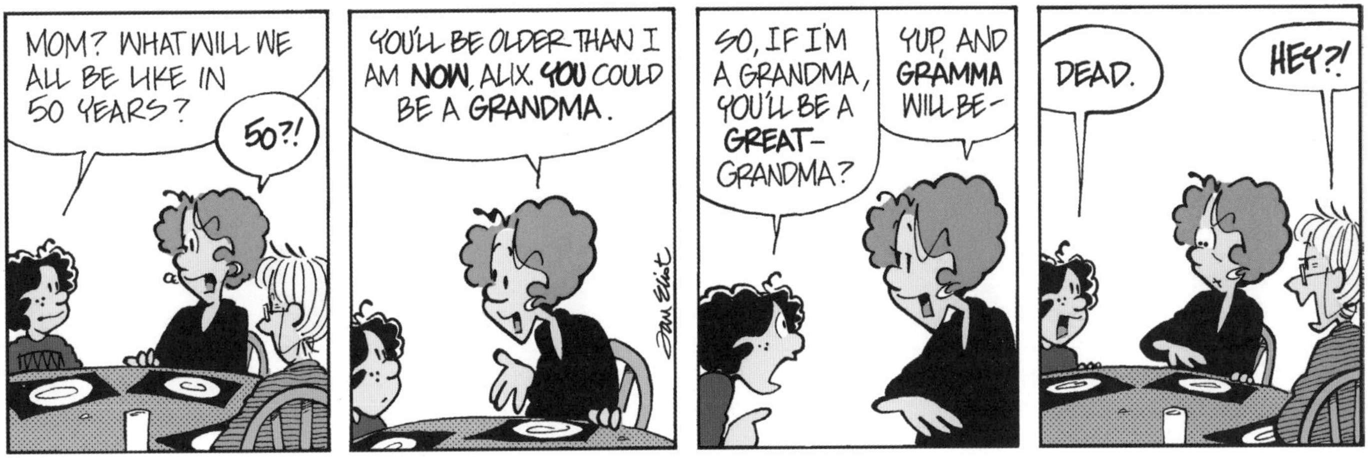
MOM? WHAT WILL WE ALL BE LIKE IN 50 YEARS?
50?!
YOU'LL BE OLDER THAN I AM **NOW**, ALIX. **YOU** COULD BE A **GRANDMA**.
SO, IF I'M A GRANDMA, YOU'LL BE A **GREAT**-GRANDMA?
YUP, AND **GRAMMA** WILL BE-
DEAD.
HEY?!

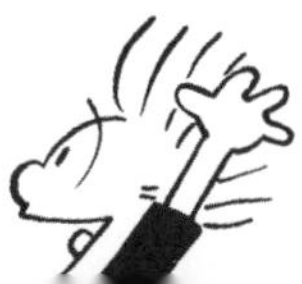

Stone Soup

MOM?! DO I HAVE TO DO MY HOME-WORK?

OF COURSE!

WHY?

SO YOU CAN BE PREPARED FOR ADULT-HOOD.

HOW DOES DOING HOMEWORK DO **THAT** ??

DON'T YOU WANT TO GO TO COLLEGE? GET A GOOD JOB? PROVIDE FOR YOUR FAMILY?? BE A RESPONSIBLE VOTER? KNOW HOW TO TAKE CARE OF THE ENVIRONMENT?!

OK OK!!

SIGH...

MAKE A TOPOGRAPHIC MAP OF CANADA USING RICE, BEANS AND MACARONI.

?

Stone Soup

HEY, WALLY! WHAT SHOULD WE DO TODAY??
THERE'S A GAME ON!
YOU'RE GOING TO WASTE ANOTHER SUNDAY WATCHING FOOTBALL?!
WE LIKE FOOTBALL!
WELL, WE'RE ALL GOING OUT.
IT'S COLD...
SO, WE'LL GO TO THE MALL... EAT IN THE FOOD COURT... ANYTHING WOULD BE BETTER THAN ANOTHER DAY OF FOOTBALL.
AND WHEN VAL GETS BACK, TELL HER SHE CAN JOIN US.

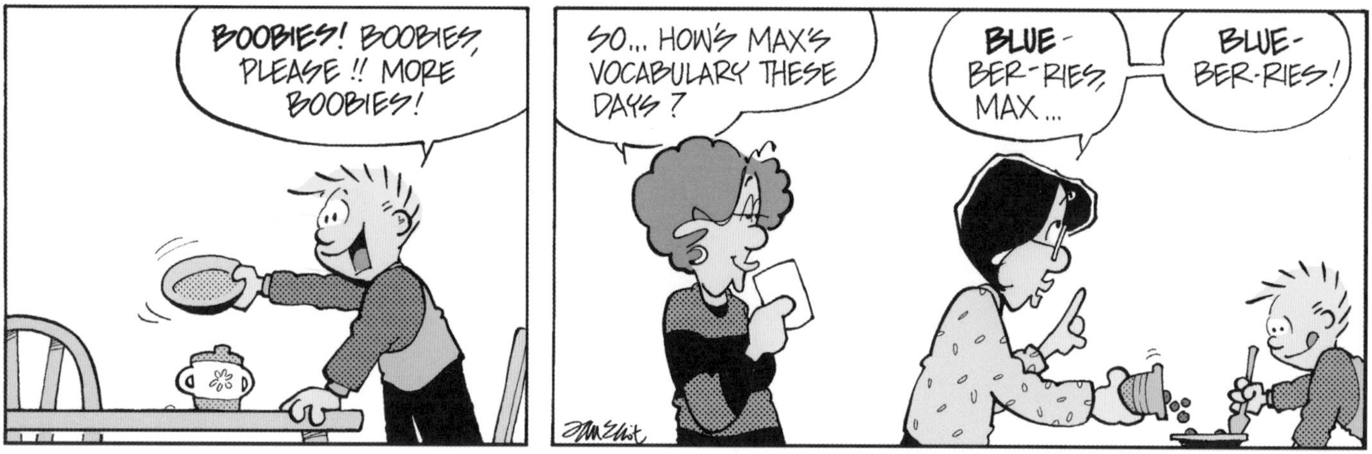
BOOBIES! BOOBIES, PLEASE !! MORE BOOBIES!
SO... HOW'S MAX'S VOCABULARY THESE DAYS ?
BLUE-BER-RIES, MAX...
BLUE-BER-RIES!

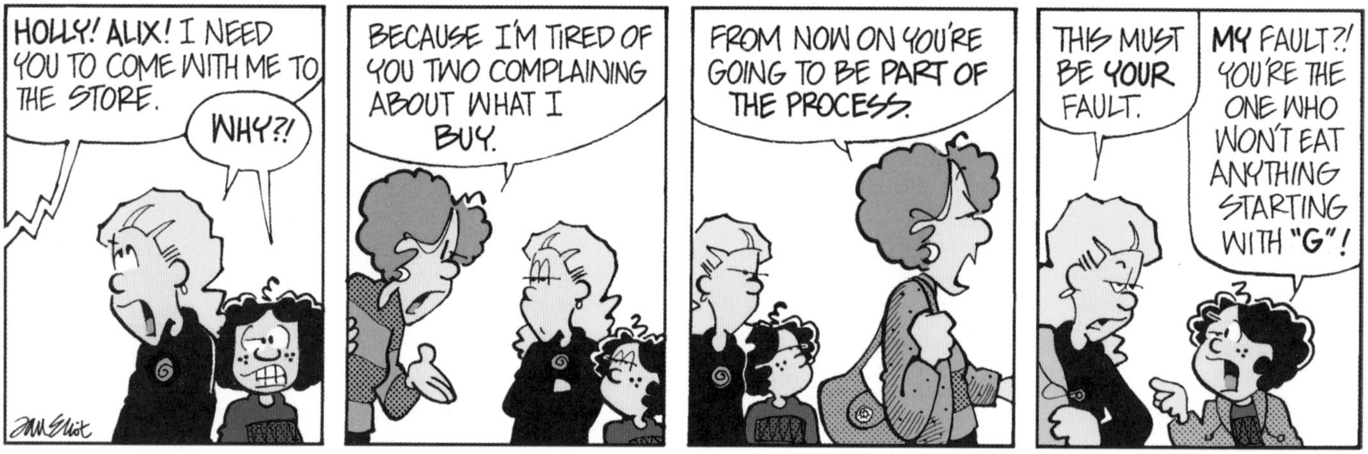
HOLLY! ALIX! I NEED YOU TO COME WITH ME TO THE STORE.
WHY?!
BECAUSE I'M TIRED OF YOU TWO COMPLAINING ABOUT WHAT I BUY.
FROM NOW ON YOU'RE GOING TO BE PART OF THE PROCESS.
THIS MUST BE YOUR FAULT.
MY FAULT?! YOU'RE THE ONE WHO WON'T EAT ANYTHING STARTING WITH "G"!

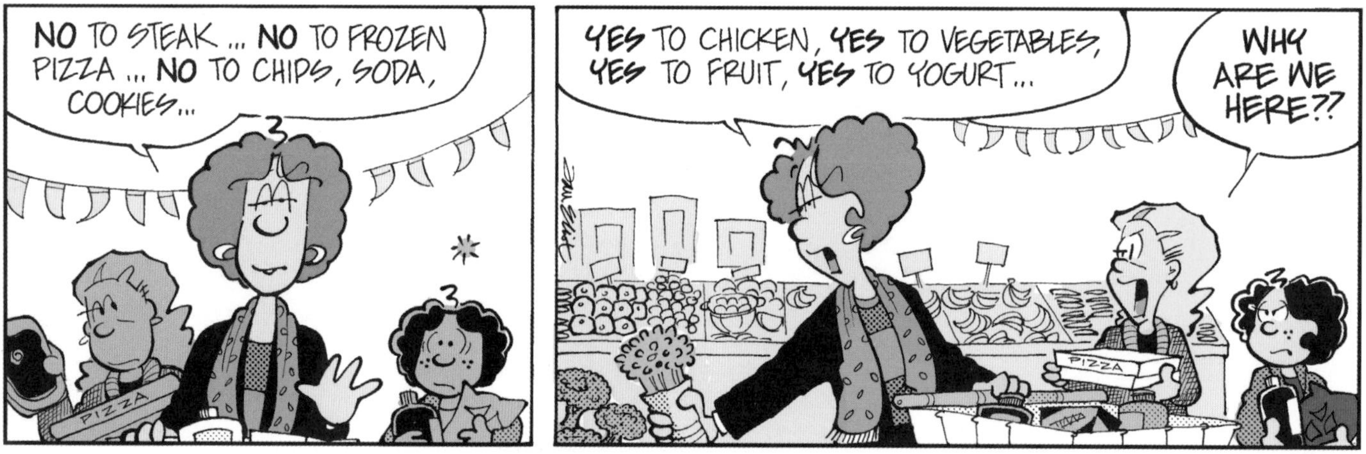
NO TO STEAK ... NO TO FROZEN PIZZA ... NO TO CHIPS, SODA, COOKIES...
PIZZA
YES TO CHICKEN, YES TO VEGETABLES, YES TO FRUIT, YES TO YOGURT...
WHY ARE WE HERE??
PIZZA

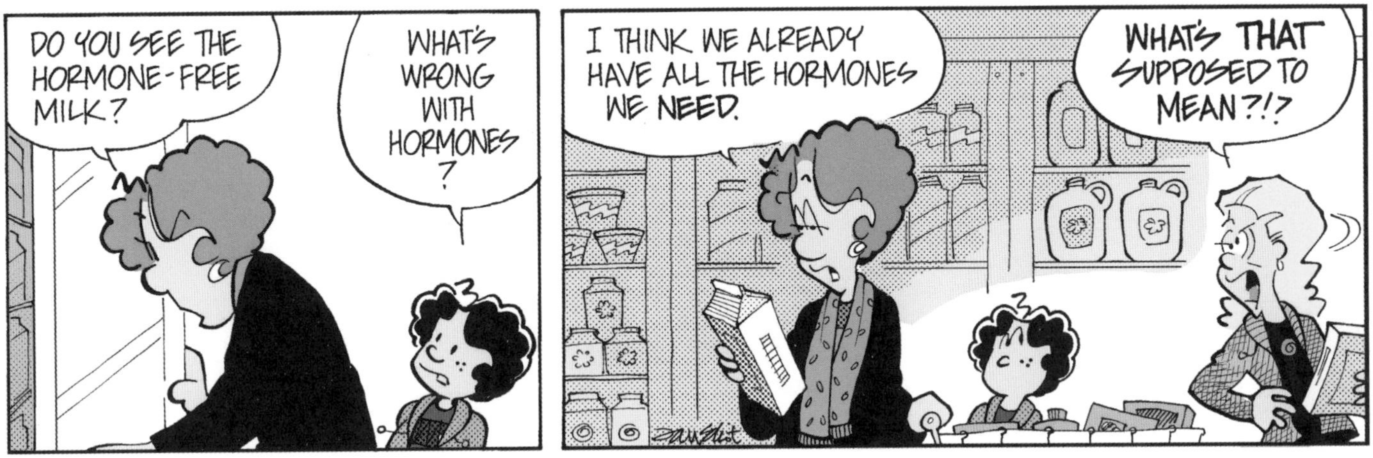
DO YOU SEE THE HORMONE-FREE MILK?
WHAT'S WRONG WITH HORMONES?
I THINK WE ALREADY HAVE ALL THE HORMONES WE NEED.
WHAT'S THAT SUPPOSED TO MEAN?!?

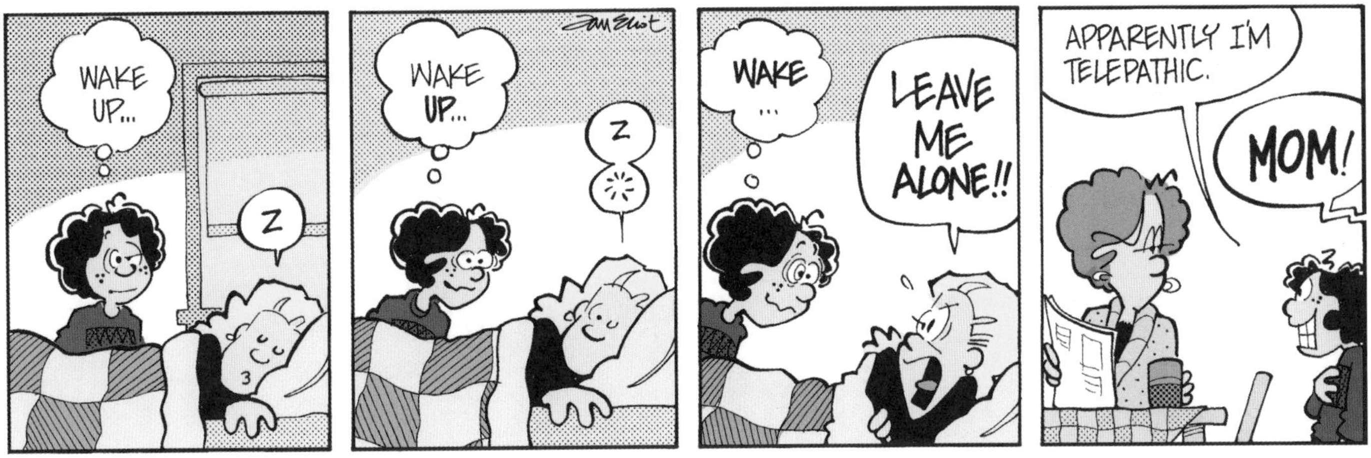
WAKE UP...
Z
WAKE UP...
Z
WAKE ...
LEAVE ME ALONE!!
APPARENTLY I'M TELEPATHIC.
MOM!

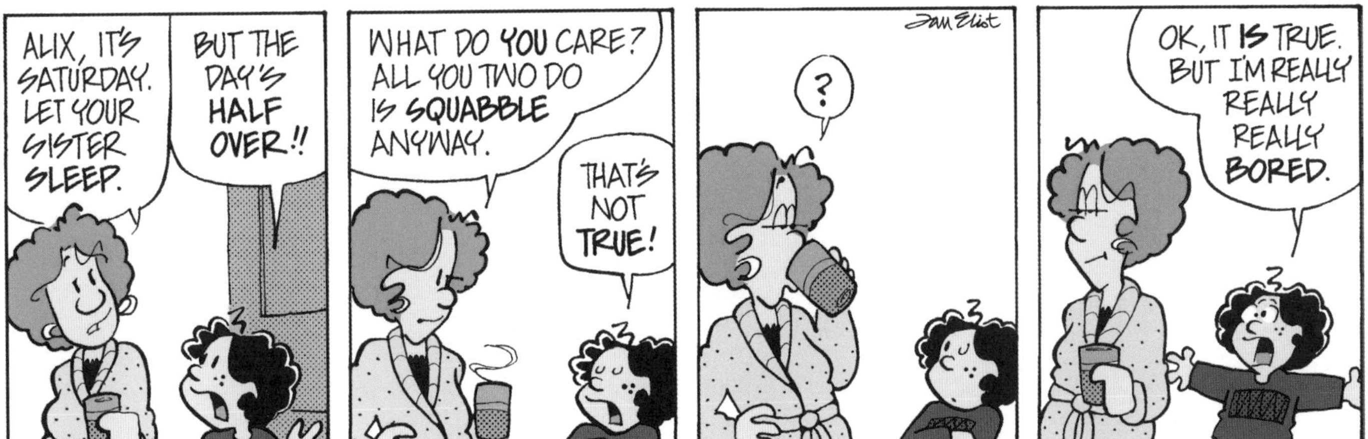
ALIX, IT'S SATURDAY. LET YOUR SISTER SLEEP.
BUT THE DAY'S HALF OVER!!
WHAT DO YOU CARE? ALL YOU TWO DO IS SQUABBLE ANYWAY.
THAT'S NOT TRUE!
?
OK, IT IS TRUE. BUT I'M REALLY REALLY REALLY REALLY BORED.

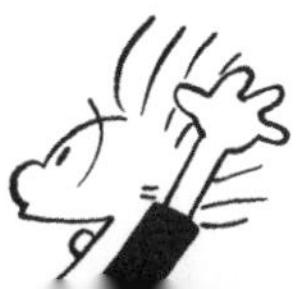

Stone Soup

SURPRISE!
YOU BOUGHT ME A **HOUSE PLANT?**
NUK NUK
IT'S AN ORCHID.
THAT SOMEONE HAS TO TAKE **CARE** OF.
IT CAN'T BE THAT HARD.
"NEEDS BRIGHT INDIRECT LIGHT."
"**AVOID DRAFTS.**"
KEEP BETWEEN **60° AND 80°**.
"FERTILIZE WEEKLY... KEEP DAMP **CONSTANTLY**..."
WEEKLY? CONSTANTLY?
I CAN'T TAKE THE **PRESSURE**!!
I THOUGHT YOU'D **LIKE** IT.
I CAN KEEP THE **KIDS** ALIVE, OR THE **PLANT**. YOU PICK.

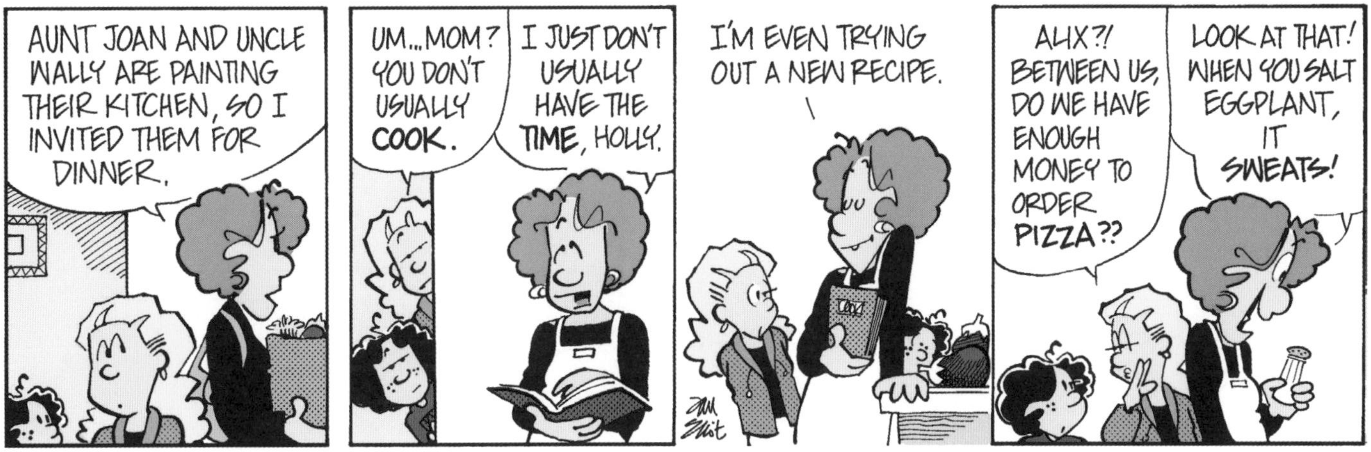
AUNT JOAN AND UNCLE WALLY ARE PAINTING THEIR KITCHEN, SO I INVITED THEM FOR DINNER.
UM...MOM? YOU DON'T USUALLY **COOK**.
I JUST DON'T USUALLY HAVE THE **TIME**, HOLLY.
I'M EVEN TRYING OUT A NEW RECIPE.
COOK
ALIX?! BETWEEN US, DO WE HAVE ENOUGH MONEY TO ORDER **PIZZA**??
LOOK AT THAT! WHEN YOU SALT EGGPLANT, IT **SWEATS**!

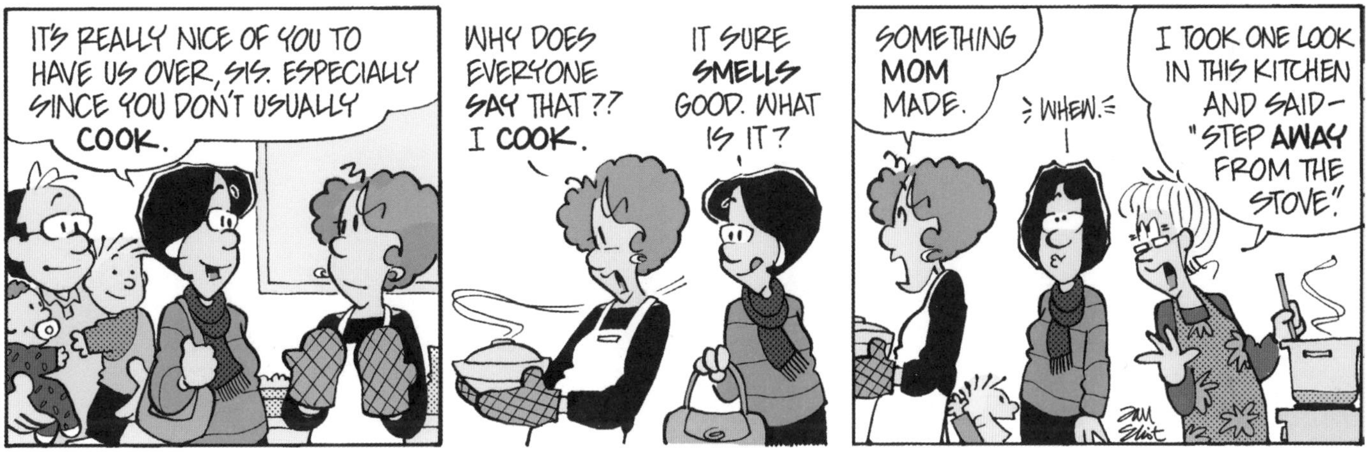
IT'S REALLY NICE OF YOU TO HAVE US OVER, SIS. ESPECIALLY SINCE YOU DON'T USUALLY **COOK**.
WHY DOES EVERYONE **SAY** THAT?? I **COOK**.
IT SURE **SMELLS** GOOD. WHAT IS IT?
SOMETHING **MOM** MADE.
WHEW.
I TOOK ONE LOOK IN THIS KITCHEN AND SAID– "STEP **AWAY** FROM THE STOVE."

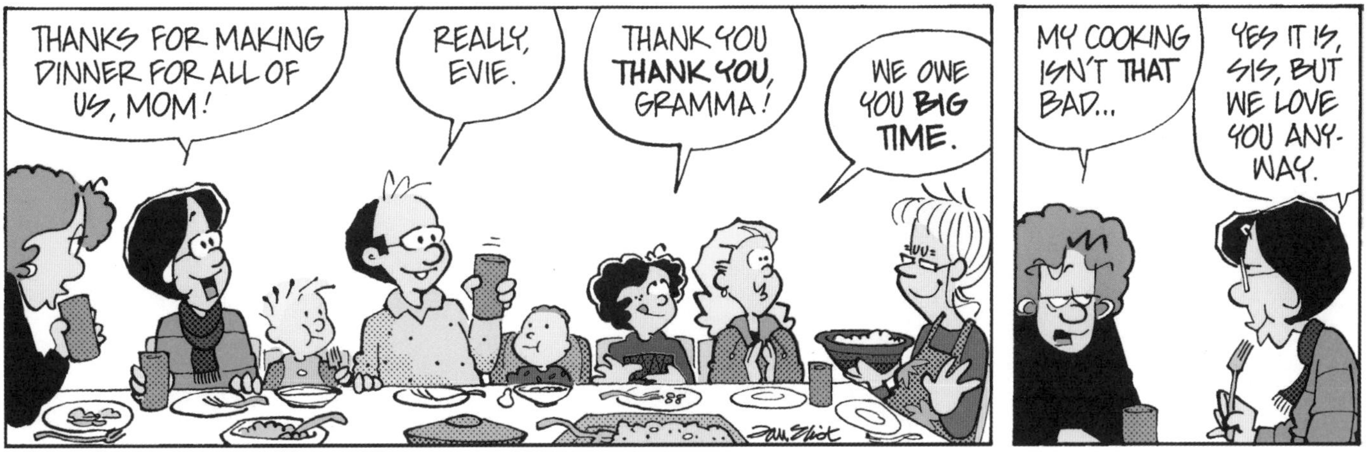
THANKS FOR MAKING DINNER FOR ALL OF US, MOM!
REALLY, EVIE.
THANK YOU **THANK YOU**, GRAMMA!
WE OWE YOU **BIG TIME**.
MY COOKING ISN'T **THAT** BAD...
YES IT IS, SIS, BUT WE LOVE YOU ANYWAY.

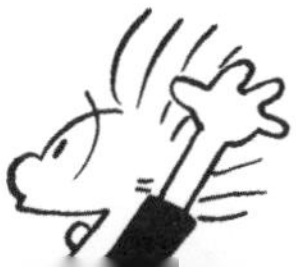

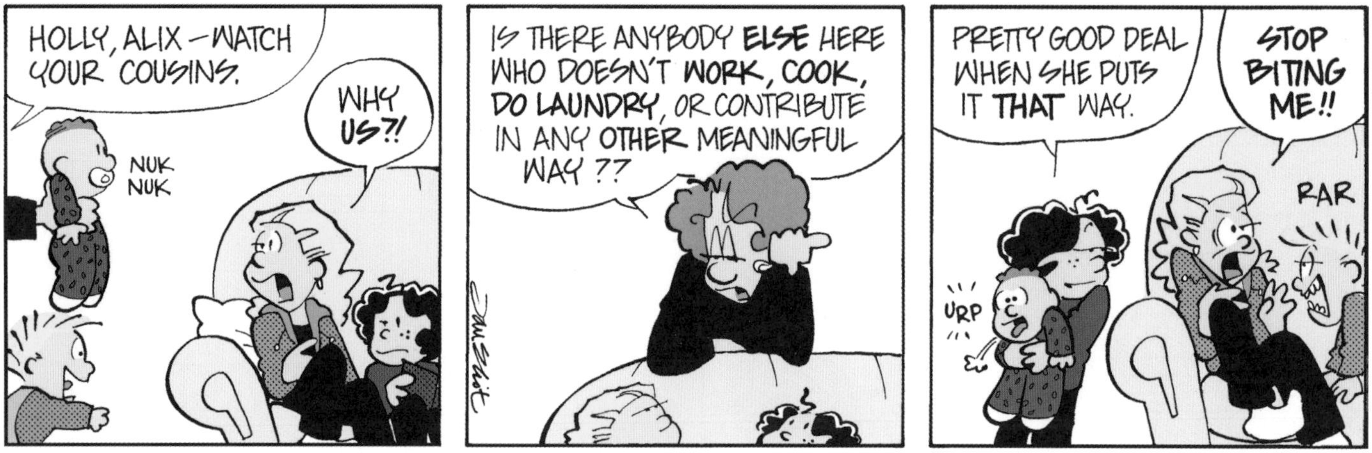
HOLLY, ALIX—WATCH YOUR COUSINS.
NUK NUK
WHY US?!
IS THERE ANYBODY **ELSE** HERE WHO DOESN'T **WORK, COOK, DO LAUNDRY**, OR CONTRIBUTE IN ANY **OTHER** MEANINGFUL WAY ??
PRETTY GOOD DEAL WHEN SHE PUTS IT **THAT** WAY.
URP
STOP BITING ME!!
RAR

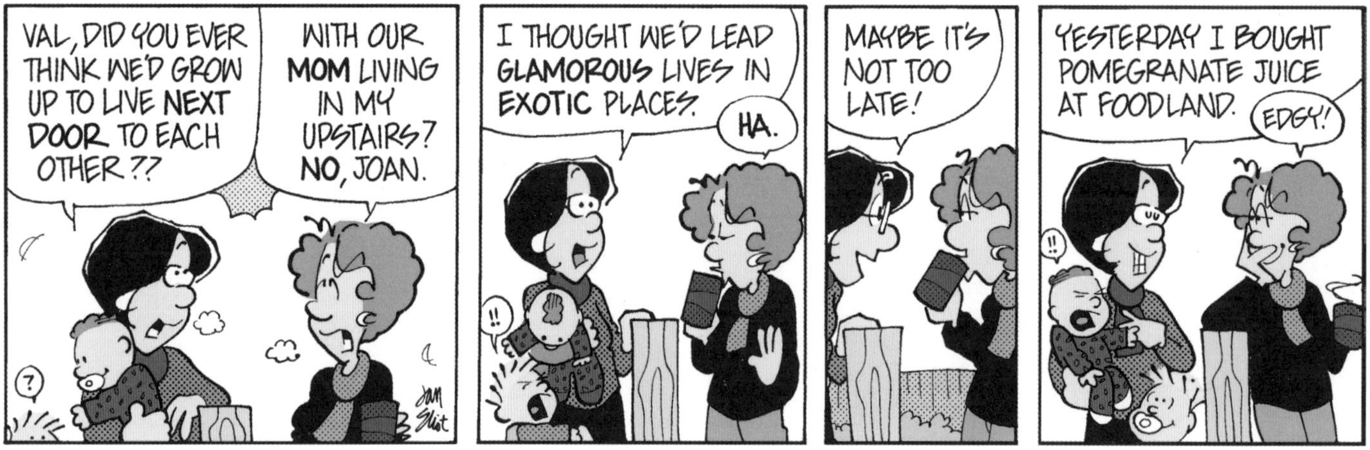
VAL, DID YOU EVER THINK WE'D GROW UP TO LIVE **NEXT DOOR** TO EACH OTHER ??
WITH OUR **MOM** LIVING IN MY UPSTAIRS? **NO**, JOAN.
?
I THOUGHT WE'D LEAD **GLAMOROUS** LIVES IN **EXOTIC** PLACES.
HA.
!!
MAYBE IT'S NOT TOO LATE!
YESTERDAY I BOUGHT POMEGRANATE JUICE AT FOODLAND.
EDGY!
!!

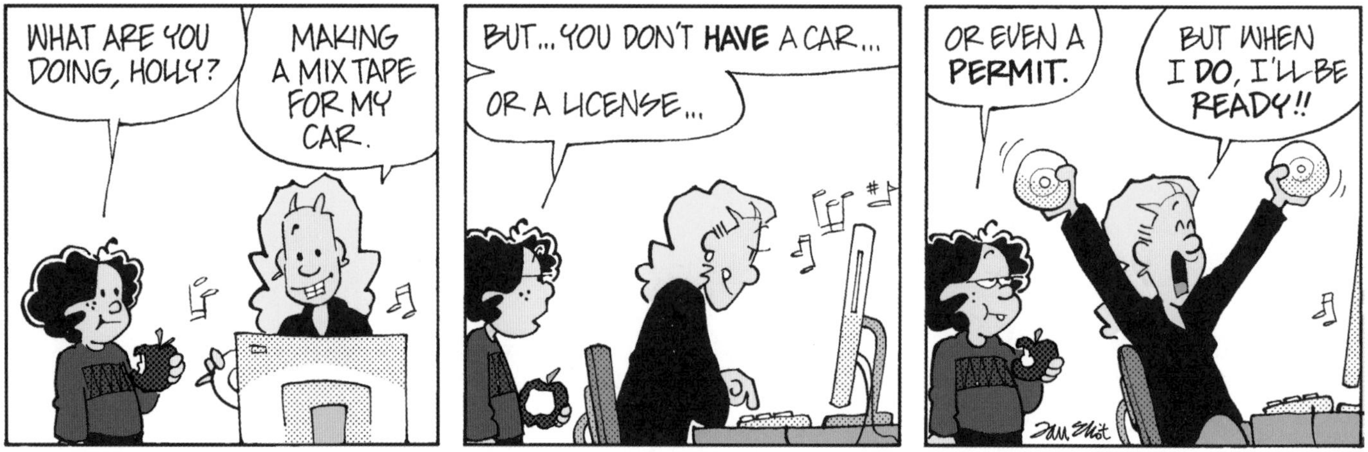
WHAT ARE YOU DOING, HOLLY?
MAKING A MIX TAPE FOR MY CAR.
BUT... YOU DON'T **HAVE** A CAR...
OR A LICENSE...
OR EVEN A **PERMIT**.
BUT WHEN I **DO**, I'LL BE **READY**!!

Stone Soup

WHO IS THAT ACTRESS?
UM... UM...
WE JUST SAW HER IN SOMETHING...
I'LL GO LOOK HER UP.
OK, HMM... QUICK EMAIL CHECK... OOH - NEW YORK TIMES STORY LINK STRANGE CREATURE IN GULF OF MEXICO?? LINK LINK PHOTOS? LINK HOW COOL IS THAT?! LINK
BANNER AD... GAP SALE LINK FOR COUPONS... ORGANIC COTTON FOR KIDS? LINK LINK LINK LINK
CLICK CLICK
JOAN?
JOAN! WHAT DID YOU FIND OUT??
JOAN??
COMING!
SO? WHO IS SHE?
WHO?

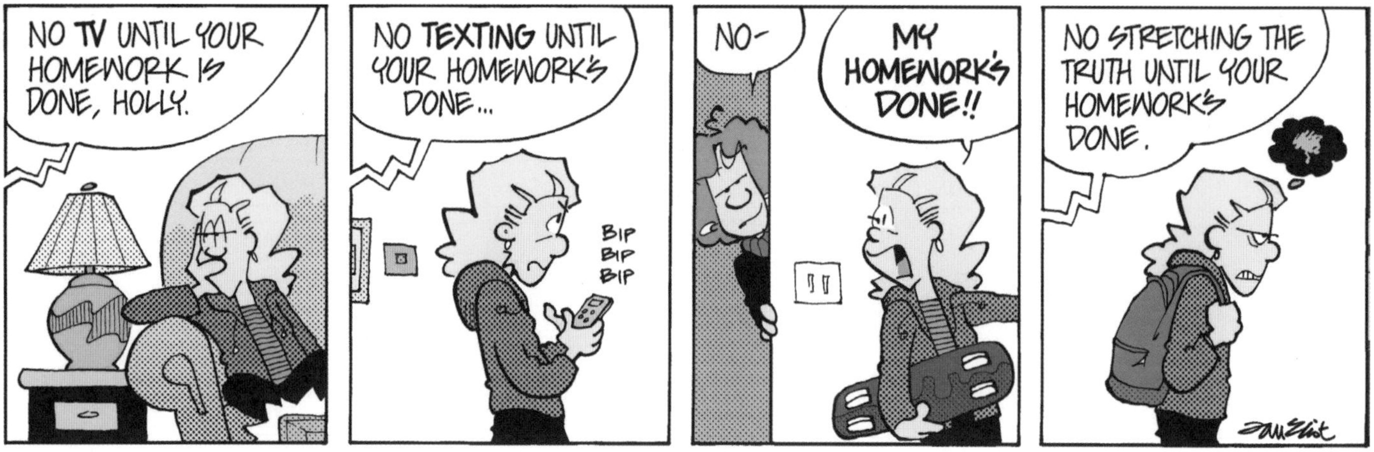
NO **TV** UNTIL YOUR HOMEWORK IS DONE, HOLLY.
NO **TEXTING** UNTIL YOUR HOMEWORK'S DONE...
BIP BIP BIP
NO-
MY HOMEWORK'S DONE!!
NO STRETCHING THE TRUTH UNTIL YOUR HOMEWORK'S DONE.

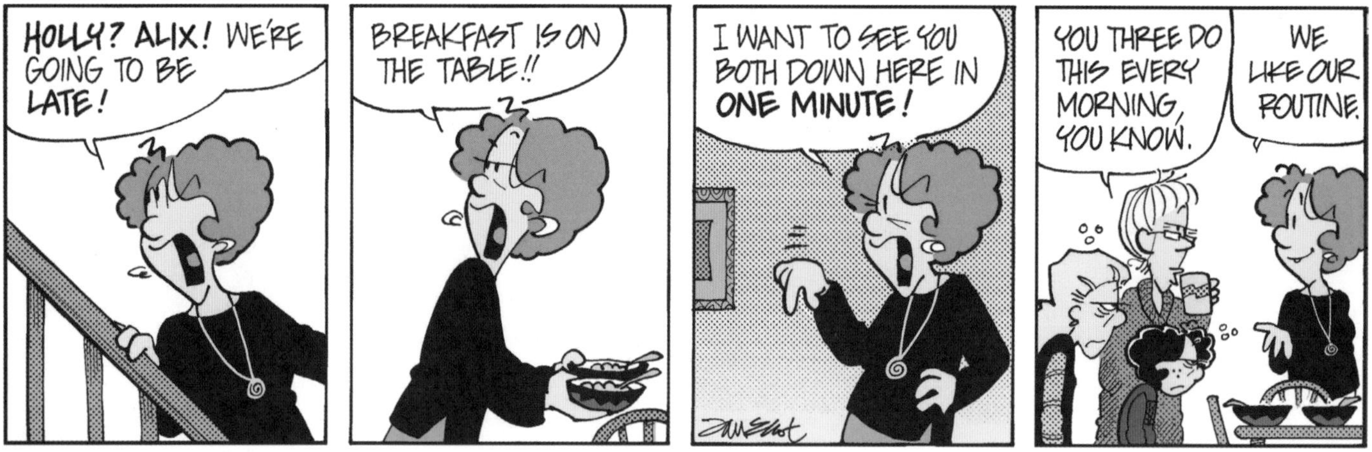
HOLLY? ALIX! WE'RE GOING TO BE **LATE**!
BREAKFAST IS ON THE TABLE!!
I WANT TO SEE YOU BOTH DOWN HERE IN **ONE MINUTE**!
YOU THREE DO THIS EVERY MORNING, YOU KNOW.
WE LIKE OUR ROUTINE.

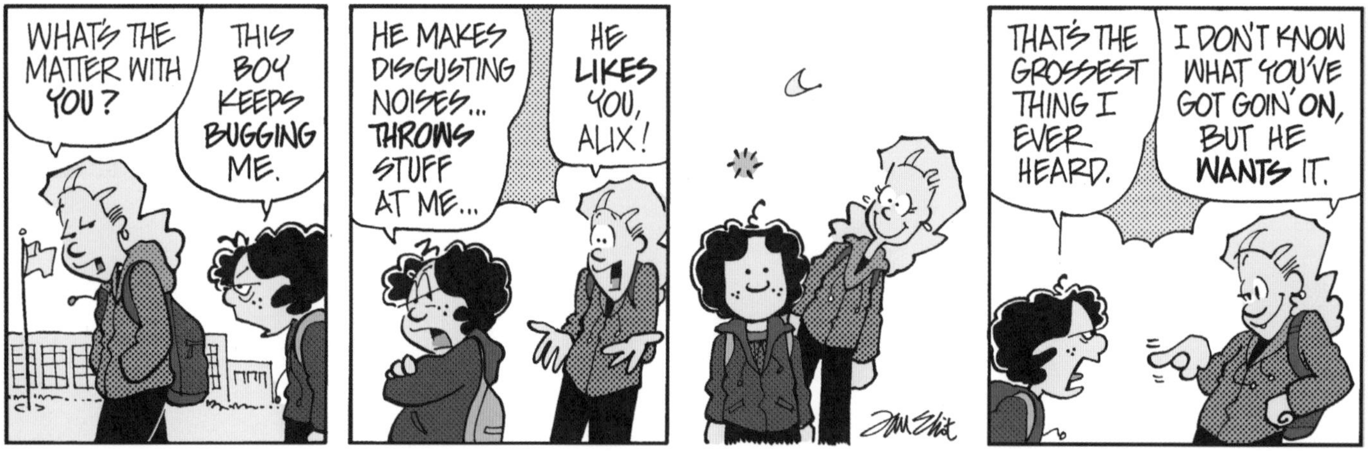
WHAT'S THE MATTER WITH **YOU**?
THIS BOY KEEPS **BUGGING** ME.
HE MAKES DISGUSTING NOISES... **THROWS** STUFF AT ME...
HE **LIKES** YOU, ALIX!
THAT'S THE GROSSEST THING I EVER HEARD.
I DON'T KNOW WHAT YOU'VE GOT GOIN' **ON**, BUT HE **WANTS** IT.

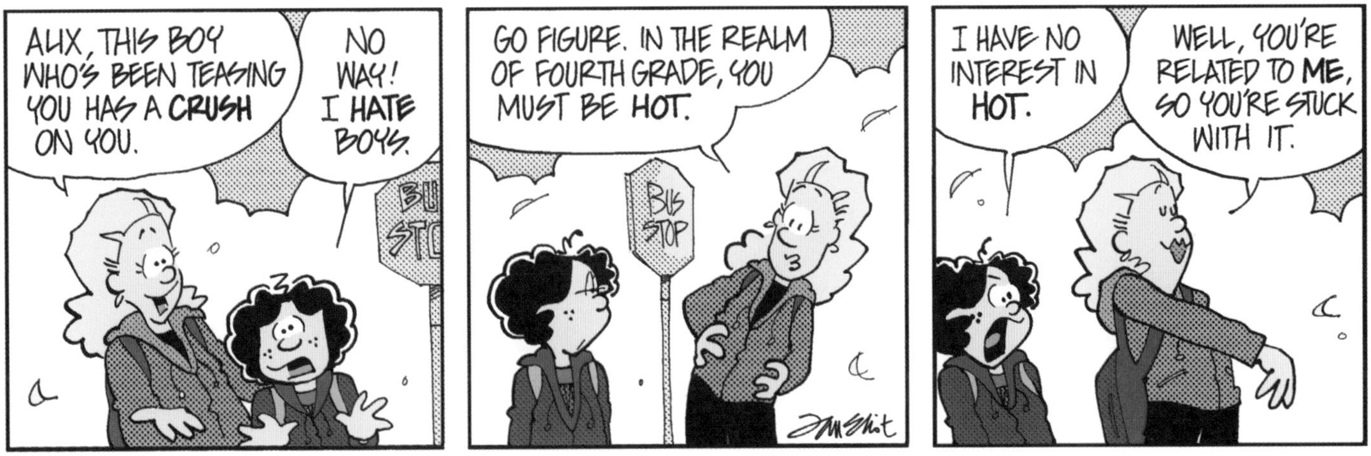
ALIX, THIS BOY WHO'S BEEN TEASING YOU HAS A **CRUSH** ON YOU.
NO WAY! I **HATE** BOYS.
GO FIGURE. IN THE REALM OF FOURTH GRADE, YOU MUST BE **HOT**.
BUS STOP
I HAVE NO INTEREST IN **HOT**.
WELL, YOU'RE RELATED TO **ME**, SO YOU'RE STUCK WITH IT.

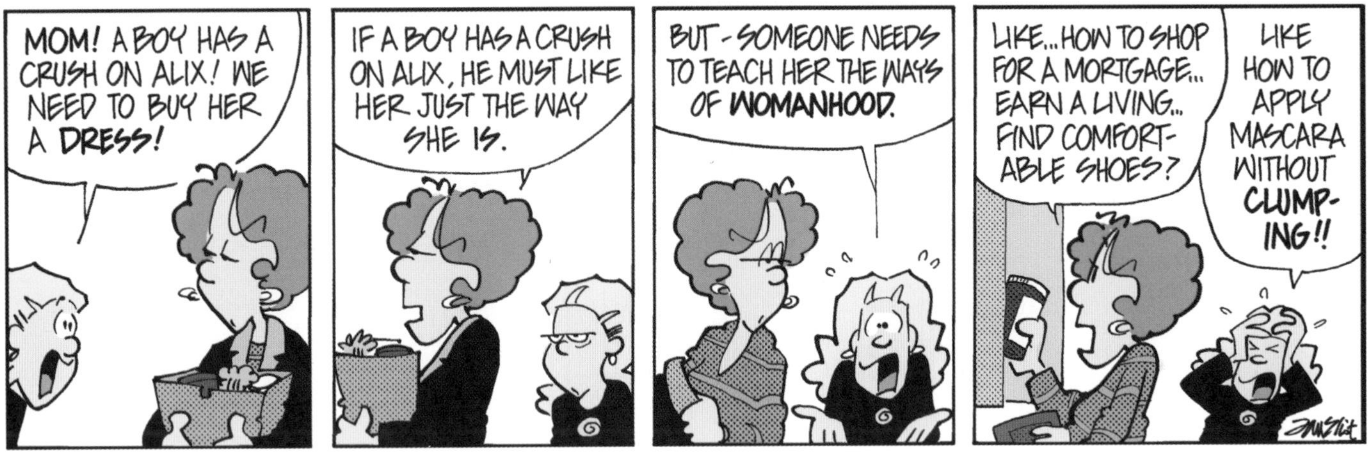
MOM! A BOY HAS A CRUSH ON ALIX! WE NEED TO BUY HER A **DRESS**!
IF A BOY HAS A CRUSH ON ALIX, HE MUST LIKE HER JUST THE WAY SHE **IS**.
BUT - SOMEONE NEEDS TO TEACH HER THE WAYS OF **WOMANHOOD**.
LIKE...HOW TO SHOP FOR A MORTGAGE... EARN A LIVING... FIND COMFORT-ABLE SHOES?
LIKE HOW TO APPLY MASCARA WITHOUT **CLUMP-ING!!**

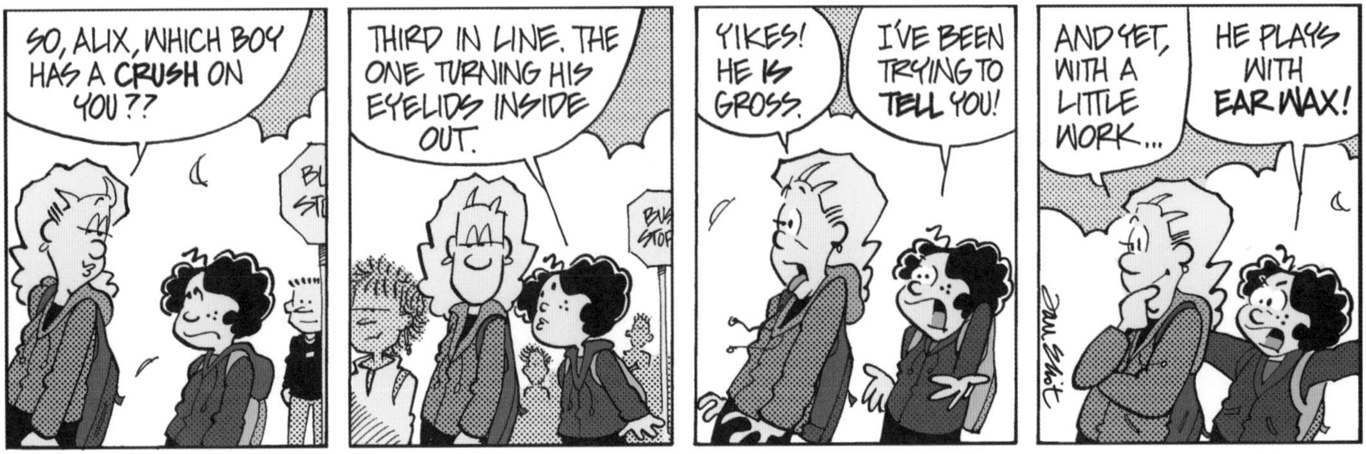
SO, ALIX, WHICH BOY HAS A **CRUSH** ON YOU??
THIRD IN LINE. THE ONE TURNING HIS EYELIDS INSIDE OUT.
YIKES! HE **IS** GROSS.
I'VE BEEN TRYING TO **TELL** YOU!
AND YET, WITH A LITTLE WORK...
HE PLAYS WITH **EAR WAX!**

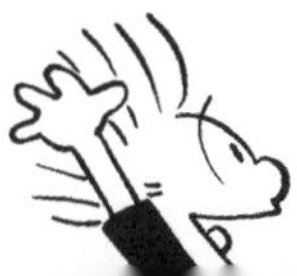

Stone Soup

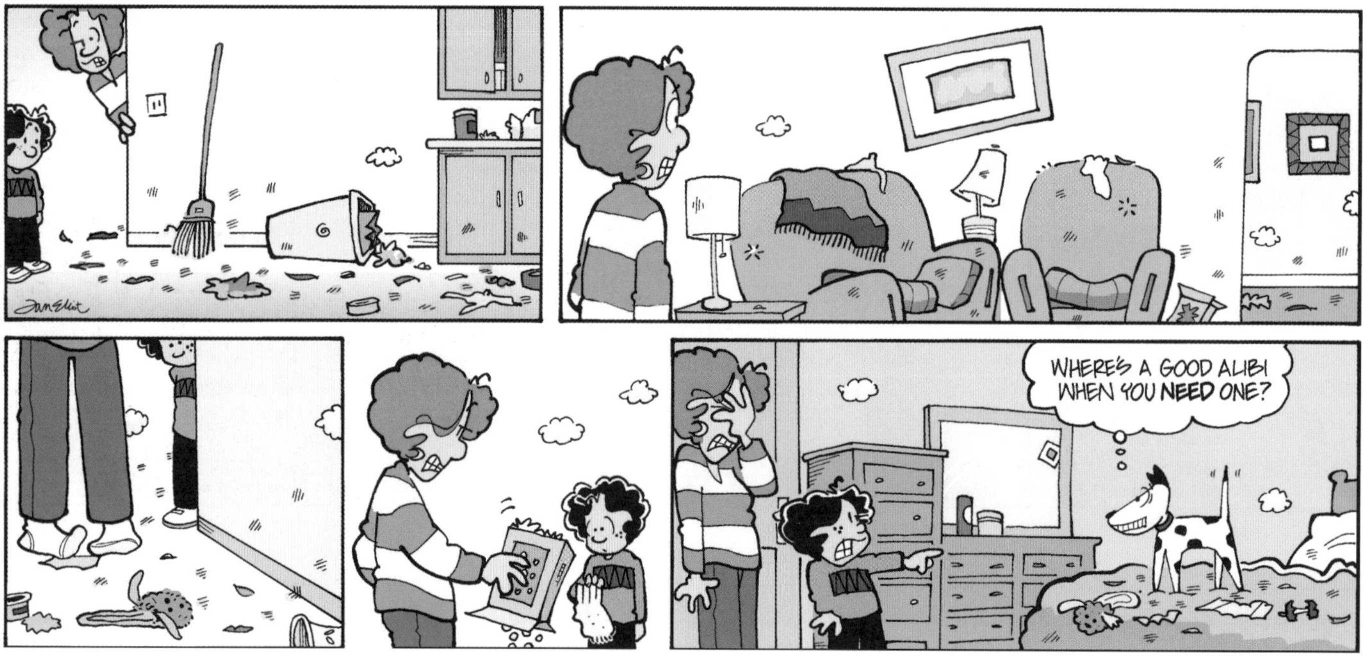
WHERE'S A GOOD ALIBI WHEN YOU **NEED** ONE?

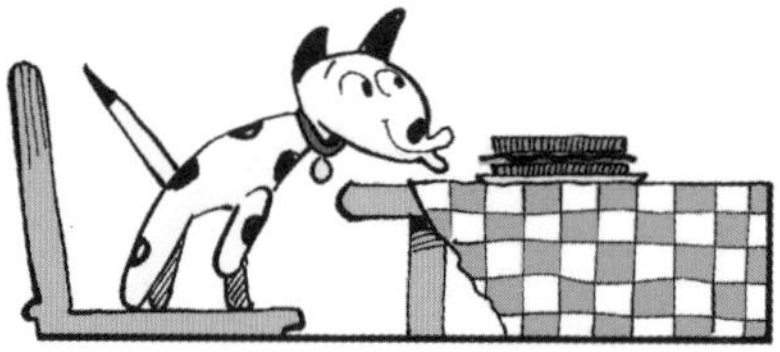

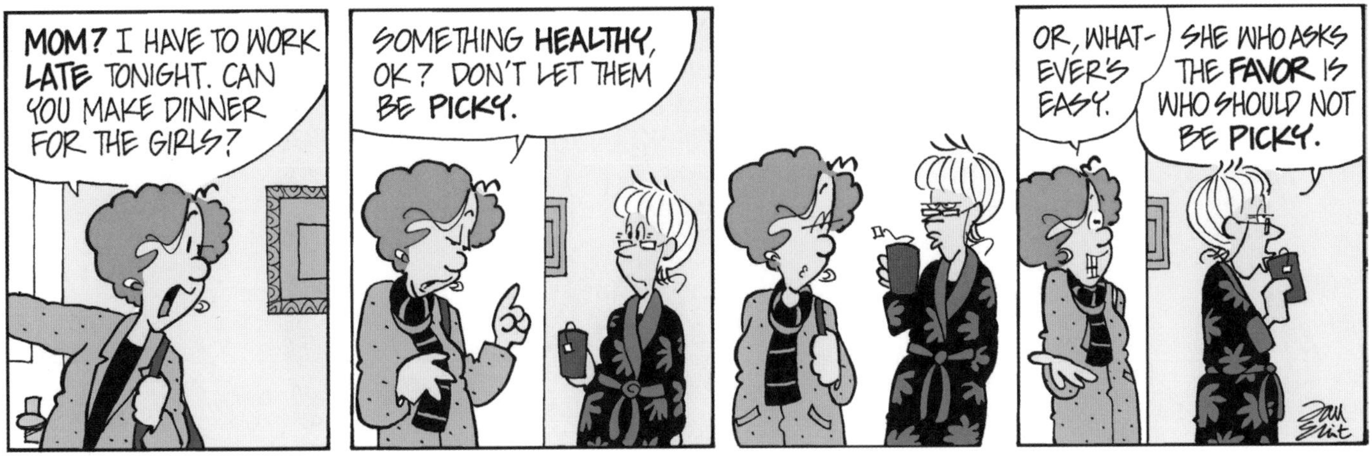
MOM? I HAVE TO WORK LATE TONIGHT. CAN YOU MAKE DINNER FOR THE GIRLS?
SOMETHING HEALTHY, OK? DON'T LET THEM BE PICKY.
OR, WHAT-EVER'S EASY.
SHE WHO ASKS THE FAVOR IS WHO SHOULD NOT BE PICKY.

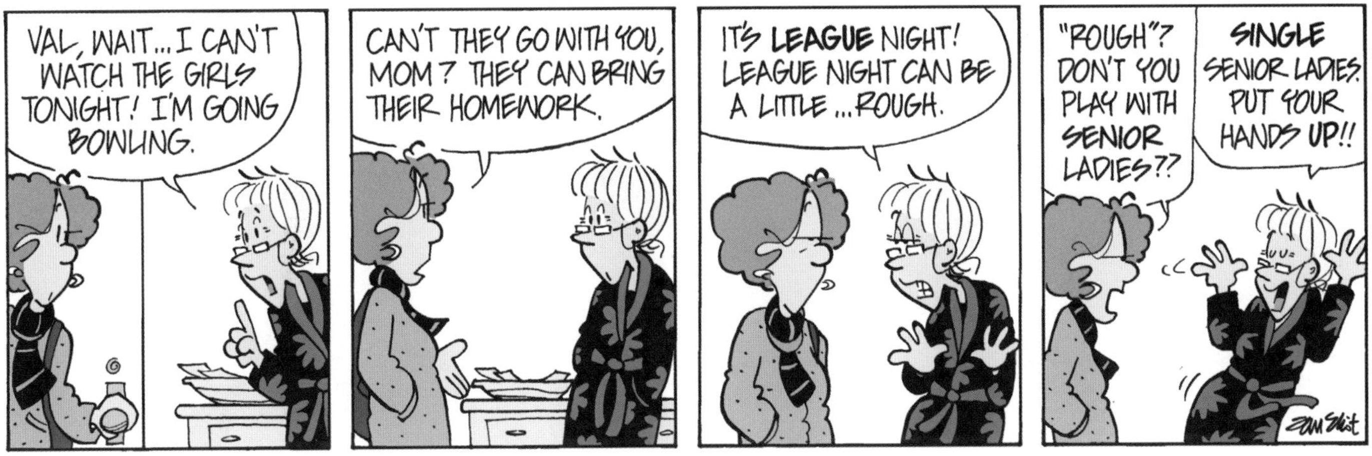
VAL, WAIT... I CAN'T WATCH THE GIRLS TONIGHT! I'M GOING BOWLING.
CAN'T THEY GO WITH YOU, MOM? THEY CAN BRING THEIR HOMEWORK.
IT'S LEAGUE NIGHT! LEAGUE NIGHT CAN BE A LITTLE ...ROUGH.
"ROUGH"? DON'T YOU PLAY WITH SENIOR LADIES??
SINGLE SENIOR LADIES. PUT YOUR HANDS UP!!

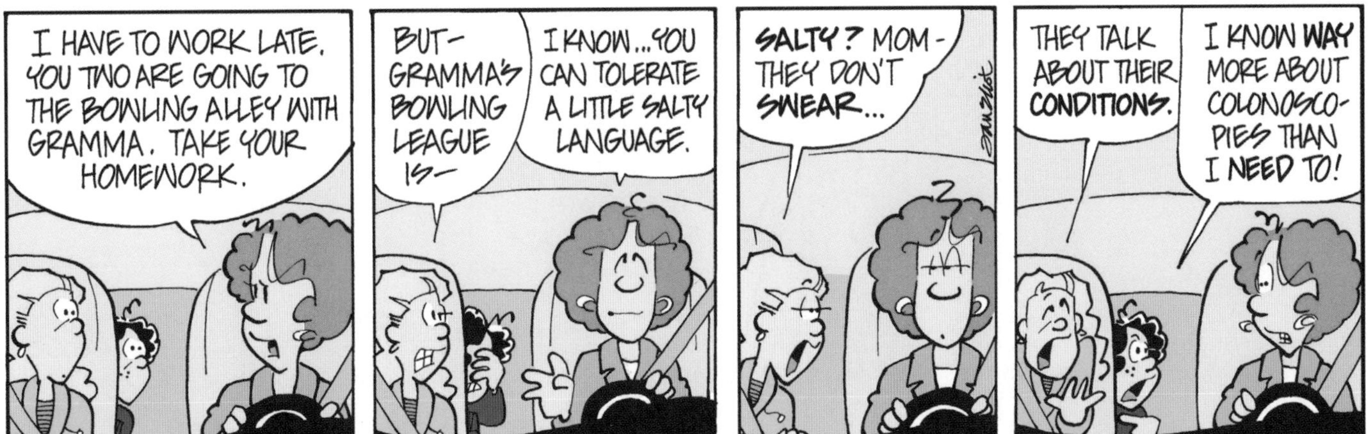
I HAVE TO WORK LATE. YOU TWO ARE GOING TO THE BOWLING ALLEY WITH GRAMMA. TAKE YOUR HOMEWORK.
BUT- GRAMMA'S BOWLING LEAGUE IS—
I KNOW...YOU CAN TOLERATE A LITTLE SALTY LANGUAGE.
SALTY? MOM- THEY DON'T SWEAR...
THEY TALK ABOUT THEIR CONDITIONS.
I KNOW WAY MORE ABOUT COLONOSCO-PIES THAN I NEED TO!

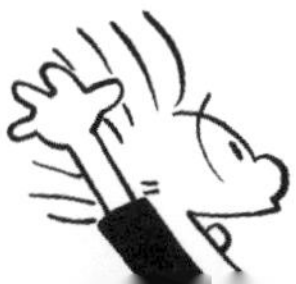

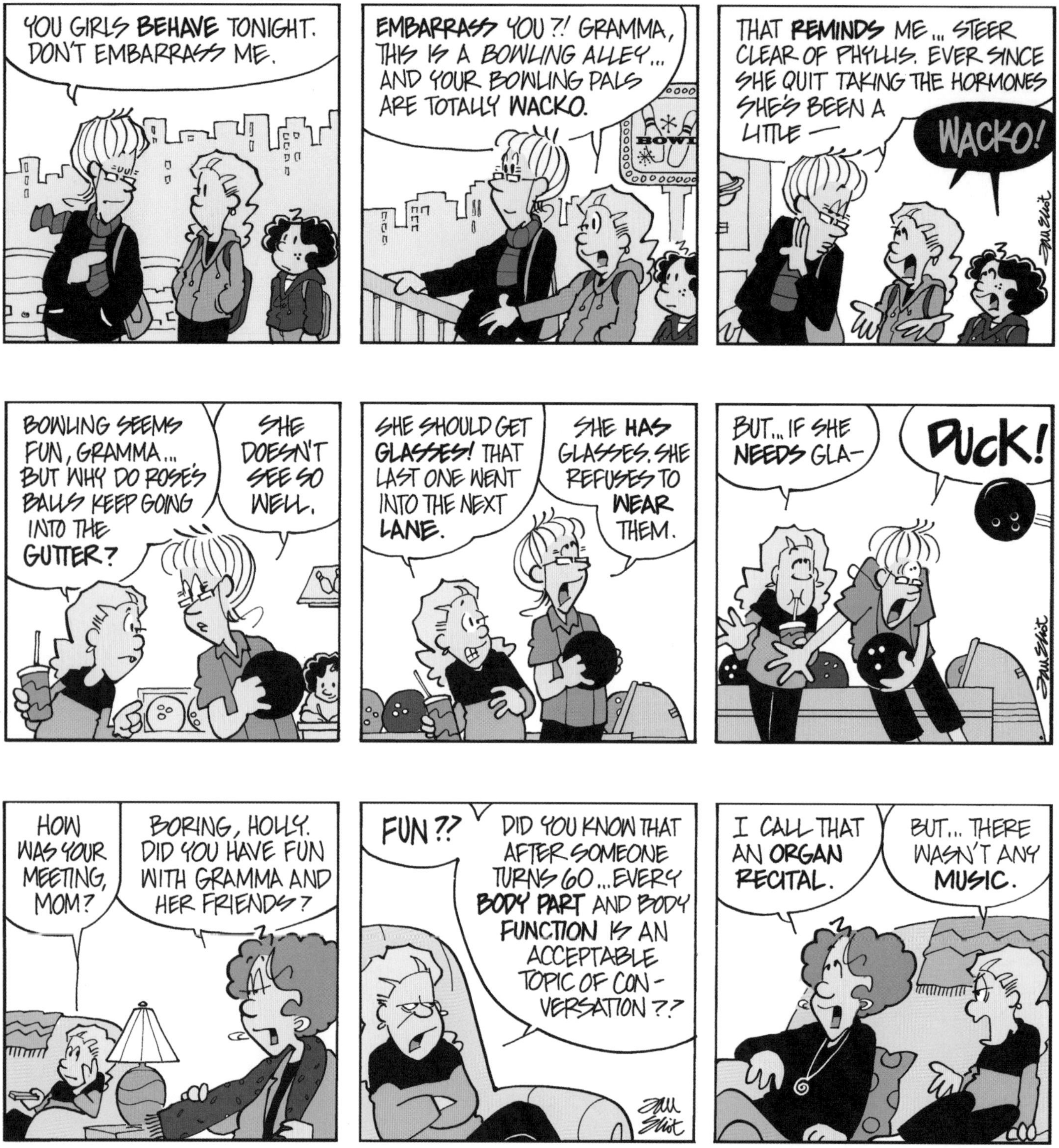
YOU GIRLS BEHAVE TONIGHT. DON'T EMBARRASS ME.
EMBARRASS YOU?! GRAMMA, THIS IS A BOWLING ALLEY... AND YOUR BOWLING PALS ARE TOTALLY WACKO.
BOWL
THAT REMINDS ME... STEER CLEAR OF PHYLLIS. EVER SINCE SHE QUIT TAKING THE HORMONES SHE'S BEEN A LITTLE —
WACKO!
BOWLING SEEMS FUN, GRAMMA... BUT WHY DO ROSE'S BALLS KEEP GOING INTO THE GUTTER?
SHE DOESN'T SEE SO WELL.
SHE SHOULD GET GLASSES! THAT LAST ONE WENT INTO THE NEXT LANE.
SHE HAS GLASSES. SHE REFUSES TO WEAR THEM.
BUT... IF SHE NEEDS GLA-
DUCK!
HOW WAS YOUR MEETING, MOM?
BORING, HOLLY. DID YOU HAVE FUN WITH GRAMMA AND HER FRIENDS?
FUN??
DID YOU KNOW THAT AFTER SOMEONE TURNS 60... EVERY BODY PART AND BODY FUNCTION IS AN ACCEPTABLE TOPIC OF CON-VERSATION??
I CALL THAT AN ORGAN RECITAL.
BUT... THERE WASN'T ANY MUSIC.

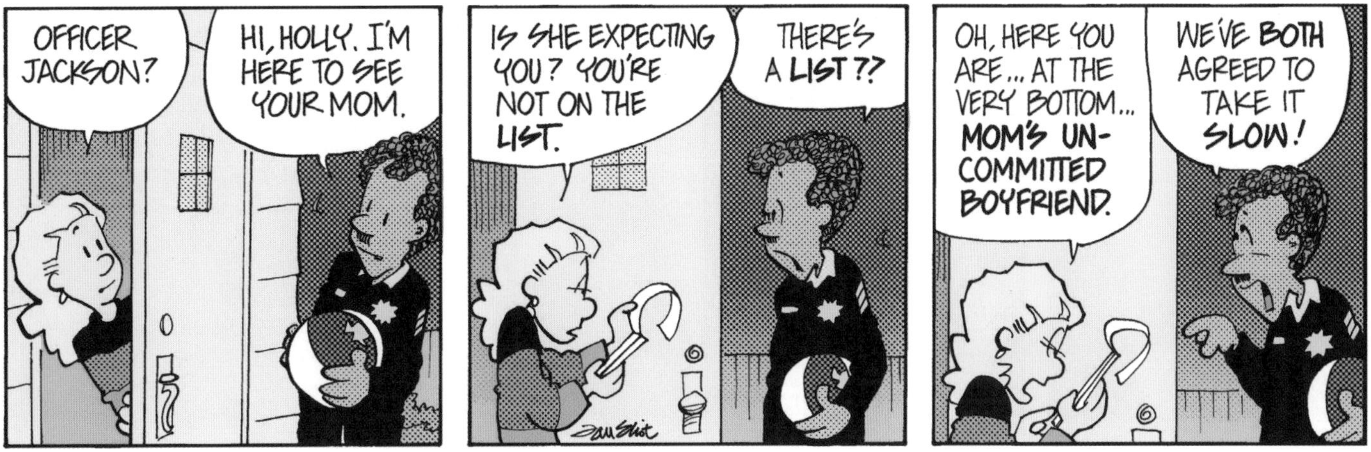
OFFICER JACKSON?
HI, HOLLY. I'M HERE TO SEE YOUR MOM.
IS SHE EXPECTING YOU? YOU'RE NOT ON THE **LIST**.
THERE'S A **LIST**??
OH, HERE YOU ARE... AT THE VERY BOTTOM... **MOM'S UN-COMMITTED BOYFRIEND.**
WE'VE **BOTH** AGREED TO TAKE IT **SLOW**!

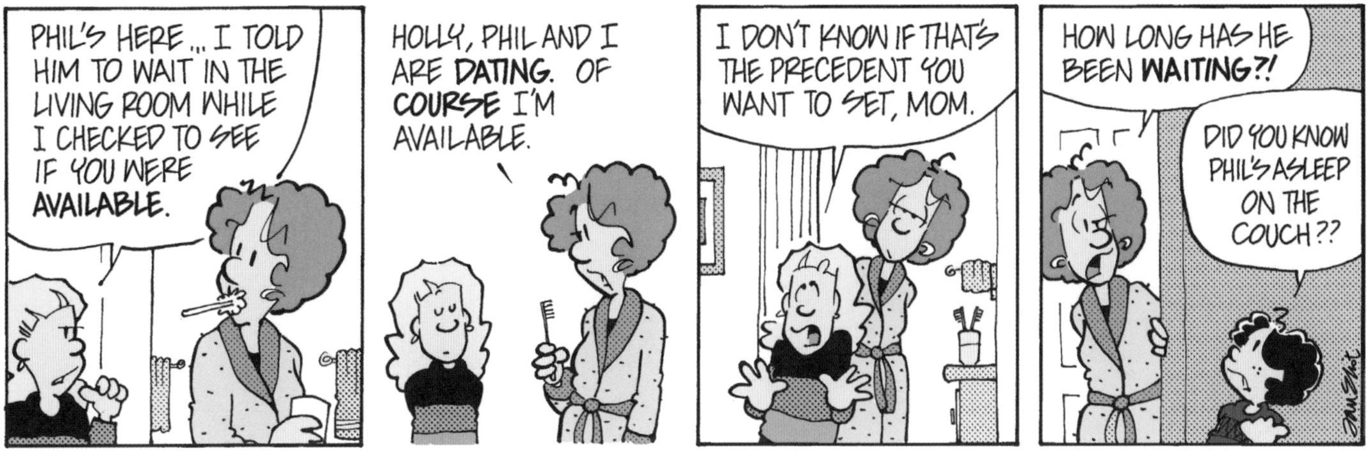
PHIL'S HERE... I TOLD HIM TO WAIT IN THE LIVING ROOM WHILE I CHECKED TO SEE IF YOU WERE **AVAILABLE**.
HOLLY, PHIL AND I ARE **DATING**. OF **COURSE** I'M AVAILABLE.
I DON'T KNOW IF THAT'S THE PRECEDENT YOU WANT TO SET, MOM.
HOW LONG HAS HE BEEN **WAITING**?!
DID YOU KNOW PHIL'S ASLEEP ON THE COUCH??

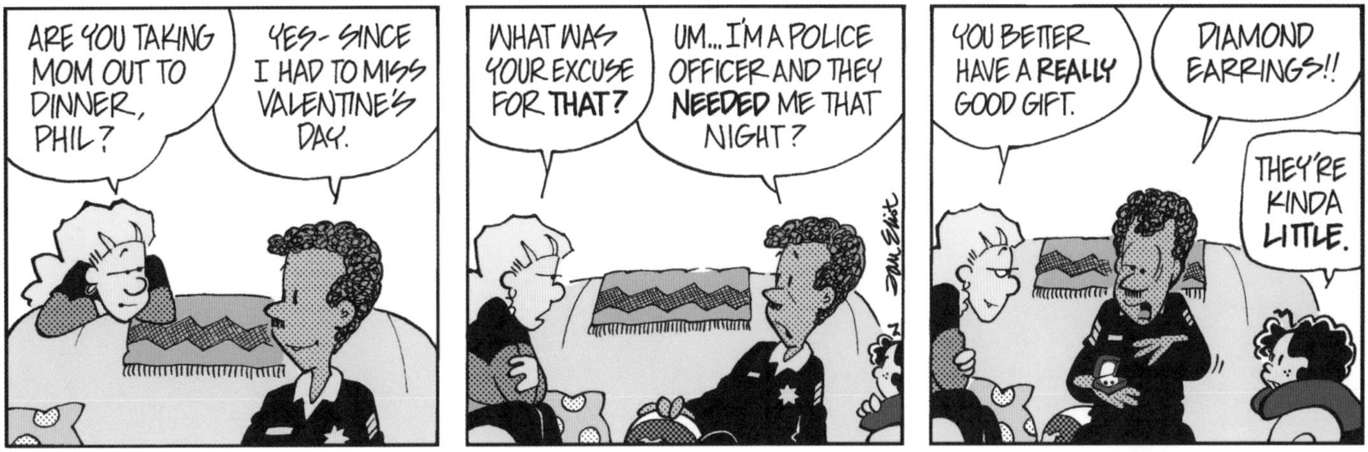
ARE YOU TAKING MOM OUT TO DINNER, PHIL?
YES- SINCE I HAD TO MISS VALENTINE'S DAY.
WHAT WAS YOUR EXCUSE FOR **THAT**?
UM... I'M A POLICE OFFICER AND THEY **NEEDED** ME THAT NIGHT?
YOU BETTER HAVE A **REALLY** GOOD GIFT.
DIAMOND EARRINGS!!
THEY'RE KINDA **LITTLE**.

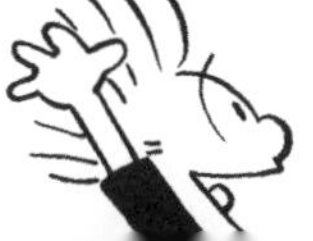

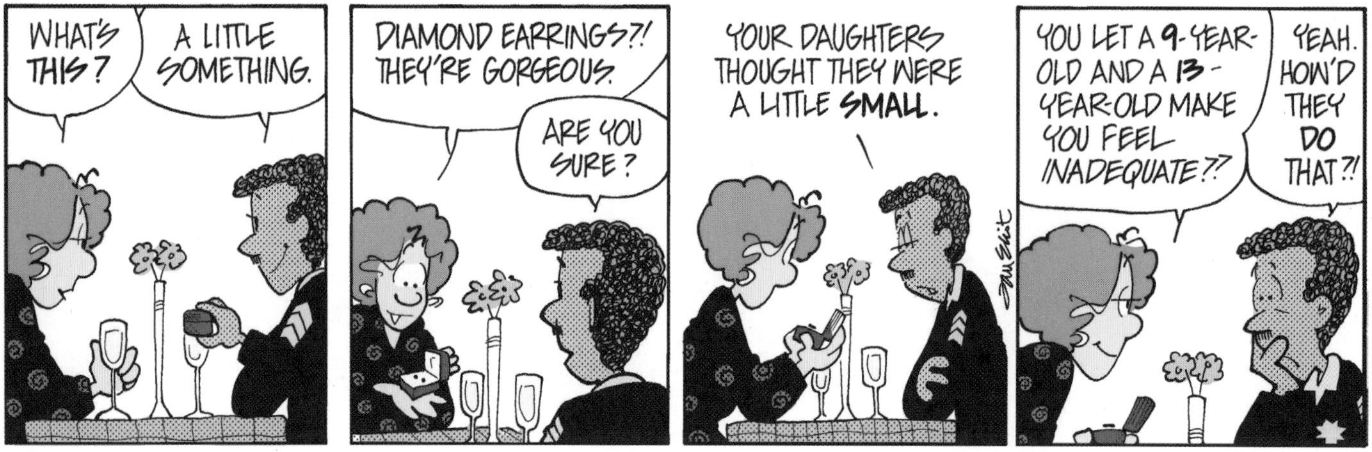
WHAT'S THIS?
A LITTLE SOMETHING.
DIAMOND EARRINGS?! THEY'RE GORGEOUS.
ARE YOU SURE?
YOUR DAUGHTERS THOUGHT THEY WERE A LITTLE SMALL.
YOU LET A 9-YEAR-OLD AND A 13-YEAR-OLD MAKE YOU FEEL INADEQUATE?!
YEAH. HOW'D THEY DO THAT?!

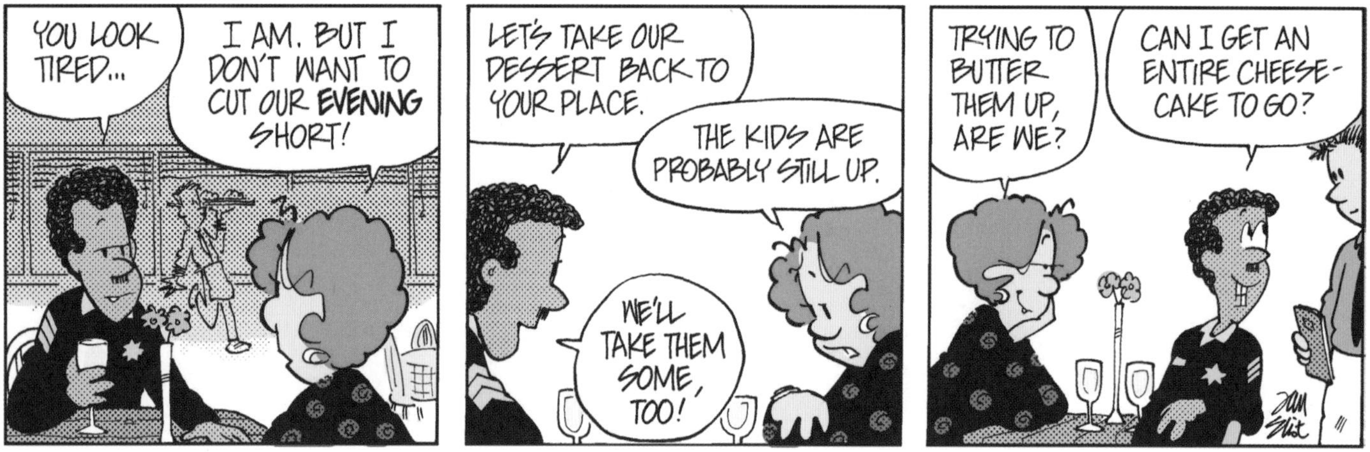
YOU LOOK TIRED...
I AM. BUT I DON'T WANT TO CUT OUR EVENING SHORT!
LET'S TAKE OUR DESSERT BACK TO YOUR PLACE.
THE KIDS ARE PROBABLY STILL UP.
WE'LL TAKE THEM SOME, TOO!
TRYING TO BUTTER THEM UP, ARE WE?
CAN I GET AN ENTIRE CHEESE-CAKE TO GO?

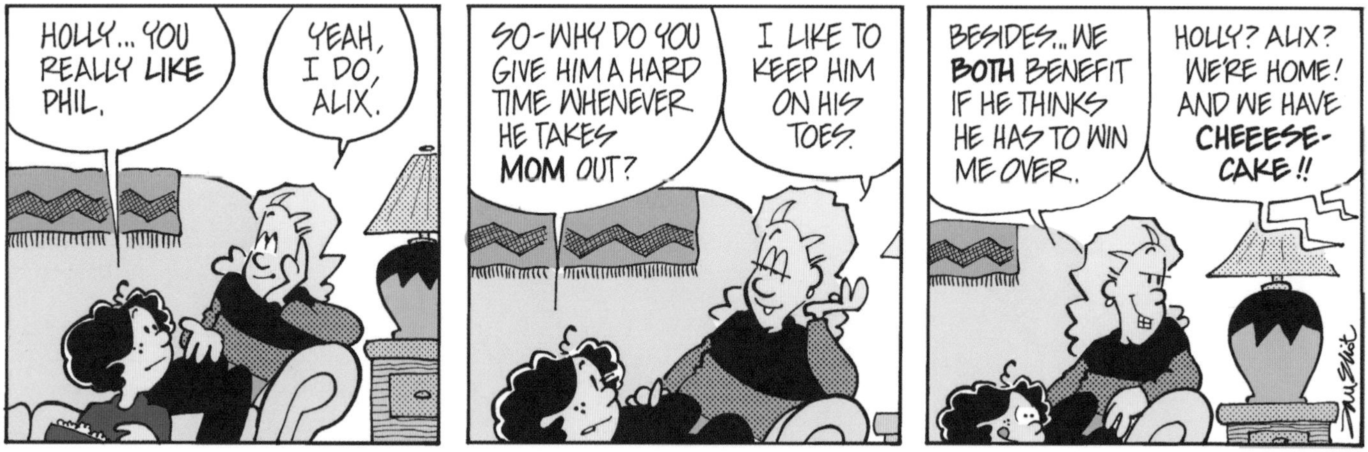
HOLLY... YOU REALLY LIKE PHIL.
YEAH, I DO, ALIX.
SO- WHY DO YOU GIVE HIM A HARD TIME WHENEVER HE TAKES MOM OUT?
I LIKE TO KEEP HIM ON HIS TOES.
BESIDES... WE BOTH BENEFIT IF HE THINKS HE HAS TO WIN ME OVER.
HOLLY? ALIX? WE'RE HOME! AND WE HAVE CHEEESE-CAKE!!

Stone Soup

GIRLS? ARE YOU EATING YOUR CEREAL?
WE'RE OUTTA MILK!
HAVE TOAST.
WE'RE OUTTA BREAD!
WE'RE LATE! HAVE A BANANA!
THEY'RE ALL BROWN AND SMOOSHY!
FINE-HAVE A POWER BAR AND SOME JUICE.
THERE'S NO—
IS THERE NOTHING TO EAT IN THIS HOUSE?!
WHY HASN'T ANYONE GONE TO THE STORE?!
I GUESS "ANYONE" WOULD BE ME.
I KEEP TELLING YOU-TEACH ME TO DRIVE.
HERE WE GO— OLIVES!

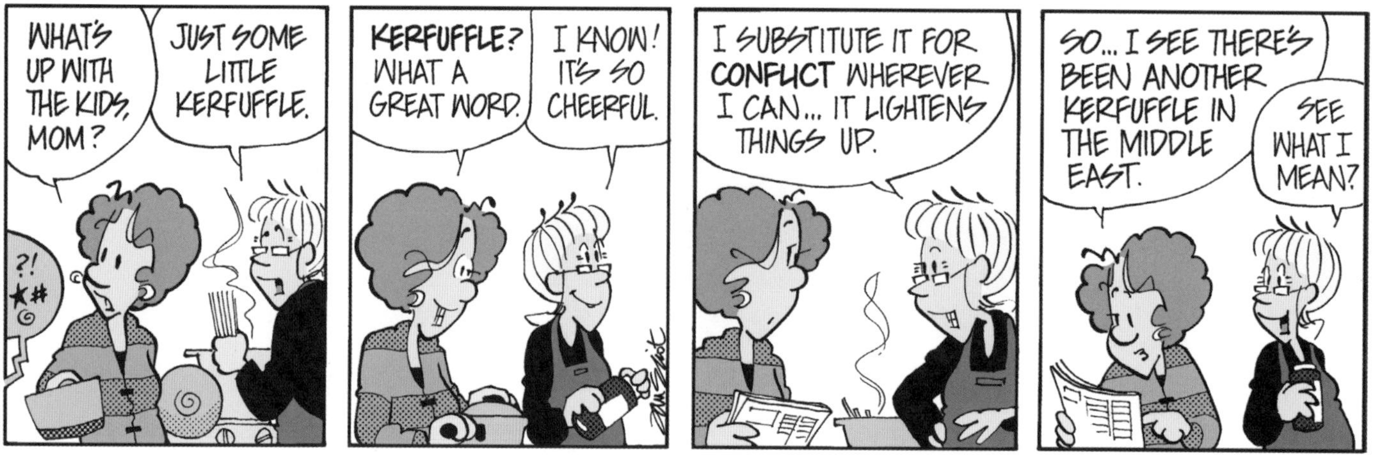
WHAT'S UP WITH THE KIDS, MOM?
JUST SOME LITTLE KERFUFFLE.
KERFUFFLE? WHAT A GREAT WORD.
I KNOW! IT'S SO CHEERFUL.
I SUBSTITUTE IT FOR **CONFLICT** WHEREVER I CAN... IT LIGHTENS THINGS UP.
SO... I SEE THERE'S BEEN ANOTHER KERFUFFLE IN THE MIDDLE EAST.
SEE WHAT I MEAN?

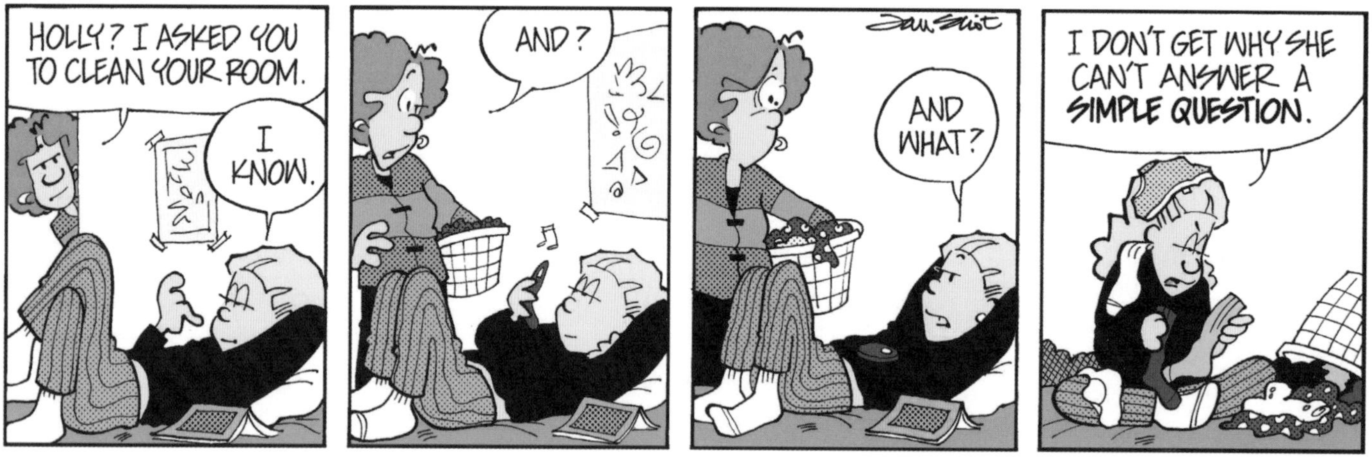
HOLLY? I ASKED YOU TO CLEAN YOUR ROOM.
I KNOW.
AND?
AND WHAT?
I DON'T GET WHY SHE CAN'T ANSWER A **SIMPLE QUESTION**.

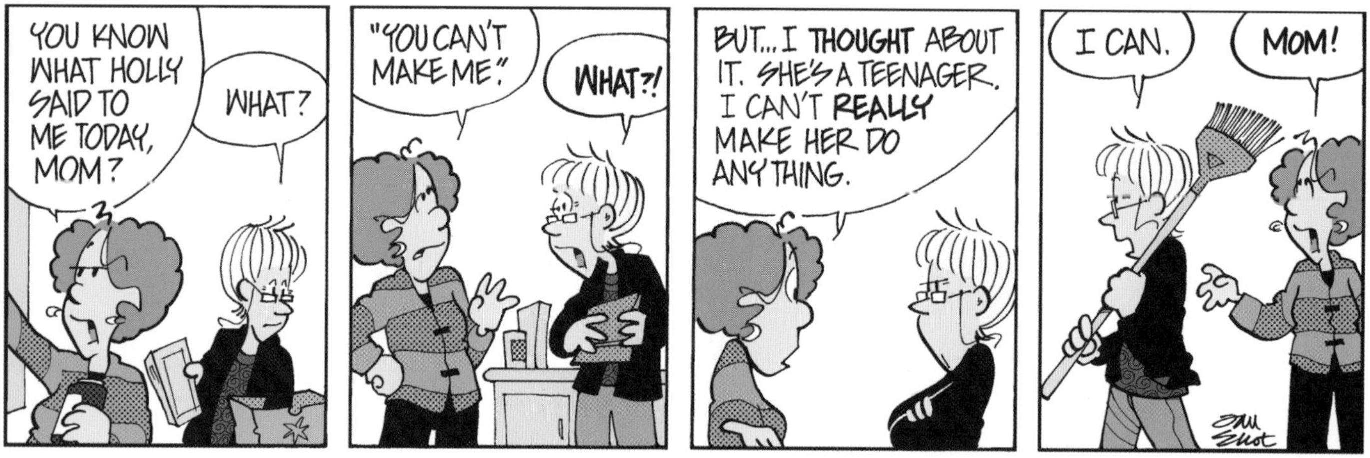
YOU KNOW WHAT HOLLY SAID TO ME TODAY, MOM?
WHAT?
"YOU CAN'T MAKE ME."
WHAT?!
BUT... I **THOUGHT** ABOUT IT. SHE'S A TEENAGER. I CAN'T **REALLY** MAKE HER DO ANYTHING.
I CAN.
MOM!

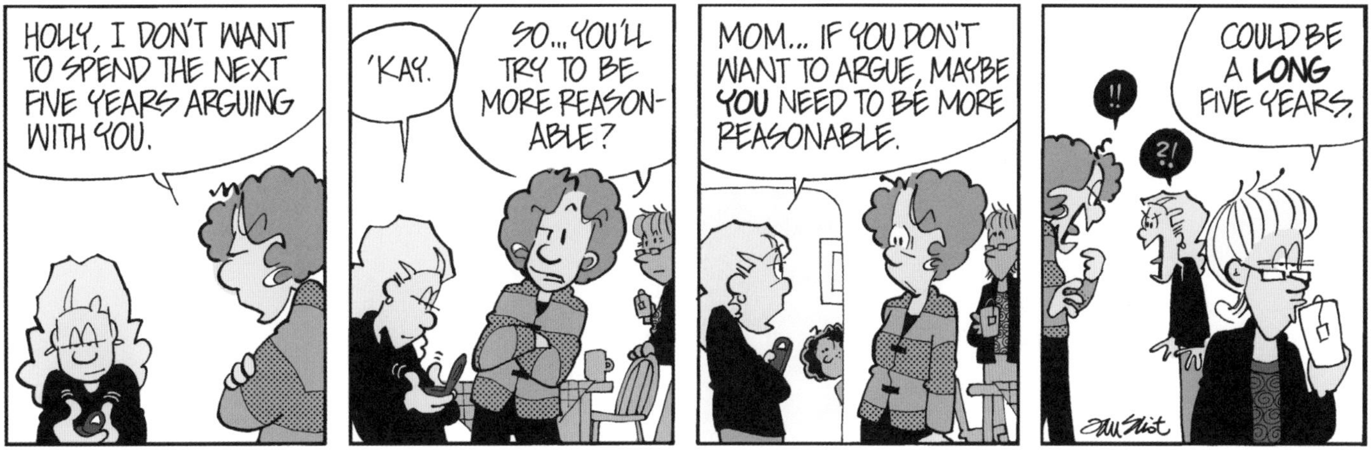
HOLLY, I DON'T WANT TO SPEND THE NEXT FIVE YEARS ARGUING WITH YOU.
'KAY.
SO... YOU'LL TRY TO BE MORE REASONABLE?
MOM... IF YOU DON'T WANT TO ARGUE, MAYBE **YOU** NEED TO BE MORE REASONABLE.
!!
?!
COULD BE A **LONG** FIVE YEARS.

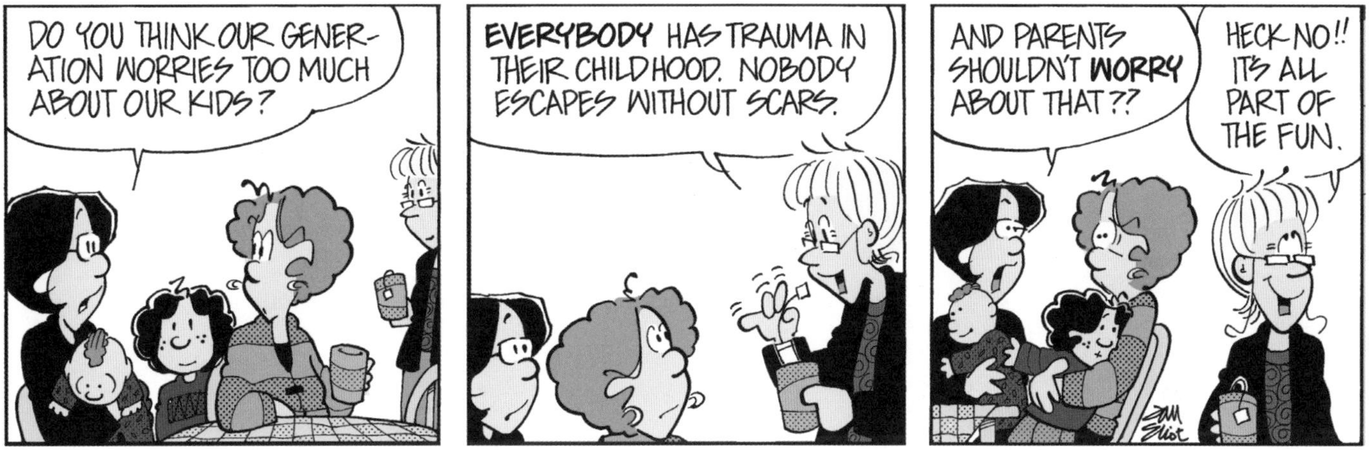
DO YOU THINK OUR GENERATION WORRIES TOO MUCH ABOUT OUR KIDS?
EVERYBODY HAS TRAUMA IN THEIR CHILDHOOD. NOBODY ESCAPES WITHOUT SCARS.
AND PARENTS SHOULDN'T **WORRY** ABOUT THAT??
HECK NO!! IT'S ALL PART OF THE FUN.

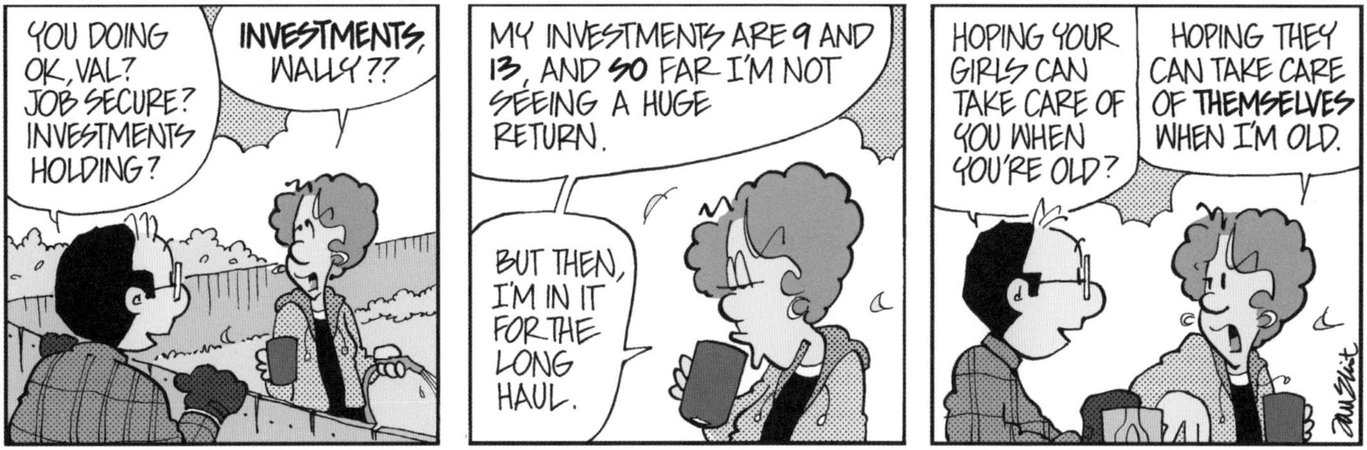
YOU DOING OK, VAL? JOB SECURE? INVESTMENTS HOLDING?
INVESTMENTS, WALLY??
MY INVESTMENTS ARE **9** AND **13**, AND **SO** FAR I'M NOT SEEING A HUGE RETURN.
BUT THEN, I'M IN IT FOR THE LONG HAUL.
HOPING YOUR GIRLS CAN TAKE CARE OF YOU WHEN YOU'RE OLD?
HOPING THEY CAN TAKE CARE OF **THEMSELVES** WHEN I'M OLD.

Stone Soup

HMM M-M-HMM
REWIND
REWIND
REWIND
I AM **NEVER** SHOWING YOU ANYTHING ON **YOUTUBE** AGAIN.
WHY?

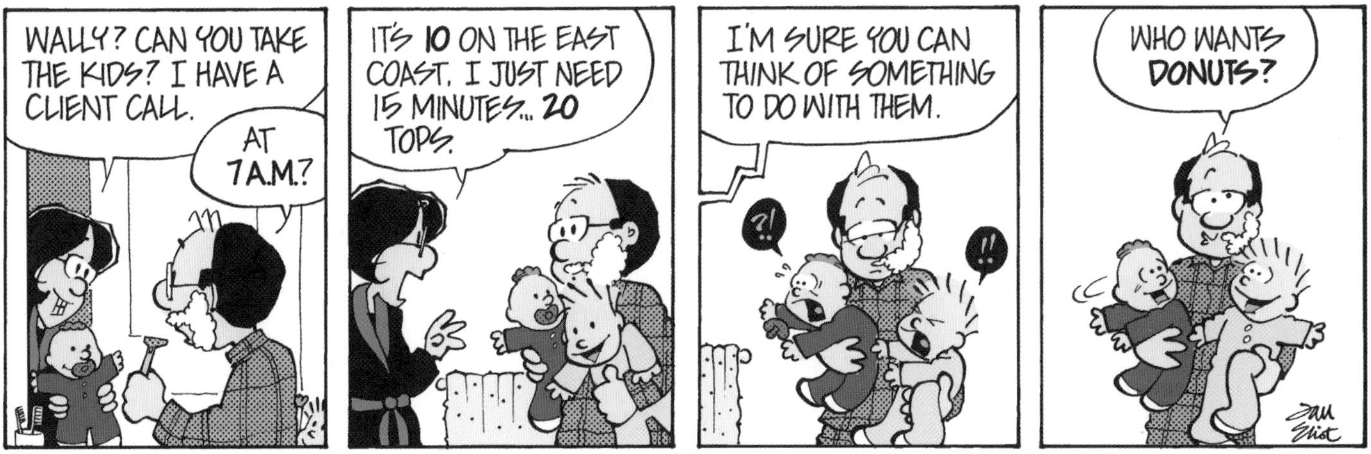
WALLY? CAN YOU TAKE THE KIDS? I HAVE A CLIENT CALL.
AT 7 A.M.?
IT'S 10 ON THE EAST COAST. I JUST NEED 15 MINUTES... 20 TOPS.
I'M SURE YOU CAN THINK OF SOMETHING TO DO WITH THEM.
?!
!!
WHO WANTS DONUTS?

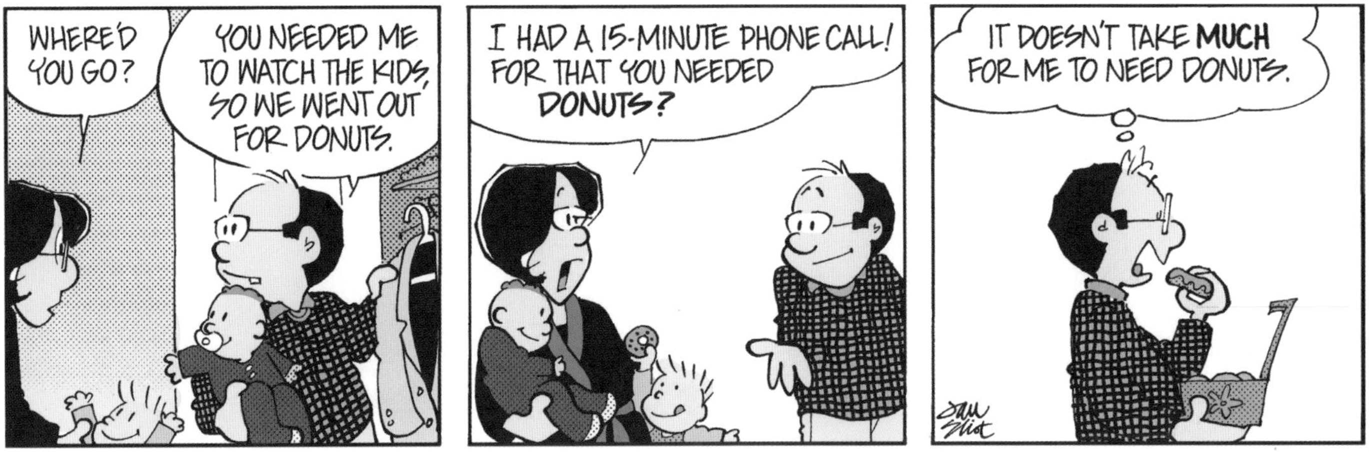
WHERE'D YOU GO?
YOU NEEDED ME TO WATCH THE KIDS, SO WE WENT OUT FOR DONUTS.
I HAD A 15-MINUTE PHONE CALL! FOR THAT YOU NEEDED DONUTS?
IT DOESN'T TAKE MUCH FOR ME TO NEED DONUTS.

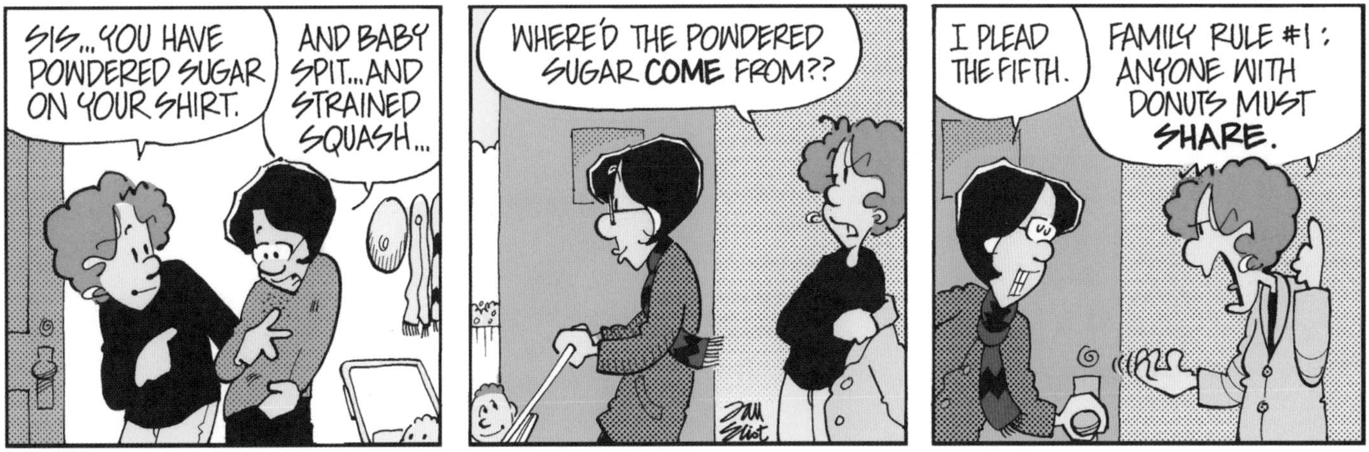
SIS... YOU HAVE POWDERED SUGAR ON YOUR SHIRT.
AND BABY SPIT... AND STRAINED SQUASH...
WHERE'D THE POWDERED SUGAR COME FROM??
I PLEAD THE FIFTH.
FAMILY RULE #1: ANYONE WITH DONUTS MUST SHARE.

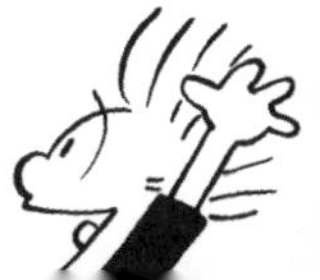

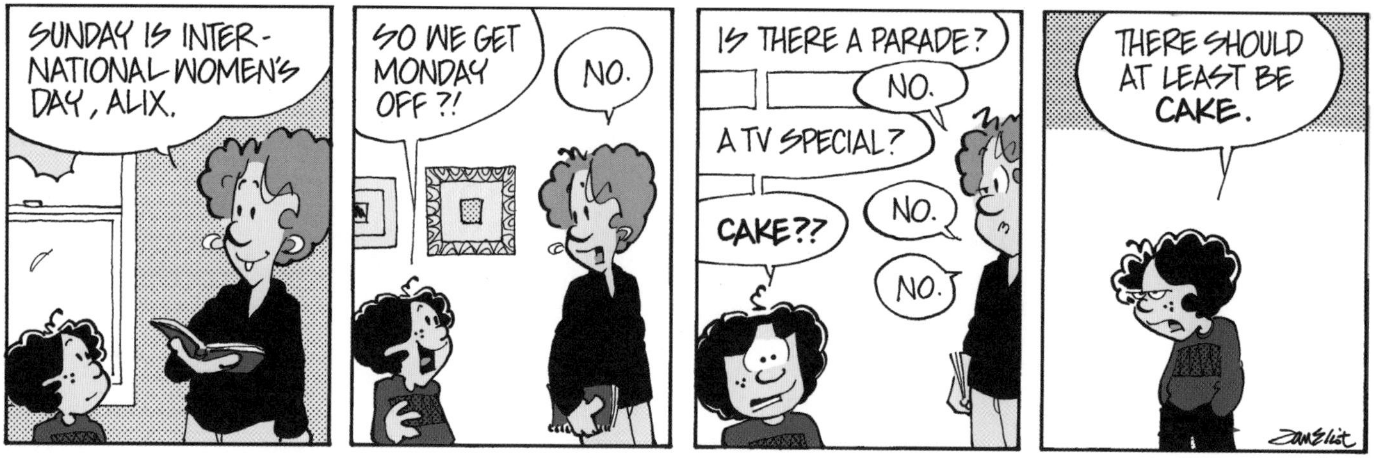
SUNDAY IS INTER-NATIONAL WOMEN'S DAY, ALIX.
SO WE GET MONDAY OFF ?!
NO.
IS THERE A PARADE?
NO.
A TV SPECIAL?
NO.
CAKE??
NO.
NO.
THERE SHOULD AT LEAST BE **CAKE**.

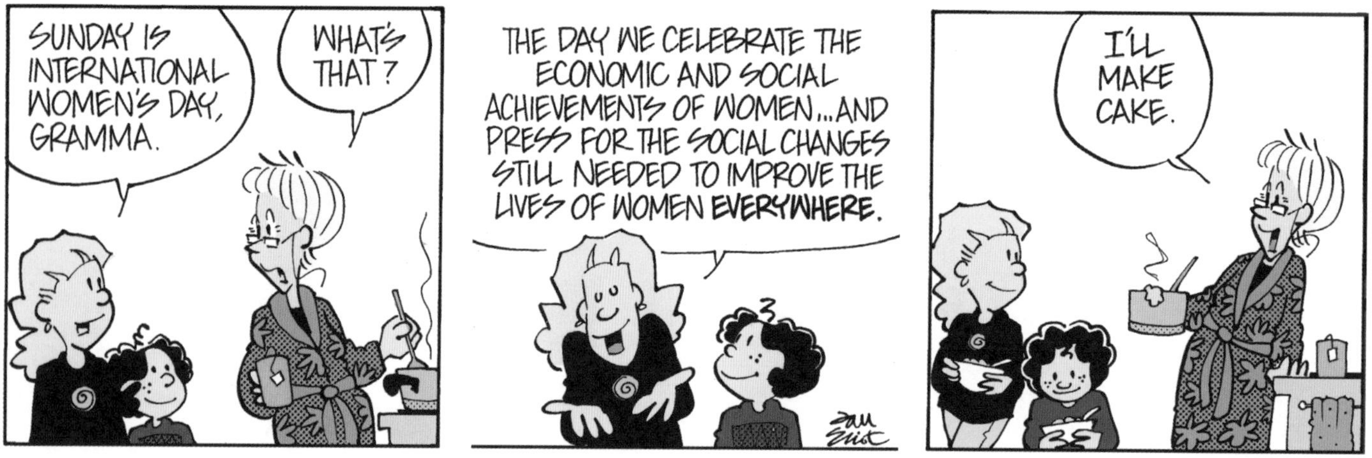
SUNDAY IS INTERNATIONAL WOMEN'S DAY, GRAMMA.
WHAT'S THAT?
THE DAY WE CELEBRATE THE ECONOMIC AND SOCIAL ACHIEVEMENTS OF WOMEN...AND PRESS FOR THE SOCIAL CHANGES STILL NEEDED TO IMPROVE THE LIVES OF WOMEN **EVERYWHERE**.
I'LL MAKE CAKE.

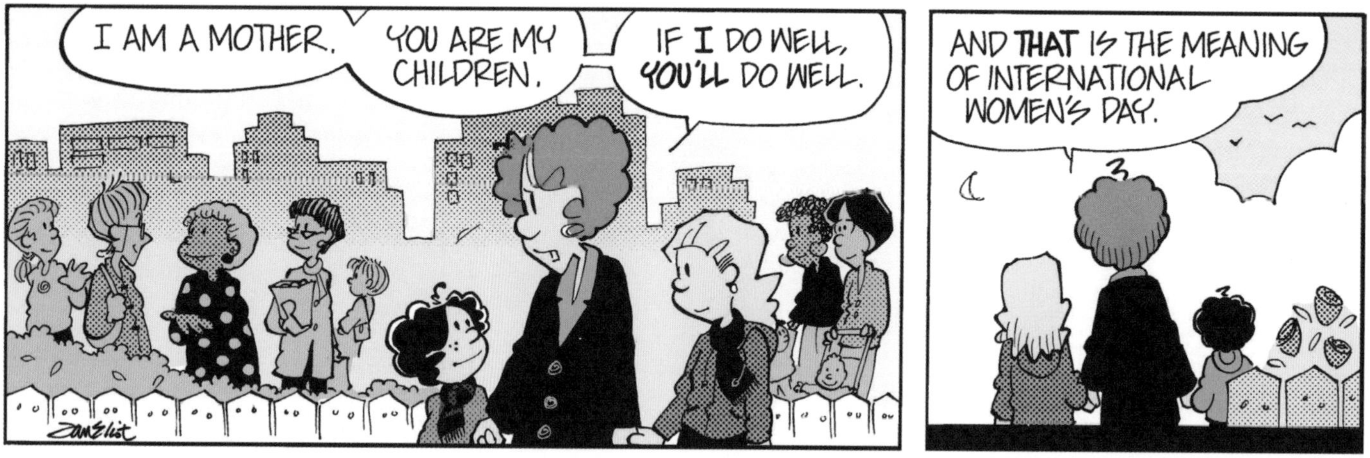
I AM A MOTHER.
YOU ARE MY CHILDREN.
IF **I** DO WELL, **YOU'LL** DO WELL.
AND **THAT** IS THE MEANING OF INTERNATIONAL WOMEN'S DAY.

Stone Soup

HOW'S IT GOING, SIS?
TRUTHFULLY? I COULD USE A DAY OFF.
TWO KIDS UNDER FIVE... I NEVER GET TO FINISH ANYTHING!!
A SENTENCE... A PHONE CONVERSATION... A PROJECT... A—
I THINK YOU ONLY HAVE MASCARA ON ONE EYE...
AND NAIL POLISH ON THREE FINGERS. I REST MY CASE.

UH·OH

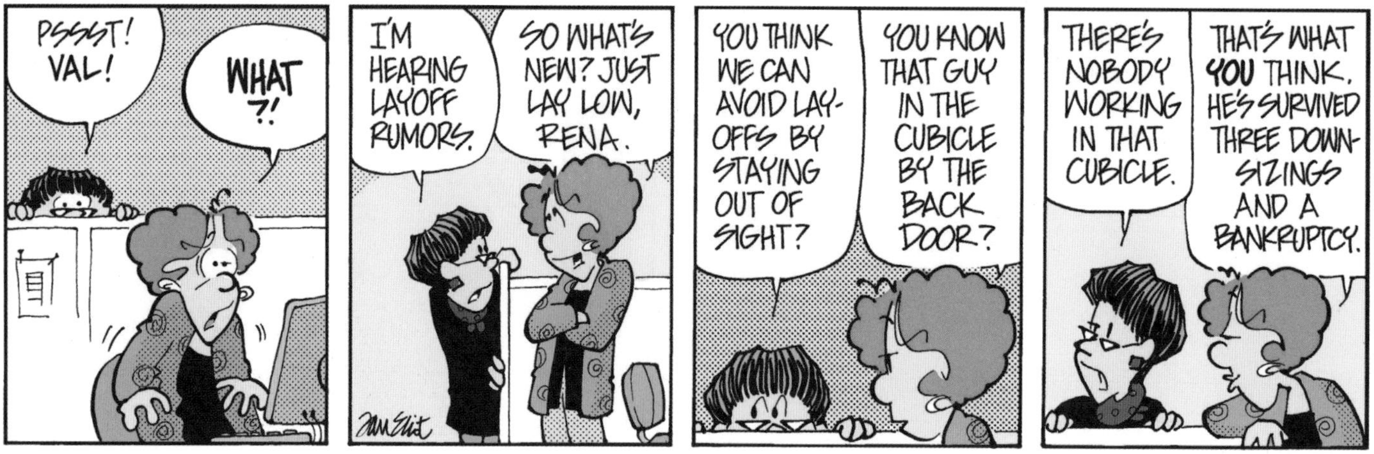
PSSST! VAL!
WHAT ?!
I'M HEARING LAYOFF RUMORS.
SO WHAT'S NEW? JUST LAY LOW, RENA.
YOU THINK WE CAN AVOID LAY-OFFS BY STAYING OUT OF SIGHT?
YOU KNOW THAT GUY IN THE CUBICLE BY THE BACK DOOR?
THERE'S NOBODY WORKING IN THAT CUBICLE.
THAT'S WHAT **YOU** THINK. HE'S SURVIVED THREE DOWN-SIZINGS AND A BANKRUPTCY.

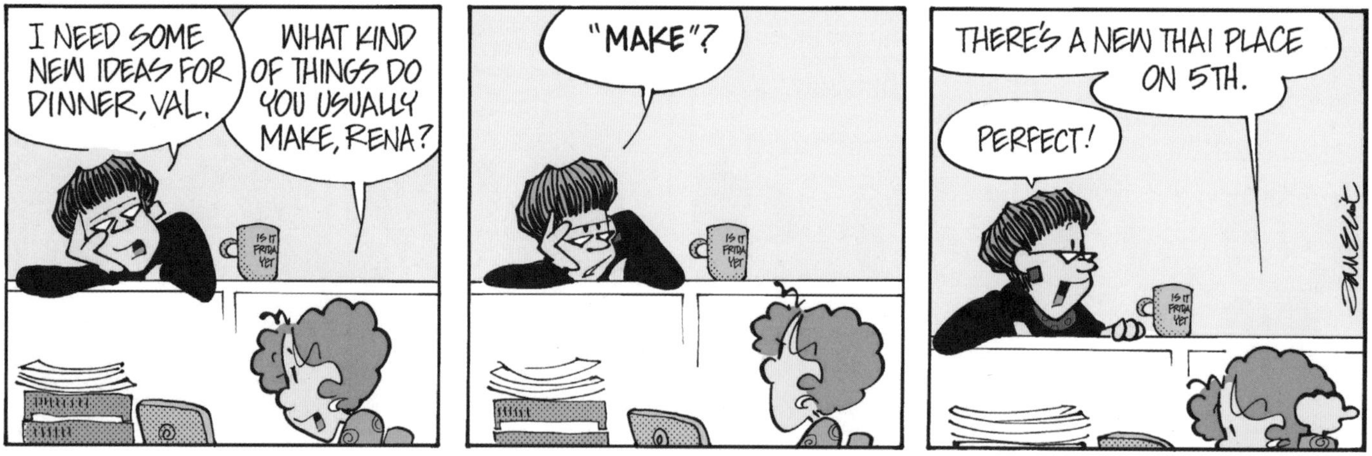
I NEED SOME NEW IDEAS FOR DINNER, VAL.
WHAT KIND OF THINGS DO YOU USUALLY MAKE, RENA?
"**MAKE**"?
THERE'S A NEW THAI PLACE ON 5TH.
PERFECT!

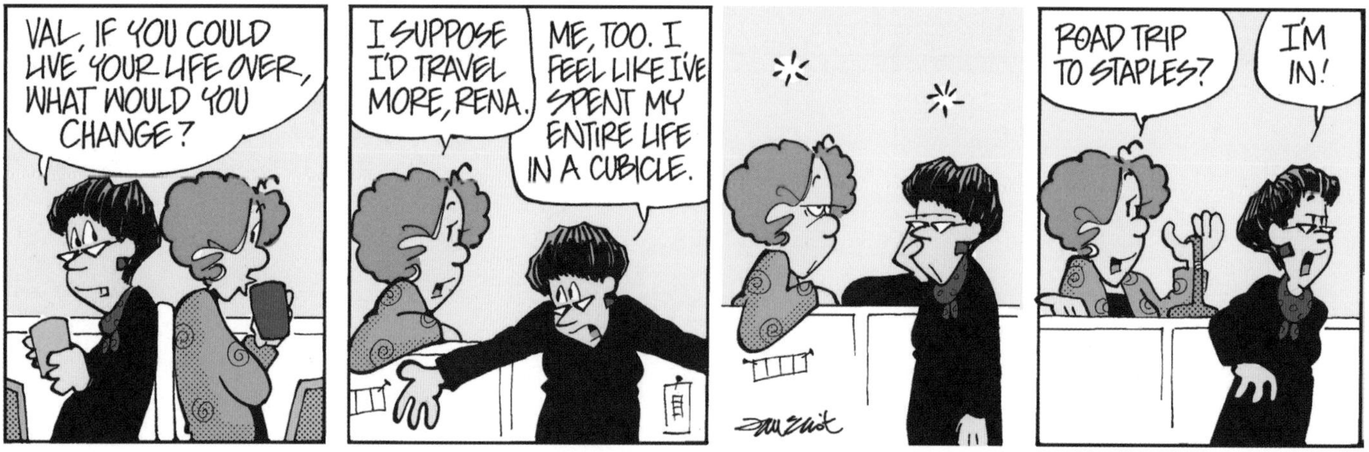
VAL, IF YOU COULD LIVE YOUR LIFE OVER, WHAT WOULD YOU CHANGE?
I SUPPOSE I'D TRAVEL MORE, RENA.
ME, TOO. I FEEL LIKE I'VE SPENT MY ENTIRE LIFE IN A CUBICLE.
ROAD TRIP TO STAPLES?
I'M IN!

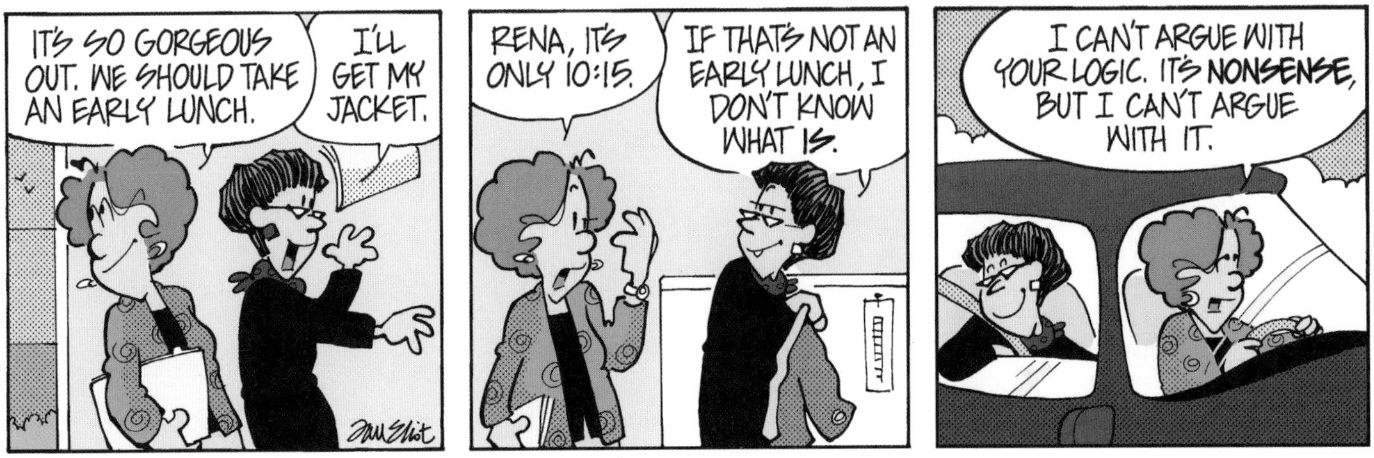
IT'S SO GORGEOUS OUT. WE SHOULD TAKE AN EARLY LUNCH.
I'LL GET MY JACKET.
RENA, IT'S ONLY 10:15.
IF THAT'S NOT AN EARLY LUNCH, I DON'T KNOW WHAT **IS**.
I CAN'T ARGUE WITH YOUR LOGIC. IT'S **NONSENSE**, BUT I CAN'T ARGUE WITH IT.

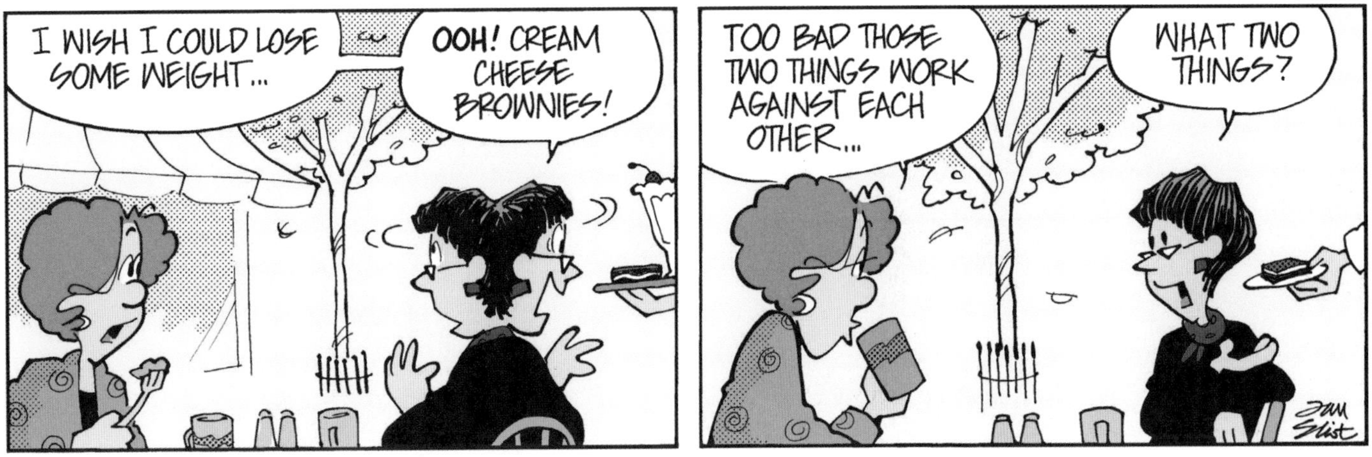
I WISH I COULD LOSE SOME WEIGHT...
OOH! CREAM CHEESE BROWNIES!
TOO BAD THOSE TWO THINGS WORK AGAINST EACH OTHER...
WHAT TWO THINGS?

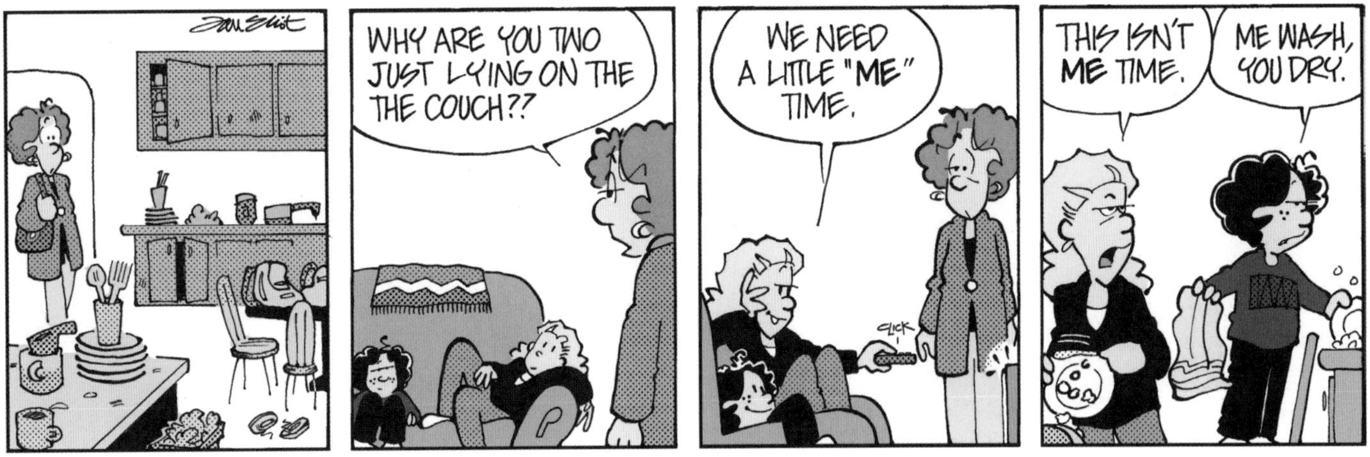
WHY ARE YOU TWO JUST LYING ON THE THE COUCH??
WE NEED A LITTLE "**ME**" TIME.
CLICK
THIS ISN'T **ME** TIME.
ME WASH, YOU DRY.

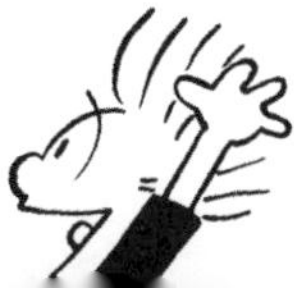

Stone Soup

I RAN INTO MY THEATER TEACHER FROM COLLEGE.
REALLY, SIS? WHERE?
IN THE CHECKOUT LINE AT SAFEWAY.
DID SHE REMEMBER YOU??
SHE DID! SHE SAID "WHAT ARE **YOU** STILL DOING HERE?"
WHERE? SAFEWAY?
NO... **HERE**. THIS TOWN.
WELL... WHERE DOES **SHE** LIVE?
CLEVELAND.
!!!
POKE POKE
MUST BE A REALLY **NICE** PART OF CLEVELAND.
WHY IS SOME-WHERE **ELSE** ALWAYS BETTER THAN **WHERE** I AM?

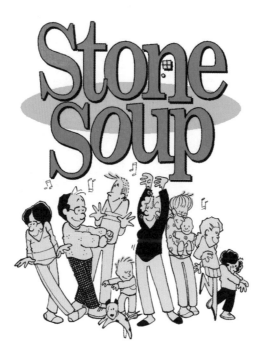

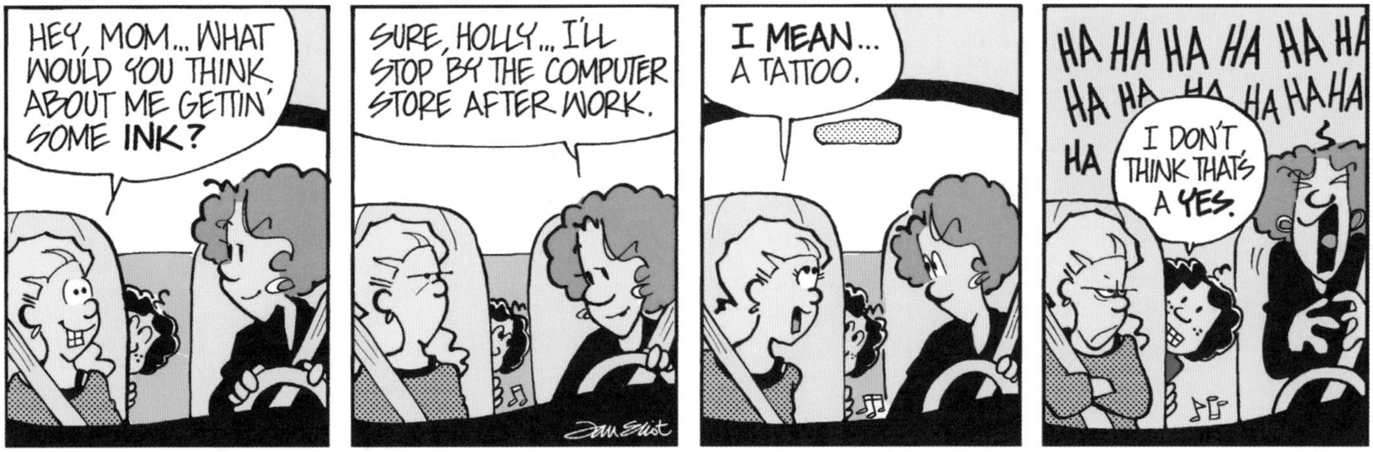
HEY, MOM... WHAT WOULD YOU THINK ABOUT ME GETTIN' SOME INK?
SURE, HOLLY... I'LL STOP BY THE COMPUTER STORE AFTER WORK.
I MEAN... A TATTOO.
HA HA HA HA HA HA HA HA HA HA HA HA HA HA
I DON'T THINK THAT'S A YES.

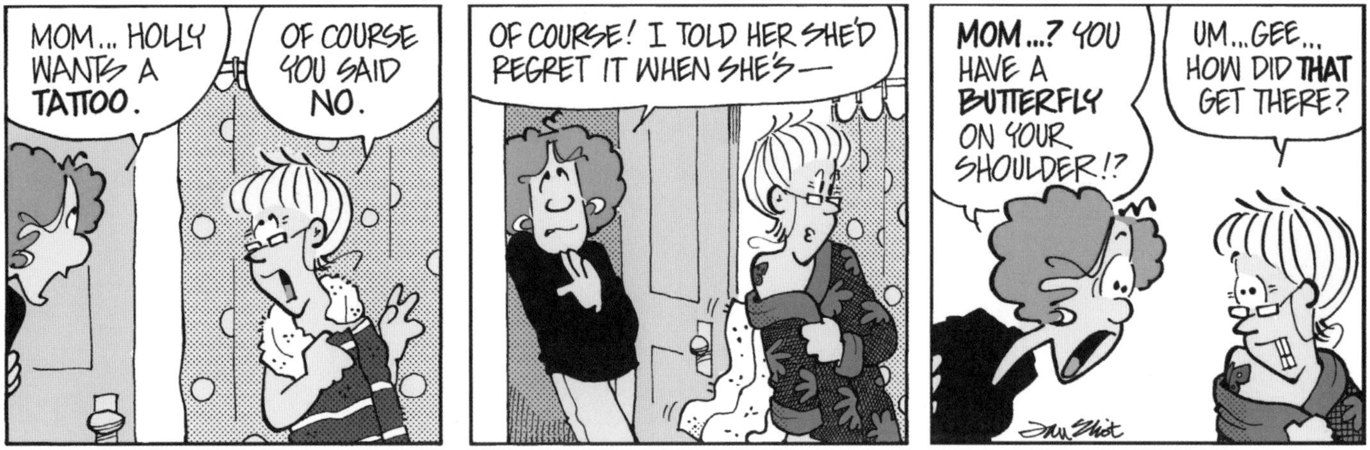
MOM... HOLLY WANTS A TATTOO.
OF COURSE YOU SAID NO.
OF COURSE! I TOLD HER SHE'D REGRET IT WHEN SHE'S—
MOM...? YOU HAVE A BUTTERFLY ON YOUR SHOULDER!?
UM...GEE... HOW DID THAT GET THERE?

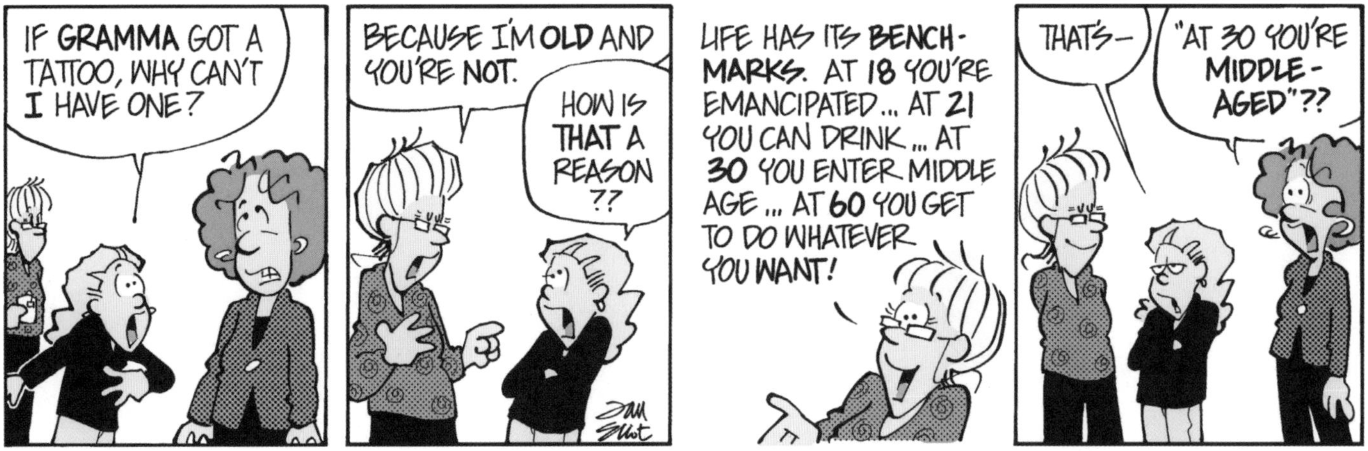
IF GRAMMA GOT A TATTOO, WHY CAN'T I HAVE ONE?
BECAUSE I'M OLD AND YOU'RE NOT.
HOW IS THAT A REASON??
LIFE HAS ITS BENCH-MARKS. AT 18 YOU'RE EMANCIPATED... AT 21 YOU CAN DRINK... AT 30 YOU ENTER MIDDLE AGE... AT 60 YOU GET TO DO WHATEVER YOU WANT!
THAT'S—
"AT 30 YOU'RE MIDDLE-AGED"??

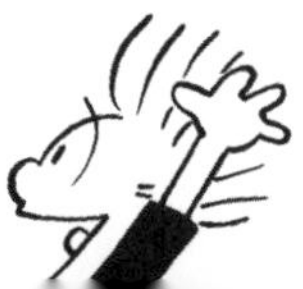

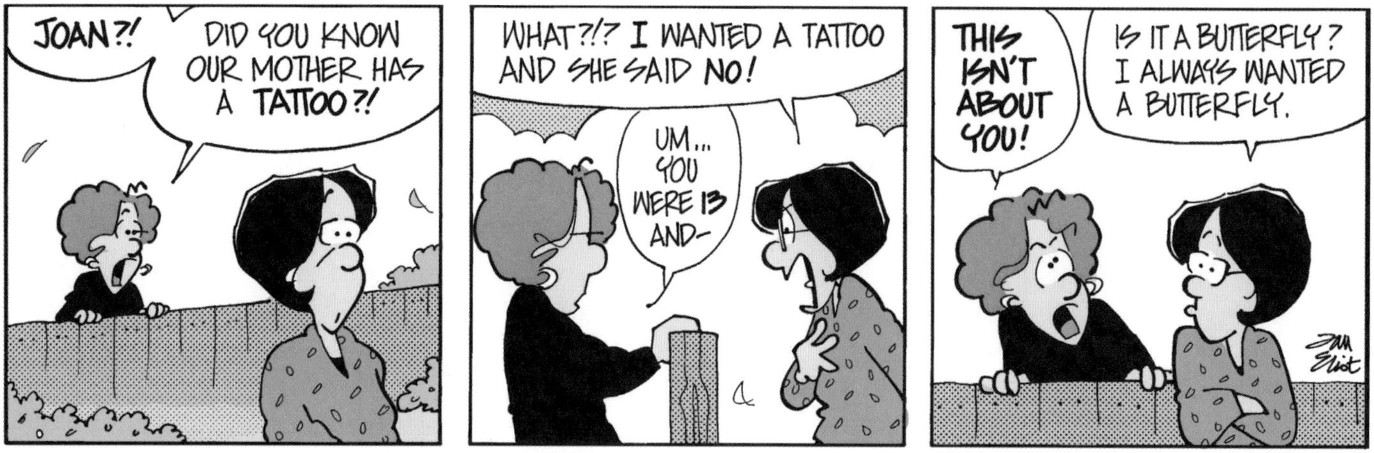
JOAN?!
DID YOU KNOW OUR MOTHER HAS A TATTOO?!
WHAT?!? I WANTED A TATTOO AND SHE SAID NO!
UM... YOU WERE 13 AND-
THIS ISN'T ABOUT YOU!
IS IT A BUTTERFLY? I ALWAYS WANTED A BUTTERFLY.

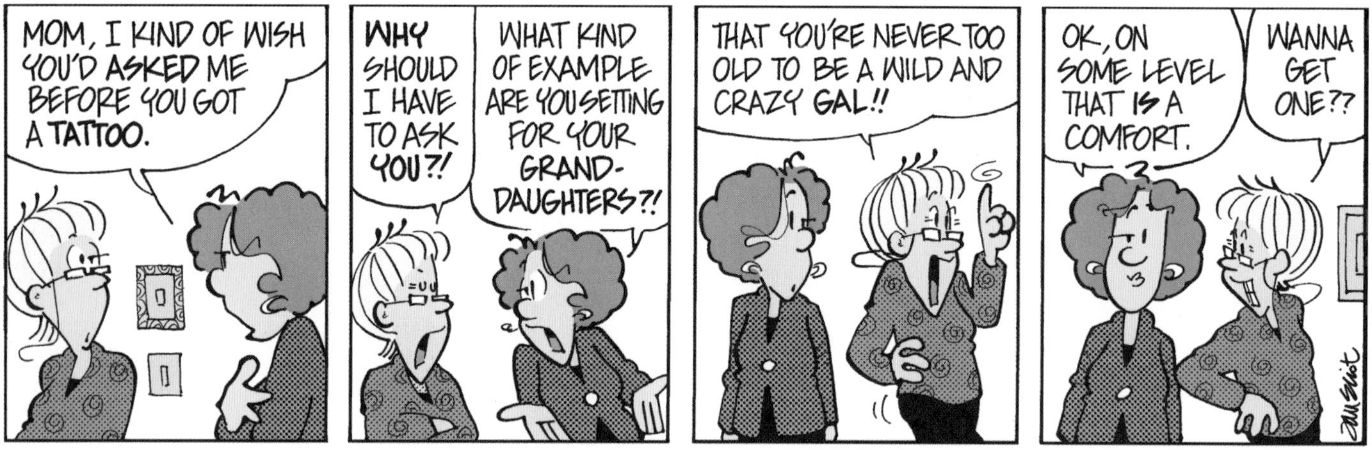
MOM, I KIND OF WISH YOU'D ASKED ME BEFORE YOU GOT A TATTOO.
WHY SHOULD I HAVE TO ASK YOU?!
WHAT KIND OF EXAMPLE ARE YOU SETTING FOR YOUR GRAND-DAUGHTERS?!
THAT YOU'RE NEVER TOO OLD TO BE A WILD AND CRAZY GAL!!
OK, ON SOME LEVEL THAT IS A COMFORT.
WANNA GET ONE??

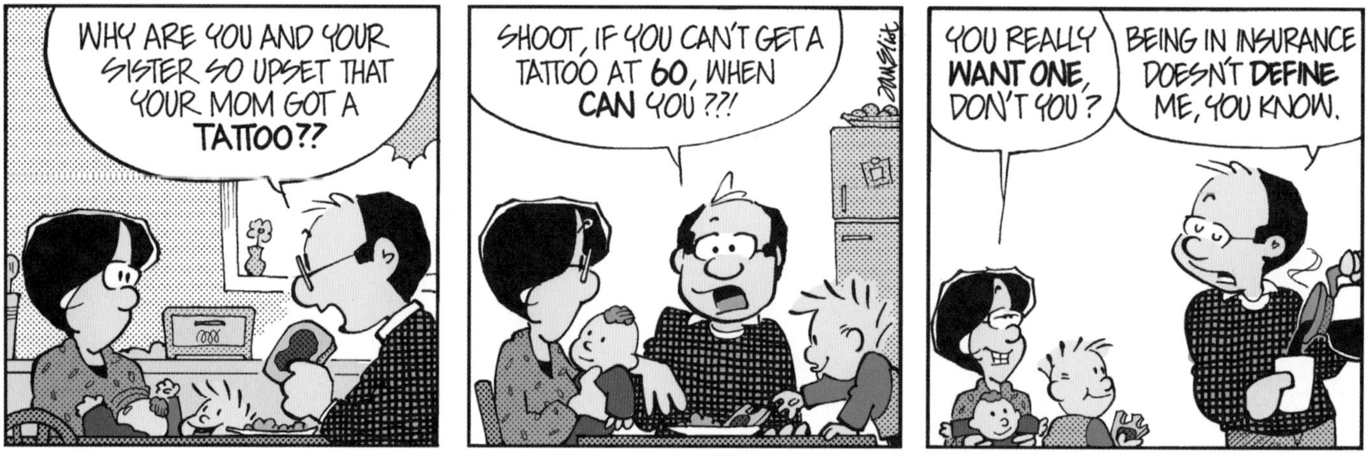
WHY ARE YOU AND YOUR SISTER SO UPSET THAT YOUR MOM GOT A TATTOO??
SHOOT, IF YOU CAN'T GET A TATTOO AT 60, WHEN CAN YOU??!
YOU REALLY WANT ONE, DON'T YOU?
BEING IN INSURANCE DOESN'T DEFINE ME, YOU KNOW.

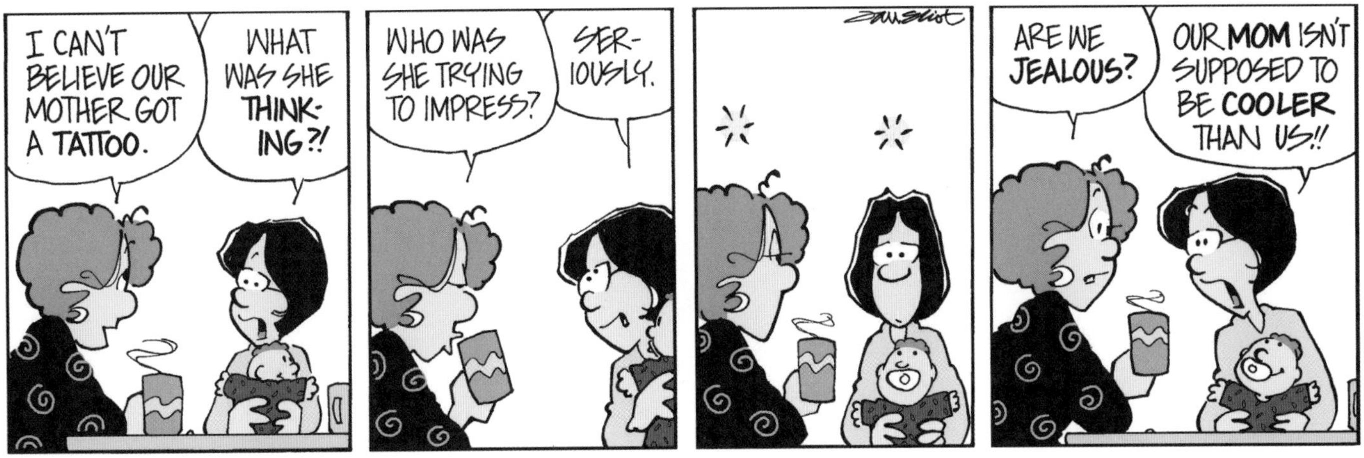
I CAN'T BELIEVE OUR MOTHER GOT A TATTOO.
WHAT WAS SHE THINKING?!
WHO WAS SHE TRYING TO IMPRESS?
SERIOUSLY.
ARE WE JEALOUS?
OUR MOM ISN'T SUPPOSED TO BE COOLER THAN US!!

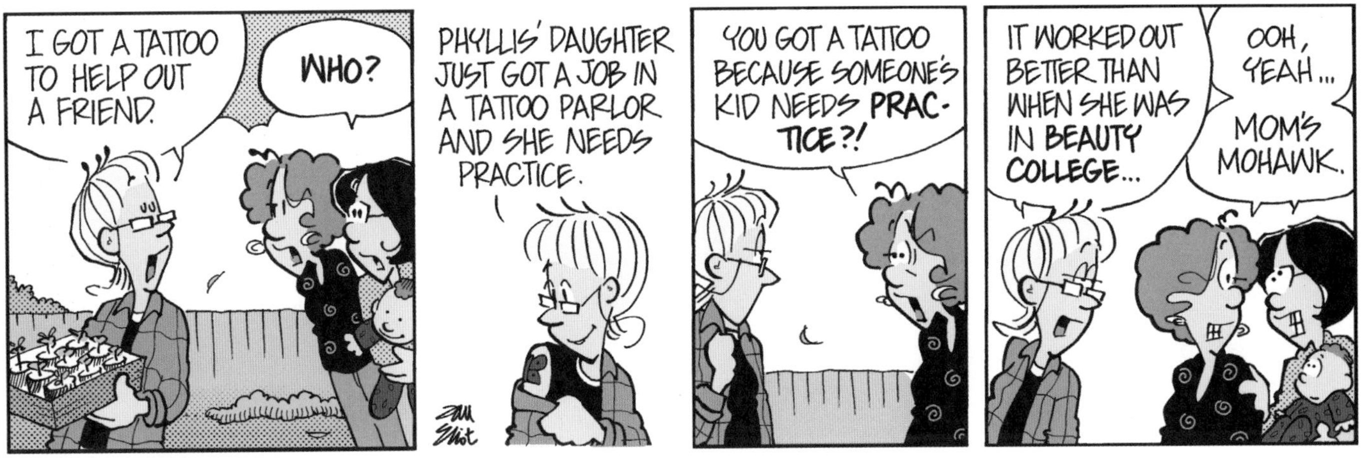
I GOT A TATTOO TO HELP OUT A FRIEND.
WHO?
PHYLLIS' DAUGHTER JUST GOT A JOB IN A TATTOO PARLOR AND SHE NEEDS PRACTICE.
YOU GOT A TATTOO BECAUSE SOMEONE'S KID NEEDS PRACTICE?!
IT WORKED OUT BETTER THAN WHEN SHE WAS IN BEAUTY COLLEGE...
OOH, YEAH...
MOM'S MOHAWK.

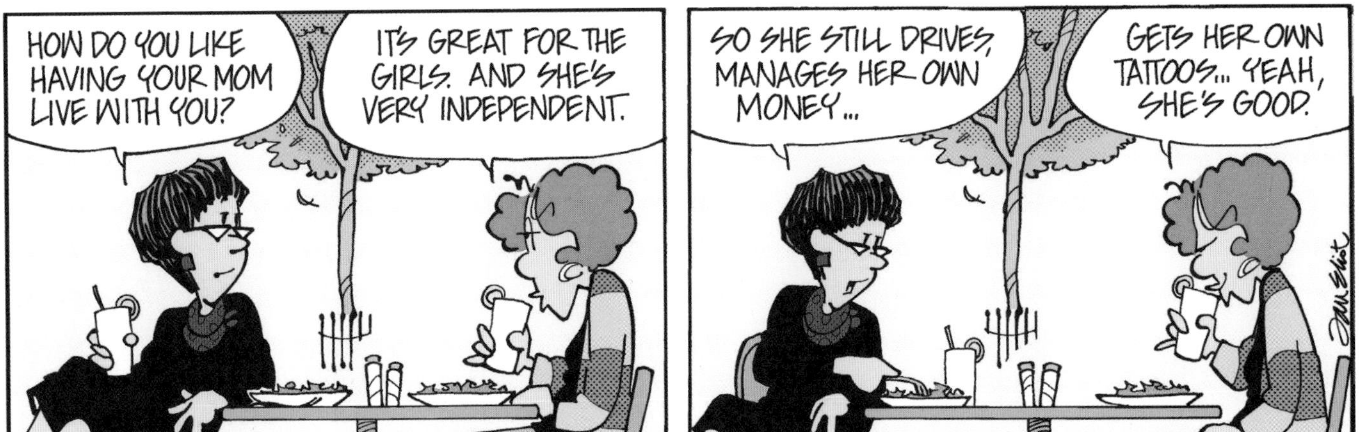
HOW DO YOU LIKE HAVING YOUR MOM LIVE WITH YOU?
IT'S GREAT FOR THE GIRLS. AND SHE'S VERY INDEPENDENT.
SO SHE STILL DRIVES, MANAGES HER OWN MONEY...
GETS HER OWN TATTOOS... YEAH, SHE'S GOOD.

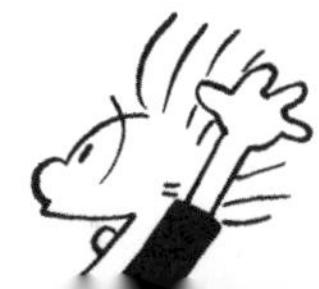

Stone Soup

RING RING
I'LL GET IT!!
NO! IT'S FOR ME!
RING
RING
HOW DO YOU KNOW?!
I HAVE WAY MORE FRIENDS THAN YOU!!
RING
RING
RING
HEY! GIMME THE PHONE, SNOT FACE!!
DORK!
RING
RING
RING!
BUGGER BREATH!
TROLL!
SLIMEBUCKET!!
BLADDA BLADDA BLADDA BLADDA
SH!!
WHAT??
IT'S FOR YOU.
?

Stone Soup

PARENTING IS EXHAUSTING, ISN'T IT?
URK

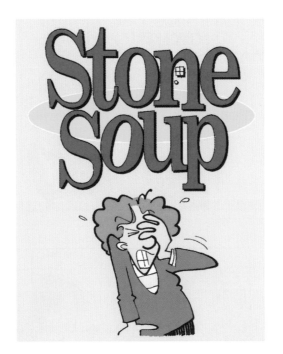

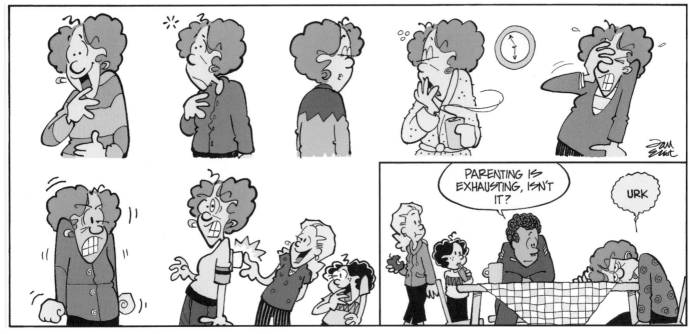

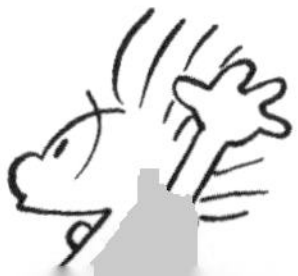

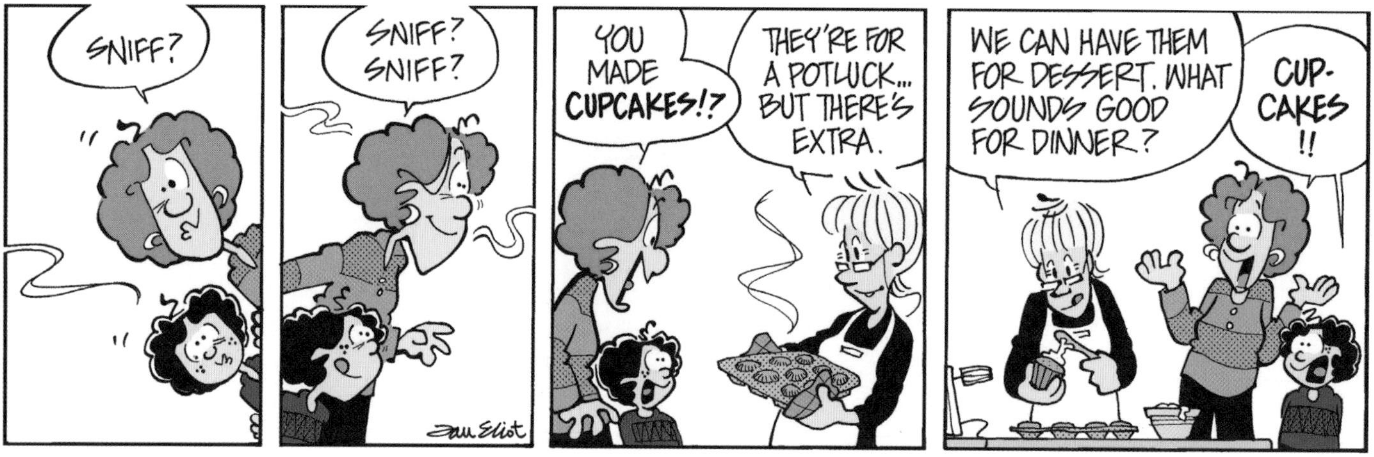
SNIFF?
SNIFF? SNIFF?
YOU MADE **CUPCAKES!?**
THEY'RE FOR A POTLUCK... BUT THERE'S EXTRA.
WE CAN HAVE THEM FOR DESSERT. WHAT SOUNDS GOOD FOR DINNER?
CUP-CAKES !!

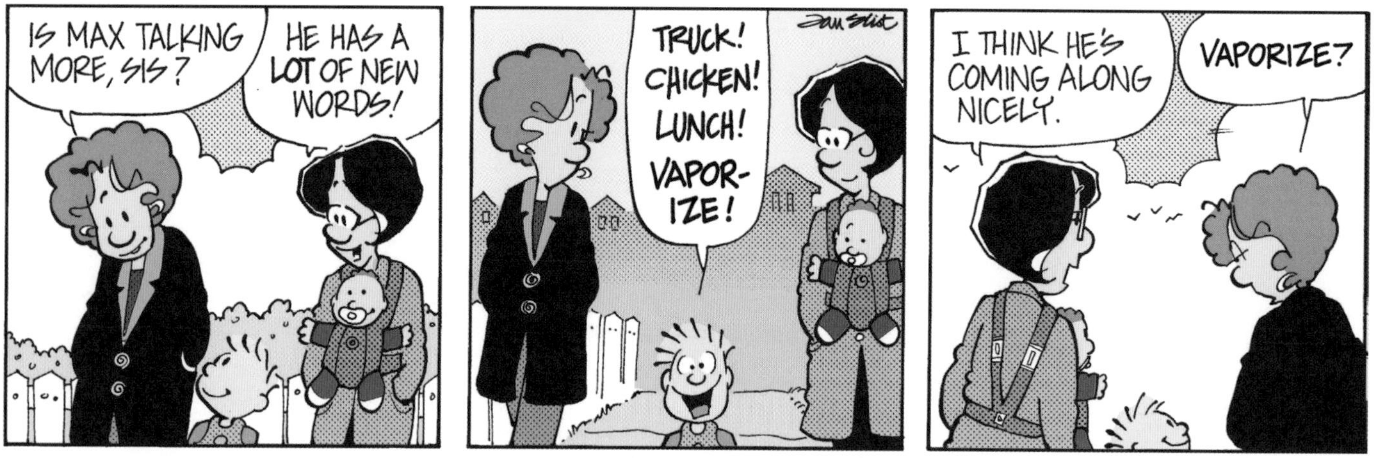
IS MAX TALKING MORE, SIS?
HE HAS A **LOT** OF NEW WORDS!
TRUCK! CHICKEN! LUNCH! VAPOR-IZE!
I THINK HE'S COMING ALONG NICELY.
VAPORIZE?

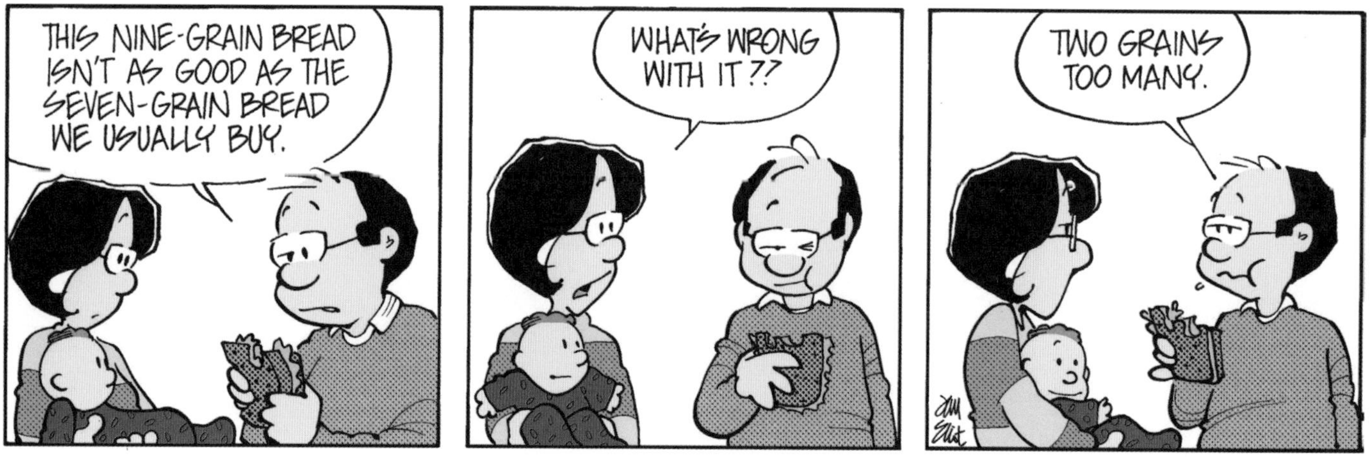
THIS NINE-GRAIN BREAD ISN'T AS GOOD AS THE SEVEN-GRAIN BREAD WE USUALLY BUY.
WHAT'S WRONG WITH IT??
TWO GRAINS TOO MANY.

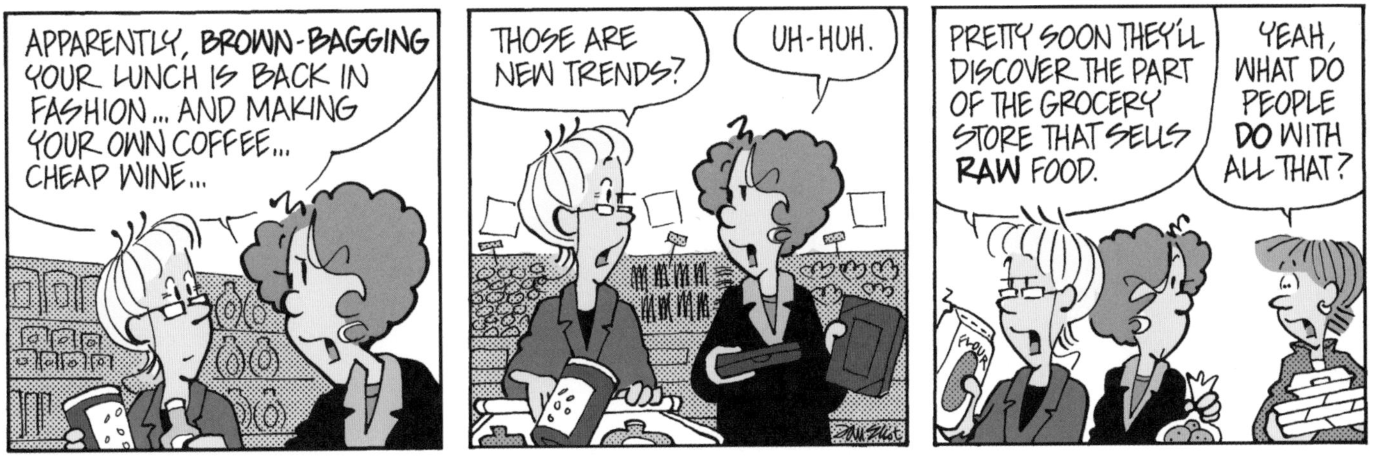
APPARENTLY, BROWN-BAGGING YOUR LUNCH IS BACK IN FASHION... AND MAKING YOUR OWN COFFEE... CHEAP WINE...
THOSE ARE NEW TRENDS?
UH-HUH.
PRETTY SOON THEY'LL DISCOVER THE PART OF THE GROCERY STORE THAT SELLS RAW FOOD.
YEAH, WHAT DO PEOPLE DO WITH ALL THAT?
FLOUR

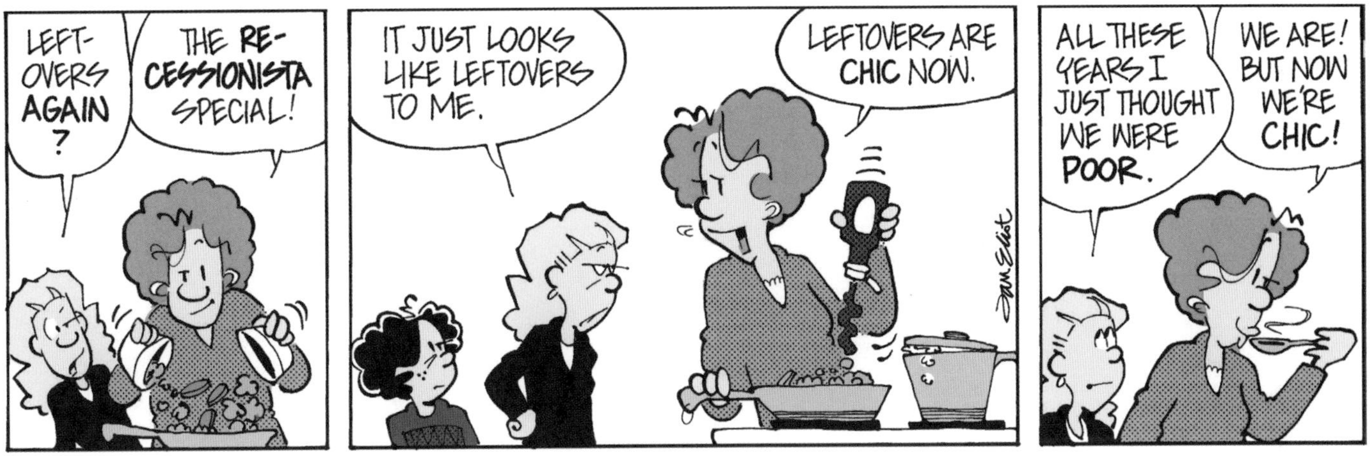
LEFT-OVERS AGAIN?
THE RE-CESSIONISTA SPECIAL!
IT JUST LOOKS LIKE LEFTOVERS TO ME.
LEFTOVERS ARE CHIC NOW.
ALL THESE YEARS I JUST THOUGHT WE WERE POOR.
WE ARE! BUT NOW WE'RE CHIC!

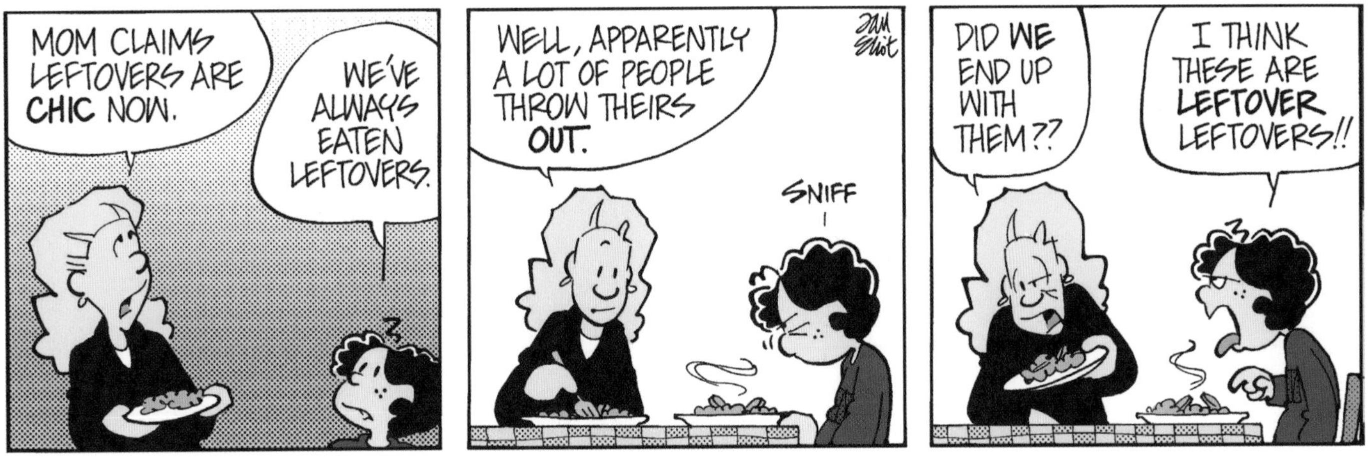
MOM CLAIMS LEFTOVERS ARE CHIC NOW.
WE'VE ALWAYS EATEN LEFTOVERS.
WELL, APPARENTLY A LOT OF PEOPLE THROW THEIRS OUT.
SNIFF
DID WE END UP WITH THEM??
I THINK THESE ARE LEFTOVER LEFTOVERS!!

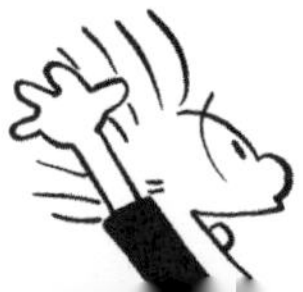

Stone Soup

WHAT IS THIS?
A BURGER.
NO IT ISN'T.
LETTUCE, TOMATO, PATTY, BUN... IT'S A **BURGER**.
YOU SAID "PATTY."
IT'S A BURGER. WHAT ELSE WOULD I SAY??
MEAT.
WITH ENOUGH KETCHUP, MUSTARD AND ONION IT TASTES **JUST THE SAME**...
WHILE LOWERING YOUR **CHOLESTEROL** AND SUPPORTING SUSTAINABLE FOOD PRACTICES ON OUR **FRAGILE PLANET**.
I WANTED A BURGER, I GOT A **CAUSE**.
MMM... YUMMY.

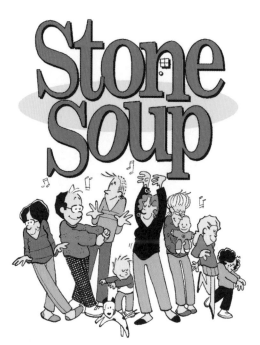

Stone Soup

OK ... OUR CHOICES ARE —

"ADULT CONTENT, SENSUALITY, BRIEF NUDITY ..."

CINEMA 15.

GASP

OR — "HEAVY ARTILLERY, TORTURE AND GLOBAL DESTRUCTION ..."

HMMM...

WE ARE SO CONFUSED.

LADY WITH NO SHIRT ... LADY WITH NO HEAD ...

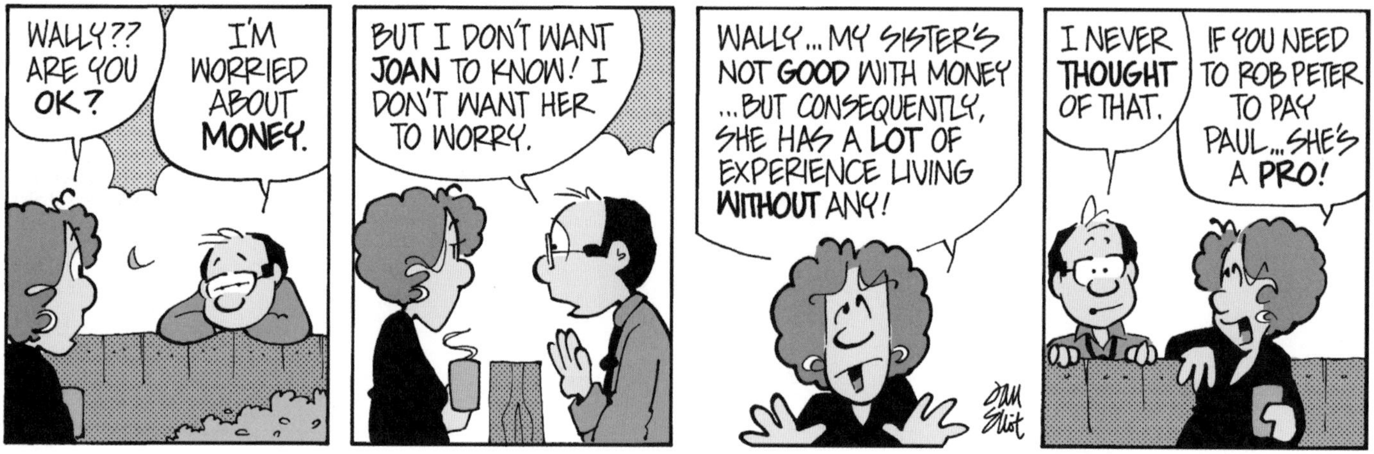
WALLY?? ARE YOU OK?
I'M WORRIED ABOUT MONEY.
BUT I DON'T WANT JOAN TO KNOW! I DON'T WANT HER TO WORRY.
WALLY... MY SISTER'S NOT GOOD WITH MONEY ...BUT CONSEQUENTLY, SHE HAS A LOT OF EXPERIENCE LIVING WITHOUT ANY!
I NEVER THOUGHT OF THAT.
IF YOU NEED TO ROB PETER TO PAY PAUL... SHE'S A PRO!

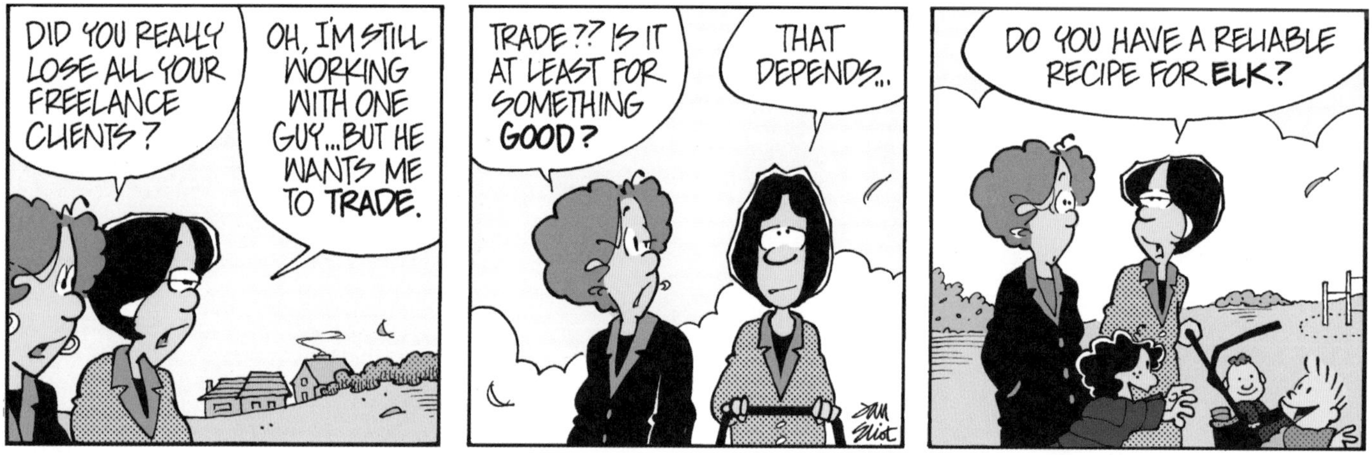
DID YOU REALLY LOSE ALL YOUR FREELANCE CLIENTS?
OH, I'M STILL WORKING WITH ONE GUY...BUT HE WANTS ME TO TRADE.
TRADE?? IS IT AT LEAST FOR SOMETHING GOOD?
THAT DEPENDS...
DO YOU HAVE A RELIABLE RECIPE FOR ELK?

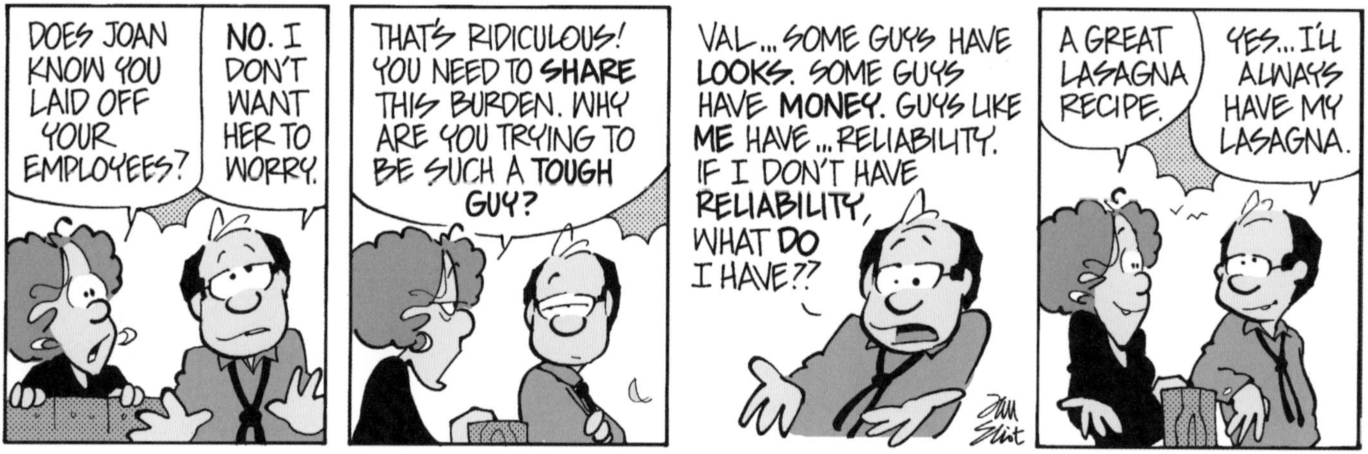
DOES JOAN KNOW YOU LAID OFF YOUR EMPLOYEES?
NO. I DON'T WANT HER TO WORRY.
THAT'S RIDICULOUS! YOU NEED TO SHARE THIS BURDEN. WHY ARE YOU TRYING TO BE SUCH A TOUGH GUY?
VAL... SOME GUYS HAVE LOOKS. SOME GUYS HAVE MONEY. GUYS LIKE ME HAVE... RELIABILITY. IF I DON'T HAVE RELIABILITY, WHAT DO I HAVE??
A GREAT LASAGNA RECIPE.
YES... I'LL ALWAYS HAVE MY LASAGNA.

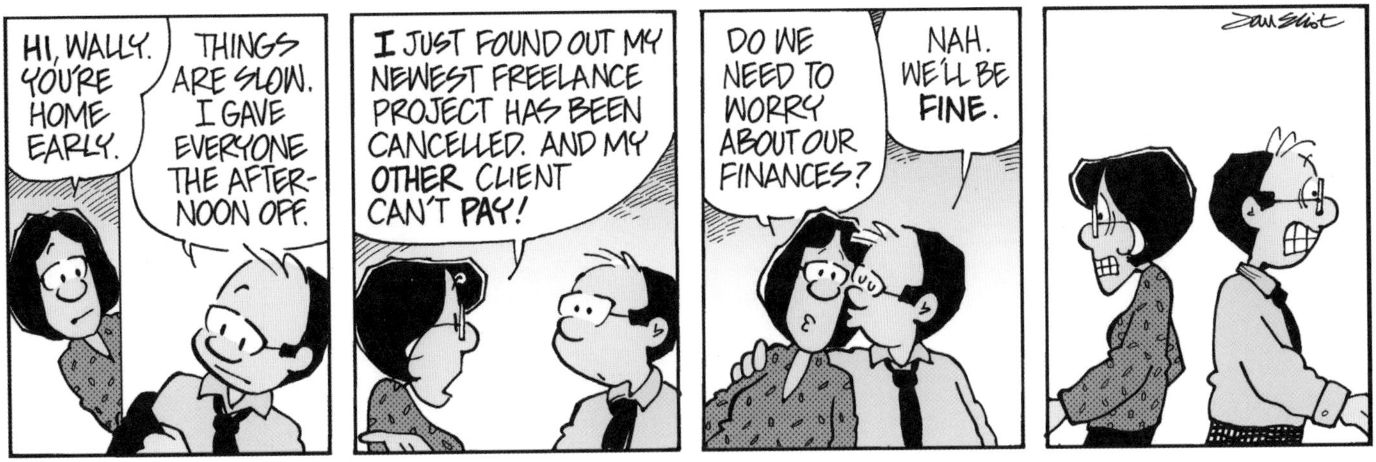
HI, WALLY. YOU'RE HOME EARLY.
THINGS ARE SLOW. I GAVE EVERYONE THE AFTER-NOON OFF.
I JUST FOUND OUT MY NEWEST FREELANCE PROJECT HAS BEEN CANCELLED. AND MY OTHER CLIENT CAN'T PAY!
DO WE NEED TO WORRY ABOUT OUR FINANCES?
NAH. WE'LL BE FINE.

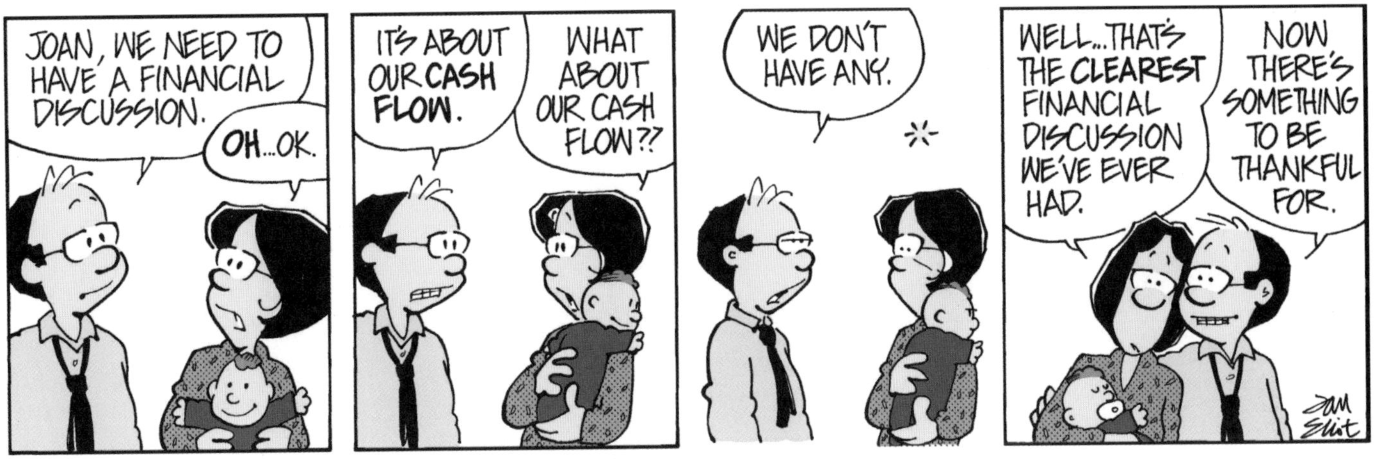
JOAN, WE NEED TO HAVE A FINANCIAL DISCUSSION.
OH...OK.
IT'S ABOUT OUR CASH FLOW.
WHAT ABOUT OUR CASH FLOW??
WE DON'T HAVE ANY.
WELL...THAT'S THE CLEAREST FINANCIAL DISCUSSION WE'VE EVER HAD.
NOW THERE'S SOMETHING TO BE THANKFUL FOR.

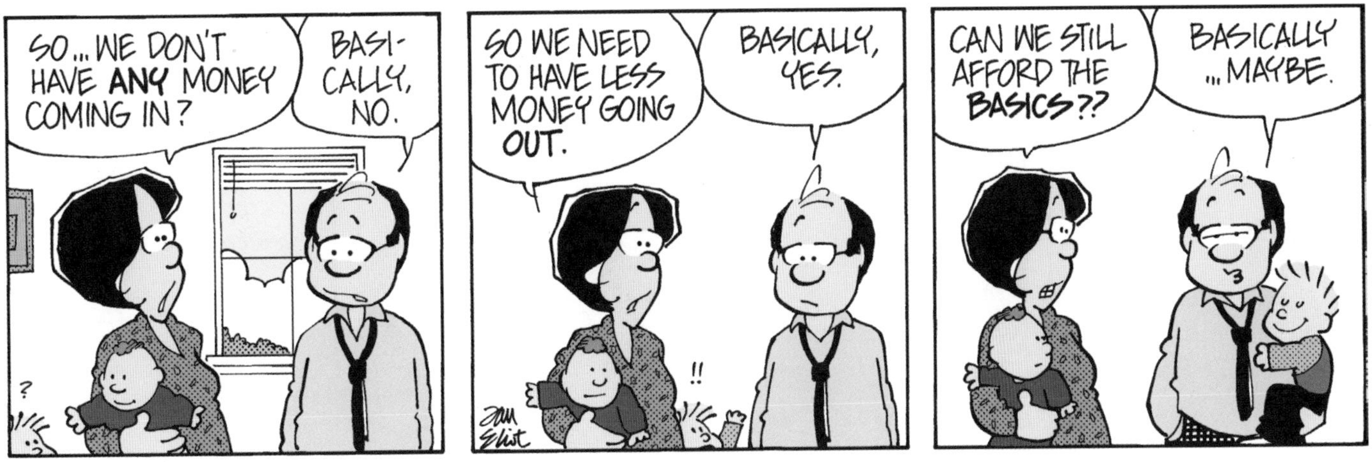
SO... WE DON'T HAVE ANY MONEY COMING IN?
BASI-CALLY, NO.
SO WE NEED TO HAVE LESS MONEY GOING OUT.
BASICALLY, YES.
CAN WE STILL AFFORD THE BASICS??
BASICALLY ...MAYBE.

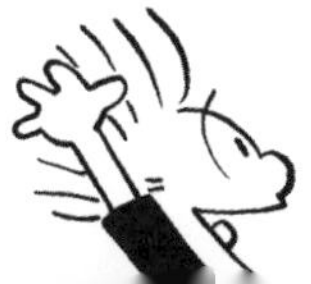

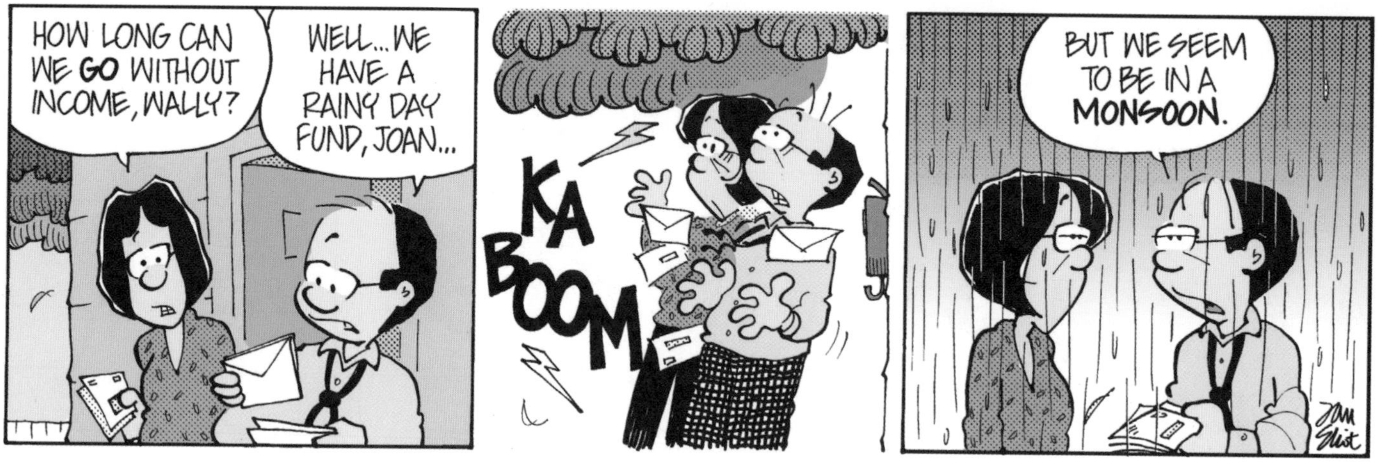
HOW LONG CAN WE **GO** WITHOUT INCOME, WALLY?
WELL... WE HAVE A RAINY DAY FUND, JOAN...
KA BOOM
BUT WE SEEM TO BE IN A **MONSOON**.

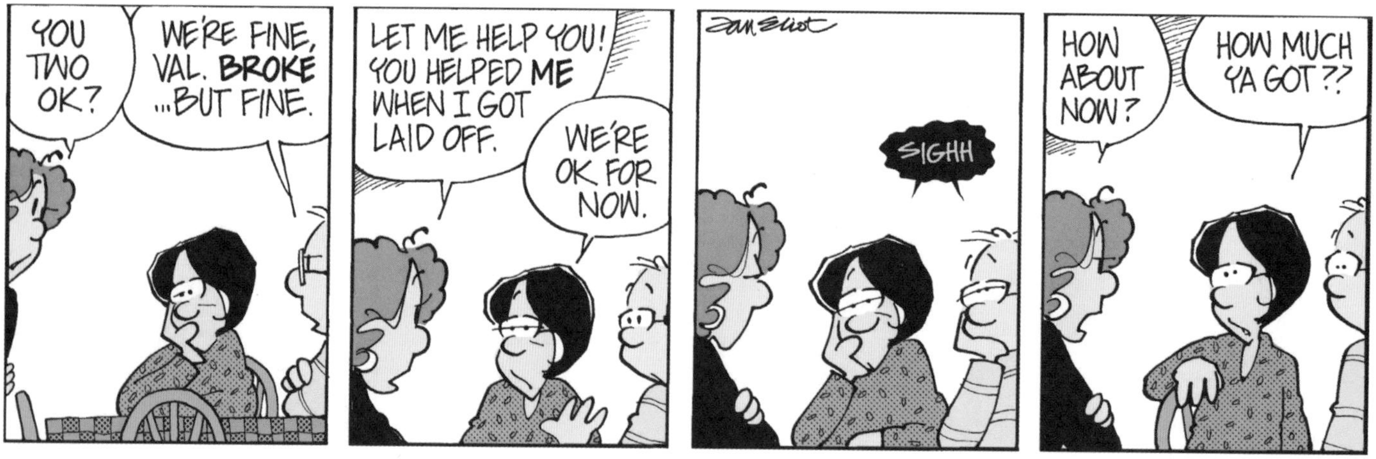
YOU TWO OK?
WE'RE FINE, VAL. **BROKE** ...BUT FINE.
LET ME HELP YOU! YOU HELPED **ME** WHEN I GOT LAID OFF.
WE'RE OK FOR NOW.
SIGHH
HOW ABOUT NOW?
HOW MUCH YA GOT??

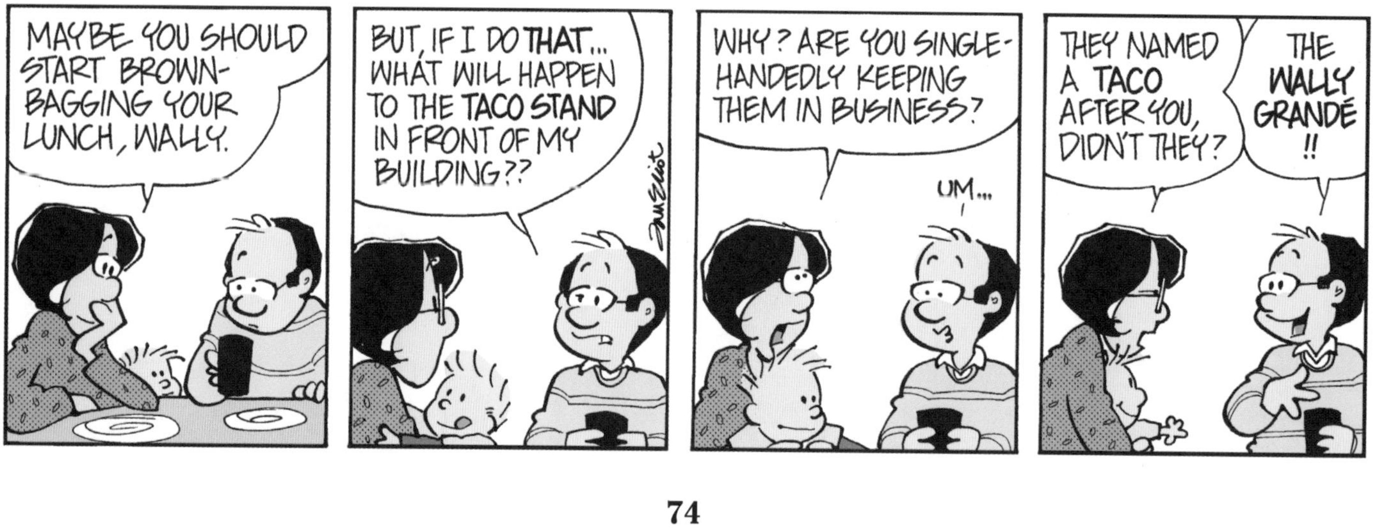
MAYBE YOU SHOULD START BROWN-BAGGING YOUR LUNCH, WALLY.
BUT, IF I DO **THAT**... WHAT WILL HAPPEN TO THE **TACO STAND** IN FRONT OF MY BUILDING??
WHY? ARE YOU SINGLE-HANDEDLY KEEPING THEM IN BUSINESS?
UM...
THEY NAMED A **TACO** AFTER YOU, DIDN'T THEY?
THE **WALLY GRANDÉ** !!

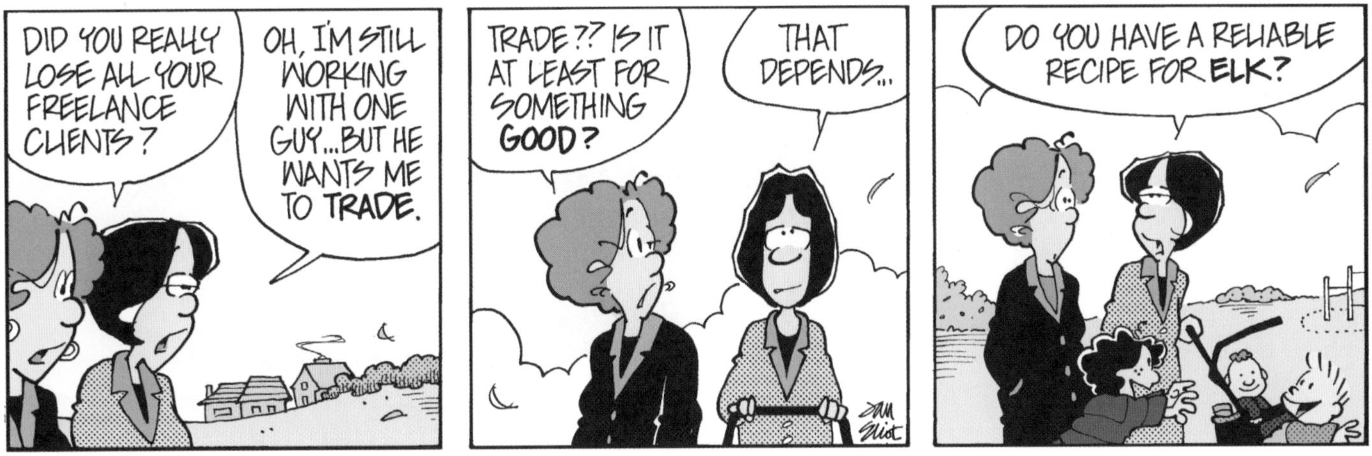
DID YOU REALLY LOSE ALL YOUR FREELANCE CLIENTS?
OH, I'M STILL WORKING WITH ONE GUY...BUT HE WANTS ME TO **TRADE**.
TRADE?? IS IT AT LEAST FOR SOMETHING **GOOD**?
THAT DEPENDS...
DO YOU HAVE A RELIABLE RECIPE FOR **ELK**?

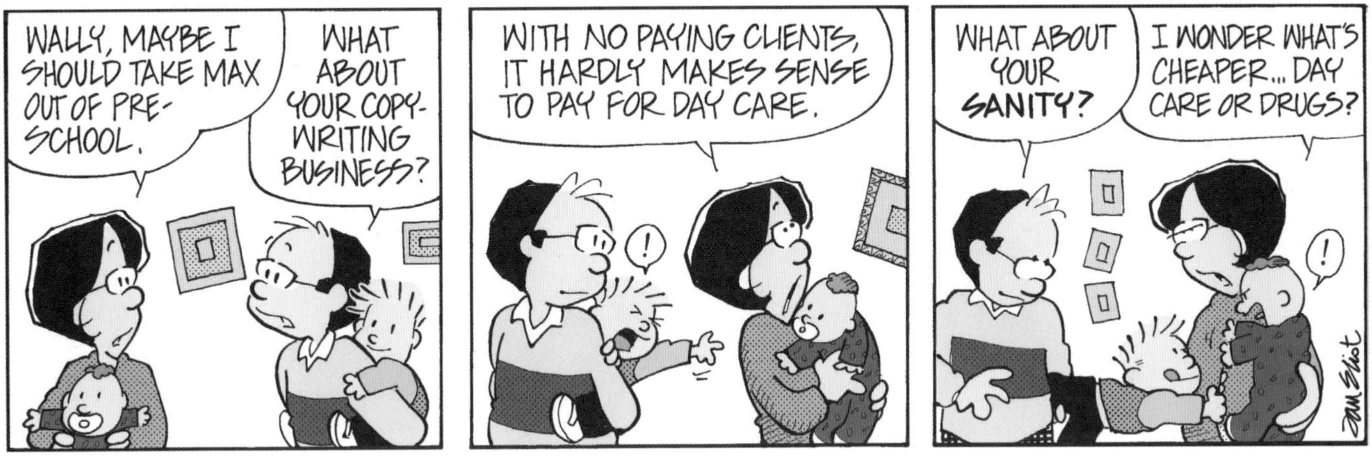
WALLY, MAYBE I SHOULD TAKE MAX OUT OF PRE-SCHOOL.
WHAT ABOUT YOUR COPY-WRITING BUSINESS?
WITH NO PAYING CLIENTS, IT HARDLY MAKES SENSE TO PAY FOR DAY CARE.
!
WHAT ABOUT YOUR **SANITY**?
I WONDER WHAT'S CHEAPER... DAY CARE OR DRUGS?
!

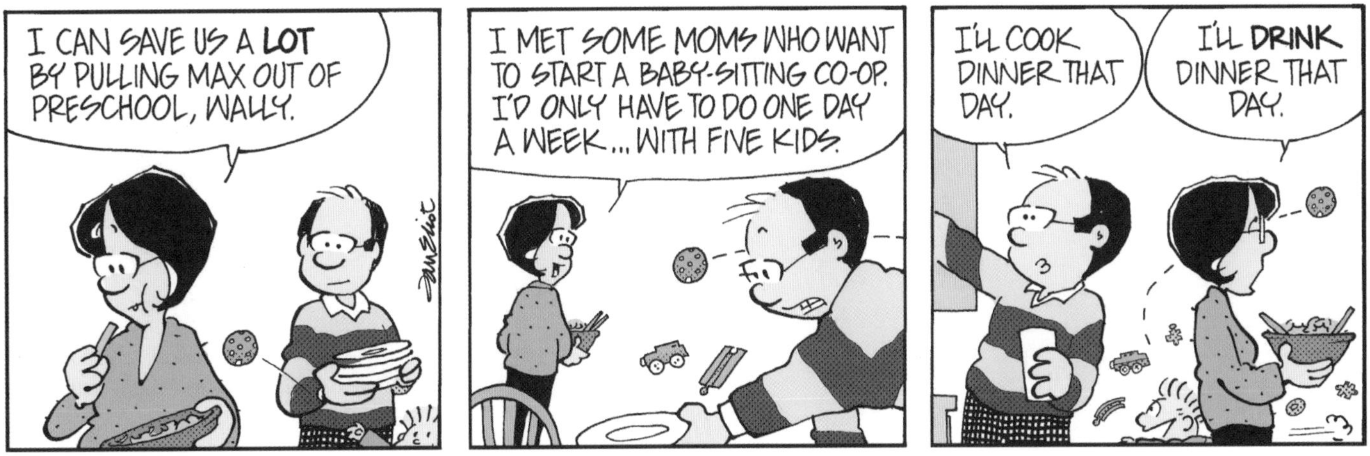
I CAN SAVE US A **LOT** BY PULLING MAX OUT OF PRESCHOOL, WALLY.
I MET SOME MOMS WHO WANT TO START A BABY-SITTING CO-OP. I'D ONLY HAVE TO DO ONE DAY A WEEK... WITH FIVE KIDS.
I'LL COOK DINNER THAT DAY.
I'LL **DRINK** DINNER THAT DAY.

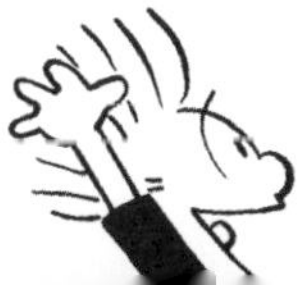

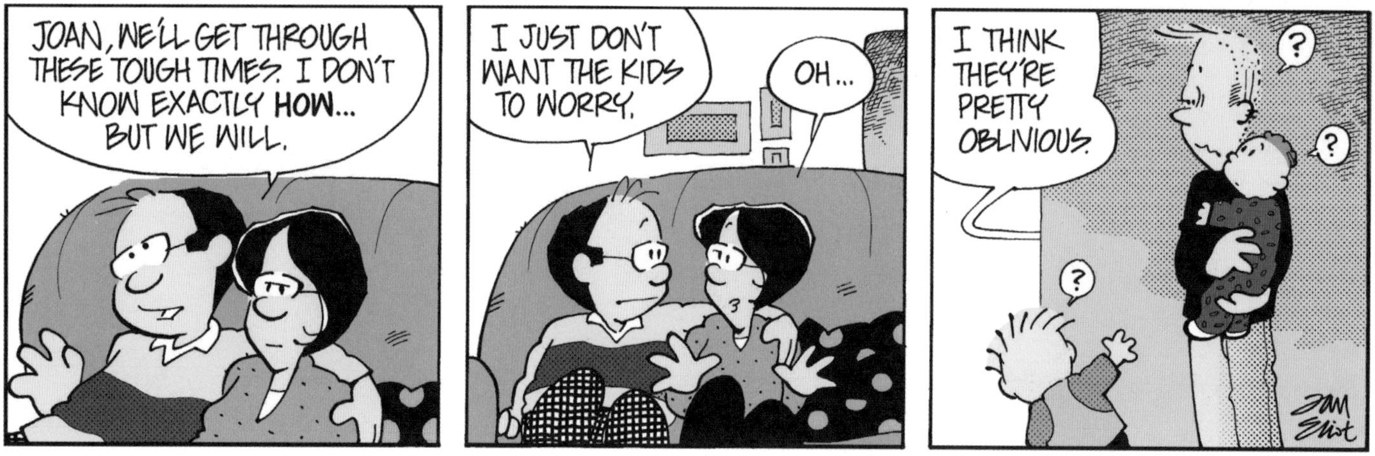
JOAN, WE'LL GET THROUGH THESE TOUGH TIMES. I DON'T KNOW EXACTLY **HOW**... BUT WE WILL.
I JUST DON'T WANT THE KIDS TO WORRY.
OH...
I THINK THEY'RE PRETTY OBLIVIOUS.
?
?
?

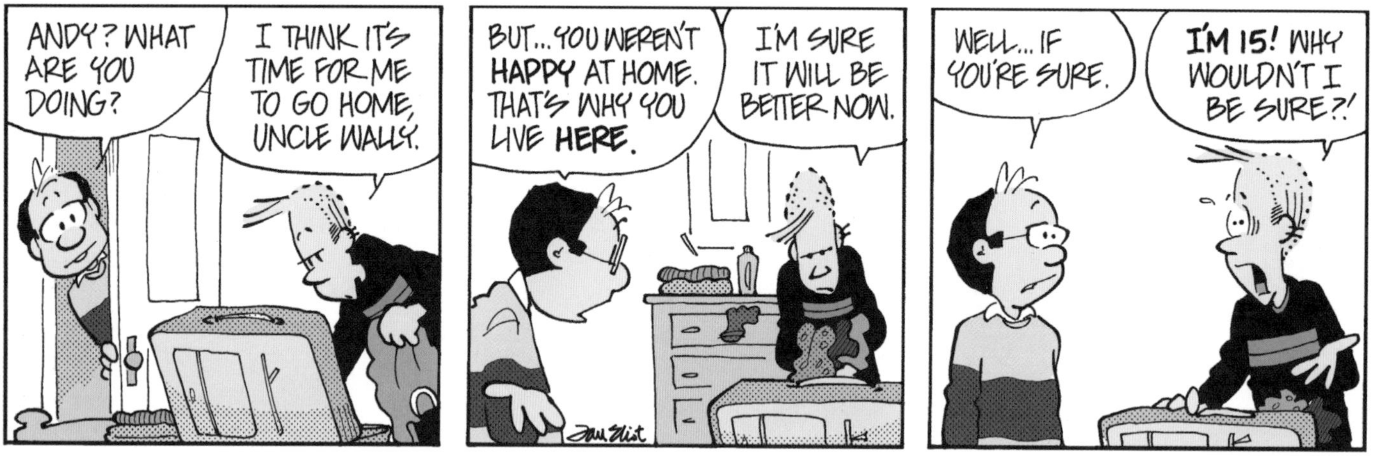
ANDY? WHAT ARE YOU DOING?
I THINK IT'S TIME FOR ME TO GO HOME, UNCLE WALLY.
BUT... YOU WEREN'T **HAPPY** AT HOME. THAT'S WHY YOU LIVE **HERE**.
I'M SURE IT WILL BE BETTER NOW.
WELL... IF YOU'RE SURE.
I'M 15! WHY WOULDN'T I BE SURE?!

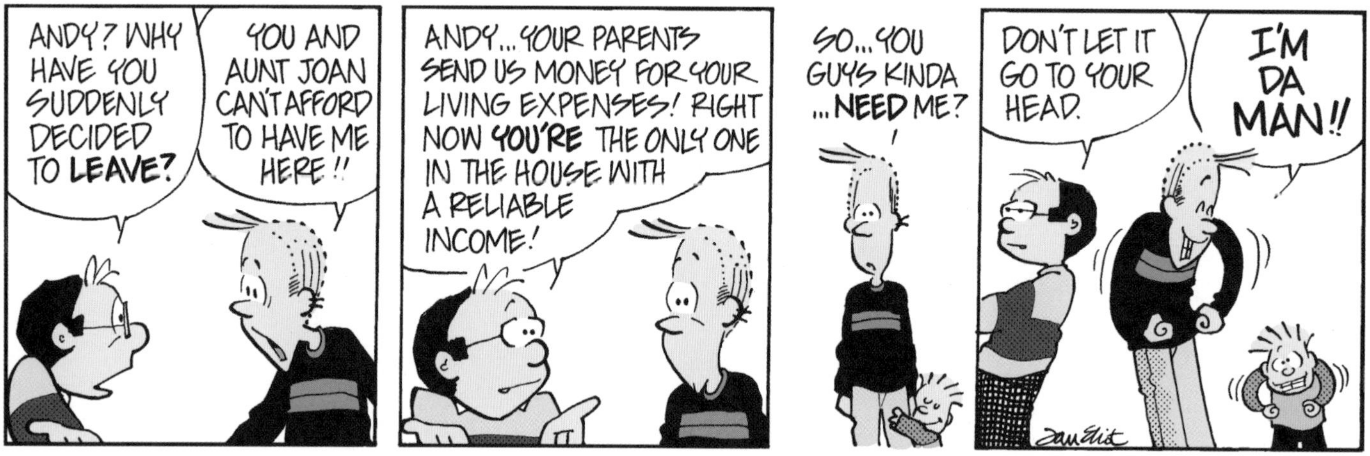
ANDY? WHY HAVE YOU SUDDENLY DECIDED TO **LEAVE**?
YOU AND AUNT JOAN CAN'T AFFORD TO HAVE ME HERE!!
ANDY... YOUR PARENTS SEND US MONEY FOR YOUR LIVING EXPENSES! RIGHT NOW **YOU'RE** THE ONLY ONE IN THE HOUSE WITH A RELIABLE INCOME!
SO... YOU GUYS KINDA ...**NEED** ME?
DON'T LET IT GO TO YOUR HEAD.
I'M DA MAN!!

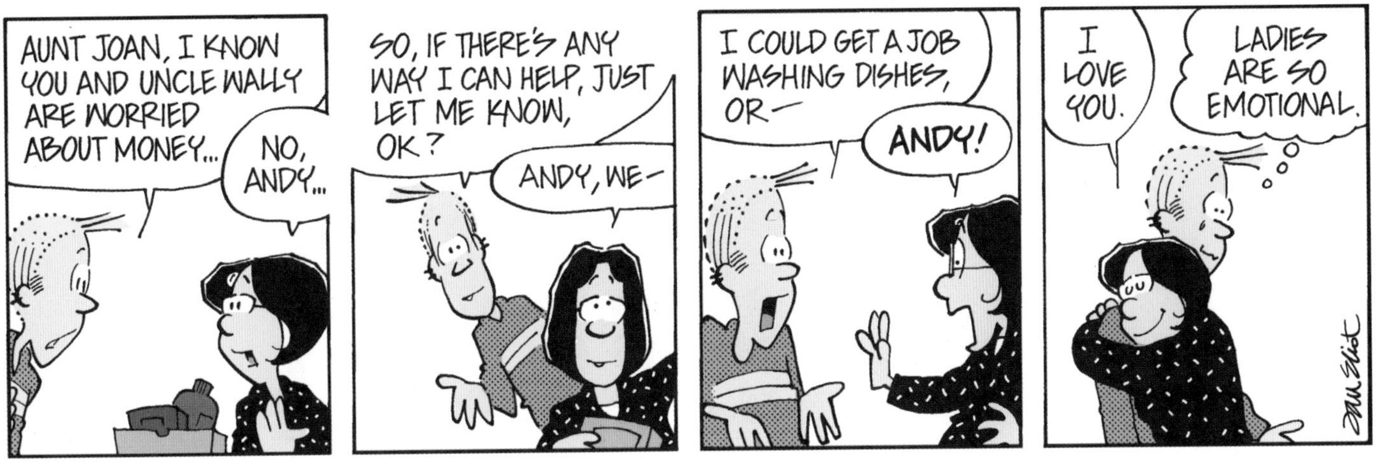
AUNT JOAN, I KNOW YOU AND UNCLE WALLY ARE WORRIED ABOUT MONEY...
NO, ANDY...
SO, IF THERE'S ANY WAY I CAN HELP, JUST LET ME KNOW, OK?
ANDY, WE-
I COULD GET A JOB WASHING DISHES, OR—
ANDY!
I LOVE YOU.
LADIES ARE SO EMOTIONAL.

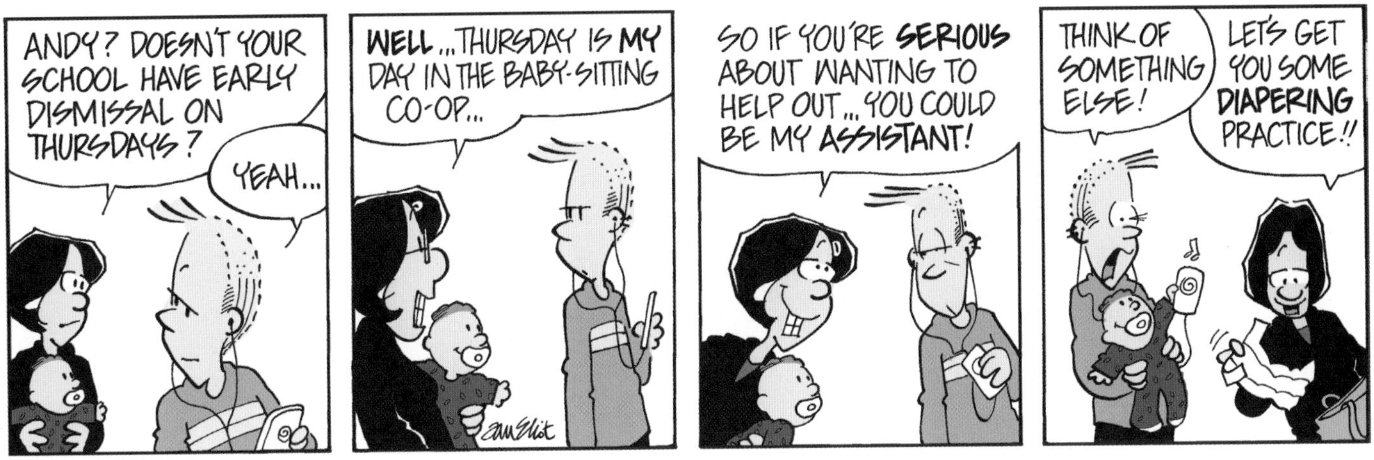
ANDY? DOESN'T YOUR SCHOOL HAVE EARLY DISMISSAL ON THURSDAYS?
YEAH...
WELL... THURSDAY IS MY DAY IN THE BABY-SITTING CO-OP...
SO IF YOU'RE SERIOUS ABOUT WANTING TO HELP OUT... YOU COULD BE MY ASSISTANT!
THINK OF SOMETHING ELSE!
LET'S GET YOU SOME DIAPERING PRACTICE!!

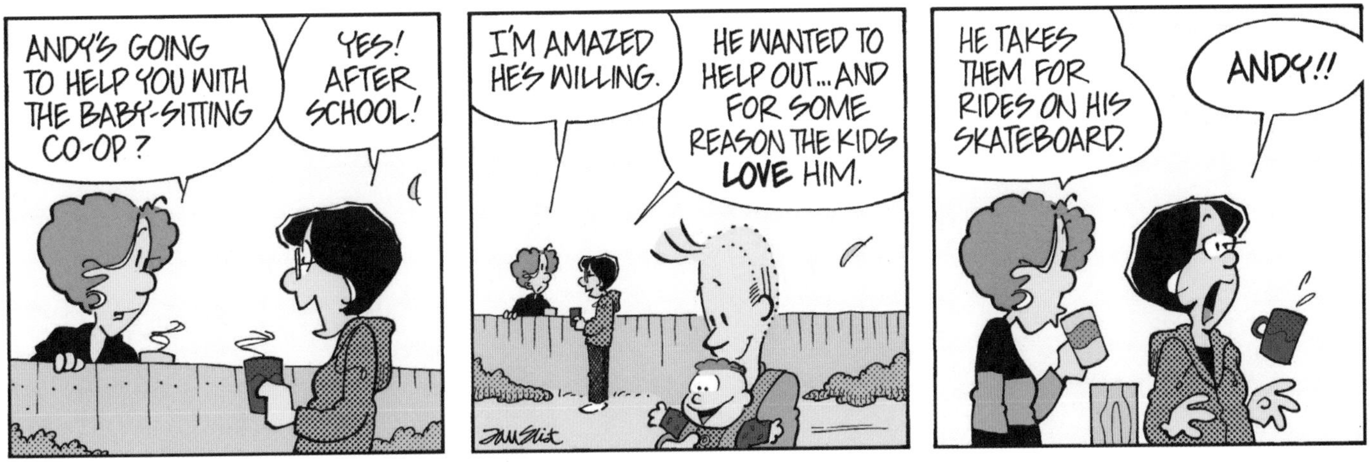
ANDY'S GOING TO HELP YOU WITH THE BABY-SITTING CO-OP?
YES! AFTER SCHOOL!
I'M AMAZED HE'S WILLING.
HE WANTED TO HELP OUT... AND FOR SOME REASON THE KIDS LOVE HIM.
HE TAKES THEM FOR RIDES ON HIS SKATEBOARD.
ANDY!!

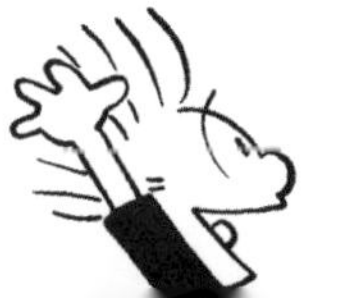

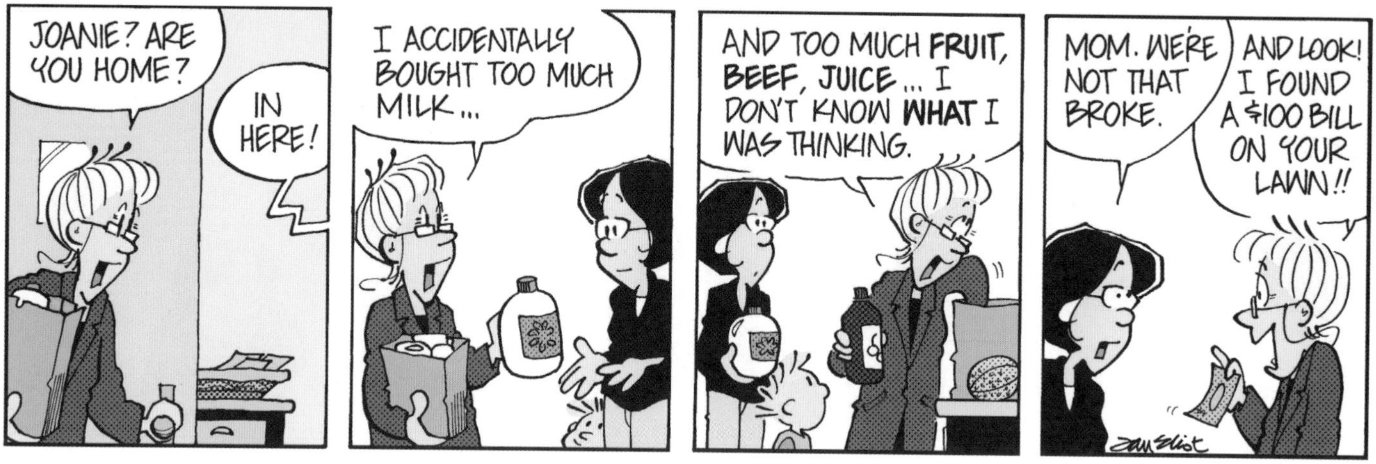
JOANIE? ARE YOU HOME?
IN HERE!
I ACCIDENTALLY BOUGHT TOO MUCH MILK...
AND TOO MUCH **FRUIT**, **BEEF**, **JUICE**... I DON'T KNOW **WHAT** I WAS THINKING.
MOM. WE'RE NOT THAT BROKE.
AND LOOK! I FOUND A $100 BILL ON YOUR LAWN!!

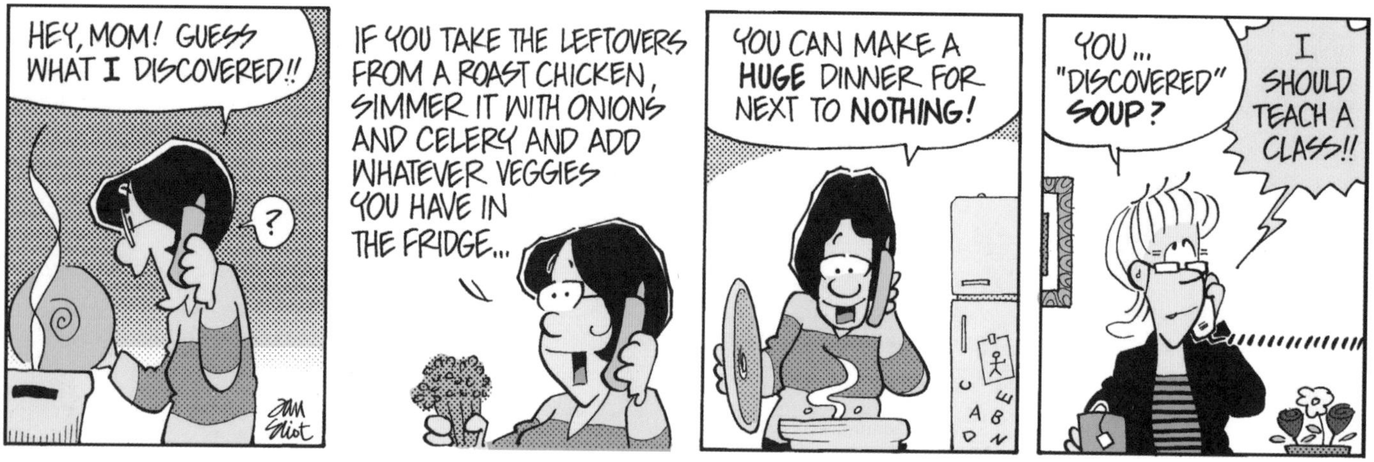
HEY, MOM! GUESS WHAT **I** DISCOVERED!!
?
IF YOU TAKE THE LEFTOVERS FROM A ROAST CHICKEN, SIMMER IT WITH ONIONS AND CELERY AND ADD WHATEVER VEGGIES YOU HAVE IN THE FRIDGE...
YOU CAN MAKE A **HUGE** DINNER FOR NEXT TO **NOTHING**!
YOU... "DISCOVERED" **SOUP**?
I SHOULD TEACH A CLASS!!

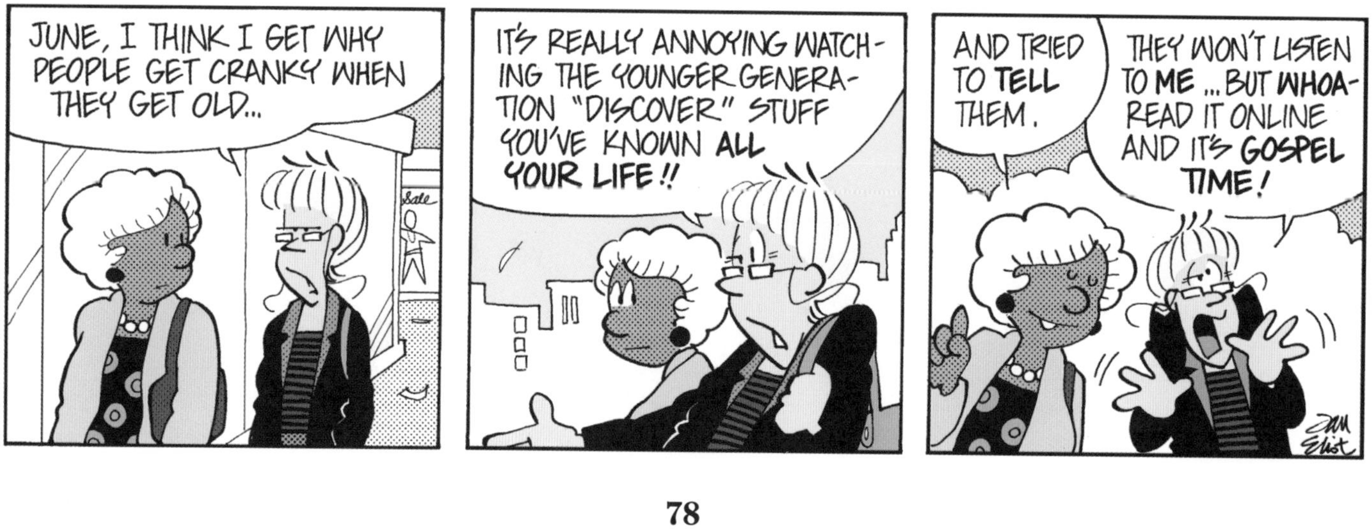
JUNE, I THINK I GET WHY PEOPLE GET CRANKY WHEN THEY GET OLD...
IT'S REALLY ANNOYING WATCHING THE YOUNGER GENERATION "DISCOVER" STUFF YOU'VE KNOWN **ALL YOUR LIFE**!!
AND TRIED TO **TELL** THEM.
THEY WON'T LISTEN TO **ME**... BUT **WHOA**-READ IT ONLINE AND IT'S **GOSPEL TIME**!

Stone Soup

LOOK! GIRL SCOUT COOKIES!
WE DON'T NEED COOKIES.
JOAN!? IT'S NOT ABOUT "NEEDING" COOKIES!
THESE GIRLS AND THEIR PARENTS STAND OUTSIDE FOR HOURS.
THEY'RE LEARNING ABOUT ENTREPRENEURSHIP... RESPONSIBILITY... LOYALTY!
THIS IS A TRADITION OLDER THAN WE ARE!!
WE HAVE TO SUPPORT THEM.
SO IT'S NOT ABOUT THE COOKIES.
NOT AT ALL!
WHAT'S YOUR FAVORITE?
OLD-FASHIONED SHORTBREAD. LET'S GET THREE BOXES.

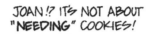

Stone Soup

SHEESH. I NEED TO GO TO **BED** EARLIER.
I USED TO SAY THAT.
I'D LOOK AT MYSELF IN THE MIRROR AND THINK —
I JUST NEED A **GOOD NIGHT'S SLEEP!**
FINALLY I REALIZED, NO... I'M JUST THAT **OLD.**
YOU GET USED TO IT.
ALL I NEED IS **SOFTER LIGHTING.**
OOH. GOOD ONE.
YAWN

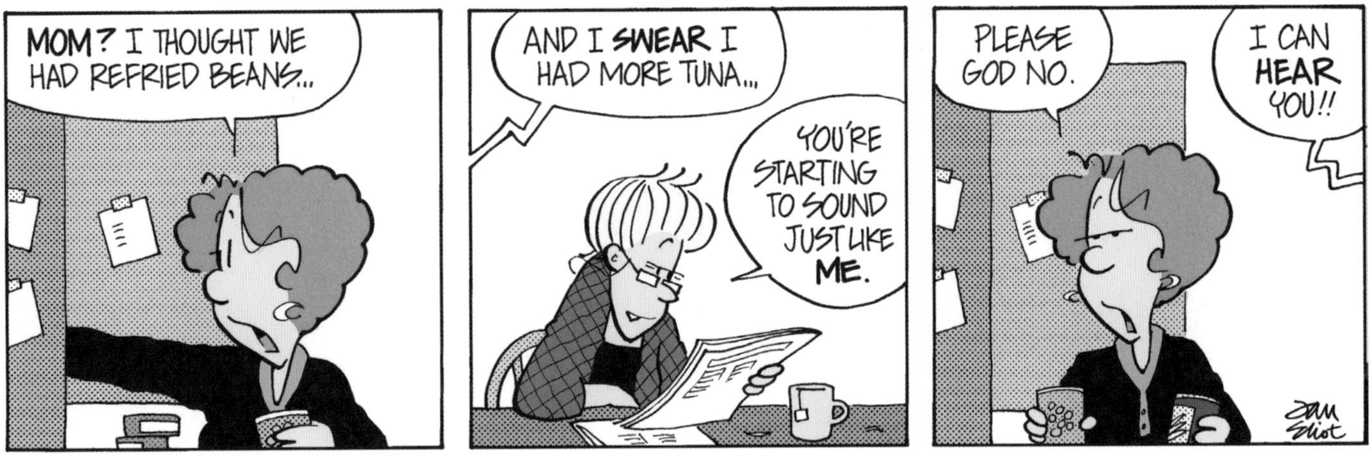
MOM? I THOUGHT WE HAD REFRIED BEANS...
AND I SWEAR I HAD MORE TUNA...
YOU'RE STARTING TO SOUND JUST LIKE ME.
PLEASE GOD NO.
I CAN HEAR YOU!!
Jan Eliot

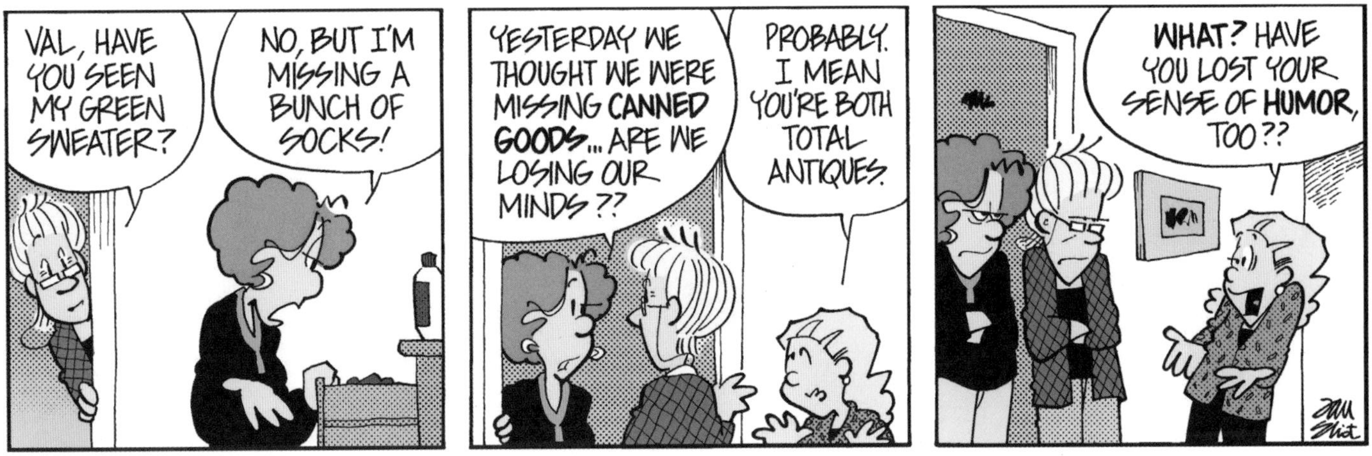
VAL, HAVE YOU SEEN MY GREEN SWEATER?
NO, BUT I'M MISSING A BUNCH OF SOCKS!
YESTERDAY WE THOUGHT WE WERE MISSING CANNED GOODS... ARE WE LOSING OUR MINDS??
PROBABLY. I MEAN YOU'RE BOTH TOTAL ANTIQUES.
WHAT? HAVE YOU LOST YOUR SENSE OF HUMOR, TOO??
Jan Eliot

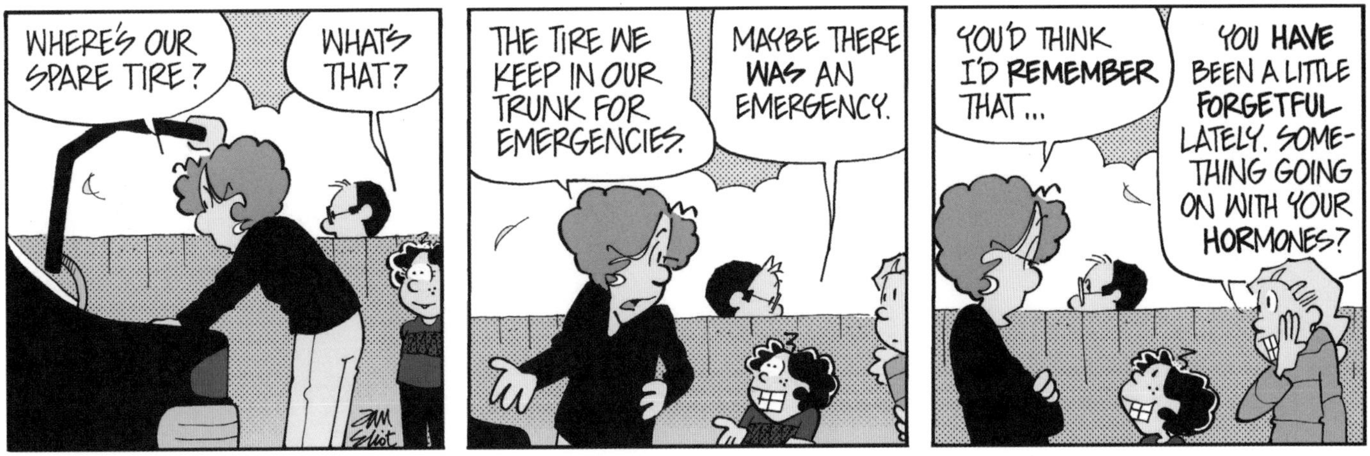
WHERE'S OUR SPARE TIRE?
WHAT'S THAT?
Jan Eliot
THE TIRE WE KEEP IN OUR TRUNK FOR EMERGENCIES.
MAYBE THERE WAS AN EMERGENCY.
YOU'D THINK I'D REMEMBER THAT...
YOU HAVE BEEN A LITTLE FORGETFUL LATELY. SOMETHING GOING ON WITH YOUR HORMONES?

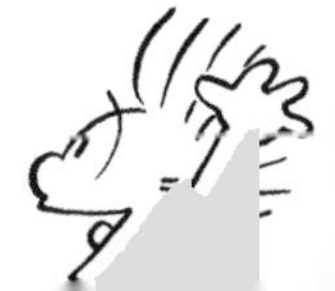

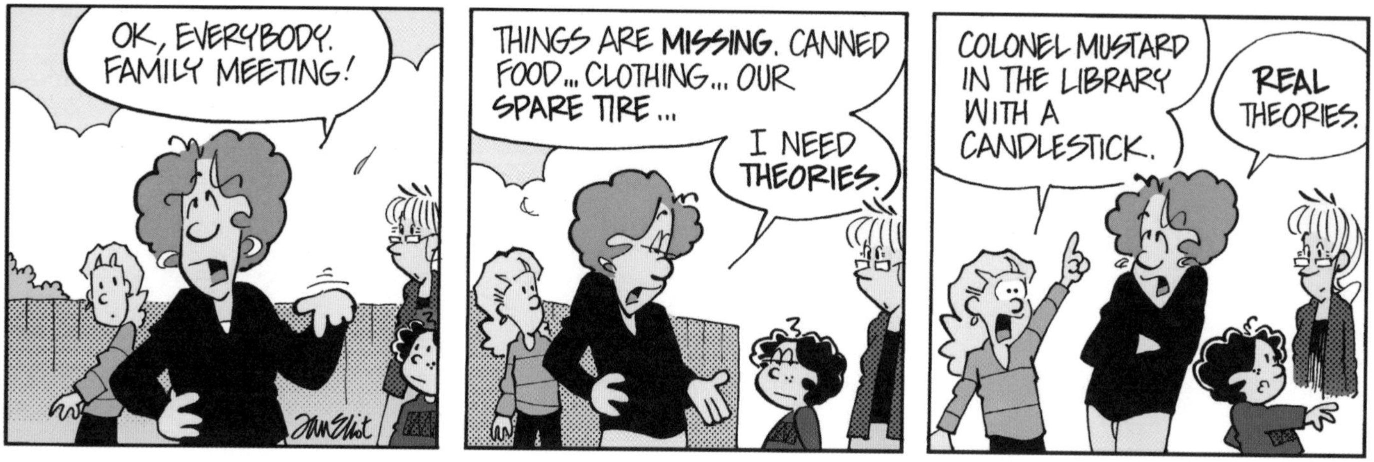
OK, EVERYBODY. FAMILY MEETING!
THINGS ARE **MISSING**. CANNED FOOD... CLOTHING... OUR **SPARE TIRE**...
I NEED **THEORIES**.
COLONEL MUSTARD IN THE LIBRARY WITH A CANDLESTICK.
REAL THEORIES.

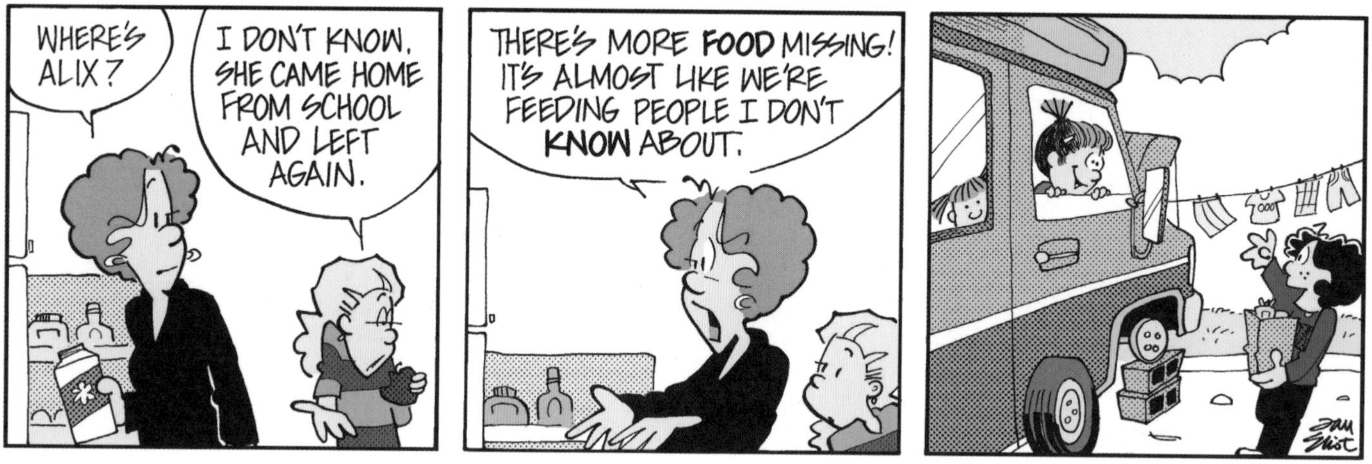
WHERE'S ALIX?
I DON'T KNOW. SHE CAME HOME FROM SCHOOL AND LEFT AGAIN.
THERE'S MORE **FOOD** MISSING! IT'S ALMOST LIKE WE'RE FEEDING PEOPLE I DON'T **KNOW** ABOUT.

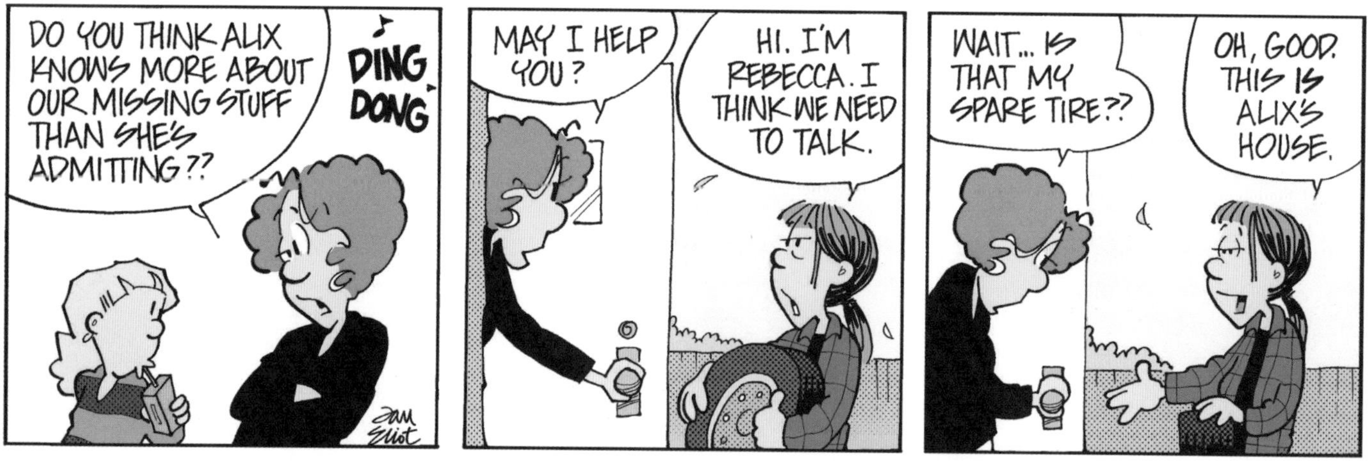
DO YOU THINK ALIX KNOWS MORE ABOUT OUR MISSING STUFF THAN SHE'S ADMITTING??
DING DONG
MAY I HELP YOU?
HI. I'M REBECCA. I THINK WE NEED TO TALK.
WAIT... IS THAT MY SPARE TIRE??
OH, GOOD. THIS **IS** ALIX'S HOUSE.

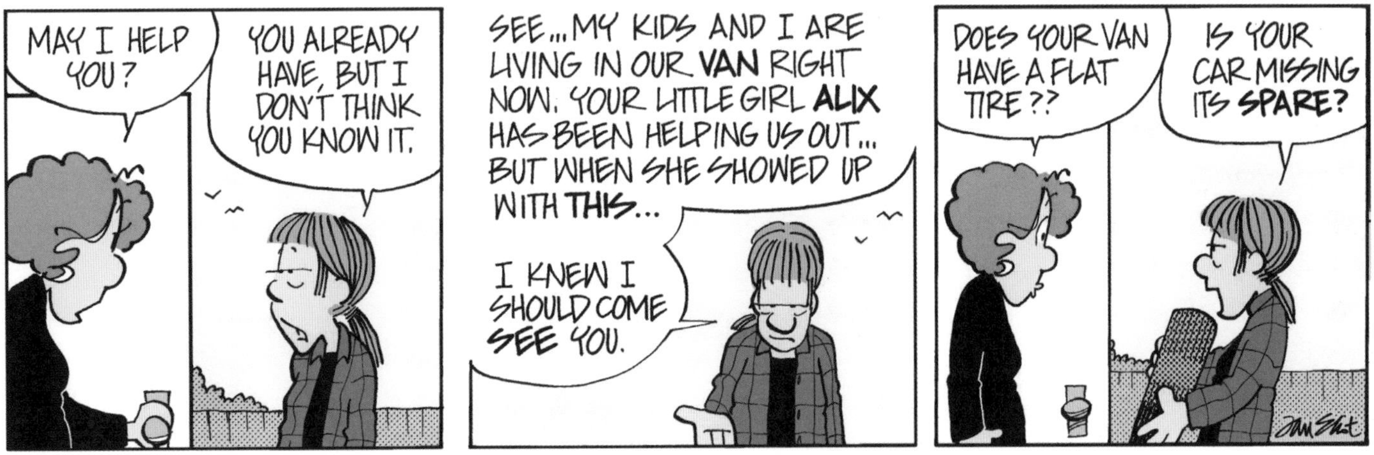

MAY I HELP YOU?
YOU ALREADY HAVE, BUT I DON'T THINK YOU KNOW IT.
SEE... MY KIDS AND I ARE LIVING IN OUR VAN RIGHT NOW. YOUR LITTLE GIRL ALIX HAS BEEN HELPING US OUT... BUT WHEN SHE SHOWED UP WITH THIS...
I KNEW I SHOULD COME SEE YOU.
DOES YOUR VAN HAVE A FLAT TIRE??
IS YOUR CAR MISSING ITS SPARE?

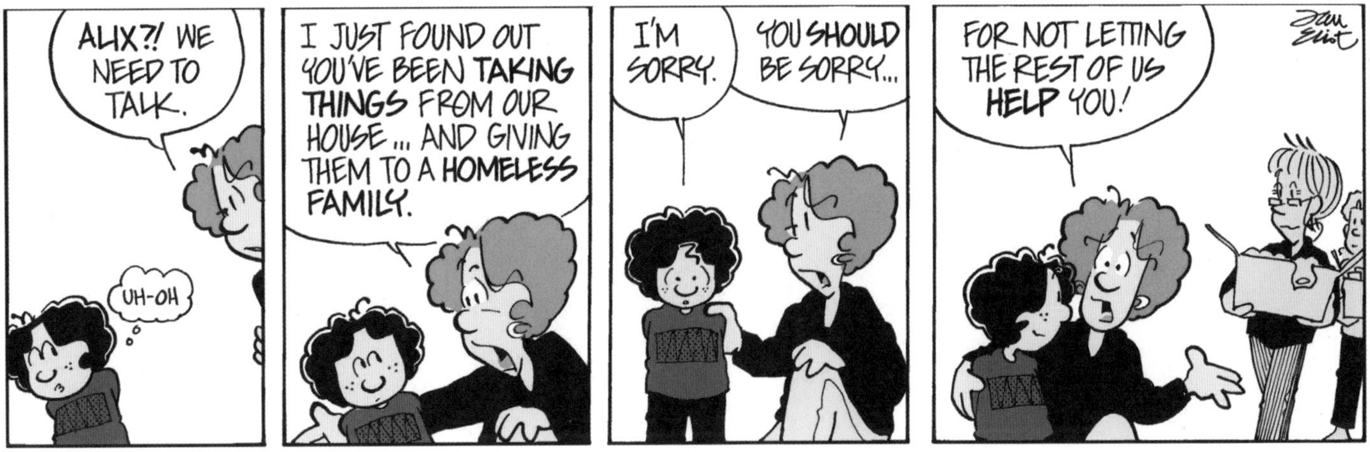

ALIX?! WE NEED TO TALK.
UH-OH
I JUST FOUND OUT YOU'VE BEEN TAKING THINGS FROM OUR HOUSE... AND GIVING THEM TO A HOMELESS FAMILY.
I'M SORRY.
YOU SHOULD BE SORRY...
FOR NOT LETTING THE REST OF US HELP YOU!

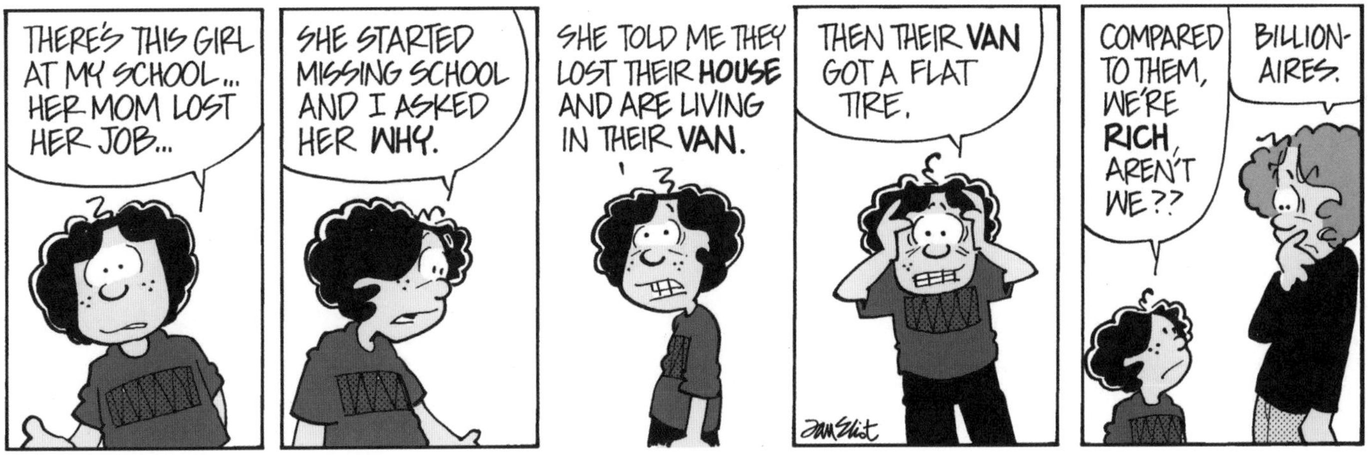

THERE'S THIS GIRL AT MY SCHOOL... HER MOM LOST HER JOB...
SHE STARTED MISSING SCHOOL AND I ASKED HER WHY.
SHE TOLD ME THEY LOST THEIR HOUSE AND ARE LIVING IN THEIR VAN.
THEN THEIR VAN GOT A FLAT TIRE.
COMPARED TO THEM, WE'RE RICH, AREN'T WE??
BILLION-AIRES.

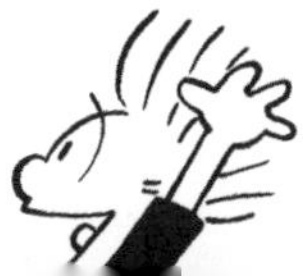

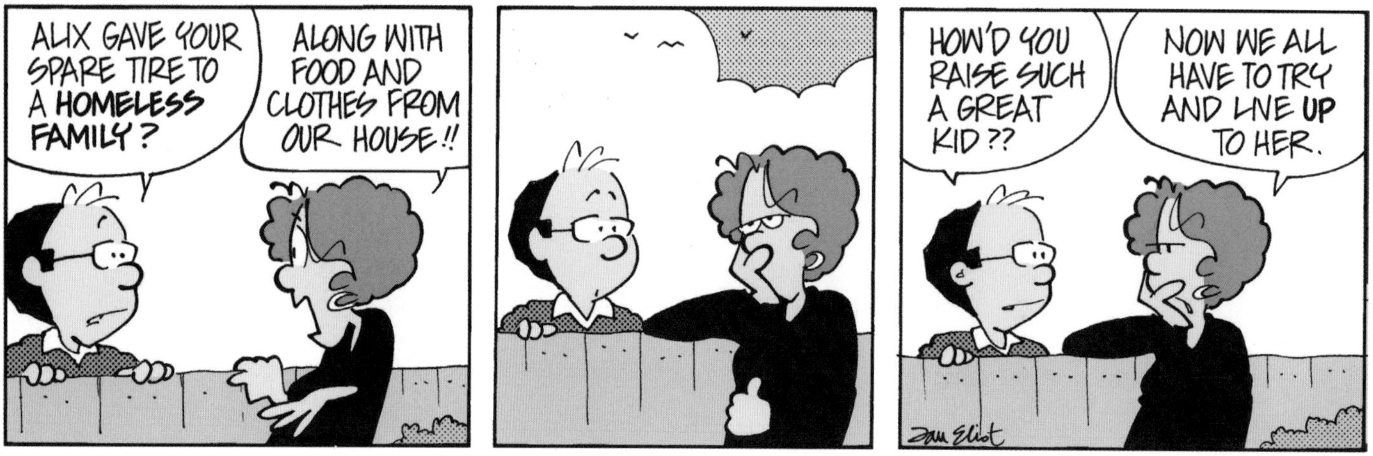
ALIX GAVE YOUR SPARE TIRE TO A **HOMELESS FAMILY**?
ALONG WITH FOOD AND CLOTHES FROM OUR HOUSE!!
HOW'D YOU RAISE SUCH A GREAT KID??
NOW WE ALL HAVE TO TRY AND LIVE **UP** TO HER.

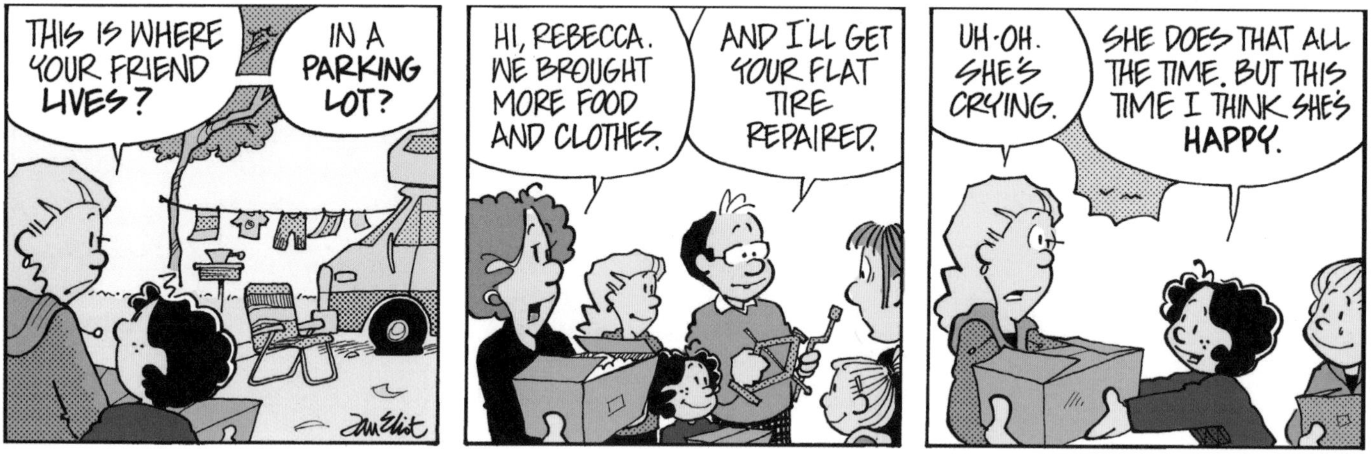
THIS IS WHERE YOUR FRIEND **LIVES**?
IN A **PARKING LOT**?
HI, REBECCA. WE BROUGHT MORE FOOD AND CLOTHES.
AND I'LL GET YOUR FLAT TIRE REPAIRED.
UH-OH. SHE'S CRYING.
SHE DOES THAT ALL THE TIME. BUT THIS TIME I THINK SHE'S **HAPPY**.

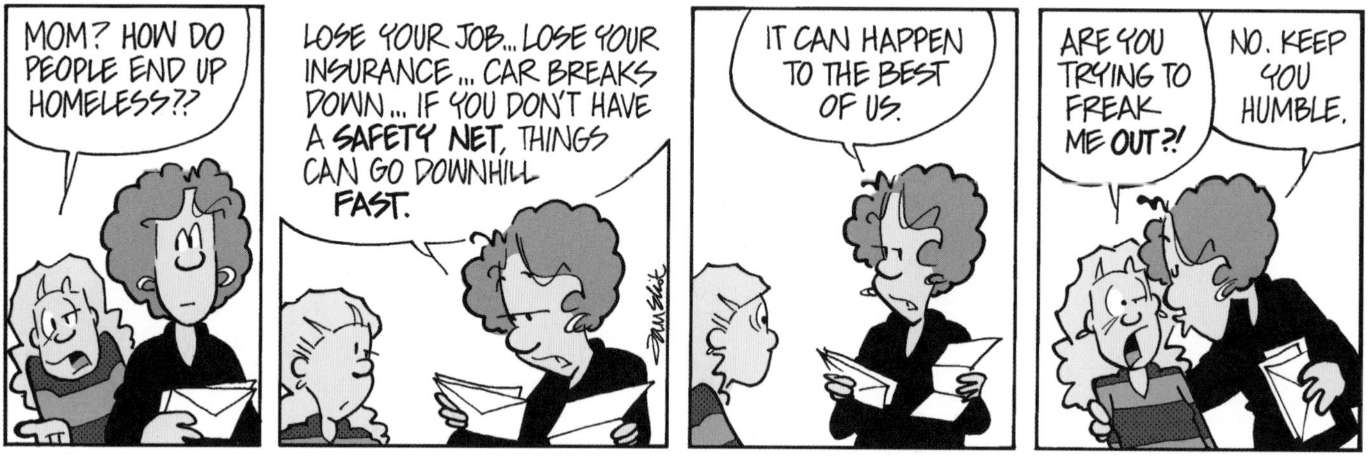
MOM? HOW DO PEOPLE END UP HOMELESS??
LOSE YOUR JOB... LOSE YOUR INSURANCE... CAR BREAKS DOWN... IF YOU DON'T HAVE A **SAFETY NET**, THINGS CAN GO DOWNHILL **FAST**.
IT CAN HAPPEN TO THE BEST OF US.
ARE YOU TRYING TO FREAK ME **OUT**?!
NO. KEEP YOU HUMBLE.

Stone Soup

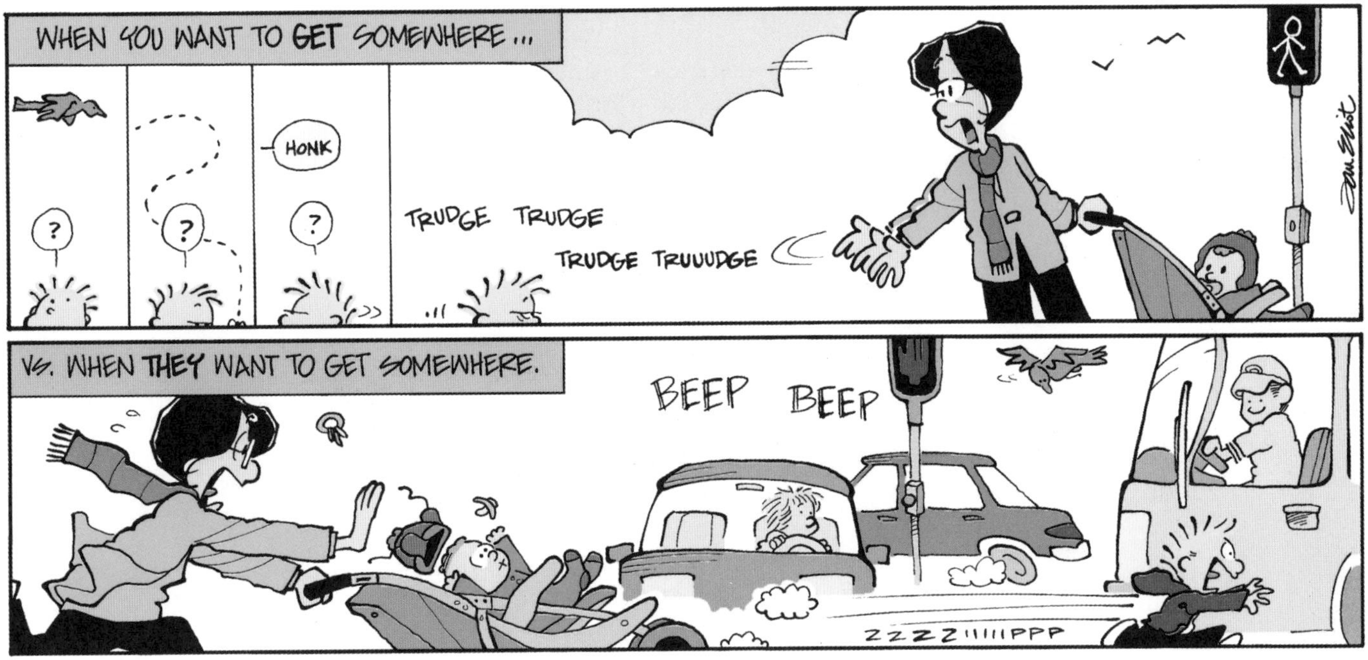

WHEN YOU WANT TO GET SOMEWHERE...
?
?
HONK
?
TRUDGE TRUDGE
TRUDGE TRUUUDGE
VS. WHEN THEY WANT TO GET SOMEWHERE.
BEEP BEEP
ZZZZIIIIIPPP

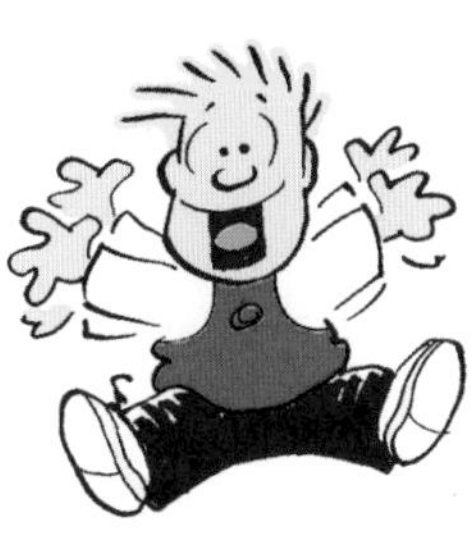

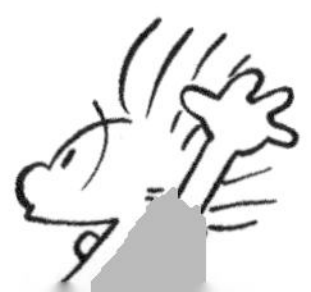

Stone Soup

Why Moms Worry...
BUT MOM!! T-REX CAN'T CATCH ME!
CHOMP
BUT MOM! EVERYBODY'S GOING!!
TITANIC
GLUB GLUB
I'M SO TAKING THIS OFF.
They Have Good Reason.

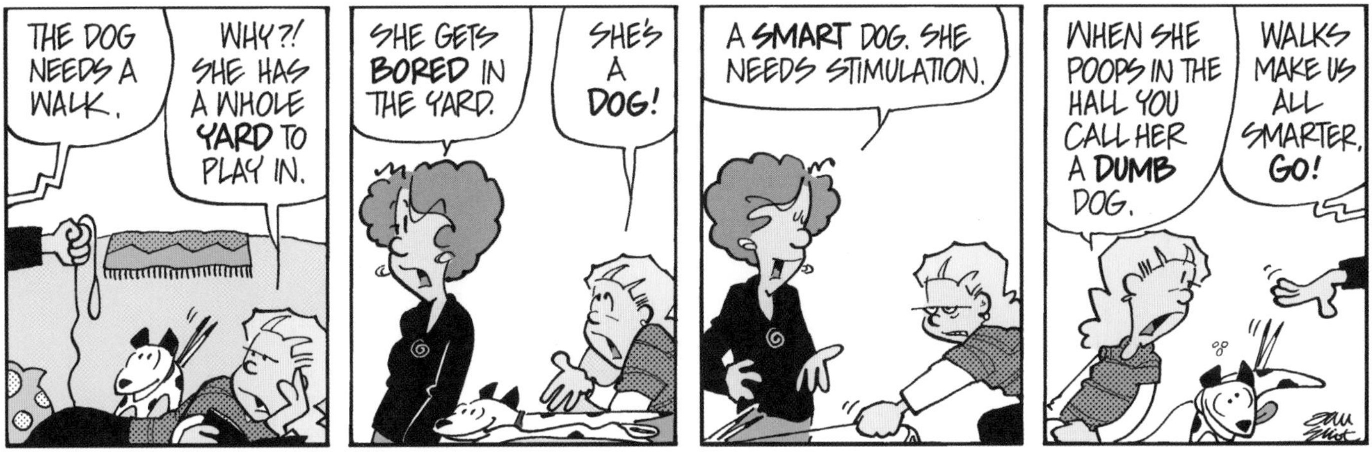
THE DOG NEEDS A WALK.
WHY?! SHE HAS A WHOLE YARD TO PLAY IN.
SHE GETS BORED IN THE YARD.
SHE'S A DOG!
A SMART DOG. SHE NEEDS STIMULATION.
WHEN SHE POOPS IN THE HALL YOU CALL HER A DUMB DOG.
WALKS MAKE US ALL SMARTER. GO!

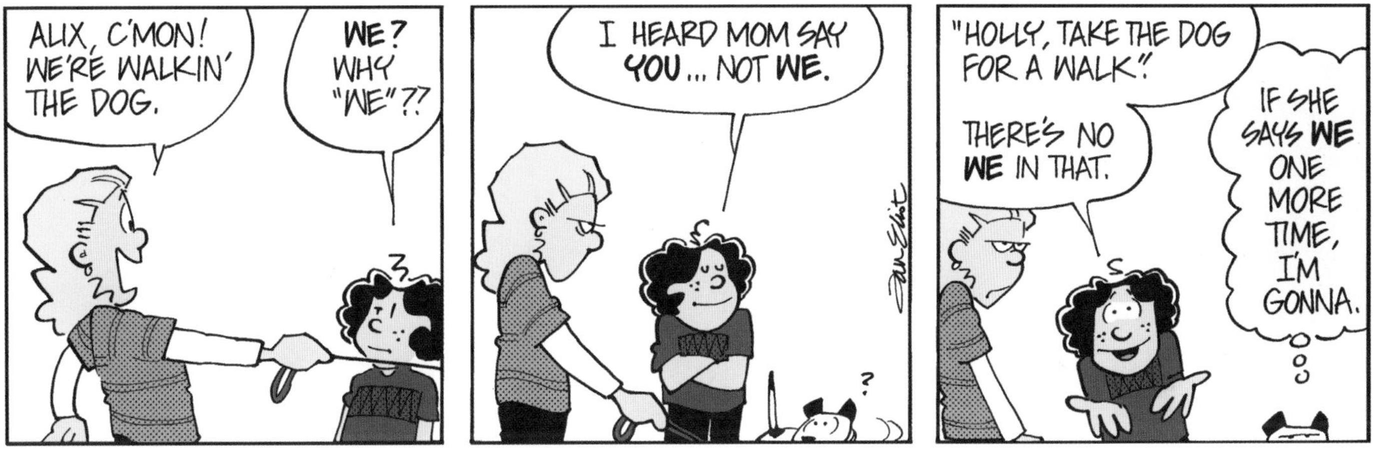
ALIX, C'MON! WE'RE WALKIN' THE DOG.
WE? WHY "WE"??
I HEARD MOM SAY YOU... NOT WE.
"HOLLY, TAKE THE DOG FOR A WALK."
THERE'S NO WE IN THAT.
IF SHE SAYS WE ONE MORE TIME, I'M GONNA.

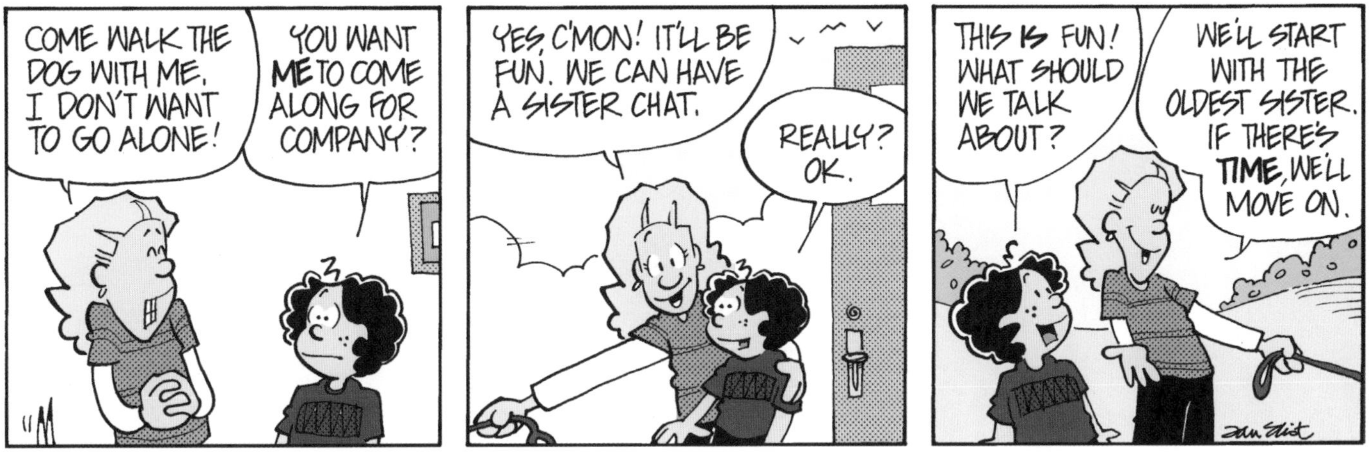
COME WALK THE DOG WITH ME. I DON'T WANT TO GO ALONE!
YOU WANT ME TO COME ALONG FOR COMPANY?
YES, C'MON! IT'LL BE FUN. WE CAN HAVE A SISTER CHAT.
REALLY? OK.
THIS IS FUN! WHAT SHOULD WE TALK ABOUT?
WE'LL START WITH THE OLDEST SISTER. IF THERE'S TIME, WE'LL MOVE ON.

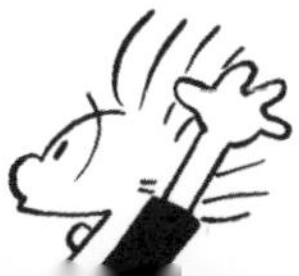

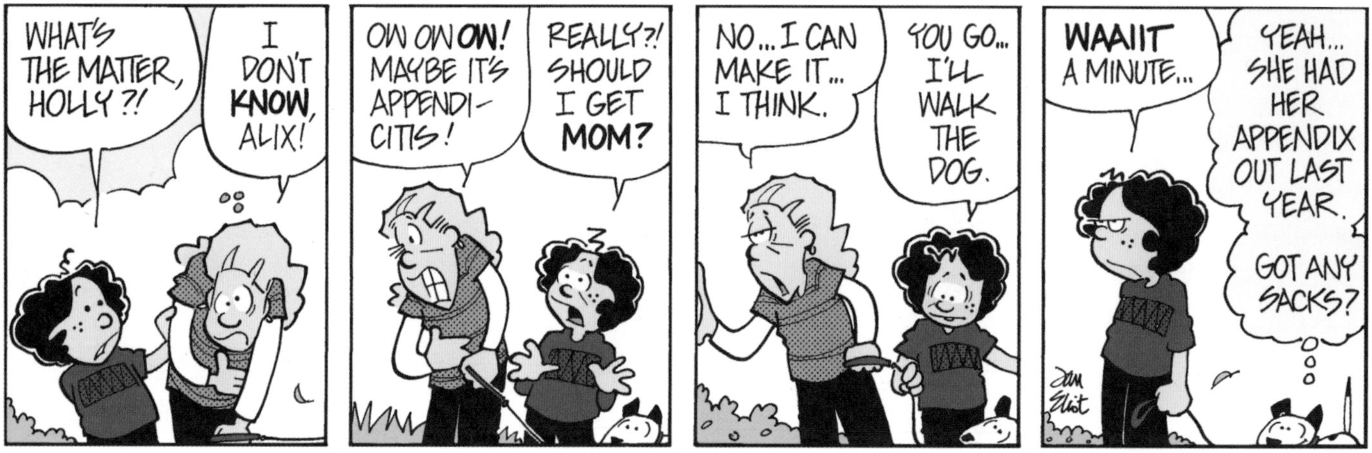

WHAT'S THE MATTER, HOLLY?!
I DON'T KNOW, ALIX!
OW OW OW! MAYBE IT'S APPENDICITIS!
REALLY?! SHOULD I GET MOM?
NO... I CAN MAKE IT... I THINK.
YOU GO... I'LL WALK THE DOG.
WAAIIT A MINUTE...
YEAH... SHE HAD HER APPENDIX OUT LAST YEAR.
GOT ANY SACKS?

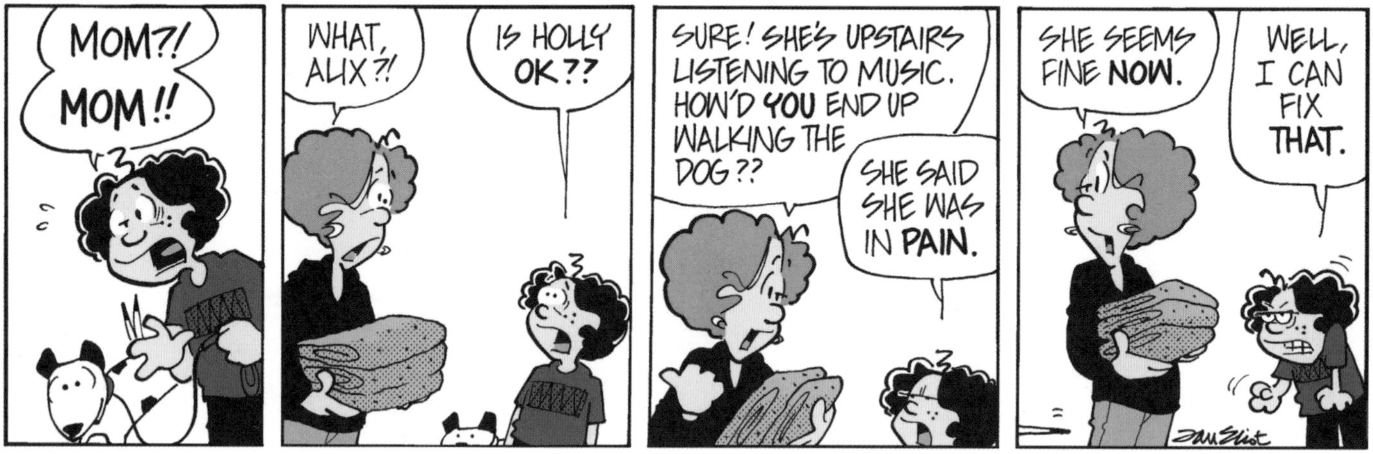

MOM?! MOM!!
WHAT, ALIX?!
IS HOLLY OK??
SURE! SHE'S UPSTAIRS LISTENING TO MUSIC. HOW'D YOU END UP WALKING THE DOG??
SHE SAID SHE WAS IN PAIN.
SHE SEEMS FINE NOW.
WELL, I CAN FIX THAT.

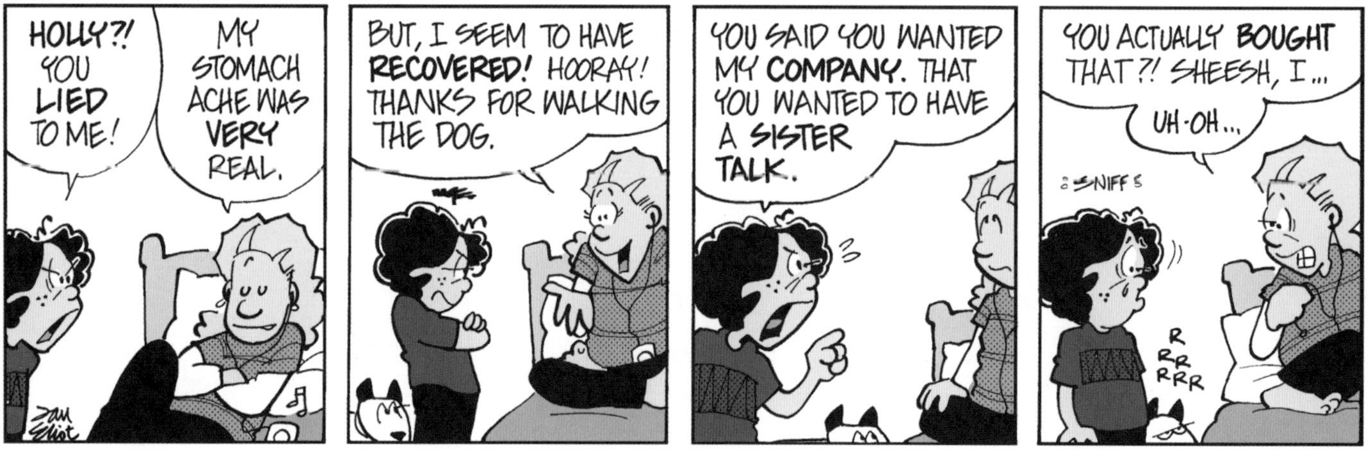

HOLLY?! YOU LIED TO ME!
MY STOMACH ACHE WAS VERY REAL.
BUT, I SEEM TO HAVE RECOVERED! HOORAY! THANKS FOR WALKING THE DOG.
YOU SAID YOU WANTED MY COMPANY. THAT YOU WANTED TO HAVE A SISTER TALK.
YOU ACTUALLY BOUGHT THAT?! SHEESH, I...
UH-OH...
SNIFF
R RR RRR

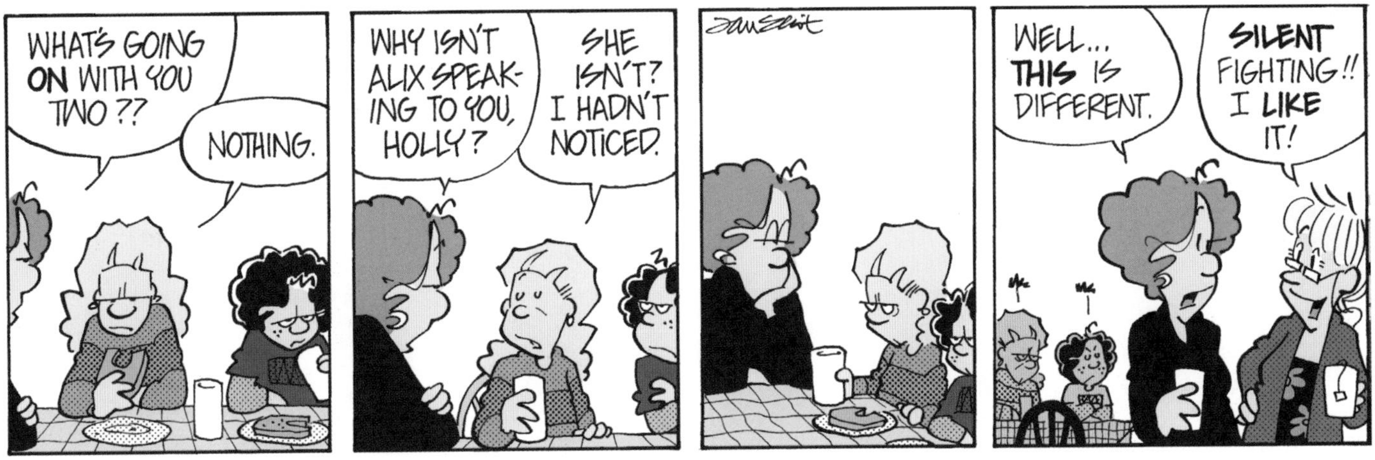
WHAT'S GOING ON WITH YOU TWO??
NOTHING.
WHY ISN'T ALIX SPEAK-ING TO YOU, HOLLY?
SHE ISN'T? I HADN'T NOTICED.
WELL... THIS IS DIFFERENT.
SILENT FIGHTING!! I LIKE IT!

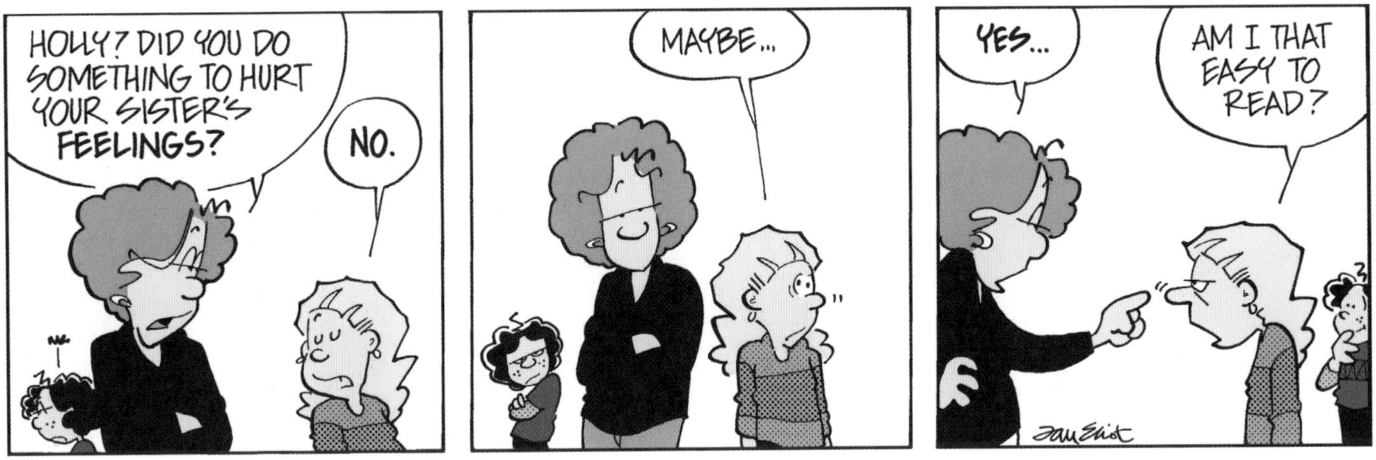
HOLLY? DID YOU DO SOMETHING TO HURT YOUR SISTER'S FEELINGS?
NO.
MAYBE...
YES...
AM I THAT EASY TO READ?

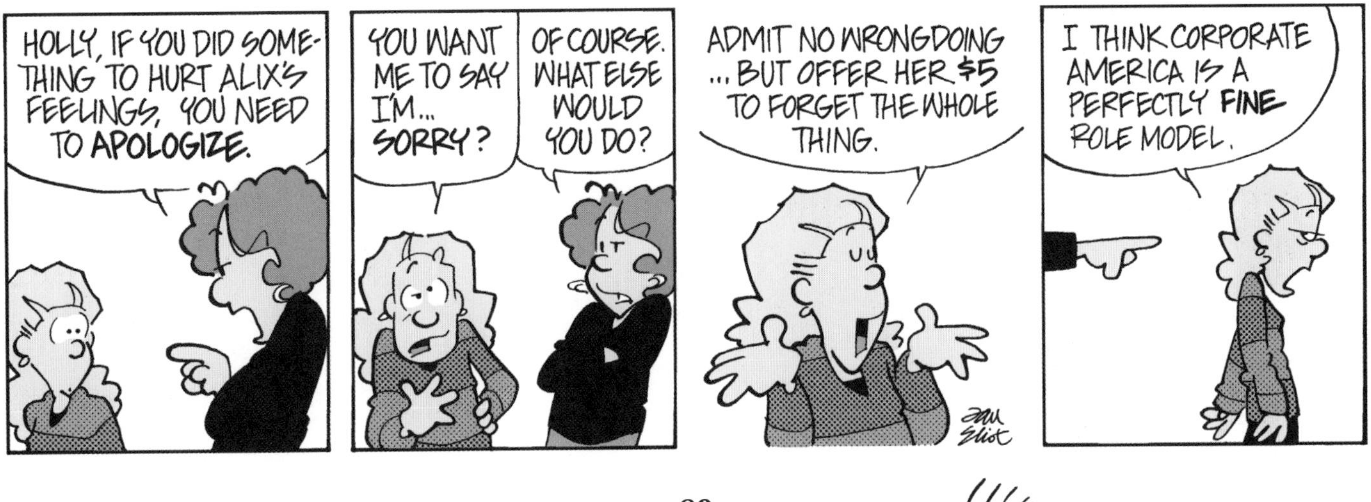
HOLLY, IF YOU DID SOME-THING TO HURT ALIX'S FEELINGS, YOU NEED TO APOLOGIZE.
YOU WANT ME TO SAY I'M... SORRY?
OF COURSE. WHAT ELSE WOULD YOU DO?
ADMIT NO WRONGDOING ... BUT OFFER HER $5 TO FORGET THE WHOLE THING.
I THINK CORPORATE AMERICA IS A PERFECTLY FINE ROLE MODEL.

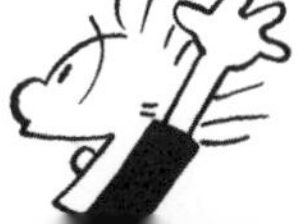

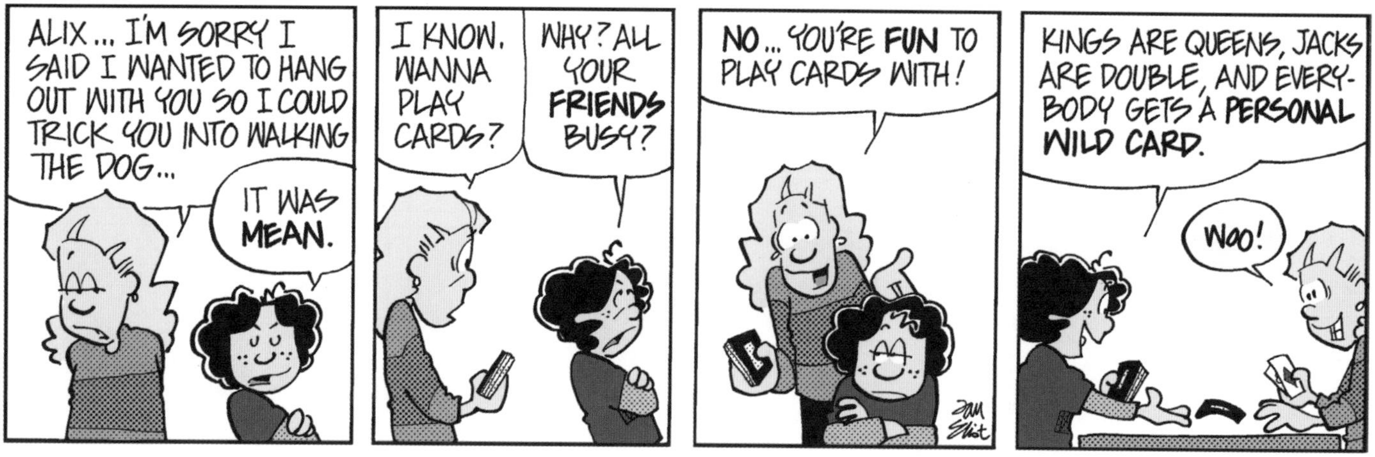
ALIX... I'M SORRY I SAID I WANTED TO HANG OUT WITH YOU SO I COULD TRICK YOU INTO WALKING THE DOG...
IT WAS **MEAN.**
I KNOW. WANNA PLAY CARDS?
WHY? ALL YOUR **FRIENDS** BUSY?
NO... YOU'RE **FUN** TO PLAY CARDS WITH!
KINGS ARE QUEENS, JACKS ARE DOUBLE, AND EVERY-BODY GETS A **PERSONAL WILD CARD.**
WOO!

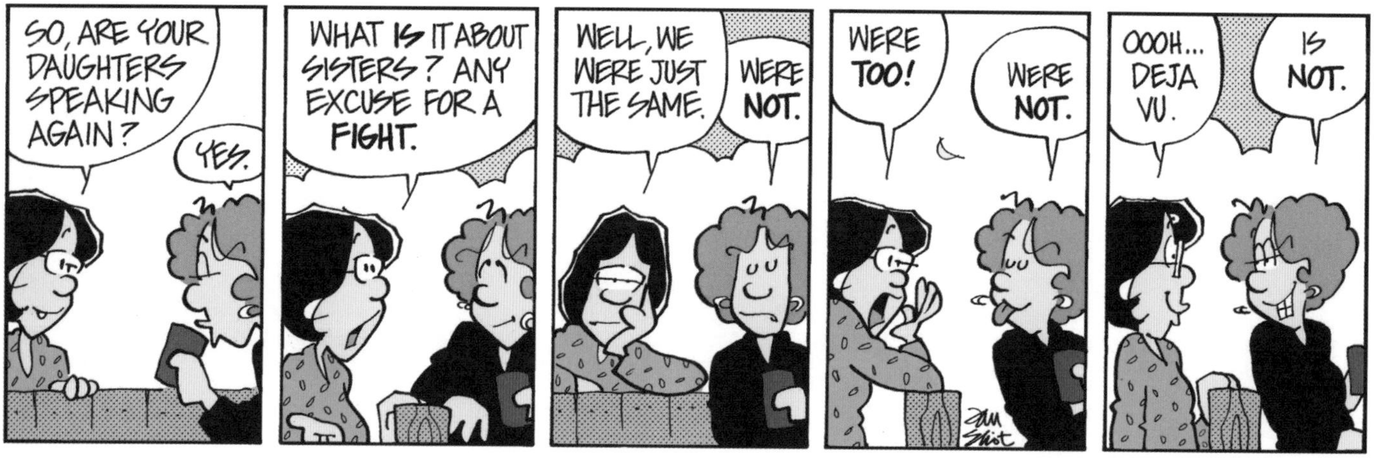
SO, ARE YOUR DAUGHTERS SPEAKING AGAIN?
YES.
WHAT **IS** IT ABOUT SISTERS? ANY EXCUSE FOR A **FIGHT.**
WELL, WE WERE JUST THE SAME.
WERE **NOT.**
WERE **TOO!**
WERE **NOT.**
OOOH... DEJA VU.
IS **NOT.**

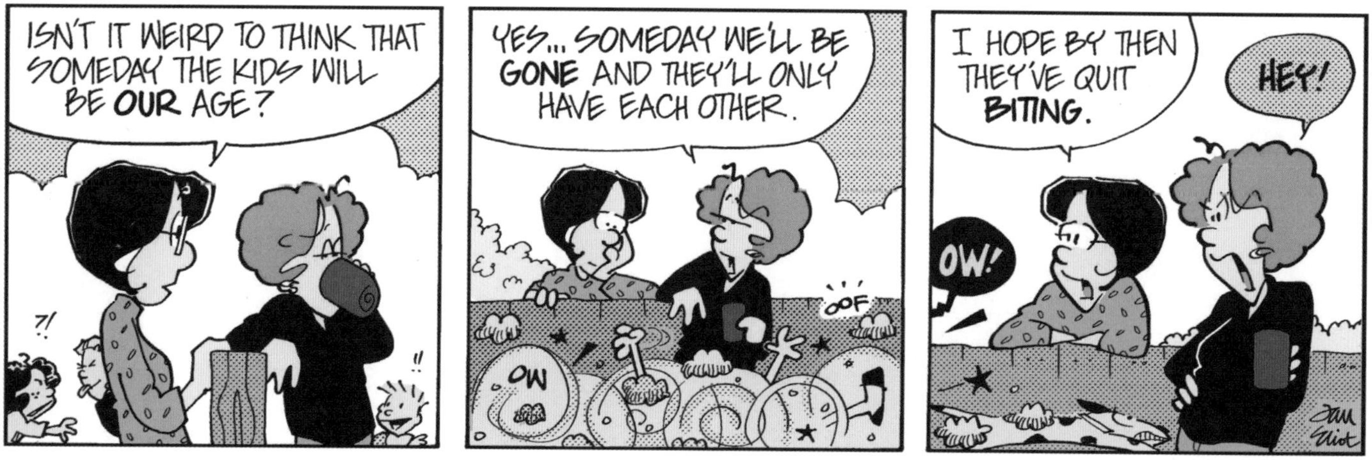
ISN'T IT WEIRD TO THINK THAT SOMEDAY THE KIDS WILL BE **OUR** AGE?
?!
!!
YES... SOMEDAY WE'LL BE **GONE** AND THEY'LL ONLY HAVE EACH OTHER.
OOF
OW
I HOPE BY THEN THEY'VE QUIT **BITING.**
HEY!
OW!

Stone Soup

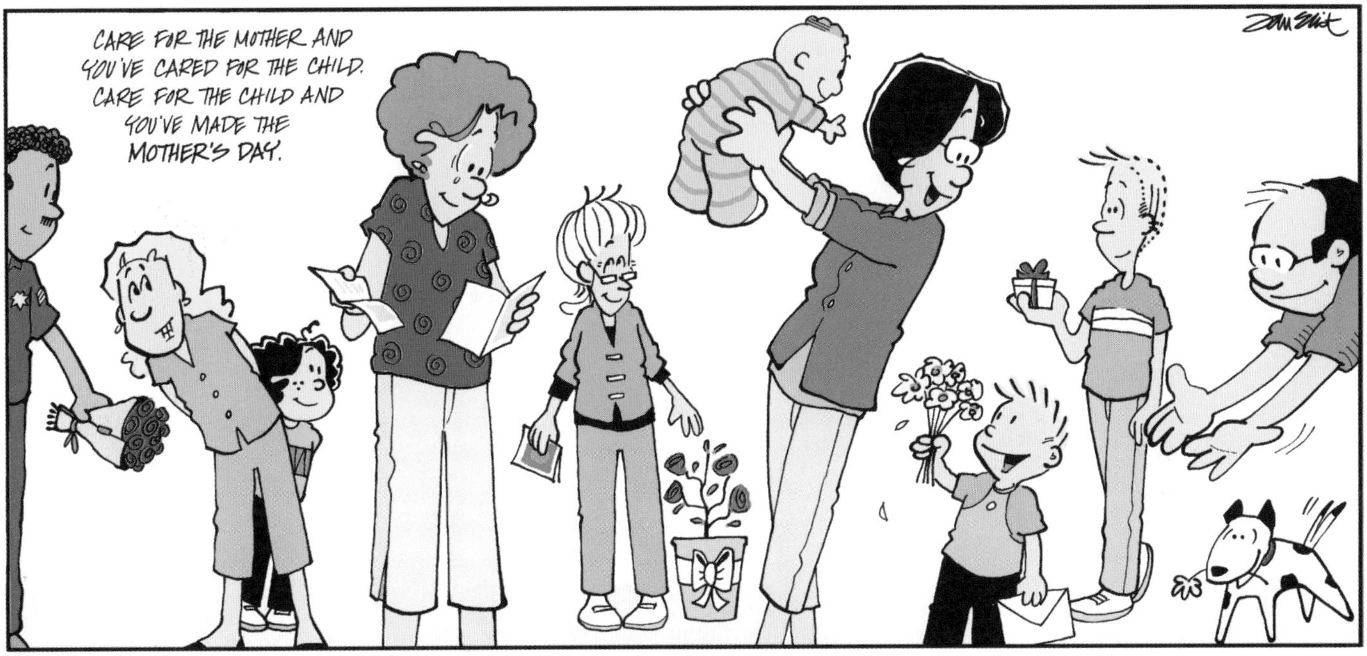
CARE FOR THE MOTHER AND YOU'VE CARED FOR THE CHILD. CARE FOR THE CHILD AND YOU'VE MADE THE MOTHER'S DAY.

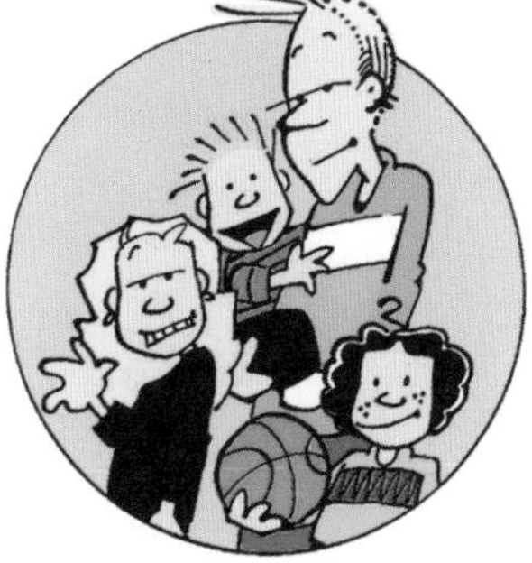

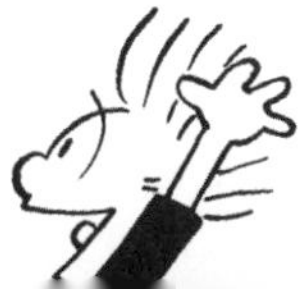

Stone Soup

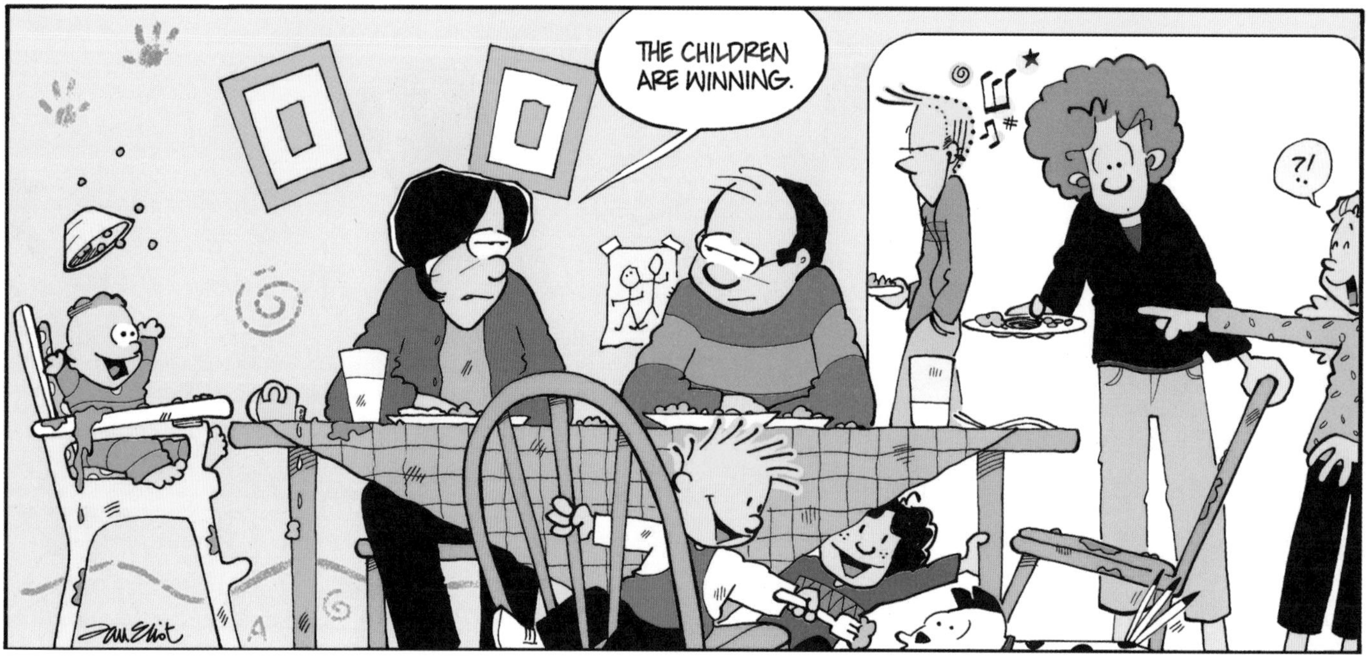
THE CHILDREN ARE WINNING.
?!

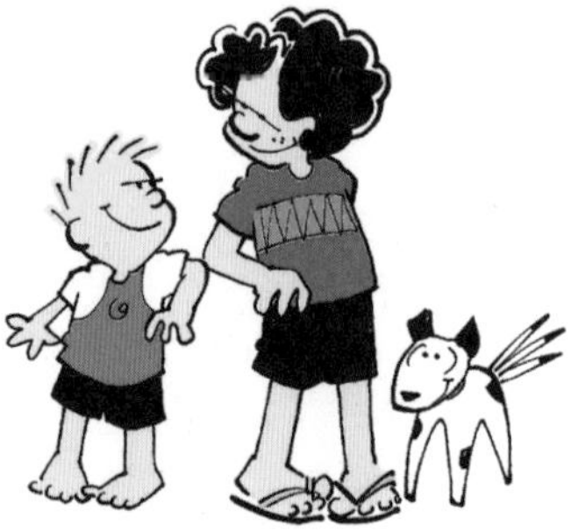

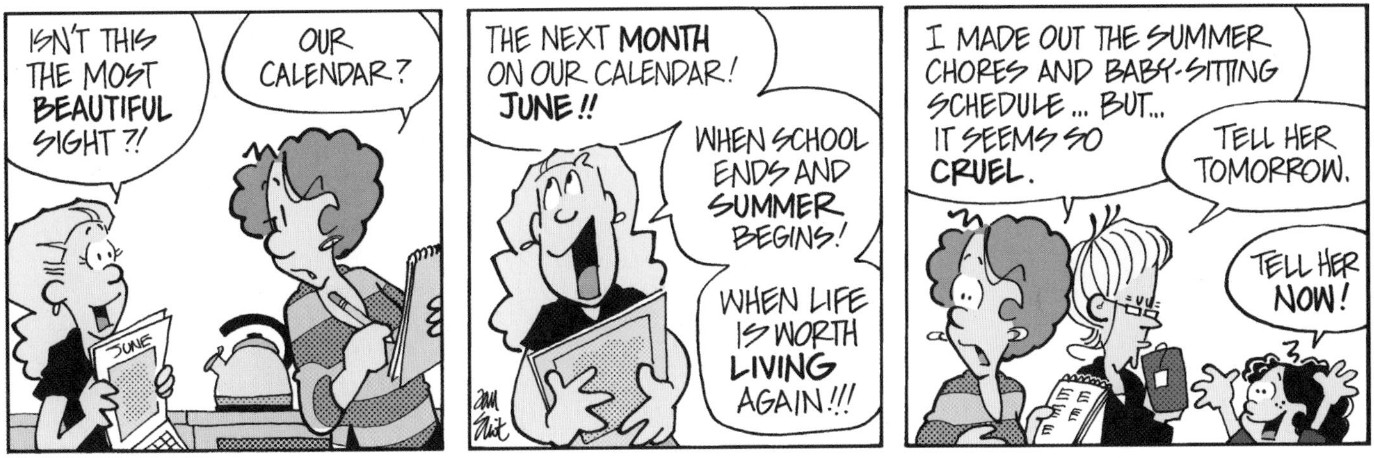
ISN'T THIS THE MOST **BEAUTIFUL** SIGHT ?!
OUR CALENDAR ?
THE NEXT **MONTH** ON OUR CALENDAR! **JUNE**!!
WHEN SCHOOL ENDS AND **SUMMER** BEGINS!
WHEN LIFE IS WORTH **LIVING** AGAIN!!!
I MADE OUT THE SUMMER CHORES AND BABY-SITTING SCHEDULE... BUT... IT SEEMS SO **CRUEL**.
TELL HER TOMORROW.
TELL HER **NOW**!

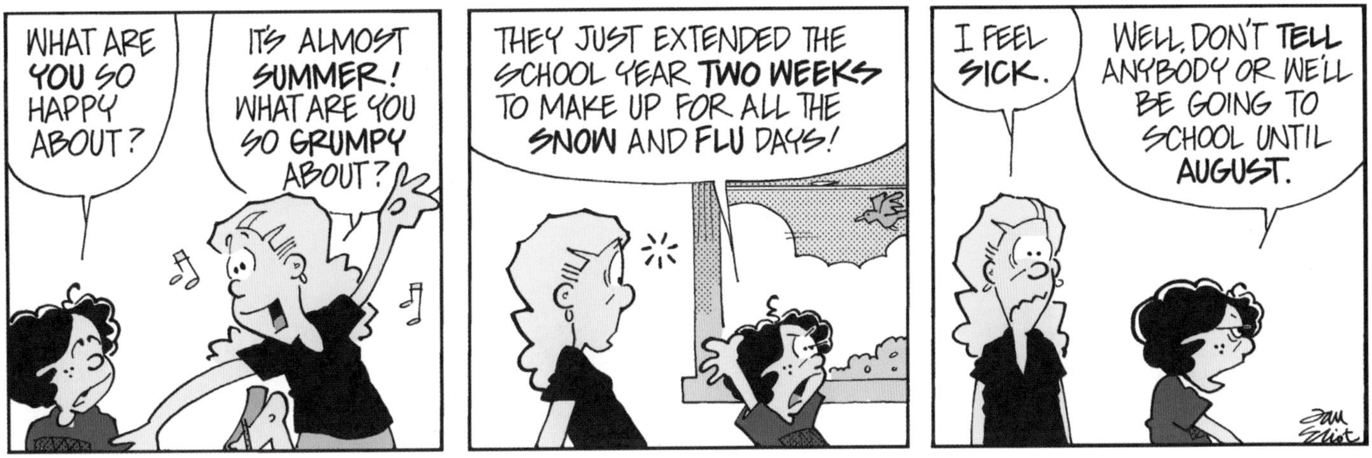
WHAT ARE **YOU** SO HAPPY ABOUT?
IT'S ALMOST **SUMMER**! WHAT ARE YOU SO **GRUMPY** ABOUT?
THEY JUST EXTENDED THE SCHOOL YEAR **TWO WEEKS** TO MAKE UP FOR ALL THE **SNOW** AND **FLU** DAYS!
I FEEL **SICK**.
WELL, DON'T **TELL** ANYBODY OR WE'LL BE GOING TO SCHOOL UNTIL **AUGUST**.

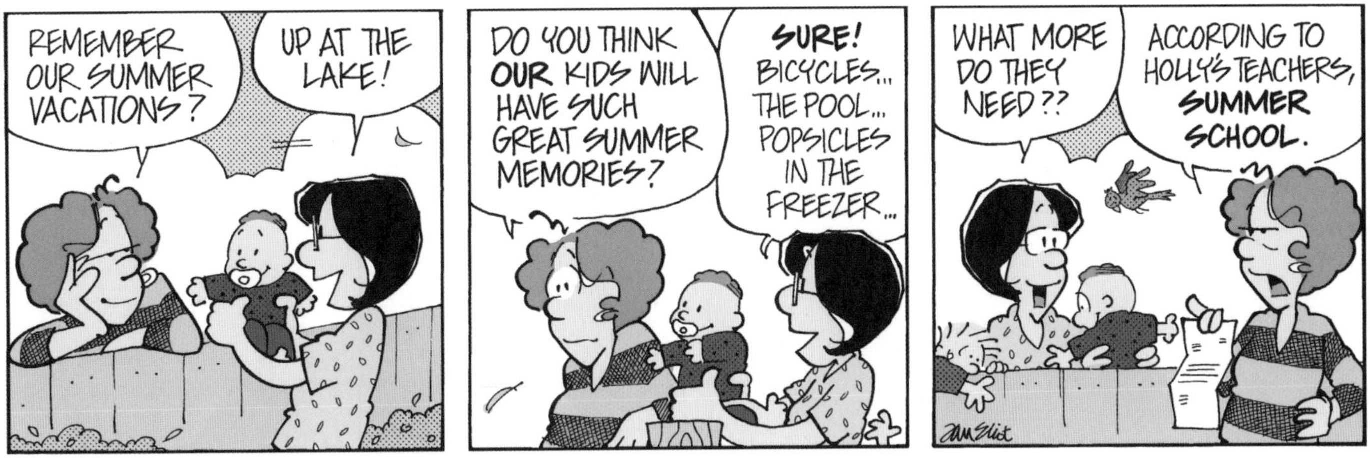
REMEMBER OUR SUMMER VACATIONS?
UP AT THE LAKE!
DO YOU THINK **OUR** KIDS WILL HAVE SUCH GREAT SUMMER MEMORIES?
SURE! BICYCLES... THE POOL... POPSICLES IN THE FREEZER...
WHAT MORE DO THEY NEED??
ACCORDING TO HOLLY'S TEACHERS, **SUMMER SCHOOL**.

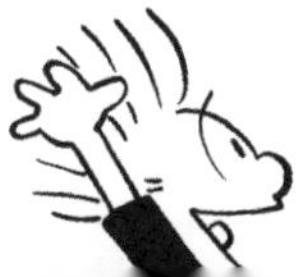

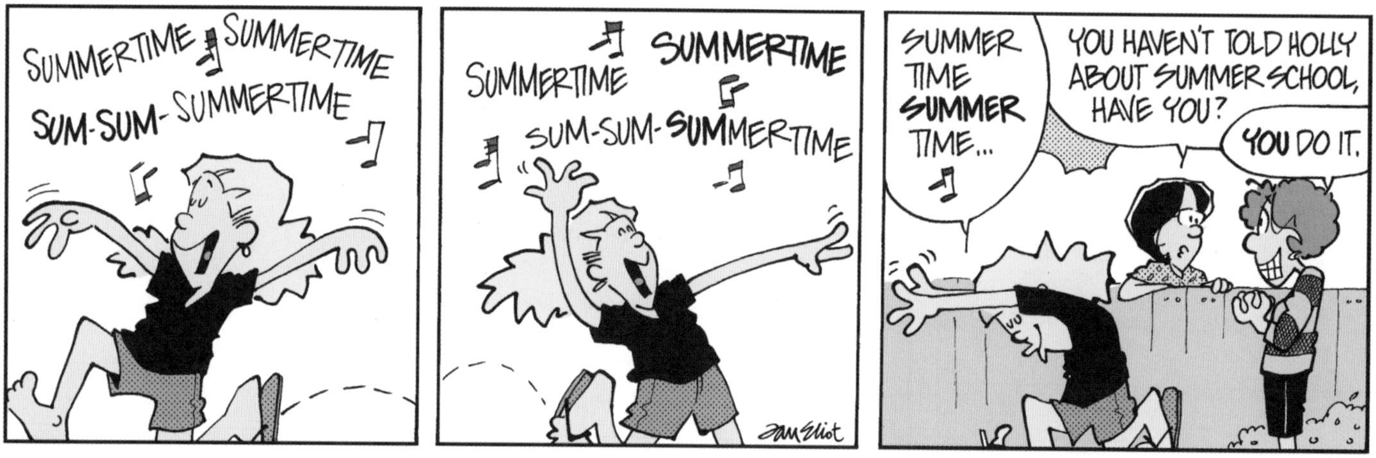
SUMMERTIME SUMMERTIME
SUM-SUM-SUMMERTIME
SUMMERTIME SUMMERTIME
SUM-SUM-SUMMERTIME
Jan Eliot
SUMMER TIME SUMMER TIME...
YOU HAVEN'T TOLD HOLLY ABOUT SUMMER SCHOOL, HAVE YOU?
YOU DO IT.

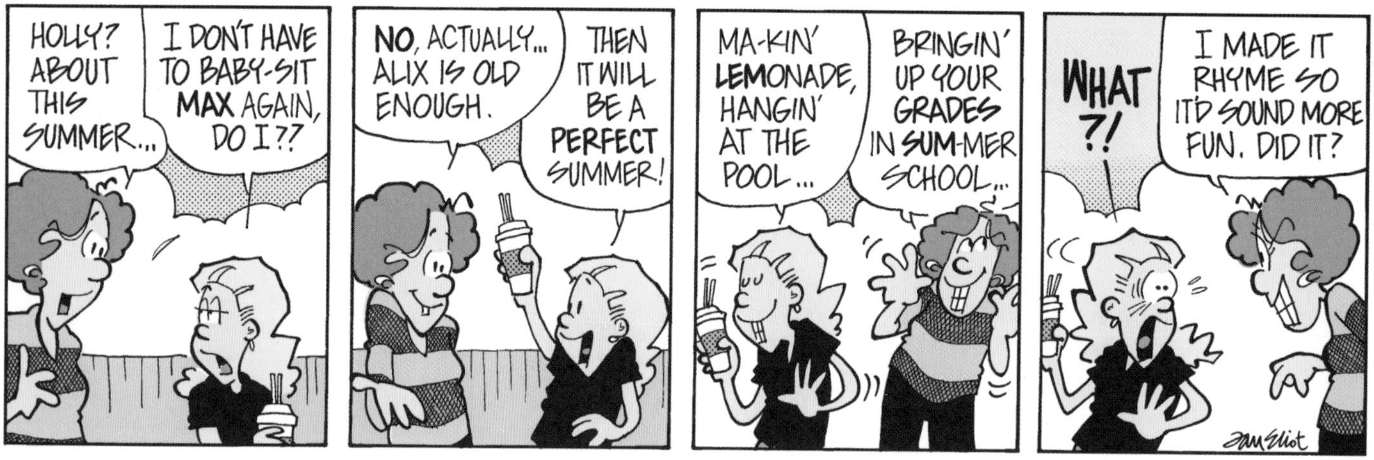
HOLLY? ABOUT THIS SUMMER...
I DON'T HAVE TO BABY-SIT MAX AGAIN, DO I??
NO, ACTUALLY... ALIX IS OLD ENOUGH.
THEN IT WILL BE A PERFECT SUMMER!
MA-KIN' LEMONADE, HANGIN' AT THE POOL...
BRINGIN' UP YOUR GRADES IN SUM-MER SCHOOL...
WHAT?!
I MADE IT RHYME SO IT'D SOUND MORE FUN. DID IT?
Jan Eliot

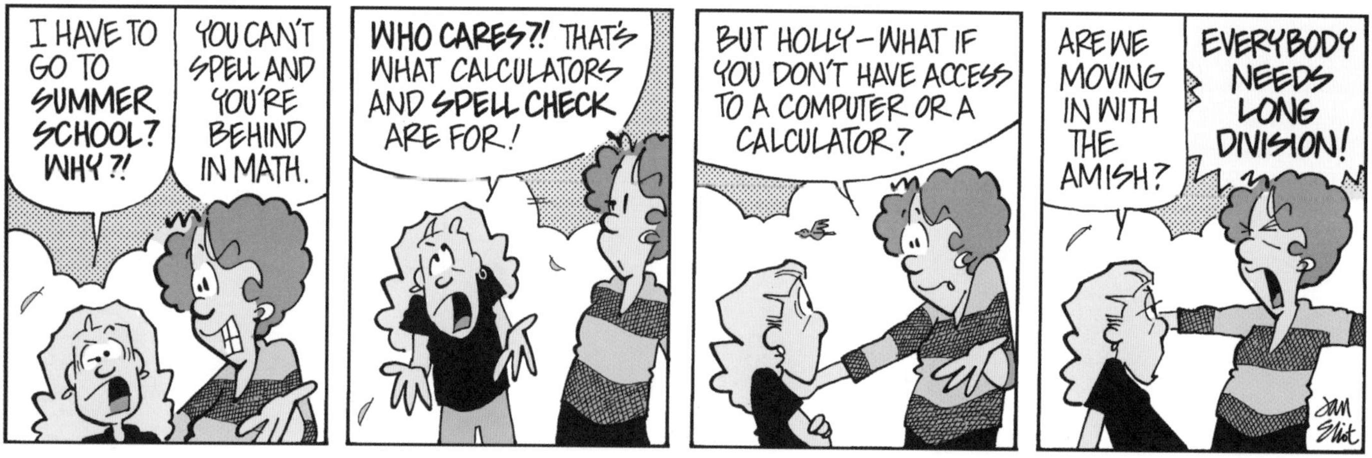
I HAVE TO GO TO SUMMER SCHOOL? WHY?!
YOU CAN'T SPELL AND YOU'RE BEHIND IN MATH.
WHO CARES?! THAT'S WHAT CALCULATORS AND SPELL CHECK ARE FOR!
BUT HOLLY—WHAT IF YOU DON'T HAVE ACCESS TO A COMPUTER OR A CALCULATOR?
ARE WE MOVING IN WITH THE AMISH?
EVERYBODY NEEDS LONG DIVISION!
Jan Eliot

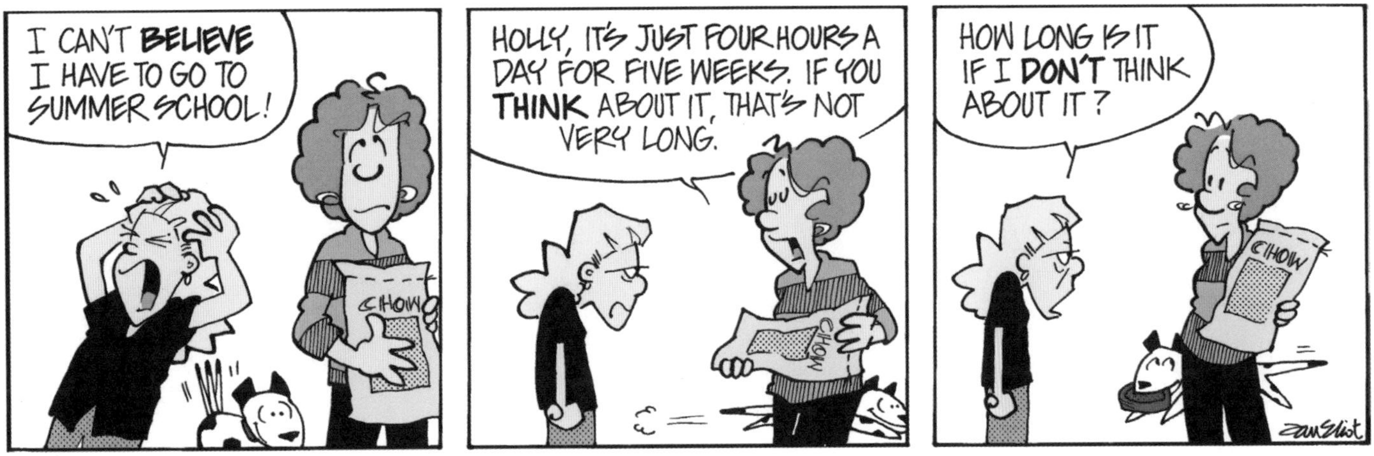
I CAN'T **BELIEVE** I HAVE TO GO TO SUMMER SCHOOL!
HOLLY, IT'S JUST FOUR HOURS A DAY FOR FIVE WEEKS. IF YOU **THINK** ABOUT IT, THAT'S NOT VERY LONG.
HOW LONG IS IT IF I **DON'T** THINK ABOUT IT?

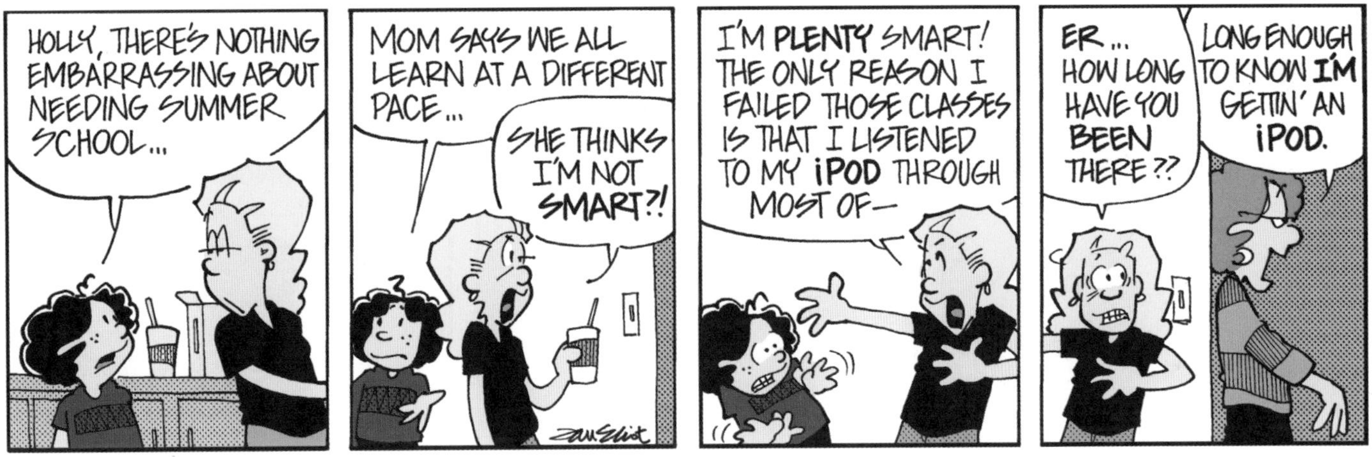
HOLLY, THERE'S NOTHING EMBARRASSING ABOUT NEEDING SUMMER SCHOOL...
MOM SAYS WE ALL LEARN AT A DIFFERENT PACE...
SHE THINKS I'M NOT **SMART**?!
I'M **PLENTY** SMART! THE ONLY REASON I FAILED THOSE CLASSES IS THAT I LISTENED TO MY **iPOD** THROUGH MOST OF—
ER... HOW LONG HAVE YOU **BEEN** THERE??
LONG ENOUGH TO KNOW **I'M** GETTIN' AN **iPOD**.

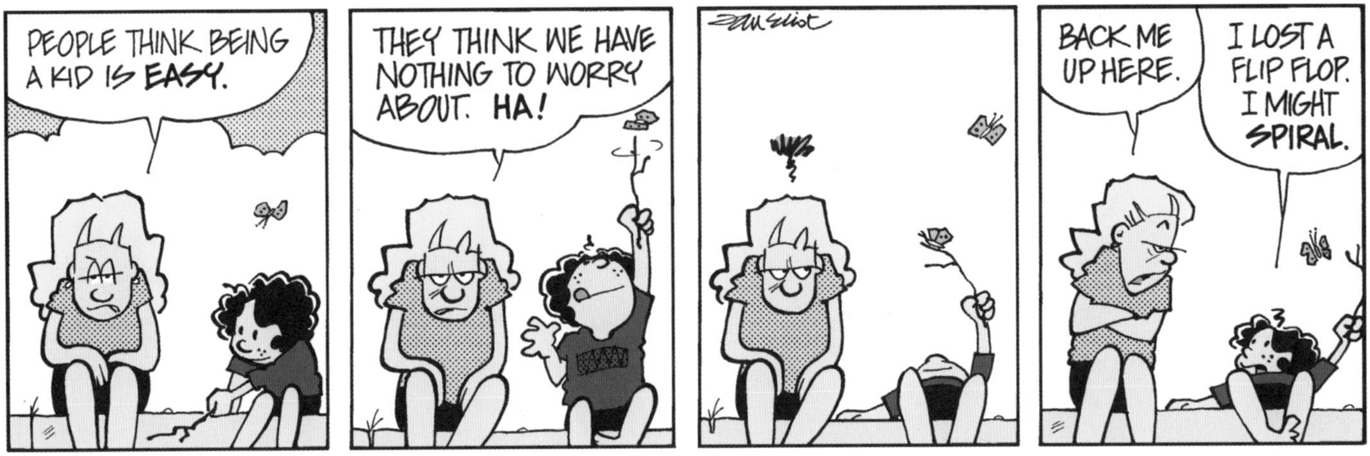
PEOPLE THINK BEING A KID IS **EASY**.
THEY THINK WE HAVE NOTHING TO WORRY ABOUT. **HA!**
BACK ME UP HERE.
I LOST A FLIP FLOP. I MIGHT **SPIRAL**.

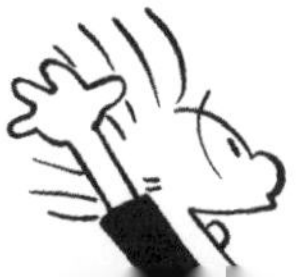

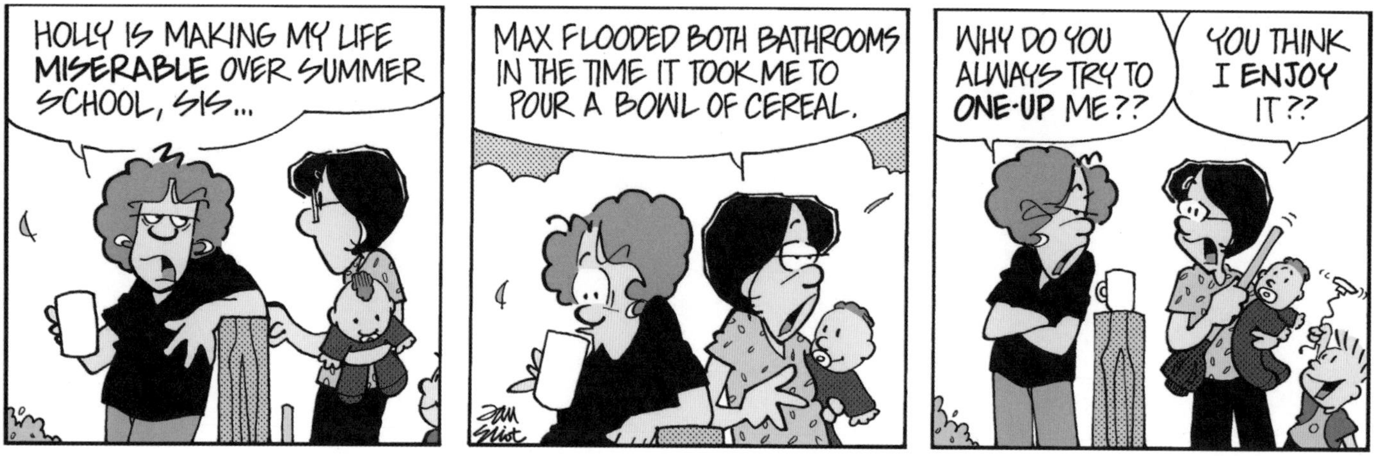
HOLLY IS MAKING MY LIFE **MISERABLE** OVER SUMMER SCHOOL, SIS...
MAX FLOODED BOTH BATHROOMS IN THE TIME IT TOOK ME TO POUR A BOWL OF CEREAL.
WHY DO YOU ALWAYS TRY TO **ONE-UP** ME??
YOU THINK I **ENJOY** IT??

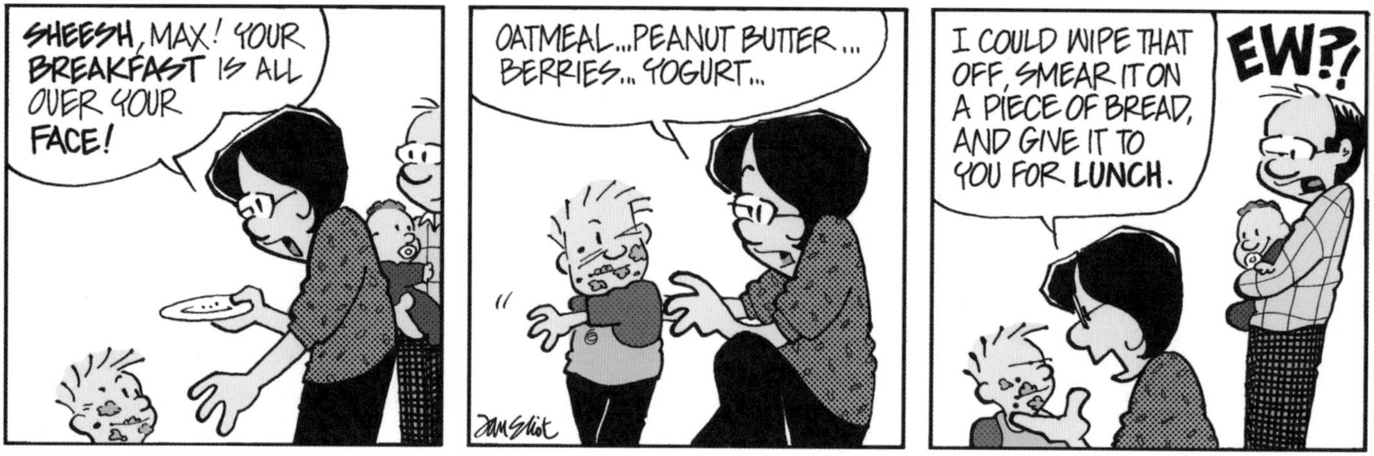
SHEESH, MAX! YOUR **BREAKFAST** IS ALL OVER YOUR **FACE**!
OATMEAL...PEANUT BUTTER... BERRIES... YOGURT...
I COULD WIPE THAT OFF, SMEAR IT ON A PIECE OF BREAD, AND GIVE IT TO YOU FOR **LUNCH**.
EW?!

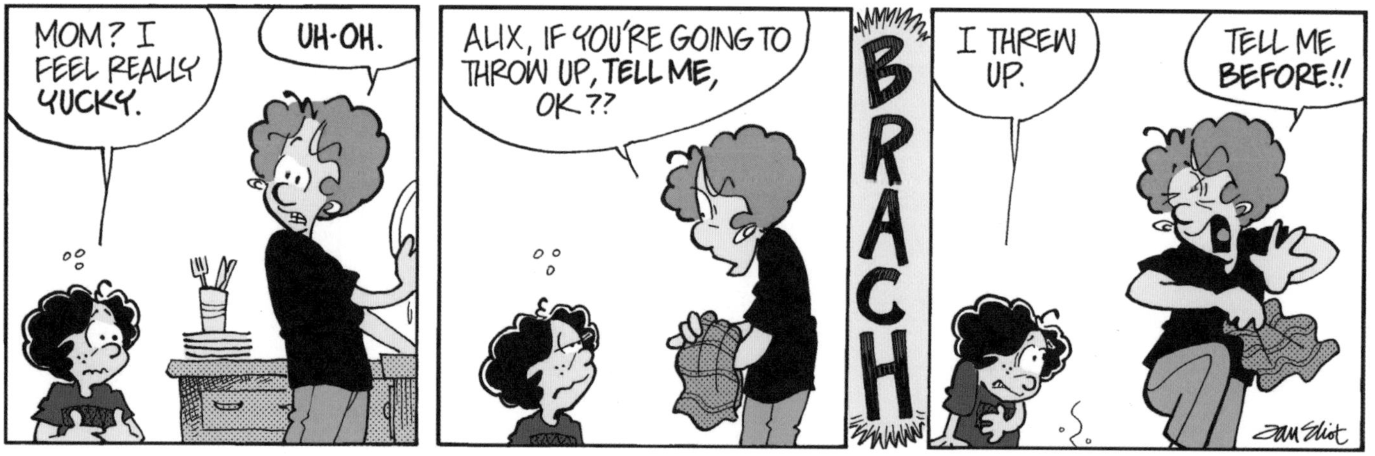
MOM? I FEEL REALLY **YUCKY**.
UH-OH.
ALIX, IF YOU'RE GOING TO THROW UP, **TELL ME**, OK??
BRACH
I THREW UP.
TELL ME **BEFORE!!**

THERE ARE NO MOVIES I CAN SEE.

WHY NOT?

WELL, I HATE VIOLENCE... THAT ELIMINATES HALF OF THEM.

I'M TIRED OF PREDICTABLE ROMANTIC COMEDIES...

WHAT'S YOUR PERFECT MOVIE?

A STRONG FEMALE LEAD AND AN INTERESTING PLOT THAT DOESN'T REVOLVE AROUND GETTING A MAN.

A WOMAN WHO EXPLORES... SERVES HUMANITY... DISCOVERS THE SECRETS OF THE UNIVERSE ...

THAT WOULD MAKE A GOOD MOVIE.

OF COURSE, SHE'D HAVE TO DO ALL THAT IN A MINISKIRT, SPIKE HEELS AND EXTREME CLEAVAGE.

WELL, SURE. YOU GOTTA SELL TICKETS.

97

Stone Soup

HEY, GRAMMA... HOW COME OLD LADIES LIKE TO GARDEN SO MUCH??
WHY DON'T YOU GO FIND AN OLD LADY AND ASK HER?
WHY? I CAN ASK YOU.
CRASH!
FOR AN OLD LADY SHE'S GOT A GOOD ARM!
INCOMING!!

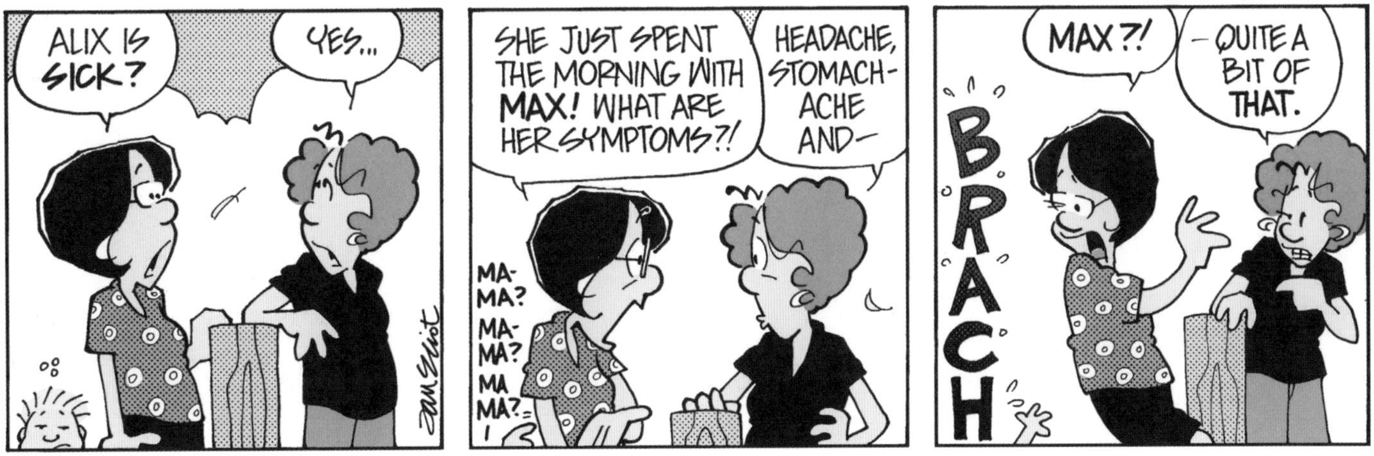
ALIX IS SICK?
YES...
SHE JUST SPENT THE MORNING WITH MAX! WHAT ARE HER SYMPTOMS?!
MA-MA? MA-MA? MA MA?!
HEADACHE, STOMACH-ACHE AND—
BRACH
MAX?!
—QUITE A BIT OF THAT.

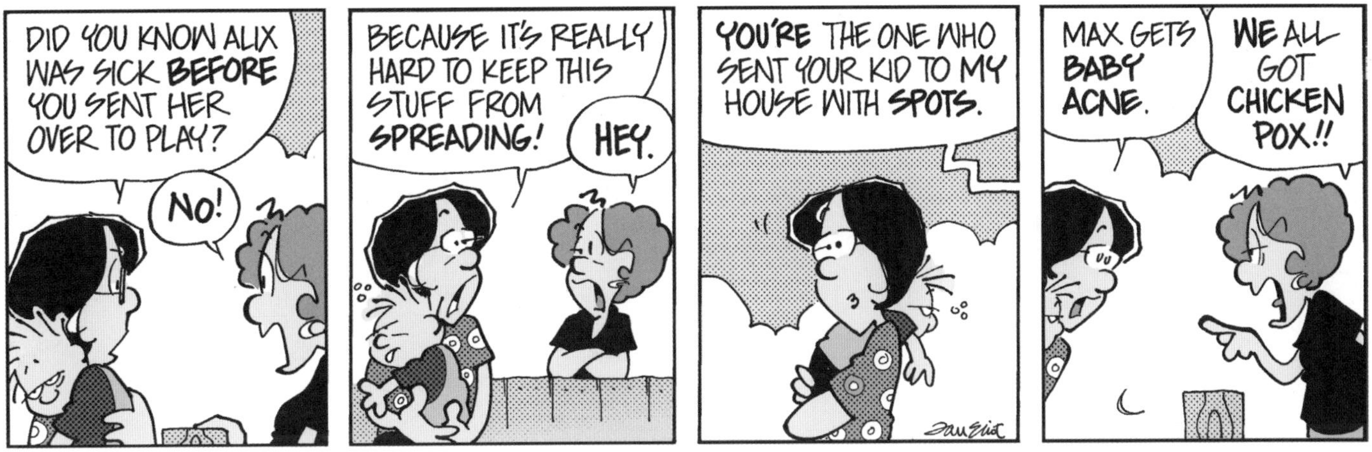
DID YOU KNOW ALIX WAS SICK BEFORE YOU SENT HER OVER TO PLAY?
NO!
BECAUSE IT'S REALLY HARD TO KEEP THIS STUFF FROM SPREADING!
HEY.
YOU'RE THE ONE WHO SENT YOUR KID TO MY HOUSE WITH SPOTS.
MAX GETS BABY ACNE.
WE ALL GOT CHICKEN POX!!

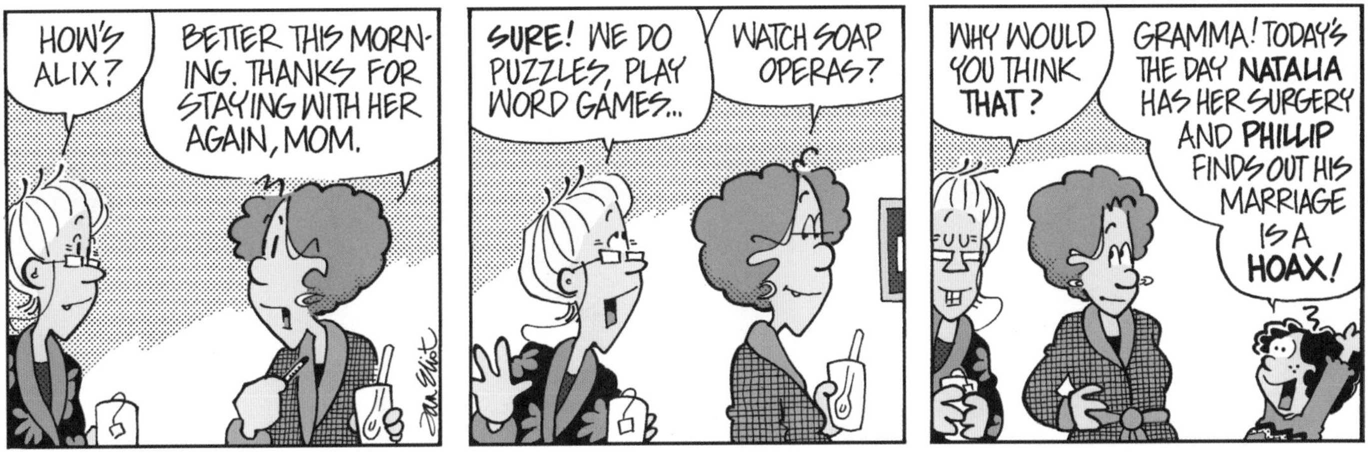
HOW'S ALIX?
BETTER THIS MORNING. THANKS FOR STAYING WITH HER AGAIN, MOM.
SURE! WE DO PUZZLES, PLAY WORD GAMES...
WATCH SOAP OPERAS?
WHY WOULD YOU THINK THAT?
GRAMMA! TODAY'S THE DAY NATALIA HAS HER SURGERY AND PHILLIP FINDS OUT HIS MARRIAGE IS A HOAX!

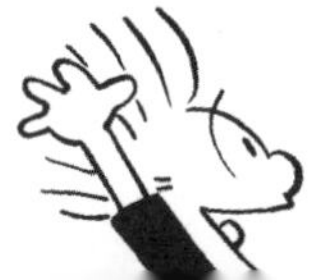

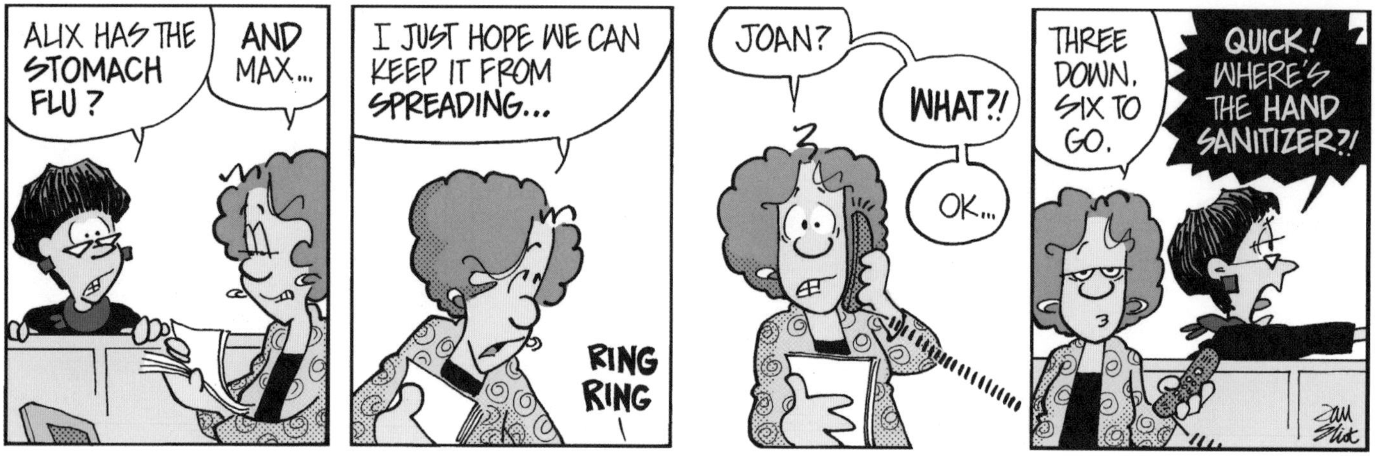
ALIX HAS THE STOMACH FLU?
AND MAX...
I JUST HOPE WE CAN KEEP IT FROM SPREADING...
RING RING
JOAN?
WHAT?!
OK...
THREE DOWN, SIX TO GO.
QUICK! WHERE'S THE HAND SANITIZER?!

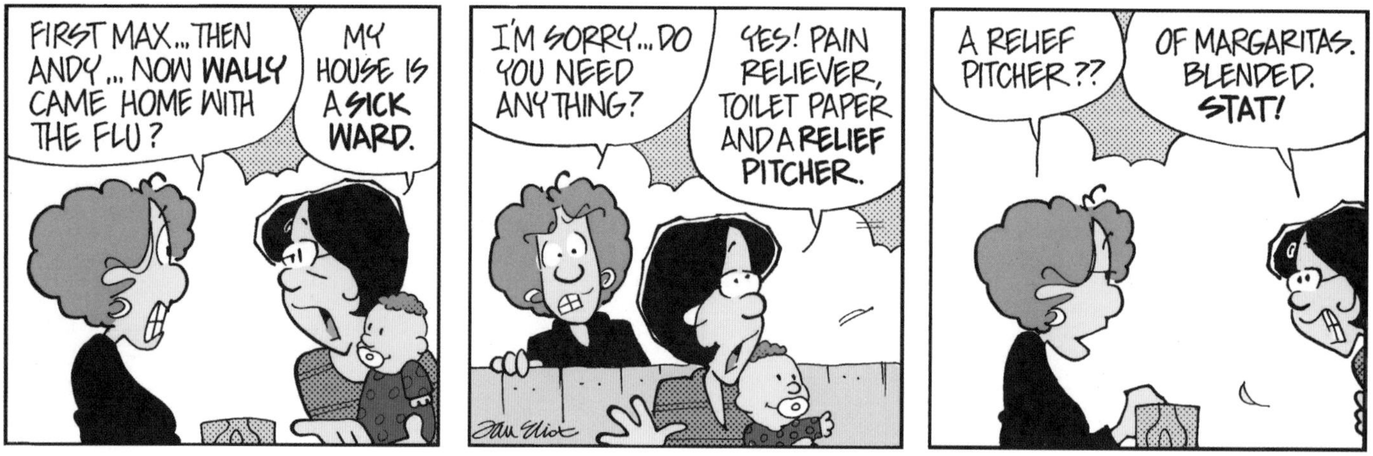
FIRST MAX... THEN ANDY... NOW WALLY CAME HOME WITH THE FLU?
MY HOUSE IS A SICK WARD.
I'M SORRY... DO YOU NEED ANYTHING?
YES! PAIN RELIEVER, TOILET PAPER AND A RELIEF PITCHER.
A RELIEF PITCHER??
OF MARGARITAS. BLENDED. STAT!

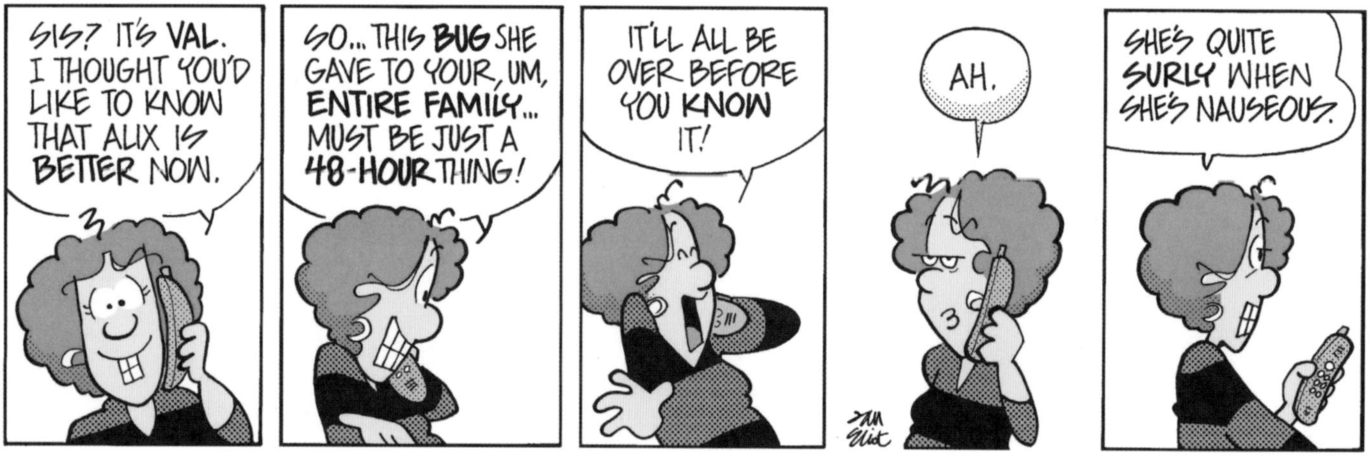
SIS? IT'S VAL. I THOUGHT YOU'D LIKE TO KNOW THAT ALIX IS BETTER NOW.
SO... THIS BUG SHE GAVE TO YOUR, UM, ENTIRE FAMILY... MUST BE JUST A 48-HOUR THING!
IT'LL ALL BE OVER BEFORE YOU KNOW IT!
AH.
SHE'S QUITE SURLY WHEN SHE'S NAUSEOUS.

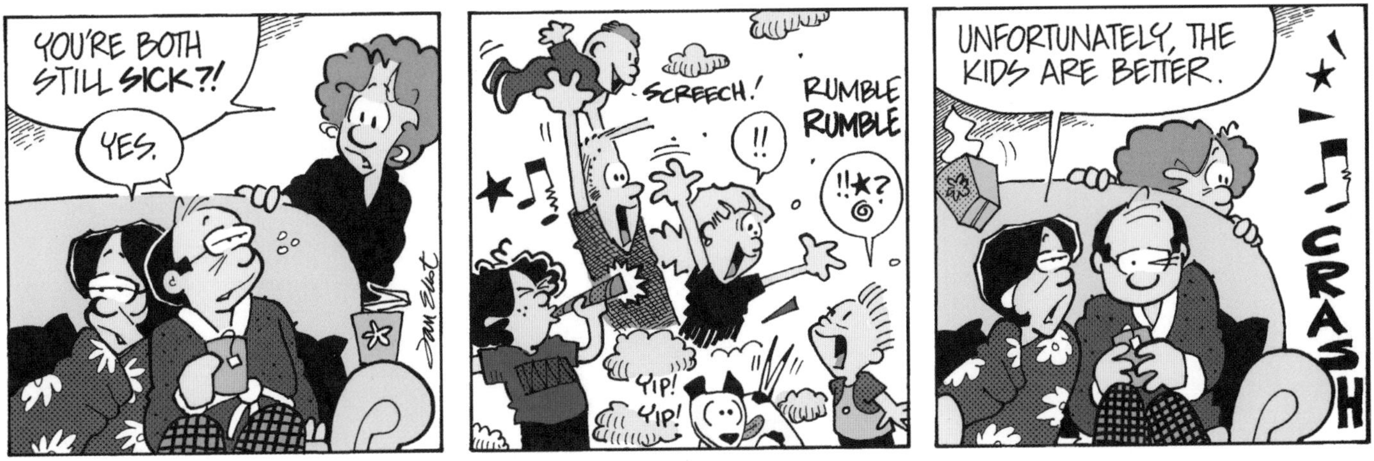
YOU'RE BOTH STILL SICK?!
YES.
SCREECH!
RUMBLE RUMBLE
!!
!!★?
YIP! YIP!
UNFORTUNATELY, THE KIDS ARE BETTER.
CRASH

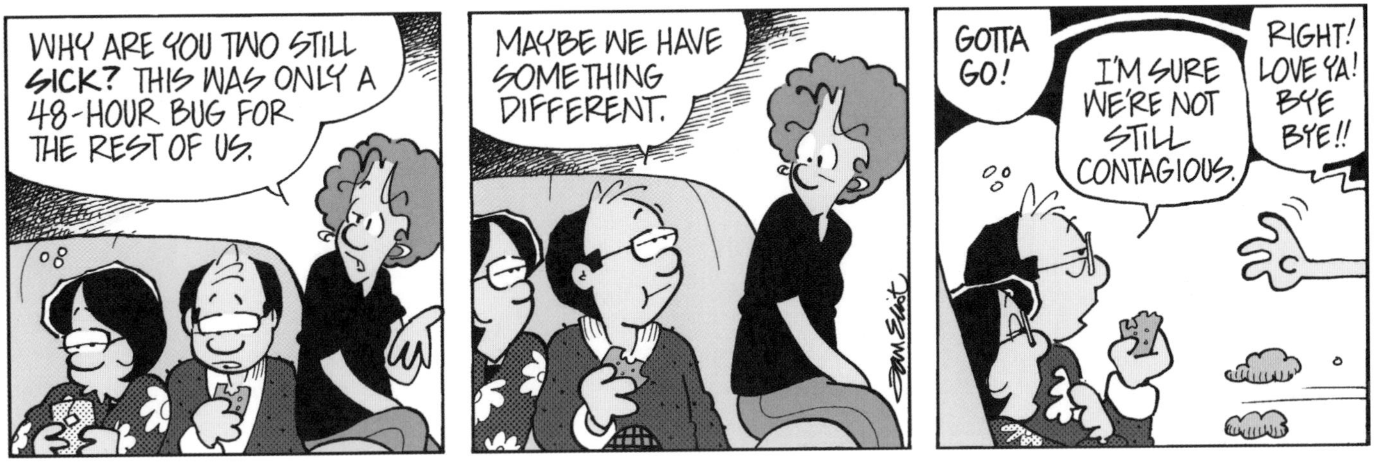
WHY ARE YOU TWO STILL SICK? THIS WAS ONLY A 48-HOUR BUG FOR THE REST OF US.
MAYBE WE HAVE SOMETHING DIFFERENT.
GOTTA GO!
I'M SURE WE'RE NOT STILL CONTAGIOUS.
RIGHT! LOVE YA! BYE BYE!!

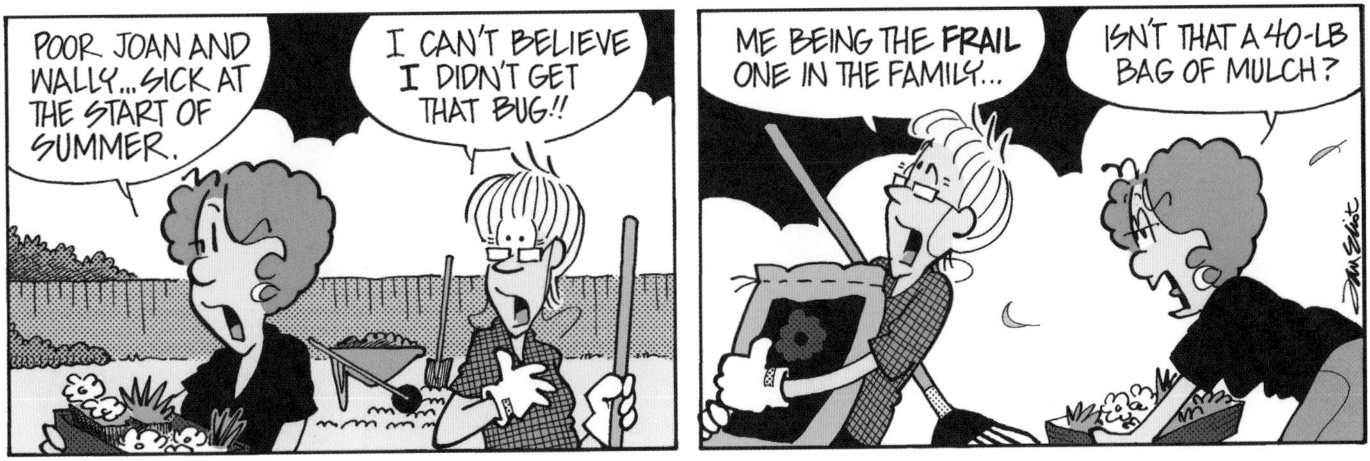
POOR JOAN AND WALLY... SICK AT THE START OF SUMMER.
I CAN'T BELIEVE I DIDN'T GET THAT BUG!!
ME BEING THE FRAIL ONE IN THE FAMILY...
ISN'T THAT A 40-LB BAG OF MULCH?

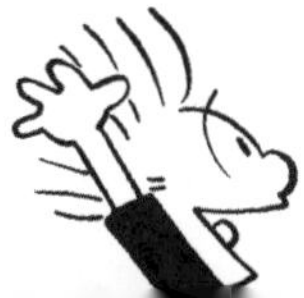

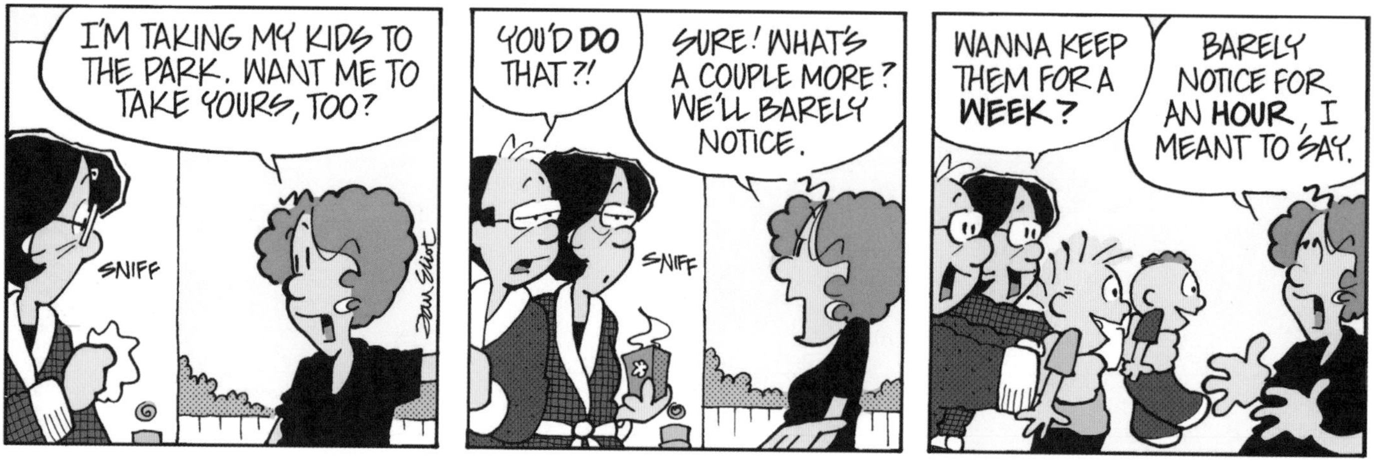
I'M TAKING MY KIDS TO THE PARK. WANT ME TO TAKE YOURS, TOO?
SNIFF
YOU'D **DO** THAT?!
SURE! WHAT'S A COUPLE MORE? WE'LL BARELY NOTICE.
SNIFF
WANNA KEEP THEM FOR A **WEEK?**
BARELY NOTICE FOR AN **HOUR**, I MEANT TO SAY.

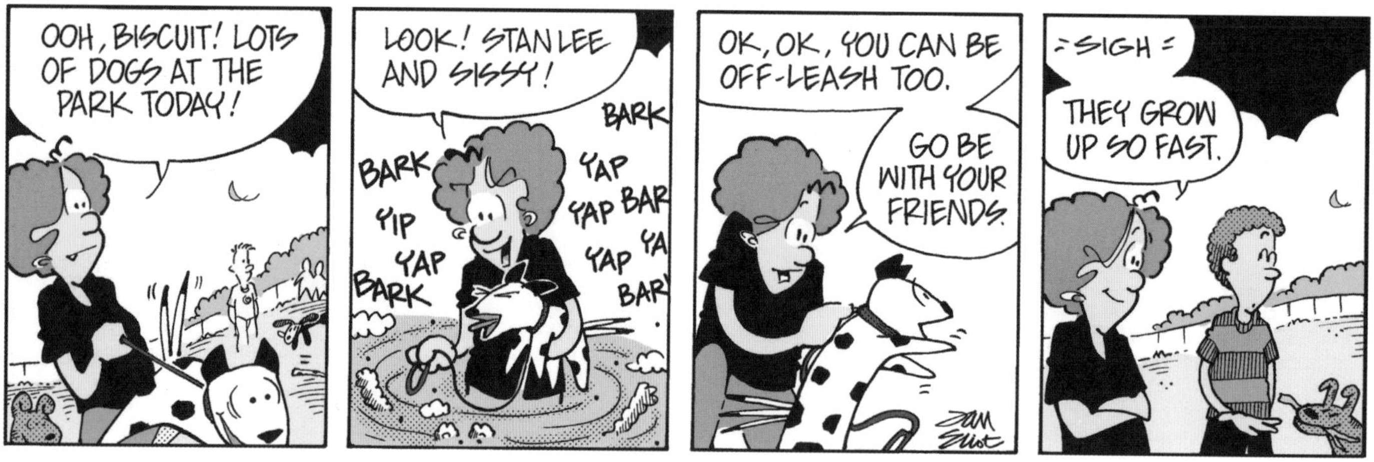
OOH, BISCUIT! LOTS OF DOGS AT THE PARK TODAY!
LOOK! STAN LEE AND SISSY!
BARK
BARK
YIP
YAP
BARK
YAP
YAP BAR
YAP
YA
BAR
OK, OK, YOU CAN BE OFF-LEASH TOO.
GO BE WITH YOUR FRIENDS.
= SIGH =
THEY GROW UP SO FAST.

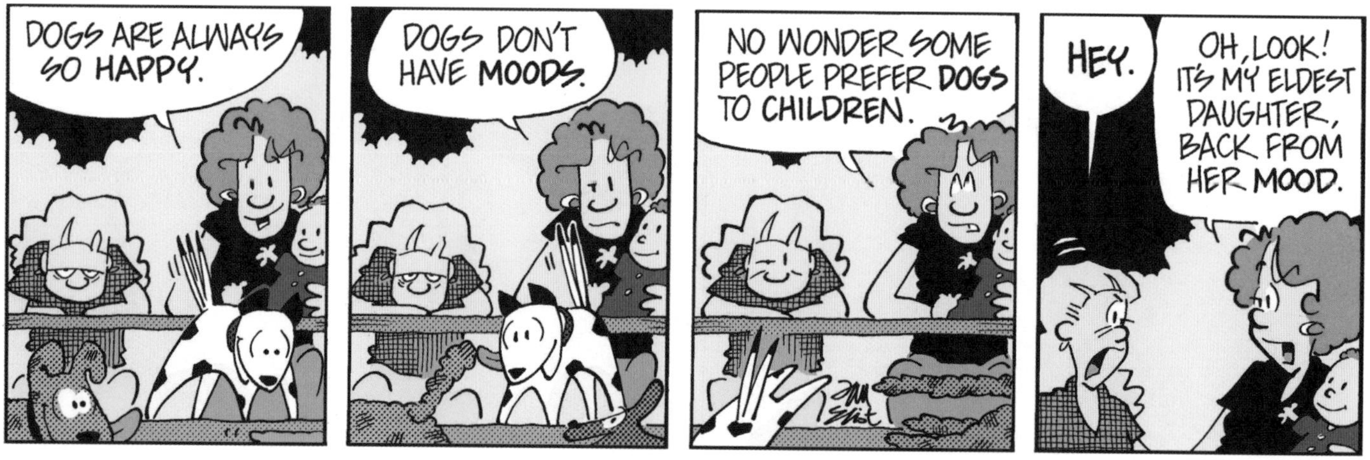
DOGS ARE ALWAYS SO **HAPPY**.
DOGS DON'T HAVE **MOODS**.
NO WONDER SOME PEOPLE PREFER **DOGS** TO **CHILDREN**.
HEY.
OH, LOOK! IT'S MY ELDEST DAUGHTER, BACK FROM HER **MOOD**.

Stone Soup

OOOH, ALIX! CAN YOU **SMELL** IT ??

WHAT? DID I STEP IN SOMETHING?!

NO ...

SUMMER!

A DELICATE BLEND OF CUT GRASS ... DANDELIONS... TANNING LOTION ...,

SHMOOSHED BUGS, POTTING SOIL, ROSES AND JUST A **HINT** OF LAWN CHAIR VINYL.

AHHHH... 2009 IS GOING TO BE A **VERY** GOOD YEAR.

YOU FORGOT CHLORINE! SUMMER'S NOT COMPLETE WITHOUT UNDERTONES OF CHLORINE.

Stone Soup

YOW! WATCH OUT FOR THE THORNY THINGS...
BIRD DOO EVERYWHERE! ICK! ICK! ICK!
UH-OH... PUDDLE OF MELTED ICE CREAM...
AAiiiiEEE! RED ANTS! THOUSANDS OF THEM!!
HOT HOT HOT HOT HOT H
WHY DON'T YOU JUST WEAR SANDALS?!
IT'S SUMMER!
I NEED TO FEEL THE EARTH BETWEEN MY TOES.
I DON'T THINK THAT'S EARTH.

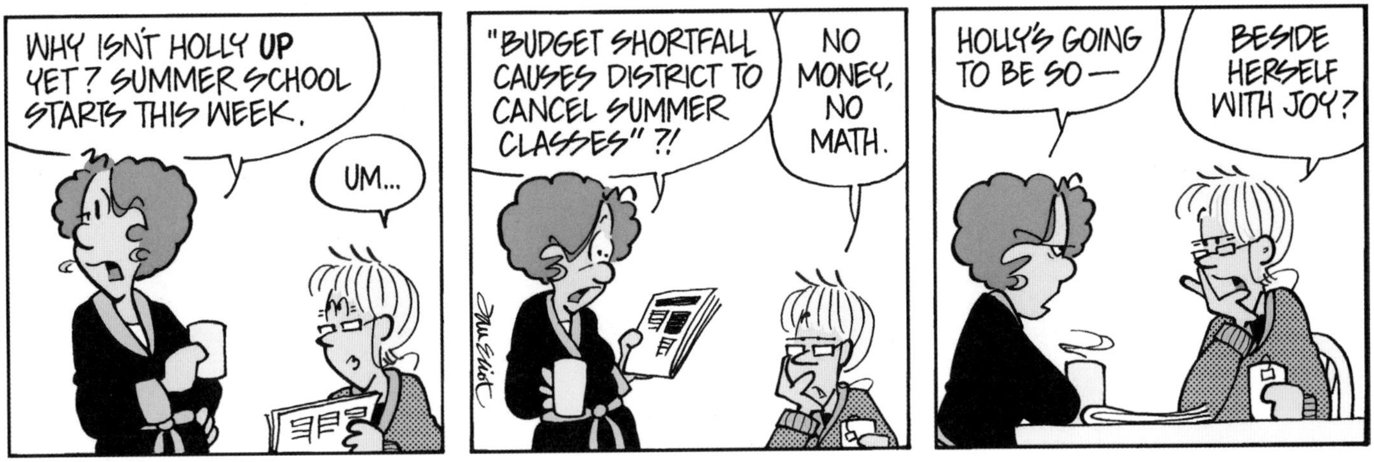
WHY ISN'T HOLLY **UP** YET? SUMMER SCHOOL STARTS THIS WEEK.
UM...
"BUDGET SHORTFALL CAUSES DISTRICT TO CANCEL SUMMER CLASSES" ?!
NO MONEY, NO MATH.
HOLLY'S GOING TO BE SO—
BESIDE HERSELF WITH JOY?

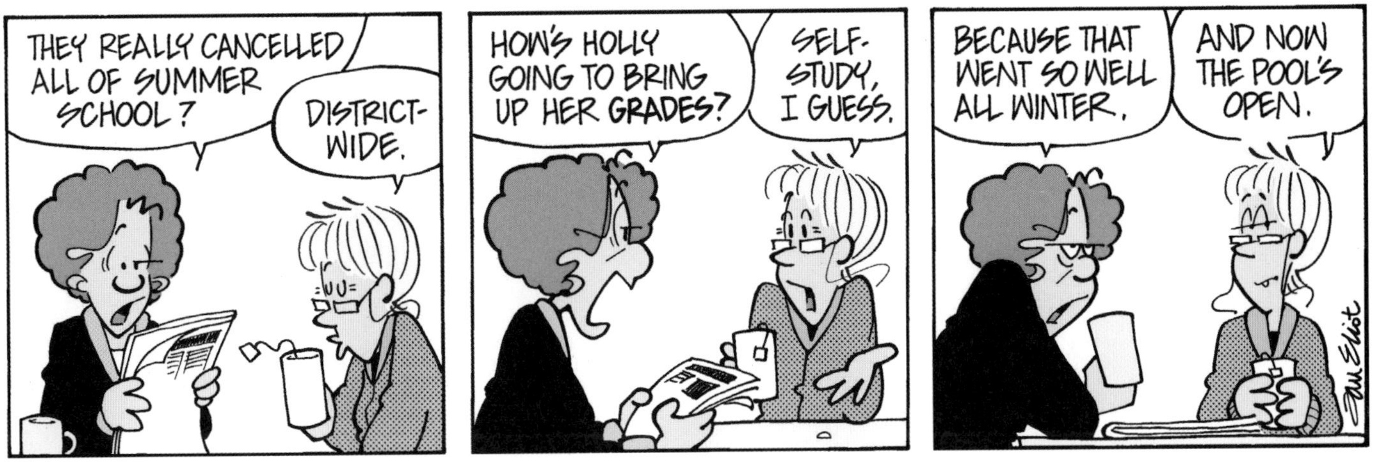
THEY REALLY CANCELLED ALL OF SUMMER SCHOOL?
DISTRICT-WIDE.
HOW'S HOLLY GOING TO BRING UP HER **GRADES**?
SELF-STUDY, I GUESS.
BECAUSE THAT WENT SO WELL ALL WINTER.
AND NOW THE POOL'S OPEN.

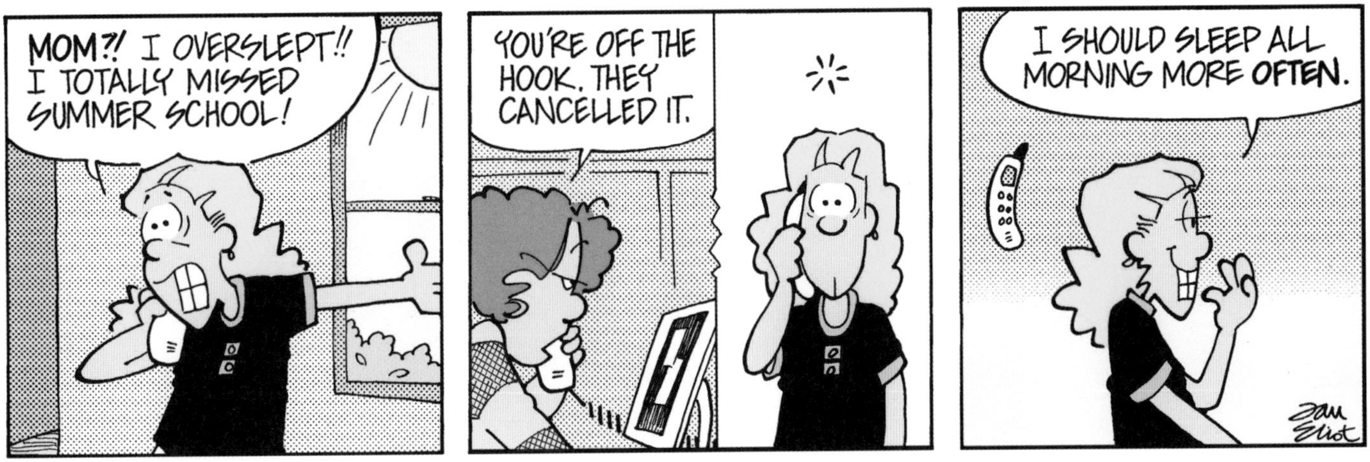
MOM?! I OVERSLEPT!! I TOTALLY MISSED SUMMER SCHOOL!
YOU'RE OFF THE HOOK. THEY CANCELLED IT.
I SHOULD SLEEP ALL MORNING MORE **OFTEN**.

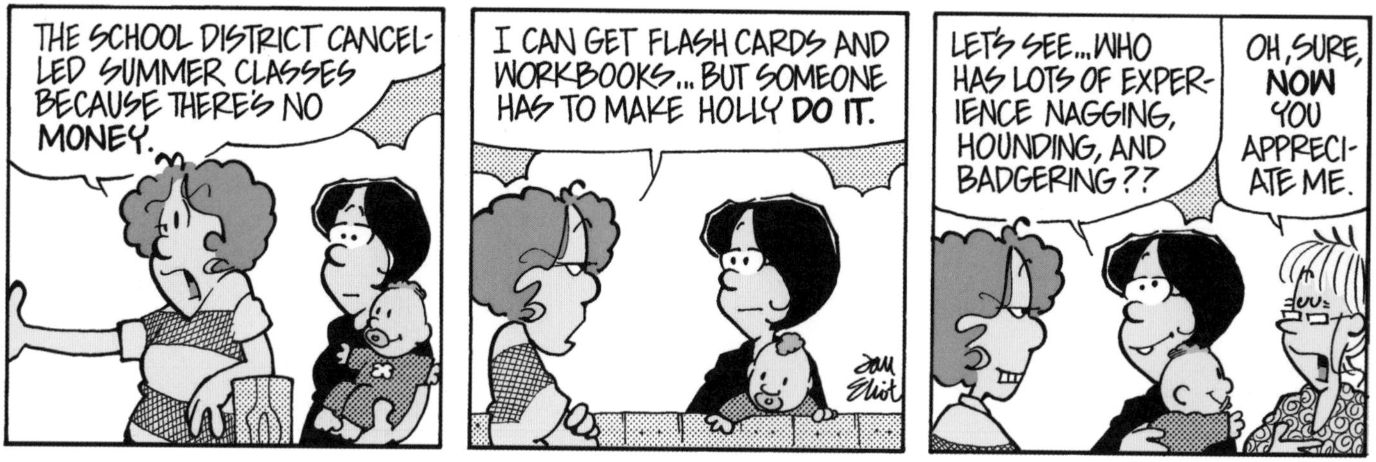
THE SCHOOL DISTRICT CANCELLED SUMMER CLASSES BECAUSE THERE'S NO MONEY.
I CAN GET FLASH CARDS AND WORKBOOKS... BUT SOMEONE HAS TO MAKE HOLLY DO IT.
LET'S SEE... WHO HAS LOTS OF EXPERIENCE NAGGING, HOUNDING, AND BADGERING??
OH, SURE, NOW YOU APPRECIATE ME.

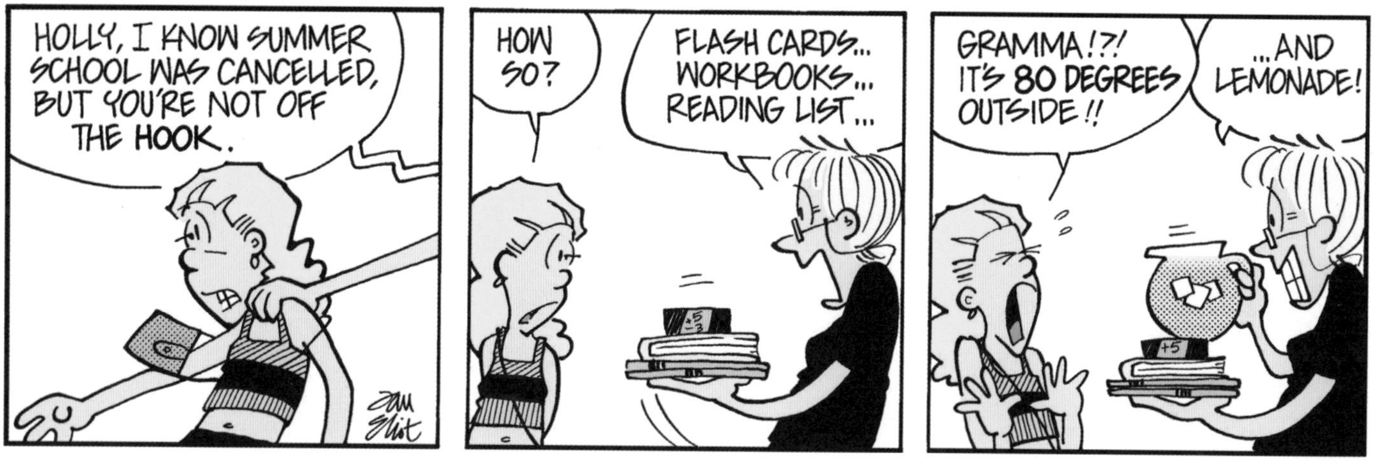
HOLLY, I KNOW SUMMER SCHOOL WAS CANCELLED, BUT YOU'RE NOT OFF THE HOOK.
HOW SO?
FLASH CARDS... WORKBOOKS... READING LIST...
GRAMMA!?! IT'S 80 DEGREES OUTSIDE!!
...AND LEMONADE!

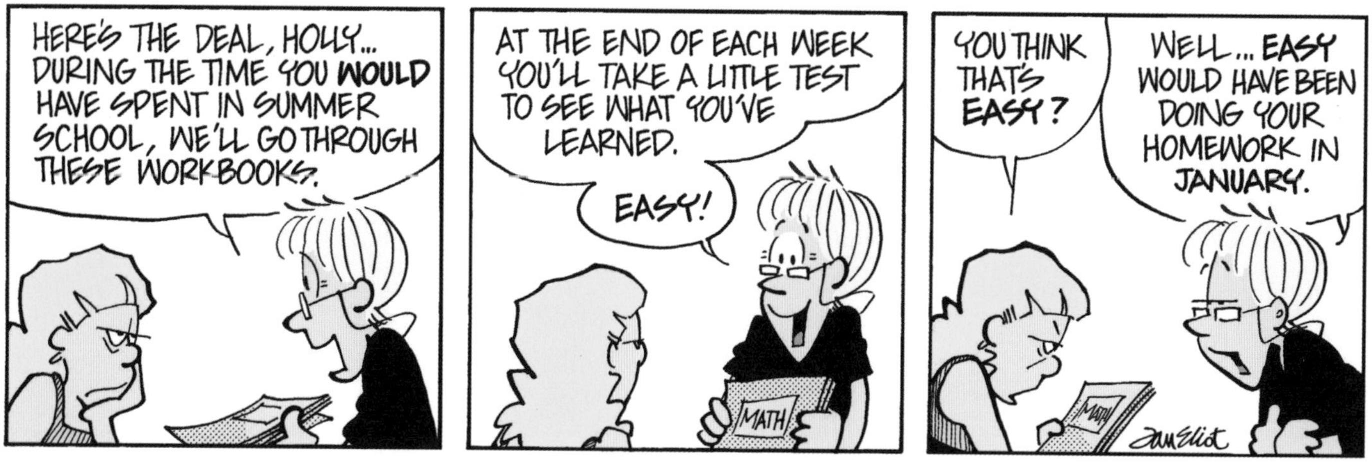
HERE'S THE DEAL, HOLLY... DURING THE TIME YOU WOULD HAVE SPENT IN SUMMER SCHOOL, WE'LL GO THROUGH THESE WORKBOOKS.
AT THE END OF EACH WEEK YOU'LL TAKE A LITTLE TEST TO SEE WHAT YOU'VE LEARNED.
EASY!
MATH
YOU THINK THAT'S EASY?
WELL... EASY WOULD HAVE BEEN DOING YOUR HOMEWORK IN JANUARY.

Stone Soup

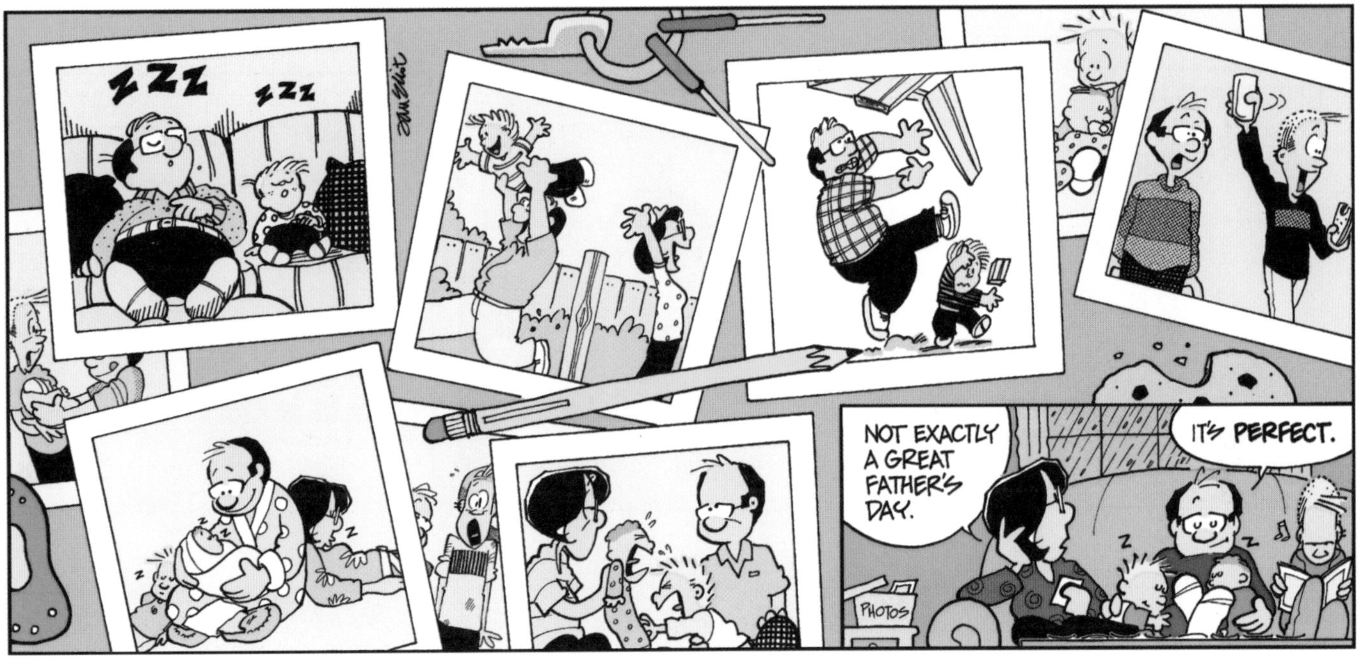
ZZZ
ZZZ
NOT EXACTLY A GREAT FATHER'S DAY.
IT'S PERFECT.
PHOTOS

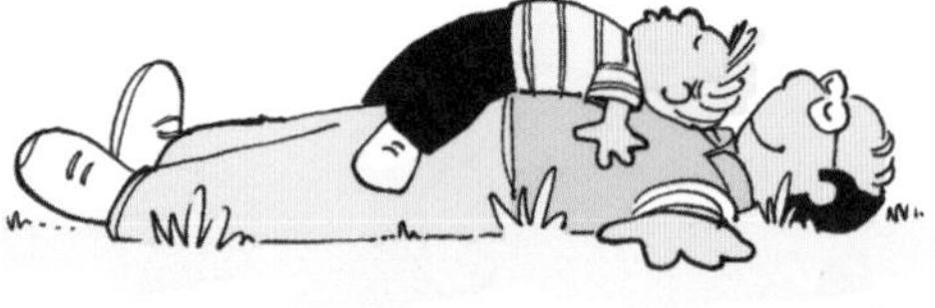

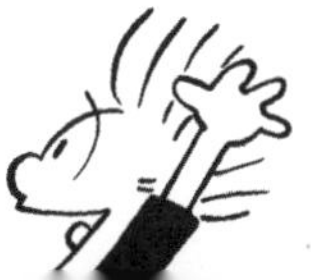

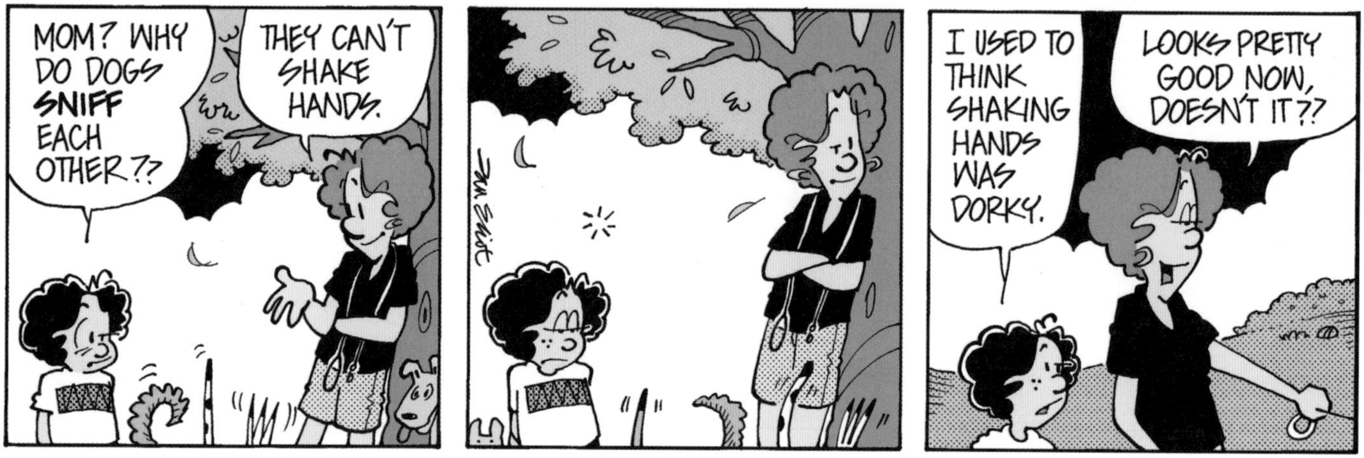
MOM? WHY DO DOGS SNIFF EACH OTHER??
THEY CAN'T SHAKE HANDS.
I USED TO THINK SHAKING HANDS WAS DORKY.
LOOKS PRETTY GOOD NOW, DOESN'T IT??

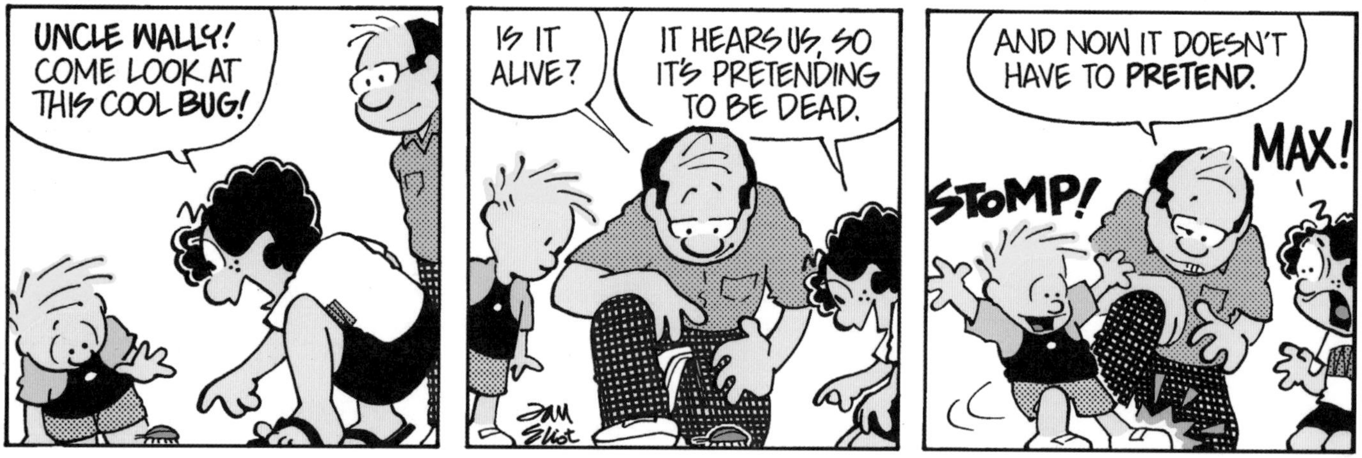
UNCLE WALLY! COME LOOK AT THIS COOL BUG!
IS IT ALIVE?
IT HEARS US, SO IT'S PRETENDING TO BE DEAD.
AND NOW IT DOESN'T HAVE TO PRETEND.
STOMP!
MAX!

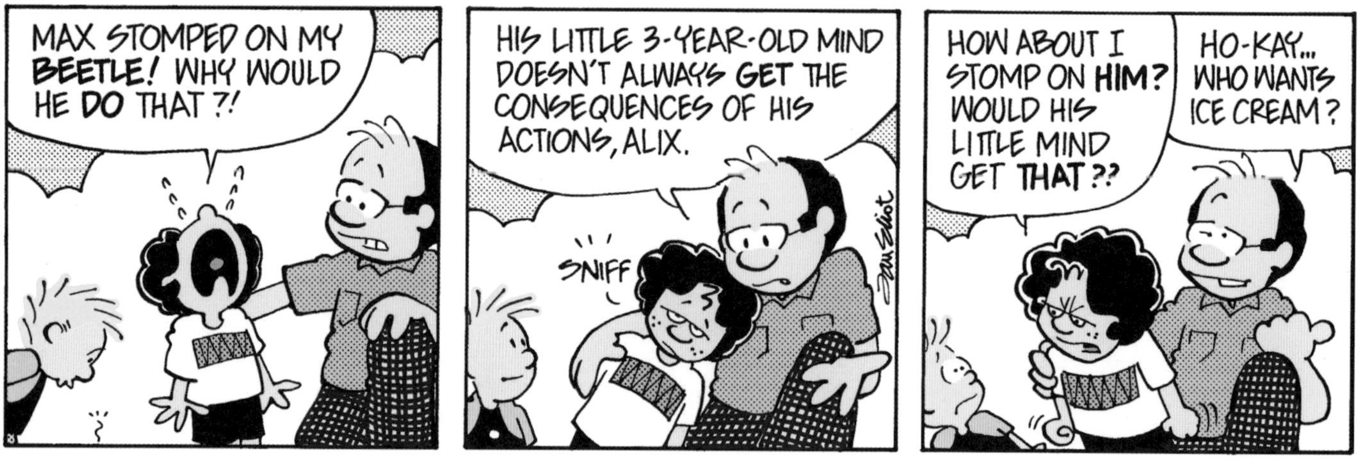
MAX STOMPED ON MY BEETLE! WHY WOULD HE DO THAT?!
HIS LITTLE 3-YEAR-OLD MIND DOESN'T ALWAYS GET THE CONSEQUENCES OF HIS ACTIONS, ALIX.
SNIFF
HOW ABOUT I STOMP ON HIM? WOULD HIS LITTLE MIND GET THAT??
HO-KAY... WHO WANTS ICE CREAM?

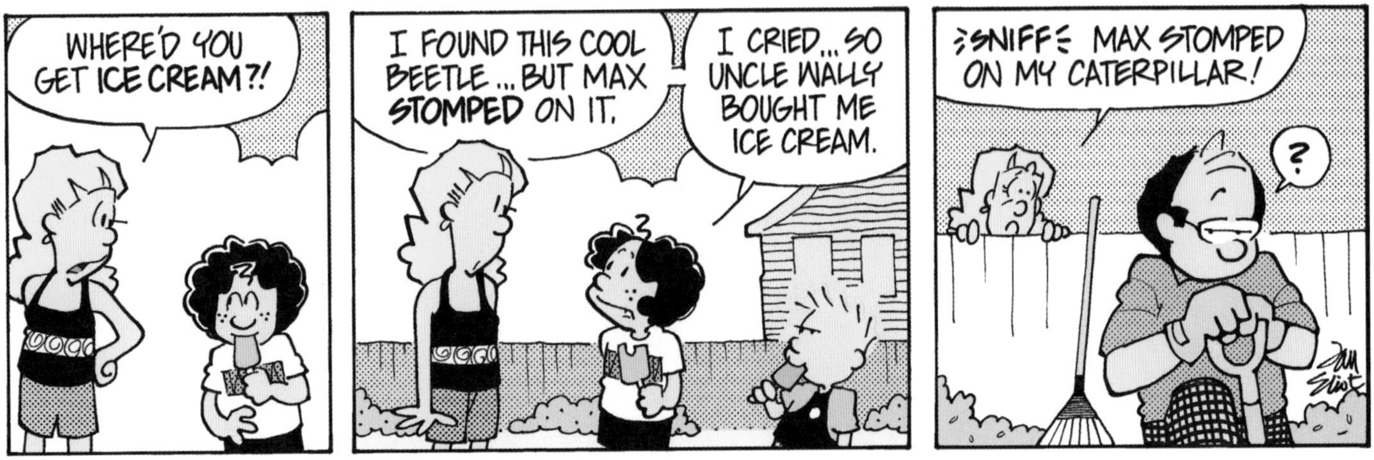
WHERE'D YOU GET ICE CREAM?!
I FOUND THIS COOL BEETLE ... BUT MAX STOMPED ON IT.
I CRIED... SO UNCLE WALLY BOUGHT ME ICE CREAM.
SNIFF MAX STOMPED ON MY CATERPILLAR!
?

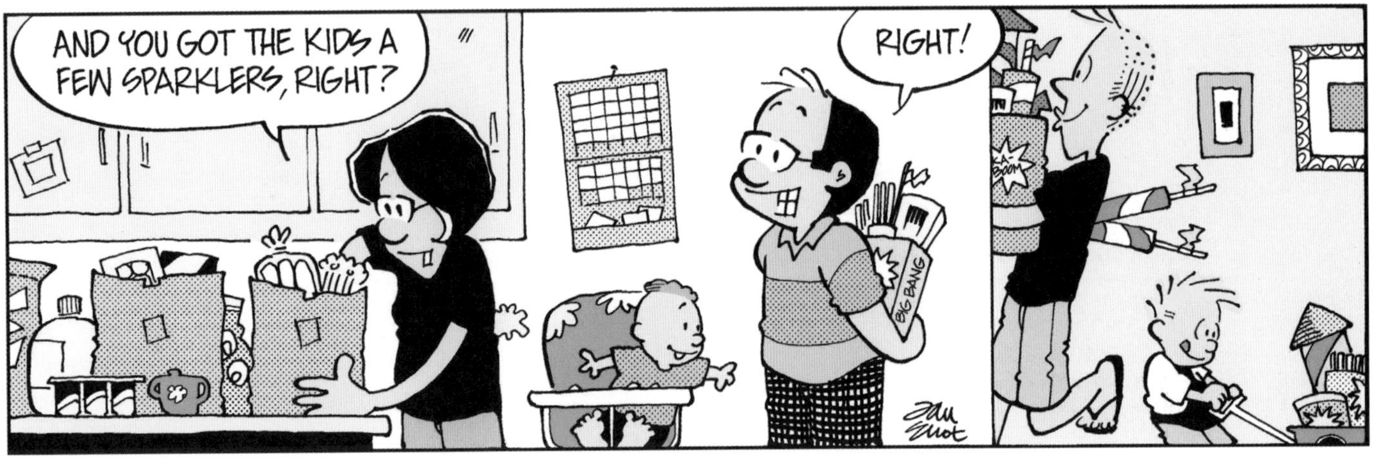
AND YOU GOT THE KIDS A FEW SPARKLERS, RIGHT?
RIGHT!
BIG BANG

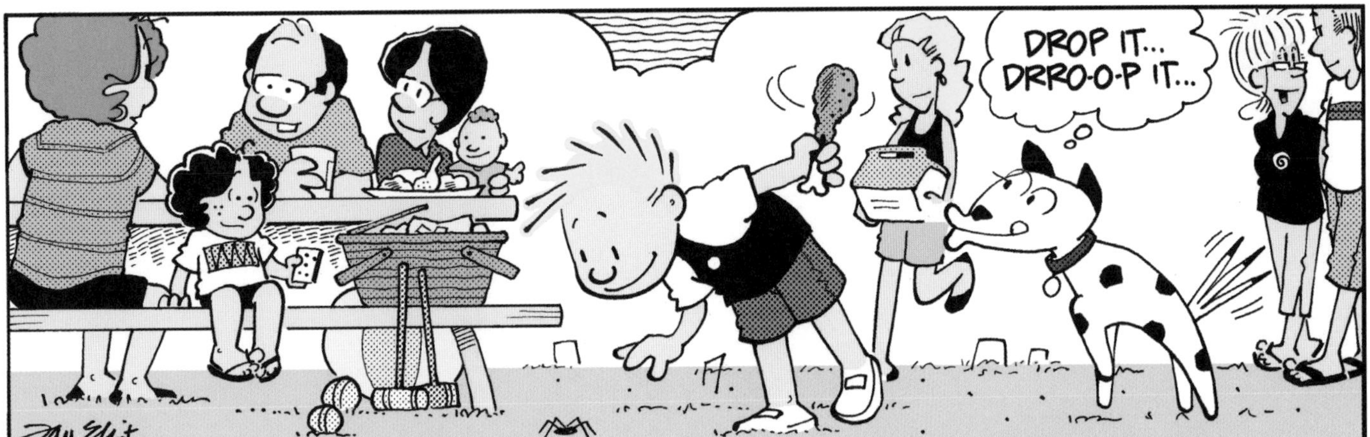
DROP IT... DRRO-O-P IT...

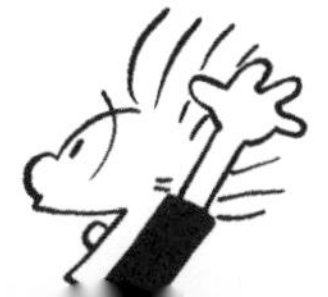

WHAT A GORGEOUS SWIMMING HOLE!

IT LOOKS DIRTY.

IT'S NATURAL!

THE STONES HURT MY FEET!

WEAR FLIP-FLOPS!

THERE ARE BUGS IN HERE!

WATER-SKIPPERS!

AREN'T YOU STAYING IN??

NOT ON YOUR LIFE! WHO KNOWS WHAT I MIGHT CATCH SWIMMING IN THAT WATER!

ISN'T THAT THE POINT?!

OOH! NICE CRAWDAD.

NICE? NICE IS A CHLORINATED POOL AND A FRAPPUCCINO!

110

Stone Soup

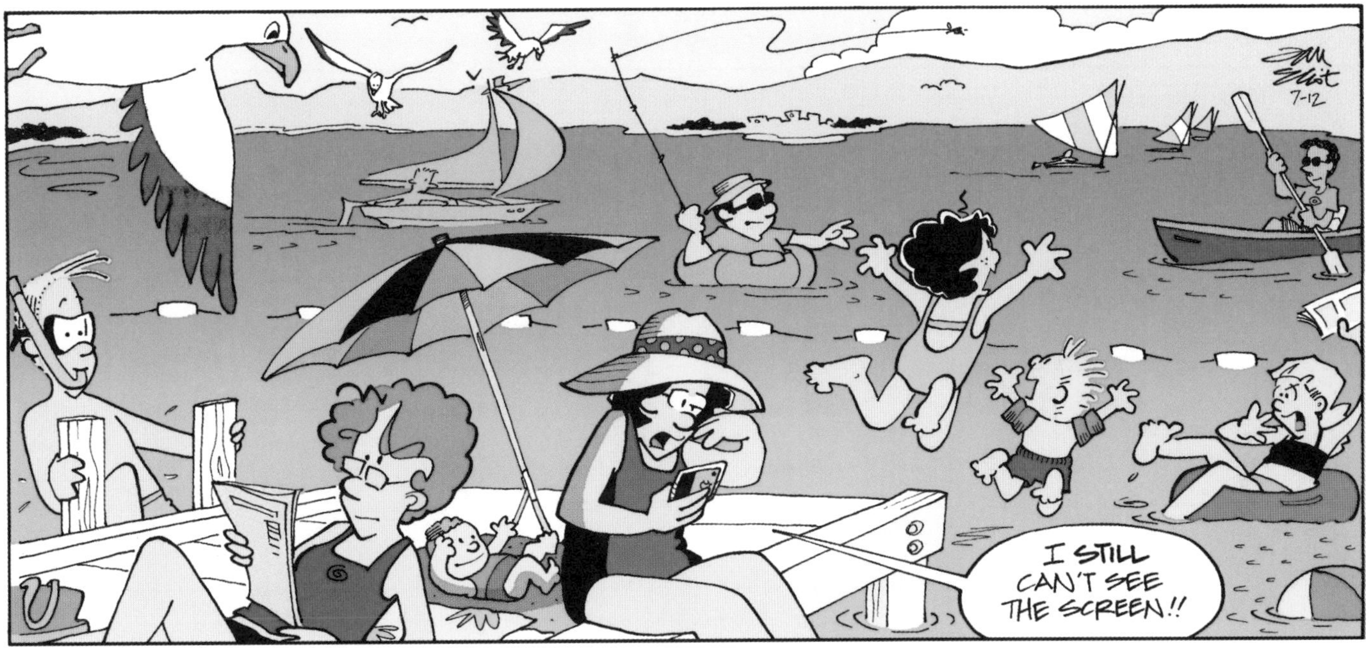
I STILL CAN'T SEE THE SCREEN!!

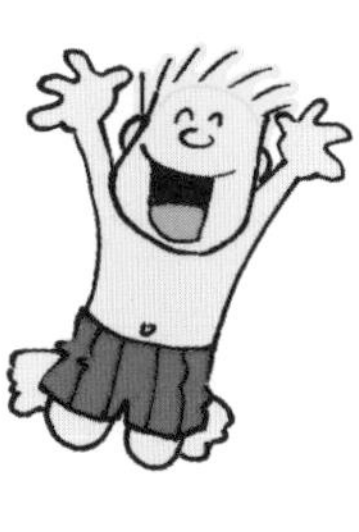

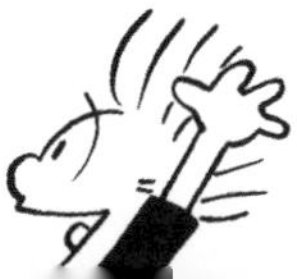

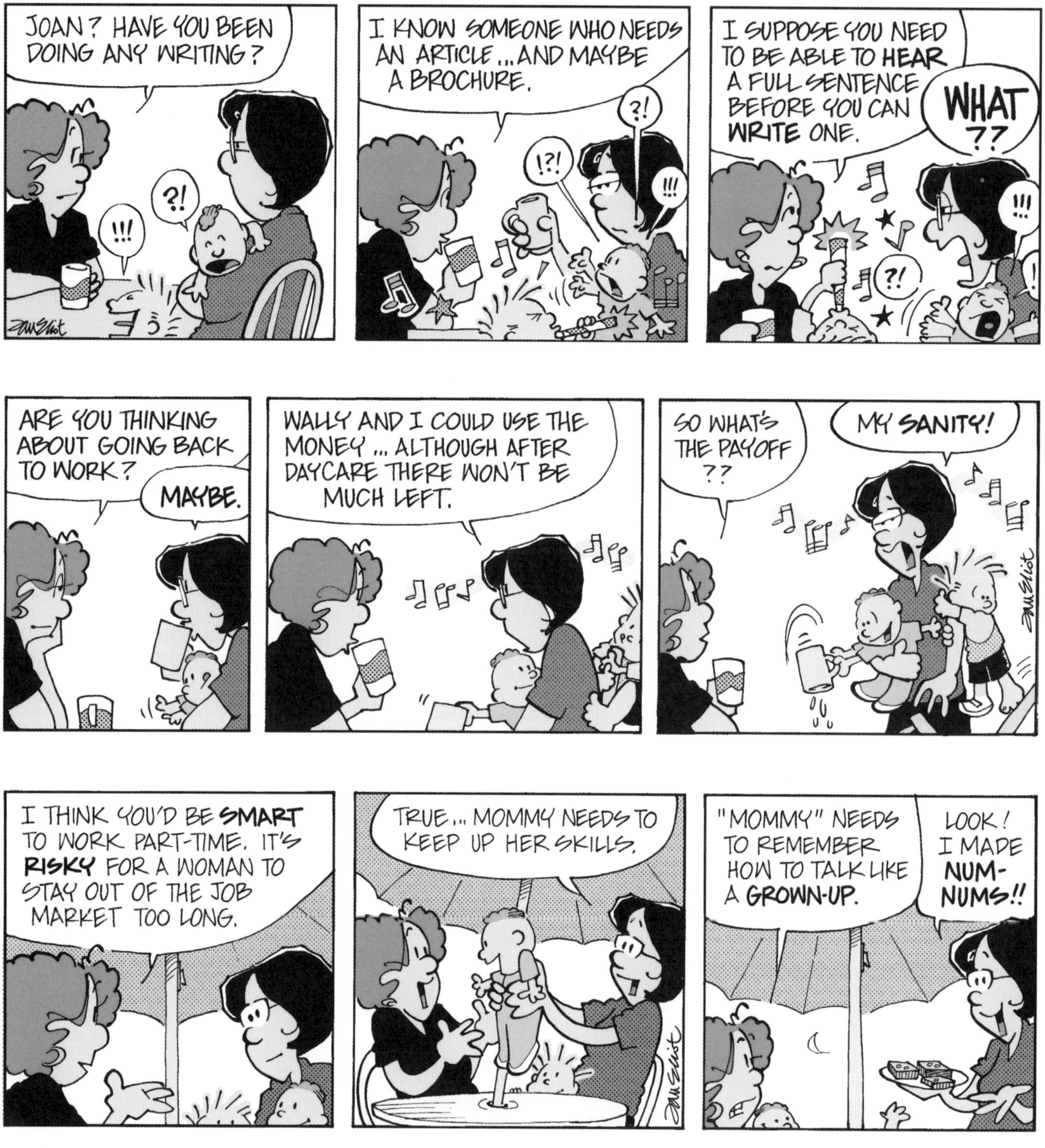
JOAN? HAVE YOU BEEN DOING ANY WRITING?
!!!
?!
I KNOW SOMEONE WHO NEEDS AN ARTICLE... AND MAYBE A BROCHURE.
!?!
?!
!!!
I SUPPOSE YOU NEED TO BE ABLE TO **HEAR** A FULL SENTENCE BEFORE YOU CAN **WRITE** ONE.
WHAT ??
!!!
?!
!
ARE YOU THINKING ABOUT GOING BACK TO WORK?
MAYBE.
WALLY AND I COULD USE THE MONEY... ALTHOUGH AFTER DAYCARE THERE WON'T BE MUCH LEFT.
SO WHAT'S THE PAYOFF ??
MY **SANITY**!
I THINK YOU'D BE **SMART** TO WORK PART-TIME. IT'S **RISKY** FOR A WOMAN TO STAY OUT OF THE JOB MARKET TOO LONG.
TRUE... MOMMY NEEDS TO KEEP UP HER SKILLS.
"MOMMY" NEEDS TO REMEMBER HOW TO TALK LIKE A **GROWN-UP**.
LOOK! I MADE **NUM-NUMS**!!

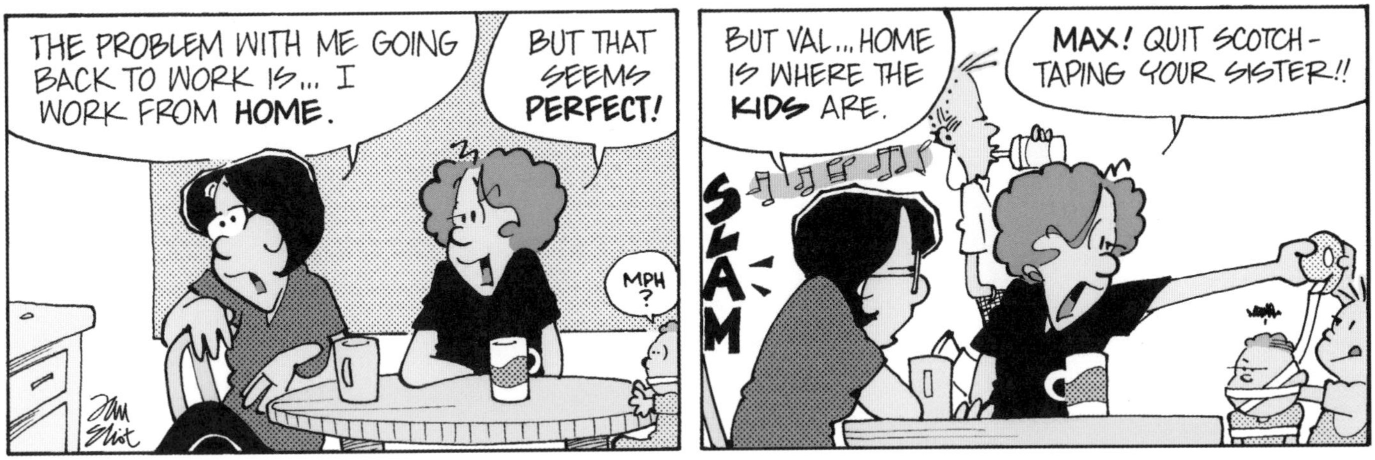
THE PROBLEM WITH ME GOING BACK TO WORK IS... I WORK FROM **HOME**.
BUT THAT SEEMS **PERFECT!**
MPH ?
BUT VAL... HOME IS WHERE THE **KIDS** ARE.
SLAM
MAX! QUIT SCOTCH-TAPING YOUR SISTER!!

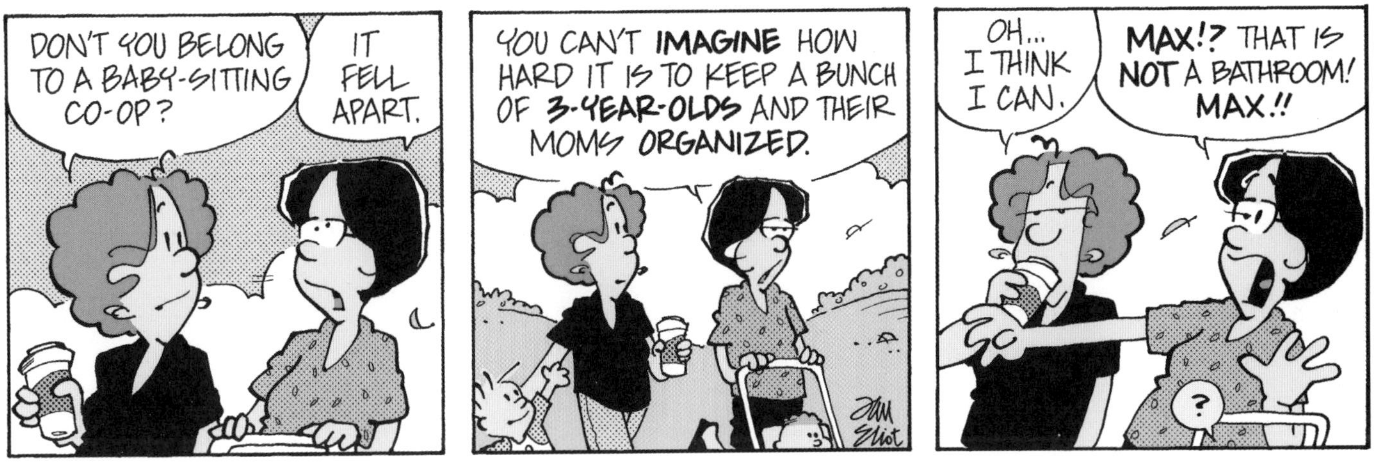
DON'T YOU BELONG TO A BABY-SITTING CO-OP?
IT FELL APART.
YOU CAN'T **IMAGINE** HOW HARD IT IS TO KEEP A BUNCH OF **3-YEAR-OLDS** AND THEIR MOMS **ORGANIZED**.
OH... I THINK I CAN.
MAX!? THAT IS **NOT** A BATHROOM! **MAX!!**
?

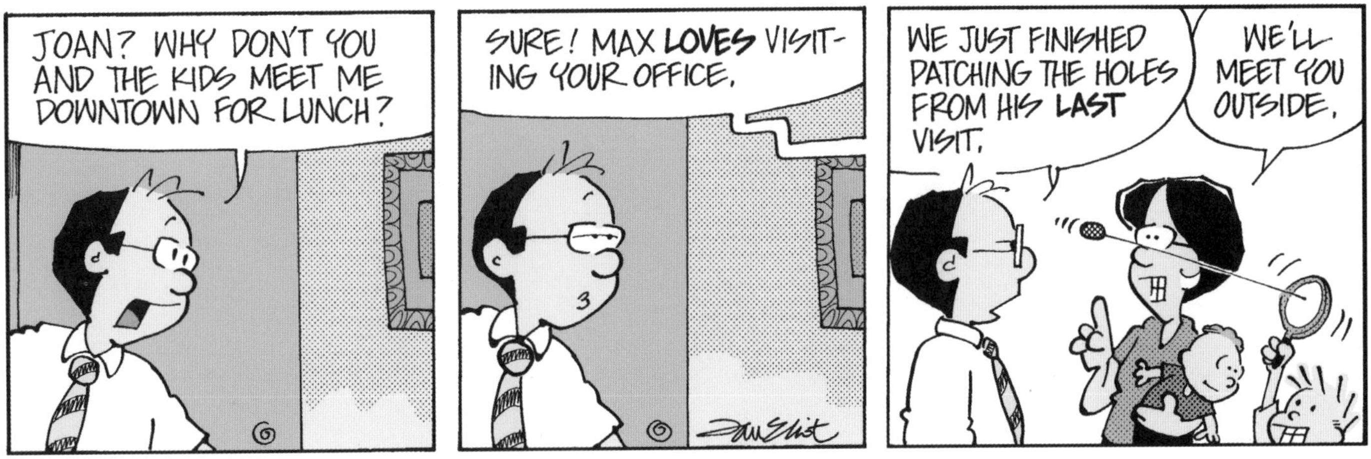
JOAN? WHY DON'T YOU AND THE KIDS MEET ME DOWNTOWN FOR LUNCH?
SURE! MAX **LOVES** VISITING YOUR OFFICE.
WE JUST FINISHED PATCHING THE HOLES FROM HIS **LAST** VISIT.
WE'LL MEET YOU OUTSIDE.

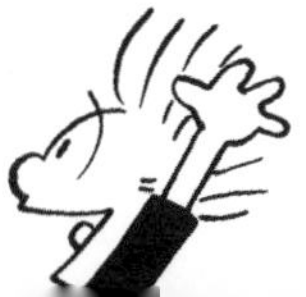

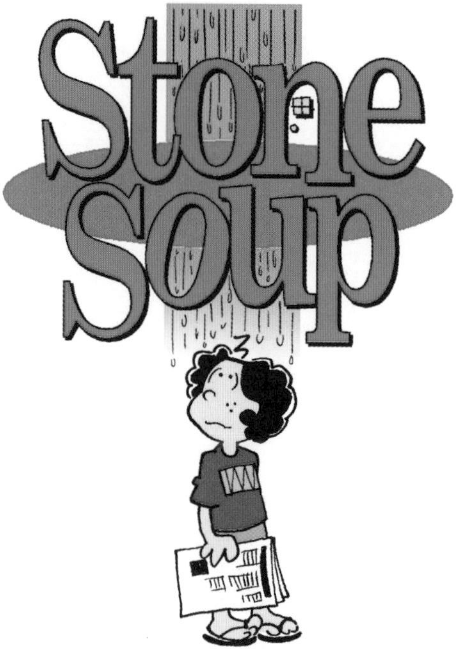
Stone Soup

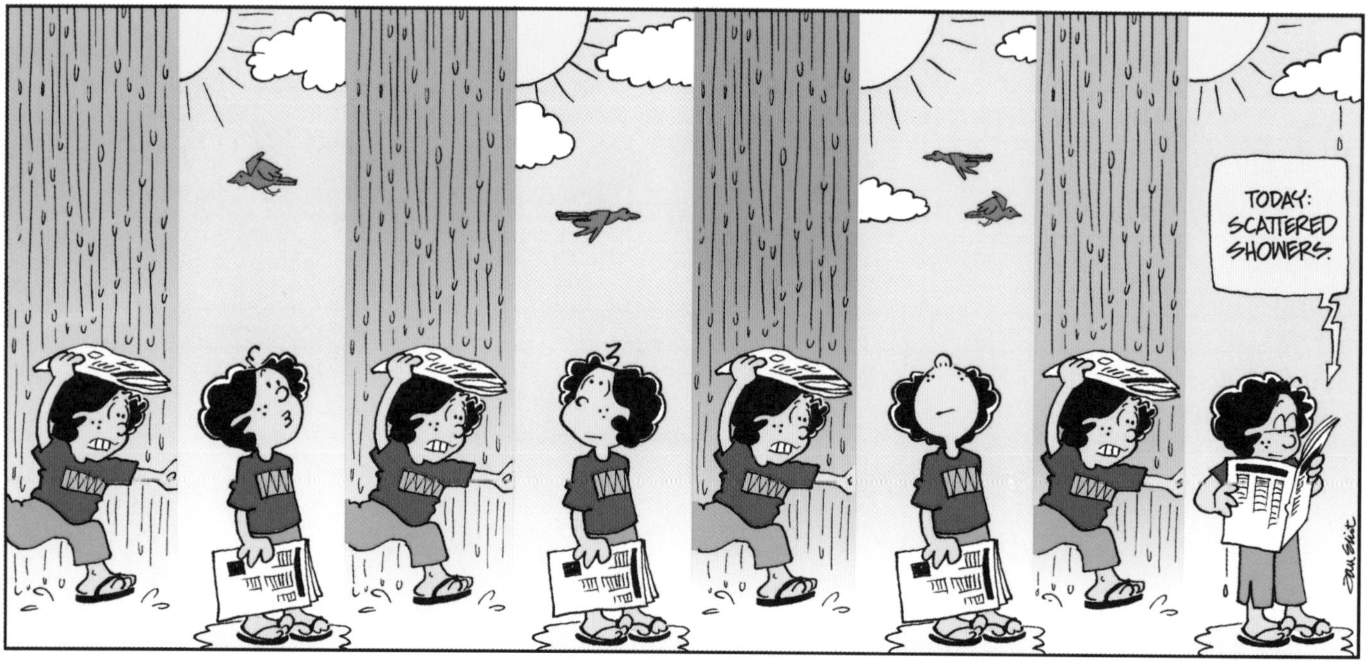
TODAY:
SCATTERED SHOWERS.

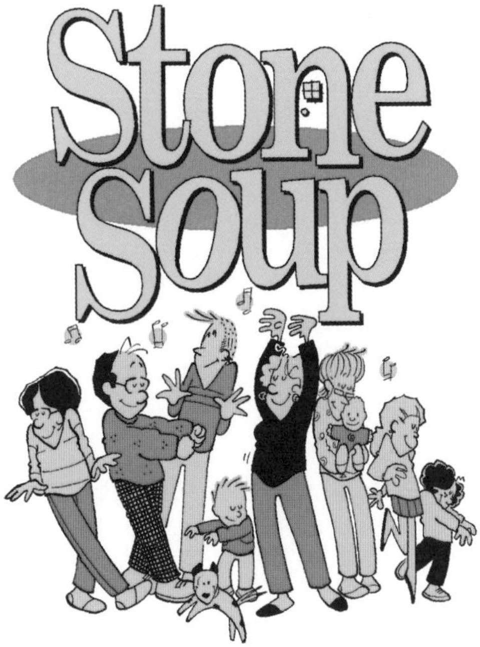
Stone Soup

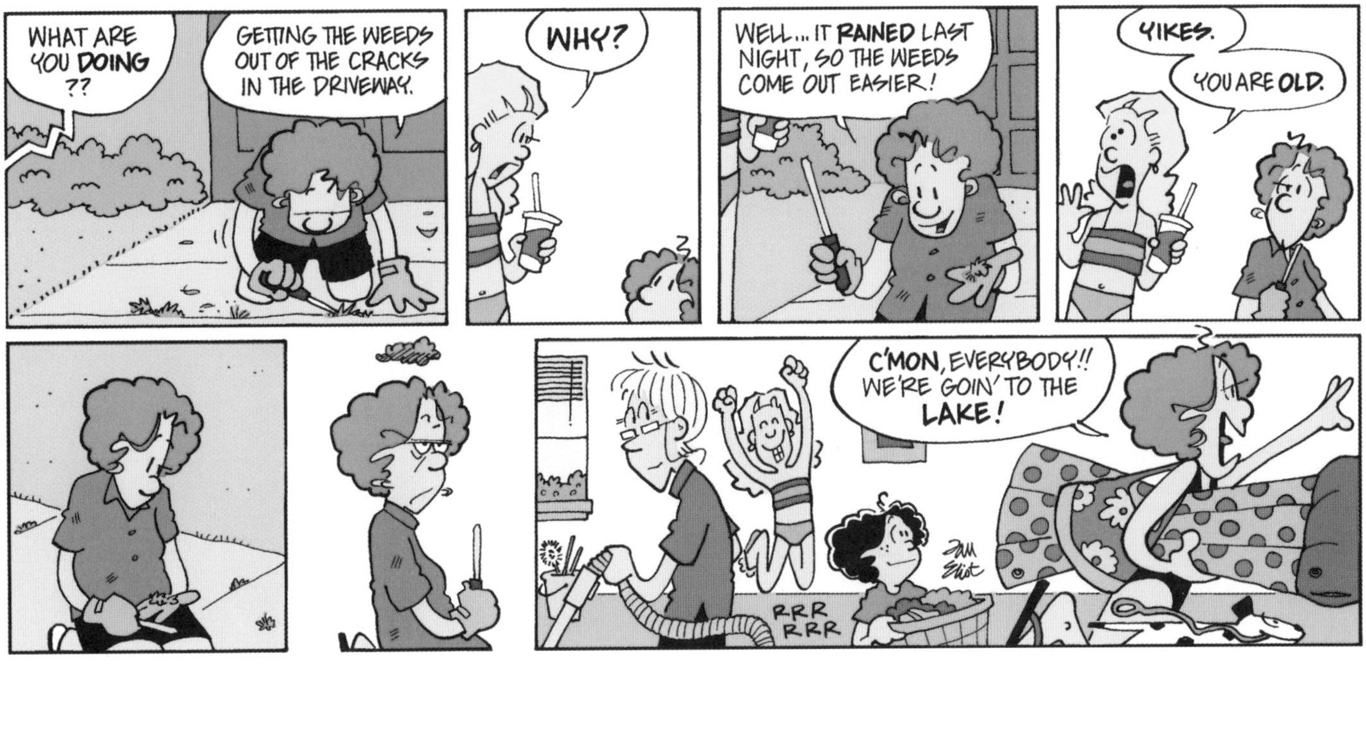
WHAT ARE YOU **DOING** ??
GETTING THE WEEDS OUT OF THE CRACKS IN THE DRIVEWAY.
WHY?
WELL... IT **RAINED** LAST NIGHT, SO THE WEEDS COME OUT EASIER!
YIKES.
YOU ARE **OLD**.
C'MON, EVERYBODY!! WE'RE GOIN' TO THE **LAKE**!
RRR RRR

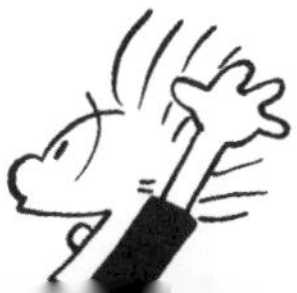

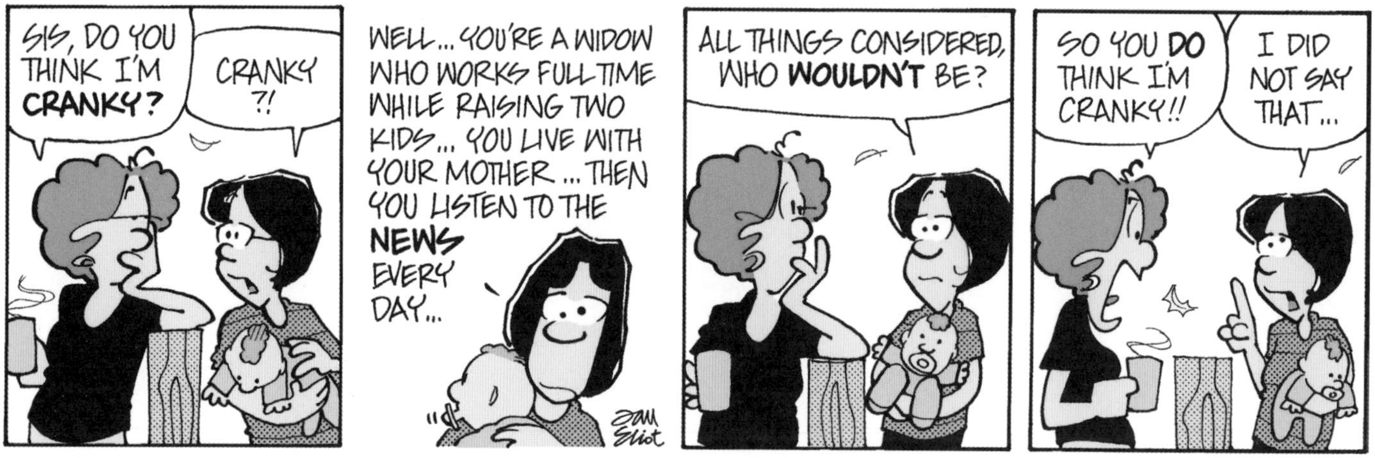
SIS, DO YOU THINK I'M **CRANKY?**
CRANKY ?!
WELL... YOU'RE A WIDOW WHO WORKS FULL TIME WHILE RAISING TWO KIDS... YOU LIVE WITH YOUR MOTHER... THEN YOU LISTEN TO THE **NEWS** EVERY DAY...
ALL THINGS CONSIDERED, WHO **WOULDN'T** BE?
SO YOU **DO** THINK I'M CRANKY!!
I DID NOT SAY THAT...

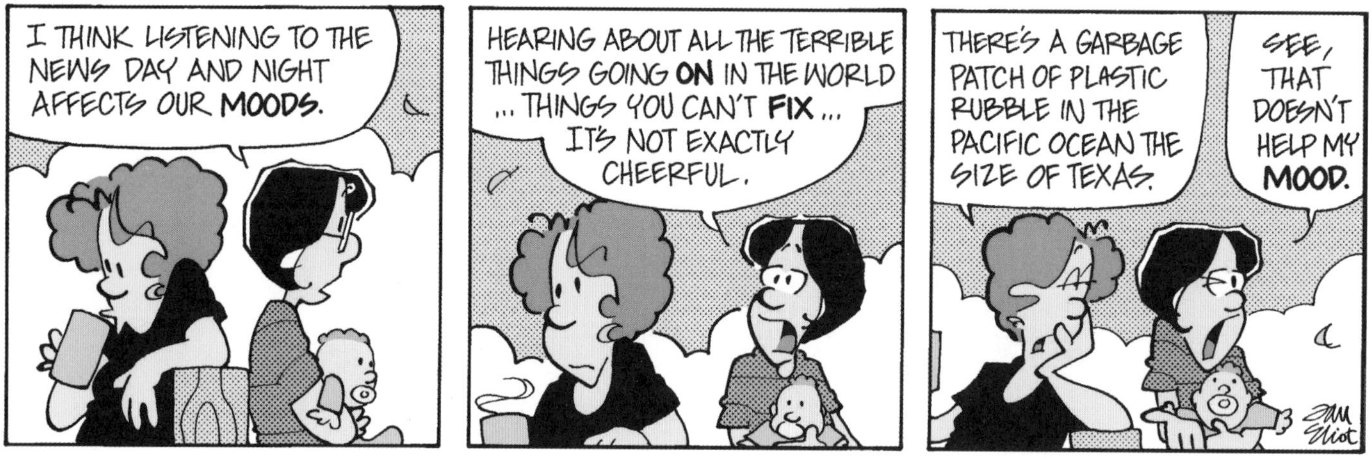
I THINK LISTENING TO THE NEWS DAY AND NIGHT AFFECTS OUR **MOODS**.
HEARING ABOUT ALL THE TERRIBLE THINGS GOING **ON** IN THE WORLD ... THINGS YOU CAN'T **FIX**... IT'S NOT EXACTLY CHEERFUL.
THERE'S A GARBAGE PATCH OF PLASTIC RUBBLE IN THE PACIFIC OCEAN THE SIZE OF TEXAS.
SEE, THAT DOESN'T HELP MY **MOOD.**

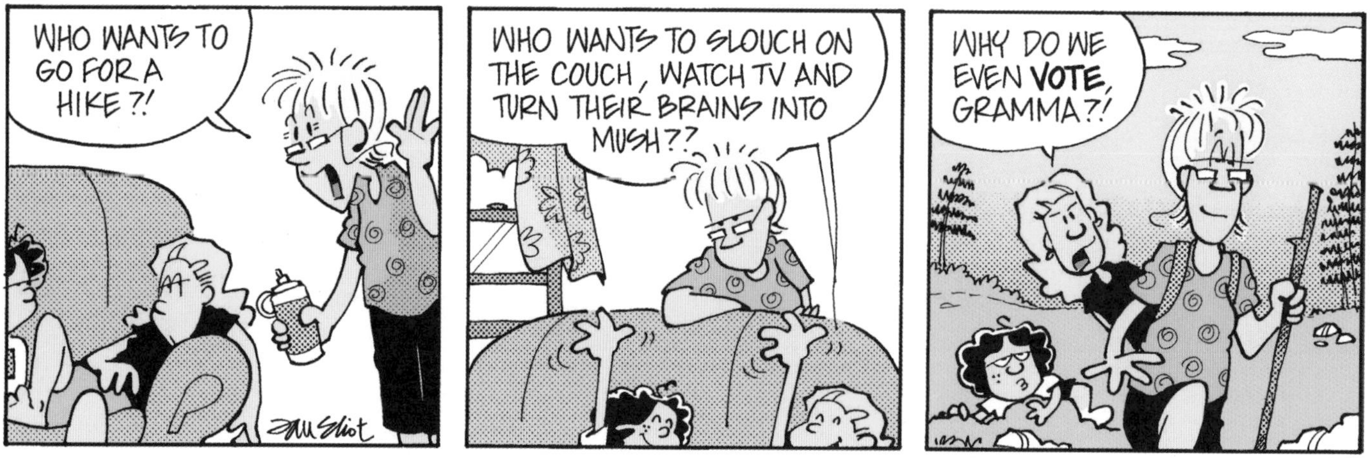
WHO WANTS TO GO FOR A HIKE ?!
WHO WANTS TO SLOUCH ON THE COUCH, WATCH TV AND TURN THEIR BRAINS INTO MUSH??
WHY DO WE EVEN **VOTE**, GRAMMA ?!

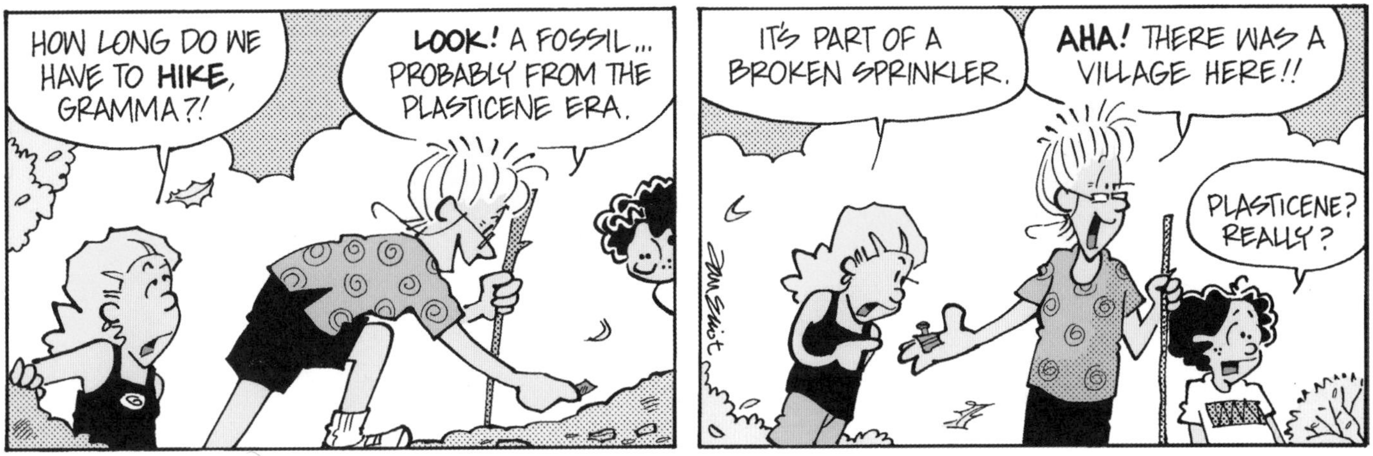
HOW LONG DO WE HAVE TO **HIKE**, GRAMMA?!
LOOK! A FOSSIL... PROBABLY FROM THE PLASTICENE ERA.
IT'S PART OF A BROKEN SPRINKLER.
AHA! THERE WAS A VILLAGE HERE!!
PLASTICENE? REALLY?

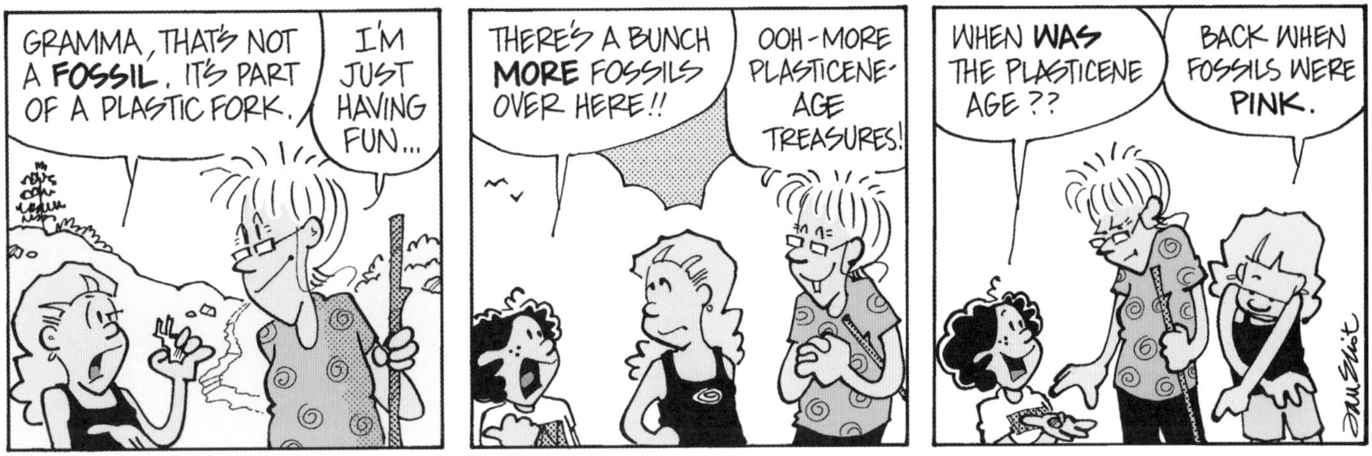
GRAMMA, THAT'S NOT A **FOSSIL**. IT'S PART OF A PLASTIC FORK.
I'M JUST HAVING FUN...
THERE'S A BUNCH **MORE** FOSSILS OVER HERE!!
OOH-MORE PLASTICENE-AGE TREASURES!
WHEN **WAS** THE PLASTICENE AGE??
BACK WHEN FOSSILS WERE **PINK**.

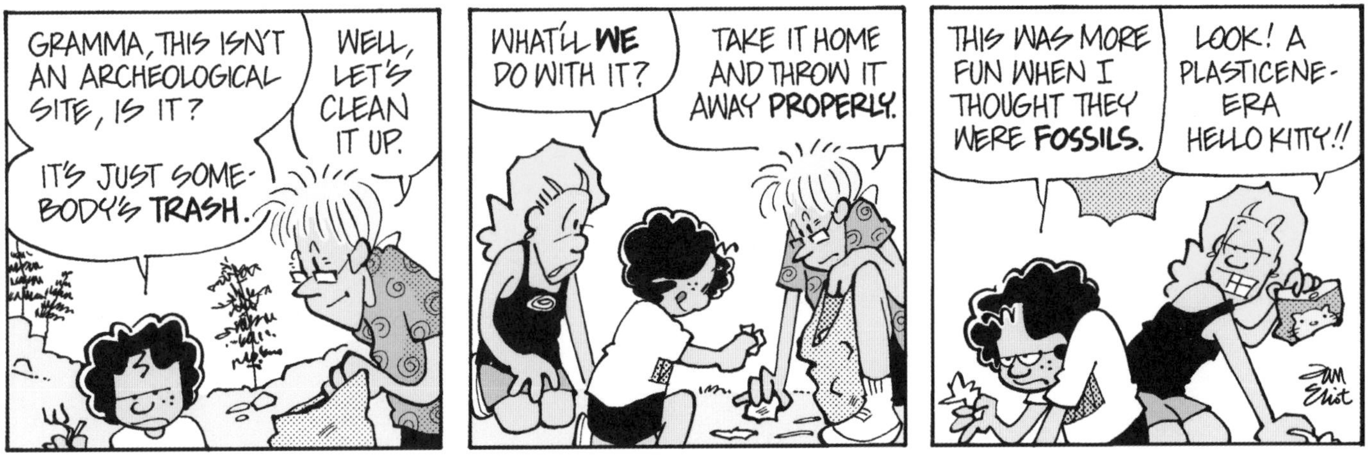
GRAMMA, THIS ISN'T AN ARCHEOLOGICAL SITE, IS IT?
IT'S JUST SOMEBODY'S **TRASH**.
WELL, LET'S CLEAN IT UP.
WHAT'LL **WE** DO WITH IT?
TAKE IT HOME AND THROW IT AWAY **PROPERLY**.
THIS WAS MORE FUN WHEN I THOUGHT THEY WERE **FOSSILS**.
LOOK! A PLASTICENE-ERA HELLO KITTY!!
JAN Eliot

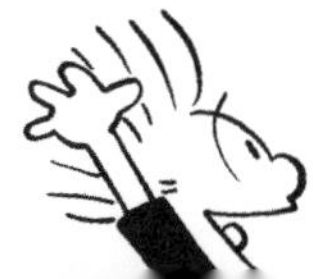

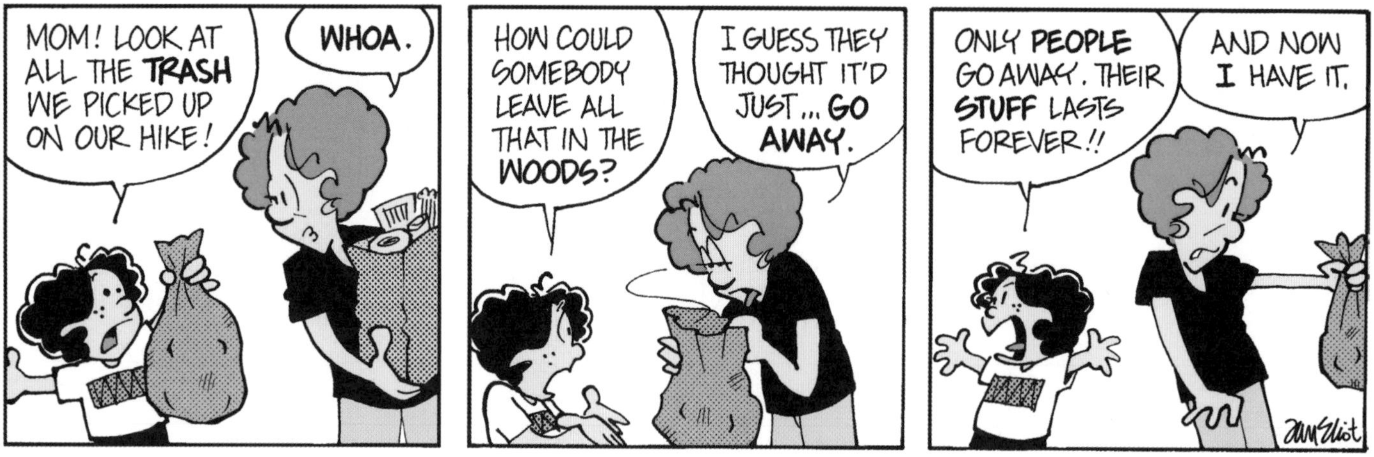
MOM! LOOK AT ALL THE TRASH WE PICKED UP ON OUR HIKE!
WHOA.
HOW COULD SOMEBODY LEAVE ALL THAT IN THE WOODS?
I GUESS THEY THOUGHT IT'D JUST... GO AWAY.
ONLY PEOPLE GO AWAY. THEIR STUFF LASTS FOREVER!!
AND NOW I HAVE IT.

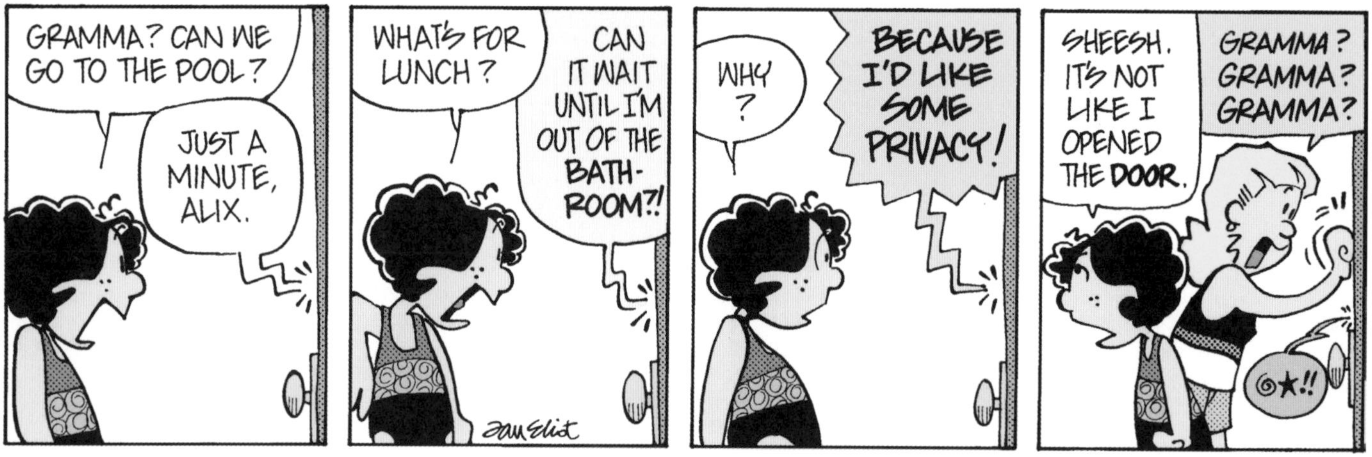
GRAMMA? CAN WE GO TO THE POOL?
JUST A MINUTE, ALIX.
WHAT'S FOR LUNCH?
CAN IT WAIT UNTIL I'M OUT OF THE BATH-ROOM?!
WHY?
BECAUSE I'D LIKE SOME PRIVACY!
SHEESH. IT'S NOT LIKE I OPENED THE DOOR.
GRAMMA? GRAMMA? GRAMMA?

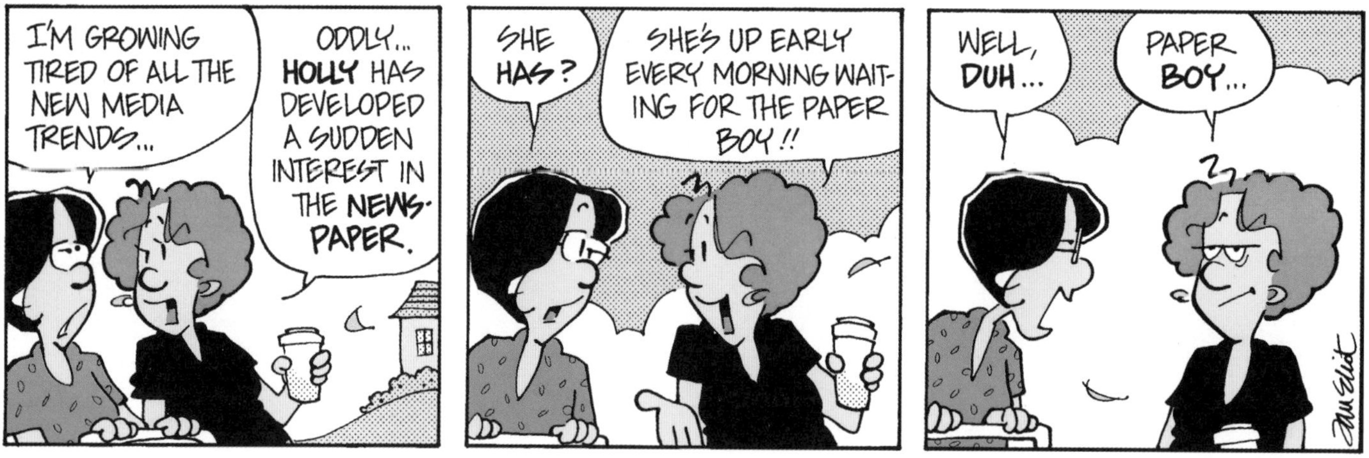
I'M GROWING TIRED OF ALL THE NEW MEDIA TRENDS...
ODDLY... HOLLY HAS DEVELOPED A SUDDEN INTEREST IN THE NEWS-PAPER.
SHE HAS?
SHE'S UP EARLY EVERY MORNING WAIT-ING FOR THE PAPER BOY!!
WELL, DUH...
PAPER BOY...

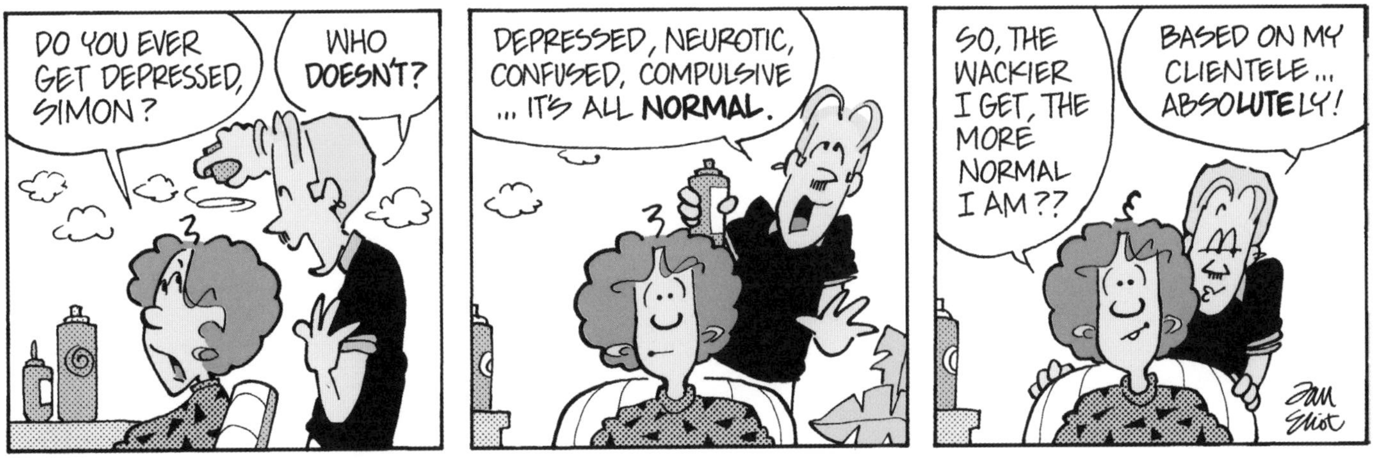
DO YOU EVER GET DEPRESSED, SIMON?
WHO **DOESN'T?**
DEPRESSED, NEUROTIC, CONFUSED, COMPULSIVE ... IT'S ALL **NORMAL**.
SO, THE WACKIER I GET, THE MORE NORMAL I AM??
BASED ON MY CLIENTELE... ABSO**LUTE**LY!
Jan Eliot

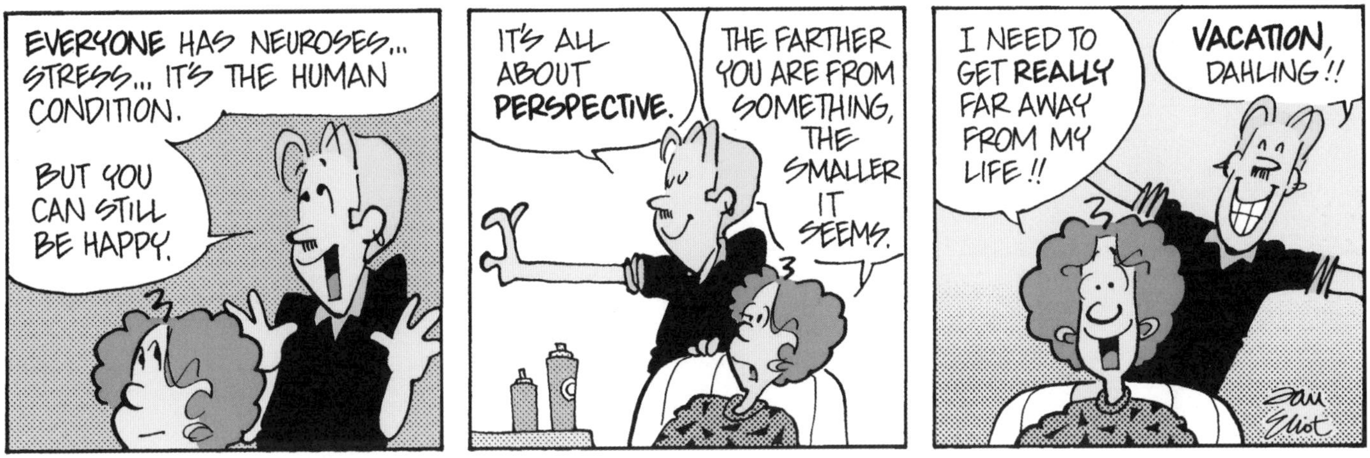
EVERYONE HAS NEUROSES... STRESS... IT'S THE HUMAN CONDITION.
BUT YOU CAN STILL BE HAPPY.
IT'S ALL ABOUT **PERSPECTIVE**.
THE FARTHER YOU ARE FROM SOMETHING, THE SMALLER IT SEEMS.
I NEED TO GET **REALLY** FAR AWAY FROM MY LIFE!!
VACATION, DAHLING!!
Jan Eliot

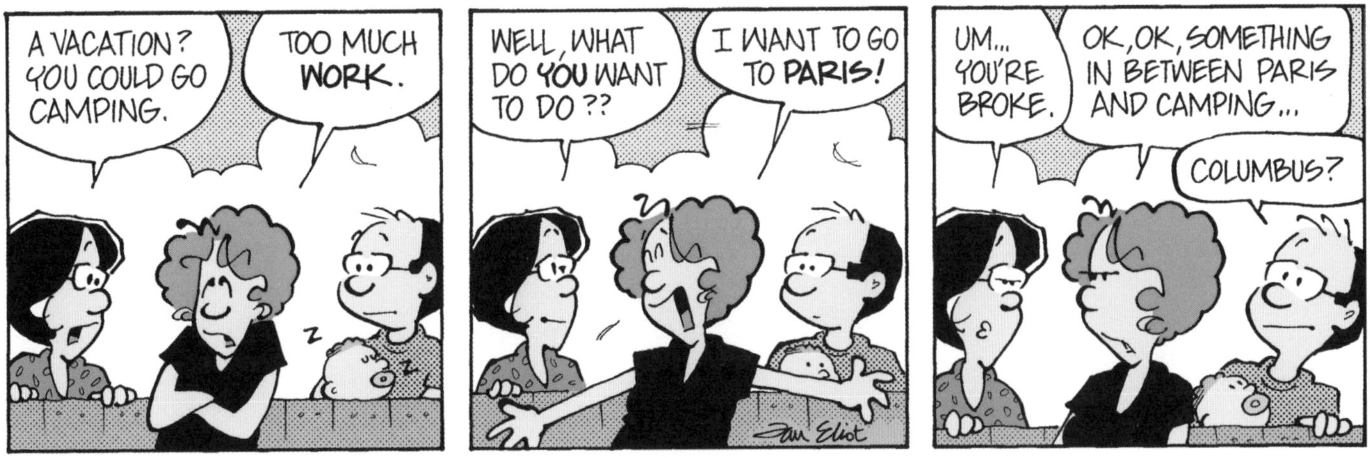
A VACATION? YOU COULD GO CAMPING.
TOO MUCH **WORK**.
WELL, WHAT DO **YOU** WANT TO DO??
I WANT TO GO TO **PARIS**!
Jan Eliot
UM... YOU'RE BROKE.
OK, OK, SOMETHING IN BETWEEN PARIS AND CAMPING...
COLUMBUS?

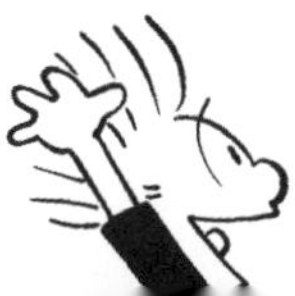

Stone Soup

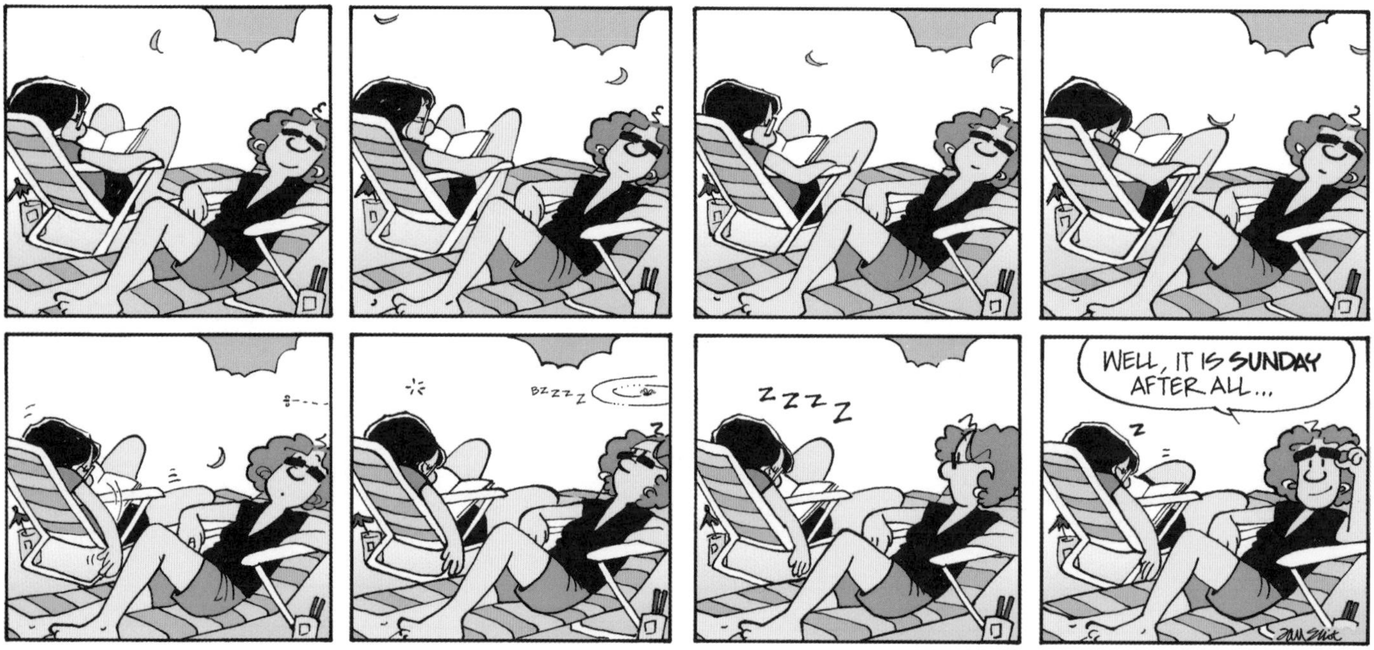
BZZZZ
ZZZZ
WELL, IT IS **SUNDAY** AFTER ALL...

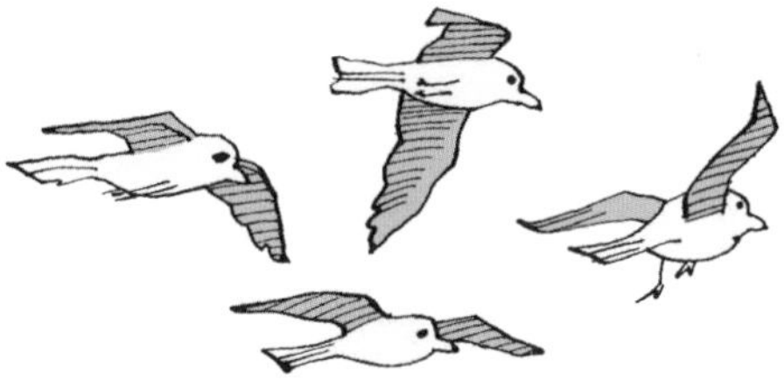

Stone Soup

HEY **ALIX**...HAS MOM EVER HAD **THE TALK** WITH YOU?
NO NEED.
WHAT DO YOU MEAN "**NO NEED**"?
WHEN SHE HAD "THE TALK" WITH **YOU**... I WAS THERE, REMEMBER?
PUBERTY? PERSONAL HYGIENE? THE FACTS OF LIFE?
I HEARD IT **ALL**.
NO FAIR.
ARE YOU **KIDDING?!**
WHEN **YOU** WERE 10, **YOU** WERE BLISSFULLY **IGNORANT**.
BUT **ME??** WEIGHED DOWN WITH THE BURDENS OF WOMANHOOD **BEFORE MY TIME**.
WOW.
THE UPSIDE IS... I'M A **HUGE** HIT AT 4TH GRADE SLUMBER PARTIES.
WWW.STONESOUPCARTOONS.COM

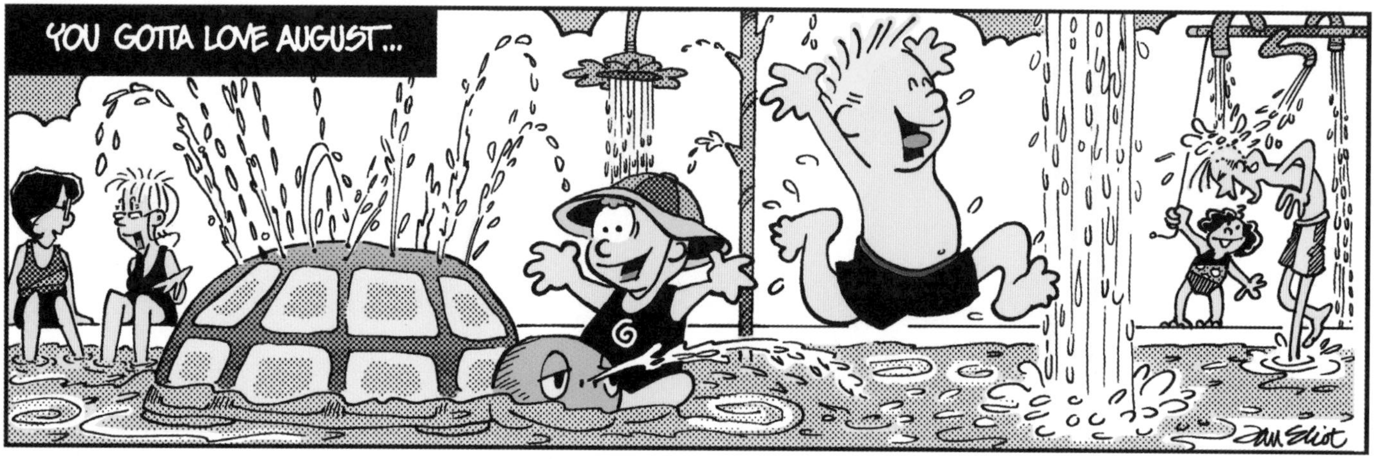
YOU GOTTA LOVE AUGUST...
Jan Eliot

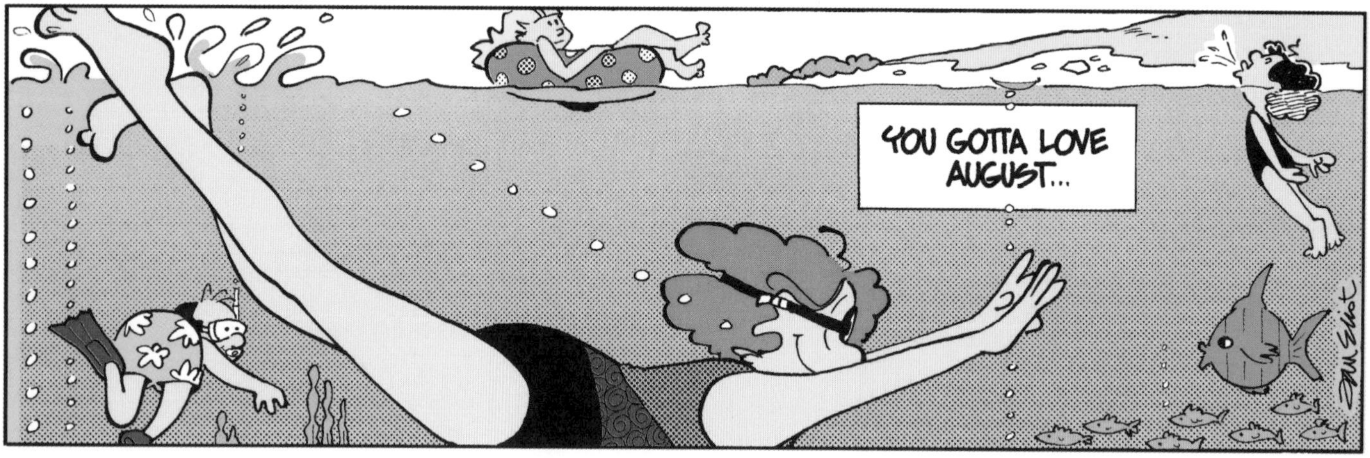
YOU GOTTA LOVE AUGUST...
Jan Eliot

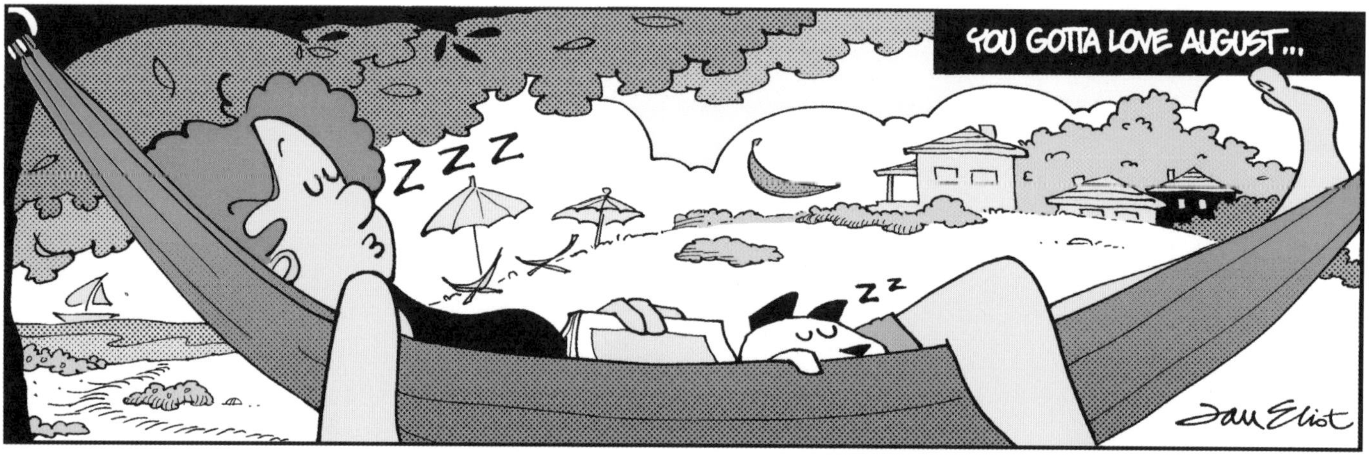
YOU GOTTA LOVE AUGUST...
Z Z Z
Z Z
Jan Eliot

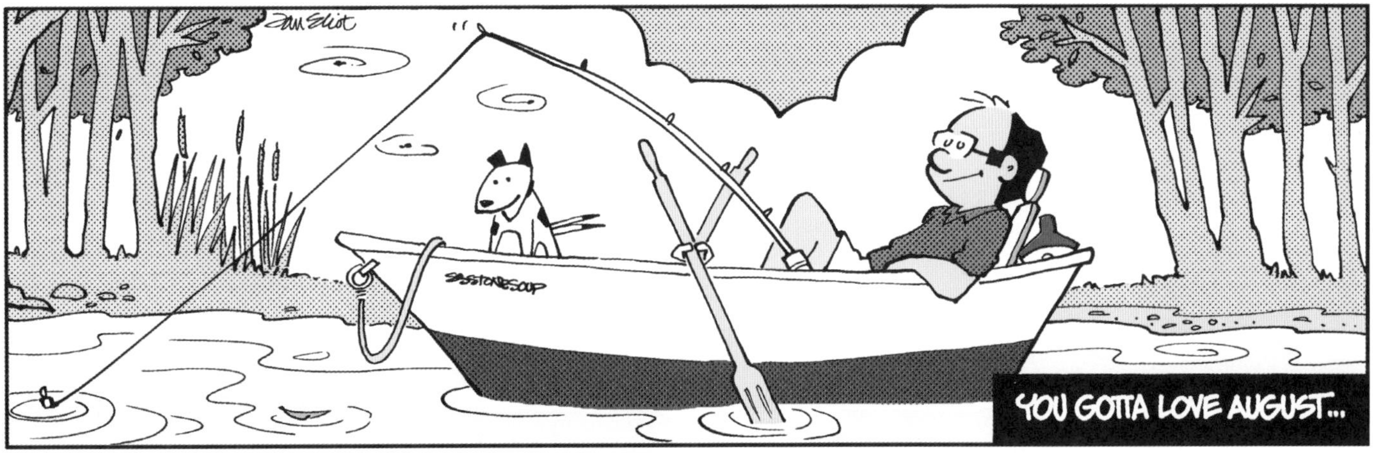
YOU GOTTA LOVE AUGUST...

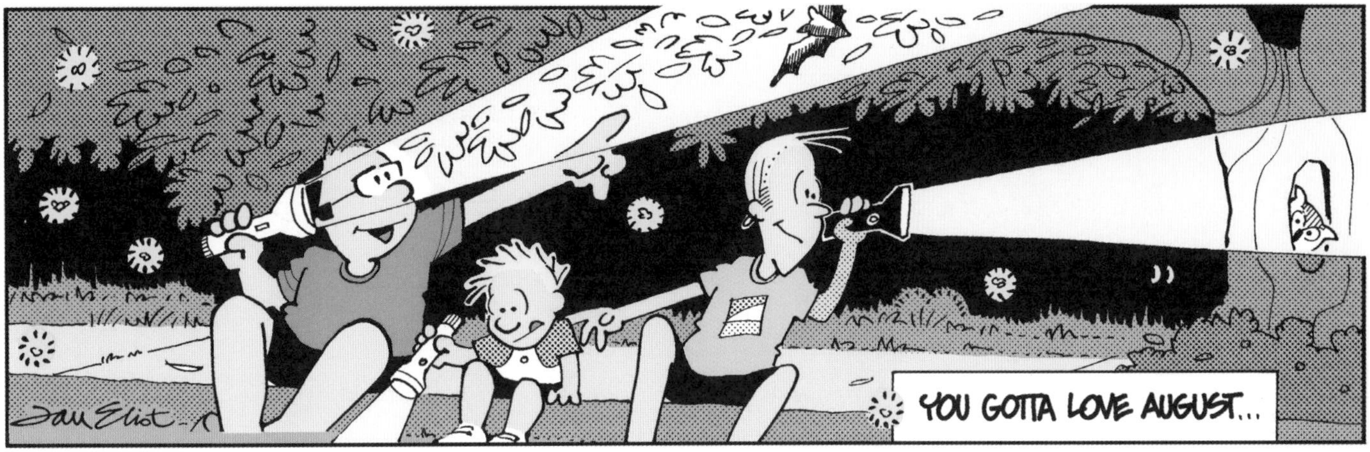
YOU GOTTA LOVE AUGUST...

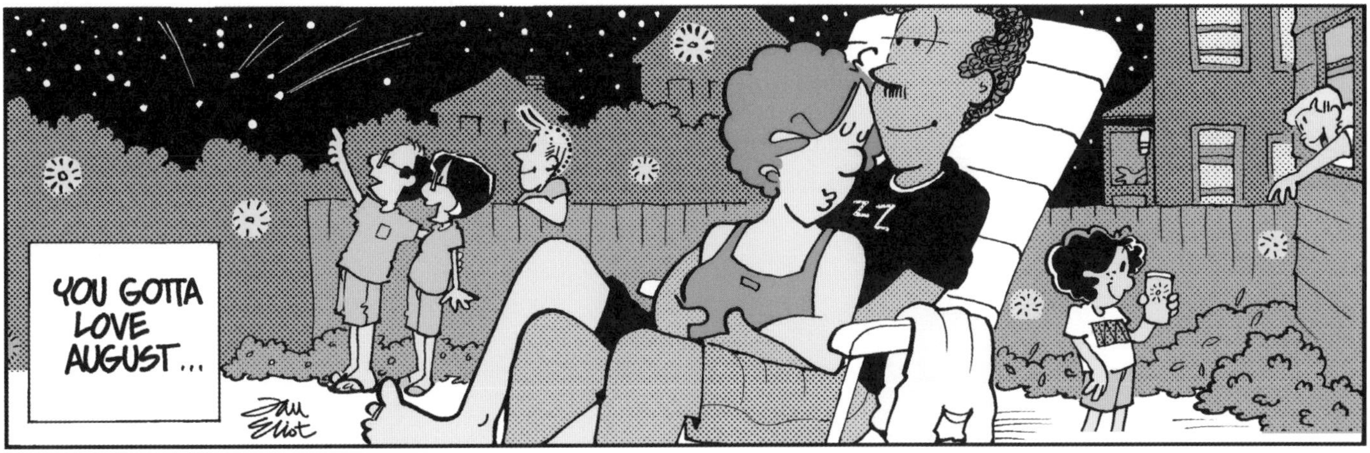
YOU GOTTA LOVE AUGUST...

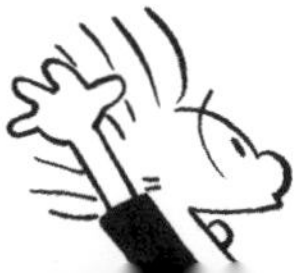

Stone Soup

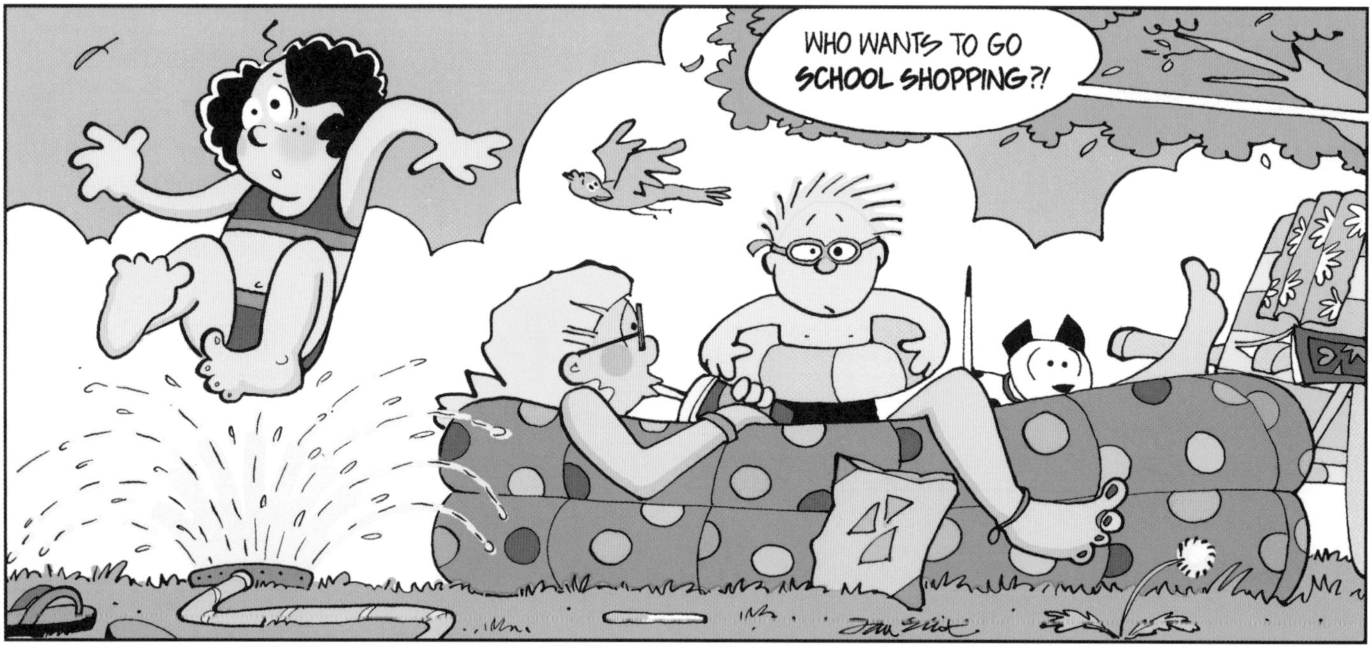
WHO WANTS TO GO SCHOOL SHOPPING?!

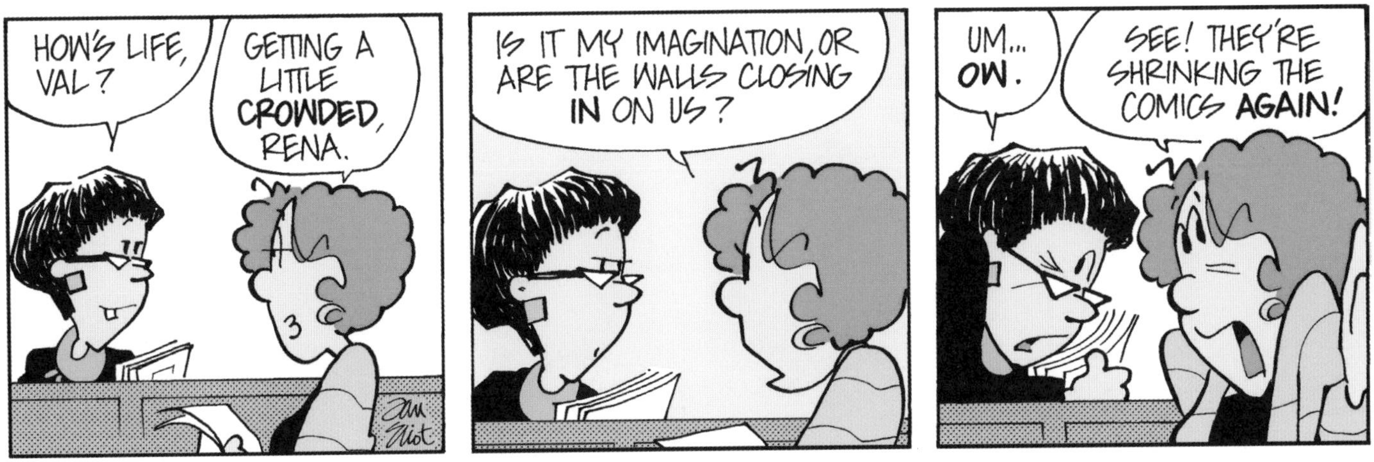
HOW'S LIFE, VAL?
GETTING A LITTLE CROWDED, RENA.
IS IT MY IMAGINATION, OR ARE THE WALLS CLOSING IN ON US?
UM... OW.
SEE! THEY'RE SHRINKING THE COMICS AGAIN!

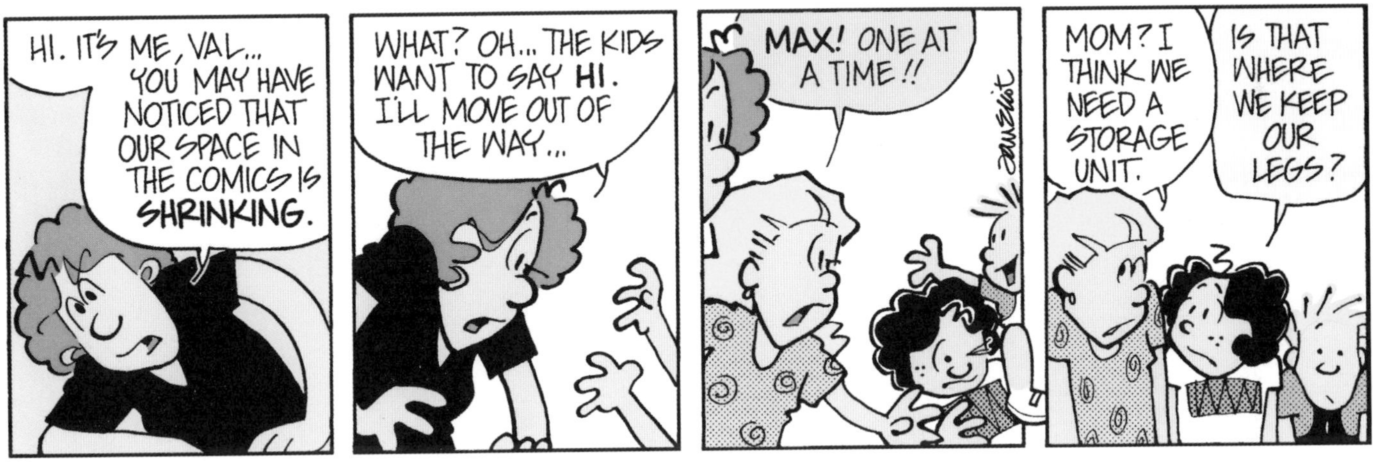
HI. IT'S ME, VAL... YOU MAY HAVE NOTICED THAT OUR SPACE IN THE COMICS IS SHRINKING.
WHAT? OH... THE KIDS WANT TO SAY HI. I'LL MOVE OUT OF THE WAY...
MAX! ONE AT A TIME!!
MOM? I THINK WE NEED A STORAGE UNIT.
IS THAT WHERE WE KEEP OUR LEGS?

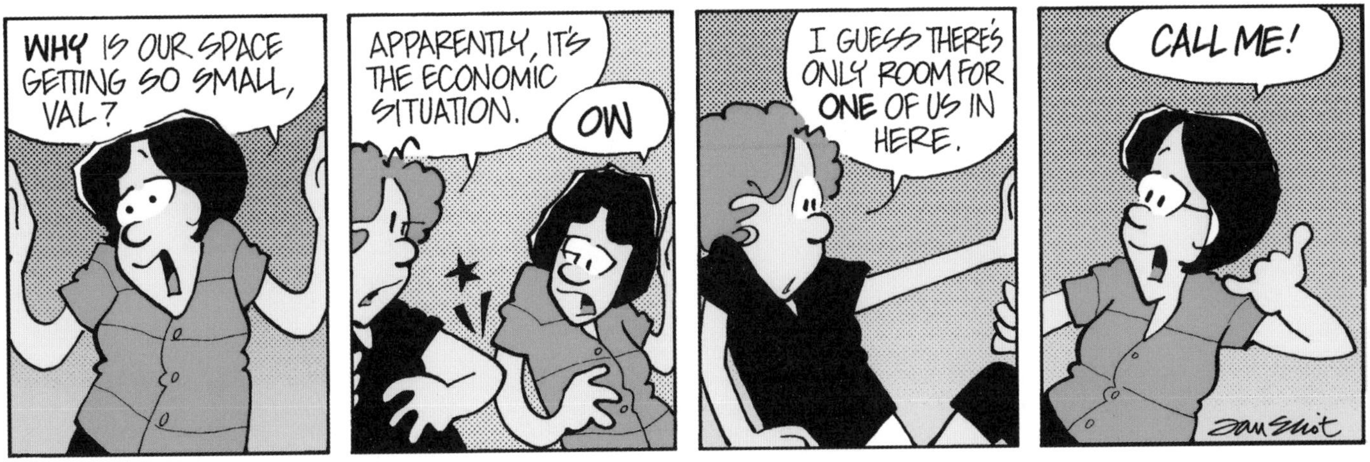
WHY IS OUR SPACE GETTING SO SMALL, VAL?
APPARENTLY, IT'S THE ECONOMIC SITUATION.
OW
I GUESS THERE'S ONLY ROOM FOR ONE OF US IN HERE.
CALL ME!

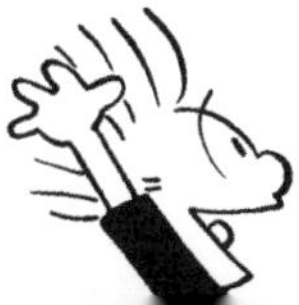

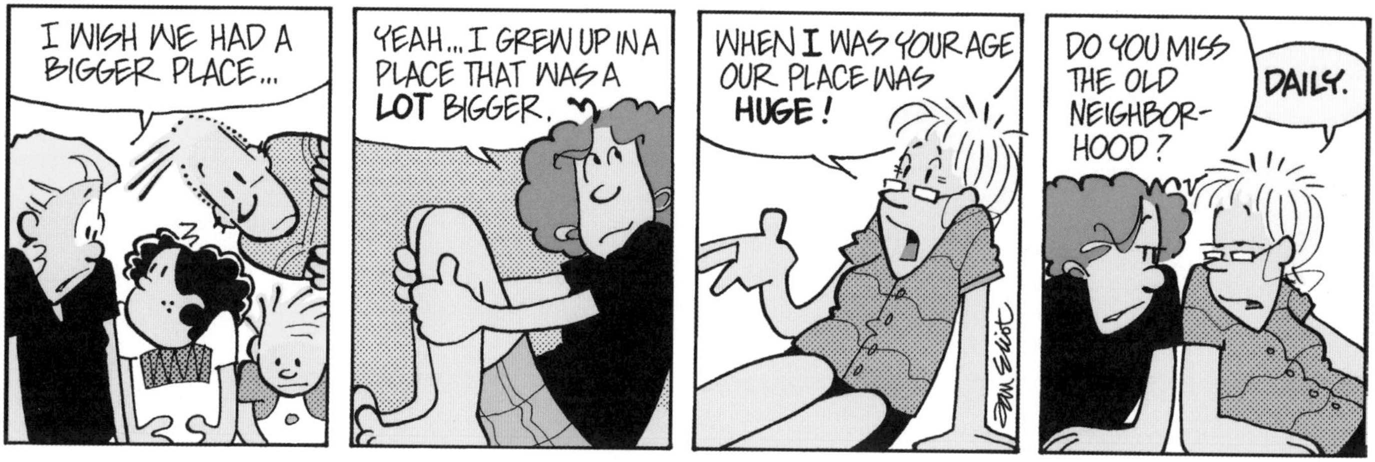
I WISH WE HAD A BIGGER PLACE...
YEAH... I GREW UP IN A PLACE THAT WAS A LOT BIGGER.
WHEN I WAS YOUR AGE OUR PLACE WAS HUGE!
DO YOU MISS THE OLD NEIGHBORHOOD?
DAILY.

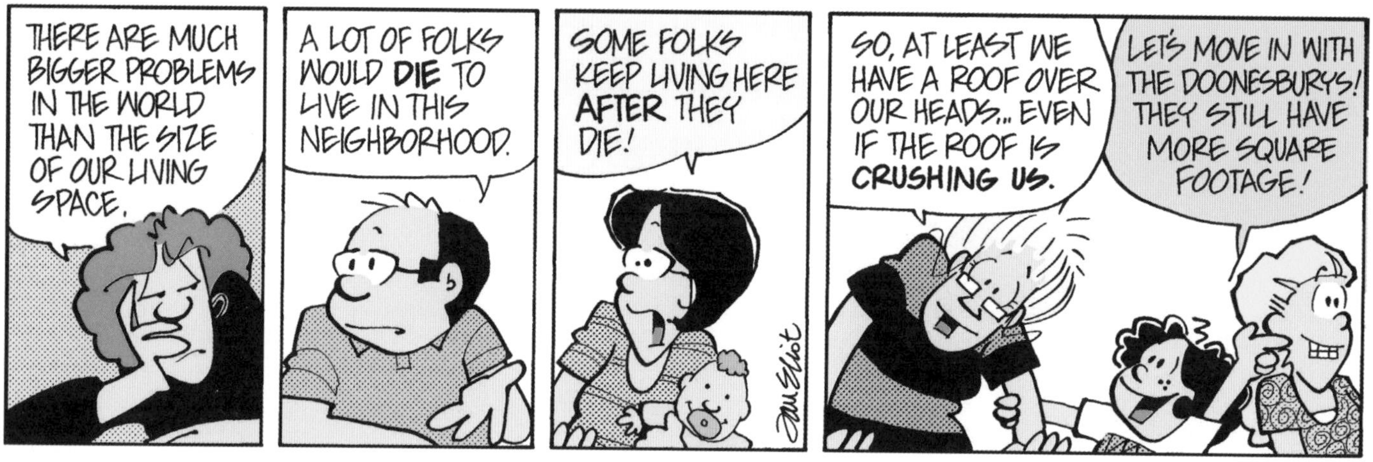
THERE ARE MUCH BIGGER PROBLEMS IN THE WORLD THAN THE SIZE OF OUR LIVING SPACE.
A LOT OF FOLKS WOULD DIE TO LIVE IN THIS NEIGHBORHOOD.
SOME FOLKS KEEP LIVING HERE AFTER THEY DIE!
SO, AT LEAST WE HAVE A ROOF OVER OUR HEADS... EVEN IF THE ROOF IS CRUSHING US.
LET'S MOVE IN WITH THE DOONESBURYS! THEY STILL HAVE MORE SQUARE FOOTAGE!

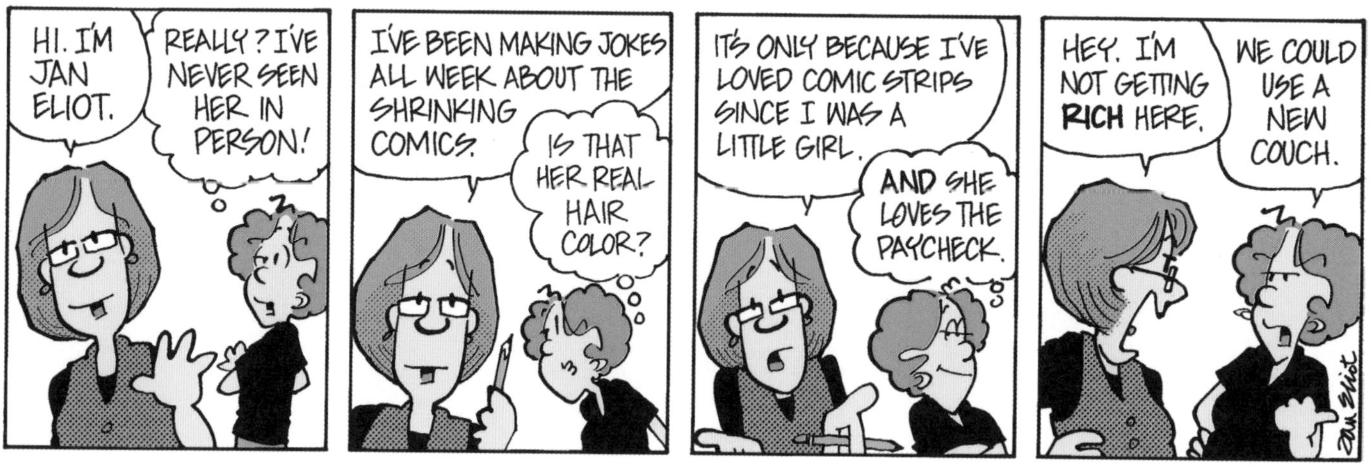
HI. I'M JAN ELIOT.
REALLY? I'VE NEVER SEEN HER IN PERSON!
I'VE BEEN MAKING JOKES ALL WEEK ABOUT THE SHRINKING COMICS.
IS THAT HER REAL HAIR COLOR?
IT'S ONLY BECAUSE I'VE LOVED COMIC STRIPS SINCE I WAS A LITTLE GIRL.
AND SHE LOVES THE PAYCHECK.
HEY. I'M NOT GETTING RICH HERE.
WE COULD USE A NEW COUCH.

Stone Soup

WOW, ALIX ... THE POOL'S **PACKED**.
THE POOL'S **CRACKED**?!
I SAID IT'S **PACKED**!!
STACKED? WHO'S STACKED?
I SAID, THERE'S TOO MANY **PEE-PUL**!!
GROSS, HOLLY.
THWEEEET!
EVERY-BODY OUT!!

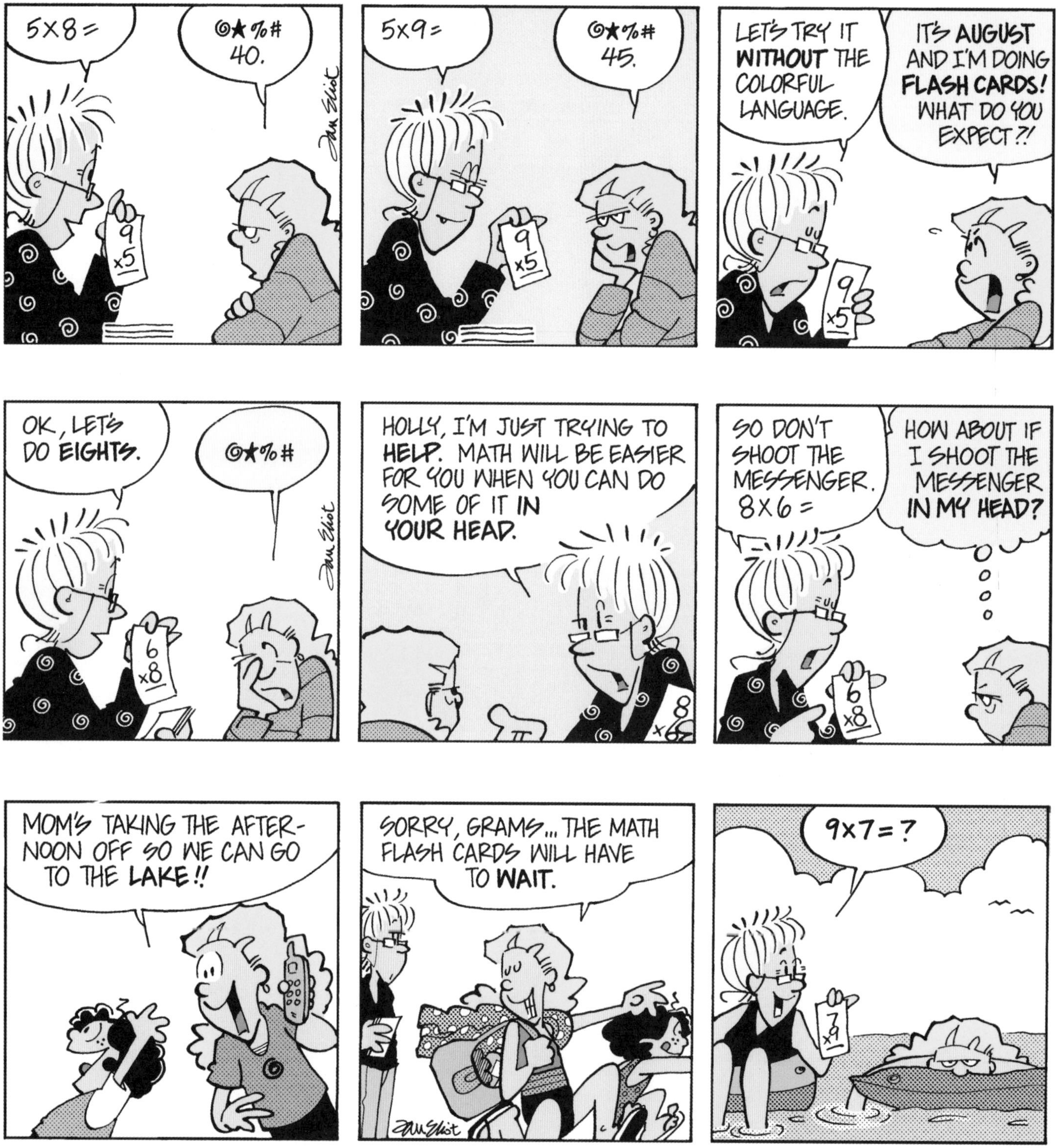
5×8=
@★%#
40.
5×9=
@★%#
45.
LET'S TRY IT WITHOUT THE COLORFUL LANGUAGE.
IT'S AUGUST AND I'M DOING FLASH CARDS! WHAT DO YOU EXPECT?!
OK, LET'S DO EIGHTS.
@★%#
HOLLY, I'M JUST TRYING TO HELP. MATH WILL BE EASIER FOR YOU WHEN YOU CAN DO SOME OF IT IN YOUR HEAD.
SO DON'T SHOOT THE MESSENGER. 8×6=
HOW ABOUT IF I SHOOT THE MESSENGER IN MY HEAD?
MOM'S TAKING THE AFTER-NOON OFF SO WE CAN GO TO THE LAKE!!
SORRY, GRAMS... THE MATH FLASH CARDS WILL HAVE TO WAIT.
9×7=?

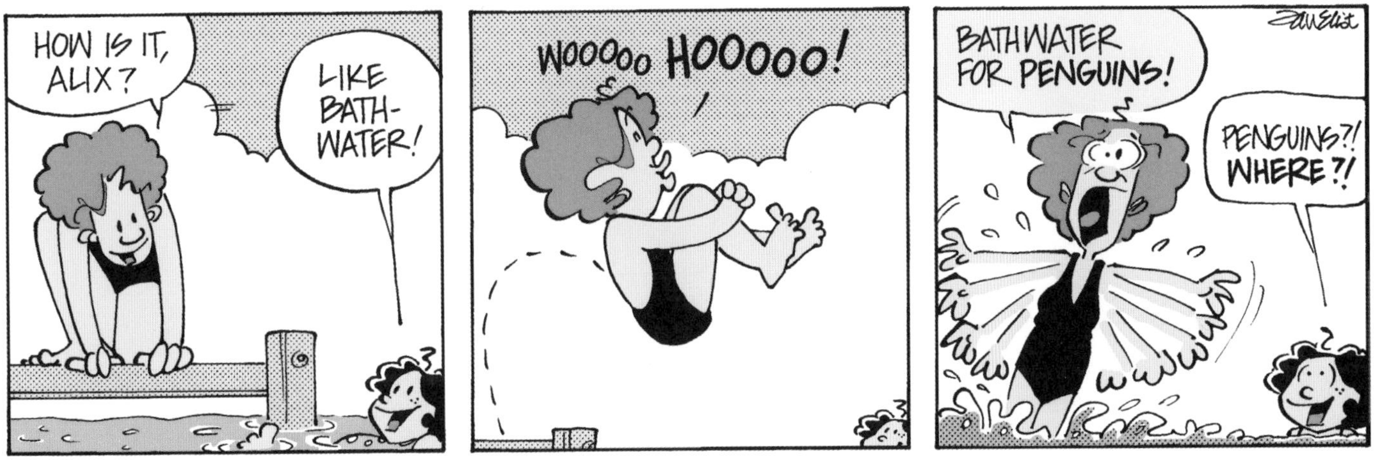
HOW IS IT, ALIX?
LIKE BATH-WATER!
WOOOOO HOOOOO!
BATHWATER FOR PENGUINS!
PENGUINS?! WHERE?!

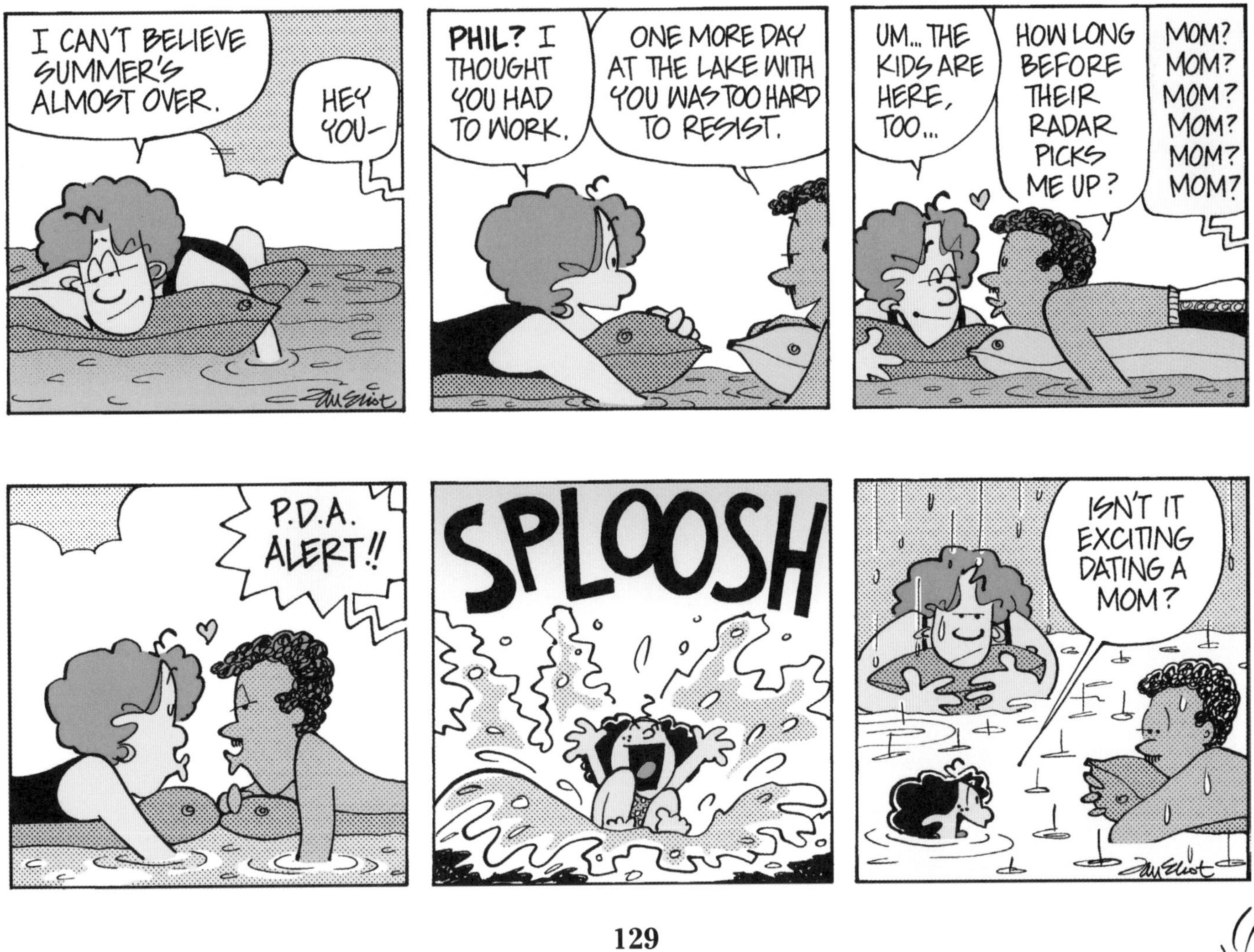
I CAN'T BELIEVE SUMMER'S ALMOST OVER.
HEY YOU-
PHIL? I THOUGHT YOU HAD TO WORK.
ONE MORE DAY AT THE LAKE WITH YOU WAS TOO HARD TO RESIST.
UM... THE KIDS ARE HERE, TOO...
HOW LONG BEFORE THEIR RADAR PICKS ME UP?
MOM? MOM? MOM? MOM? MOM? MOM?
P.D.A. ALERT!!
SPLOOSH
ISN'T IT EXCITING DATING A MOM?

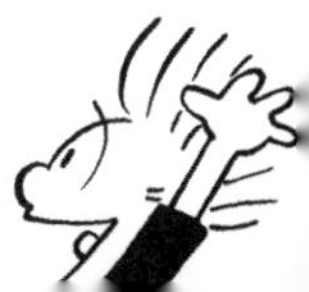

Stone Soup

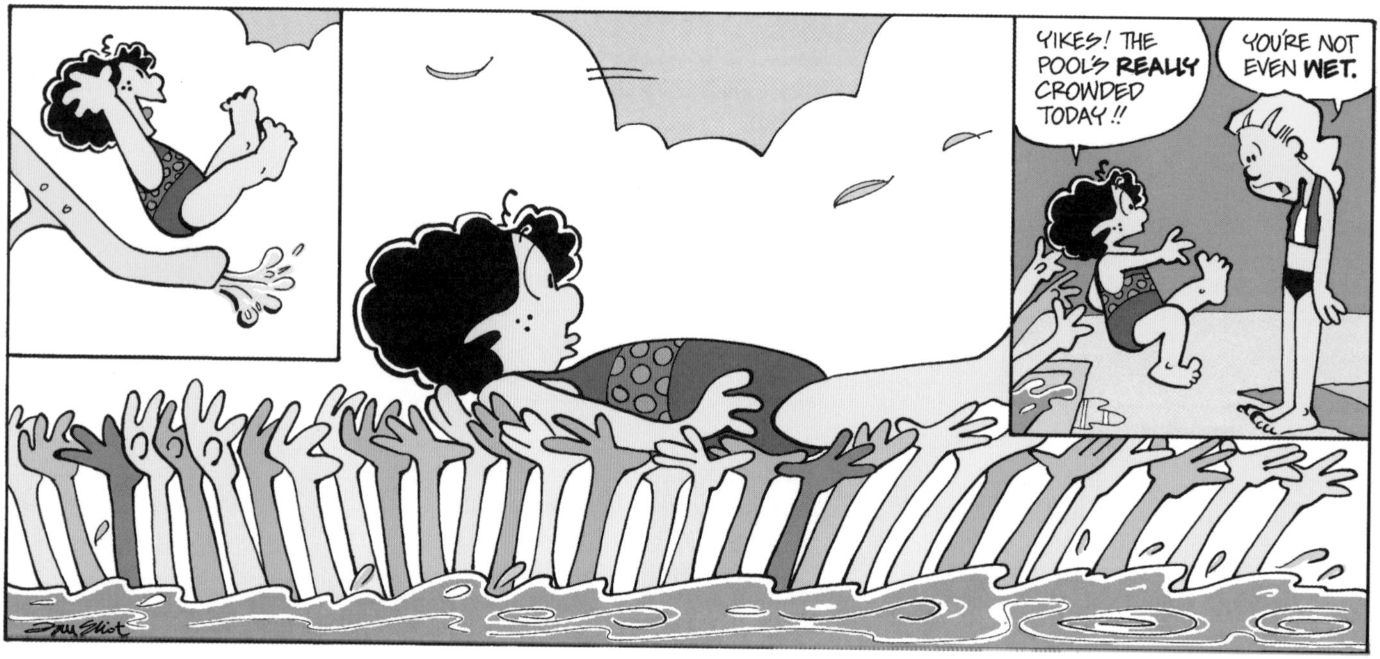
YIKES! THE POOL'S **REALLY** CROWDED TODAY!!
YOU'RE NOT EVEN **WET.**

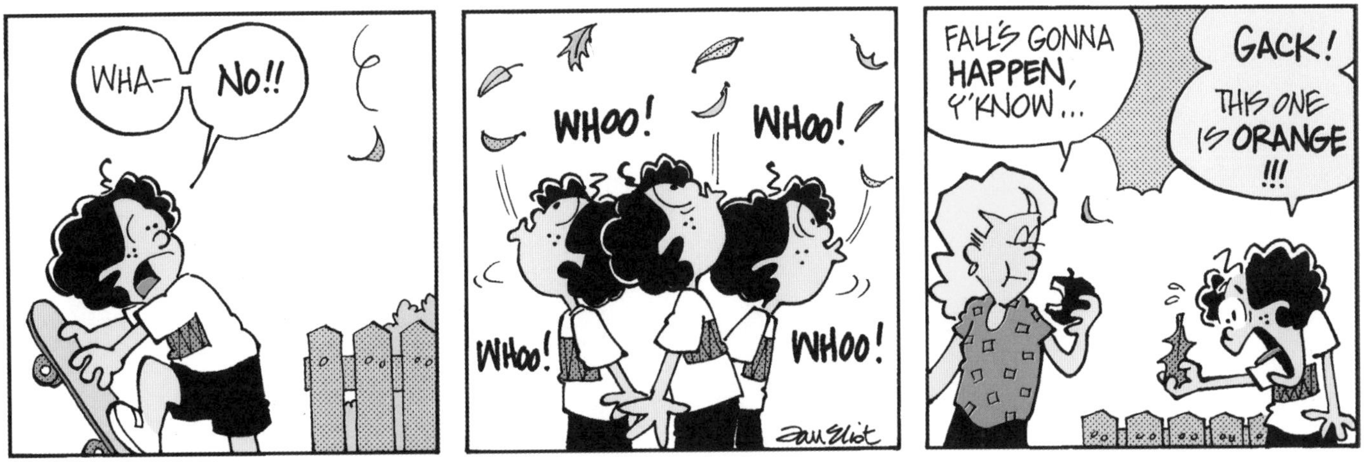
WHA—
NO!!
WHOO! WHOO!
WHOO! WHOO!
FALL'S GONNA HAPPEN, Y'KNOW...
GACK! THIS ONE IS ORANGE !!!

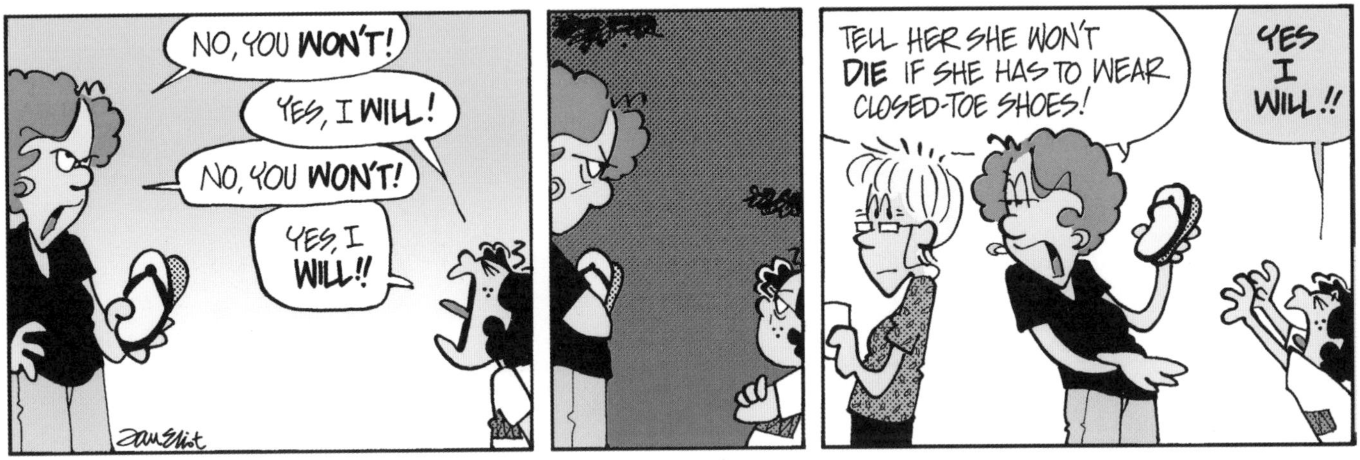
NO, YOU WON'T!
YES, I WILL!
NO, YOU WON'T!
YES, I WILL!!
TELL HER SHE WON'T DIE IF SHE HAS TO WEAR CLOSED-TOE SHOES!
YES I WILL!!

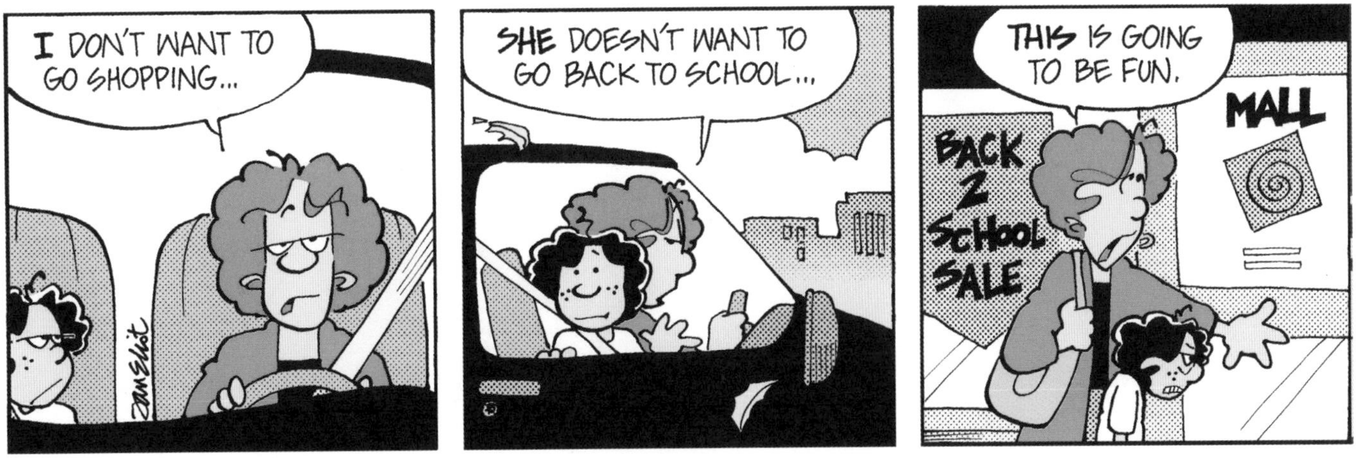
I DON'T WANT TO GO SHOPPING...
SHE DOESN'T WANT TO GO BACK TO SCHOOL...
THIS IS GOING TO BE FUN.
BACK 2 SCHOOL SALE
MALL

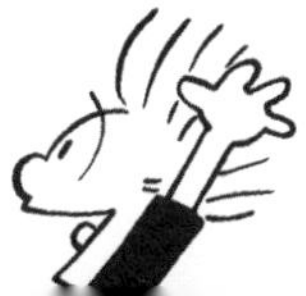

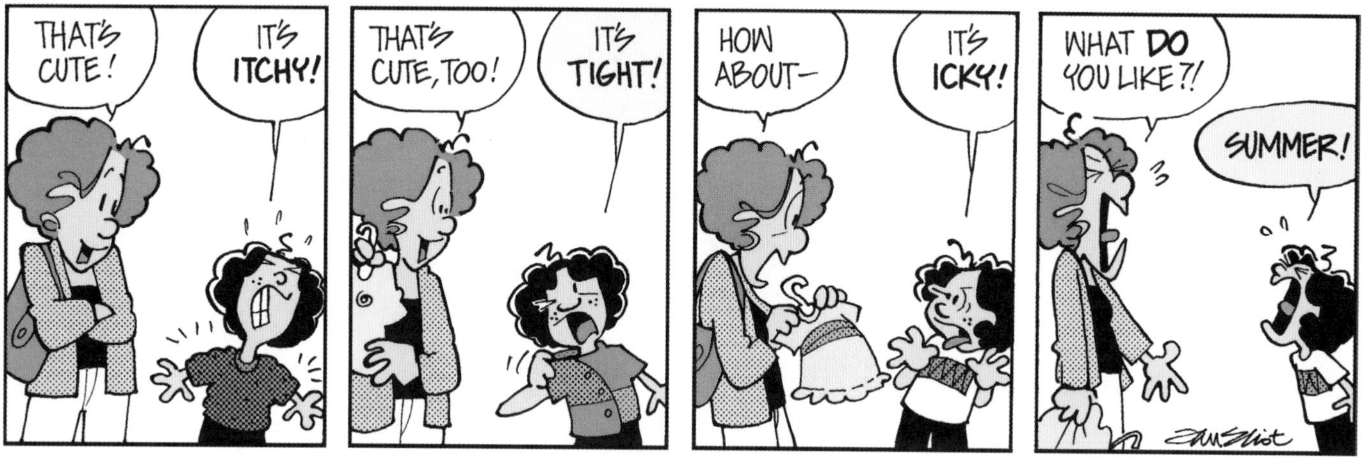
THAT'S CUTE!
IT'S ITCHY!
THAT'S CUTE, TOO!
IT'S TIGHT!
HOW ABOUT—
IT'S ICKY!
WHAT DO YOU LIKE?!
SUMMER!

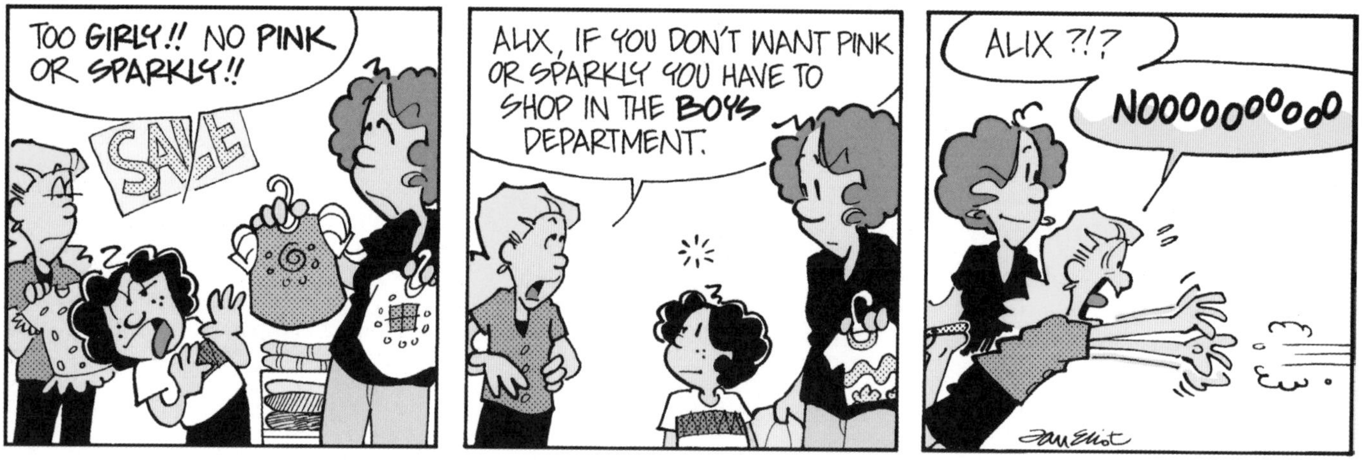
TOO GIRLY!! NO PINK OR SPARKLY!!
SALE
ALIX, IF YOU DON'T WANT PINK OR SPARKLY YOU HAVE TO SHOP IN THE BOYS DEPARTMENT.
ALIX?!?
NOOOOOOOOOO

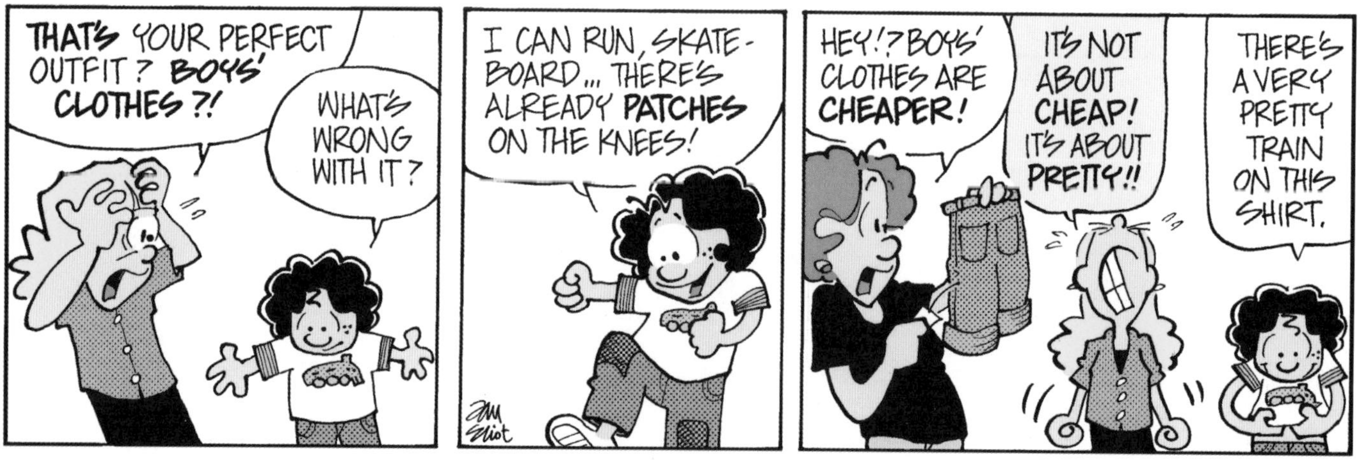
THAT'S YOUR PERFECT OUTFIT? BOYS' CLOTHES?!
WHAT'S WRONG WITH IT?
I CAN RUN, SKATE-BOARD... THERE'S ALREADY PATCHES ON THE KNEES!
HEY!? BOYS' CLOTHES ARE CHEAPER!
IT'S NOT ABOUT CHEAP! IT'S ABOUT PRETTY!!
THERE'S A VERY PRETTY TRAIN ON THIS SHIRT.

Stone Soup

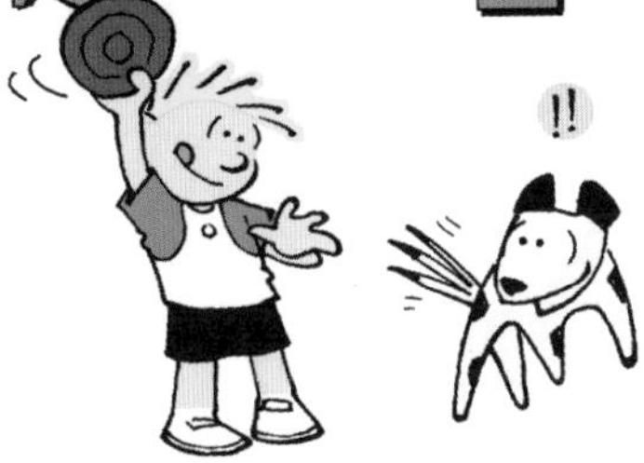

!!

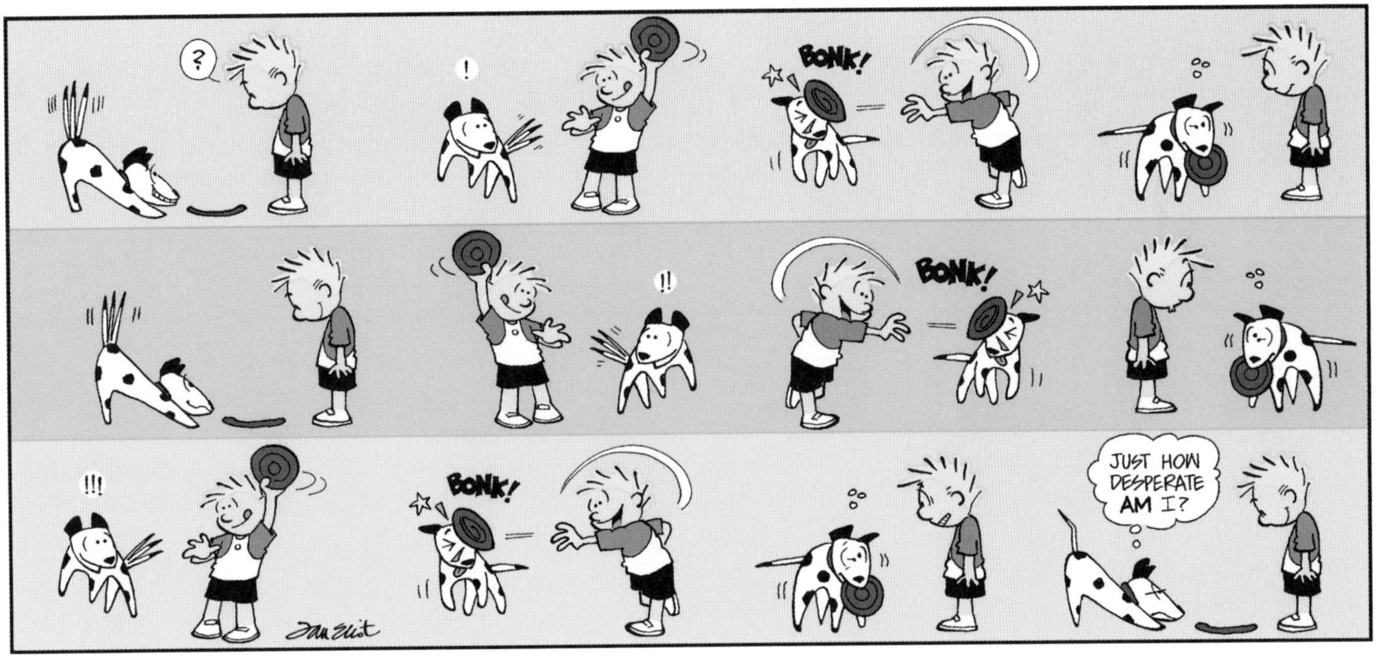

?
!
BONK!
!!
BONK!
!!!
BONK!
JUST HOW DESPERATE AM I?

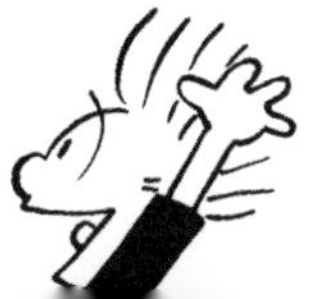

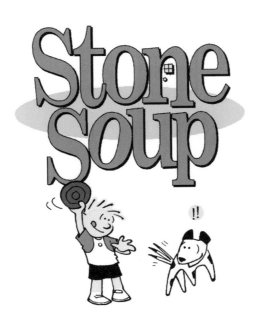

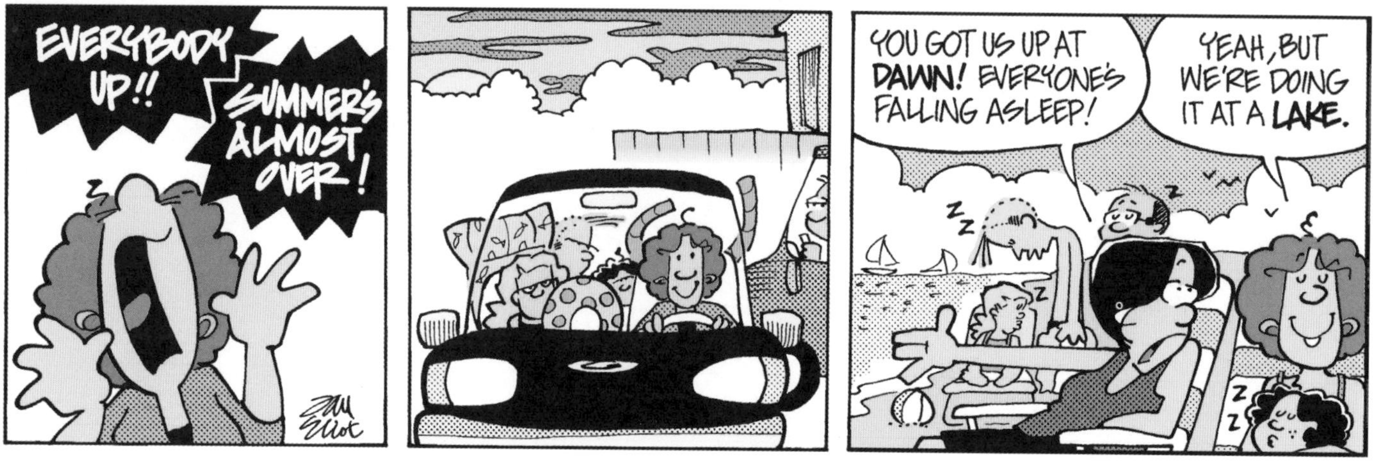
EVERYBODY UP!!
SUMMER'S ALMOST OVER!
YOU GOT US UP AT DAWN! EVERYONE'S FALLING ASLEEP!
YEAH, BUT WE'RE DOING IT AT A LAKE.

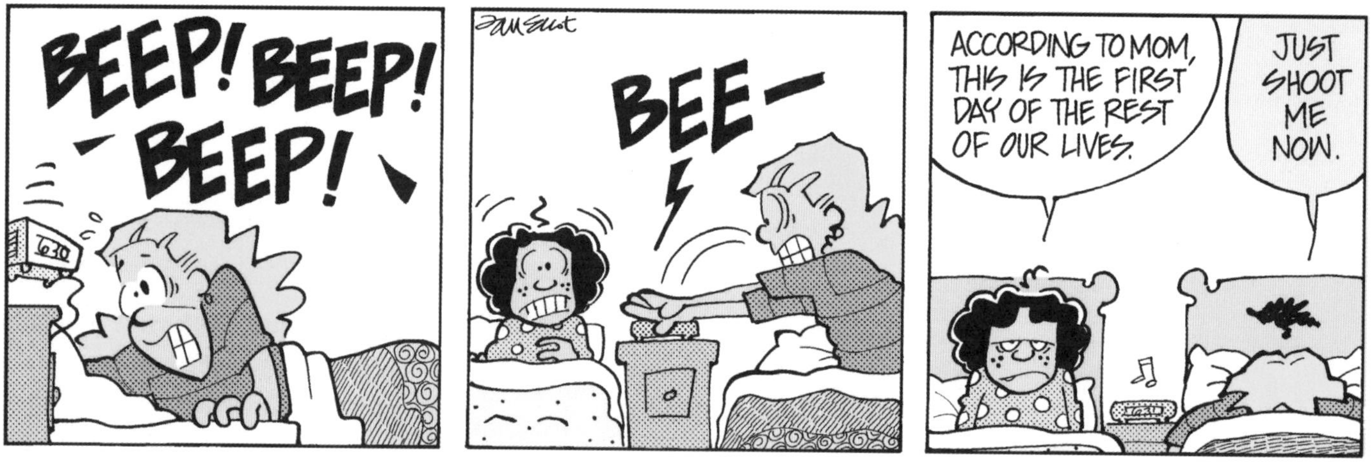
BEEP! BEEP! BEEP!
BEE—
ACCORDING TO MOM, THIS IS THE FIRST DAY OF THE REST OF OUR LIVES.
JUST SHOOT ME NOW.

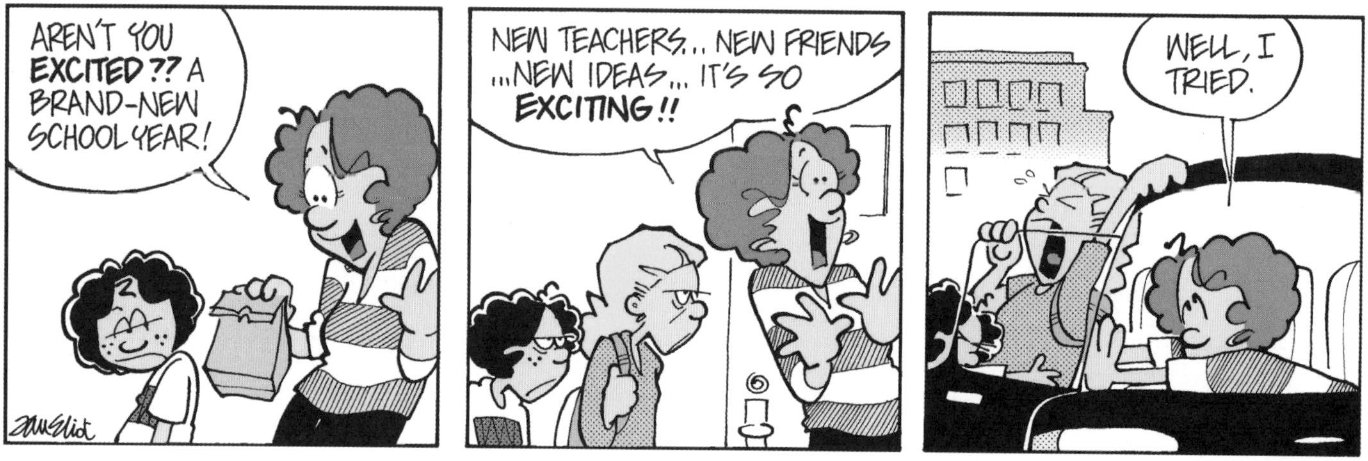
AREN'T YOU EXCITED?? A BRAND-NEW SCHOOL YEAR!
NEW TEACHERS... NEW FRIENDS ...NEW IDEAS... IT'S SO EXCITING!!
WELL, I TRIED.

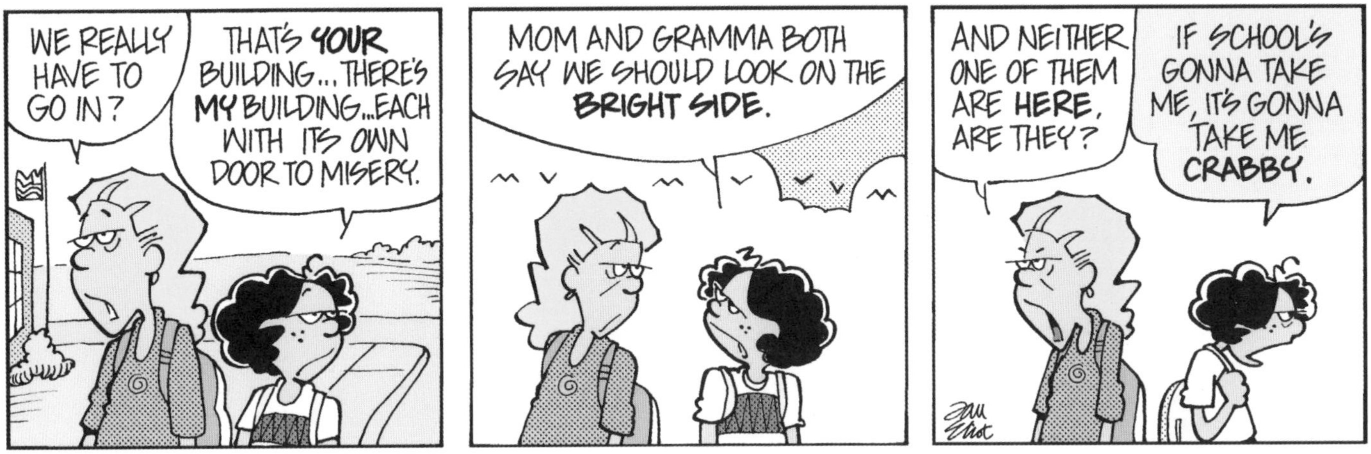
WE REALLY HAVE TO GO IN?
THAT'S **YOUR** BUILDING... THERE'S **MY** BUILDING...EACH WITH ITS OWN DOOR TO MISERY.
MOM AND GRAMMA BOTH SAY WE SHOULD LOOK ON THE **BRIGHT SIDE**.
AND NEITHER ONE OF THEM ARE **HERE**, ARE THEY?
IF SCHOOL'S GONNA TAKE ME, IT'S GONNA TAKE ME **CRABBY**.

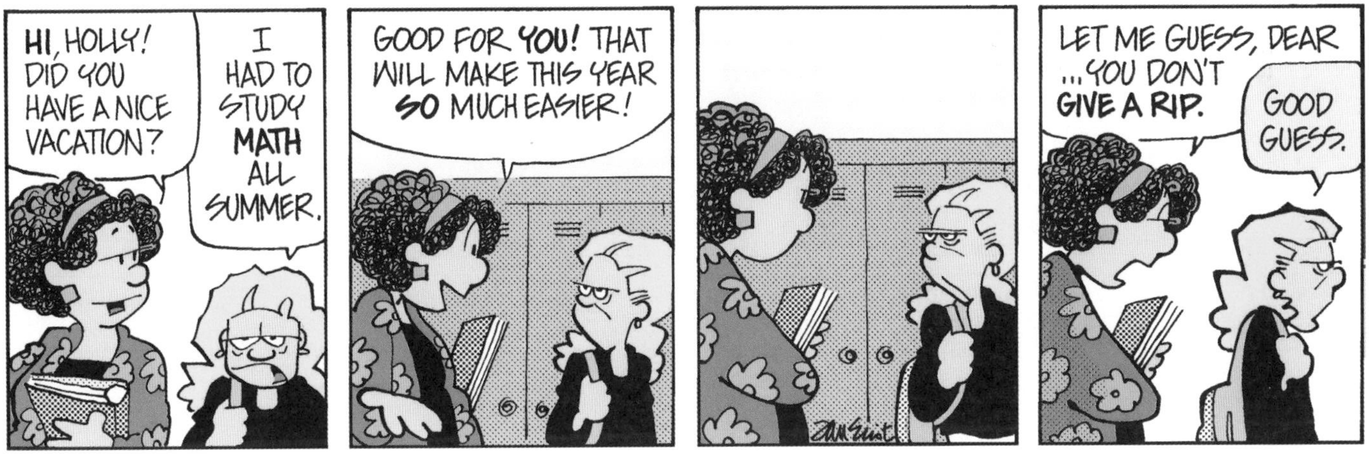
HI, HOLLY! DID YOU HAVE A NICE VACATION?
I HAD TO STUDY **MATH** ALL SUMMER.
GOOD FOR **YOU!** THAT WILL MAKE THIS YEAR **SO** MUCH EASIER!
LET ME GUESS, DEAR ...YOU DON'T **GIVE A RIP**.
GOOD GUESS.

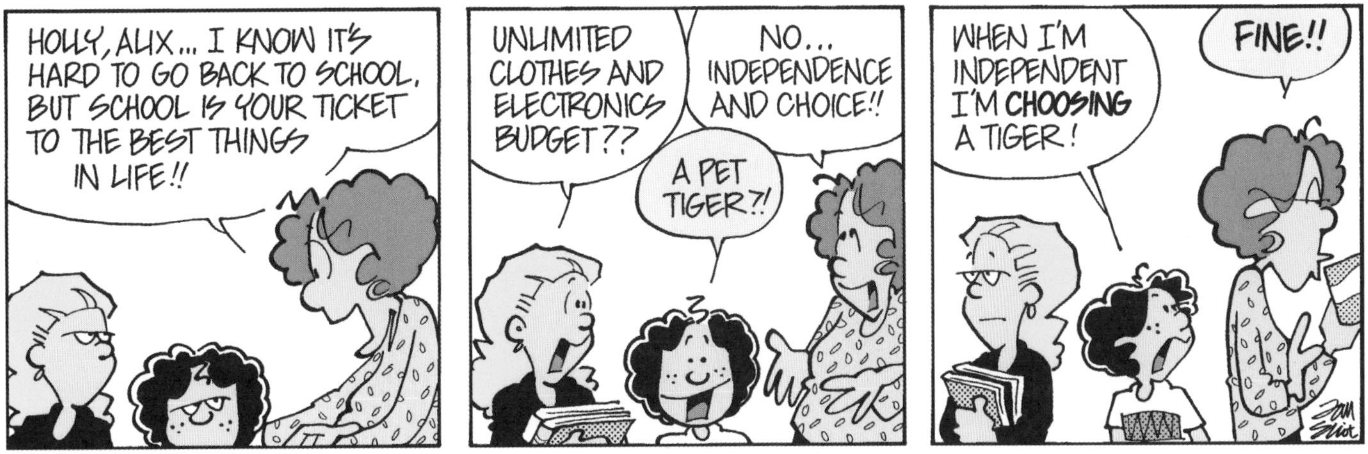
HOLLY, ALIX... I KNOW IT'S HARD TO GO BACK TO SCHOOL, BUT SCHOOL IS YOUR TICKET TO THE BEST THINGS IN LIFE!!
UNLIMITED CLOTHES AND ELECTRONICS BUDGET??
NO... INDEPENDENCE AND CHOICE!!
A PET TIGER?!
WHEN I'M INDEPENDENT I'M **CHOOSING** A TIGER!
FINE!!

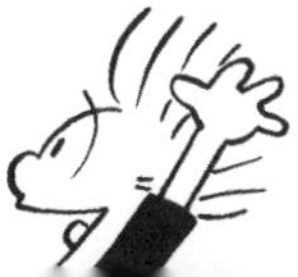

Stone Soup

RENA! IF SOMEONE FROM WORK SEES US, WE'RE **TOAST**!
RELAX, VAL!!
THESE COULD BE THE LAST DAYS OF SUMMER!
WE **DESERVE** A MID-AFTERNOON TREAT IN AN OUTDOOR CAFE.
BESIDES... WE'RE WORKING — "OFF SITE."
REALLY? WORKING ON **WHAT**?
UM... THE VALUE-ADDED EFFECTS OF **PROPS** IN PRODUCT PRESENTATION!
WE'RE DOING MARKET RESEARCH ON **DRINK UMBRELLAS**??
SOMEBODY HAS TO!

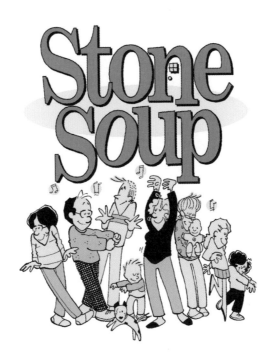

Stone Soup

HELLO? MAX WANTS TO TALK WITH HIS AUNTIE VAL!

UM...

BAGEL! LUCI! FIRE-TRUCK!

GOOD TIMES, MAX. NOW PUT MOMMY BACK ON THE PHONE.

POTTY! OUTSIDE! COOO-KIE!

CONGRATULATIONS. SIS?! ARE YOU THERE?? I'M AT WORK!!

ELMO MAMA NIGHT-NIGHT!

TRUCK! TRUCK! MAMA DADA ICE CREAM!

SORRY, BIG GUY. I HAVE A MEETING.

?

HI! HI?

HI?

PLEASE TELL ME THAT'S NOT A CLIENT.

PO PO! CAH CAH! LUNCH!

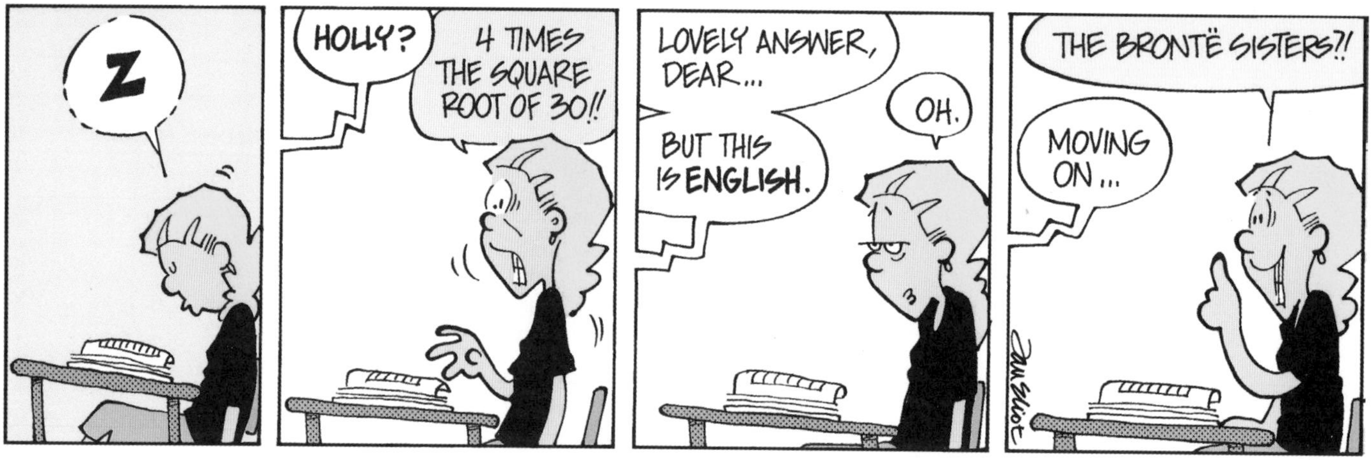
Z
HOLLY?
4 TIMES THE SQUARE ROOT OF 30!!
LOVELY ANSWER, DEAR...
BUT THIS IS **ENGLISH**.
OH.
THE BRONTË SISTERS?!
MOVING ON...

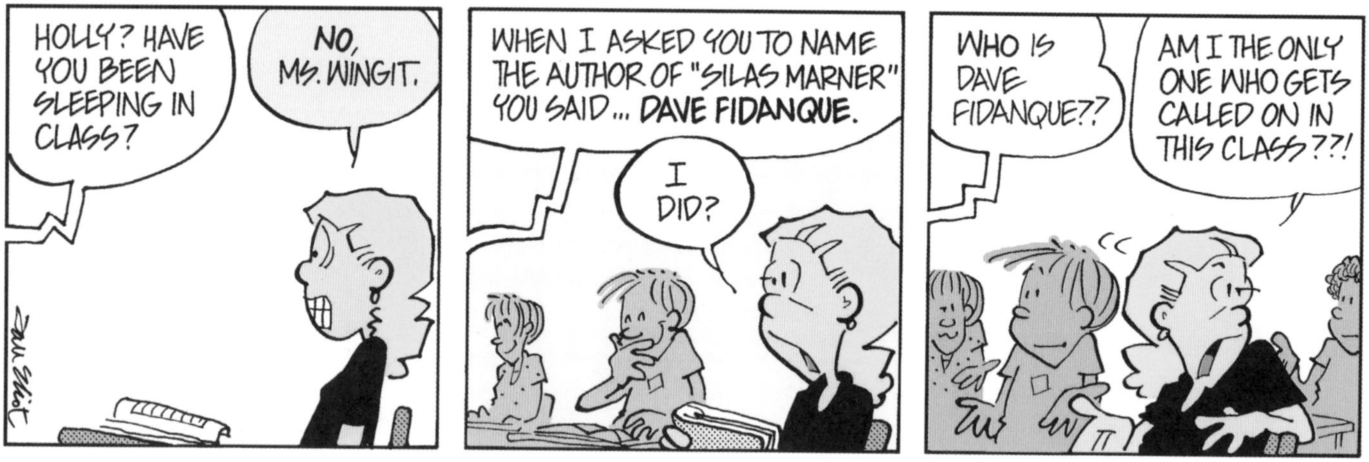
HOLLY? HAVE YOU BEEN SLEEPING IN CLASS?
NO, MS. WINGIT.
WHEN I ASKED YOU TO NAME THE AUTHOR OF "SILAS MARNER" YOU SAID... **DAVE FIDANQUE.**
I DID?
WHO IS DAVE FIDANQUE??
AM I THE ONLY ONE WHO GETS CALLED ON IN THIS CLASS??!

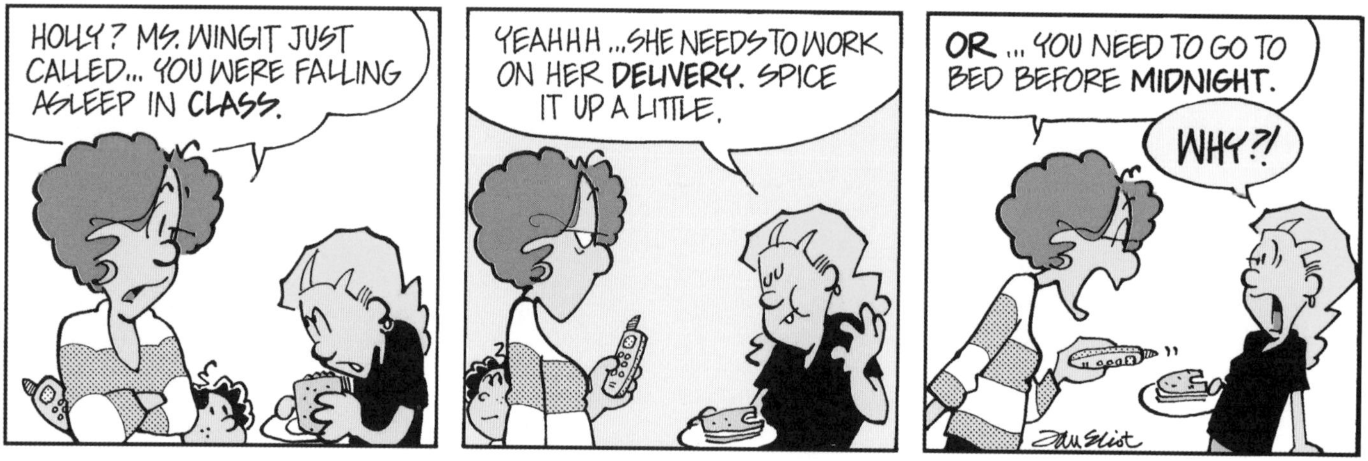
HOLLY? MS. WINGIT JUST CALLED... YOU WERE FALLING ASLEEP IN **CLASS**.
YEAHHH... SHE NEEDS TO WORK ON HER **DELIVERY**. SPICE IT UP A LITTLE.
OR ... YOU NEED TO GO TO BED BEFORE **MIDNIGHT**.
WHY?!

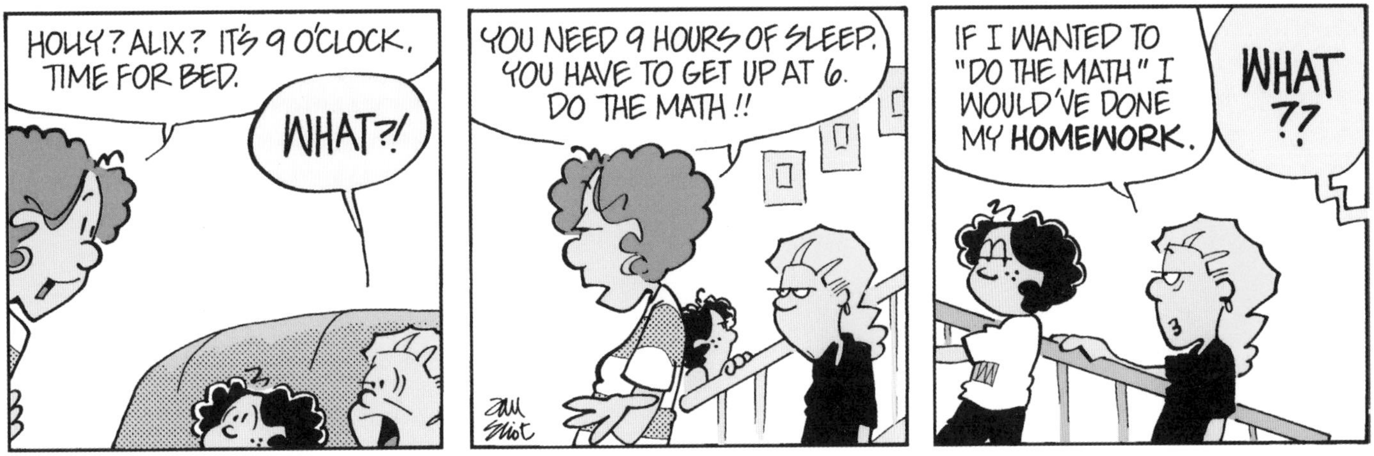
HOLLY? ALIX? IT'S 9 O'CLOCK. TIME FOR BED.
WHAT?!
YOU NEED 9 HOURS OF SLEEP. YOU HAVE TO GET UP AT 6. DO THE MATH!!
IF I WANTED TO "DO THE MATH" I WOULD'VE DONE MY **HOMEWORK**.
WHAT??

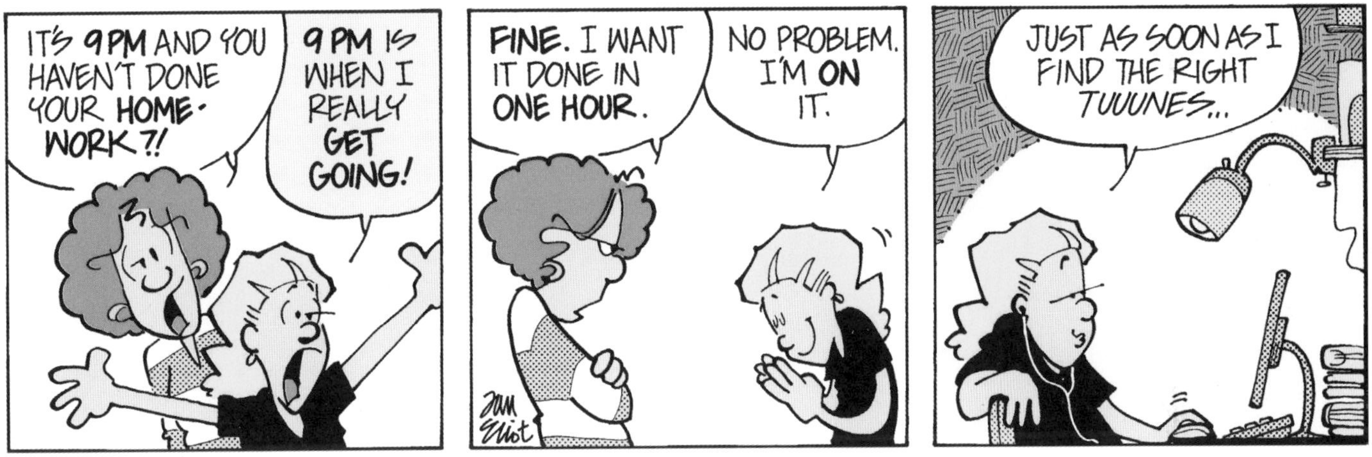
IT'S **9 PM** AND YOU HAVEN'T DONE YOUR **HOME-WORK**?!
9 PM IS WHEN I REALLY **GET GOING!**
FINE. I WANT IT DONE IN **ONE HOUR**.
NO PROBLEM. I'M **ON** IT.
JUST AS SOON AS I FIND THE RIGHT *TUUUNES*...

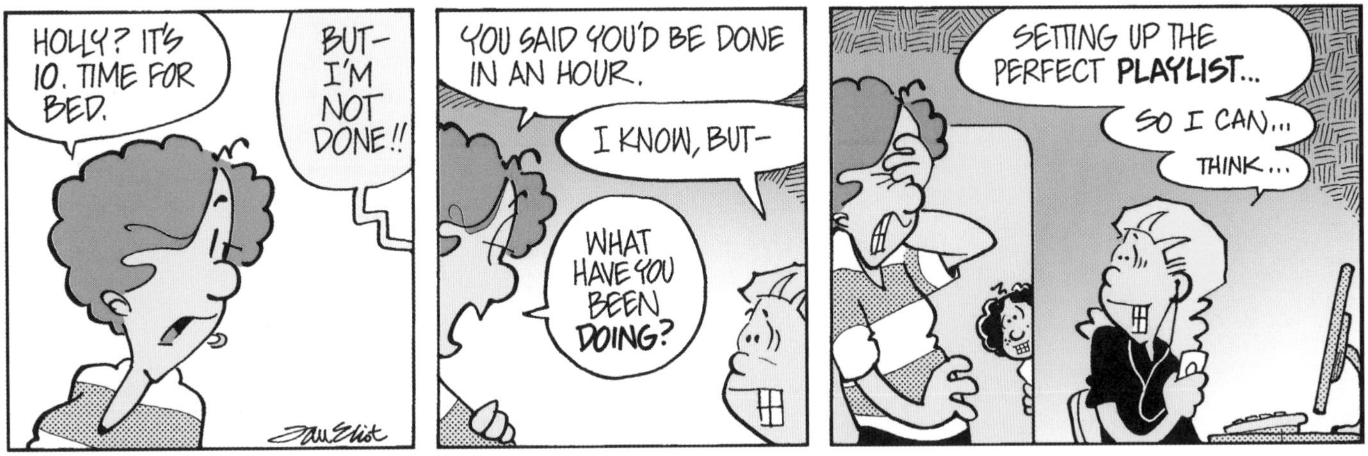
HOLLY? IT'S 10. TIME FOR BED.
BUT- I'M NOT DONE!!
YOU SAID YOU'D BE DONE IN AN HOUR.
I KNOW, BUT-
WHAT HAVE YOU BEEN **DOING**?
SETTING UP THE PERFECT **PLAYLIST**...
SO I CAN...
THINK...

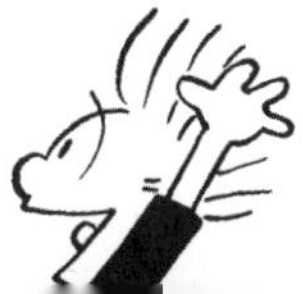

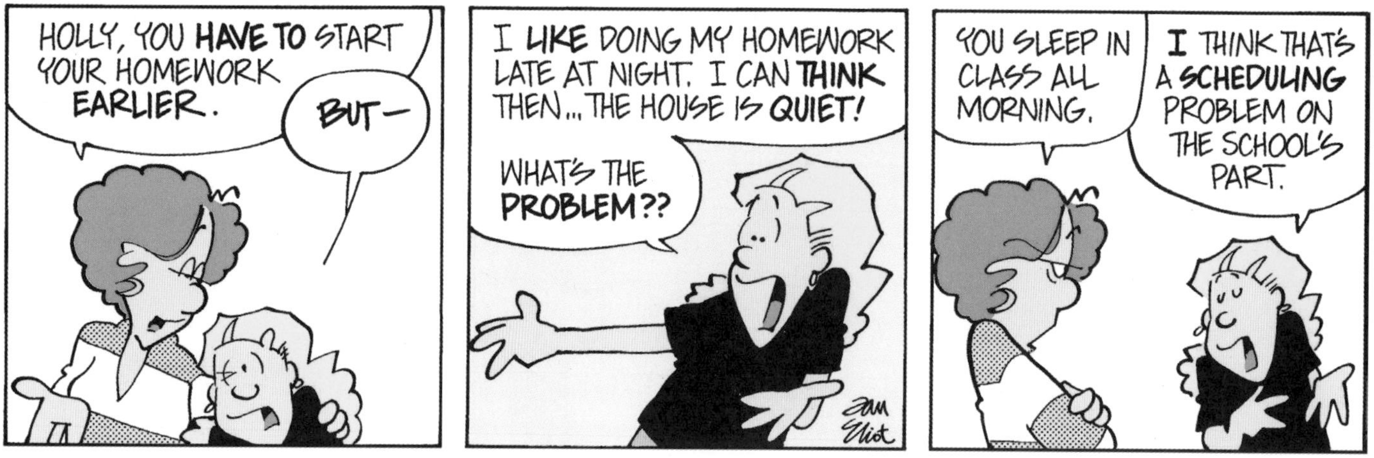
HOLLY, YOU **HAVE TO** START YOUR HOMEWORK **EARLIER**.
BUT—
I **LIKE** DOING MY HOMEWORK LATE AT NIGHT. I CAN **THINK** THEN... THE HOUSE IS **QUIET**!
WHAT'S THE **PROBLEM**??
YOU SLEEP IN CLASS ALL MORNING.
I THINK THAT'S A **SCHEDULING** PROBLEM ON THE SCHOOL'S PART.

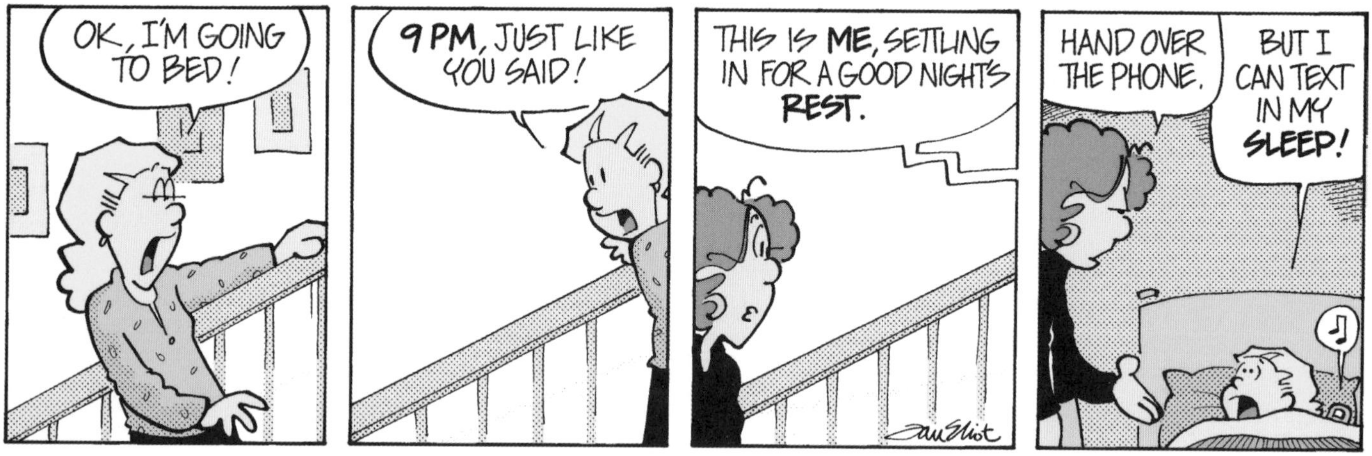
OK, I'M GOING TO BED!
9 PM, JUST LIKE YOU SAID!
THIS IS **ME**, SETTLING IN FOR A GOOD NIGHT'S **REST**.
HAND OVER THE PHONE.
BUT I CAN TEXT IN MY **SLEEP**!

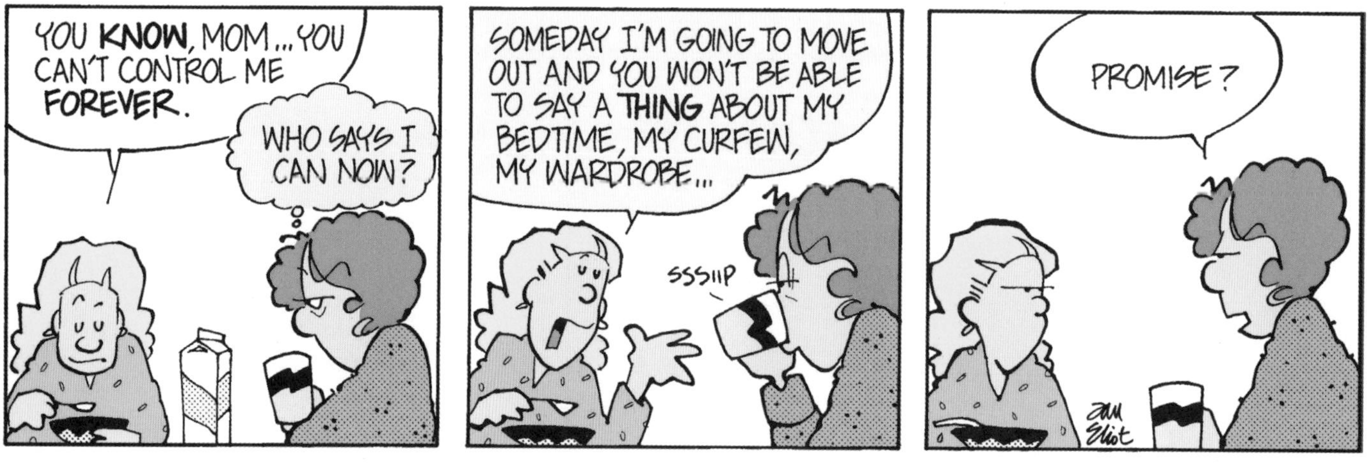
YOU **KNOW**, MOM... YOU CAN'T CONTROL ME **FOREVER**.
WHO SAYS I CAN NOW?
SOMEDAY I'M GOING TO MOVE OUT AND YOU WON'T BE ABLE TO SAY A **THING** ABOUT MY BEDTIME, MY CURFEW, MY WARDROBE...
SSSIIP
PROMISE?

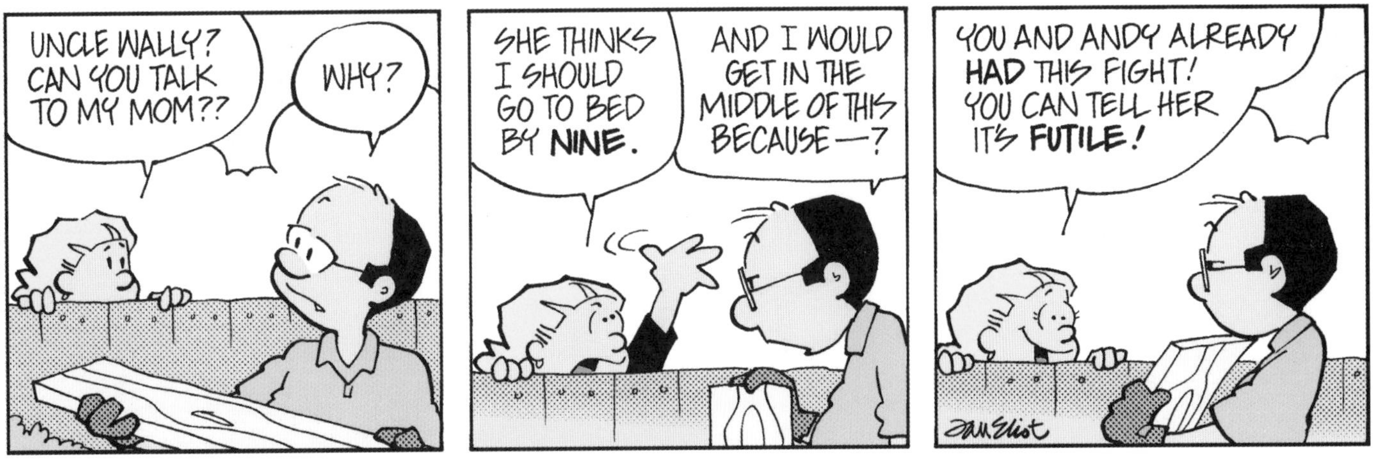
UNCLE WALLY? CAN YOU TALK TO MY MOM??
WHY?
SHE THINKS I SHOULD GO TO BED BY **NINE.**
AND I WOULD GET IN THE MIDDLE OF THIS BECAUSE —?
YOU AND ANDY ALREADY **HAD** THIS FIGHT! YOU CAN TELL HER IT'S **FUTILE!**

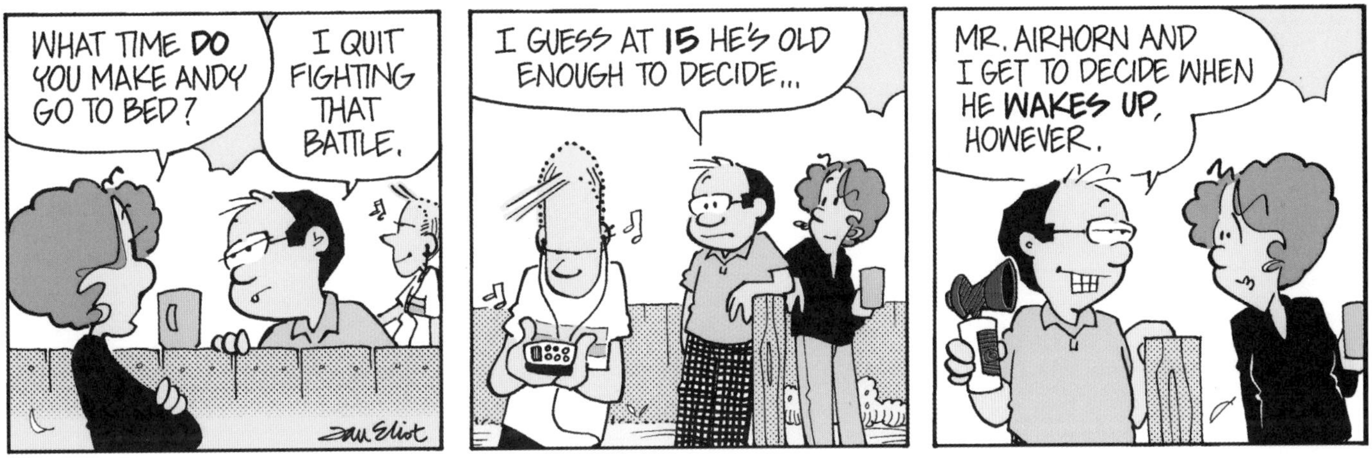
WHAT TIME **DO** YOU MAKE ANDY GO TO BED?
I QUIT FIGHTING THAT BATTLE.
I GUESS AT **15** HE'S OLD ENOUGH TO DECIDE...
MR. AIRHORN AND I GET TO DECIDE WHEN HE **WAKES UP**, HOWEVER.

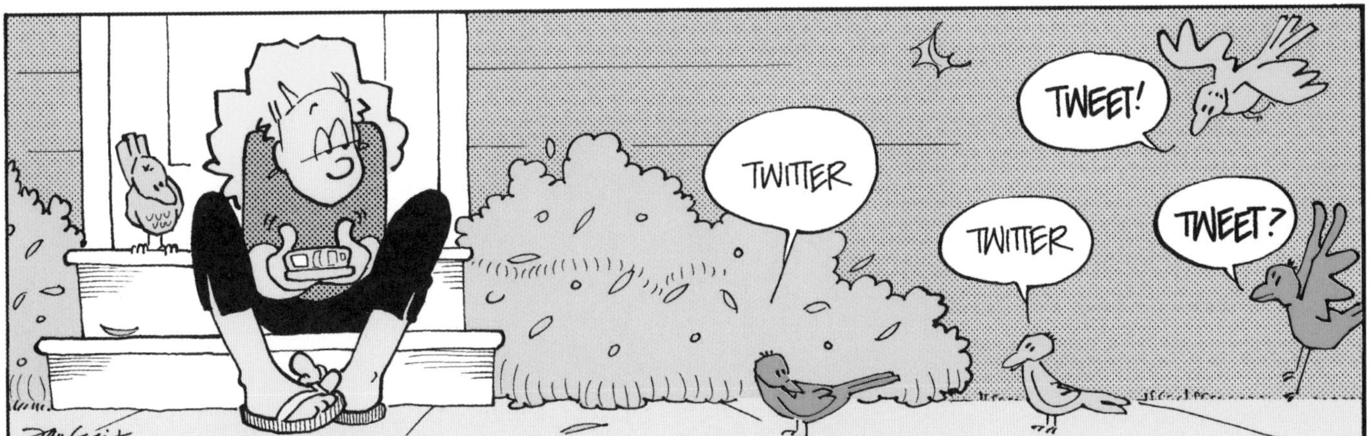
TWEET!
TWITTER
TWITTER
TWEET?

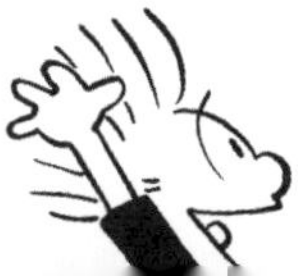

Stone Soup

WELCOME...
TO ENSURE QUALITY CUSTOMER SERVICE WE NOW HAVE AN **AUTOMATED** SYSTEM...
PLEASE **SAY** OR **ENTER** YOUR ACCOUNT NUMBER.
BIP
BIP
BARK BARK BARK BAR
BARK BARK BARK
SORRY, I DIDN'T UNDERSTAND YOU. PLEASE **SAY** OR **ENTER** YOUR ACCOUNT NUMBER...
SH!!
BIP
BIP
BIP
BARK
BARK
BARK
BARK
BARK
I **THINK** YOU SAID—
©★#!!
BARK
BARK
BARK
BARK
BAR—
FOR **ENGLISH** PRESS ONE... FOR **SPANISH** PRESS TWO...
I **COULD** PUT YOU OUTSIDE... BUT THIS IS KIND OF ENTERTAIN-ING...

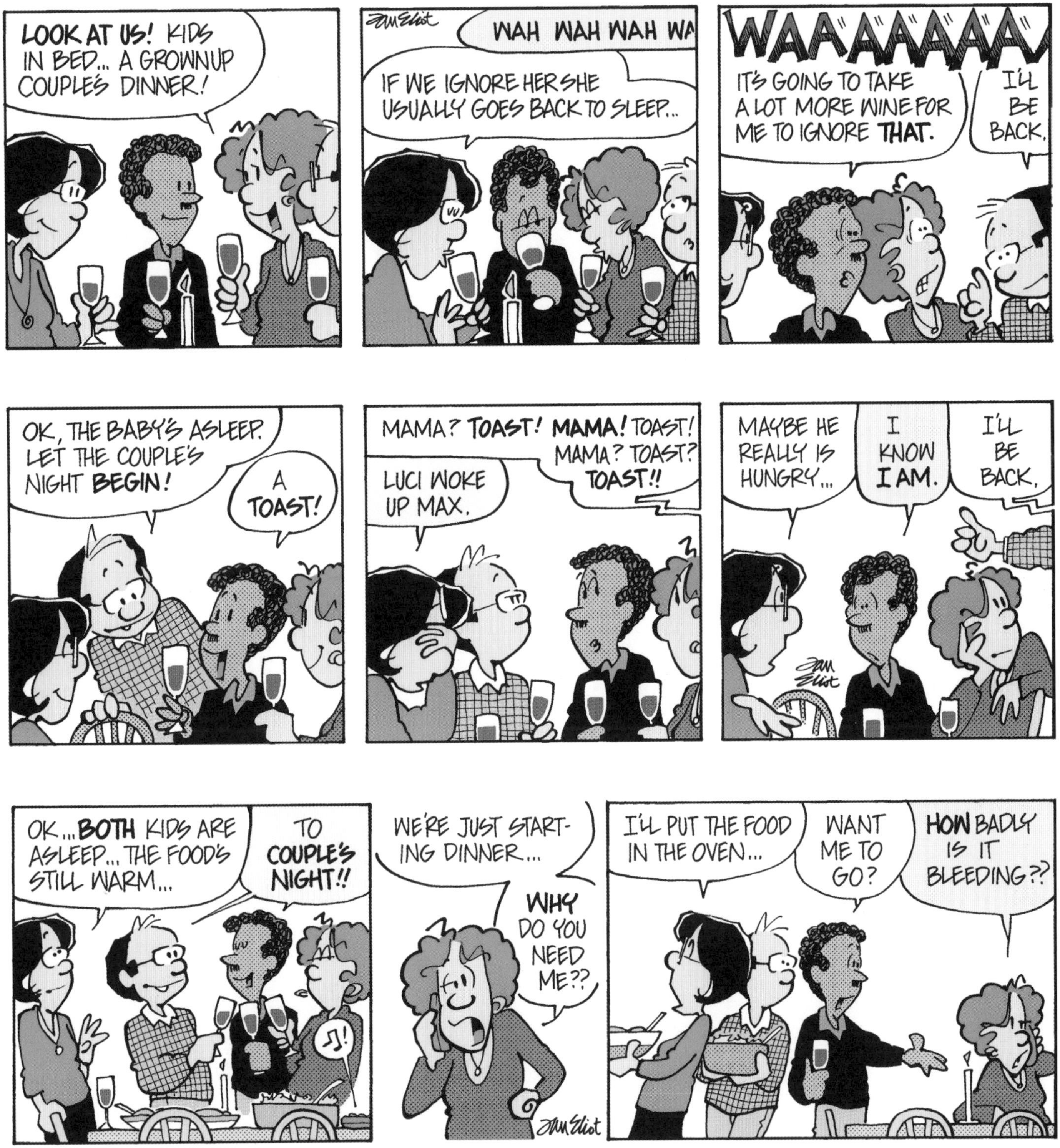
LOOK AT US! KIDS IN BED... A GROWNUP COUPLE'S DINNER!
WAH WAH WAH WA
IF WE IGNORE HER SHE USUALLY GOES BACK TO SLEEP...
WAAAAAAA
IT'S GOING TO TAKE A LOT MORE WINE FOR ME TO IGNORE THAT.
I'LL BE BACK.
OK, THE BABY'S ASLEEP. LET THE COUPLE'S NIGHT BEGIN!
A TOAST!
MAMA? TOAST! MAMA! TOAST! MAMA? TOAST? TOAST!!
LUCI WOKE UP MAX.
MAYBE HE REALLY IS HUNGRY...
I KNOW I AM.
I'LL BE BACK.
OK... BOTH KIDS ARE ASLEEP... THE FOOD'S STILL WARM...
TO COUPLE'S NIGHT!!
WE'RE JUST STARTING DINNER...
WHY DO YOU NEED ME??
I'LL PUT THE FOOD IN THE OVEN...
WANT ME TO GO?
HOW BADLY IS IT BLEEDING??

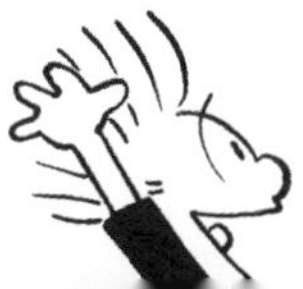

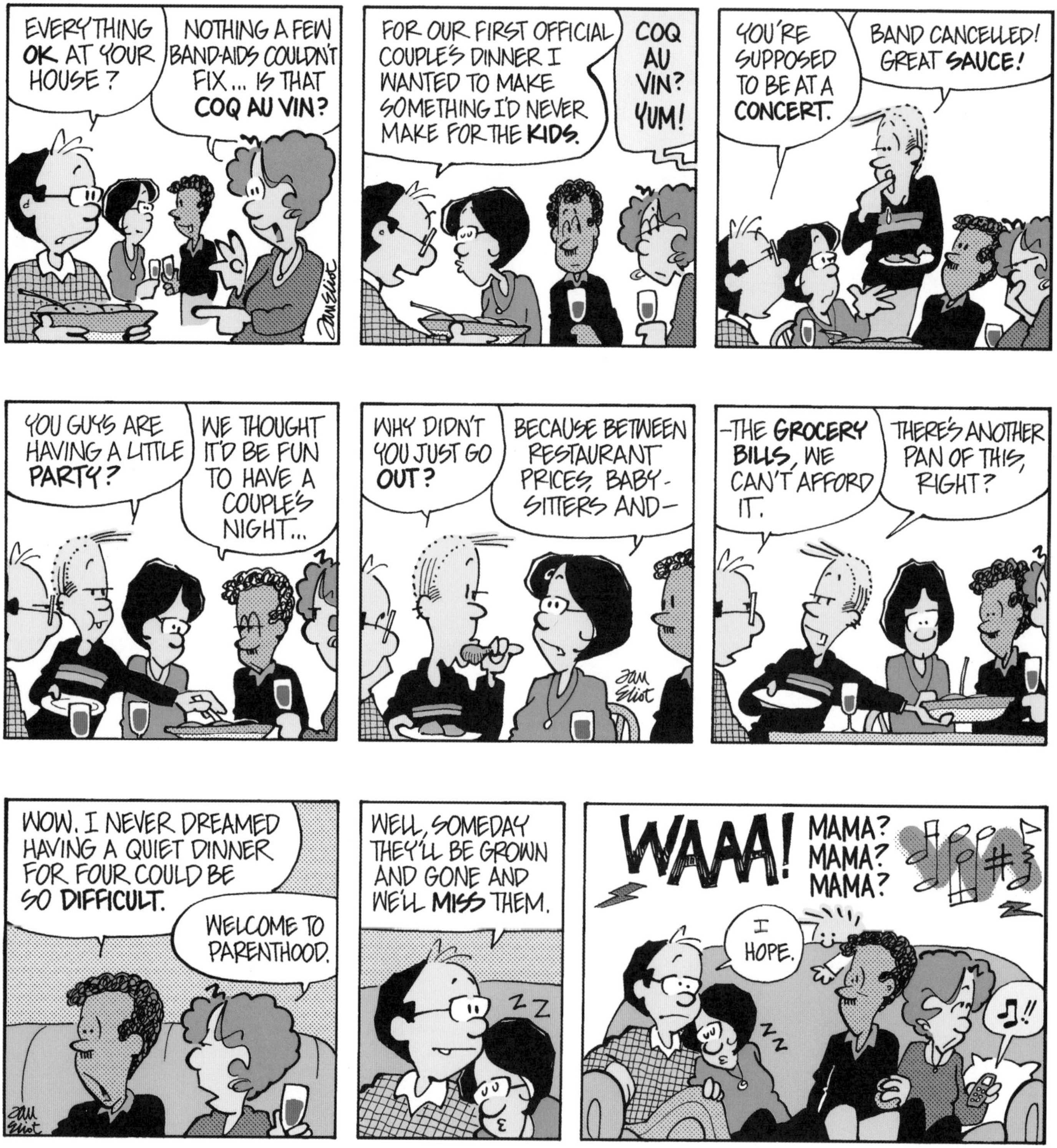
EVERYTHING OK AT YOUR HOUSE?
NOTHING A FEW BAND-AIDS COULDN'T FIX... IS THAT COQ AU VIN?
FOR OUR FIRST OFFICIAL COUPLE'S DINNER I WANTED TO MAKE SOMETHING I'D NEVER MAKE FOR THE KIDS.
COQ AU VIN? YUM!
YOU'RE SUPPOSED TO BE AT A CONCERT.
BAND CANCELLED! GREAT SAUCE!
YOU GUYS ARE HAVING A LITTLE PARTY?
WE THOUGHT IT'D BE FUN TO HAVE A COUPLE'S NIGHT...
WHY DIDN'T YOU JUST GO OUT?
BECAUSE BETWEEN RESTAURANT PRICES, BABY-SITTERS AND—
—THE GROCERY BILLS, WE CAN'T AFFORD IT.
THERE'S ANOTHER PAN OF THIS, RIGHT?
WOW. I NEVER DREAMED HAVING A QUIET DINNER FOR FOUR COULD BE SO DIFFICULT.
WELCOME TO PARENTHOOD.
WELL, SOMEDAY THEY'LL BE GROWN AND GONE AND WE'LL MISS THEM.
WAAA!
MAMA? MAMA? MAMA?
I HOPE.

Stone Soup

WE'RE GOING FROM WHINERY TO WINERY FOR MY BIRTHDAY.
HOW NICE. WHAT OTHER WINERIES HAVE YOU VISITED?
VISITED?! I LIVE IN A WHINERY!
I SEE... WHAT'S YOUR SPECIALTY?
THAT'S A GREAT WAY TO PUT IT. I THINK OUR MOST POPULAR WHINES ARE...
"I'M NOT TIRED!!"
"I DON'WANNA!"
"MAMAMAMA MAMAMAMA MAMA!!"
AND THE EVER POPULAR-
"EAEAEAEAEAHHH!"
THAT'S A VERY COMPLEX SELECTION.
IT'S EVOLVED OVER TIME.
WAIT 'TIL YOU GET...
"EVERYBODY HAS A CELLLL PHHONNNE!!"
THAT'S A SLIGHTLY MORE MATURE GRAPE. I MEAN GRIPE...

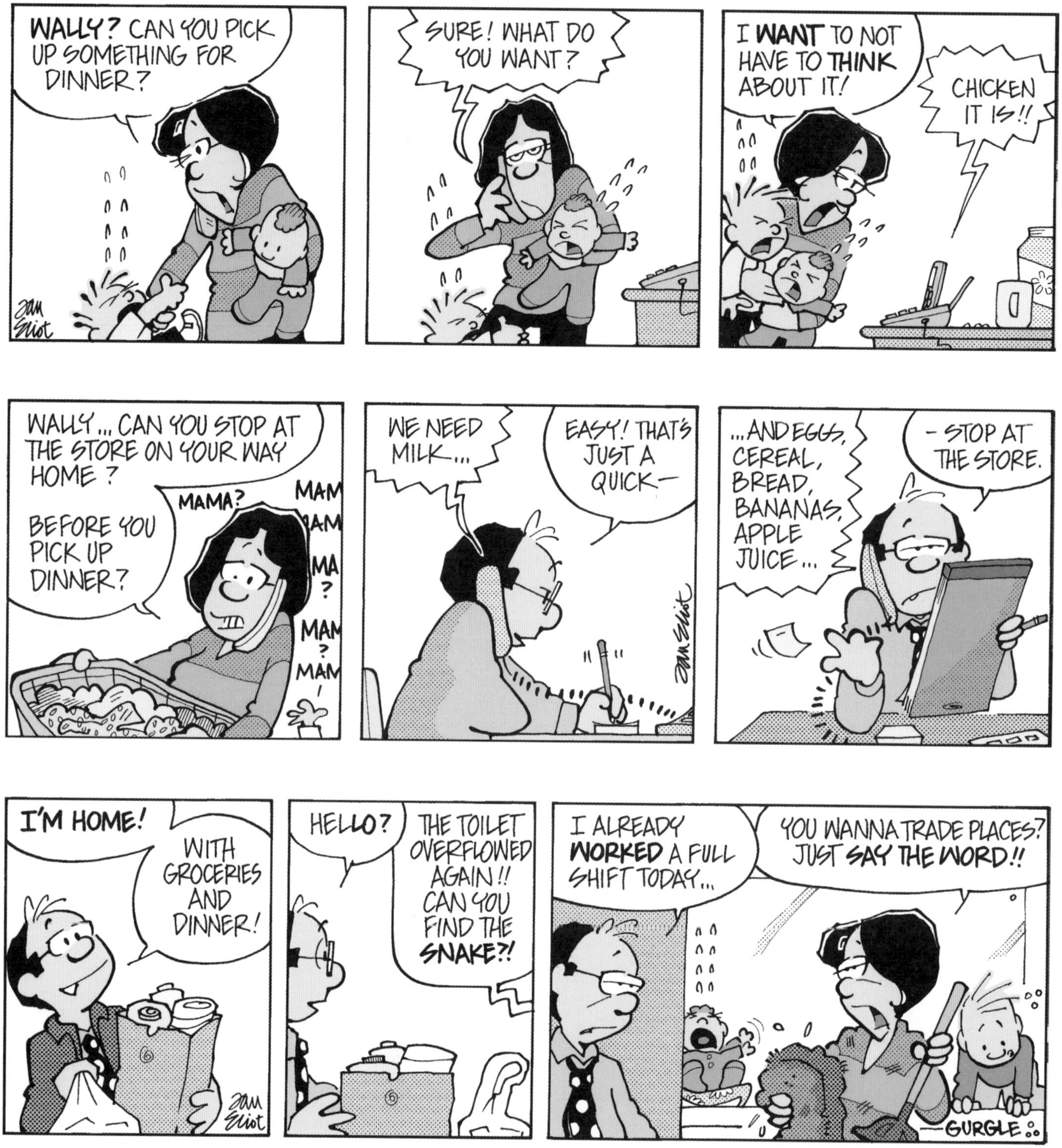
WALLY? CAN YOU PICK UP SOMETHING FOR DINNER?
SURE! WHAT DO YOU WANT?
I WANT TO NOT HAVE TO THINK ABOUT IT!
CHICKEN IT IS!!
WALLY... CAN YOU STOP AT THE STORE ON YOUR WAY HOME?
BEFORE YOU PICK UP DINNER?
MAMA?
MAM
MAM
MA ?
MAM ? MAM !
WE NEED MILK...
EASY! THAT'S JUST A QUICK—
...AND EGGS, CEREAL, BREAD, BANANAS, APPLE JUICE...
–STOP AT THE STORE.
I'M HOME!
WITH GROCERIES AND DINNER!
HELLO?
THE TOILET OVERFLOWED AGAIN!! CAN YOU FIND THE SNAKE?!
I ALREADY WORKED A FULL SHIFT TODAY...
YOU WANNA TRADE PLACES? JUST SAY THE WORD!!
—GURGLE

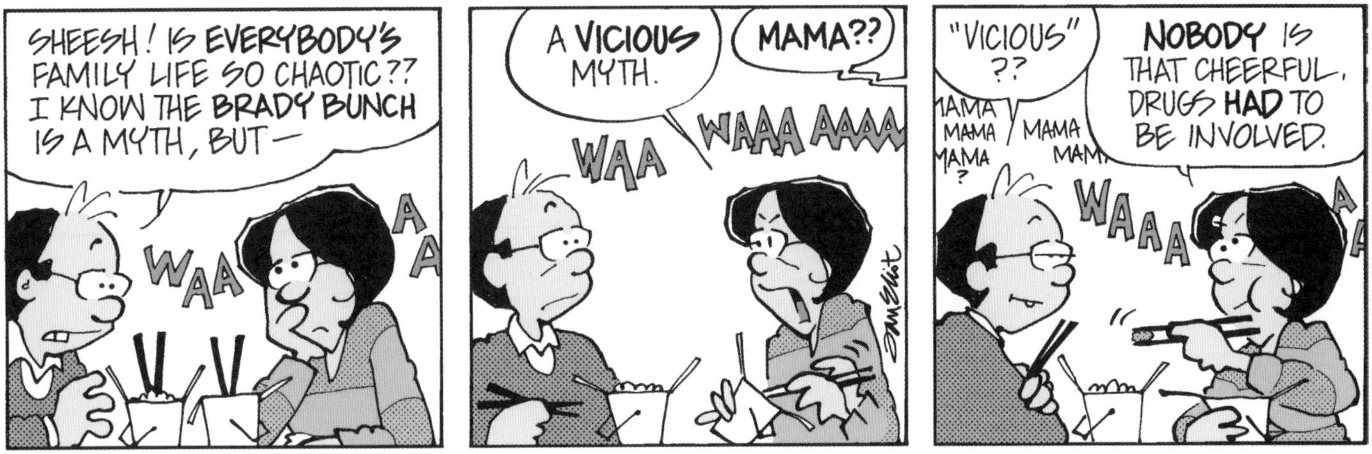
SHEESH! IS EVERYBODY'S FAMILY LIFE SO CHAOTIC?? I KNOW THE BRADY BUNCH IS A MYTH, BUT—
WAA
AA
A VICIOUS MYTH.
MAMA??
WAA
WAAA AAAA
"VICIOUS" ??
MAMA
MAMA
MAMA
?
MAMA
NOBODY IS THAT CHEERFUL. DRUGS HAD TO BE INVOLVED.
WAAAA
AA

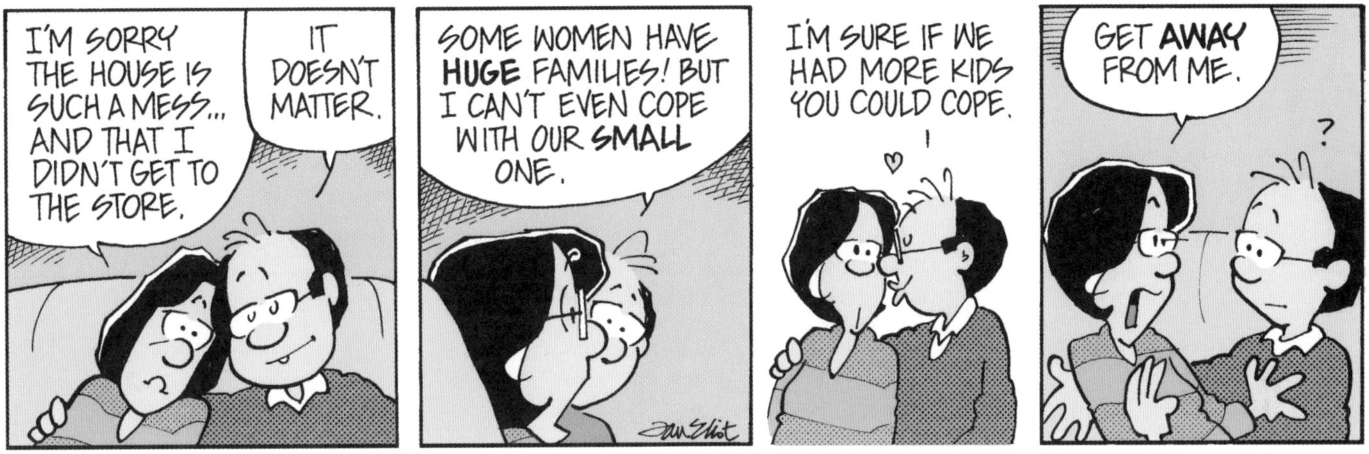
I'M SORRY THE HOUSE IS SUCH A MESS... AND THAT I DIDN'T GET TO THE STORE.
IT DOESN'T MATTER.
SOME WOMEN HAVE HUGE FAMILIES! BUT I CAN'T EVEN COPE WITH OUR SMALL ONE.
I'M SURE IF WE HAD MORE KIDS YOU COULD COPE.
!
GET AWAY FROM ME.
?

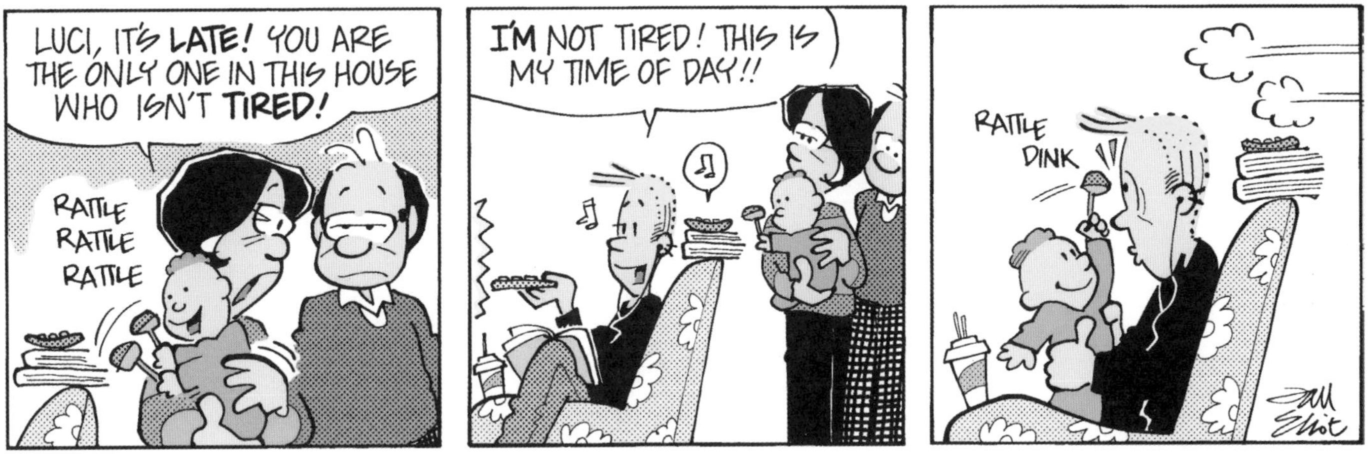
LUCI, IT'S LATE! YOU ARE THE ONLY ONE IN THIS HOUSE WHO ISN'T TIRED!
RATTLE
RATTLE
RATTLE
I'M NOT TIRED! THIS IS MY TIME OF DAY!!
RATTLE
DINK

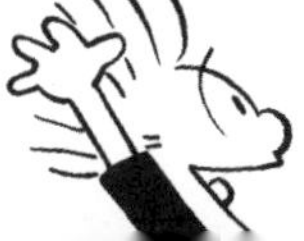

Stone Soup

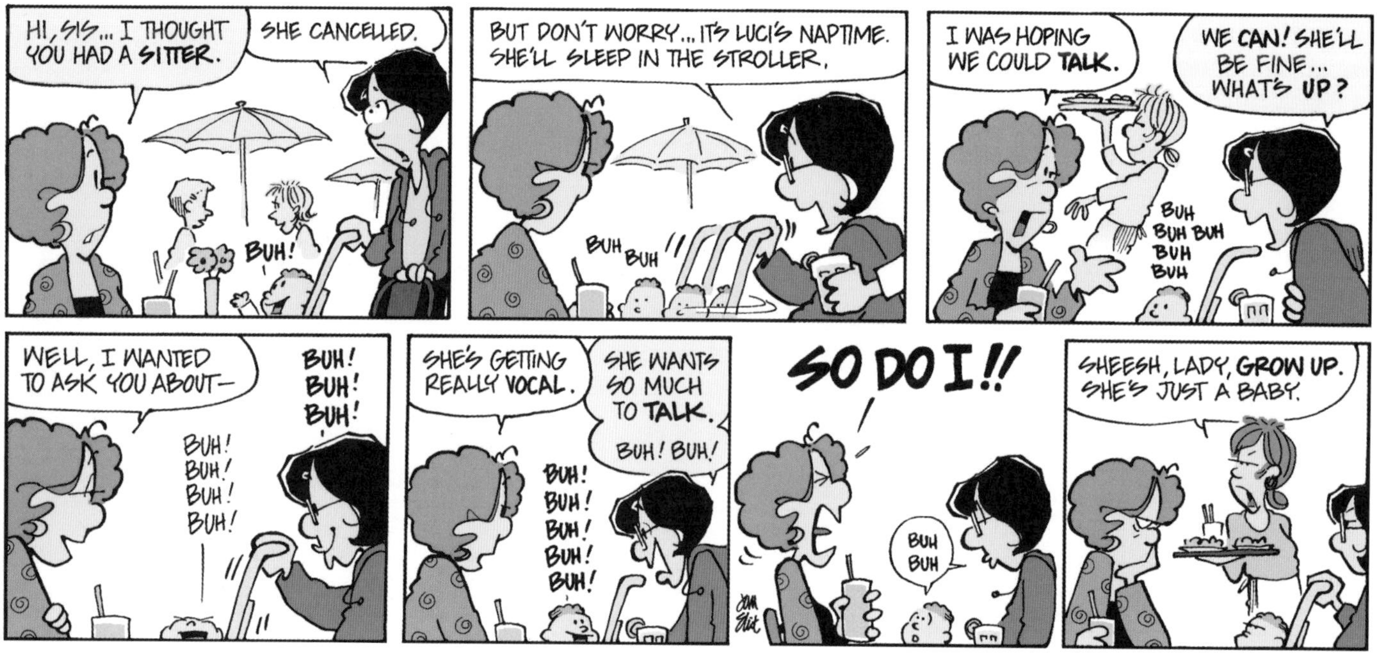

HI, SIS... I THOUGHT YOU HAD A SITTER.
SHE CANCELLED.
BUH!
BUT DON'T WORRY... IT'S LUCI'S NAPTIME. SHE'LL SLEEP IN THE STROLLER.
BUH BUH
I WAS HOPING WE COULD TALK.
WE CAN! SHE'LL BE FINE... WHAT'S UP?
BUH BUH BUH BUH BUH
WELL, I WANTED TO ASK YOU ABOUT—
BUH! BUH! BUH!
BUH! BUH! BUH! BUH!
SHE'S GETTING REALLY VOCAL.
SHE WANTS SO MUCH TO TALK.
BUH! BUH!
BUH! BUH! BUH! BUH! BUH!
SO DO I!!
BUH BUH
SHEESH, LADY, GROW UP. SHE'S JUST A BABY.

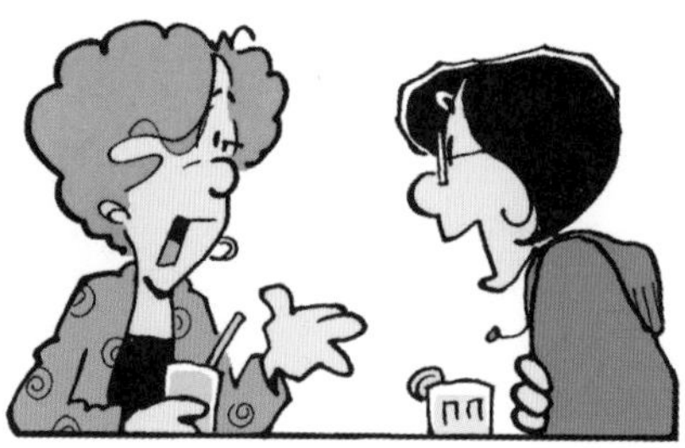

Stone Soup

OCTOBER SUN...
GET IT WHILE YOU CAN.

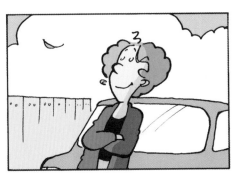

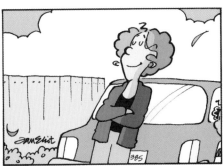

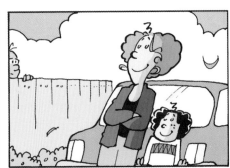

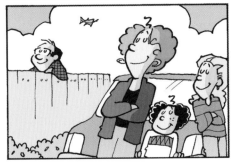

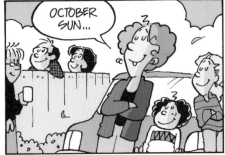

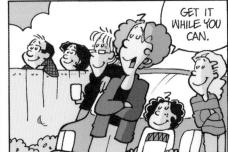

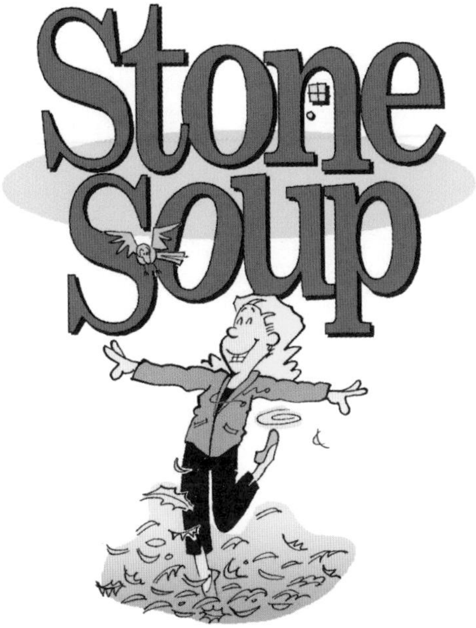

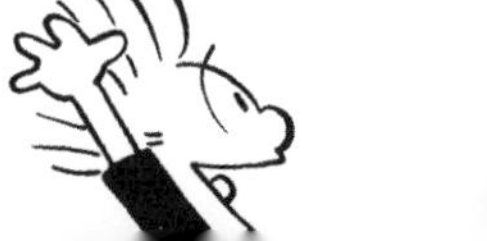

Stone Soup

MAMA?! MAMA?! MAMA?!
MAX! YOU AND HENRY JUST PLAY. I'LL BE OUT IN A—
—MINUTE.
CAN I HAVE A LITTLE PRIVACY, PLEASE?
OK!
SLAM
UM... PERFECT.
WHATCHA DOIN'?

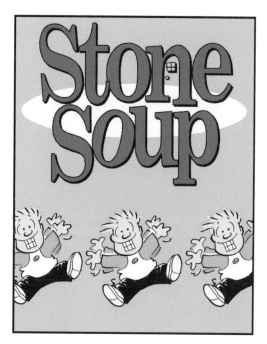

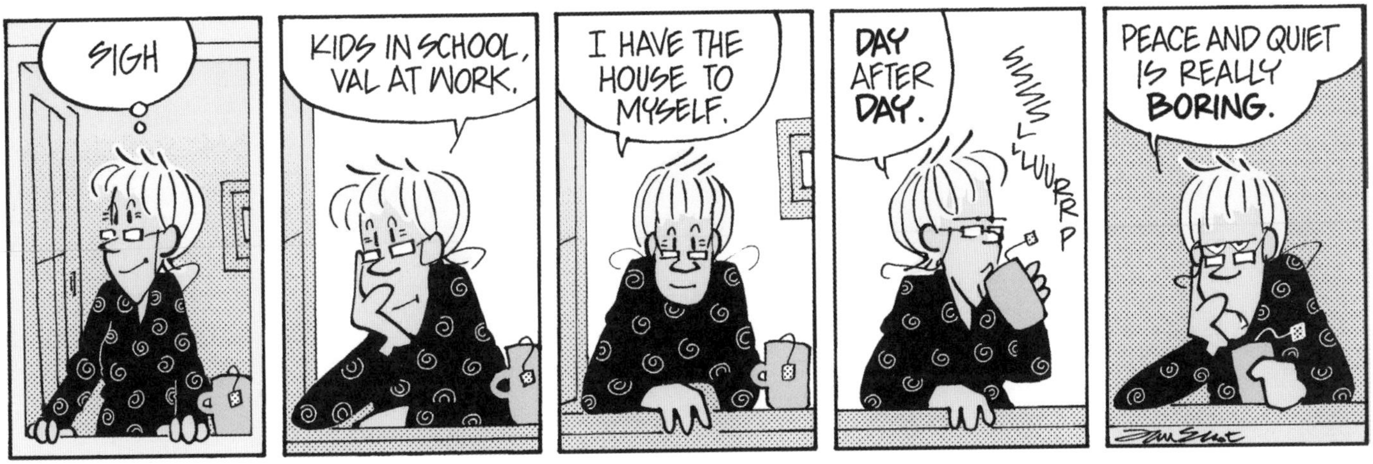
SIGH
KIDS IN SCHOOL, VAL AT WORK.
I HAVE THE HOUSE TO MYSELF.
DAY AFTER DAY.
SSSSS LUUURRP
PEACE AND QUIET IS REALLY BORING.

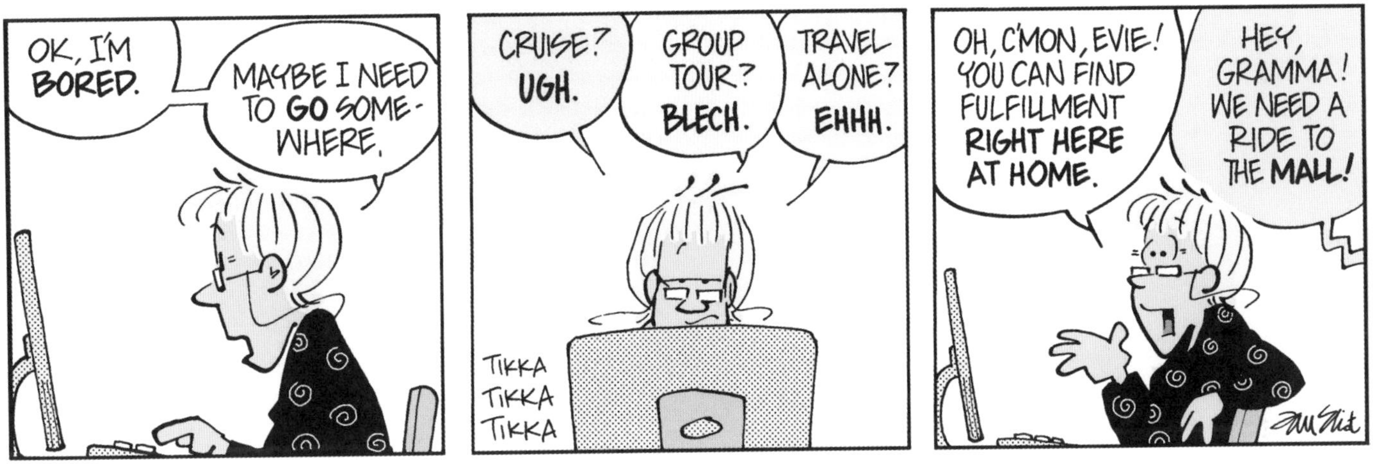
OK, I'M BORED.
MAYBE I NEED TO GO SOMEWHERE.
CRUISE? UGH.
GROUP TOUR? BLECH.
TRAVEL ALONE? EHHH.
TIKKA TIKKA TIKKA
OH, C'MON, EVIE! YOU CAN FIND FULFILLMENT RIGHT HERE AT HOME.
HEY, GRAMMA! WE NEED A RIDE TO THE MALL!

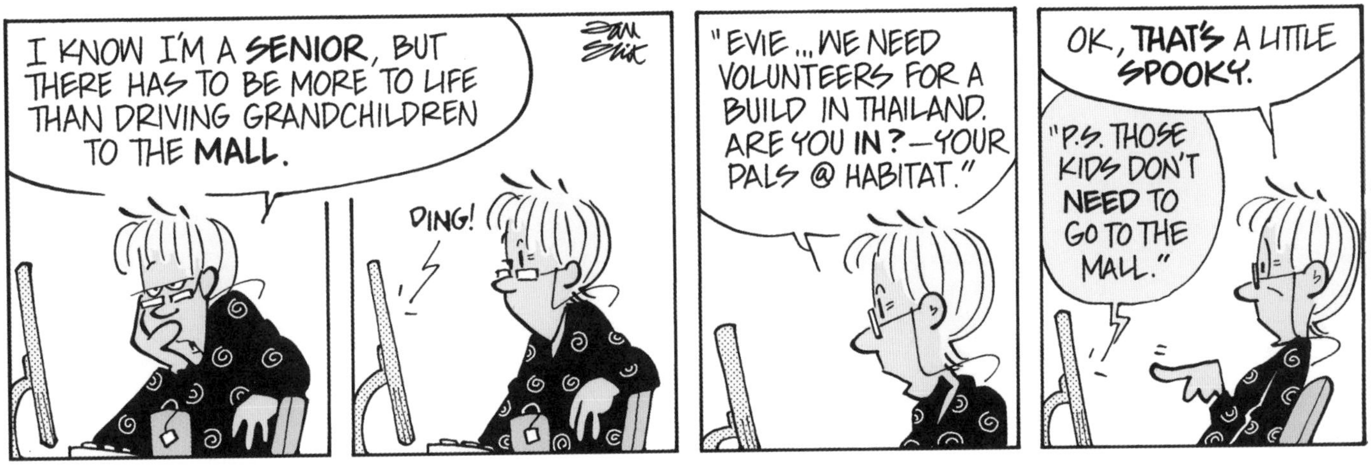
I KNOW I'M A SENIOR, BUT THERE HAS TO BE MORE TO LIFE THAN DRIVING GRANDCHILDREN TO THE MALL.
DING!
"EVIE... WE NEED VOLUNTEERS FOR A BUILD IN THAILAND. ARE YOU IN? —YOUR PALS @ HABITAT."
OK, THAT'S A LITTLE SPOOKY.
"P.S. THOSE KIDS DON'T NEED TO GO TO THE MALL."

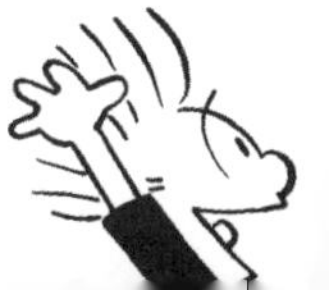

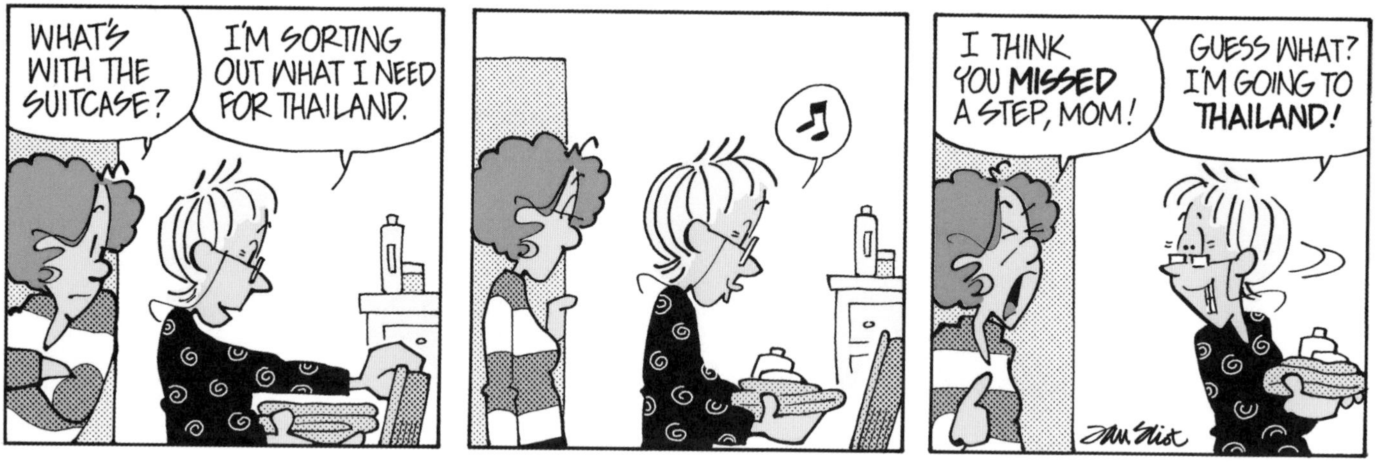
WHAT'S WITH THE SUITCASE?
I'M SORTING OUT WHAT I NEED FOR THAILAND.
I THINK YOU **MISSED** A STEP, MOM!
GUESS WHAT? I'M GOING TO **THAILAND**!

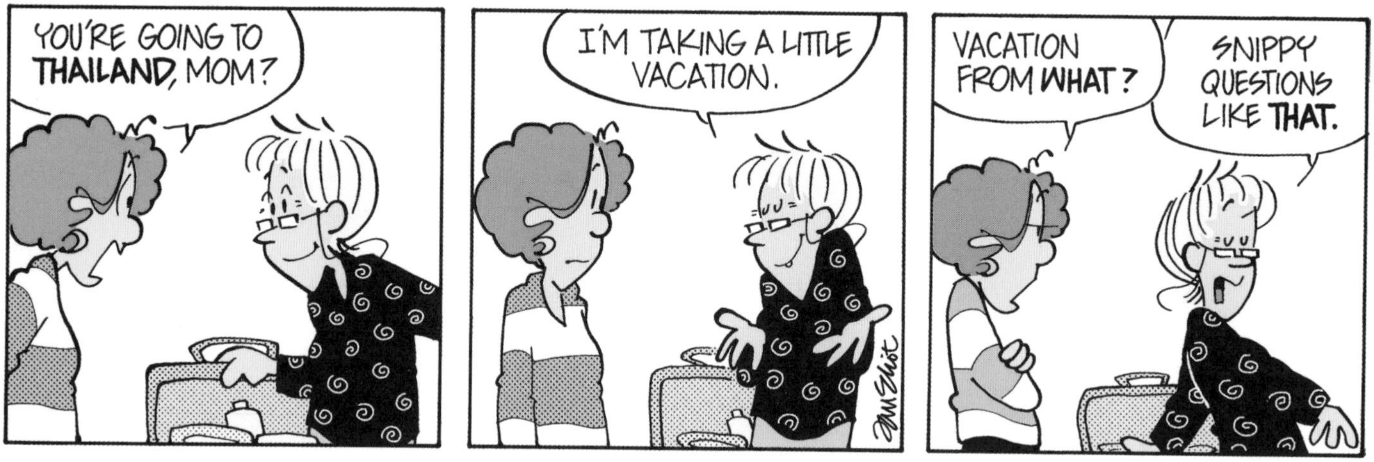
YOU'RE GOING TO **THAILAND**, MOM?
I'M TAKING A LITTLE VACATION.
VACATION FROM **WHAT**?
SNIPPY QUESTIONS LIKE **THAT**.

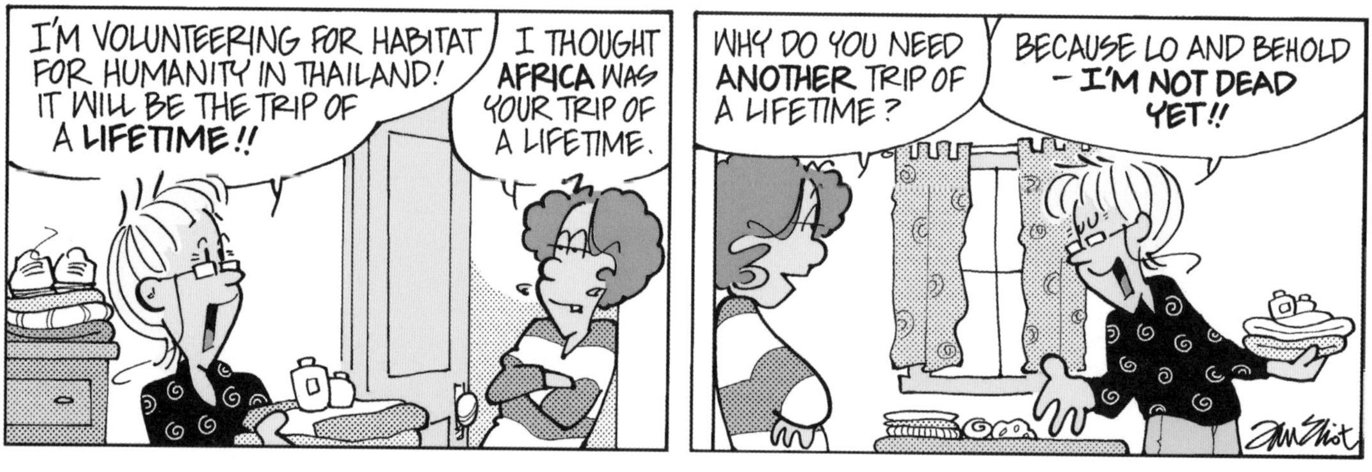
I'M VOLUNTEERING FOR HABITAT FOR HUMANITY IN THAILAND! IT WILL BE THE TRIP OF A **LIFETIME**!!
I THOUGHT **AFRICA** WAS YOUR TRIP OF A LIFETIME.
WHY DO YOU NEED **ANOTHER** TRIP OF A LIFETIME?
BECAUSE LO AND BEHOLD – **I'M NOT DEAD YET**!!

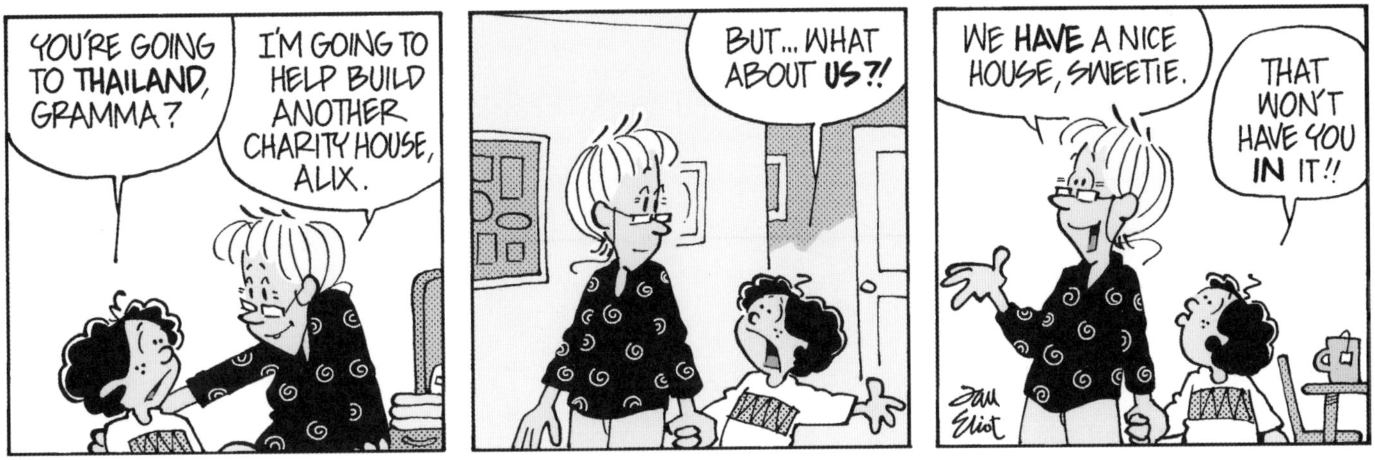
YOU'RE GOING TO **THAILAND**, GRAMMA?
I'M GOING TO HELP BUILD ANOTHER CHARITY HOUSE, ALIX.
BUT... WHAT ABOUT **US**?!
WE **HAVE** A NICE HOUSE, SWEETIE.
THAT WON'T HAVE YOU **IN** IT!!
Jan Eliot

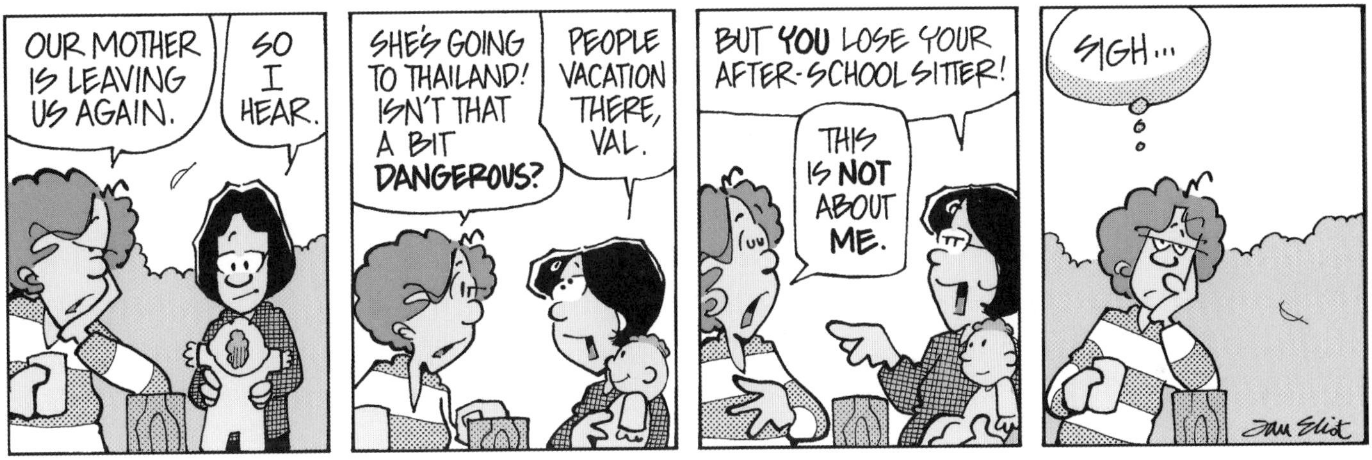
OUR MOTHER IS LEAVING US AGAIN.
SO I HEAR.
SHE'S GOING TO THAILAND! ISN'T THAT A BIT **DANGEROUS**?
PEOPLE VACATION THERE, VAL.
BUT **YOU** LOSE YOUR AFTER-SCHOOL SITTER!
THIS IS **NOT** ABOUT **ME**.
SIGH...
Jan Eliot

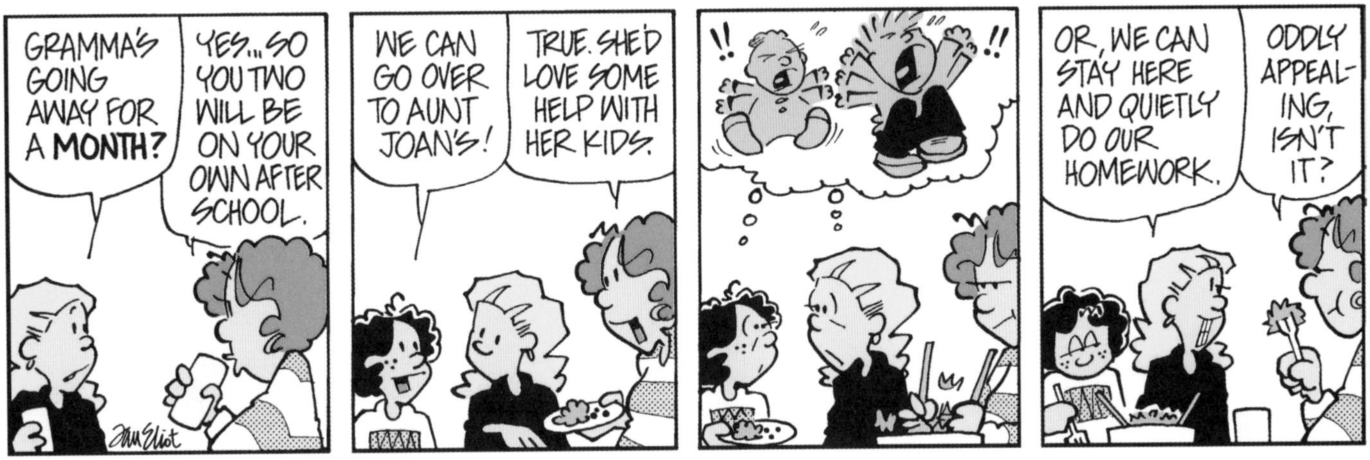
GRAMMA'S GOING AWAY FOR A **MONTH**?
YES... SO YOU TWO WILL BE ON YOUR OWN AFTER SCHOOL.
Jan Eliot
WE CAN GO OVER TO AUNT JOAN'S!
TRUE. SHE'D LOVE SOME HELP WITH HER KIDS.
!!
!!
OR, WE CAN STAY HERE AND QUIETLY DO OUR HOMEWORK.
ODDLY APPEALING, ISN'T IT?

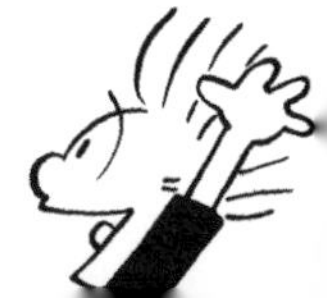

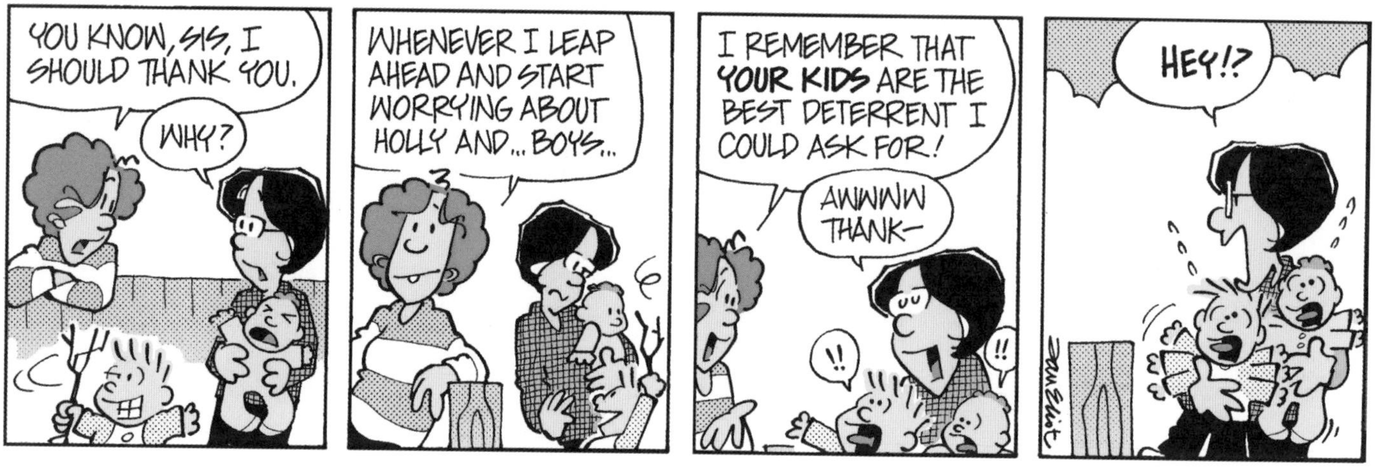
YOU KNOW, SIS, I SHOULD THANK YOU.
WHY?
WHENEVER I LEAP AHEAD AND START WORRYING ABOUT HOLLY AND... BOYS...
I REMEMBER THAT **YOUR KIDS** ARE THE BEST DETERRENT I COULD ASK FOR!
AWWWW THANK—
!!
!!
HEY!?

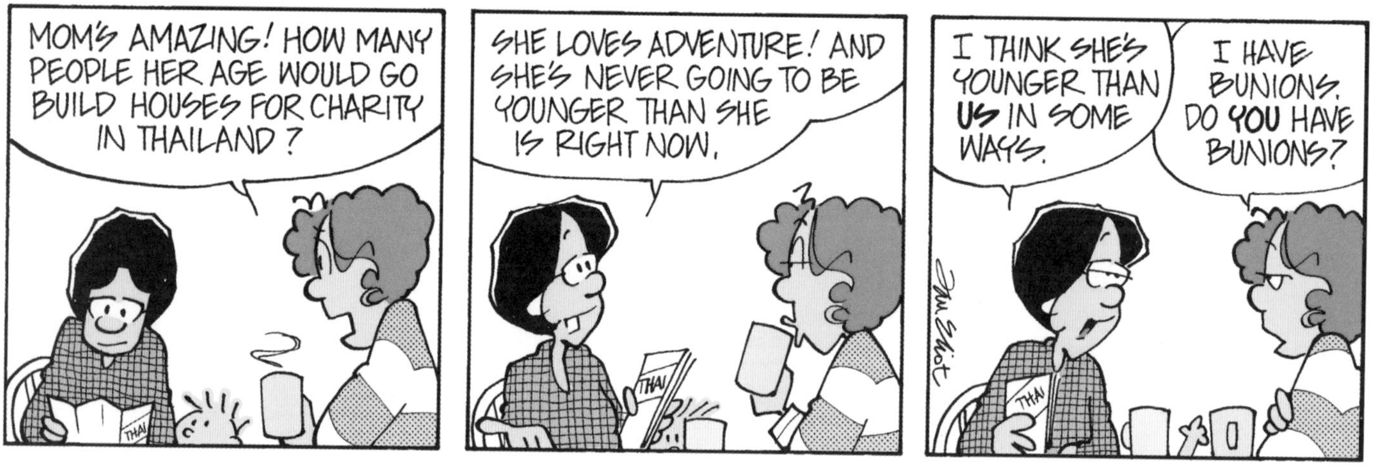
MOM'S AMAZING! HOW MANY PEOPLE HER AGE WOULD GO BUILD HOUSES FOR CHARITY IN THAILAND?
THAI
SHE LOVES ADVENTURE! AND SHE'S NEVER GOING TO BE YOUNGER THAN SHE IS RIGHT NOW.
THAI
I THINK SHE'S YOUNGER THAN **US** IN SOME WAYS.
I HAVE BUNIONS. DO **YOU** HAVE BUNIONS?
THAI

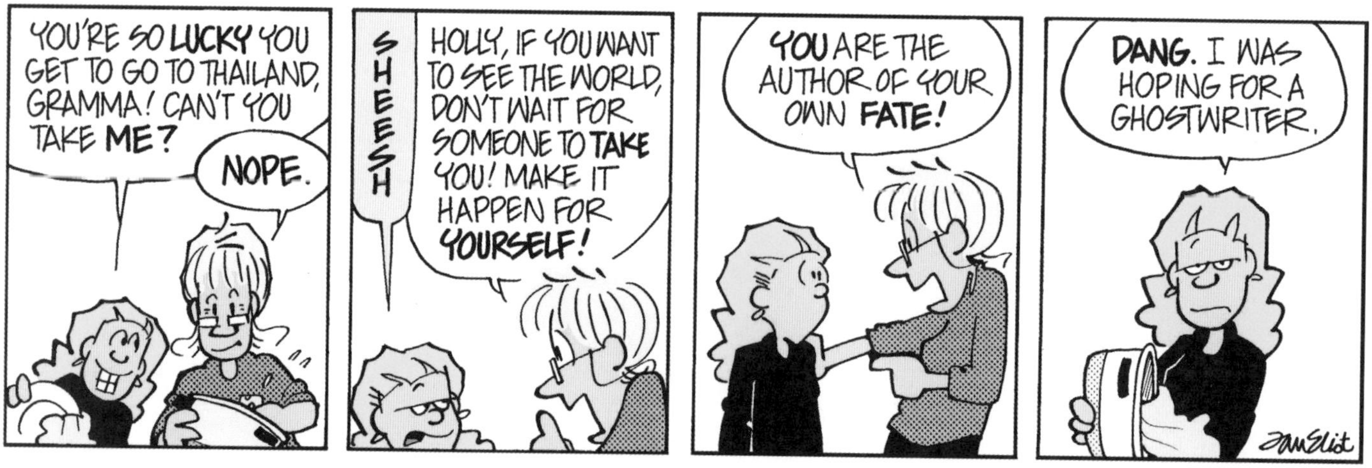
YOU'RE SO **LUCKY** YOU GET TO GO TO THAILAND, GRAMMA! CAN'T YOU TAKE **ME**?
NOPE.
SHEESH
HOLLY, IF YOU WANT TO SEE THE WORLD, DON'T WAIT FOR SOMEONE TO **TAKE** YOU! MAKE IT HAPPEN FOR **YOURSELF**!
YOU ARE THE AUTHOR OF YOUR OWN **FATE**!
DANG. I WAS HOPING FOR A GHOSTWRITER.

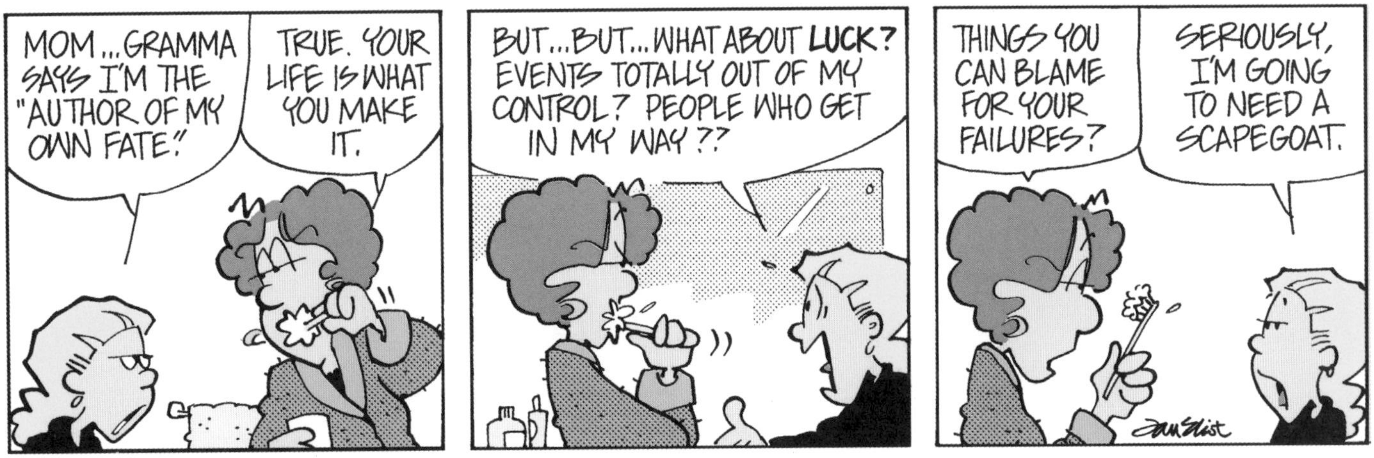
MOM... GRAMMA SAYS I'M THE "AUTHOR OF MY OWN FATE."
TRUE. YOUR LIFE IS WHAT YOU MAKE IT.
BUT... BUT... WHAT ABOUT LUCK? EVENTS TOTALLY OUT OF MY CONTROL? PEOPLE WHO GET IN MY WAY??
THINGS YOU CAN BLAME FOR YOUR FAILURES?
SERIOUSLY, I'M GOING TO NEED A SCAPEGOAT.

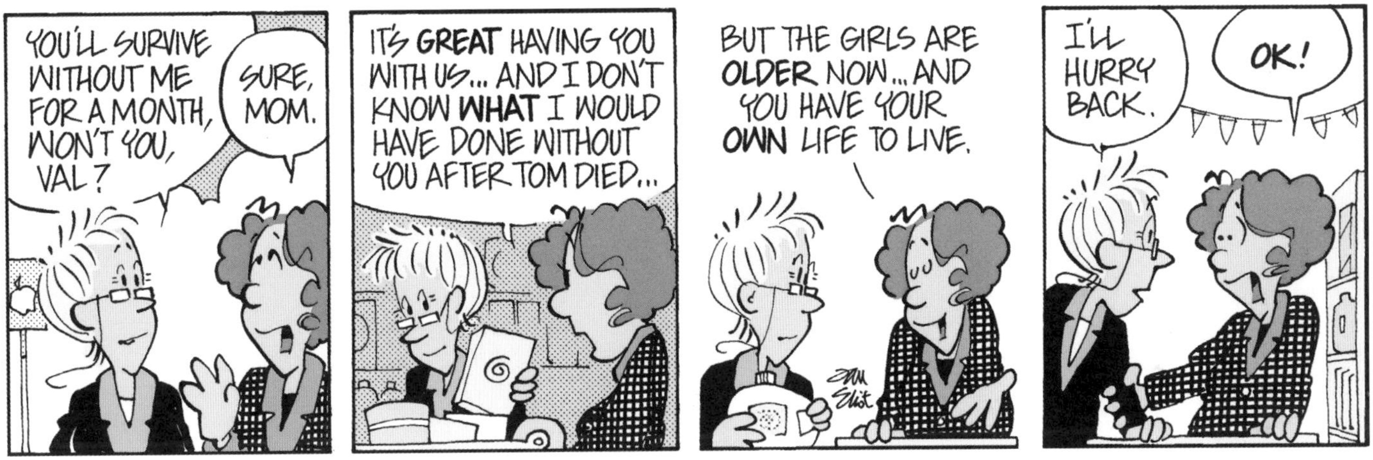
YOU'LL SURVIVE WITHOUT ME FOR A MONTH, WON'T YOU, VAL?
SURE, MOM.
IT'S GREAT HAVING YOU WITH US... AND I DON'T KNOW WHAT I WOULD HAVE DONE WITHOUT YOU AFTER TOM DIED...
BUT THE GIRLS ARE OLDER NOW... AND YOU HAVE YOUR OWN LIFE TO LIVE.
I'LL HURRY BACK.
OK!

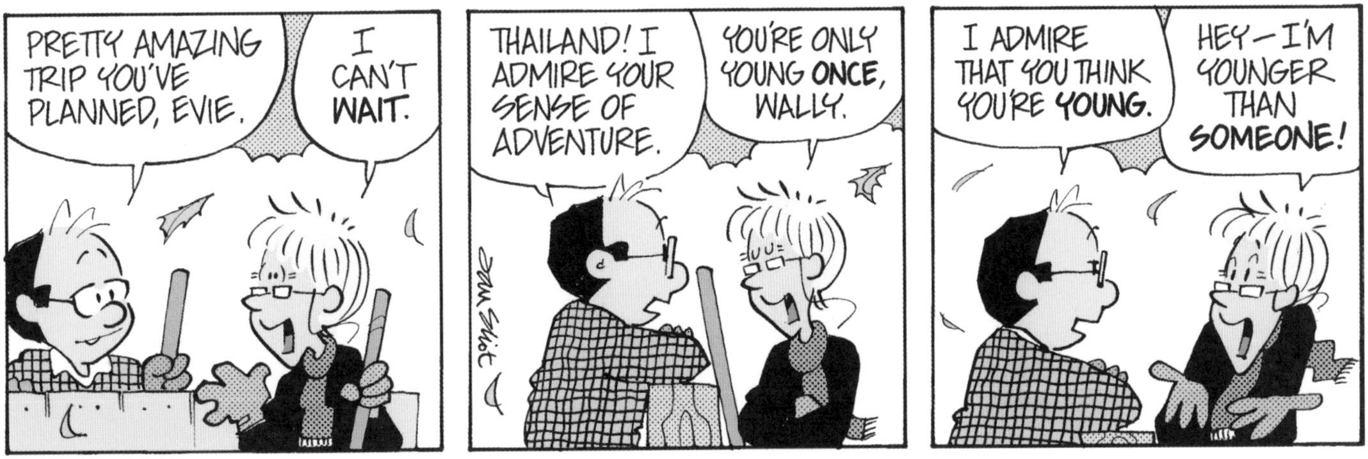
PRETTY AMAZING TRIP YOU'VE PLANNED, EVIE.
I CAN'T WAIT.
THAILAND! I ADMIRE YOUR SENSE OF ADVENTURE.
YOU'RE ONLY YOUNG ONCE, WALLY.
I ADMIRE THAT YOU THINK YOU'RE YOUNG.
HEY—I'M YOUNGER THAN SOMEONE!

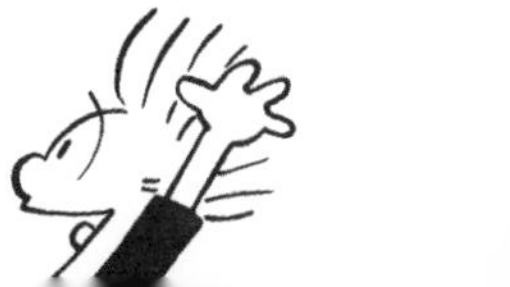

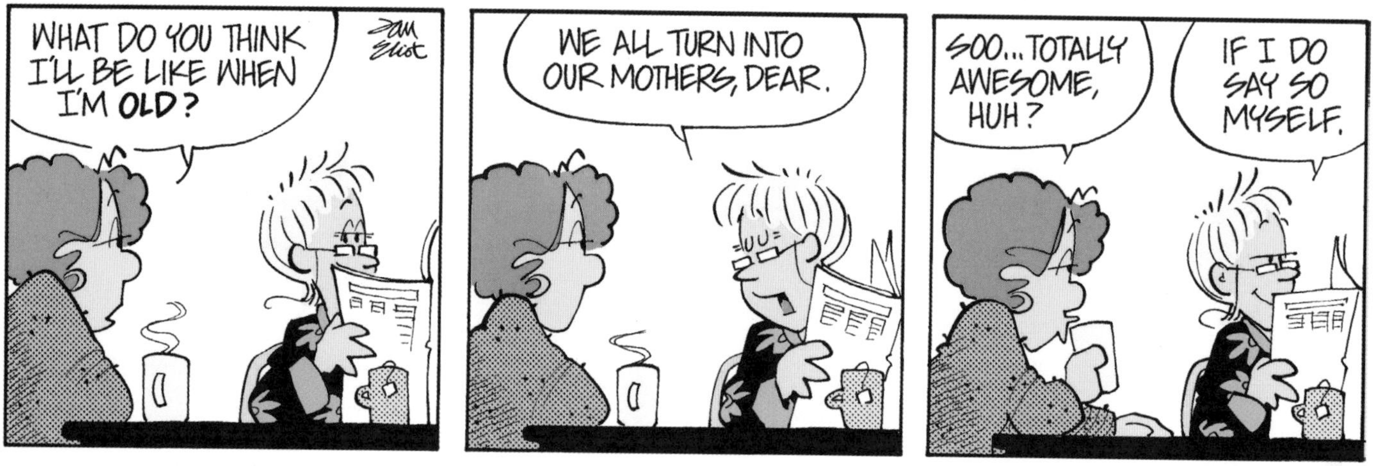
WHAT DO YOU THINK I'LL BE LIKE WHEN I'M **OLD**?
Jan Eliot
WE ALL TURN INTO OUR MOTHERS, DEAR.
SOO... TOTALLY AWESOME, HUH?
IF I DO SAY SO MYSELF.

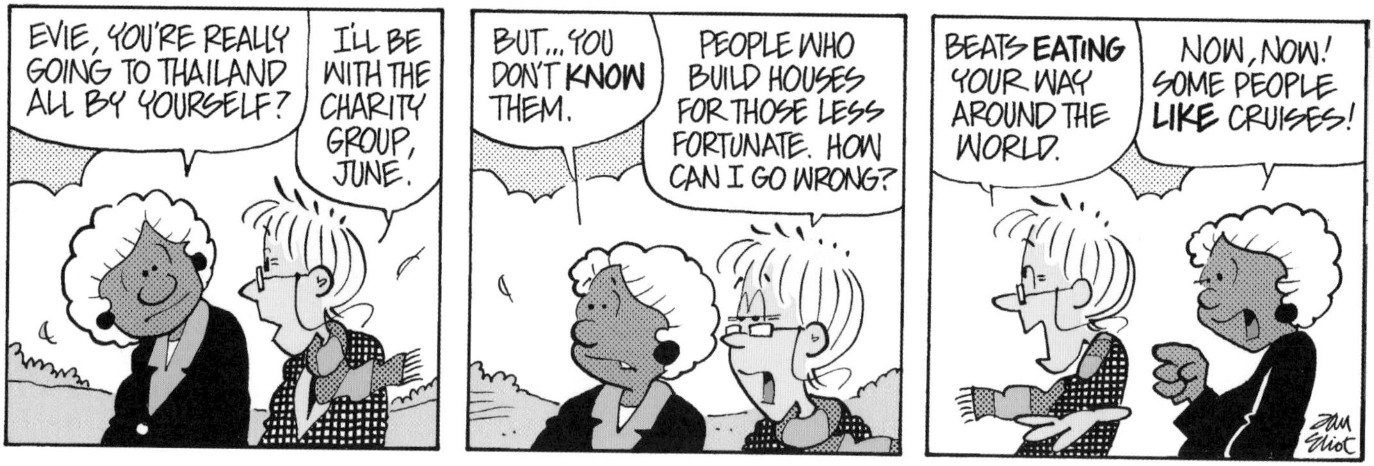
EVIE, YOU'RE REALLY GOING TO THAILAND ALL BY YOURSELF?
I'LL BE WITH THE CHARITY GROUP, JUNE.
BUT... YOU DON'T **KNOW** THEM.
PEOPLE WHO BUILD HOUSES FOR THOSE LESS FORTUNATE. HOW CAN I GO WRONG?
BEATS **EATING** YOUR WAY AROUND THE WORLD.
NOW, NOW! SOME PEOPLE **LIKE** CRUISES!
Jan Eliot

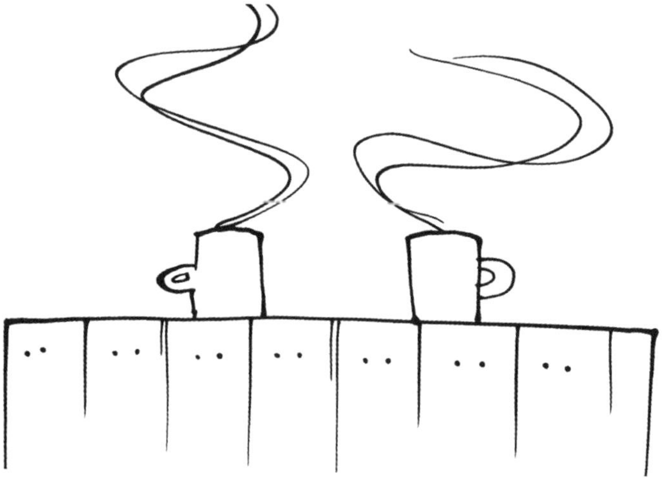

Stone Soup

WALLY? ARE YOU READY?
JUST A SEC —
WHAT ARE YOU **DOING?**
I'M MAKING MYSELF "**PRESENTABLE.**"
UNCLE WALLY?! LOOKIN' **GOOD** FOR PARENTS' NIGHT!!
YOU POOR **NERD.**
I CAN'T **WAIT** TO GET BACK HOME SO I CAN PUT MY **BELT** BACK ON.

Stone Soup

IS IT REALLY **NOVEMBER** ?!
NO KIDDING. WHAT A GREAT DAY!
SOOO... WHAT'S THE LATEST ON GLOBAL WARMING?
"THE JURY'S STILL OUT..."
DO YOU THINK WE SHOULD WATER THE LAWN??

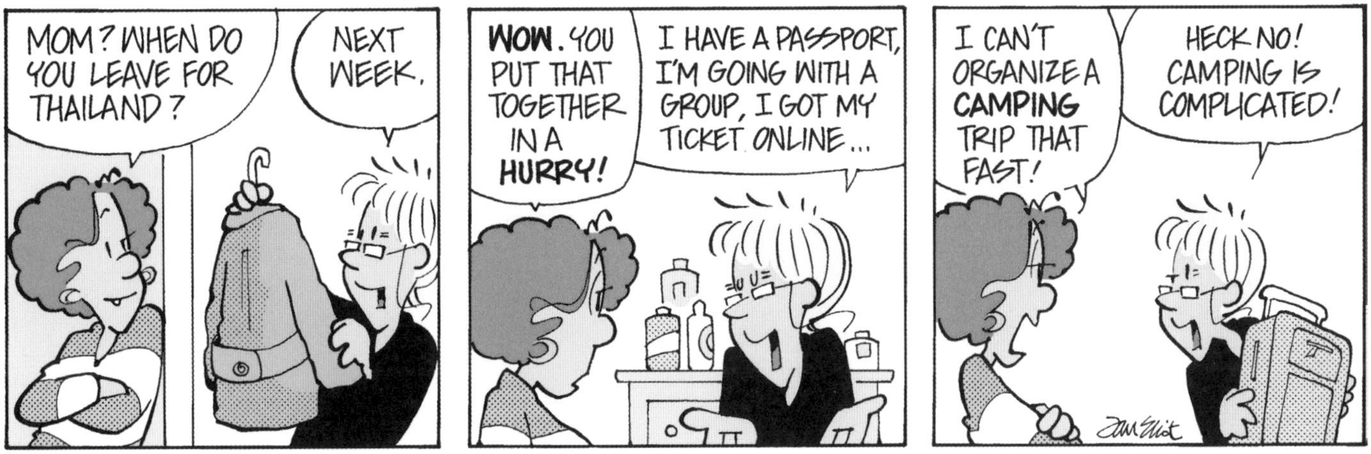
MOM? WHEN DO YOU LEAVE FOR THAILAND?
NEXT WEEK.
WOW. YOU PUT THAT TOGETHER IN A **HURRY!**
I HAVE A PASSPORT, I'M GOING WITH A GROUP, I GOT MY TICKET ONLINE...
I CAN'T ORGANIZE A **CAMPING** TRIP THAT FAST!
HECK NO! CAMPING IS COMPLICATED!

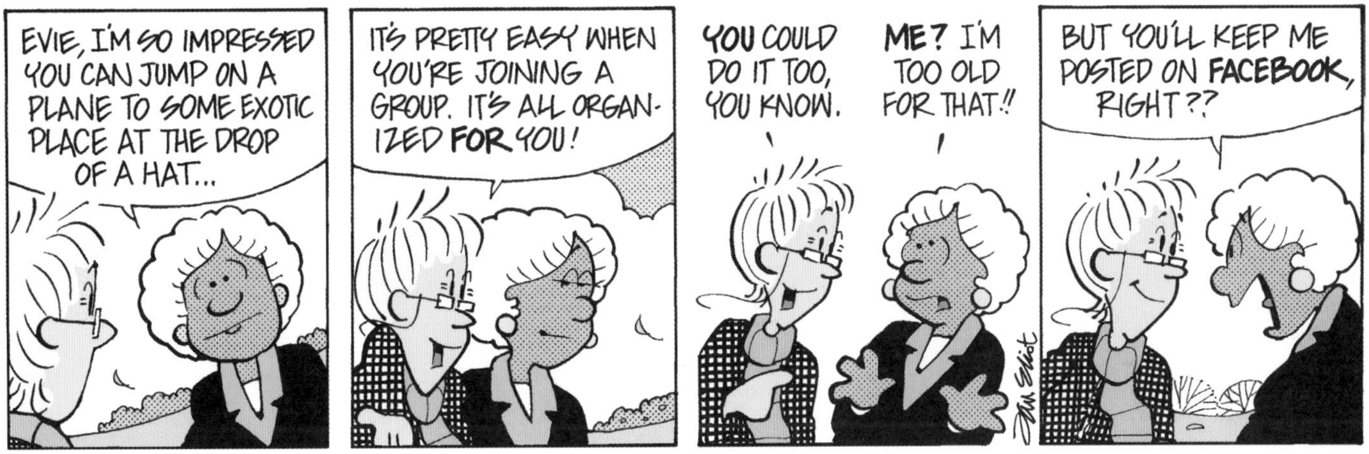
EVIE, I'M SO IMPRESSED YOU CAN JUMP ON A PLANE TO SOME EXOTIC PLACE AT THE DROP OF A HAT...
IT'S PRETTY EASY WHEN YOU'RE JOINING A GROUP. IT'S ALL ORGANIZED **FOR** YOU!
YOU COULD DO IT TOO, YOU KNOW.
ME? I'M TOO OLD FOR THAT!!
BUT YOU'LL KEEP ME POSTED ON **FACEBOOK**, RIGHT??

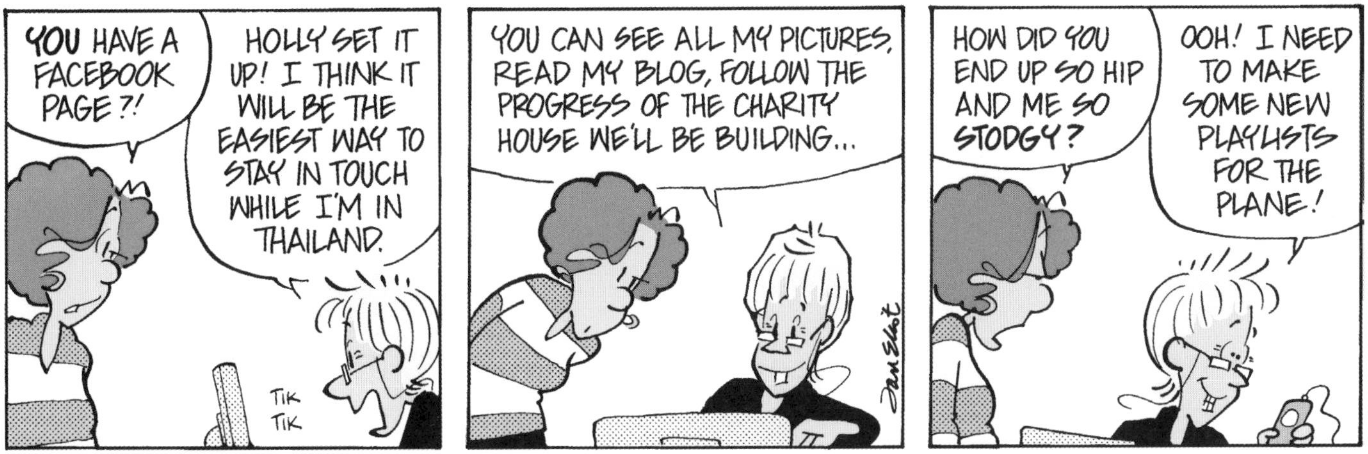
YOU HAVE A FACEBOOK PAGE?!
HOLLY SET IT UP! I THINK IT WILL BE THE EASIEST WAY TO STAY IN TOUCH WHILE I'M IN THAILAND.
TIK TIK
YOU CAN SEE ALL MY PICTURES, READ MY BLOG, FOLLOW THE PROGRESS OF THE CHARITY HOUSE WE'LL BE BUILDING...
HOW DID YOU END UP SO HIP AND ME SO **STODGY?**
OOH! I NEED TO MAKE SOME NEW PLAYLISTS FOR THE PLANE!

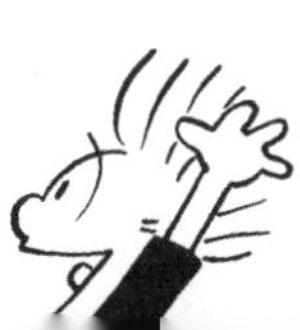

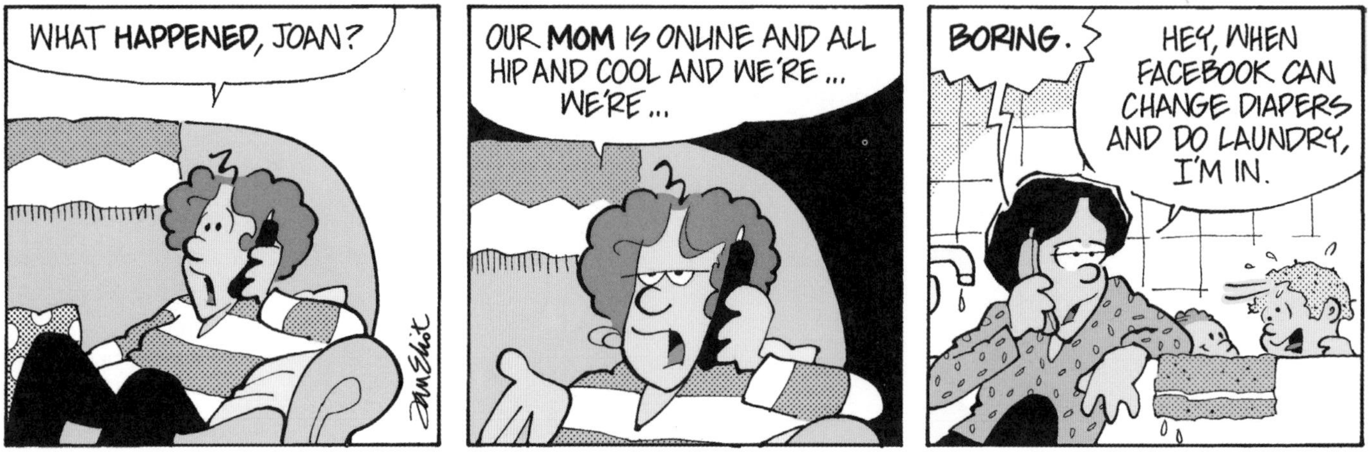
WHAT HAPPENED, JOAN?
OUR MOM IS ONLINE AND ALL HIP AND COOL AND WE'RE ... WE'RE ...
BORING.
HEY, WHEN FACEBOOK CAN CHANGE DIAPERS AND DO LAUNDRY, I'M IN.

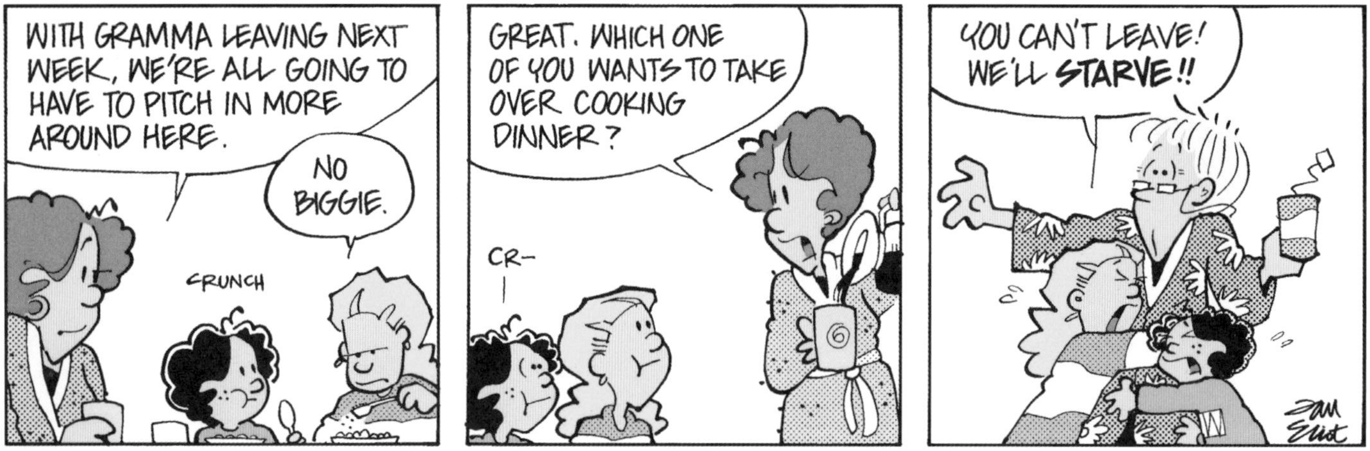
WITH GRAMMA LEAVING NEXT WEEK, WE'RE ALL GOING TO HAVE TO PITCH IN MORE AROUND HERE.
CRUNCH
NO BIGGIE.
GREAT. WHICH ONE OF YOU WANTS TO TAKE OVER COOKING DINNER?
CR–
YOU CAN'T LEAVE! WE'LL STARVE!!

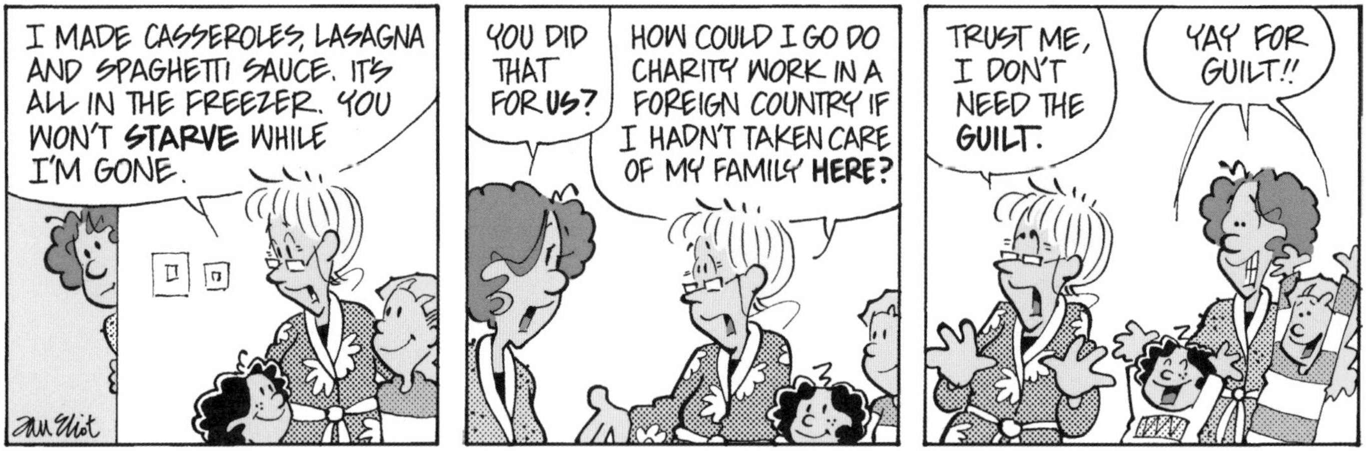
I MADE CASSEROLES, LASAGNA AND SPAGHETTI SAUCE. IT'S ALL IN THE FREEZER. YOU WON'T STARVE WHILE I'M GONE.
YOU DID THAT FOR US?
HOW COULD I GO DO CHARITY WORK IN A FOREIGN COUNTRY IF I HADN'T TAKEN CARE OF MY FAMILY HERE?
TRUST ME, I DON'T NEED THE GUILT.
YAY FOR GUILT!!

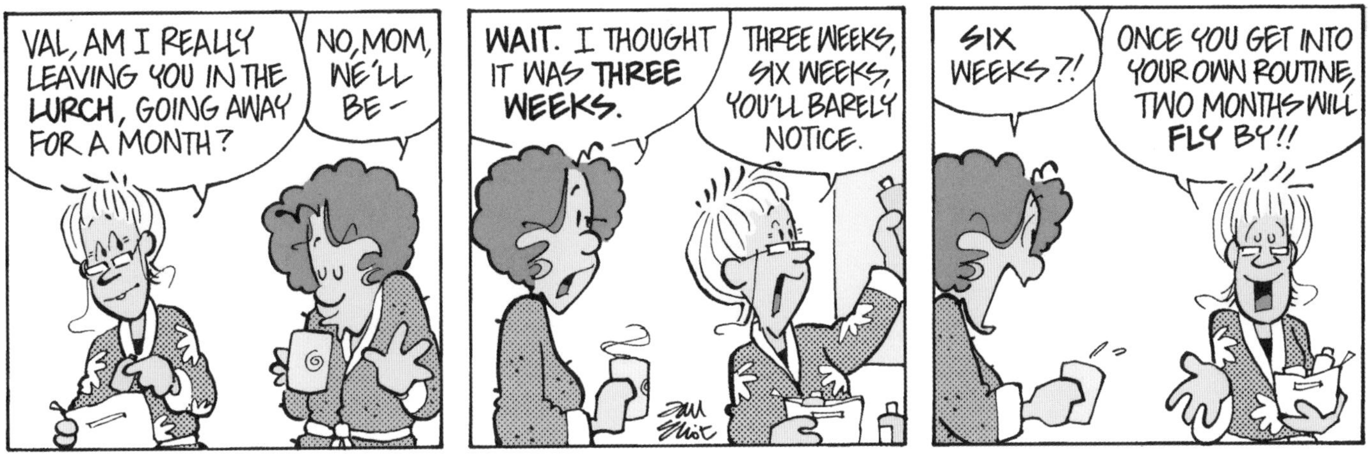
VAL, AM I REALLY LEAVING YOU IN THE **LURCH**, GOING AWAY FOR A MONTH?
NO, MOM, WE'LL BE -
WAIT. I THOUGHT IT WAS **THREE WEEKS.**
THREE WEEKS, SIX WEEKS, YOU'LL BARELY NOTICE.
SIX WEEKS?!
ONCE YOU GET INTO YOUR OWN ROUTINE, TWO MONTHS WILL **FLY** BY!!

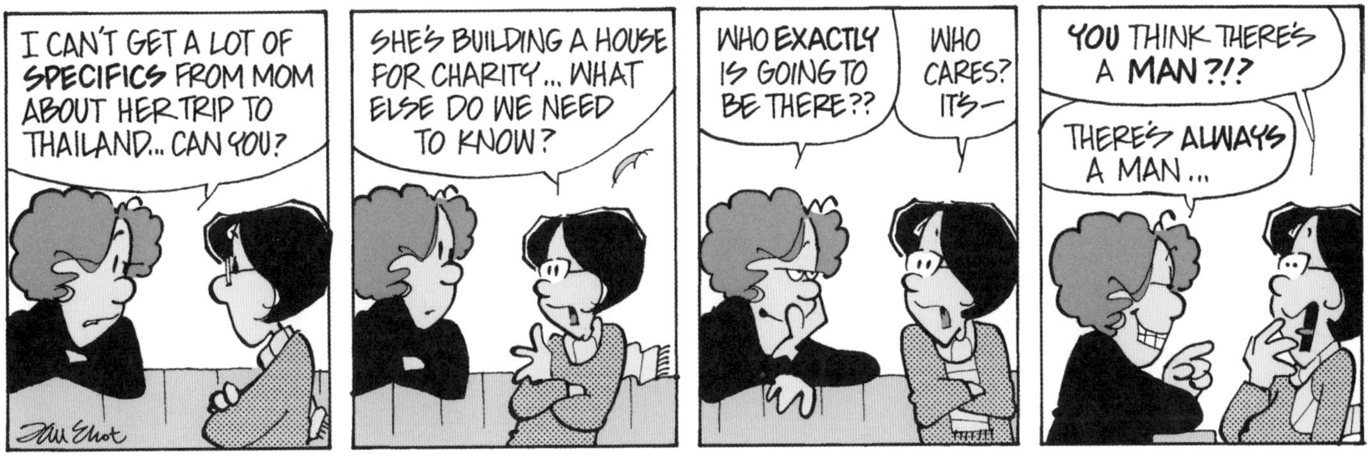
I CAN'T GET A LOT OF **SPECIFICS** FROM MOM ABOUT HER TRIP TO THAILAND... CAN YOU?
SHE'S BUILDING A HOUSE FOR CHARITY... WHAT ELSE DO WE NEED TO KNOW?
WHO **EXACTLY** IS GOING TO BE THERE??
WHO CARES? IT'S —
YOU THINK THERE'S A **MAN**?!?
THERE'S **ALWAYS** A MAN...

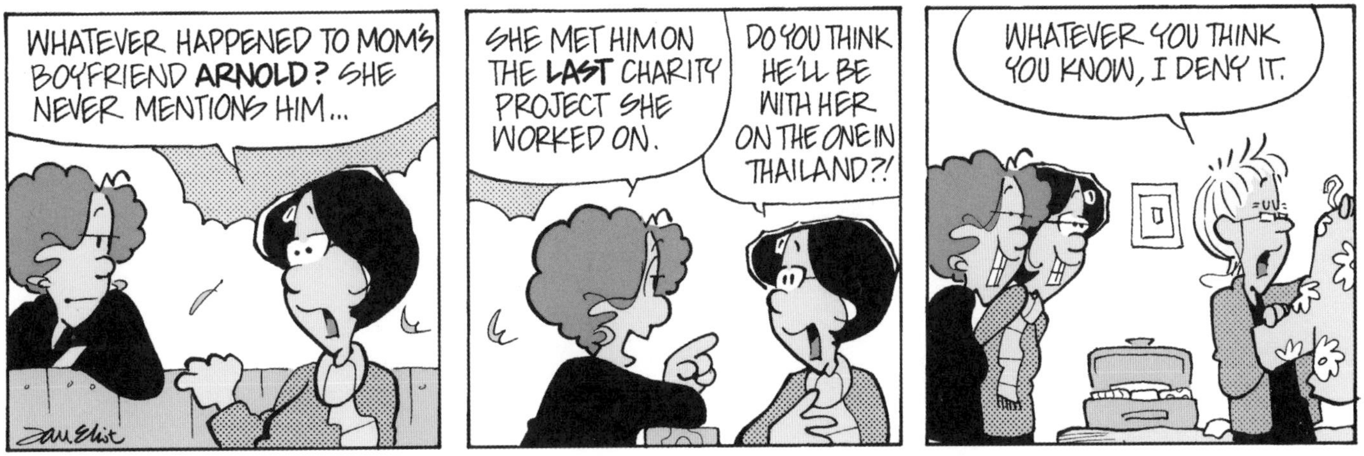
WHATEVER HAPPENED TO MOM'S BOYFRIEND **ARNOLD**? SHE NEVER MENTIONS HIM...
SHE MET HIM ON THE **LAST** CHARITY PROJECT SHE WORKED ON.
DO YOU THINK HE'LL BE WITH HER ON THE ONE IN THAILAND?!
WHATEVER YOU THINK YOU KNOW, I DENY IT.

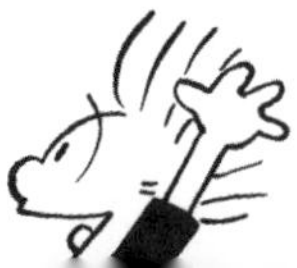

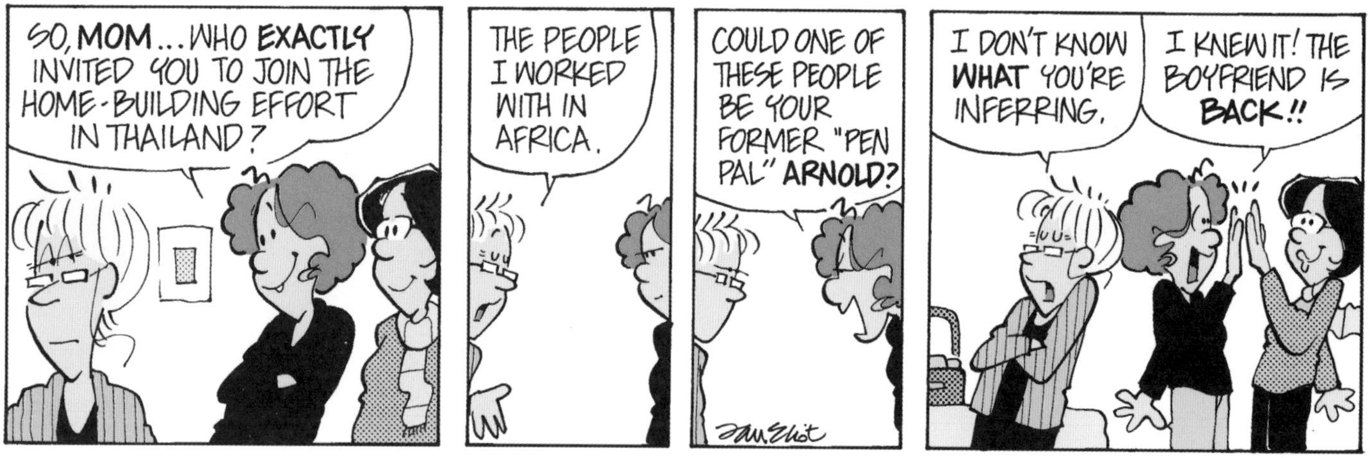
SO, MOM... WHO EXACTLY INVITED YOU TO JOIN THE HOME-BUILDING EFFORT IN THAILAND?
THE PEOPLE I WORKED WITH IN AFRICA.
COULD ONE OF THESE PEOPLE BE YOUR FORMER "PEN PAL" ARNOLD?
I DON'T KNOW WHAT YOU'RE INFERRING.
I KNEW IT! THE BOYFRIEND IS BACK!!

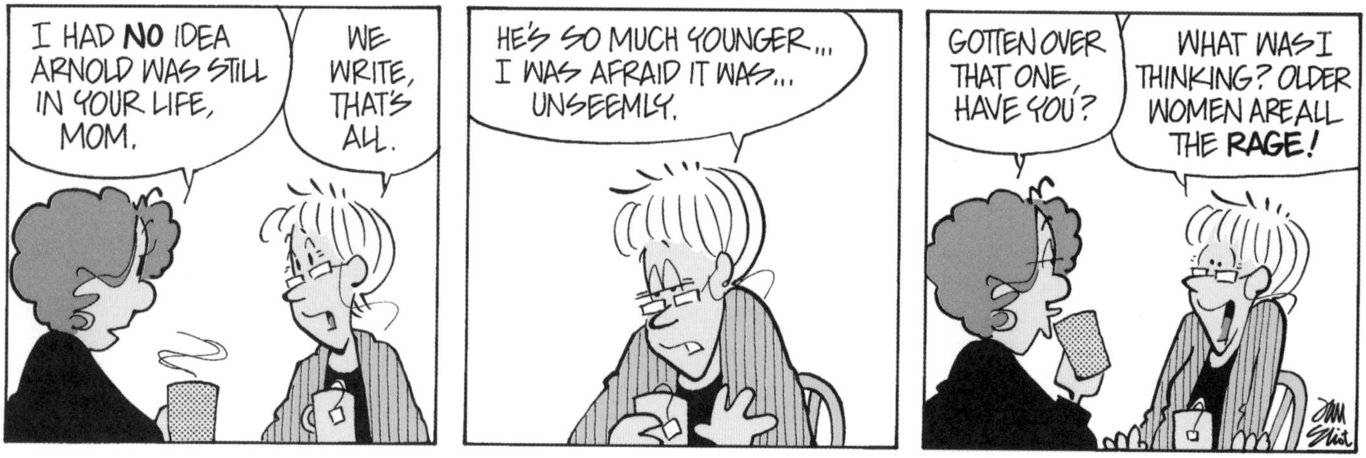
I HAD NO IDEA ARNOLD WAS STILL IN YOUR LIFE, MOM.
WE WRITE, THAT'S ALL.
HE'S SO MUCH YOUNGER... I WAS AFRAID IT WAS... UNSEEMLY.
GOTTEN OVER THAT ONE, HAVE YOU?
WHAT WAS I THINKING? OLDER WOMEN ARE ALL THE RAGE!

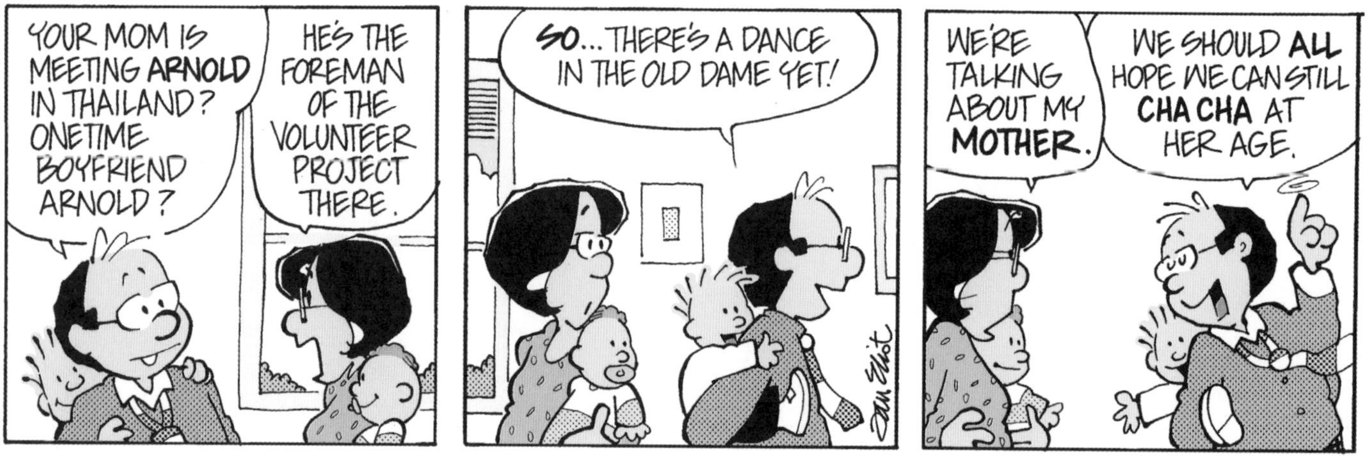
YOUR MOM IS MEETING ARNOLD IN THAILAND? ONETIME BOYFRIEND ARNOLD?
HE'S THE FOREMAN OF THE VOLUNTEER PROJECT THERE.
SO... THERE'S A DANCE IN THE OLD DAME YET!
WE'RE TALKING ABOUT MY MOTHER.
WE SHOULD ALL HOPE WE CAN STILL CHA CHA AT HER AGE.

Stone Soup

HEY, ANDY...HOW'S SCHOOL GOING?

'K.

ANY NEW FRIENDS?

COUPLE.

ANY OF THEM **GIRLS**?

NOT **GOIN'** THERE, AUNT VAL.

SHEESH. CAN'T GET MUCH OUT OF HIM, CAN YOU?

WHAT DO YOU MEAN?

HIS GRADES ARE FINE, HE HAS A GREAT GROUP OF FRIENDS, HE HAS A GIRLFRIEND BUT IT'S NOT SERIOUS.

YOU GOT ALL **THAT** FROM SEVEN MUMBLED WORDS?

I'M THE **COOL** AUNT, I SPEAK **DUDE**.

Stone Soup

ANOTHER THANKSGIVING... HOW MANY HAVE WE SPENT TOGETHER NOW?
I'VE LOST COUNT.
ALL THOSE YEARS OF TURKEY AND GRAVY AND DRESSING JUST FLOW TOGETHER IN MY MIND...
AND WIND UP HERE.
THERE? NO, THAT'S PIE.

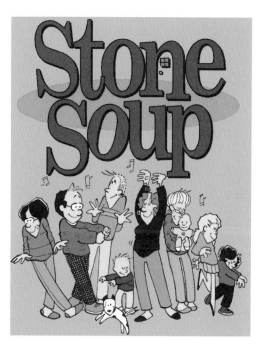

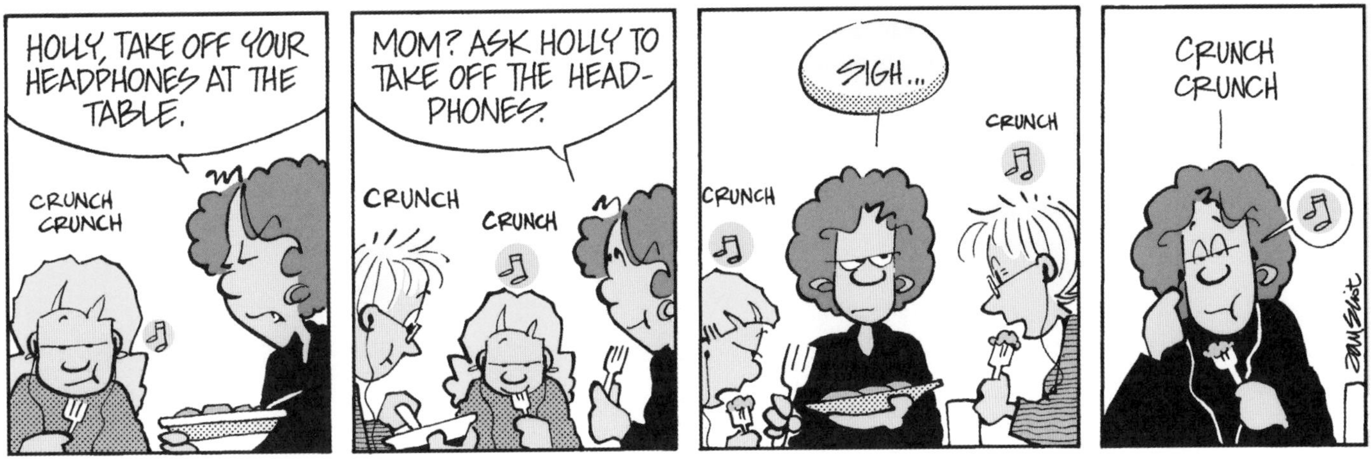
HOLLY, TAKE OFF YOUR HEADPHONES AT THE TABLE.
CRUNCH CRUNCH
MOM? ASK HOLLY TO TAKE OFF THE HEAD-PHONES.
CRUNCH
CRUNCH
SIGH...
CRUNCH
CRUNCH
CRUNCH CRUNCH

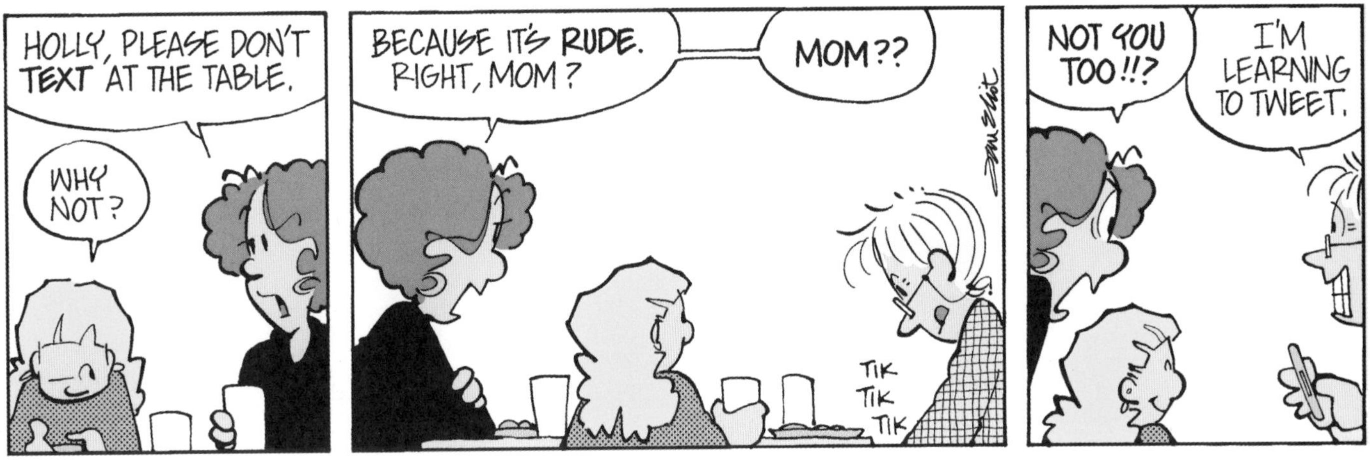
HOLLY, PLEASE DON'T **TEXT** AT THE TABLE.
WHY NOT?
BECAUSE IT'S **RUDE.** RIGHT, MOM?
MOM??
TIK TIK TIK
NOT YOU TOO!!?
I'M LEARNING TO TWEET.

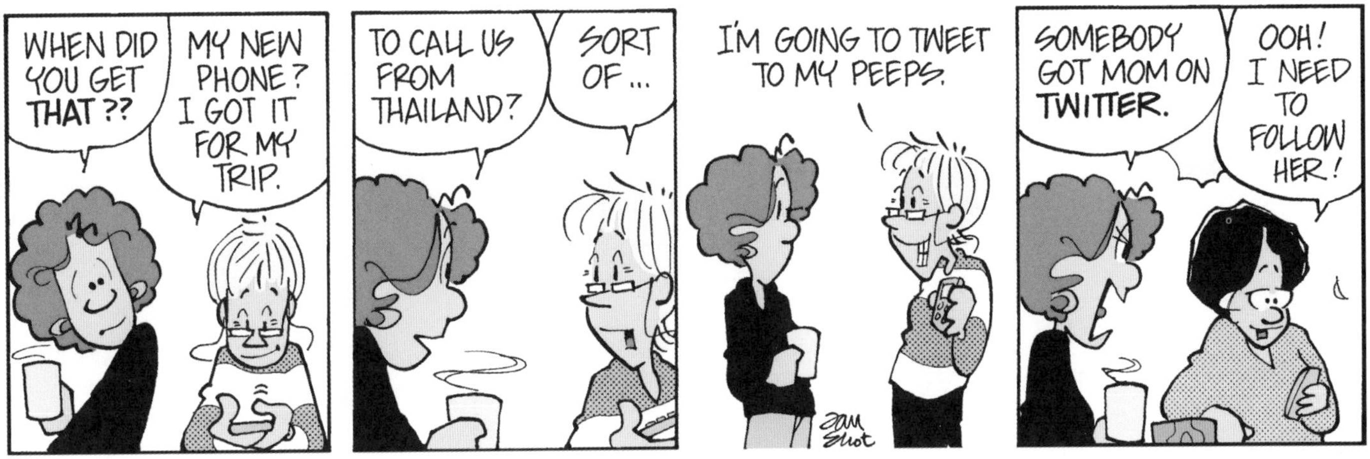
WHEN DID YOU GET **THAT**??
MY NEW PHONE? I GOT IT FOR MY TRIP.
TO CALL US FROM THAILAND?
SORT OF...
I'M GOING TO TWEET TO MY PEEPS.
SOMEBODY GOT MOM ON **TWITTER.**
OOH! I NEED TO FOLLOW HER!

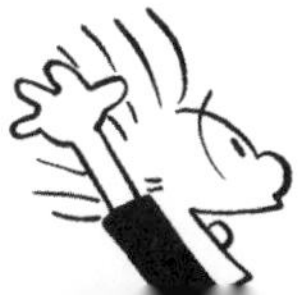

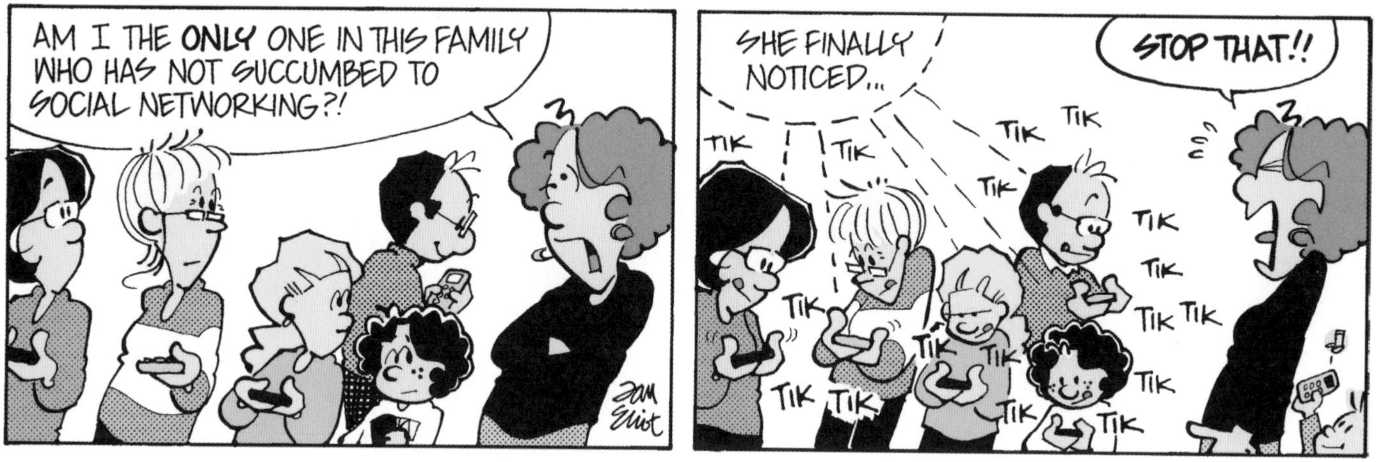
AM I THE **ONLY** ONE IN THIS FAMILY WHO HAS NOT SUCCUMBED TO SOCIAL NETWORKING?!
SHE FINALLY NOTICED...
TIK TIK TIK TIK TIK TIK TIK TIK TIK TIK TIK TIK TIK TIK TIK
STOP THAT!!

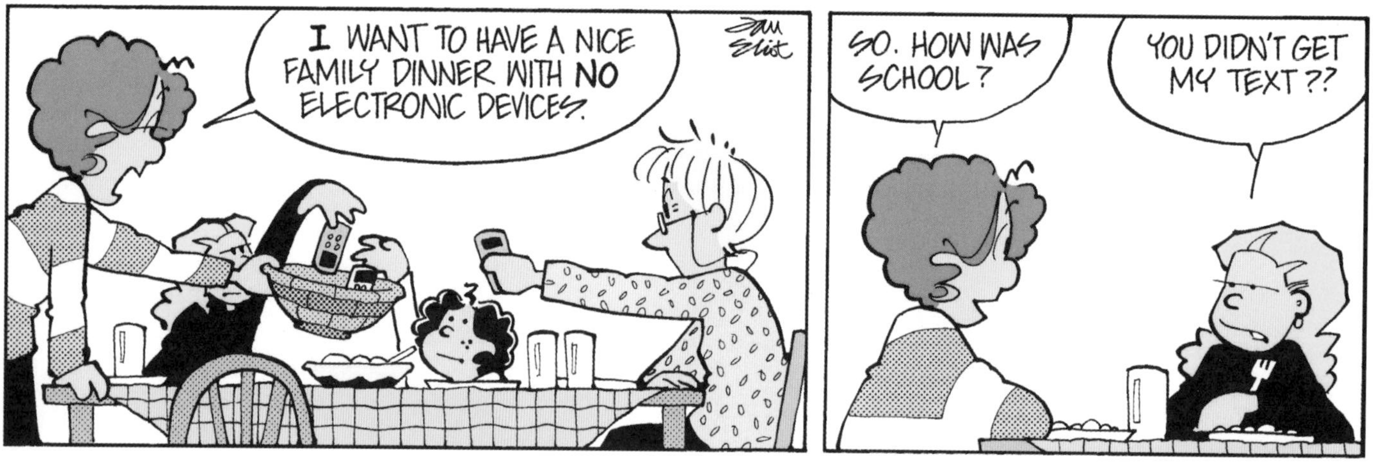
I WANT TO HAVE A NICE FAMILY DINNER WITH **NO** ELECTRONIC DEVICES.
SO. HOW WAS SCHOOL?
YOU DIDN'T GET MY TEXT??

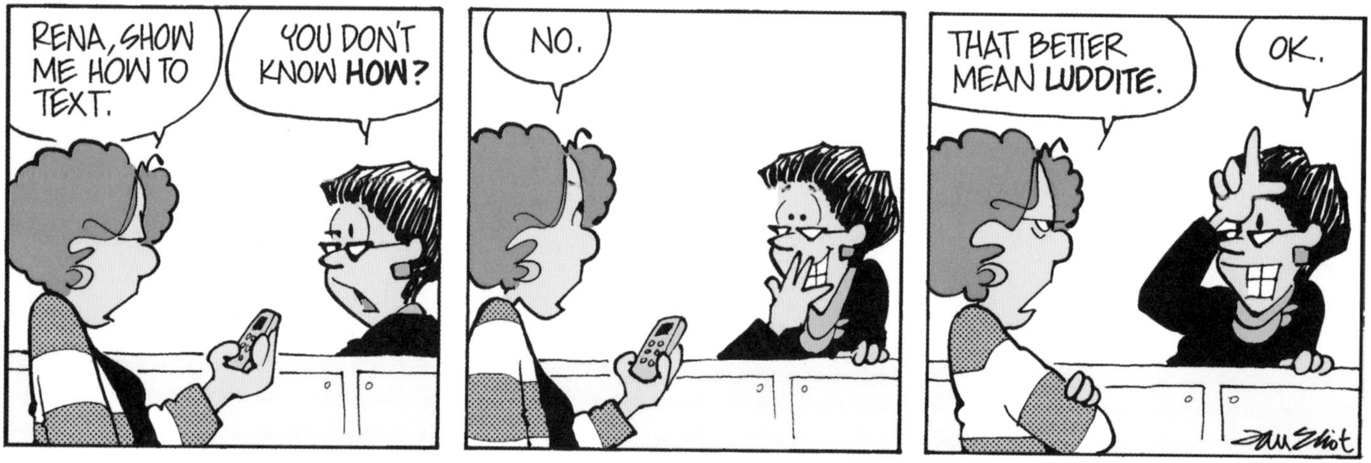
RENA, SHOW ME HOW TO TEXT.
YOU DON'T KNOW **HOW**?
NO.
THAT BETTER MEAN **LUDDITE**.
OK.

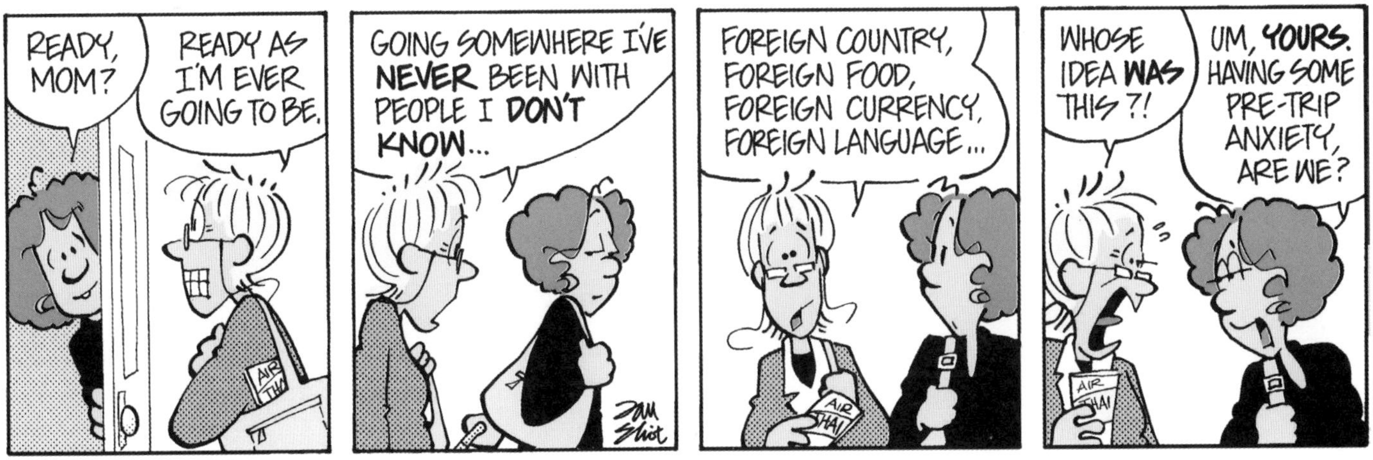
READY, MOM?
READY AS I'M EVER GOING TO BE.
GOING SOMEWHERE I'VE **NEVER** BEEN WITH PEOPLE I **DON'T KNOW**...
AIR THAI
FOREIGN COUNTRY, FOREIGN FOOD, FOREIGN CURRENCY, FOREIGN LANGUAGE...
WHOSE IDEA **WAS** THIS?!
UM, **YOURS.** HAVING SOME PRE-TRIP ANXIETY, ARE WE?

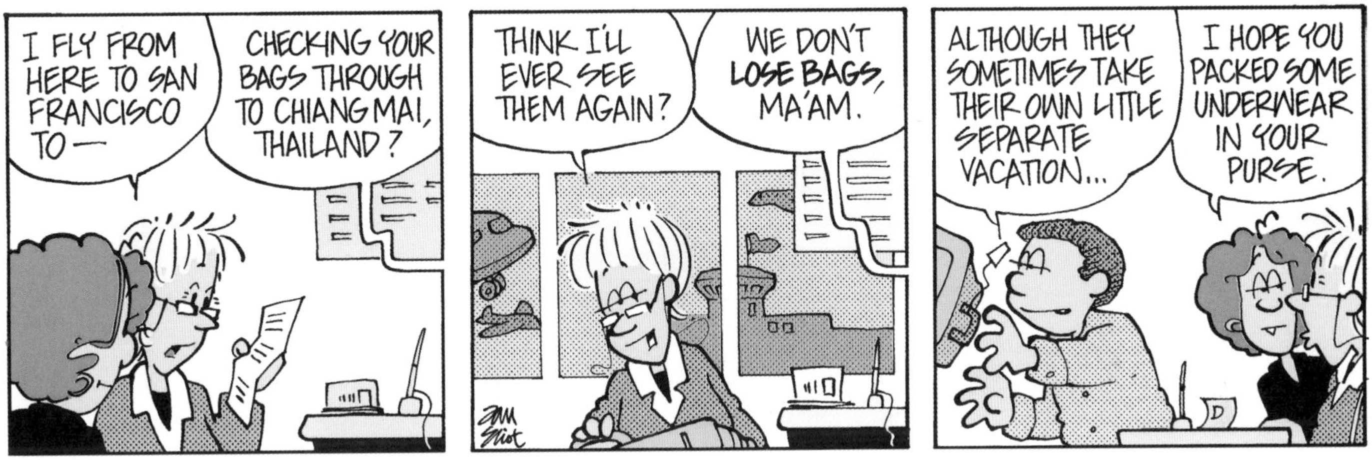
I FLY FROM HERE TO SAN FRANCISCO TO—
CHECKING YOUR BAGS THROUGH TO CHIANG MAI, THAILAND?
THINK I'LL EVER SEE THEM AGAIN?
WE DON'T **LOSE BAGS**, MA'AM.
ALTHOUGH THEY SOMETIMES TAKE THEIR OWN LITTLE SEPARATE VACATION...
I HOPE YOU PACKED SOME UNDERWEAR IN YOUR PURSE.

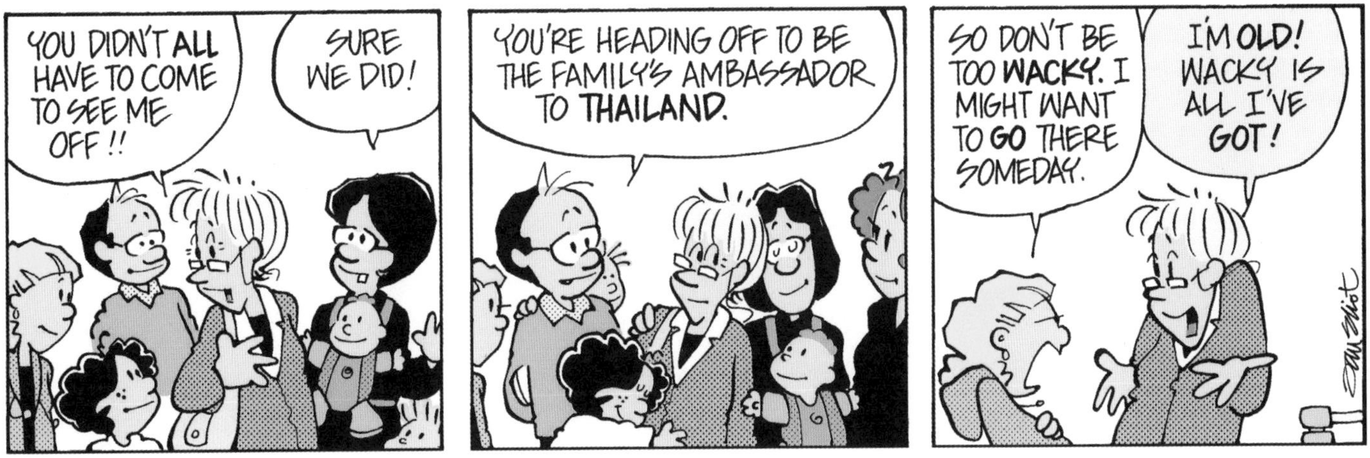
YOU DIDN'T **ALL** HAVE TO COME TO SEE ME OFF!!
SURE WE DID!
YOU'RE HEADING OFF TO BE THE FAMILY'S AMBASSADOR TO **THAILAND**.
SO DON'T BE TOO **WACKY**. I MIGHT WANT TO **GO** THERE SOMEDAY.
I'M **OLD**! WACKY IS ALL I'VE **GOT**!

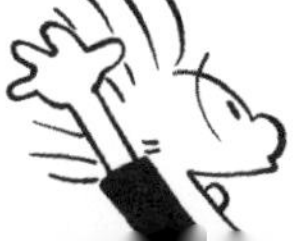

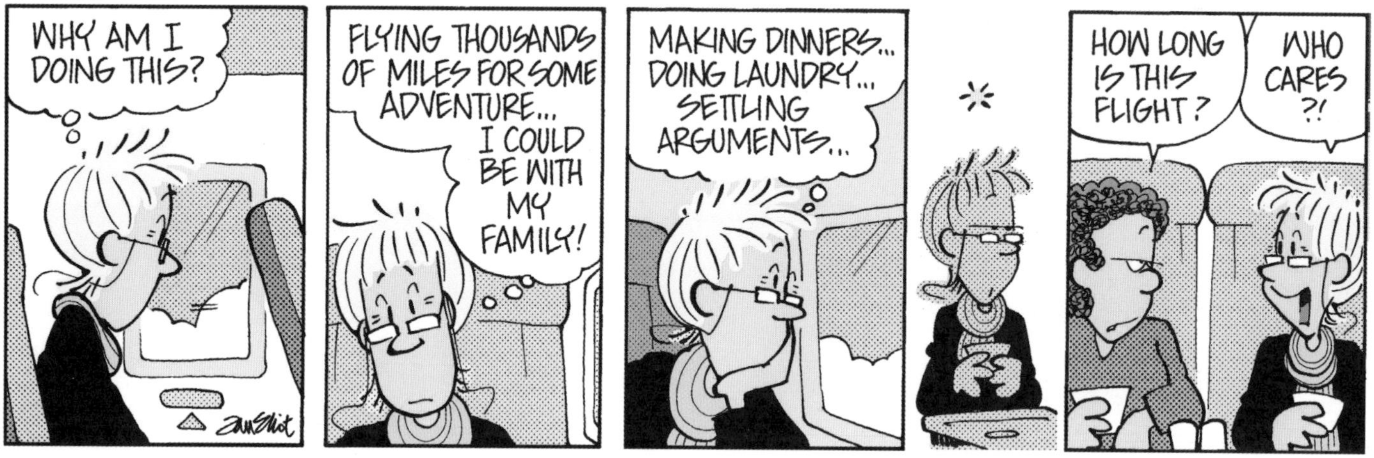
WHY AM I DOING THIS?
FLYING THOUSANDS OF MILES FOR SOME ADVENTURE...
I COULD BE WITH MY FAMILY!
MAKING DINNERS... DOING LAUNDRY... SETTLING ARGUMENTS...
HOW LONG IS THIS FLIGHT?
WHO CARES ?!

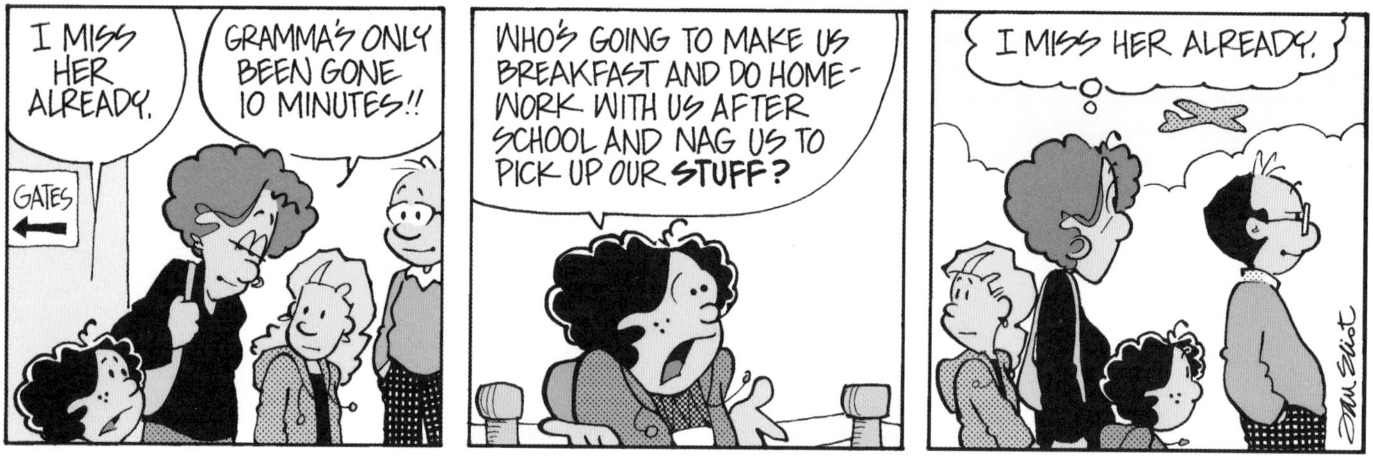
I MISS HER ALREADY.
GRAMMA'S ONLY BEEN GONE 10 MINUTES!!
GATES
WHO'S GOING TO MAKE US BREAKFAST AND DO HOMEWORK WITH US AFTER SCHOOL AND NAG US TO PICK UP OUR STUFF?
I MISS HER ALREADY.

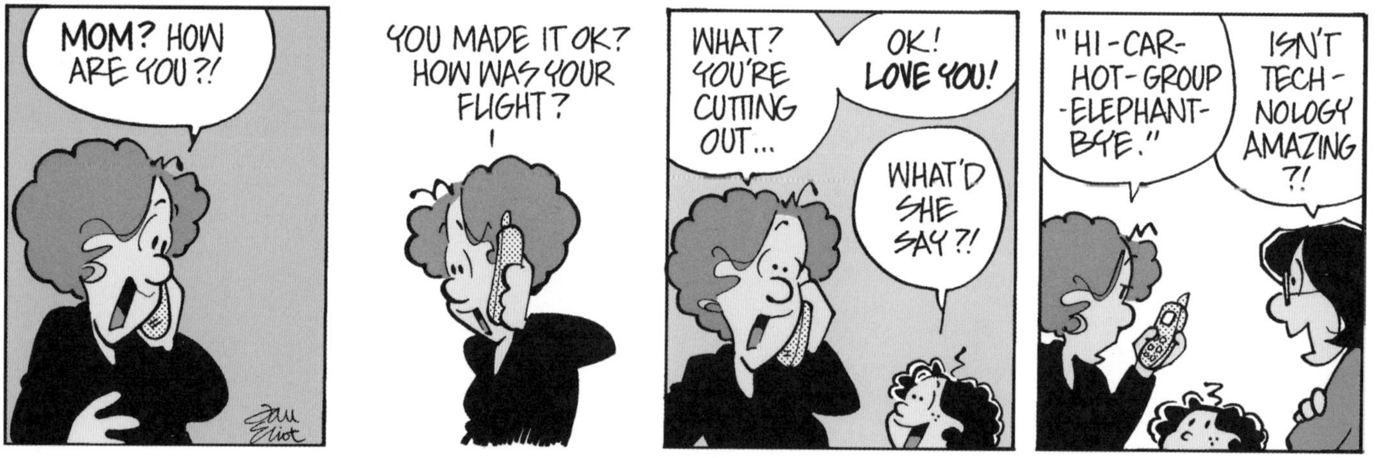
MOM? HOW ARE YOU?!
YOU MADE IT OK? HOW WAS YOUR FLIGHT?
WHAT? YOU'RE CUTTING OUT...
OK! LOVE YOU!
WHAT'D SHE SAY?!
"HI-CAR-HOT-GROUP-ELEPHANT-BYE."
ISN'T TECHNOLOGY AMAZING ?!

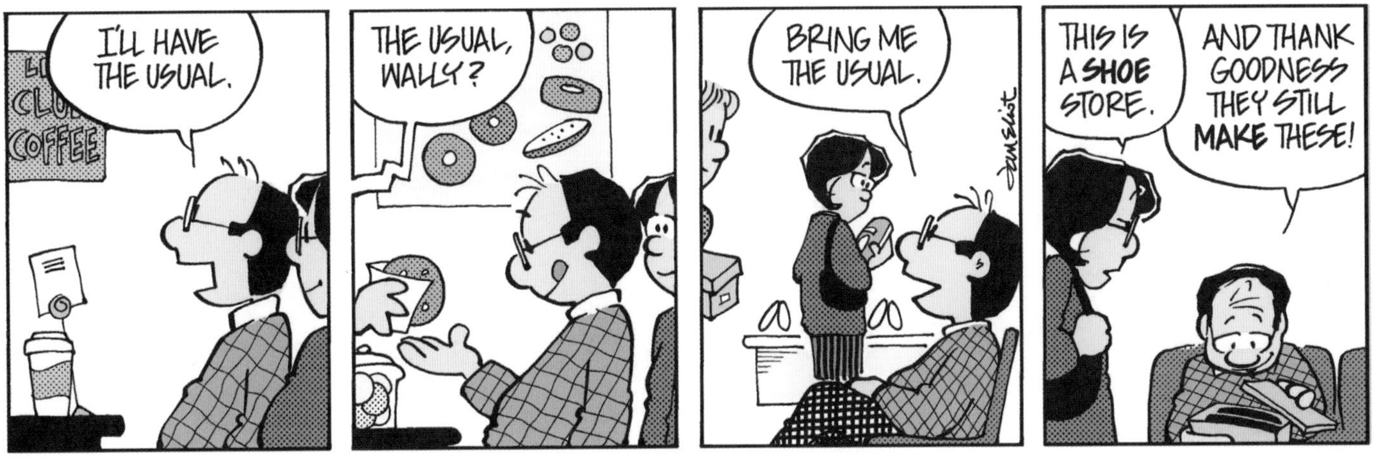
I'LL HAVE THE USUAL.
COFFEE
THE USUAL, WALLY?
BRING ME THE USUAL.
THIS IS A **SHOE** STORE.
AND THANK GOODNESS THEY STILL **MAKE** THESE!

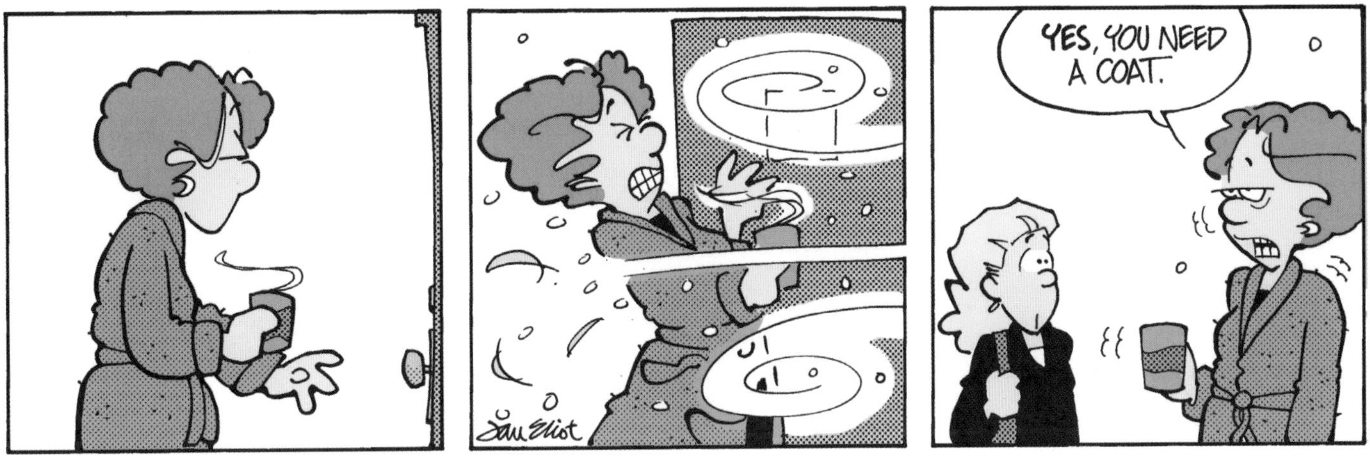
YES, YOU NEED A COAT.

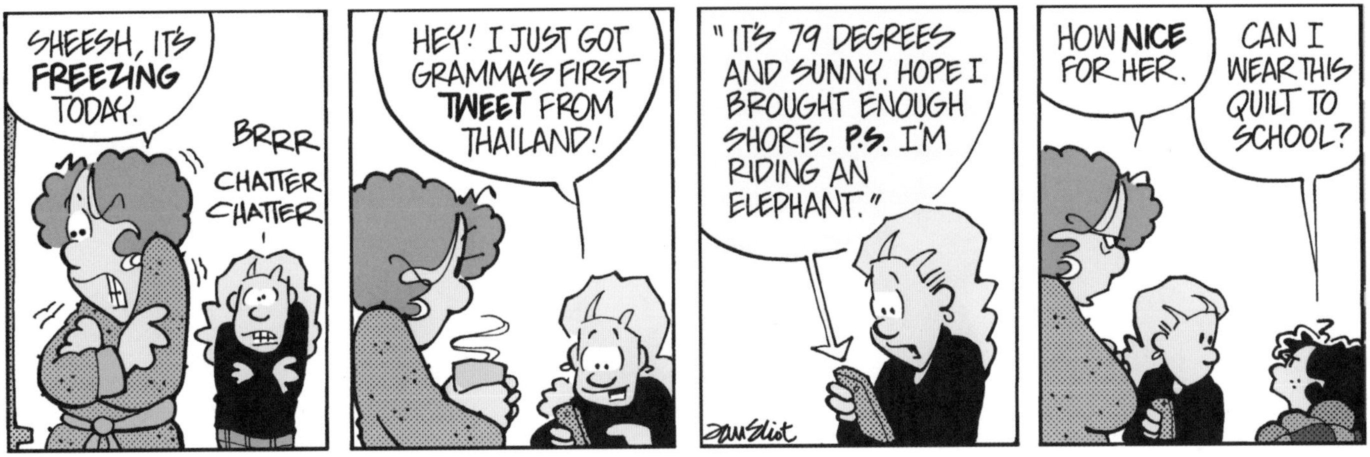
SHEESH, IT'S **FREEZING** TODAY.
BRRR
CHATTER CHATTER
HEY! I JUST GOT GRAMMA'S FIRST **TWEET** FROM THAILAND!
"IT'S 79 DEGREES AND SUNNY. HOPE I BROUGHT ENOUGH SHORTS. **P.S.** I'M RIDING AN ELEPHANT."
HOW **NICE** FOR HER.
CAN I WEAR THIS QUILT TO SCHOOL?

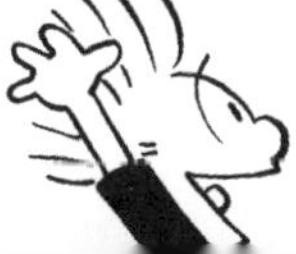

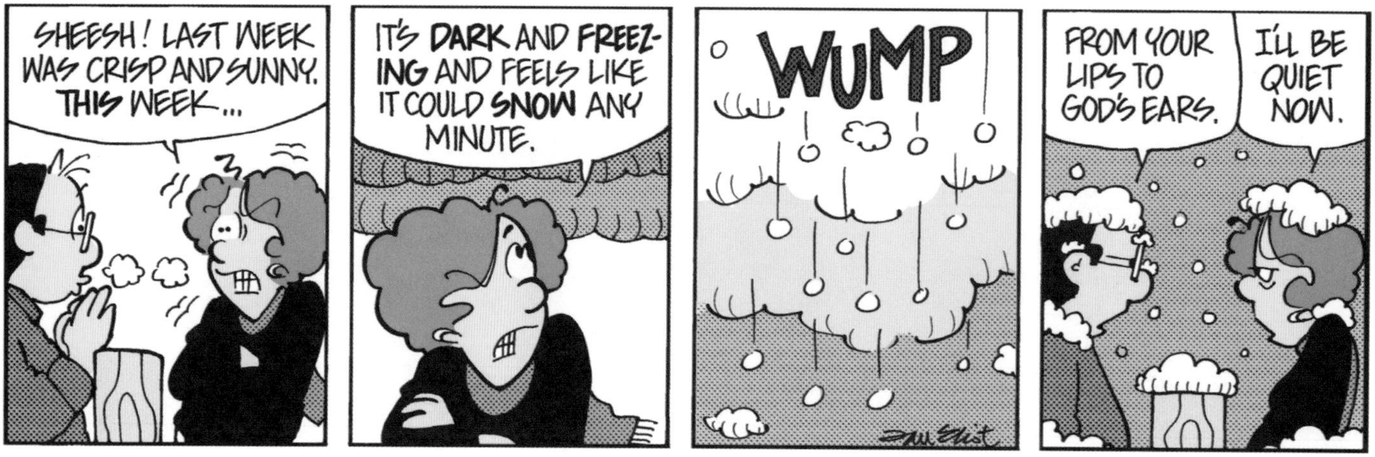
SHEESH! LAST WEEK WAS CRISP AND SUNNY. THIS WEEK...
IT'S DARK AND FREEZING AND FEELS LIKE IT COULD SNOW ANY MINUTE.
WUMP
FROM YOUR LIPS TO GOD'S EARS.
I'LL BE QUIET NOW.

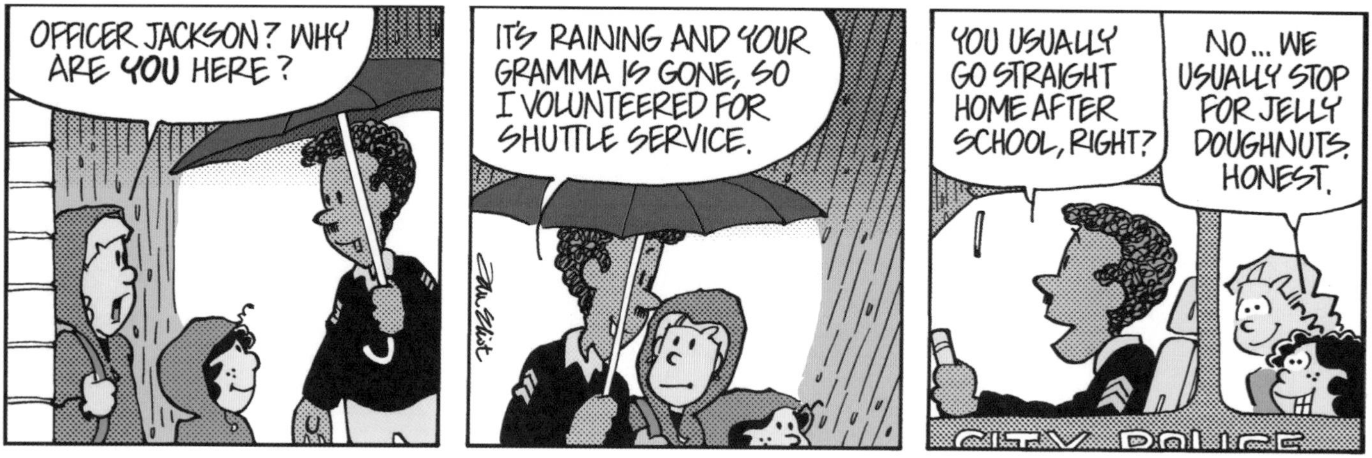
OFFICER JACKSON? WHY ARE YOU HERE?
IT'S RAINING AND YOUR GRAMMA IS GONE, SO I VOLUNTEERED FOR SHUTTLE SERVICE.
YOU USUALLY GO STRAIGHT HOME AFTER SCHOOL, RIGHT?
NO... WE USUALLY STOP FOR JELLY DOUGHNUTS. HONEST.

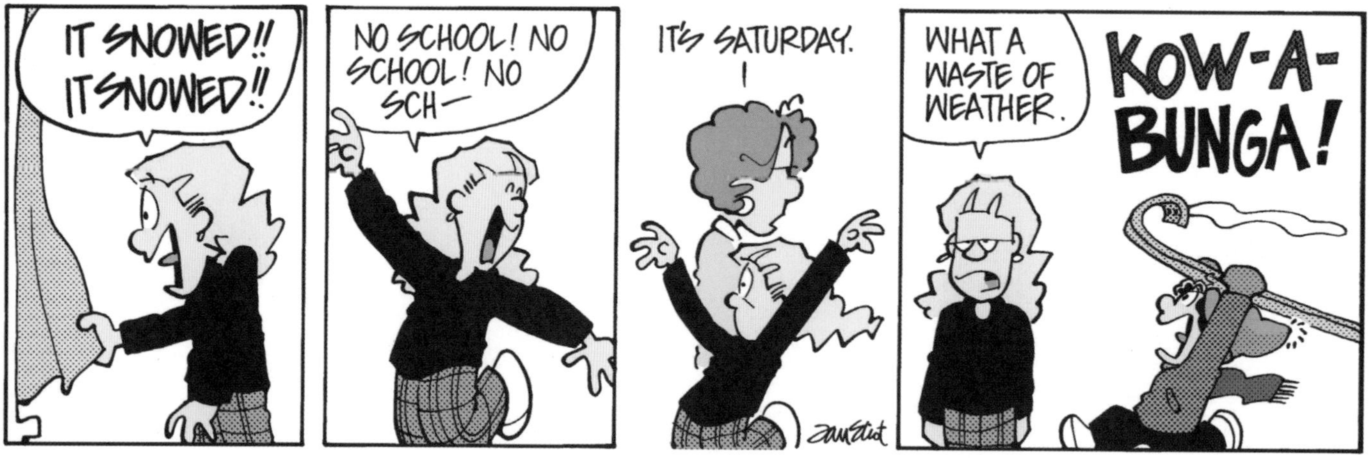
IT SNOWED!! IT SNOWED!!
NO SCHOOL! NO SCHOOL! NO SCH—
IT'S SATURDAY.
WHAT A WASTE OF WEATHER.
KOW-A-BUNGA!

Stone Soup

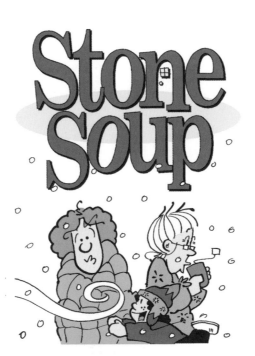

BRRR

FIRST BIG STORM OF THE SEASON!

UNCLE WALLY AND ANDY AND MAX ARE GETTING OUT THE SLEDS...

ME TOO! ME TOO!

POP!

BY FEBRUARY WE'RE GOING TO **HATE** SNOW.

YEAH, BUT THAT'S **THEN**. COCOA??

Stone Soup

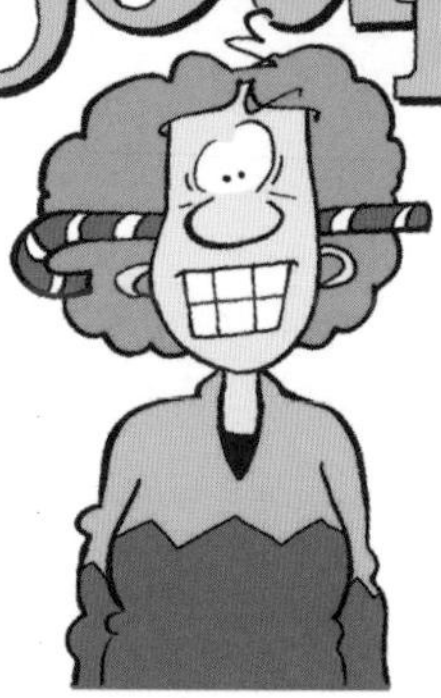

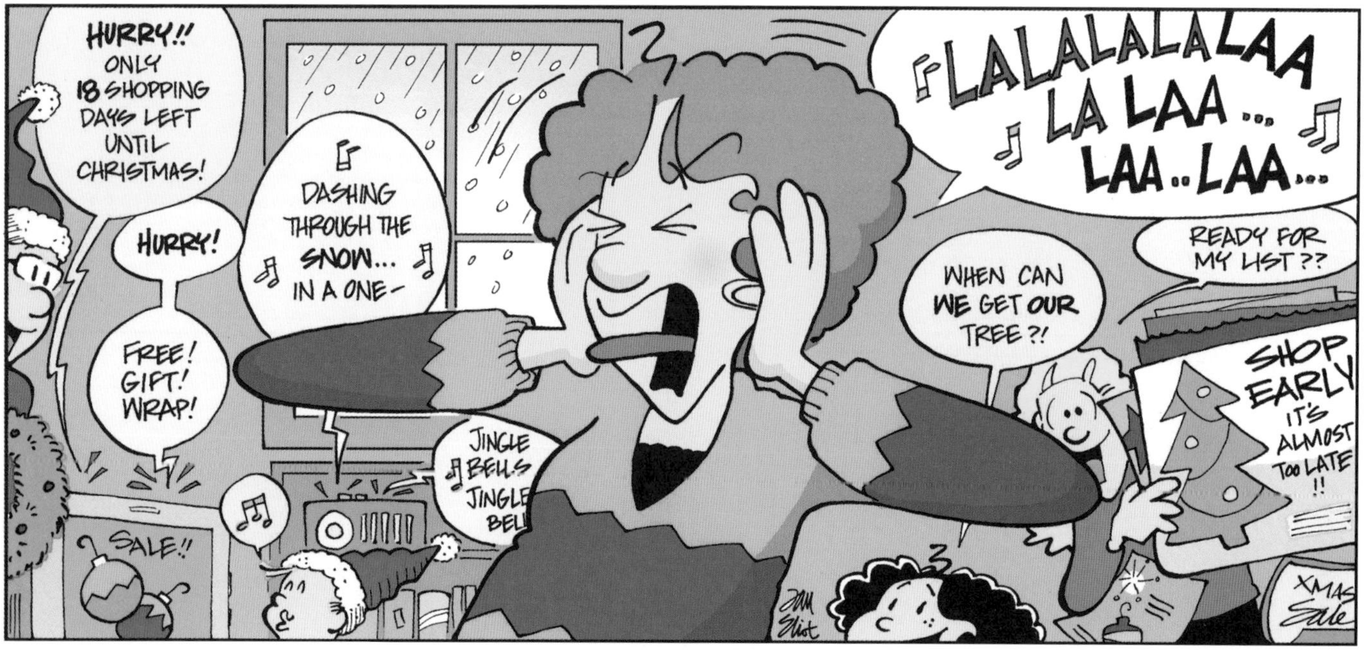

HURRY!! ONLY 18 SHOPPING DAYS LEFT UNTIL CHRISTMAS!
HURRY!
FREE! GIFT! WRAP!
DASHING THROUGH THE SNOW... IN A ONE-
JINGLE BELLS JINGLE BEL
LALALALALALAA LA LAA... LAA.. LAA...
READY FOR MY LIST??
WHEN CAN WE GET OUR TREE?!
SHOP EARLY IT'S ALMOST TOO LATE!!
SALE!!
XMAS Sale

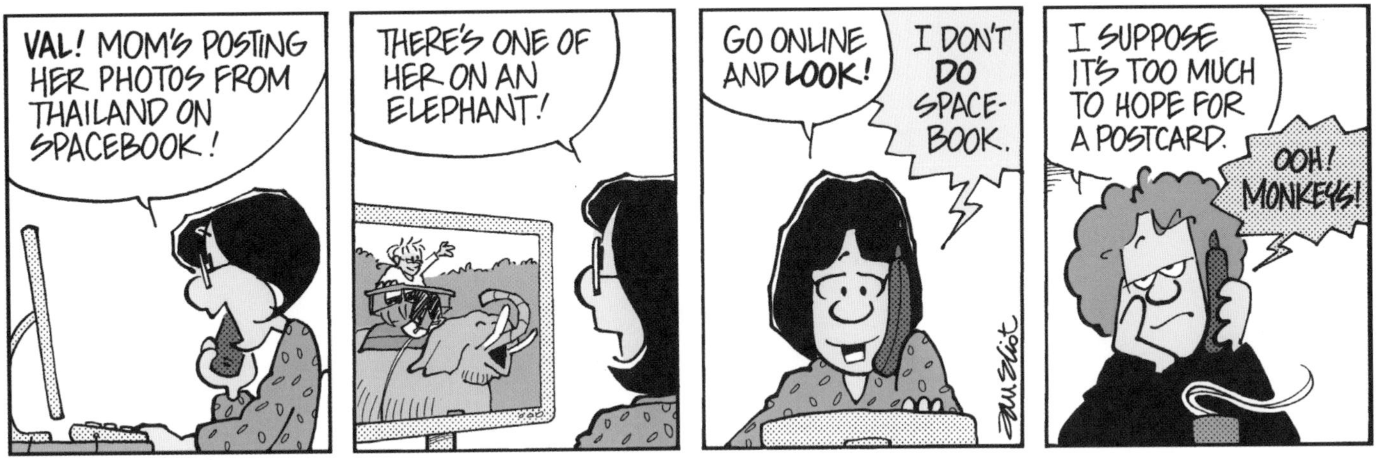
VAL! MOM'S POSTING HER PHOTOS FROM THAILAND ON SPACEBOOK!
THERE'S ONE OF HER ON AN ELEPHANT!
GO ONLINE AND LOOK!
I DON'T DO SPACE-BOOK.
I SUPPOSE IT'S TOO MUCH TO HOPE FOR A POSTCARD.
OOH! MONKEYS!

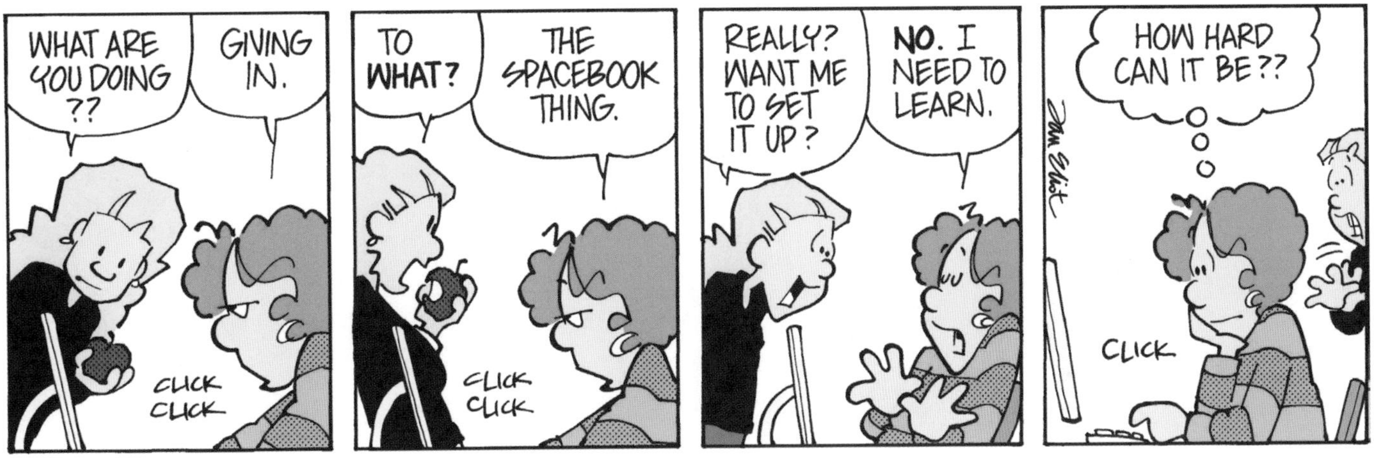
WHAT ARE YOU DOING ??
GIVING IN.
CLICK CLICK
TO WHAT?
THE SPACEBOOK THING.
CLICK CLICK
REALLY? WANT ME TO SET IT UP?
NO. I NEED TO LEARN.
HOW HARD CAN IT BE??
CLICK

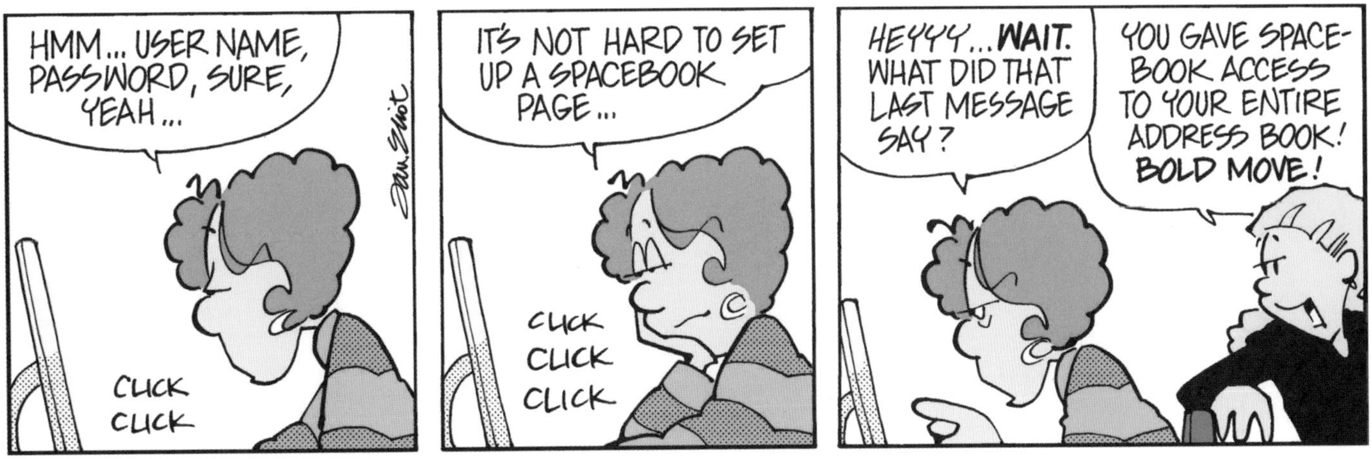
HMM... USER NAME, PASSWORD, SURE, YEAH...
CLICK CLICK
IT'S NOT HARD TO SET UP A SPACEBOOK PAGE...
CLICK CLICK CLICK
HEYYY... WAIT. WHAT DID THAT LAST MESSAGE SAY?
YOU GAVE SPACE-BOOK ACCESS TO YOUR ENTIRE ADDRESS BOOK! BOLD MOVE!

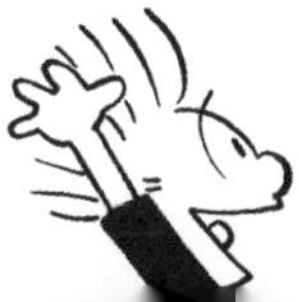

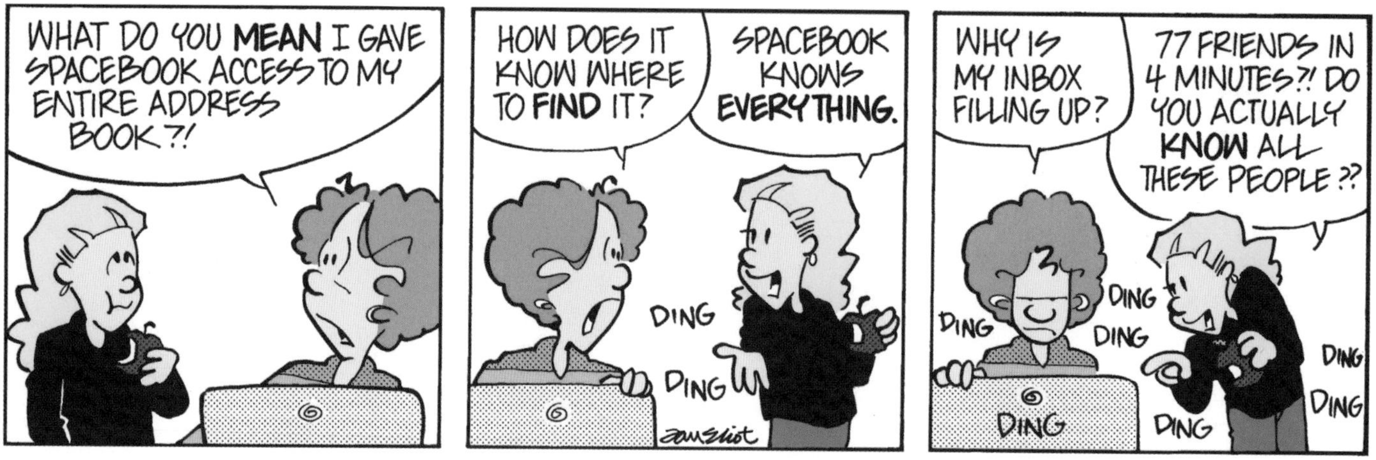
WHAT DO YOU **MEAN** I GAVE SPACEBOOK ACCESS TO MY ENTIRE ADDRESS BOOK?!
HOW DOES IT KNOW WHERE TO **FIND** IT?
SPACEBOOK KNOWS **EVERYTHING.**
DING
DING
WHY IS MY INBOX FILLING UP?
77 FRIENDS IN 4 MINUTES?! DO YOU ACTUALLY **KNOW** ALL THESE PEOPLE??
DING
DING
DING
DING
DING
DING
DING
DING

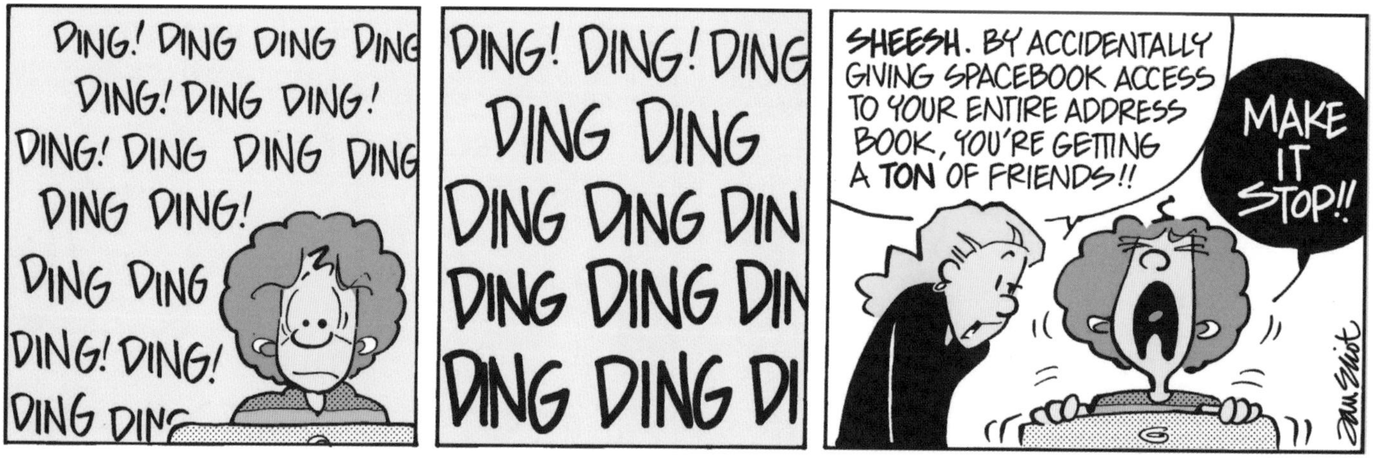
DING! DING DING DING
DING! DING DING!
DING! DING DING DING
DING DING!
DING DING
DING! DING!
DING DING
DING! DING! DING
DING DING
DING DING DIN
DING DING DIN
DING DING DI
SHEESH. BY ACCIDENTALLY GIVING SPACEBOOK ACCESS TO YOUR ENTIRE ADDRESS BOOK, YOU'RE GETTING A **TON** OF FRIENDS!!
MAKE IT STOP!!

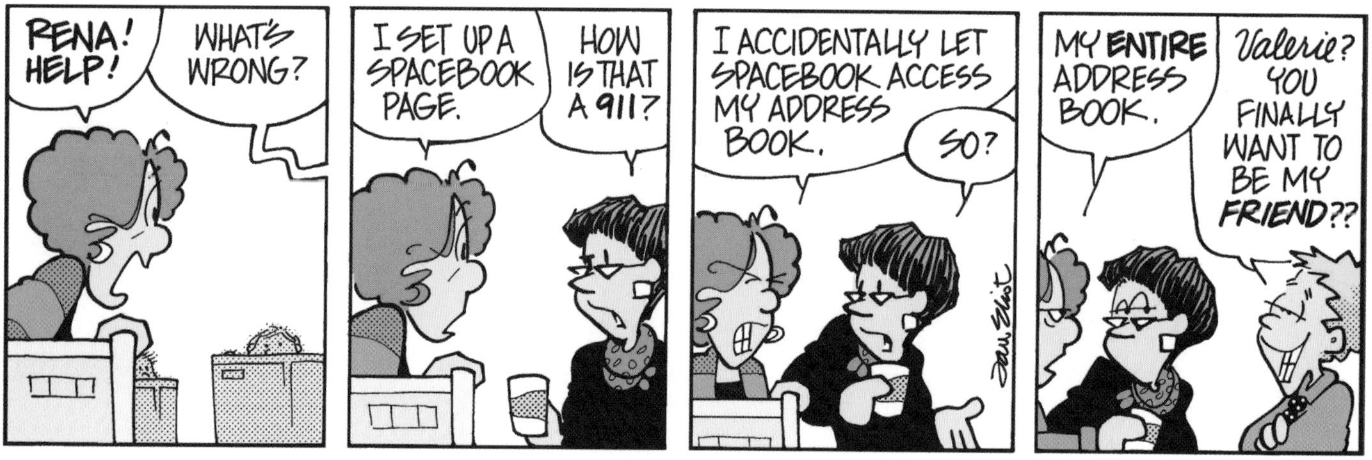
RENA! HELP!
WHAT'S WRONG?
I SET UP A SPACEBOOK PAGE.
HOW IS THAT A **911**?
I ACCIDENTALLY LET SPACEBOOK ACCESS MY ADDRESS BOOK.
SO?
MY **ENTIRE** ADDRESS BOOK.
Valerie? YOU FINALLY WANT TO BE MY ***FRIEND***??

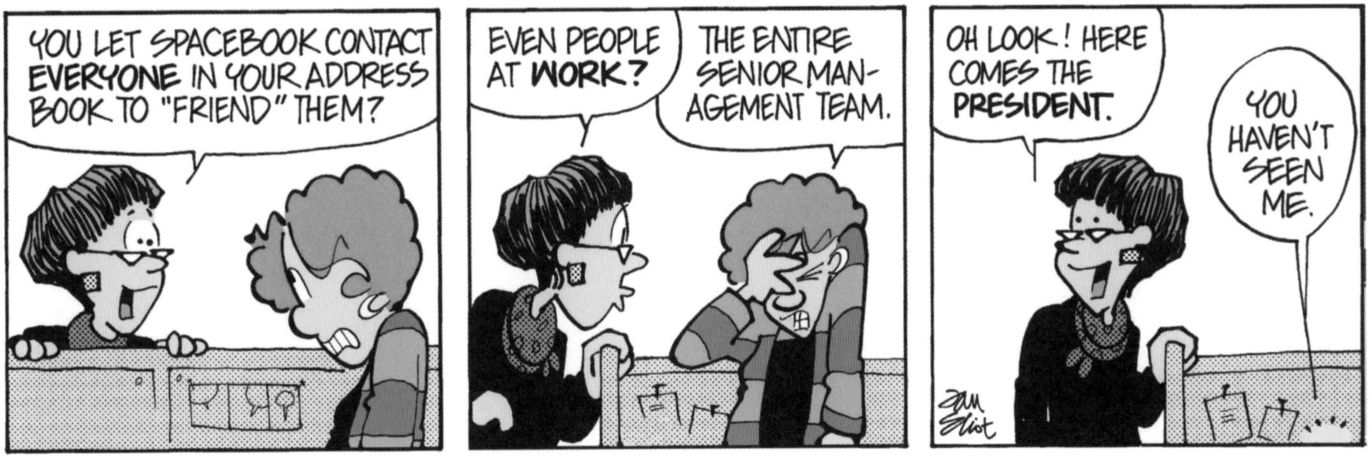
YOU LET SPACEBOOK CONTACT **EVERYONE** IN YOUR ADDRESS BOOK TO "FRIEND" THEM?
EVEN PEOPLE AT **WORK?**
THE ENTIRE SENIOR MANAGEMENT TEAM.
OH LOOK! HERE COMES THE **PRESIDENT.**
YOU HAVEN'T SEEN ME.

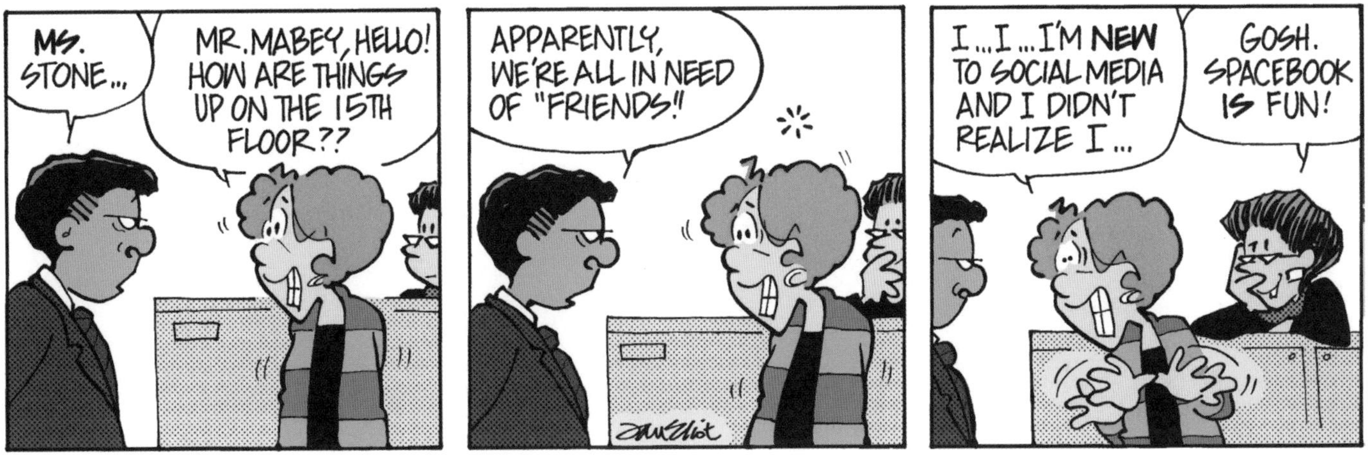
MS. STONE...
MR. MABEY, HELLO! HOW ARE THINGS UP ON THE 15TH FLOOR??
APPARENTLY, WE'RE ALL IN NEED OF "FRIENDS!"
I... I... I'M **NEW** TO SOCIAL MEDIA AND I DIDN'T REALIZE I...
GOSH. SPACEBOOK **IS** FUN!

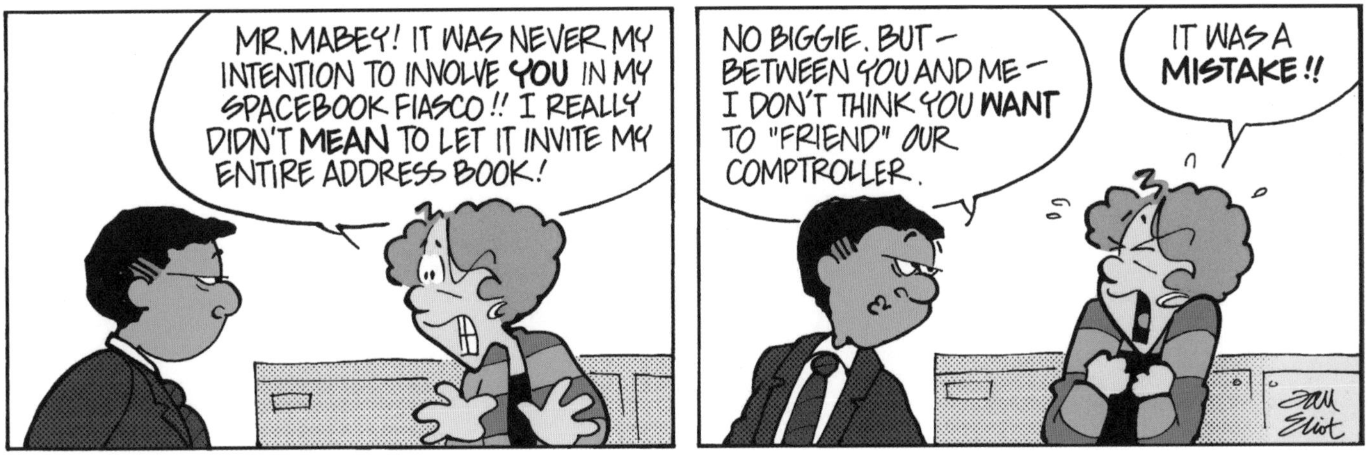
MR. MABEY! IT WAS NEVER MY INTENTION TO INVOLVE **YOU** IN MY SPACEBOOK FIASCO!! I REALLY DIDN'T **MEAN** TO LET IT INVITE MY ENTIRE ADDRESS BOOK!
NO BIGGIE. BUT — BETWEEN YOU AND ME — I DON'T THINK YOU **WANT** TO "FRIEND" OUR COMPTROLLER.
IT WAS A **MISTAKE!!**

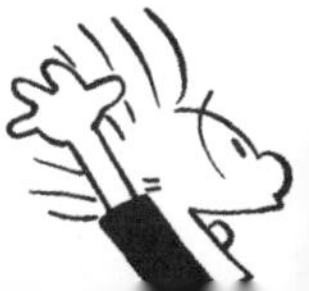

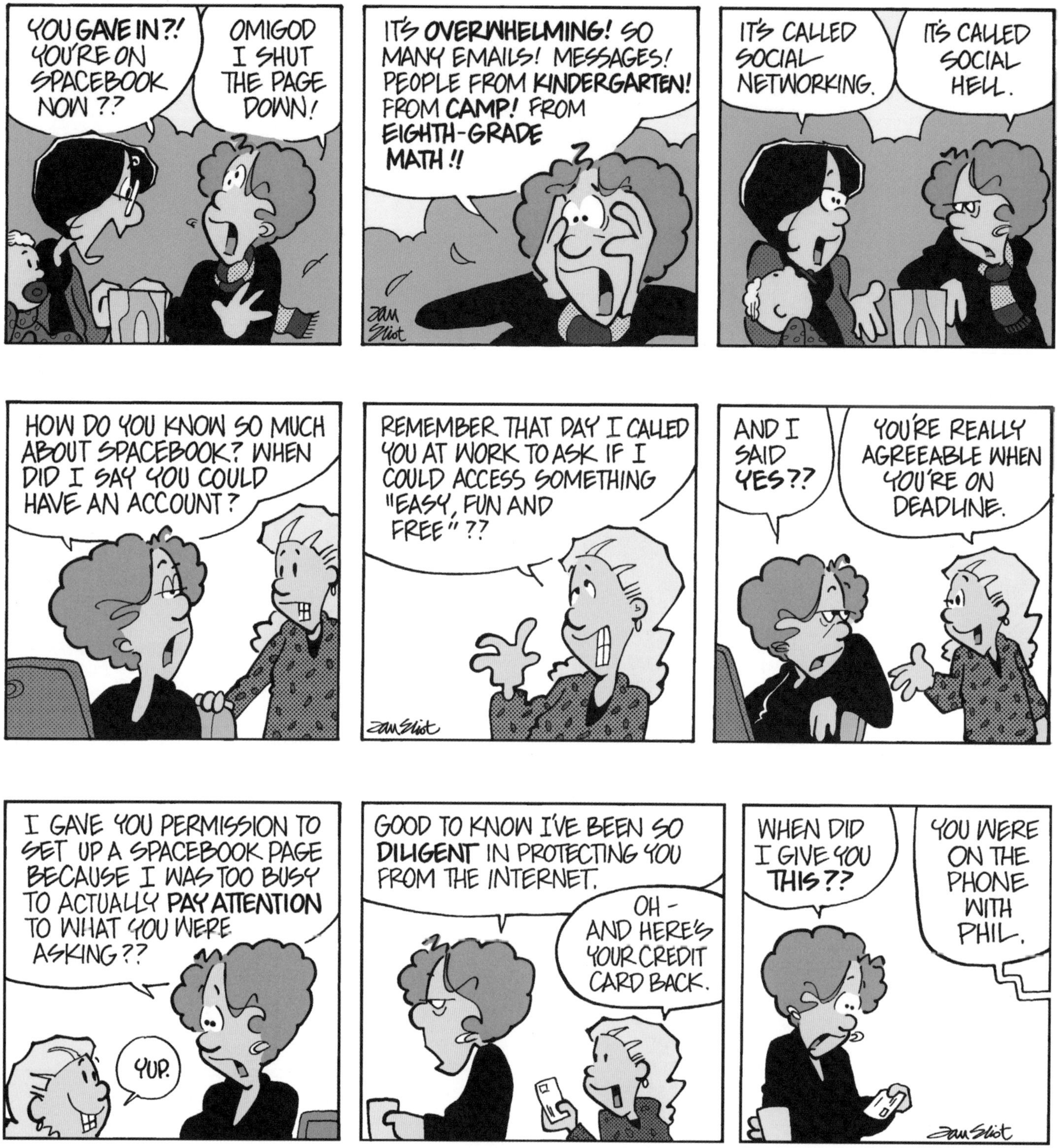

YOU GAVE IN?! YOU'RE ON SPACEBOOK NOW??
OMIGOD I SHUT THE PAGE DOWN!
IT'S OVERWHELMING! SO MANY EMAILS! MESSAGES! PEOPLE FROM KINDERGARTEN! FROM CAMP! FROM EIGHTH-GRADE MATH!!
IT'S CALLED SOCIAL NETWORKING.
IT'S CALLED SOCIAL HELL.
HOW DO YOU KNOW SO MUCH ABOUT SPACEBOOK? WHEN DID I SAY YOU COULD HAVE AN ACCOUNT?
REMEMBER THAT DAY I CALLED YOU AT WORK TO ASK IF I COULD ACCESS SOMETHING "EASY, FUN AND FREE"??
AND I SAID YES??
YOU'RE REALLY AGREEABLE WHEN YOU'RE ON DEADLINE.
I GAVE YOU PERMISSION TO SET UP A SPACEBOOK PAGE BECAUSE I WAS TOO BUSY TO ACTUALLY PAY ATTENTION TO WHAT YOU WERE ASKING??
YUP.
GOOD TO KNOW I'VE BEEN SO DILIGENT IN PROTECTING YOU FROM THE INTERNET.
OH - AND HERE'S YOUR CREDIT CARD BACK.
WHEN DID I GIVE YOU THIS??
YOU WERE ON THE PHONE WITH PHIL.

WHY WOULD SOMEONE WANT TEN LORDS A-LEAPING AND A BUNCH OF **BIRDS**?

FOR THE SAME REASON THEY EAT **PIGGY** PUDDING.

FIGGY PUDDING.

AND WHAT DOES FRANKENSTEIN HAVE TO DO WITH CHRISTMAS?

FRANKINCENSE!

LET'S TURN OFF THE CHRISTMAS CAROLS FOR A WHILE.

FROSTY **DIES!** ISN'T THAT KIND OF DEPRESSING!?

STOP!!

Stone Soup

UNCLE WALLY? WHY DO YOU GET A CHRISTMAS TREE?
YOU CELEBRATE HANUKKAH.
BECAUSE AUNT JOAN CELEBRATES CHRISTMAS.
WE HONOR EACH OTHER'S HOLIDAYS.
SOOO... LATKES AND SUGAR COOKIES.
RUGELACH AND GINGERBREAD.
DOUGHNUTS AND CANDY CANES.
CHOCOLATE GELT AND CHOCOLATE SANTAS...
RELIGIOUS TOLERANCE HAS ITS PERKS.
AND ITS PUDGE.

Stone Soup

'MORNING...
HMMM...
IT'S ONLY 7AM AND SOMEBODY HAS COOKIE BREATH.
WE LOVE THE HOLIDAYS.

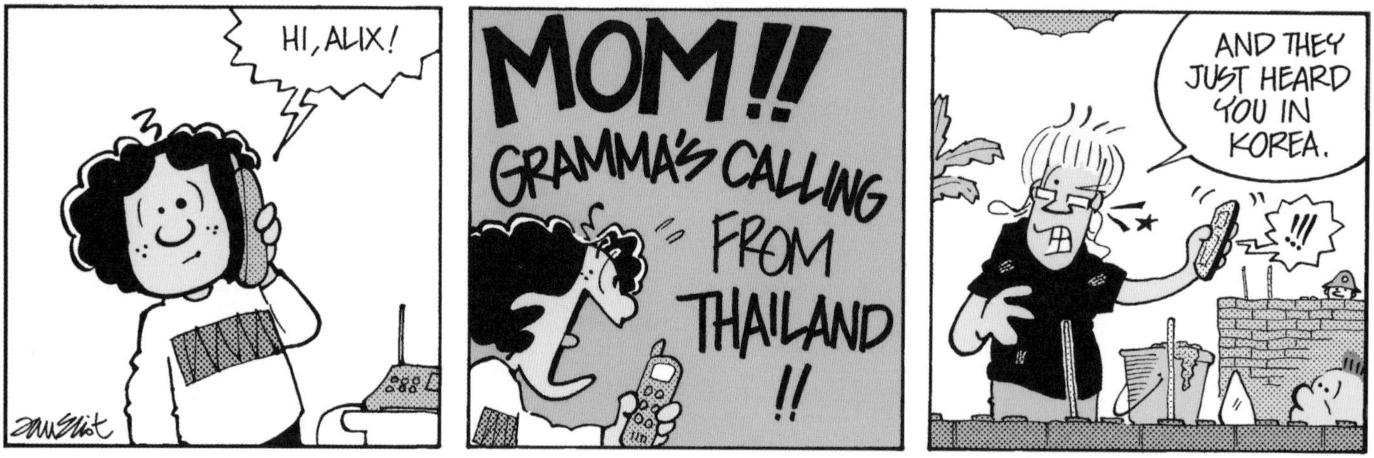
HI, ALIX!
MOM!! GRAMMA'S CALLING FROM THAILAND !!
AND THEY JUST HEARD YOU IN KOREA.

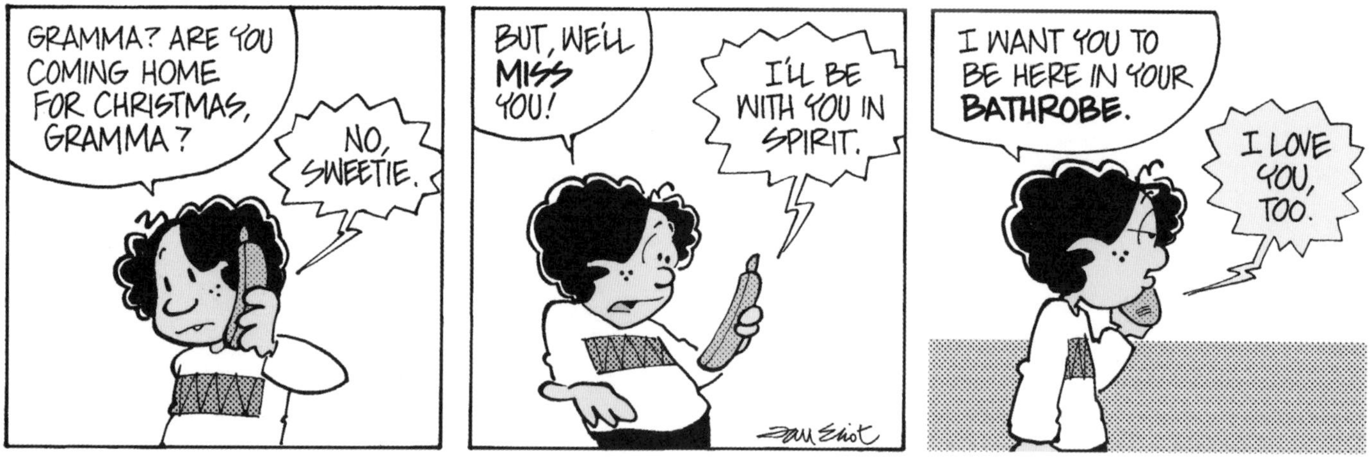
GRAMMA? ARE YOU COMING HOME FOR CHRISTMAS, GRAMMA?
NO, SWEETIE.
BUT, WE'LL **MISS** YOU!
I'LL BE WITH YOU IN SPIRIT.
I WANT YOU TO BE HERE IN YOUR **BATHROBE.**
I LOVE YOU, TOO.

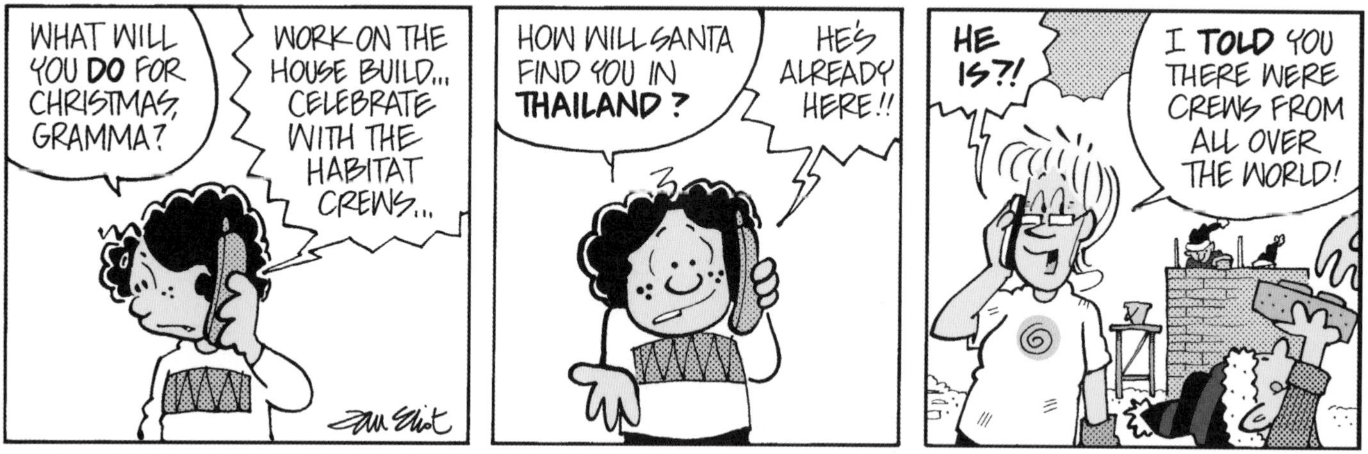
WHAT WILL YOU **DO** FOR CHRISTMAS, GRAMMA?
WORK ON THE HOUSE BUILD... CELEBRATE WITH THE HABITAT CREWS...
HOW WILL SANTA FIND YOU IN **THAILAND?**
HE'S ALREADY HERE!!
HE IS?!
I **TOLD** YOU THERE WERE CREWS FROM ALL OVER THE WORLD!

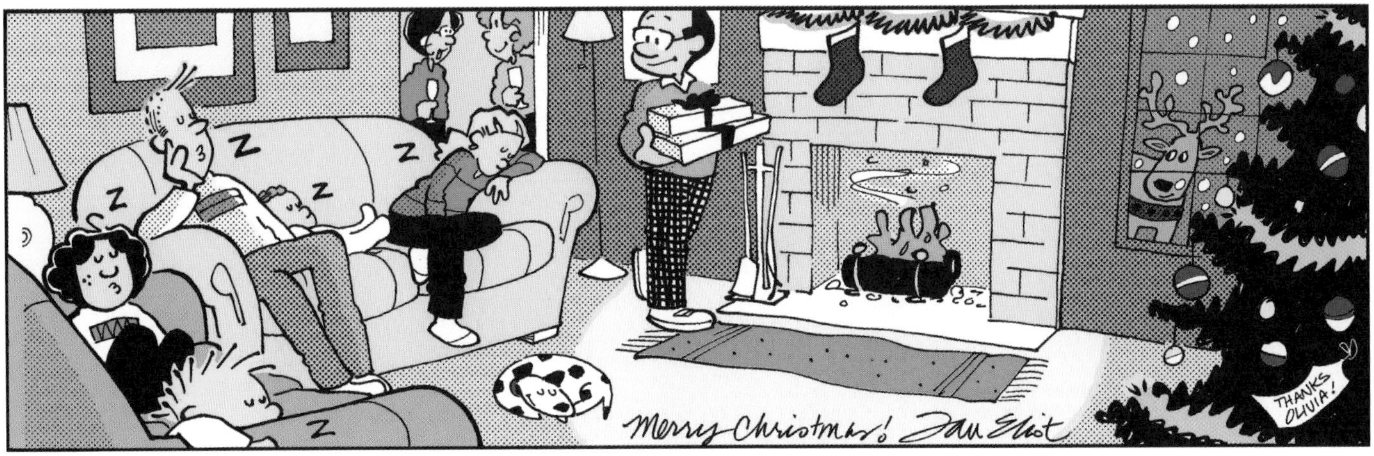
THANKS OLIVIA!
Merry Christmas! Jan Eliot

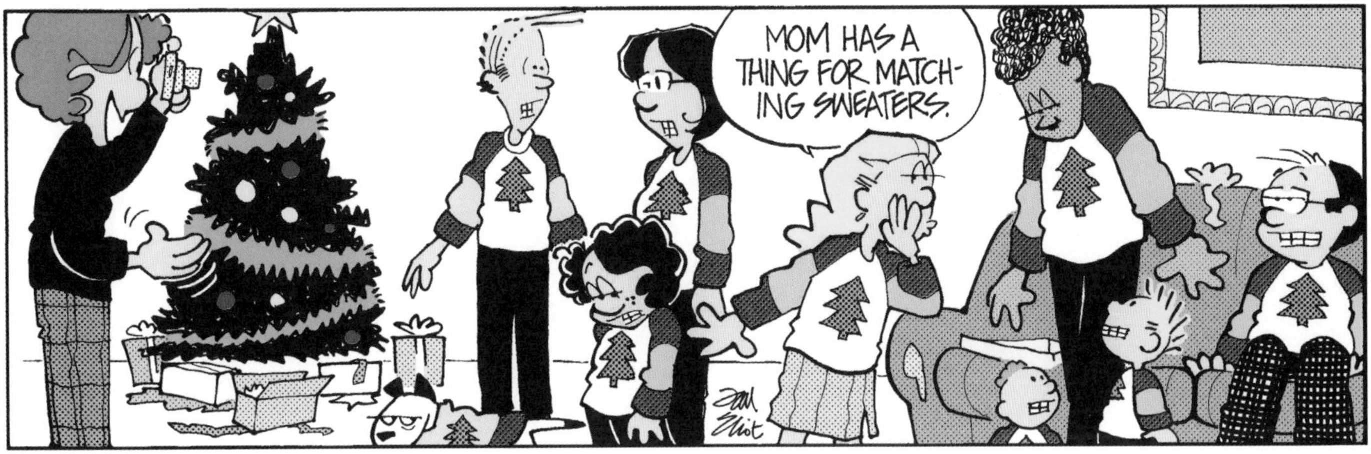
MOM HAS A THING FOR MATCHING SWEATERS.
Jan Eliot

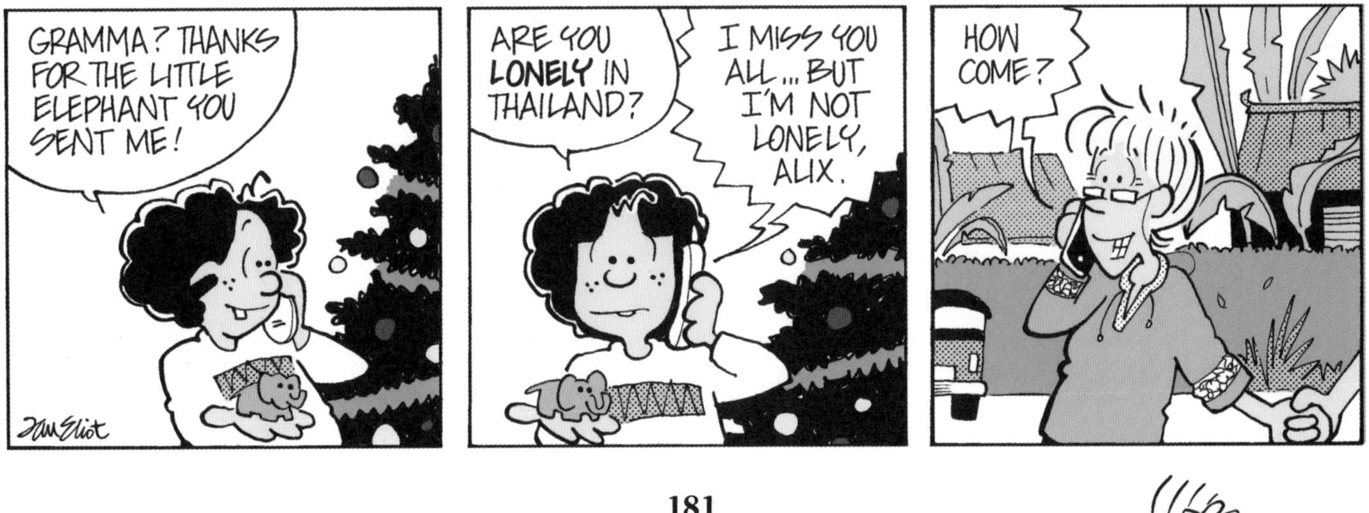
GRAMMA? THANKS FOR THE LITTLE ELEPHANT YOU SENT ME!
Jan Eliot
ARE YOU **LONELY** IN THAILAND?
I MISS YOU ALL... BUT I'M NOT LONELY, ALIX.
HOW COME?

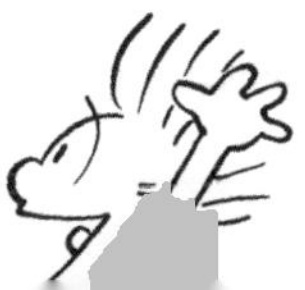

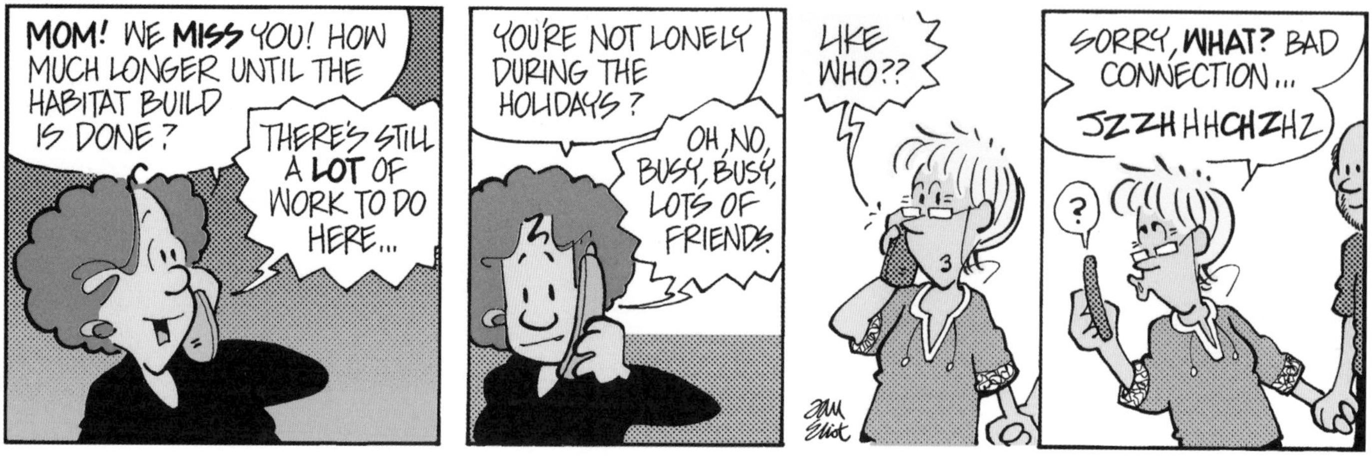
MOM! WE MISS YOU! HOW MUCH LONGER UNTIL THE HABITAT BUILD IS DONE?
THERE'S STILL A LOT OF WORK TO DO HERE...
YOU'RE NOT LONELY DURING THE HOLIDAYS?
OH, NO, BUSY, BUSY, LOTS OF FRIENDS.
LIKE WHO??
SORRY, WHAT? BAD CONNECTION...
JZZH HHCHZHZ
?

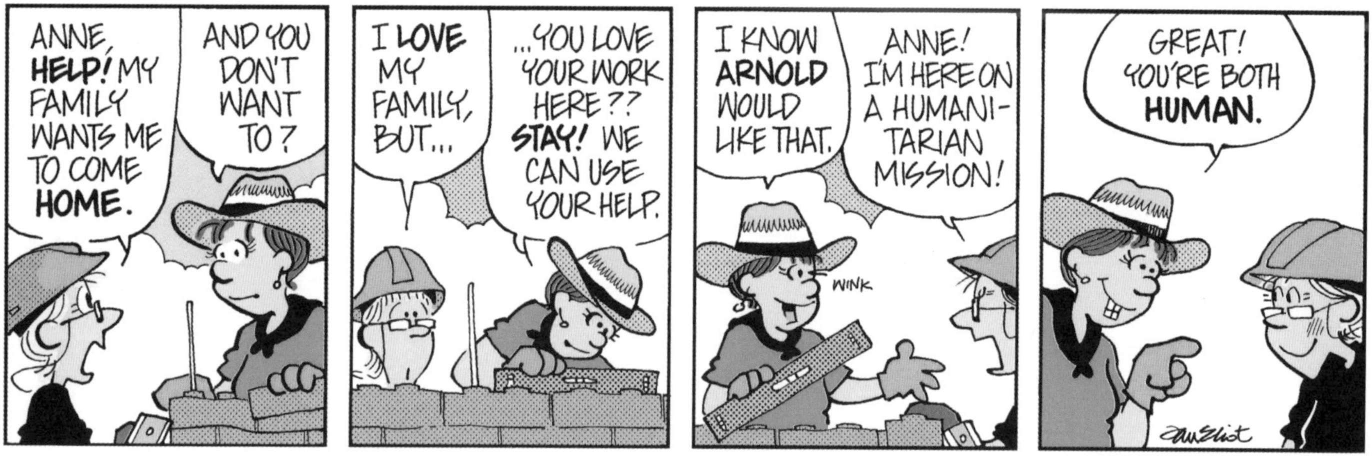
ANNE, HELP! MY FAMILY WANTS ME TO COME HOME.
AND YOU DON'T WANT TO?
I LOVE MY FAMILY, BUT...
...YOU LOVE YOUR WORK HERE?? STAY! WE CAN USE YOUR HELP.
I KNOW ARNOLD WOULD LIKE THAT.
WINK
ANNE! I'M HERE ON A HUMANITARIAN MISSION!
GREAT! YOU'RE BOTH HUMAN.

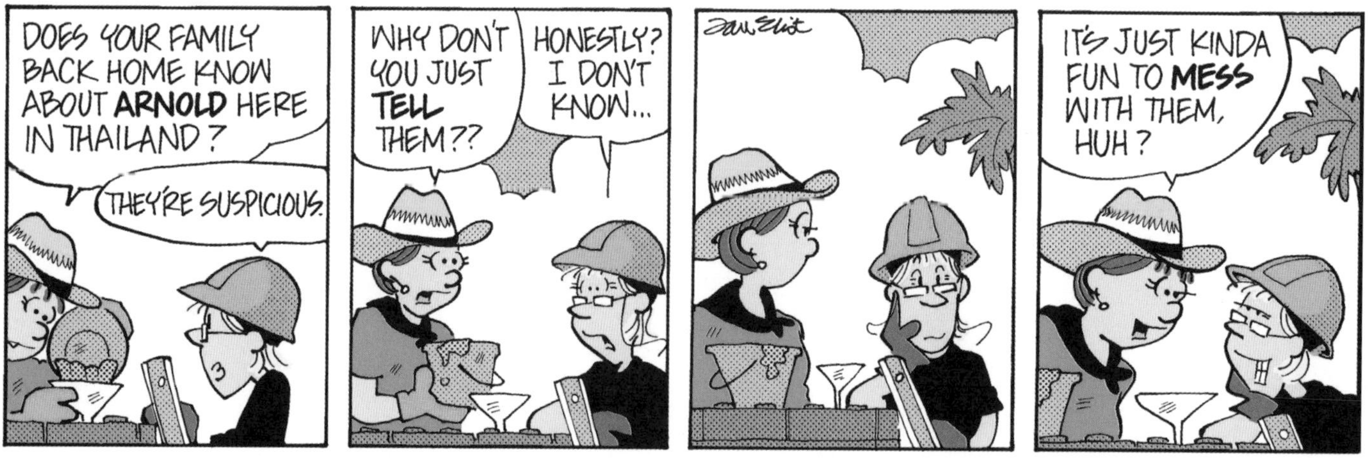
DOES YOUR FAMILY BACK HOME KNOW ABOUT ARNOLD HERE IN THAILAND?
THEY'RE SUSPICIOUS.
WHY DON'T YOU JUST TELL THEM??
HONESTLY? I DON'T KNOW...
IT'S JUST KINDA FUN TO MESS WITH THEM, HUH?

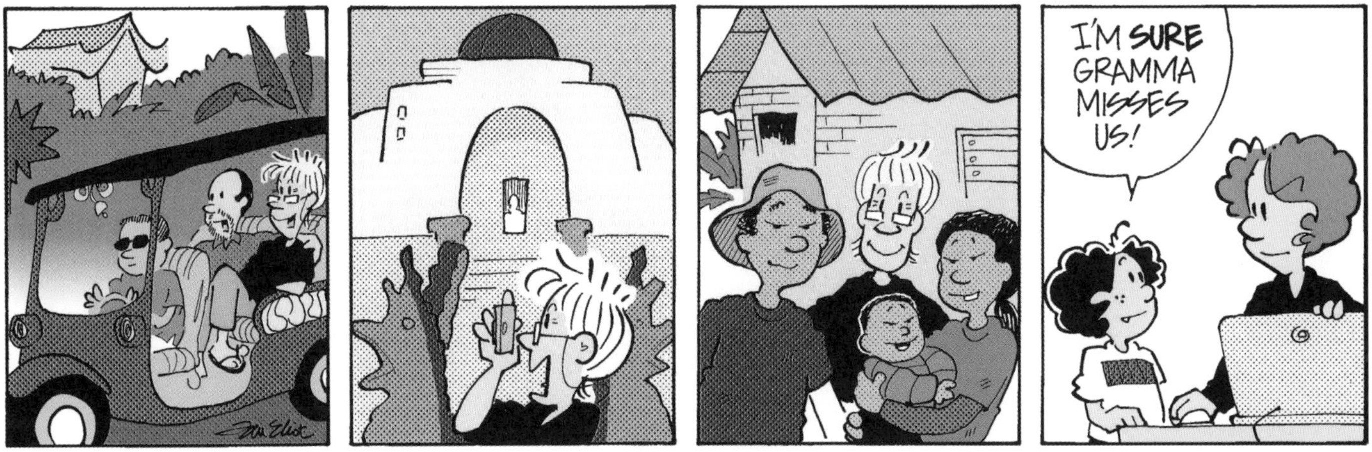
I'M SURE GRAMMA MISSES US!

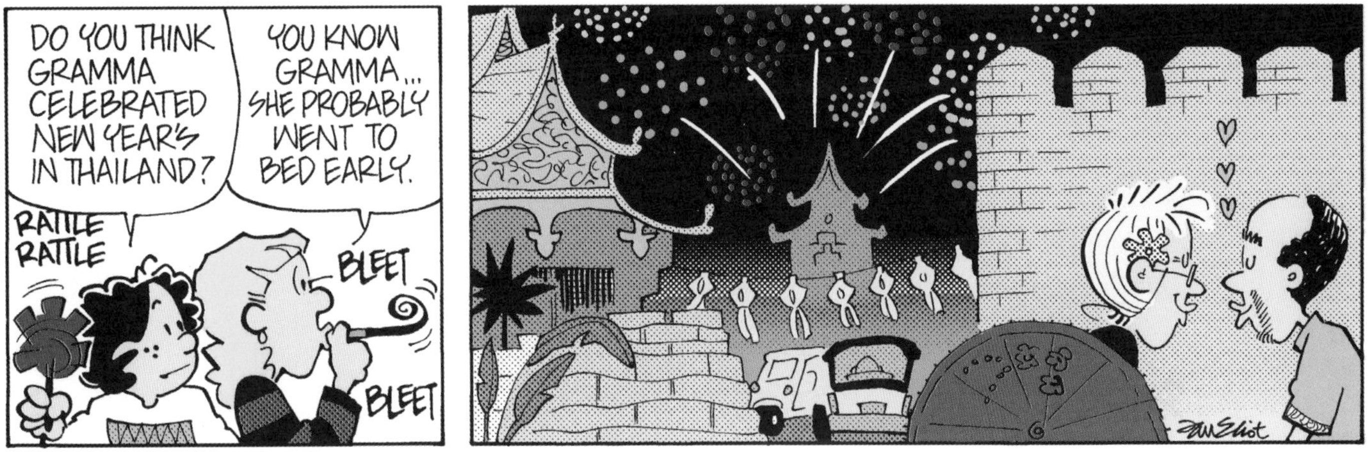
DO YOU THINK GRAMMA CELEBRATED NEW YEAR'S IN THAILAND?
YOU KNOW GRAMMA... SHE PROBABLY WENT TO BED EARLY.
RATTLE RATTLE
BLEET
BLEET

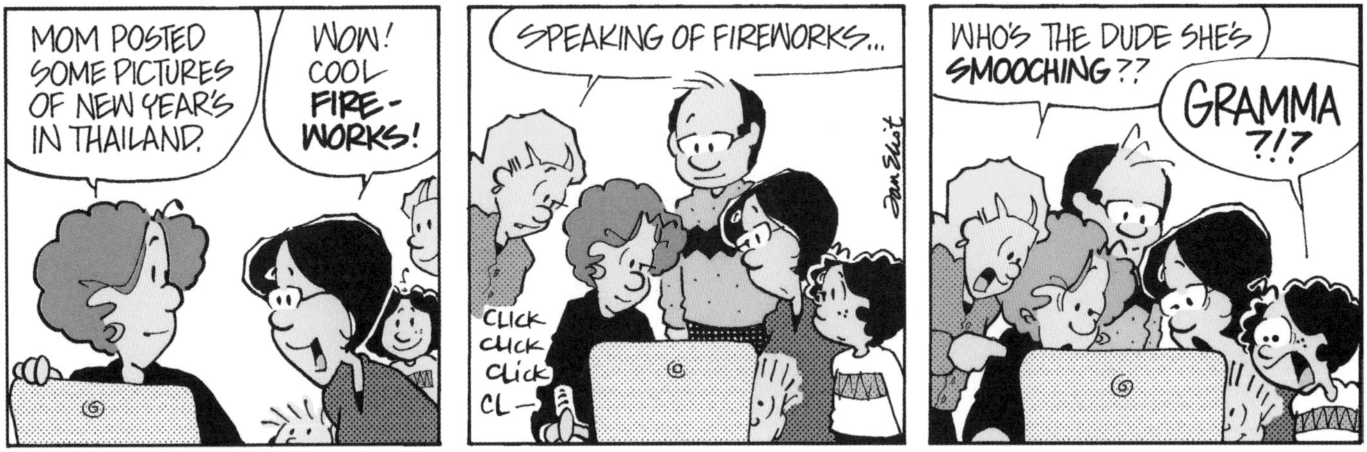
MOM POSTED SOME PICTURES OF NEW YEAR'S IN THAILAND.
WOW! COOL FIRE-WORKS!
SPEAKING OF FIREWORKS...
CLICK CLICK CLICK CL—
WHO'S THE DUDE SHE'S SMOOCHING??
GRAMMA ?!?

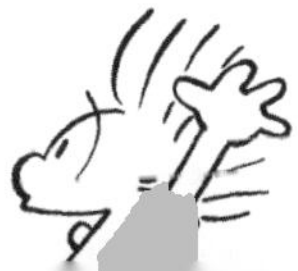

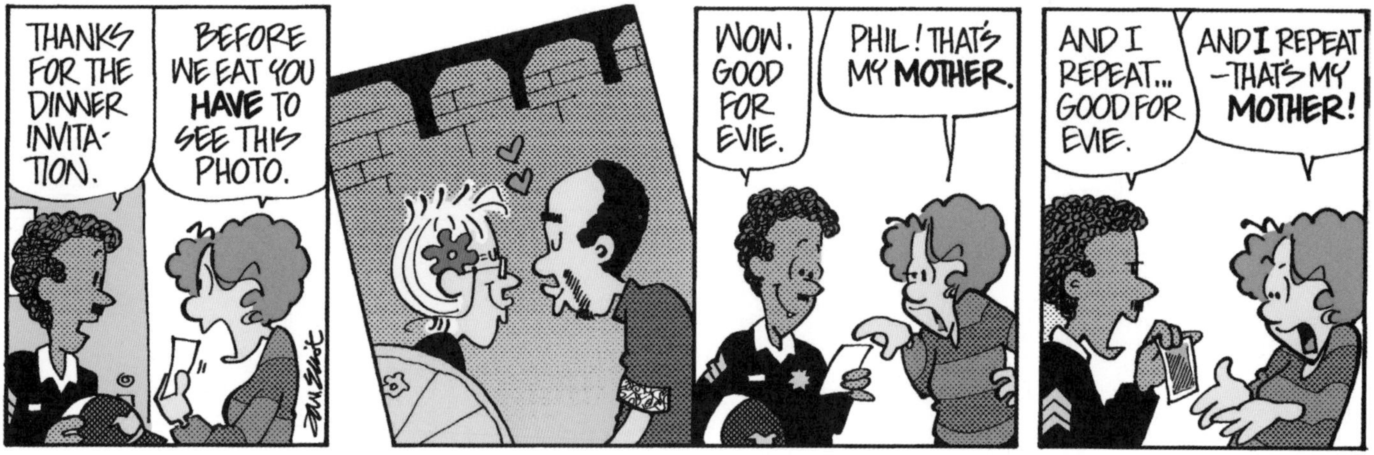
THANKS FOR THE DINNER INVITATION.
BEFORE WE EAT YOU **HAVE** TO SEE THIS PHOTO.
WOW. GOOD FOR EVIE.
PHIL! THAT'S MY **MOTHER**.
AND I REPEAT... GOOD FOR EVIE.
AND **I** REPEAT —THAT'S MY **MOTHER**!

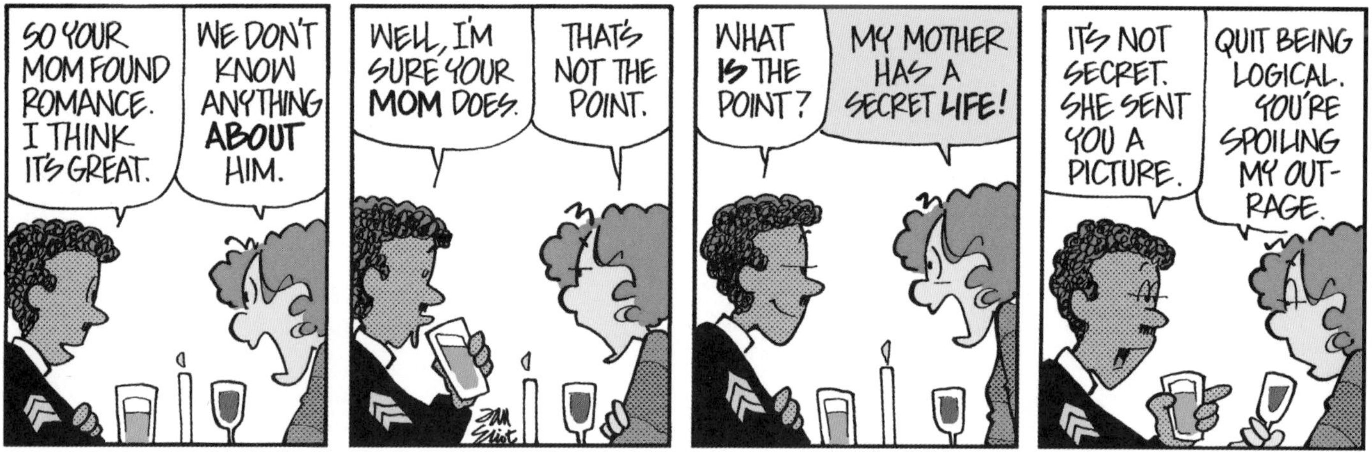
SO YOUR MOM FOUND ROMANCE. I THINK IT'S GREAT.
WE DON'T KNOW ANYTHING **ABOUT** HIM.
WELL, I'M SURE YOUR **MOM** DOES.
THAT'S NOT THE POINT.
WHAT **IS** THE POINT?
MY MOTHER HAS A SECRET **LIFE**!
IT'S NOT SECRET. SHE SENT YOU A PICTURE.
QUIT BEING LOGICAL. YOU'RE SPOILING MY OUTRAGE.

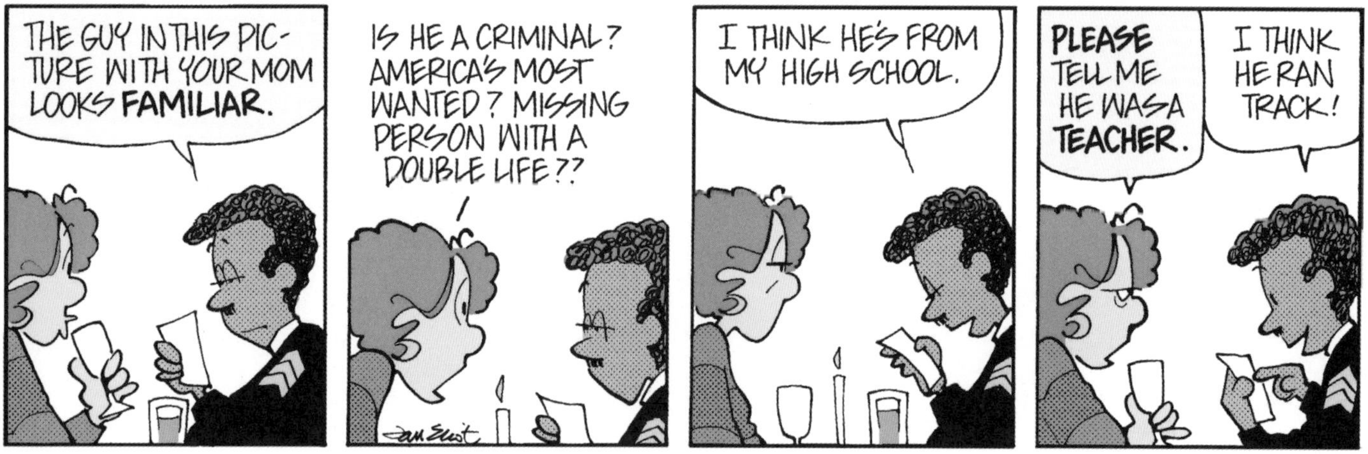
THE GUY IN THIS PICTURE WITH YOUR MOM LOOKS **FAMILIAR**.
IS HE A CRIMINAL? AMERICA'S MOST WANTED? MISSING PERSON WITH A DOUBLE LIFE??
I THINK HE'S FROM MY HIGH SCHOOL.
PLEASE TELL ME HE WAS A **TEACHER**.
I THINK HE RAN TRACK!

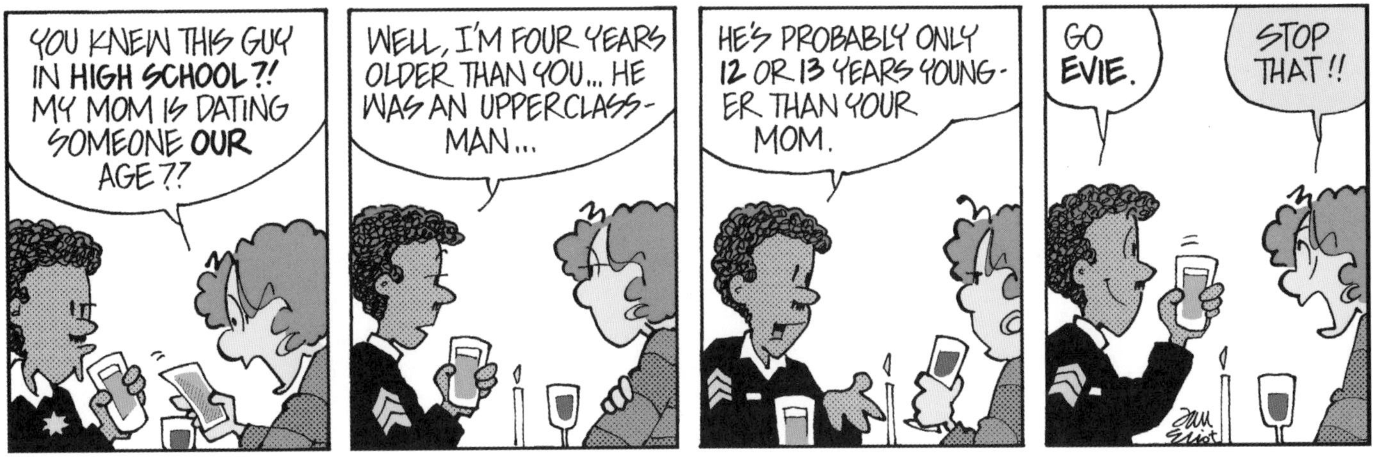
YOU KNEW THIS GUY IN **HIGH SCHOOL**?! MY MOM IS DATING SOMEONE **OUR** AGE??
WELL, I'M FOUR YEARS OLDER THAN YOU... HE WAS AN UPPERCLASSMAN...
HE'S PROBABLY ONLY **12** OR **13** YEARS YOUNGER THAN YOUR MOM.
GO **EVIE**.
STOP THAT!!

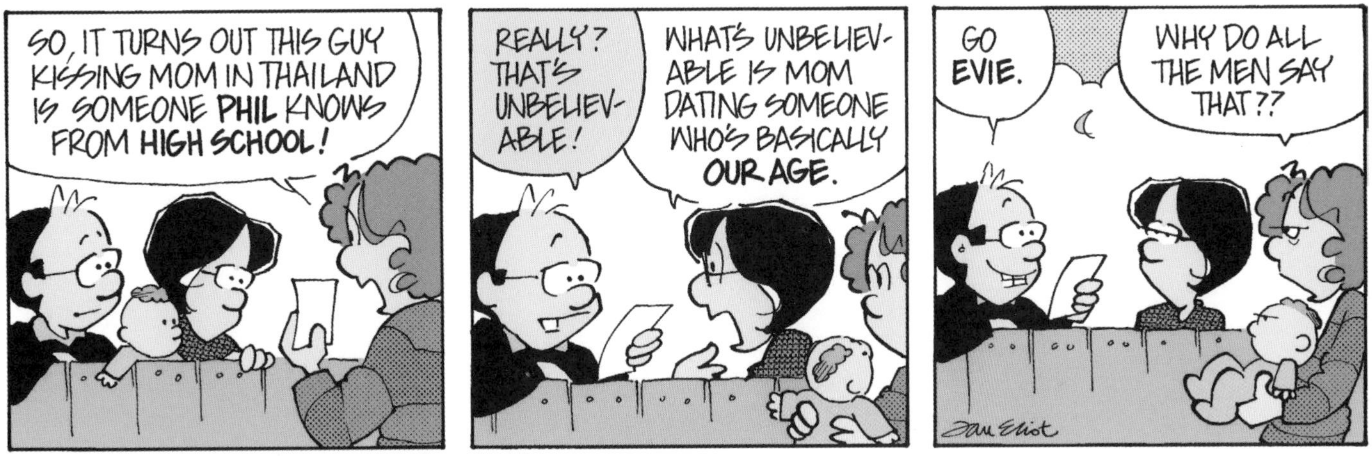
SO, IT TURNS OUT THIS GUY KISSING MOM IN THAILAND IS SOMEONE **PHIL** KNOWS FROM **HIGH SCHOOL**!
REALLY? THAT'S UNBELIEVABLE!
WHAT'S UNBELIEVABLE IS MOM DATING SOMEONE WHO'S BASICALLY **OUR AGE**.
GO **EVIE**.
WHY DO ALL THE MEN SAY THAT??

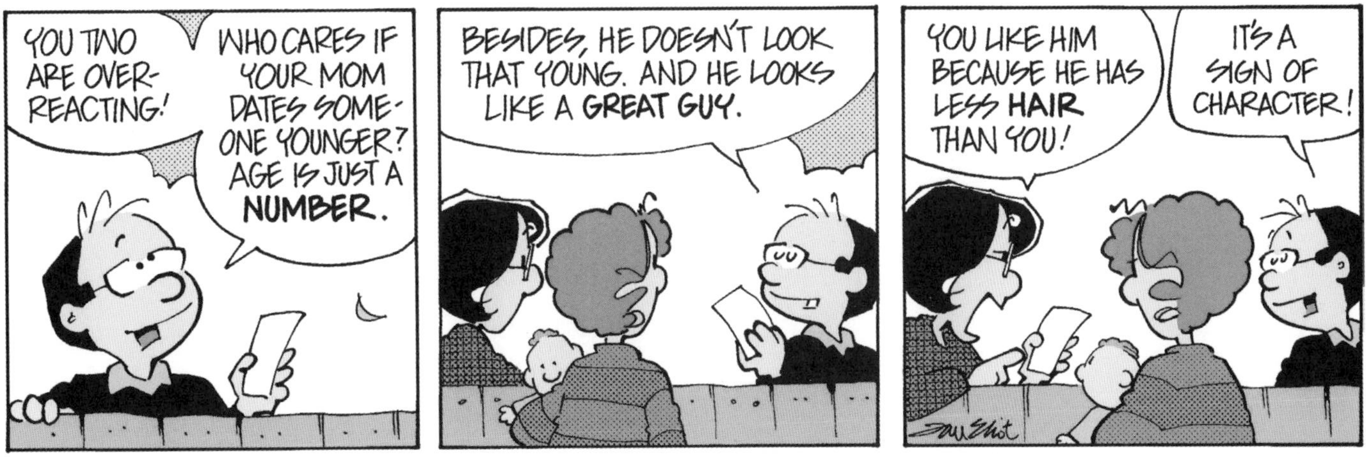
YOU TWO ARE OVER-REACTING!
WHO CARES IF YOUR MOM DATES SOMEONE YOUNGER? AGE IS JUST A **NUMBER**.
BESIDES, HE DOESN'T LOOK THAT YOUNG. AND HE LOOKS LIKE A **GREAT GUY**.
YOU LIKE HIM BECAUSE HE HAS LESS **HAIR** THAN YOU!
IT'S A SIGN OF CHARACTER!

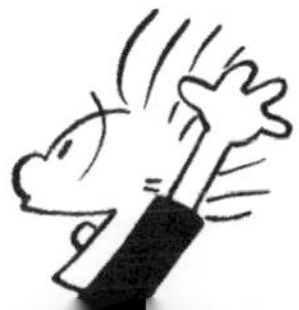

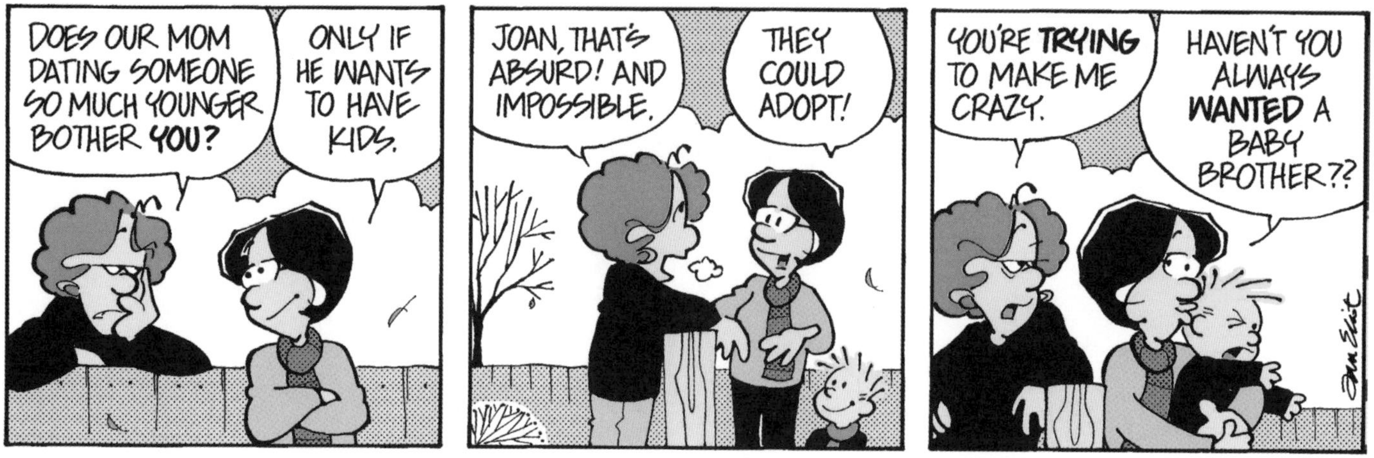
DOES OUR MOM DATING SOMEONE SO MUCH YOUNGER BOTHER **YOU?**
ONLY IF HE WANTS TO HAVE KIDS.
JOAN, THAT'S ABSURD! AND IMPOSSIBLE.
THEY COULD ADOPT!
YOU'RE **TRYING** TO MAKE ME CRAZY.
HAVEN'T YOU ALWAYS **WANTED** A BABY BROTHER??

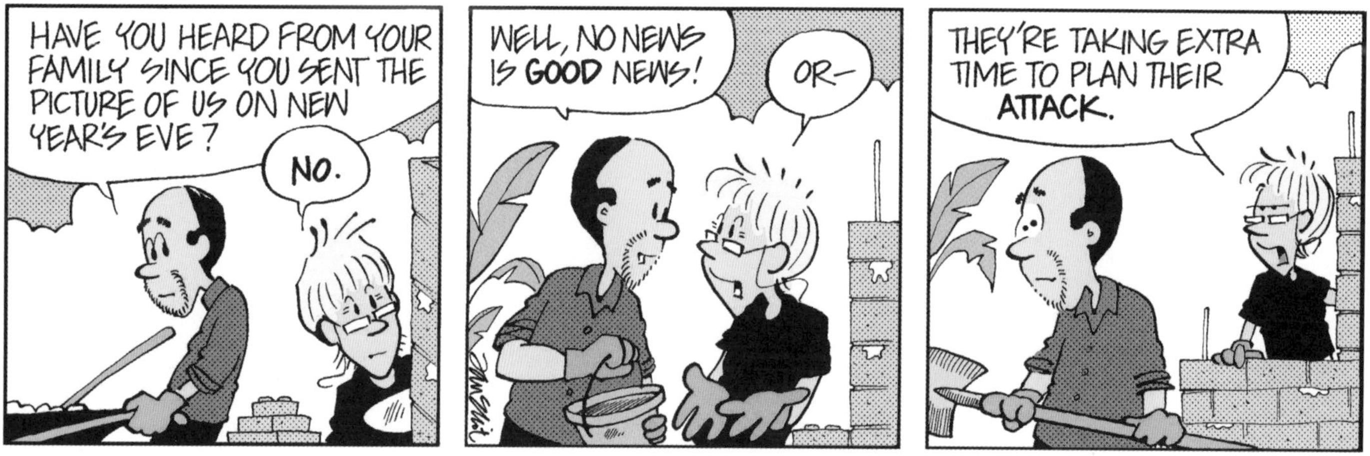
HAVE YOU HEARD FROM YOUR FAMILY SINCE YOU SENT THE PICTURE OF US ON NEW YEAR'S EVE?
NO.
WELL, NO NEWS IS **GOOD** NEWS!
OR–
THEY'RE TAKING EXTRA TIME TO PLAN THEIR **ATTACK**.

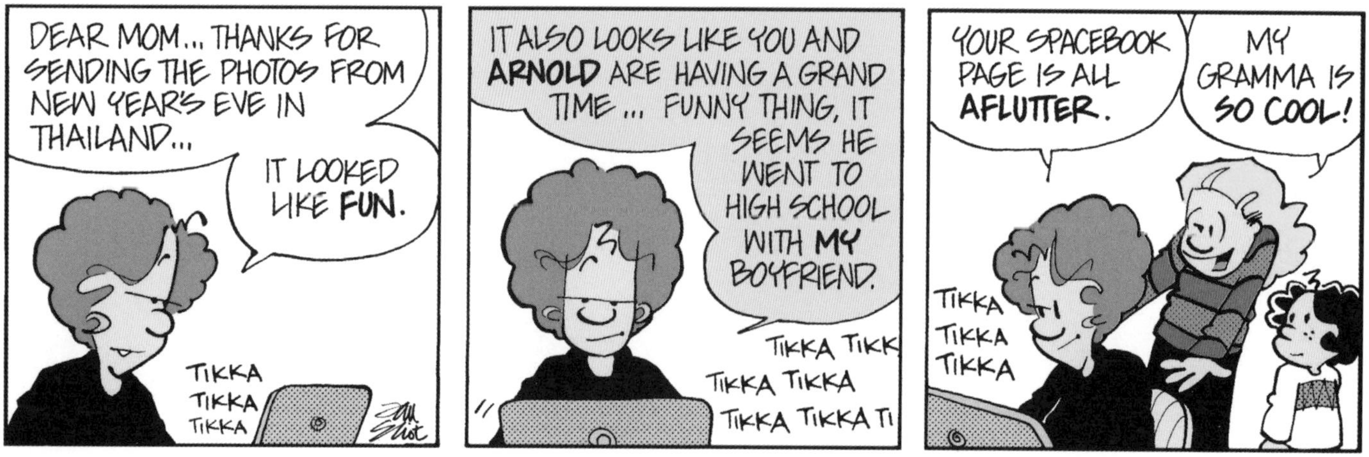
DEAR MOM... THANKS FOR SENDING THE PHOTOS FROM NEW YEAR'S EVE IN THAILAND...
IT LOOKED LIKE **FUN**.
TIKKA TIKKA TIKKA
IT ALSO LOOKS LIKE YOU AND **ARNOLD** ARE HAVING A GRAND TIME... FUNNY THING, IT SEEMS HE WENT TO HIGH SCHOOL WITH **MY** BOYFRIEND.
TIKKA TIKK
TIKKA TIKKA
TIKKA TIKKA TI
YOUR SPACEBOOK PAGE IS ALL **AFLUTTER**.
MY GRAMMA IS **SO COOL!**
TIKKA TIKKA TIKKA

ARNOLD, MY DAUGHTER'S BOYFRIEND THINKS HE KNEW YOU IN **HIGH SCHOOL**...

IS THAT **POSSIBLE?**

HOW OLD ARE YOU?!

\\\\...

WELL ZIPPIDY DOO-DAH.

ARNOLD, WHAT WILL I DO WHEN OUR WORK IN THAILAND IS DONE?

MUCH AS I MISS MY FAMILY... IT'S HARD TO IMAGINE GOING BACK TO MY OLD LIFE.

DON'T! THERE ARE VOLUNTEER OPPORTUN-ITIES ALL OVER THE WORLD. COME WITH ME TO THE **NEXT** ONE.

REALLY?

DEAR DAUGHTERS...

INTERNET CAFE open

IT SEEMS THERE ARE ENDLESS VOLUNTEER OPPORTUNITIES HERE IN THAILAND...

TIKKA TIKKA TIKKA

I COULD STAY LONGER, HELP BUILD A SCHOOL. I **MISS** YOU ALL, BUT—

TIKKA TIKKA TIK

I LOVE WHO I AM HERE.

UH-OH.

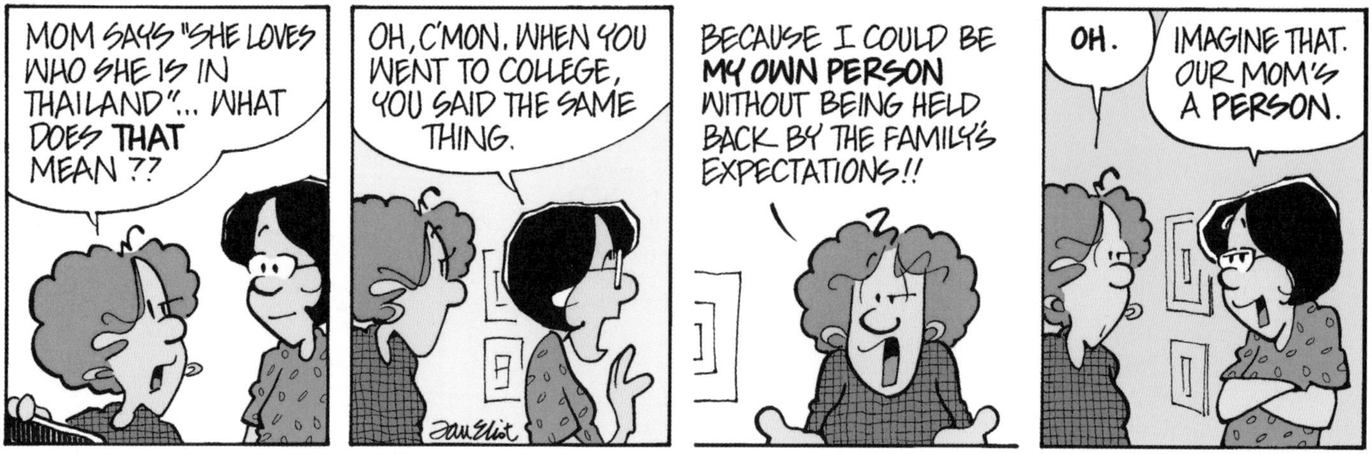
MOM SAYS "SHE LOVES WHO SHE IS IN THAILAND"... WHAT DOES **THAT** MEAN ??
OH, C'MON. WHEN YOU WENT TO COLLEGE, YOU SAID THE SAME THING.
BECAUSE I COULD BE **MY OWN PERSON** WITHOUT BEING HELD BACK BY THE FAMILY'S EXPECTATIONS!!
OH.
IMAGINE THAT. OUR MOM'S A **PERSON**.

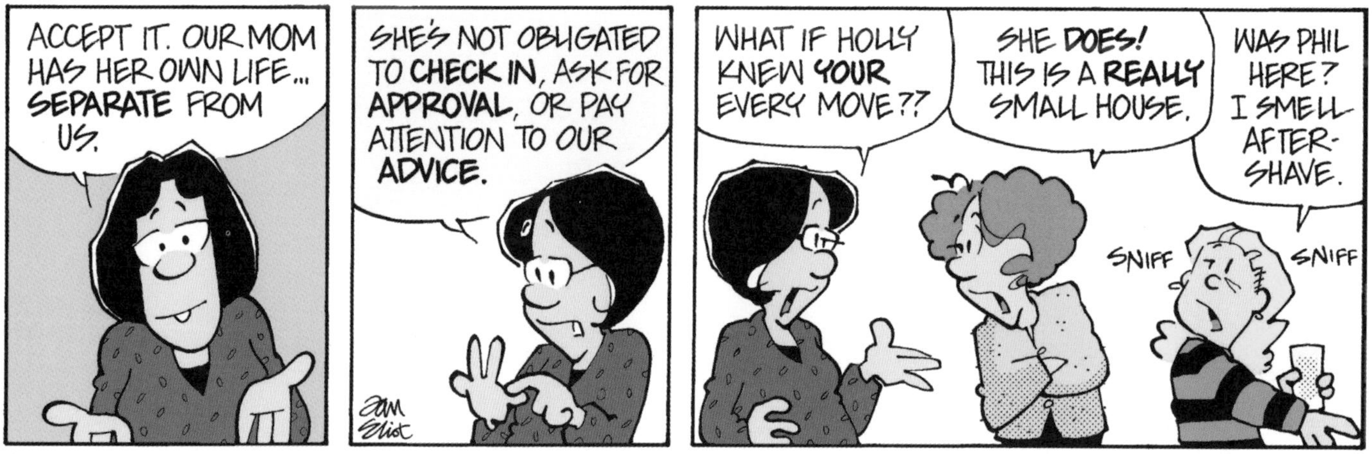
ACCEPT IT. OUR MOM HAS HER OWN LIFE... **SEPARATE** FROM US.
SHE'S NOT OBLIGATED TO **CHECK IN**, ASK FOR **APPROVAL**, OR PAY ATTENTION TO OUR **ADVICE.**
WHAT IF HOLLY KNEW **YOUR** EVERY MOVE ??
SHE **DOES!** THIS IS A **REALLY** SMALL HOUSE.
WAS PHIL HERE ? I SMELL AFTER-SHAVE.
SNIFF
SNIFF

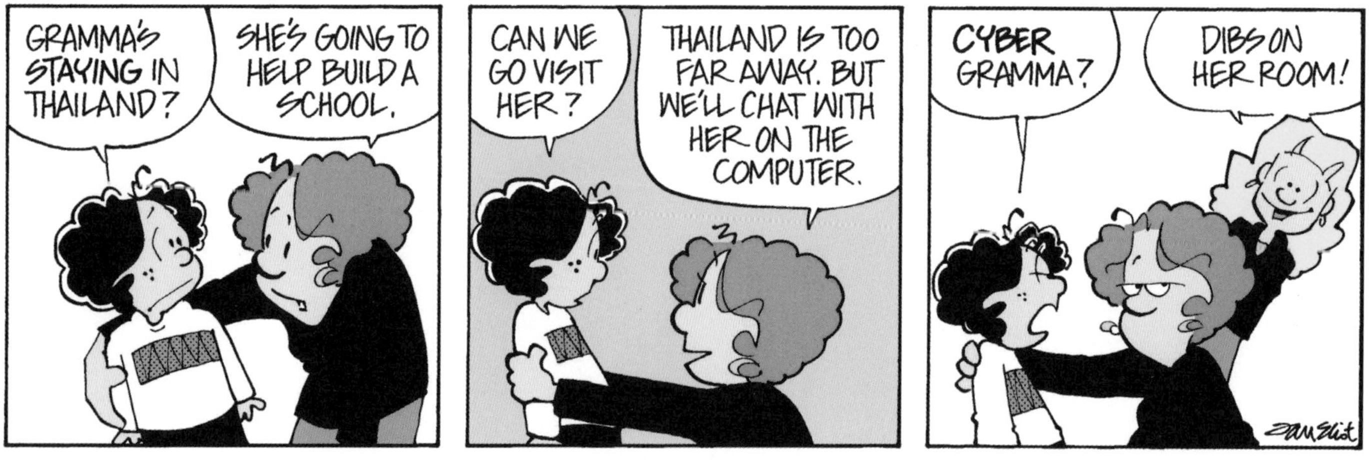
GRAMMA'S **STAYING** IN THAILAND ?
SHE'S GOING TO HELP BUILD A SCHOOL.
CAN WE GO VISIT HER ?
THAILAND IS TOO FAR AWAY. BUT WE'LL CHAT WITH HER ON THE COMPUTER.
CYBER GRAMMA ?
DIBS ON HER ROOM!

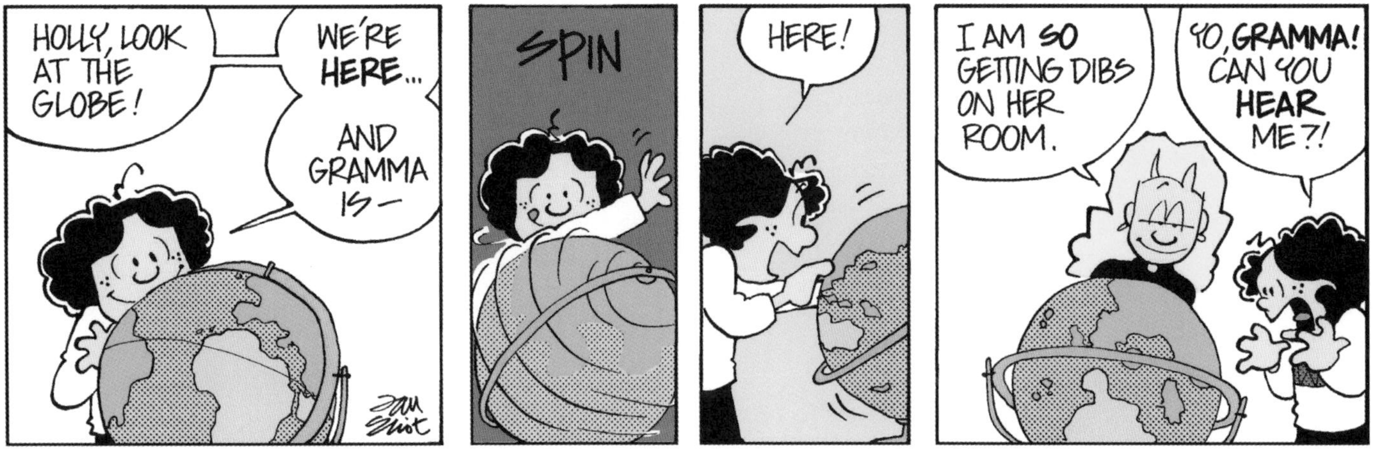
HOLLY, LOOK AT THE GLOBE!
WE'RE **HERE**...
AND GRAMMA IS—
SPIN
HERE!
I AM **SO** GETTING DIBS ON HER ROOM.
YO, **GRAMMA!** CAN YOU **HEAR** ME?!

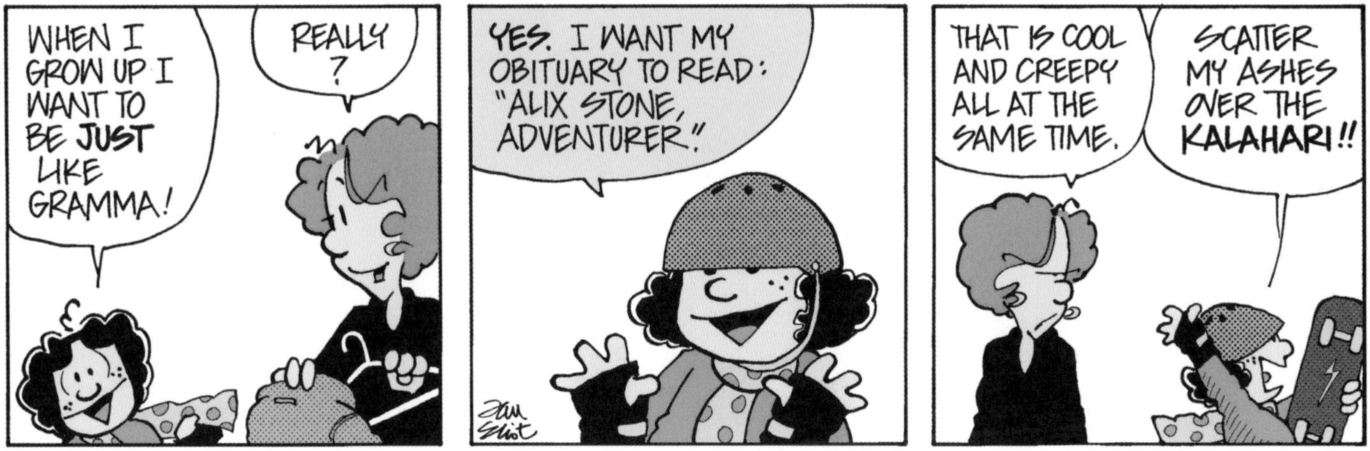
WHEN I GROW UP I WANT TO BE **JUST** LIKE GRAMMA!
REALLY?
YES. I WANT MY OBITUARY TO READ: "ALIX STONE, ADVENTURER."
THAT IS COOL AND CREEPY ALL AT THE SAME TIME.
SCATTER MY ASHES OVER THE **KALAHARI!!**

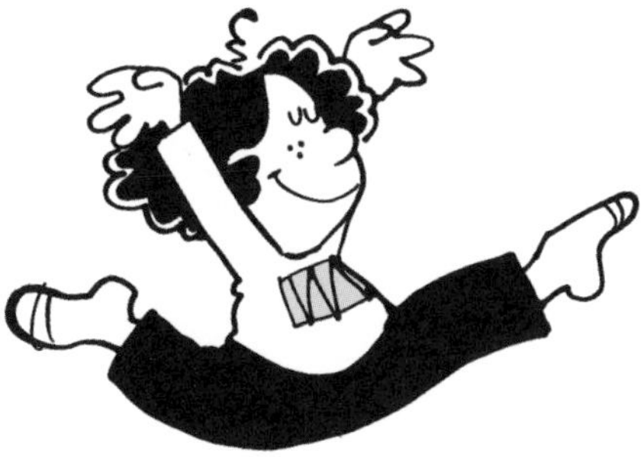

Other *Stone Soup*® Collections:

Stone Soup

You Can't Say Boobs On Sunday

Stone Soup the Comic Strip

Road Kill in the Closet

Not So Picture Perfect

Desperate Households

This Might Not Be Pretty

We'll Be Really Careful

Brace Yourself

It Seemed Like a Good Idea at the Time

All *Stone Soup* books are available through your
favorite local or online bookstores, or at
stonesoupcartoons.com or fourpanelpress.com.